READINGS IN
PERSONNEL MANAGEMENT

SECOND EDITION

HERBERT J. CHRUDEN

Professor of Business Administration
Sacramento State College

ARTHUR W. SHERMAN, JR.

Professor of Psychology
Sacramento State College

Published by

SOUTH-WESTERN PUBLISHING COMPANY

Cincinnati
Chicago

New Rochelle, N. Y.

Burlingame, Calif.
Dallas

P26

Library of Congress Catalog Card Number: 66-12625
H367

PREFACE

Students and practitioners of personnel management are well aware of the dynamic characteristics of this field. Personnel management is not only changing constantly but its horizons are continuing to expand as a result of the research and experience that is accumulating steadily. If one is to keep abreast of current changes and developments, he must review the literature that is being published in the professional journals. The problem of remaining current in the field is, however, a sizable task because of the volume of articles that are published and the varying quality and repetitious content of many of the articles. An extensive amount of professional reading, therefore, is required just to maintain contact with what is being published and to uncover those articles that may contain new and challenging ideas or that synthesize or reorganize existing knowledge more effectively.

Although it is desirable for students in personnel management courses to review the current literature, adequate copies of the journals often are not available to serve the needs of large numbers of students. The purpose of this book is to make available in a single volume those articles that, in the opinion of the authors, represent some of the more significant contributions in the field. The articles that appeared in the first edition of this book were screened from an original list of over 2,000 articles, the majority of which were published in leading professional journals during the preceding five years.

In order to keep the length of this second edition within reasonable limits and still permit the addition of more recent articles, it has not been possible to retain some of the articles that appeared in the first edition. Neither has it been possible to include many other excellent articles that have appeared in the literature since the first edition of this book was published. A number of the articles that we would like to have included in this edition are listed at the end of each chapter. These articles are recommended as additional reading and are available in bound volumes or on microfilm in college and industrial libraries.

Since it is envisioned that this book in many instances will be used as a supplement to a basic personnel management text, many of the articles were selected for the purpose of covering a particular topic more intensively than can be done in a textbook chapter. Other articles were selected because they contained a provocative viewpoint that differs from the theory commonly expressed in most personnel texts. Every effort has also been made to cover as many of the functional areas of personnel management as possible by selecting some of the best contributions from each area.

In compiling this book we have tried to include the writings of a variety of recognized authorities in the personnel management field. We acknowledge with gratitude the individual contributions that each of these authors has made to the value of this volume.

Although the articles in this book have been selected from a variety of journals, the largest number of them have been taken from *Personnel Administration*, the *Harvard Business Review*, and the publications of the American Management Association, including *Personnel, Management Review,* and *Supervisory Management.* We are particularly grateful to the publishers of these journals for permitting us to reproduce these articles. We would like to thank also the publishers of the following journals for permitting us to reproduce the articles that were selected:

Academy of Management Journal
Advanced Management
Advanced Management Journal
Advanced Management—Office Executive
Business Horizons
Business Topics
California Management Review
Connecticut Industry
Dun's Review and Modern Industry
Industrial and Labor Relations Review
Journal of the Academy of Management
Labor Law Journal
Management of Personnel Quarterly
Management Record
Menninger Quarterly
National Association of Suggestion Systems Quarterly
Nation's Business
Personnel Journal
Personnel Psychology

The authors are grateful to the staff of the Sacramento State College Library for its generous assistance. Certainly this book would not have been possible without the cooperation and valued assistance of our wives, Marie Chruden and Leneve Sherman. Their many contributions are gratefully acknowledged.

Herbert J. Chruden
Arthur W. Sherman, Jr.

CONTENTS

CHAPTER I. PERSONNEL MANAGEMENT IN PERSPECTIVE

CHAPTER 2. DEVELOPING HUMAN RESOURCES

Page

CHAPTER 3. ACHIEVING EFFICIENT PERFORMANCE

CHAPTER 4. PROVIDING EFFECTIVE LEADERSHIP

CHAPTER 5. ORGANIZATIONAL BEHAVIOR

CHAPTER 6. ECONOMIC INCENTIVES AND SECURITY

CHAPTER 7. UNION RELATIONS

CHAPTER 8. PERSONNEL MANAGEMENT: MEETING TODAY'S PROBLEMS

CHAPTER 1

Personnel Management in Perspective

Personnel management in some form has existed since man first discovered the advantage of group endeavor and of working with and through others to accomplish civil and military objectives. As a specialized body of knowledge, however, personnel management has been the subject of study only in relatively recent years. The personnel department, furthermore, has come into being only during the past fifty years. In spite of its rapid growth, personnel management is still in a state of development and much more knowledge remains to be acquired about the subject. Further research, for example, is needed in the areas of organizational theory and human behavior. The exact role of the personnel department and the nature of its relationship to the other departments and their personnel, moreover, is currently the subject of considerable study and debate. Many of the tools and processes of personnel management, as will be revealed in this and the chapters that follow, need to be refined still further.

The main purpose of this chapter is to provide the reader with a selected number of articles that provide him with some perspective of the field and with the thinking of current authors concerning it. It is hoped that by reading these articles he will gain a greater appreciation of the progress that has occurred in the field and of some of the issues that are the subject of current debate.

The first article by Eitington discusses a few of the pioneers in personnel management and the contributions that each has made to it. In addition to these pioneers, another well-known leader, who has become known as the "father of scientific management," was Frederick W. Taylor. His work, his views, and his philosophy have been the subject of interpretation as well as misinterpretation and debate by scores of writers for the past fifty years. By now, probably as much has been written about him as was written by him. In order that the reader may analyze for himself Taylor's views relating to the management of people, one of the last articles ever written by him has been included in this chapter.

The article by Colonel Urwick discusses some of the problems that exist in terms of melding of theories and terminology relating to the fields of organization and management with those relating to the emerging emphasis on the behavioral sciences. Colonel Urwick, who is an internationally recognized authority in the field of management, offers a very frank view of what he regards to be some of the erroneous concepts that have been advanced in the writings of some contemporary researchers in the behavioral science field. In the article that follows, however, the reader is afforded the opportunity to study the views of Chris Argyris, a behavioral scientist, who points out some of the weaknesses of contemporary personnel management theory based upon his research in the behavioral sciences. The next article by Peter Drucker also calls attention to certain weaknesses in personnel management that he feels should be corrected. While most personnel managers undoubtedly will take exception to some of Drucker's criticisms, his article can serve to remind them that their programs probably are subject to improvement.

The article by Anderson is concerned with the subject of authority. This article points up some of the difficulties that exist in differentiating functional authority from staff authority within an organization. The difficulty of defining and making the distinction between such types of authority constitutes the basis for one of the major problems encountered by the personnel department in its relations with other departments. The article by Cyril O'Donnell which discusses the role of committees is included because of the important role that committees exercise in the management of personnel. It summarizes most effectively how committees can be used to an advantage within an organization.

It is hoped that the articles selected for this chapter will stimulate the readers to view the field of personnel management more critically. Since this field is a dynamic one, it is essential that one continue to examine and question personnel theories and practices with the view of refining and improving them still further.

1. PIONEERS OF MANAGEMENT *

Julius E. Eitington

Personnel management is a multi-faceted discipline to which distinguished individuals from a number of disciplines have made contributions. Therefore, no two observers of the personnel management scene would agree on one or even on several contributors who meet the criterion of "outstanding." This lack of agreement is understandable when one considers that the past fifty years have been a period marked by movements and counter-movements, by diverse philosophies and great innovations.

To a large extent, the problem is complicated further by the definition of personnel management. Does the term involve, for example, solely the traditional functions of a personnel office, such as job evaluation, recruitment, training, employee and union relations, employee services, etc.? Or might it include, too, the advancing concepts contained in terms such as human relations and organizational behavior?

The category of personnel management is also used broadly. Thus in a discussion of the pioneers of or outstanding contributors to personnel management it is just as significant to include the pioneer of the group dynamics movement as it is to identify the most influential authority in the personnel testing field. Further, although personnel management is ordinarily conceived of as a staff function, two line managers whose work and thought have greatly influenced the personnel function seem also worthy of mention.

When assessing "contribution," it is not always easy to assert categorically that an individual was the creator of an idea, the innovator of a technique, or the founder of a movement. Obviously ideas and techniques come from several sources. For example, Dr. Carl Rogers is considered to be the prime developer of the technique of nondirective counseling, but Freud's work in psychoanalysis is certainly basic to that technique. Also, authorities differ as to who was the father of a particular movement. An example is Kurt Lewin versus J. L. Moreno in group dynamics.

* From *Advanced Management—Office Executive*, Vol. 2, No. 1 (January, 1963), pp. 16-19. Reprinted with permission.

Be that as it may, here are 12 individuals who, many persons believe, have greatly influenced personnel management during the past 50 years.

In the early part of this period, Dr. Walter Dill Scott (1869-1955), educator and psychologist, was a long-time key figure in personnel management. He is noted for having set up the World War I Army testing program. He was awarded the Distinguished Service Medal for "devising, installing, and supervising the personnel system in the U. S. Army." His work in testing influenced personnel management significantly in industry and government. He was also the joint author of an early textbook, *Personnel Management* (1923).

Dr. Walter Van Dyke Bingham (1880-1952) is considered by many to have been the dean of American personnel psychologists. He worked with Walter Dill Scott and other pioneers in the testing field on the Army testing program in World War I.

In that period Dr. Bingham was Executive Secretary, Committee on Classification of Personnel in the Army (1917-18), and then a Lieutenant Colonel, Personnel Branch, Army General Staff (1918-19). His text, *Aptitudes and Aptitude Testing* (1937), is still a classic in the field. His *How to Interview* (1931), written with B. V. Moore, is a standard text too. He was also joint author of the widely used text, *Procedures in Employment Psychology* (1937). Toward the latter part of his long career, he was Chief Psychologist, Adjutant General's Office, U. S. War Department (1940-47).

Dr. Warner W. Stockberger (1872-1944), a scientist by profession, was the first Personnel Director (1925-38) of the U. S. Department of Agriculture and of the Federal Government. He was also the first President of the Society for Personnel Administration, Washington, D. C. (1937). He was an early pioneer in Federal personnel management, and he had a keen appreciation of the human factor in management.

Dr. Stockberger's work, which included training of many personnel workers who ultimately moved on to other Federal agencies, helped to influence the character of Federal personnel management generally. His efforts were instrumental in changing Federal personnel work from a clerical to a substantive function.

Internationally recognized

Dr. Leonard D. White (1891-1958) was an internationally recognized figure in public personnel administration. He was a teacher at the University of Chicago, a scholar, writer, thinker, idealist, and practitioner. He is credited with many "firsts": he was the author of the first text on public administration (a text which also contained considerable information on personnel management); he was the first to teach public administration in a university classroom; he pioneered in starting the Junior Civil Service Examiner Examination, which attracted liberal arts and social science majors to careers in the Federal Government.

While in Washington with the Civil Service Commission in the 1930's, Dr. White taught a course in Public Personnel Administration at American University. In his class was born an idea which led to the establishment of the Society for Personnel Administration.

More recently, Dr. White served with distinction on the two Hoover Commissions which recommended improvements in Federal personnel management (1948-49, 1953-55). Some of his widely known works include *Introduction to Public Administration* (1926), *The City Manager* (1927), and *Prestige Value of Public Employment* (1929).

Dr. White's work on organization and personnel management was influenced by the scientific management movement. Some of his students, principally Herbert Simon, later challenged Dr. White's adherence to "principles" of organization. The work of the "behavioral scientists" presented many insights about management and organizational behavior, ones which Dr. White and others in his era had not explored.

In retrospect, then, Dr. White's major contributions to personnel management lay in his support to the merit system; his having facilitated the entry of college graduates from *all* disciplines into the Federal service, rather than from the recognized professions only; his having encouraged the building of a personnel "profession"; and his concern with augmenting the prestige of the public service.

The Hawthorne experiments

During the middle period of the past 50 years, the first intensive human relations research study was the Hawthorne experiments. These experiments were conducted at the Hawthorne plant of the Western Electric Co. for twelve years, starting November 1924, by the research staff of Harvard University's Graduate School of Business.

Leader of the world-famous Hawthorne Experiments was Dr. Elton Mayo (1880-1949). Whereas Taylor and his contemporaries viewed management and organization primarily from the standpoint of engineering, Dr. Mayo and his staff applied socio-psychological techniques to managerial problems. From this research, a new theory of human behavior in organizations was created. The research also sparked what has become known as the "human relations" school.

The Hawthorne Experiments led to, among other things, the creation of employee counseling programs in the 1930's, a phase of personnel management which is operative in most organizations today.

The basic account of Dr. Mayo's experiments at the Hawthorne Plant is in *Management and the Worker* (1939) by Fritz J. Roethlisberger and W. J. Dickson. This publication is regarded as a classic, combining research and outstanding social theory and philosophy. As these researchers found it, there is a world of logic of cost and efficiency and a world of logic of sentiment and emotion.

In his *The Human Problem of an Industrial Civilization* (1933) and his *Social Problems of an Industrial Civilization* (1954), Dr. Mayo gave us his scholarly interpretation of the significance of human factors in our industrial culture. His thesis related to the advantages to be derived from involving the worker in the decision-making process. He questioned strongly the "rabble hypothesis"—that materialistic goals are the only motivating force and that authoritarian leadership is essential to get the lazy to work and to keep the grasping in line.

Dr. Mayo, in his *Social Problems of an Industrial Civilization*, said: "For all of us the feeling of security and certainty derives always from assured membership of a group. If this is lost, no monetary gain, no job guarantee can be sufficient compensation."

Another solid contributor to the personnel field is Dr. Ordway Tead (1891-   ). Dr. Tead taught personnel administration, and at Columbia, 1917-18, he was in charge of war emergency employment management courses of the War Department. He continued at Columbia as a lecturer in personnel administration during 1920-50, and from 1951-56 he was Adjunct Professor of Industrial Relations. He was also a faculty member of the Department of Industry at the New York School of Social Work, 1920-29.

Stressed democratic principles

Dr. Tead is widely known as an educator, an editor, a publisher (McGraw Hill Book Co.), an author. His writings, which stressed democratic principles of management, have not been dimmed by more recent research. His better known works are *The Art of Leadership* (1935) and *The Art of Administration* (1951). He also co-authored with Henry C. Metcalf a pioneer personnel textbook, called *Personnel Administration: Its Principles and Practices* (1920).

Dr. Tead's career is a unified one in the sense that in the fields of administrating, editing, and writing, and in teaching of social science and in educational themes he has shown the interrelation of theory and practice in management, higher education, and publishing.

Dr. Chester I. Barnard (1886-1961), an eminent industrialist, is a former president of the New Jersey Bell Telephone Co. and later of the Rockefeller Foundation. In his much-quoted classic, *The Functions of the Executive* (1938), Dr. Barnard analyzed and stressed the sociopsychological and ethical aspects of managerial organization and functions. His book is an early, if not the first, recognition of the import of the informal as well as the formal organizational structure. He viewed organization as a social system.

This view necessitates a high degree of cooperation as opposed to emphasis upon authority and order-giving; the relegation of economic factors as motivators to a secondary role; the individual's identification with the organization based on a strong belief in its codes, as opposed to compliance imposed from without.

Communication responsibilities

Dr. Barnard was also one of the first management authorities to stress the communication responsibilities of executives, to analyze the role of status in organizational endeavor, and to develop systematically an analysis of incentive systems in organizations.

Charles P. McCormick (1896-   ), Chairman of the Board at McCormick and Co.—a Baltimore concern which sells tea, spices, and extracts—is the founder of "Multiple Management" (1932). He conceived the idea of establishing several boards—senior, junior, factory, and sales—as a means of securing participation, and thus ideas, to save the firm from the adverse effects of the Big Depression. Some 500 U. S. organizations now use this means of securing participation, manager development, problem-solving, morale building.

His plan and philosophy are described in *Multiple Management* (1938) and *Power of People* (1949).

To tie together the work and thinking of the early and middle periods, a quotation from John M. Pfiffner and Frank P. Sherwood is appropriate. In their *Administrative Organization* (1960), these men said:

> It seems ironic that during the period when the credos of formal organization were receiving their most literate conceptualization (by Mooney, Urwick, White, Willoughby, and Gulick), the seeds for its decline were being laid by Mayo, Roethlisberger, and Barnard. It was as though a patriarch was being prepared for burial at the time of his birth. However, the point should be made here that the patriarch did not die; he merely metamorphosed (footnote, p. 63).

Tested his ideas about groups

Among the leaders of the more current period, Dr. Kurt Lewin (1890-47) is regarded by many social psychologists as the founder of contemporary group dynamics. Dr. Lewin tested his ideas about groups after he left Germany in 1932 and settled in the United States. His pioneer study on group leadership was carried out at the University of Iowa.

Dr. Lewin found in a classic experiment on 10-year-old boys that democratic leadership was superior to either authoritarian or laissez-faire styles (reported in *Journal of Social Psychology*, 1939). When he moved to the Massachusetts Institute of Technology he conducted research in industry, results of which pointed up the direct relationship between production and participation in the decision-making process.

Also, Dr. Lewin showed during World War II the superiority of group discussion and group decision over lectures in getting Iowa housewives to try less desirable cuts of meat.

Dr. Lewin should be credited, too, with being the father of "sensitivity training." He was probably the first to experiment with discussion groups which were unstructured—that is, they functioned without a leader and without procedures or agenda, all elements of a sensitivity training situation.

In general, Dr. Lewin's ideas and studies on group behavior and social climate have provided industry, education, and government with tremendous insights about groups at work, particularly with reference to authority, decision-making, motivation, and introduction of change.

A disciple of Dr. Lewin, Dr. Leland P. Bradford (1905-), established in 1947 at Bethel, Maine, the first "sensitivity" or human relations laboratory. Since that time his efforts have spawned such training at some thirty-four universities and in a number of regular organizations as well. This has been a uniquely significant contribution to group leadership, and it has a tremendous potential for organizational health. Dr. Bradford is Director, National Training Laboratories, National Education Assn., Washington, D. C. He has served in this post since 1947.

Sensitivity training is a "gut" level experience. It provides the participants with insight into their own behavior. This insight is gained by receiving candid "feedback" from group members as they perceive one's behavior. The method holds great promise for improving interpersonal relations—if conducted on a vertical basis within organizations—for in the leveling process, helpful data are generated on communication difficulties, authority problems, and similar problems. An early summation of the work at Bethel is contained in Bradford's *Explanations in Human Relations Training: An Assessment of Experience*, 1947-53.

Researcher, teacher, consultant

Industrial Psychologist Norman R. F. Maier (1900-), University of Michigan, is a unique and prolific writer, a researcher, teacher, trainer, lecturer, and consultant. His unusually creative work emphasizes the importance of group decisions, employee participation, causation, motivation, and frustration.

As a practical trainer of supervisors, Dr. Maier has stimulated the wide use of "group-in-action" training methods by training specialists. His *Principles of Human Relations* (1952), *Psychology of Industry* (1946), and *Supervisory and Executive Development: A Manual for Role Playing* (1957) have enriched the personnel field immensely.

Dr. Rensis Likert (1903-), who is Director (since 1948) of the Institute of Social Research, University of Michigan, has conducted highly significant human relations research since the 40's. He has pointed up that the old concept of high morale meaning high productivity is much too simple, for, in fact, all kinds of combinations are possible. Dr. Likert's research demonstrates the value to productivity of (1) "supportive" as opposed to threatening supervision and (2) "participative" as opposed to hierarchically-controlled management.

Reports his basic conclusions

In general, supervisory attitudes—that is, those which are "employee centered" as opposed to "production centered"—are basic to productivity. Dr. Likert's findings cast doubt on the long-range success of organizations which use people for short-range goals. His book, *New Patterns of Management* (1961), reports his basic findings and conclusions.

We must also recognize that the contemporary scene can boast a good number of other top-flight thinkers, writers, and researchers. Examples are Carroll Shartle (from Ohio State) who has conducted highly significant studies in leadership; Charles R. Walker and Robert H. Guest (from Yale University) and their work on the human aspects of technology; E. Wright Bakke and Chris Argyris (Yale) and their analysis of the processes by which the individual and the organization adapt to one another's needs.

Still other examples include William Foote Whyte (Cornell) who has analyzed the psychology of groups; Douglas McGregor (M.I.T.) and his ideas on leadership theory, motivation, and goal setting; Melville Dalton (U.C.L.A.) and his sociological analysis of organizations and the men who manage them, including concern with line and staff conflict, power, status, influence maneuvering, and the "implicit and the explicit" organization; Herbert A. Simon (Carnegie) and his analysis of organizational behavior from the standpoint of decision-making, particularly its nonrational character.

All these men are representative of the rapidly expanding field of today's personnel administration.

Questions

1. Why is it difficult to single out a particular group of individuals as having made the most significant contributions to the development of the field of personnel management?
2. What other individuals would you include in your list of contributors who were not mentioned in this article?
3. Who is considered to be the founder of the field of group dynamics? What type of training is an outgrowth of this field?
4. What major contributions did Elton Mayo render to the field of personnel management?

2. THE PRINCIPLES OF SCIENTIFIC MANAGEMENT *

Frederick Winslow Taylor [1]

By far the most important fact which faces the industries of our country, the industries, in fact, of the civilized world, is that not only the average worker, but nineteen out of twenty workmen throughout the civilized world firmly believe that it is for their best interests to go slow instead of to go fast. They firmly believe that it is for their interest to give as little work in return for the money that they get as is practical. The reasons for this belief are two-fold, and I do not believe that the workingmen are to blame for holding these fallacious views.

If you will take any set of workmen in your own town and suggest to those men that it would be a good thing for them in their trade if they were to double their output in the coming year, each man turn out twice as much work and become twice as efficient, they would say, "I do not know anything about other people's trades; what you are saying about increasing efficiency being a good thing may be good for other trades, but I know that the only result if you come to our trade would be that half of us would be out of a job before the year was out." That to the average workingman is an axiom; it is not a matter subject to debate at all. And even among the average business men of this country that opinion is almost universal. They firmly believe that that would be the result of a great increase in efficiency, and yet directly the opposite is true.

The effect of labor-saving devices

Whenever any labor-saving device of any kind has been introduced into any trade—go back into the history of any trade and see it—

* From the *Bulletin of the Taylor Society*, December, 1916, as reproduced in *Advanced Management Journal* (September, 1963), pp. 30-39. Reprinted with permission.

[1] An abstract of an address given by the late Dr. Taylor before the Cleveland Advertising Club, March 3, 1915, two weeks prior to his death. It was repeated the following day at Youngstown, Ohio, and this presentation was Dr. Taylor's last public appearance.

· 11 ·

even though that labor-saving device may turn out ten, twenty, thirty times that output that was originally turned out by men in that trade, the result has universally been to make work for more men in that trade, not work for less men.

Let me give you one illustration. Let us take one of the staple businesses, the cotton industry. About 1840 the power loom succeeded the old hand loom in the cotton industry. It was invented many years before, somewhere about 1780 or 1790, but it came in very slowly. About 1840 the weavers of Manchester, England, saw that the power loom was coming, and they knew it would turn out three times the yardage of cloth in a day that the hand loom turned out. And what did they do, these five thousand weavers of Manchester, England, who saw starvation staring them in the face? They broke into the establishments into which those machines were being introduced, they smashed them, they did everything possible to stop the introduction of the power loom. And the same result followed that follows every attempt to interfere with the introduction of any labor-saving device, if it is really a labor-saving device. Instead of stopping the introduction of the power loom, their opposition apparently accelerated it, just as opposition to scientific management all over the country, bitter labor opposition today, is accelerating the introduction of it instead of retarding it. History repeats itself in that respect. The power loom came right straight along.

And let us see the result in Manchester. Just what follows in every industry when any labor-saving device is introduced. Less than a century has gone by since 1840. The population of England in that time has not more than doubled. Each man in the cotton industry in Manchester, England, now turns out, at a restricted estimate ten yards of cloth for every yard of cloth that was turned out in 1840. In 1840 there were 5,000 weavers in Manchester. Now there are 265,000. Has that thrown men out of work? Has the introduction of labor-saving machinery, which has multiplied the output per man by tenfold, thrown men out of work?

What is the real meaning of this? All that you have to do is to bring wealth into this world and the world uses it. That is the real meaning. The meaning is that wherein 1840 cotton goods were a luxury to be worn only by rich people when they were hardly ever seen on the street, now every man, woman and child all over the world wears cotton goods as a daily necessity.

Nineteen-twentieths of the real wealth of this world is used by the poor people, and not the rich, so that the workingman who sets out as a steady principle to restrict output is merely robbing his own kind. That group of manufacturers which adopts as a permanent principle restriction of output, in order to hold up prices, is robbing the world. The one great thing that marks the improvement of this world is measured by the enormous increase in output of the individuals in this world. There is fully twenty times the output per man now that there was three hundred years ago. That marks the increase in the real wealth of the world; that marks the increase of the happiness of the world, that gives us the opportunity for shorter hours, for better education, for amusement, for art, for music, for everything that is worthwhile in this world—goes right straight back to this increase in the output of the individual. The workingmen of today live better than the king did three hundred years ago. From what does the progress the world has made come? Simply from the increase in the output of the individual all over the world.

The development of soldiering

The second reason why the workmen of this country and of Europe deliberately restrict output is a very simple one. They, for this reason, are even less to blame than they are for the other. If, for example, you are manufacturing a pen, let us assume for simplicity that a pen can be made by a single man. Let us say that the workman is turning out ten pens per day, and that he is receiving $2.50 a day for his wages. He has a progressive foreman who is up to date, and that foreman goes to the workman and suggests, "Here, John, you are getting $2.50 a day, and you are turning out ten pens. I would suggest that I pay you 25 cents for making that pen." The man takes the job, and through the help of his foreman, through his own ingenuity, through his increased work, through his interest in his business, through the help of his friends, at the end of the year he finds himself turning out twenty pens instead of ten. He is happy, he is making $5, instead of $2.50 a day. His foreman is happy because, with the same room, with the same men he had before, he has doubled the output of his department, and the manufacturer himself is sometimes happy, but not often. Then someone on the board of directors asks to see the payroll, and he finds that we are paying $5 a day where other similar mechanics are only getting $2.50, and in no uncertain terms he announces that we must stop ruining the labor market. We cannot pay $5 a day when the standard rate of wages is $2.50; how can we hope to compete with surrounding towns? What is the result? Mr. Foreman is sent for, and he is told that he has got to stop ruining the labor market of Cleveland. And the foreman goes back to his workman in sadness, in depression, and tells his workman, "I am sorry, John, but I have got to cut the price down for that pen; I cannot let you earn $5 a day; the board of directors has got on to it, and it is ruining the labor market; you ought to be willing to have the price reduced. You cannot earn more than $3 or $2.75 a day, and I will have to cut your wages so that you will only get $3 a day." John, of necessity accepts the cut, but he sees to it that he never makes enough pens to get another cut.

Characteristics of the union workman

There seem to be two divergent opinions about the workmen of this country. One is that a lot of the trade unions' workmen, particularly in this country, have become brutal, have become dominating, careless of any interests but their own, and are a pretty poor lot. And the other opinion which those same trade unionists hold of themselves is that they are pretty close to little gods. Whichever view you may hold of the workingmen of this country, and my personal view of them is that they are a pretty fine lot of fellows, they are just about the same as you and I. But whether you hold the bad opinion or the good opinion, it makes no difference. Whatever the workingmen of this country are or whatever they are not, they are not fools. And all that is necessary is for a workingman to have but one object lesson, like that I have told you, and he soldiers for the rest of his life.

There are a few exceptional employers who treat their workmen differently, but I am talking about the rule of the country. Soldiering is the absolute rule with all workmen who know their business. I am not saying it is for their interest to soldier. You cannot blame them for it. You cannot expect them to be large enough minded men to look at the proper view of the matter. Nor is the man who cuts the wages necessarily to blame. It is simply a misfortune in industry.

The development of scientific management

There has been, until comparatively recently, no scheme promulgated by which the evils of rate cutting could be properly avoided, so soldiering has been the rule.

Now the first step that was taken toward the development of those methods, of those principles, which rightly or wrongly have come to be known under the name of scientific management—the first step that was taken in an earnest endeavor to remedy the evils of soldiering; an earnest endeavor to make it unnecessary for workmen to be hypocritical in this way, to deceive themselves, to deceive their employers, to live day in and day out a life of deceit, forced upon them by conditions—the very first step that was taken toward the development was to overcome that evil. I want to emphasize that, because I wish to emphasize the one great fact relating to scientific management, the greatest factor: namely, that scientific management is no new set of theories that has been tried on by any one at every step. Scientific management at every step has been an evolution, not a theory. In all cases the practice has preceded the theory, not succeeded it. In every case one measure after another has been tried out, until the proper remedy has been found. That series of proper eliminations, that evolution, is what is called scientific management. Every element of it has had to fight its way against the elements that preceded it, and prove itself better or it would not be there tomorrow.

All the men that I know of who are in any way connected with scientific management are ready to abandon any scheme, any theory in favor of anything else that could be found that is better. There is nothing in scientific management that is fixed. There is no one man, or group of men, who have invented scientific management.

What I want to emphasize is that all of the elements of scientific management are an evolution, not an invention. Scientific management is in use in an immense range and variety of industries. Almost every type of industry in this country has scientific management working successfully. I think I can safely say that on the average in those establishments in which scientific management has been introduced, the average workman is turning out double the output he was before. I think that is a conservative statement.

What scientific management is

What is scientific management? It is no efficiency device, nor is it any group or collection of efficiency devices. Scientific management is no new scheme for paying men, it is no bonus system, no piece-work system, no premium system of payment; it is no new method of figuring costs. It is no one of the various elements by which it is commonly known, by which people refer to it. It is not time study nor man study. It is not the printing of a ton or two of blanks and unloading them on a company and saying, "There is your system, go ahead and use it." Scientific management does not exist and cannot exist until there has been a complete mental revolution on the part of the workmen working under it, as to their duties toward themselves and toward their employers, and a complete mental revolution in the outlook of the employers, toward their duties, toward themselves, and toward their workmen. And until this great mental change takes place, scientific management does not exist. Do you think you can make a great mental revolution in a large group of workmen in a year, or do you think you can make it in a large group of foremen and superintendents in a year? If you do, you are very much mistaken. All of us hold mighty close to our ideas and prin-ciples in life, and we change very slowly toward the new, and very properly too.

Let me give you an idea of what I mean by this change in mental outlook. If you are manufacturing a hammer or a mallet, into the cost of that mallet goes a certain amount of raw materials, a certain amount of wood and metal. If you will take the cost of the raw materials and then add to it that cost which is frequently called by various names—overhead expenses, general expense, indirect expense; that is, the proper share of taxes, insurance, light, heat, salaries of officers and advertising—and you have a sum of money. Subtract that sum from the selling price, and what is left over is called the surplus. It is over this surplus that all of the labor disputes in the past have occurred. The workman naturally wants all he can get. His wages come out of that surplus. The manufacturer wants all he can get in the shape of profits, and it is from the division of this surplus that all the labor disputes have come in the past—the equitable division.

The new outlook that comes under scientific management is this: The workmen, after many object lessons, come to see and the manage-ment come to see that this surplus can be made so great, providing both sides will stop their pulling apart, will stop their fighting and will push as hard as they can to get as cheap an output as possible, that there is no occasion to quarrel. Each side can get more than ever before. The acknowledgment of this fact represents a complete mental revolution.

What scientific management will do

I am going to try to prove to you that the old style of management has not a ghost of a chance in competition with the principles of scientific management. Why? In the first place, under scientific management, the initiative of the workmen, their hard work, their good-will, their best endeavors are obtained with absolute regularity. There are cases all the time where men will soldier, but they become the exception, as a rule, and they give their true initiative under scientific management. That is the least of the two sources of gain. The greatest source of gain under scientific management comes from the new and almost unheard-of duties and burdens which are voluntarily assumed, not by the workmen, but by the men on the management side. These are the things which make scientific management a success. These new duties, these new burdens undertaken by the management have rightly or wrongly been divided into four groups, and have been called the principles of scientific management.

The first of the great principles of scientific management, the first of the new burdens which are voluntarily undertaken by those on the management side is the deliberate gathering together of the great mass of traditional knowledge which, in the past, has been in the heads of the workmen, recording it, tabulating it, reducing it in most cases to rules, laws, and in many cases to mathematical formulae, which, with these new laws, are applied to the co-operation of the management to the work of the workmen. This results in an immense increase in the output, we may say, of the two. The gathering in of this great mass of traditional knowledge, which is done by the means of motion study, time study, can be truly called the science.

Let me make a prediction. I have before me the first book, so far as I know, that has been published on motion study and on time study. That is, the motion study and time study of the cement and concrete trades. It contains everything relating to concrete work. It is of about seven hundred pages and embodies the motions of men, the time and the best way of doing that sort of work. It is the first case in which a trade has been reduced to the same condition that engineering data of all kinds have been reduced, and it is this sort of data that is bound to sweep the world.

I have before me something which has been gathering for about fourteen years, the time or motion study of the machine shop. It will take probably four or five years more before the first book will be ready to publish on that subject. There is a collection of sixty or seventy thousand elements affecting machine-shop work. After a few years, say three, four or five years more, some one will be ready to publish the first book giving the laws of the movements of men in the machine shop—all the laws, not only a few of them. Let me predict, just as sure as the sun shines, that is going to come in every trade. Why? Because it pays, for no other reason. That results in doubling the output in any shop. Any device which results in an increased output is bound to come in spite of all opposition, whether we want it or not. It comes automatically.

The selection of the workman

The next of the four principles of scientific management is the scientific selection of the workman, and then his progressive development. It becomes the duty under scientific management of not one, but of a group of men on the management side, to deliberately study the workmen who are under them; study them in the most careful, thorough and painstaking way; and not just leave it to the poor, overworked foreman to go out and say, "Come on, what do you want? If you are cheap enough I will give you a trial."

That is the old way. The new way is to take a great deal of trouble in selecting the workmen. The selection proceeds year after year. And it becomes the duty of those engaged in scientific management to know something about the workmen under them. It becomes their duty to set out deliberately to train the workmen in their employ to be able to do a better and still better class of work than ever before, and to then pay them higher wages than ever before. This deliberate selection of the workmen is the second of the great duties that devolve on the management under scientific management.

Bringing together the science and the man

The third principle is the bringing together of this science of which I have spoken and the trained workmen. I say bringing because they don't come together unless some one brings them. Select and train your workmen all you may, but unless there is some one who will make the men and the science come together, they will stay apart. The "make" involves a great many elements. They are not all disagreeable elements. The most important and largest way of "making" is to do something nice for the man whom you wish to make come together with the science. Offer him a plum, something that is worthwhile. There are many plums offered to those who come under scientific management—better treatment, more kindly treatment, more consideration for their wishes, and an opportunity for them to express their wants freely. That is one side of the "make." An equally important side is, whenever a man will not do what he ought, to either make him do it or stop it. If he will not do it, let him get out. I am not talking of any mollycoddle. Let me disabuse your minds of any opinion that scientific management is a mollycoddle scheme.

I have a great many union friends. I find they look with especial bitterness on this word "make." They have been used to doing the "making" in the past. That is the attiude of the trade unions, and it softens matters greatly when you can tell them the facts, namely, that in our making the science and the men come together, nine-tenths of our trouble comes with the men on the management side in making them do their new duties. I am speaking of those who have been trying to change from the old system to the new. Nine-tenths of our troubles come in trying to make the men on the management side do what they ought to do, to make them do the new duties, and take on these new burdens, and give up their old duties. That softens this word "make."

The principle of the division of work

The fourth principle is the plainest of all. It involves a complete re-division of the work of the establishment. Under the old scheme of management, almost all of the work was done by the workmen. Under the new, the work of the establishment is divided into two large parts. All of that work which formerly was done by the workmen alone is divided into two large sections, and one of those sections is handed over to the management. They do a whole division of the work formerly done by the workmen. It is this real cooperation, this genuine division of the work between the two sides, more than any other element which accounts for the fact that there never will be strikes under scientific management. When the workman realizes that there is hardly a thing he does that does not have to be preceded by some act of preparation on the part of management, and when that workman realizes when the management falls down and does not do its part, that he is not only entitled to a kick, but that he can register that kick in the most forcible possible way, he cannot quarrel with the men over him. It is team work. There are more complaints made every day on the part of the workmen that the men on the management side fail to do their duties than are made by the management that the men fail. Every one of the complaints of the men have to be heeded, just as much as the complaints from the management that the workmen do not do their share. That is characteristic of scientific management. It represents a democracy, co-operation, a genuine division of work which never existed before in this world.

The proof of the theory

I am through now with the theory. I will try to convince you of the value of these four principles by giving you some practical illustrations. I hope that you will look for these four elements in the illustrations. I shall begin by trying to show the power of these four elements when applied to the greatest kind of work I know of that is done by man. The reason I have heretofore chosen pig-iron for an illustration is that it is the lowest form of work that is known.

A pig of iron weighs about ninety-two pounds on an average. A man stoops down and, with no other implement than his hands, picks up a pig of iron, walks a few yards with it, and drops it on a pile. A large part of the community has the impression that scientific management is chiefly handling pig-iron. The reason I first chose pig-iron for an illustration is that, if you can prove to any one the strength, the effect, of those four principles when applied to such rudimentary work as handling pig-iron, the presumption is that it can be applied to something better. The only way to prove it is to start at the bottom and show those four principles all along the line. I am sorry I cannot, because of lack of time, give you the illustration of handling pig-iron. Many of you doubt whether there is much of any science in it. I am going to try to prove later with a high class mechanic that the workman who is fit to work at any type of work is almost universally incapable of understanding the principles without the help of some one else. I will use shoveling because it is a shorter illustration, and I will try to show what I mean by the science of shoveling, and the power which comes to the man who knows the science of shoveling. It is a high art compared with pig-iron handling.

The science of shoveling

When I went to the Bethlehem Steel Works, the first thing I saw was a gang of men unloading rice coal. They were a splendid set of fellows, and they shoveled fast. There was no loafing at all. They shoveled as hard as you could ask any man to work. I looked with the greatest of interest for a long time, and finally they moved off rapidly down into the yard to another part of the yard and went right at handling iron ore. One of the main facts connected with that shoveling was that the work those men were doing was that, in handling the rice coal, they had on their shovels a load of 3¾ pounds, and when the same men went to handling ore with the same shovel, they had over 38 pounds on their shovels. Is it asking too much of anyone to inquire whether 3¾ pounds is the right load for a shovel, or whether 38 pounds is the right load for a shovel? Surely if one is right the other must be wrong. I think that is a self-evident fact, and yet I am willing to bet that that is what workmen are doing right now in Cleveland.

That is the old way. Suppose we notice that fact. Most of us do not notice it because it is left to the foreman. At the Midvale works, we had to find out these facts. What is the old way of finding them out? The old way was to sit down and write one's friends and ask them the question. They got answers from contractors about what they thought it ought to be, and then they averaged them up, or took the most reliable man, and said, "That is all right; now we have a shovel load of so much." The more common way is to say, "I want a good shovel foreman." They will send for the foreman of the shovelers and put the job up to him to find what is the proper load to put on a shovel. He will tell you right off the bat. I want to show you the difference under scientific management.

Under scientific management you ask no one. Every little trifle,— there is nothing too small,—becomes the subject of experiment. The experiments develop into a law; they save money; they increase the output of the individual and make the thing worthwhile. How is this done? What we did in shoveling experiments was to deliberately select two first class shovelers, the best we knew how to get. We brought them into the office and said, "Jim and Mike, you two fellows are both good shovelers. I have a proposition to make to you. I am going to pay you double wages if you fellows will go out and do what I want you to do. There will be a young chap go along with you with a pencil and a piece of paper, and he will tell you to do a lot of fool things, and you will do them, and he will write down a lot of fool things, and you will think it is a joke, but it is nothing of the kind. Let me tell you one thing: if you fellows think that you can fool that chap you are very much mistaken, you cannot fool him at all. Don't get it through your heads you can fool him. If you take this double wages, you will be straight and do what you are told." They both promised and did exactly what they were told. What we told them was this: "We want you to start in and do whatever shoveling you are told to do, and work at just the pace, all day long, that when it comes night you are going to be good and tired, but not tired out. I do not want you exhausted or anything like that, but properly tired. You know what a good day's work is. In other words, I do not want any loafing business or any overwork business. If you find yourself overworked and getting too tired, slow down." Those men did that and did it in the most splendid kind of way day in and day out. We proved their co-operation because they were in different parts of the yard, and they both got near enough the same results. Our results were duplicated.

I have found that there are a lot of schemes among my working friends, but no more among them than among us. They are good, straight fellows if you only treat them right, and put the matter up squarely to them. We started in at a pile of material, with a very large shovel. We kept innumerable accurate records of all kinds, some of them useless. Thirty or forty different items were carefully observed about the work of those two men. We counted the number of shovelfuls thrown in a day. We found with a weight of between thirty-eight and thirty-nine pounds on the shovel, the man made a pile of material of a certain height. We then cut off the shovel, and he shoveled again and with a thirty-four pound load his pile went up and he shoveled more in a day. We again cut off the shovel to thirty pounds, and the pile went up again. With twenty-six pounds on the shovel, the pile again went up, and at twenty-one and one-half pounds the men could do their best. At twenty pounds the pile went down, at eighteen it went down, and at fourteen it went down, so that they were at the peak at twenty-one and one-half pounds. There is a scientific fact. A first class shoveler ought to take twenty-one and one-half pounds on his shovel in order to work to the best possible advantage. You are not giving that man a chance unless you **give him a shovel which will hold twenty-one pounds.**

The men in the yard were run by the old fashioned foreman. He simply walked about with them. We at once took their shovels away from them. We built a large labor tool room which held ten to fifteen different kinds of shoveling implements so that for each kind of material that was handled in that yard, all the way from rice coal, ashes, coke, all the way up to ore, we would have a shovel that would just hold twenty-one pounds, or average twenty-one. One time it would hold eighteen, the next twenty-four, but it will average twenty-one.

When you have six hundred men laboring in the yard, as we had there, it becomes a matter of quite considerable difficulty to get, each day, for each one of those six hundred men, engaged in a line one and one-half to two miles long and a half mile wide, just the right shovel for shoveling material. That requires organization to lay out and plan for those men in advance. We had to lay out the work each day. We had to have large maps on which the movements of the men were plotted out a day in advance. When each workman came in the morning, he took out two pieces of paper. One of the blanks gave them a statement of the implements which they had to use, and the part of the yard in which they had to work. That required organization planning in advance.

One of the first principles we adopted was that no man in that labor gang could work on the new way unless he earned sixty per cent higher wages than under the old plan. It is only just to the workman that he shall know right off whether he is doing his work right or not. He must not be told a week or month after, that he fell down. He must know it the next morning. So the next slip that came out of the pigeon hole was either a white or yellow slip. We used the two colors because some of the men could not read. The yellow slip meant that he had not earned his sixty per cent higher wages. He knew that he could not stay in that gang and keep on getting yellow slips.

Teaching the men

I want to show you again the totally different outlook there is under scientific management by illustrating what happened when that man got his yellow slips. Under the old scheme, the foreman could say to him, "You are no good, get out of this; no time for you, you cannot earn sixty per cent higher wages; get out of this! Go!" It was not done politely, but the foreman had no time to palaver. Under the new scheme what happened? A teacher of shoveling went down to see that man. A teacher of shoveling is a man who is handy with a shovel, who has made his mark in life with a shovel, and yet who is a kindly fellow and knows how to show the other fellow what he ought to do. When that teacher went there he said, "See here, Jim, you have a lot of those yellow slips, what is the matter with you? What is up? Have you been drunk? Are you tired? Are you sick? Anything wrong with you? Because if you are tired or sick we will give you a show somewhere else." Well, no, I am all right." "Then if you are not sick, or there is nothing wrong with you, you have forgotten how to shovel. I showed you how to shovel. You have forgotten something, now go ahead and shovel and I will show you what is the matter with you." Shoveling is a pretty big science, it is not a little thing.

If you are going to use the shovel right you should always shovel off an iron bottom; if not an iron bottom, a wooded bottom; and if not a wooden bottom a hard dirt bottom. Time and again the conditions are such that you have to go right into the pile. When that is the case, with nine out of ten materials it takes more trouble and more time and more effort to get the shovel into the pile than to do all the rest of the shoveling. That is where the effort comes. Those of you again who have taught the art of shoveling will have taught your workmen to do this. There is only one way to do it right. Put your forearm down onto the upper part of your leg, and when you push into the pile, throw your weight against it. That relieves your arm of work. You then have an automatic push, we will say, about eighty pounds, the weight of your body thrown on to it. Time and again we would find men whom we had taught to shovel right were going at it in the old way, and of course they could not do a day's work. The teacher would simply stand over that fellow and say, "There is what is the matter with you, Jim, you have forgotten to shovel into the pile."

You are not interested in shoveling, you are not interested in whether one way or the other is right, but I do hope to interest you in the difference of the mental attitude of the men who are teaching under the new system. Under the new system, if a man falls down, the presumption is that it is our fault at first, that we probably have not taught the man right, have not given him a fair show, have not spent time enough in showing him how to do his work.

Let me tell you another thing that is characteristic of scientific management. In my day, we were smart enough to know when the boss was coming, and when he came up we were apparently really working. Under scientific management, there is none of that pretense. I cannot say that in the old days we were delighted to see the boss coming around. We always expected some kind of roast if he came too close. Under the new, the teacher is welcomed; he is not an enemy, but a friend. He comes there to try to help the man get bigger wages, to show him how to do something. It is the great mental change, the change in the outlook that comes, rather than the details of it.

Does scientific management pay?

It took the time of a number of men for about three years to study the art of shoveling in that yard at the Bethlehem Steel Works alone. They were carefully trained college men, and they were busy all the time. That costs money, the tool room costs money, the clerks we had to keep there all night figuring up how much the men did the day before cost money, the office in which the men laid out and planned the work cost money. The very fair and proper question, the only question to ask is "Does it pay?" because if scientific management does not pay, there is nothing in it; if it does not pay in dollars and cents, it is the rankest kind of nonsense. There is nothing philanthropic about it. It has got to pay, because business which cannot be done on a profitable basis ought not to be done on a philanthropic basis, for it will not last. At the end of three and one-half years we had a very good chance to know whether or not it paid.

Fortunately in the Bethlehem Steel Works they had records of how much it cost to handle the materials under the old system, where the single foreman led a group of men around the works. It costs them between seven and eight cents a ton to handle materials, on an average throughout the year. After paying for all this extra work I have told you about, it cost between three and four cents a ton to handle materials, and there was a profit of between seventy-five and eighty thousand dollars a year in that yard by handling those materials in the new way. What the men got out of it was this: Under the old system there were between four and six hundred men handling the material in that yard, and when we got through there were about one hundred and forty. Each one was earning a great deal more money. We made careful investigation and found they were almost all saving money, living better, happier; they are the most contented set of laborers to be seen anywhere. It is only by this kind of justification, justification of a profit for both sides, an advantage to both sides, that scientific management can exist.

I would like to give you one more illustration. I want to try to prove to you that even the highest class mechanic cannot possibly understand the philosophy of his work, cannot possibly understand the laws under which he has to operate. There is a man who has had a high school education, an ingenious fellow who courts variety in life, to whom it is pleasant to change from one kind of work to another. He is not a cheap man, he is rather a high grade man among the machinists of this country. The case of which I am going to tell you is one in which my friend Barth went to introduce scientific management in the works of an owner, who, at between 65 and 70 years of age, had built up his business from nothing to almost five thousand men. They had a squabble, and after they got through, Mr. Barth made the proposition, "I will take any machine that you use in your shop, and I will show you that I can double the output of that machine." A very fair machine was selected. It was a lathe on which the workman had been working about twelve years. The product of that shop is a patented machine with a good many parts, 350 men working making those parts year in and year out. Each man had ten or a dozen parts a year.

The first thing that was done was in the presence of the foreman, the superintendent and the owner of the establishment. Mr. Barth laid down the way in which all of the parts were to be machined on that machine by the workman. Then Mr. Barth, with one of his small slide rules, proceeded to analyze the machine. With the aid of this analysis, which embodies the laws of cutting metals, Mr. Barth was able to take his turn at the machine; his gain was from two and one-half times to three times the amount of work turned out by the other man. This is what can be done by science as against the old rule of thumb knowledge. That is not exaggeration; the gain is as great as that in many cases.

The effect on the workman

Almost every one says, "Why, yes, that may be a good thing for the manufacturer, but how about the workmen? You are taking all the initiative away from that workman, you are making a machine out of him; what are you doing for him? He becomes merely a part of the machine." That is the almost universal impression. Again let me try to sweep aside the fallacy of that view by an illustration. The modern surgeon without a doubt is the finest mechanic in the world. He combines the greatest manual dexterity with the greatest knowledge of implements and the greatest knowledge of the materials on which he is working. He is a true scientist, and he is a very highly skilled mechanic.

How does the surgeon teach his trade to the young men who come to the medical school? Does he say to them, "Now, young men, we belong to an older generation than you do, but the new generation is going to far outstrip anything that has been done in our generation; therefore, what we want of you is your initiative. We must have your brains, your thought, with your initiative. Of course, you know we old fellows have certain prejudices. For example, if we were going to amputate a leg, when we come down to the bone we are accustomed to take a saw, and we use it in that way and saw the bone off. But, gentlemen, do not let that fact one minute interfere with your originality, with your initiative, if you prefer an axe or a hatchet." Does the surgeon say this? He does not. He says, "You young men are going to outstrip us, but we will show you how. You shall not use a single implement in a single way until you know just which one to use, and we will tell you which one to use, and until you know how to use it, we will tell you how to use that implement, and after you have learned to use that implement our way, if you then see any defects in the implements, any defects in the method, then invent; but, invent so that you can invent upwards. Do not go inventing things which we discarded years ago."

That is just what we say to our young men in the shops. Scientific Management makes no pretense that there is any finality in it. We merely say that the collective work of thirty or forty men in this trade through eight or ten years has gathered together a large amount of data. Every man in the establishment must start that way, must start our way, then if he can show us any better way, I do not care what it is, we will make an experiment to see if it is better. It will be named after him, and he will get a prize for having improved on one of our standards. There is the way we make progress under scientific management. There is your justification for all this. It does not dwarf initiative, it makes true initiative. Most of our progress comes through our workmen, but it comes in a legitimate way.

Questions

1. To what extent, if any, is Taylor's article applicable to conditions in industry today?
2. What did Taylor feel were the factors that encouraged workers to restrict their production?
3. What personnel functions did the author feel should receive special attention in the approach to management that he recommended?
4. Taylor, in his scientific approach to management, has been criticized for having not given adequate recognition to the "human factor." What is your reaction to this criticism after having read this article?
5. How did Taylor feel that the initiative of the worker would be affected by scientific management?

3. HAVE WE LOST OUR WAY IN THE JUNGLE OF MANAGEMENT THEORY? *

Lyndall F. Urwick

Businessmen today are aware that there exists a body of knowledge about managing that can be applied to their affairs with advantage. But when they turn to the theorists for guidance, they are too often met with what Professor Harold Koontz has aptly called "a kind of confused and destructive 'jungle warfare.'" Academic writers in particular, Professor Koontz goes on to say, in their eagerness to carve out an original approach to management "seem to have become overly concerned with downrating, and sometimes misrepresenting, what anyone else has said, or thought, or done." [1]

The idea that new developments in knowledge gain in stature and significance if it can be shown that they supersede previous knowledge is as misguided as the practice of attacking the products of one's competitors. The businessman who follows this course merely undermines public confidence in the whole range of similar products, including his own. In the same way, students of management who attack the work of their predecessors merely diminish confidence in management theory generally, while doing nothing to enhance the acceptability of what they are trying to say. They are reactionaries in the "mental revolution" initiated by Frederick W. Taylor more than half-a-century ago.

Ironically enough, this situation appears to have developed, at least in part, out of the work of the late Professor Elton Mayo and his famous experiments at the Hawthorne plant of the Western Electric Company. Mayo was not a sociologist. Initially, he was trained in medicine; subsequently, he took a degree in philosophy and psychology. During World War I, he became intensely interested in the treatment of "shell shock" cases. Later, his study of members of the "extreme Left" convinced him that, in certain cases, their failure to adjust to society was psychopathological. Throughout his life his approach to problems was that of the clinician.

* From *Personnel*, Vol. 42, No. 3 (May-June, 1965), pp. 8-18. Reprinted with permission.
[1] H. Koontz, "Making Sense of Management Theory," *Harvard Business Review*, July-August, 1962.

But in proving that many of the factors that lower morale and reduce productivity in primary working groups are social in character, the Hawthorne findings trespassed on territory that the social psychologists and the sociologists regarded as their province. Thus, they detonated what was, in effect, a demarcation dispute between a trade union and a worker who had no membership card. It was conducted with all the bitterness characteristic of demarcation disputes. As F. J. Roethlisberger, one of Mayo's collaborators and himself a sociologist, later recalled:

> To have to admit that this war was waged by intellectuals and academics and by men called political and social scientists makes me still blush with shame for my "reference group." That men who called themselves scientists should understand so little the nature of scientific questions and evidence appalled me.[2]

The irony was that, in their attacks on Mayo's work, the sociologists and social psychologists directly confirmed his criticism of their "disciplines." "When one turns," Mayo once wrote, "from the successful sciences—chemistry, physics, physiology—to the unsuccessful sciences—sociology, psychology, political science—one cannot fail to be struck by the failure of the latter to communicate to students a skill that is directly usable in human situations." [3]

Nevertheless, since that date there has developed what can only be described as a take-over bid by some representatives of the so-called "behavioral sciences" to be the main, if not the sole, source of knowledge about managing. As a result, the semantics of the subject are now in a state of great confusion.

One term, for example, that has ceased to have any meaning whatsoever as a result of the attentions of the behavioral scientists is the word *organization*. Earlier students of the subject attempted to analyze the process of managing, and hence the body of knowledge about it that is called management, into definite functions or aspects. Henri Fayol, for instance, divided it into the functions of planning, organizing, directing, coordinating, and controlling.

But this did not suit the new school. They fall back on the popular use of *organization*, preceded by *an* or *the*, as a synonym for the institution, the corporation, the undertaking *as a whole*. Thus, Professor Herbert A. Simon writes:

[2] F. J. Roethlisberger, Foreword to paperback edition of E. Mayo's *The Human Problems of an Industrial Civilization* (New York: Viking Press, 1960).
[3] E. Mayo, *The Social Problems of an Industrial Civilization* (Boston, Mass.: Division of Research, Graduate School of Business Administration, Harvard University, 1945), pp. 19-20.

> An organization is a system of interrelated social behaviors of a number of persons whom we shall call the participants in the organization.[4]

To be sure, that is one thing that any human institution is. Man is a social animal. But the definition is simply destructive of all previous attempts to give more precise content and meaning to the term *organization*. All human existence, save that of Robinson Crusoe on his desert island before he met Friday, is "a system of interrelated social behavior." The definition does not define; its purpose appears to be to emphasize the term *behavior*.

If the General Motors Corporation is described as "the organization," then the phrase "the organization of the General Motors Corporation" has no meaning. Yet many leading American corporations have departments assigned to undertake "organization planning." Do these departments plan *all* the operations of the undertaking or a specific aspect of those operations? Would it be enlightening if citizens began using "the Constitution" as a synonym for the United States as a whole?

A second confusion deriving from this use of "the organization" is that people forget that the term "corporation," for which it becomes a synonym, is abstract. It represents a legal fiction. Though we can talk about "The General Motors Corporation," there is nothing in the real world we can point to and say, "That is the General Motors Corporation." We can see the plants and buildings *it* occupies, or the automobiles *it* makes, or the personnel *it* employs. But this *it* has no concrete existence. *It* is merely an agreement on a piece of paper between certain people to do thus and so. To be sure, this fictitious personality has enormous assets and tremendous power. But that power is exercised by people. And one of the dangers of personalizing an abstraction is that individuals who should be and feel responsible for their acts shelter behind the fictitious personality.

Professor Argyris, of Yale, has written two books that fall into this trap. The first, *Personality and Organization*, is full of such sentences as, "There are some basic incongruences between the growth trends of a healthy personality and the requirements of the formal organization." This is an example of the error known technically as animism—attributing human characteristics to an inanimate object. The "formal organization" as such cannot have

---

[4] J. G. March and H. A. Simon, *Organizations* (New York: John Wiley & Sons, Inc., 1958).

"requirements." It is merely a plan, a wiring diagram. The "requirements" are those of persons who, for the time being, occupy positions indicated by the plan.

The title of another book by Professor Argyris, *Integrating the Individual and the Organization,* compounds the confusion. You cannot integrate a human being with a fictitious personality. You can only integrate the ideas or actions of two or more people.

A failure of focus

Professor Argyris writes excellent good sense on such questions as how people who occupy positions of authority ought to behave toward subordinates. But, by personifying "the organization," he has taken a backward step. His failure to focus clearly one of the central problems of modern management—how to lead a bureaucracy so that it is both effective and efficient—leaves him tilting at the inevitable.

A modern business enterprise of any size is necessarily a bureaucracy. Any method of organization that aims at efficiency and economy is bound to become so in part. According to one British student of management, a bureaucracy has four main characteristics—specialization, a hierarchy of authority, a system of rules, and impersonality.[5] The problem is that individuals react unfavorably when those in authority over them rely on bureaucracy alone.

But this potential conflict between officials and the individual is nothing new. It has long been recognized that officials of the juggernaut we call the state can treat the citizen with gross injustice if his liberty as an individual is not secured. In large-scale business enterprises, where the individual lacks the safeguards provided by a separate judiciary, this can occur just as readily.

But the remedy is not to water down bureaucracy; it is to insure that those appointed to positions of authority are trained as leaders. The requirement of impersonality and the fact that few individuals occupy the same post for more than a comparatively brief period compel the student of organization to consider the structure of positions or posts *first* in order of time, and the assignment and behavior of individuals second. Like F. W. Taylor, he must begin with the analysis of work. If for no other reason, it is impossible to plan an executive development program without first having a reasonably

---

[5] R. Stewart, *The Reality of Management* (London: Heinemann Publishers, Ltd., 1963), p. 6.

clear picture of the requirements of the positions for which individuals are being developed. No man can build an institution by improvising as he goes alone. He must design it first.

To charge a business leader, for this reason, with indifference to human motives and human values is to misinterpret completely what he is trying to accomplish. And the use of "the" or "an" organization as a synonym for the undertaking as a whole facilitates this distortion. Scientific medicine began with the study of anatomy. We do not criticize the early anatomists because they knew little about the biochemistry of the nervous system. Should the Founding Fathers be stigmatized as indifferent to human values because they created the Presidency instead of thinking up a job for George Washington?

A semantic waste

A third objection to using "the organization" or "an organization" as a synonym for the institution as a whole is that it is semantically wasteful. There are half-a-dozen other terms that can be used—the enterprise, the undertaking, the corporation, and so on. Why rob the study of management of an established technical term, merely to add to an already ample list?

A second source of confusion arises from the tendency of the latter-day management theorists to use such epithets as "classical" or "traditional" to describe the work of earlier students of management. Thus, the late Professor Douglas McGregor, in his excellent book *The Human Side of Enterprise*, asserted, "The principles of organization which comprise the bulk of the literature of management could only have been derived from assumptions such as those of Theory *X*." [6] By Theory *X*, as is probably now well known, McGregor meant a concept of management that relied exclusively on detailed measurement and the exercise of authority, in order to get people to work. But just what "literature of management" he was referring to in making this generalization, I do not know.

Admittedly, as a young lead man Taylor started by trying to secure output through the use of authority. But the struggle that resulted offended his deepest beliefs, and it was precisely this failure of undiluted "authority" that started him to develop scientific management. Thus he tried the alternatives of analyzing operations

---

[6] D. McGregor, *The Human Side of Enterprise* (New York: McGraw-Hill Book Company, Inc., 1960), p. 35.

accurately, removing those obstacles to better output that were the fault of management, rewarding men adequately, and eliminating autocracy from supervision. He was particularly cautious and considerate about introducing changes. He did not believe in issuing instructions and arguing with his men. His method was to persuade one worker to try a new system, in the belief that when the other men saw him working differently and earning much more, they would also want to "have a go." Ultimately, he held, the whole shop would come around voluntarily to the new method.

When asked if less considerate managers might not imitate his methods of work analysis and use them to drive men, Taylor always maintained that this was not "scientific management" as he understood the term. In fact, he insisted that if the "mental revolution" had not taken place on *both sides*, then it was misleading to talk about any undertaking as being scientifically managed.[7]

The study of motives

Taylor also foresaw the interest in the behavioral sciences that has developed in the last 25 years. "There is another type of scientific investigation," he once wrote, "which should receive special attention, namely, the accurate study of the motives which influence men."[8] But in his time psychology was only just beginning to emerge into a modern inductive discipline. The first book on the application of psychology to industrial problems, I believe—Hugo Munsterberg's *Psychology and Industrial Efficiency*—was published in 1913, less than two years before Taylor's death.

If the literature of management were indeed, as McGregor suggested, based on the assumptions of Theory *X*, how did it happen that at least two employers who were among the earliest supporters of scientific management, both in Great Britain and in the United States, were unquestionably among the most humane and far-seeing industrialists of their day in either country—Benjamin Seebohm Rowntree and Henry Dennison? I knew both these men intimately and can affirm that their styles of leadership approximated McGregor's Theory *Y* much more closely than his Theory *X*.

---

[7] F. W. Taylor, *Scientific Management* (New York: Harper & Row, Inc., 1947), "Testimony," p. 26.
[8] *Ibid.*, "Principles," p. 119.

Rensis Likert draws the same misleading antithesis in his *New Patterns of Management*, though his book is based on a tremendous amount of research:

> The highest producing managers use all the technical resources of the classical theories of management, such as time and motion study, budgeting and financial controls. They use these resources at least as completely as do the low producing managers, but in quite different ways. . . . The low producing managers, in keeping with traditional practice, feel that the way to motivate and direct behavior is to exercise control through authority.[9]

And again, he observes:

> Those supervisors and managers whose pattern of leadership yields consistently favorable attitudes more often think of employees as "human beings" rather than just as persons to get the work done. Consistently, in study after study, the data show that treating people as "human beings" rather than as "cogs in a machine" is a variable highly related to the attitudes and motivation of the subordinate at every level in the organization.[10]

Such statements leave the impression that "scientific managment" was just a bundle of control techniques, and that "traditional practice" in the U.S. knows of nothing but authority. I find it well-nigh incredible that scientific management should be so described, when I recollect that Seebohm Rowntree's treatise, *The Human Factor in Business*, was published in 1921. In any case, it is not really true of the U.S., where Dr. Lillian Gilbreth's *Psychology of Management* appeared as far back as 1914.

Surely, what Dr. Likert is really saying is not that the "traditional theory" of scientific management ignores the importance of enlisting the enthusiasm and creativeness in every individual. It is that a full understanding of Taylor's philosophy has not yet penetrated to any but a small minority of American managers. Just as Taylor feared might happen, they have imitated some of his techniques without appreciating the basic ideas underlying them. There is nothing "new" in Likert's theory to any serious student of scientific management. But we can all be grateful to him for collecting so much evidence that much managing is still to a great extent prescientific.

A conspicuous example of the tendency to make "semantic hay" of the work of previous writers is to be found in Chapters 1 and 2 of *Organizations*, by James G. March and Herbert A. Simon. This is to

---

[9] R. Likert, *New Patterns of Management* (New York: McGraw-Hill Book Company, Inc., 1961), p. 99.
[10] *Ibid.*, p. 101.

be regretted, since the rest of the book contains much useful analysis and summation of the work of the behavioral science school.

Two or one and the same?

The text of these two chapters is a curious jumble. The authors single out two strands—as a matter of fact there were a great many more than two—in the earlier study of management. The two on which they concentrate are time study, or what they call, "physiological organization theory," and something that they label "administrative management theory." But, while distinguishing between them, they seem anxious at the same time to leave readers with the impression that they may be regarded as one. "They share, particularly in their more formal versions, a preoccupation with the simpler neurophysiological properties of humans and the simpler kinds of tasks that are handled in organizations." [11]

However, they add, "the administrative management theorists tended to carry their analysis, at least at the level of wisdom and insight, beyond the boundaries set by their formal models." It may be presumed that they did. One of the exponents of "administrative management theory" cited by March and Simon, for instance, was the late Lord Haldane, whom Haig described as "the greatest Secretary of State for War England ever had." Certainly, it may be questioned whether the complete reorganization of the British Army and its preparation for war could have been carried through on the basis of "a preoccupation with the simpler neuro-physiological properties of humans and the simpler kinds of tasks that are handled in organizations."

Then again, we learn from March and Simon that "Taylor and his associates studied primarily the use of men as adjuncts to machines in the performance of routine productive tasks." [12] Moreover, they assert that, in administrative management theory, there is "a tendency to view the employee as an inert instrument performing the tasks assigned to him" and "as a given rather than a variable in the system. The grand theories of organizational structure have largely ignored factors associated with individual behavior and particularly its motivational bases." [13]

---

[11] March and Simon, *op. cit.*, p. 22.
[12] *Ibid.*, p. 13.
[13] *Ibid.*, p. 29.

Out of these statements is constructed a phrase—"the machine-model of human behavior"—that is used as a catch-all throughout the book to explain almost any circumstance in which the use of bureaucratic rules, unaccompanied by humane leadership, produces negative reactions. Of course, if men are treated like machines they will react, not like machines, but like mules: They will kick. But this has nothing to do with Taylor or his ideas. In one of his earliest papers on management Taylor said quite categorically, "No system of management, however good, should be applied in a wooden way."

Nor is the suggestion that Taylor studied men "as adjuncts to machines" even factually correct. Some of his best-known studies, e.g., the yard labor at Bethlehem Steel or the bicycle-ball sorters, were not on machine processes. Frank B. Gilbreth, who was for some years one of his most enthusiastic admirers and collaborators, was a construction man. Nearly all his early studies were on hand processes, such as bricklaying. Taylor quoted them frequently. Actually, Taylor wrote at least as much about foremen and managers and their jobs as he did about workers and their jobs.

A whale of a conscience

Apparently, what Professors March and Simon are saying is that Taylor was wrong in *starting* with the analysis of work. But Taylor had a remarkably acute sense of scientific integrity. His biographer, F. B. Copley, described him as possessing "the *whale* of a New England conscience." He started with the element in the problem he could measure accurately, namely, the work. And to see that work could be analyzed and measured accurately was in itself a tremendous step forward.

In dealing with people Taylor recognized that the techniques of psychology as developed up to his time were not a reliable basis for theorizing about social behavior. Hence, he relied on his own personal sympathy and his extremely sensitive social conscience. Despite his original ideas there was never a strike in any plant where he himself was in charge of the reorganization. So his assumptions about human behavior cannot have been so glaringly wide of the mark.

Elsewhere, Professor Simon has written, "We have a rapidly expanding body of empirical knowledge about how decisions are actually made in organizations, including in recent years successful attempts to simulate some kinds of middle management decision making quite accurately with digital computers." [14]   In the light of his enthusiasm for the computer, who is Professor Simon to criticize other writers for adopting a "machine-model of human behavior"?

The computer is a machine and, like any other machine, it can do only what it is programed to do by an individual human being. It cannot be programed to include any of the factors that matter most in decisions, even at the middle management level. Creativity, compassion, sympathy—these are the qualities that really determine whether decisions will be accepted happily and constructively by those on whose *positive* collaboration managers depend to get things done. For decisions must not only be right; they must be seen to be right.

Indeed, the phrase "decision making" itself raises a number of problems. Professor Simon opened a series of lectures at New York University in 1960 by saying, "I shall find it convenient to take mild liberties with the English language by using 'decision making' as though it were synonymous with managing." [15]   He then went on to explain that he regarded all the processes leading up to and emanating from a decision as part of decision making.

Nondefining definition

But, like describing an organization as a "system of social behaviors," this definition, too, does not define. Almost all human activities consist of processes leading up to or emanating from decisions. If I take my bath or eat my breakfast I am implementing a decision. Thus, there is no particular activity that this definition distinguishes as managing.

Reversing Simon's sentence to make it operational, we get: "Managers spend all their time making decisions; when they are not making decisions, they are not managing." But whether this is so or not, we do not know. We need far more information than we presently have as to how, in fact, managers do spend their time. On the whole, managers have displayed a virginal modesty in making this part of the anatomy of management available to public scrutiny. Meanwhile, the phrase "decision making" is, of course, flattering to managers. As the late Mary Parker Follett observed in 1926, "I have

---

[14] *Toward a Unified Theory of Management*, ed. H. Koontz (New York: McGraw-Hill Book Company, Inc., 1964), p. 103.

[15] H. A. Simon, *The New Science of Management Decision* (New York: Harper & Row, Inc., 1960), p. 1.

seen an executive look a little self-important over a decision he had made, when that decision had really come to him ready-made. An executive decision is a moment in a process." [16]

But the central issue is whether research into management can start effectively with studies of human behavior at large. Surely, if we wish to study human behavior in the context of a particular activity we must start with the purpose of that activity, just as Taylor started by analyzing and measuring work, or as the students of organization started, by analyzing functions.

Behind this difficulty of where to start lies a wider difficulty as to the nature and purpose of science itself. Professors March and Simon write of their predecessors: "The great bulk of this wisdom and lore has never been subjected to the rigorous scrutiny of scientific method. The literature contains many assertions, but little evidence to determine—by the usual scientific standards of public testability and reproducibility—whether these assertions really hold up in the world of fact." [17] It's worth examining for a moment the two assumptions in this statement.

First, it assumes that it is desirable that the whole truth about human behavior in organizational situations should be published. Personally, I am extremely dubious about this. In many instances, ordinary decency and kindliness would suggest that a veil of obscurity, or at least of anonymity, be drawn over individual failures and insufficiencies. The fictitious personality, the corporation, is theoretically immortal, or hopes to be. But an unkind public does not always distinguish between mistakes that have been discovered and corrected and current performance; then, the "image" of the corporation suffers. Considerations such as these explain the extreme reluctance of managers to expose the internal working of their corporations or their own activities to academic investigators who may well lack the practical experience in such matters to appreciate the possible repercussions of public discussion of their affairs.

Second, the statement assumes that our present knowledge of social psychology and its techniques of investigation admit group situations to be reproduced with accuracy. This also is questionable. Even with an identical group performing an identical activity on Monday and Tuesday, the investigator cannot possibly be sure that it

[16] M. P. Follett, "The Illusion of Final Authority," in *Freedom and Coordination* (London: Sir Isaac Pitman & Sons, Ltd., 1949), p. 1. Lecture originally given to the Taylor Society, 1926.
[17] March and Simon, *op. cit.*, p. 5.

is identical or that he is aware of *all* the factors influencing performance. The mere fact that the group is performing an identical activity argues a "practice" effect. Moreover, one member of the group may have had a row with his wife on Monday night. A second may be basking in the glow of a lucky game of poker. A third may have waited in the cold for a bus and has caught a cold.

Henri le Chatelier, the physicist who introduced the work of Frederick Taylor to France, once said that scientific method consists of six steps—definition, analysis, measurement, hypothesis, experiment, and proof, *in that order*. As far as I can see the claims of some representatives of the behavioral sciences to a lion's share of the contribution to our knowledge of managing and their anxiety to embark on step three—measurement—have served only to confuse the progress made in the first four decades of this century in the first two steps, definition and analysis. In particular, they have made the terminology of the subject extremely disorderly.

Aside from being quite unnecessary, this is an embarrassment to practicing managers, who have to use such knowledge as we possess here and now. In fact, it merely endorses Mayo's castigation of such sciences as "unsuccessful," on the grounds of their failure to convey skills that are "directly usable in human situations."

Questions

1. In what way does the author feel that the term "organization" is the subject of misuse?
2. What term does he feel should be used instead of "the organizations"? Do you agree or disagree with his argument?
3. What are Colonel Urwick's reactions to the position taken by the late Dr. McGregor in his concept of "Theory X"? (Theory X is discussed by McGregor in Article No. 15 of Chapter 3.)
4. What is the author's reaction to the views expressed by some of the current researchers in the field of behavioral sciences?

4. A NEW ERA IN PERSONNEL RELATIONS *

Chris Argyris

Forty-five years ago the whole idea of personnel administration in American industry was viewed as nonsense by the vast majority of employers. Their attitudes in the years just before World War I have been characterized as "employment by crook of the finger" and "dictatorship and autocratic paternalism."

It was into this atmosphere that the pioneers of personnel administration moved. And they moved in, as Thomas Spates puts it in his book *Human Values Where People Work*, with a determination to eliminate the "brutal disregard for human values at the workplace" and to substitute "a code of civilized treatment of employees."

The second era of personnel administration began just before World War II. This second generation of personnel administrators seemed to be concerned less with new ideas and more with defending the gains of the pioneers and expanding them wherever possible. Services were expanded to make up for, or even to push into the background, those negative working conditions that could not be alleviated. Cafeterias, recreational programs, clubs and parties became hallmarks of "good human relations."

Management kept needling personnel people because their function seemed to be no more than trying to keep people happy. And personnel managers sought to defend themselves by trying to make personnel activities more scientific and thus more respectable.

The end result of the first- and second-era personnel programs has been to satisfy the employees' basic needs for food, shelter, clothing, as well as their needs for security. But now that satisfaction of these needs is, to a degree, guaranteed, the old personnel policies no longer tend to motivate productive behavior.

Now a new, third era in personnel relations is about to begin. And despite the gains of the last 45 years, it will bring an urgently needed change.

* Reprinted by special permission from *Dun's Review & Modern Industry*, June 1962. Copyright 1965, Dun & Bradstreet Publications Corp.

Personnel administration, in its new form, seeks to meet needs that have been called "self-realizing." Simply put, these needs motivate human beings to strive to enlarge and express their full potentialities, and this process of striving is in itself rewarding. As self-realization increases, responsibility, commitment, competence and a respect for oneself and others also tend to increase. And these qualities are important sources of productiveness and effective leadership.

Tackling this new job promises to be one of the toughest tasks that personnel administrators have taken on. For there seems to be a basic incongruence between the nature of formal organizations like corporations and managerial controls on the one hand and mature individuals on the other. Corporations require employees, especially at the lower levels, to be dependent upon others and submissive to them. These requirements are antithetical to mature human beings who aspire to be relatively independent, self-responsible and self-controlled.

Formal organization and managerial controls by their very nature assume that human beings, out of a sense of loyalty, will act rationally, and that they will accept, for a fair set of rewards, a world in which they are required to be dependent and subordinate. But research suggests that such an assumption runs counter to the nature of mature individuals. In an attempt to live within the organization and produce what is expected of them, they either tend to fight the organization or to accept it by becoming apathetic and noninvolved.

Management can readily recognize the "fight" reaction. But it has a lot more difficulty discerning acceptance of the organization by the employee when it is based on apathy and noninvolvement. Yet it often happens that after years of apathy and indifference, the individual's capacity for productive, creative work decreases. He no longer even looks for challenging work.

This, of course, often leads management heads to believe that an employee is lazy and not highly responsible. But the fact is that management may well create many of the conditions that cause these problems.

Personnel men are supposed to make top management aware of the causes of these problems and to help solve the problems. But what have the personnel men contributed? The fair answer is: not very much.

Fields of failure

Their present communications programs may tend to increase
employee mistrust of management and increase executive isolation.
Their human relations programs, emphasizing the equality of everyone, may help some management men to use the authority they have
to hide their incompetence. Their programs of employee participation
may, in fact, frustrate employees. Their programs designed to increase the employee's identification with his job and with his company may actually decrease his sense of identification.

Programs that attempt to teach basic economics and the importance of cost-cutting and profit making may discourage, frustrate
and indeed insult some employees. Leadership training (of the
traditional classroom variety) tends to increase the foreman's internal tension, his feeling of hostility toward management and his
sense of separateness from the organization. Many management
performance reviews, at best, tend to create dependence of the
subordinate upon the superior; at worst they breed an incipient conformity. Coaching, as typically carried out by many top managements, tends to block self-development and increase "image development." Executive-development programs can intensify the illness
of a corporation by providing a rationalization for the organization
not to face its own problems.

In short, many personnel programs simply reinforce the causes
of a company's personnel problems and increase an employee's feelings of dependence and conformity. At best, personnel programs
protect employees from the tensions of self-realization and responsibility while hopefully "making him happy."

The painstaking statistical research conducted by many personnel men may merely prolong the ineffectiveness of these programs. For one consequence of this research is to eliminate the
bias of the human element.

One company's personnel researcher, for instance, not long ago
sought to improve his company's rating system by evading the fact
that different supervisors used different "internal scales" to measure
people. The personnel man suggested a quartile system by which the
supervisor had to place 25% of his group in each quartile. Statistically, this makes sense, for it minimizes the differences among
supervisors. But it also protects the supervisor from having to come
to grip with their biases.

Wage and salary programs tend to reward the average, penalize the outstanding (by not rewarding him adequately) and support the less competent. Selection programs may tend to select accurately for the first job but are not designed to say much about an employee's long-range potential for commitment, responsibility and contribution to organization growth. Top-management training of the classroom variety tends to skirt these human problems and protect the executives from having to face them. All these conditions build up the internal forces that have made personnel administration a defensive operation. Programs are continually developed that are safe and do not rock the boat.

Indeed, some personnel programs that have been cited as examples of "the finest" by such organizations as the American Management Association and the National Industrial Conference Board have this defensiveness built into them. Not long ago the top executives of one large corporation whose personnel program had received just such accolades made a thorough examination of their program, and reached a disturbing conclusion. They knew that the major characteristics of their organization's future were change and growth. Yet they found that their personnel policies were geared to maintaining the status quo. They began to realize that their personnel policies had done precious little to prepare the employees to participate fully in the organization's growth. Nor were their first- and middle-line management any better prepared. The corporation clearly was likely to explode with personnel problems.

Unprepared for change

Another of America's industrial giants recently found that its employees "walked" in the direction of an extremely militant union, while at the same time the very same employees reported that they were receiving excellent wages and benefits. An analysis suggested one of the major problems was the company's personnel philosophy of "taking care of the workers" and protecting them from stresses, strains and pressures.

Finally, it became apparent that the company could not survive unless it made some dramatic changes, including deep cuts in costs. Neither employees nor management were prepared for such actions, and both groups found it difficult to adapt to the new stress. Management defended itself by being unexpectedly severe and harsh.

The employees responded similarly. Again, it makes clear that protective and defensive personnel policies are not enough, for they will not support growth and development.

And that is why a new era in personnel administration is beginning. We are learning that man is free when he is responsible. Making people "happy" or "secure" will no longer be the main philosophy.

Human productivity and growth on the one hand and the idea of pleasure and happiness on the other are not necessarily correlated. To emphasize happiness and pleasure is to overlook the enormous significance of tension for self-realization. And to meet this need I believe that human relations policies will need to be significantly shifted.

The policies of the future will have to emphasize internal commitment, self-responsibility and productiveness. The policy makers must assume that individuals are but one part of the organization and that their importance varies under different conditions. They must also realize that no one can develop anyone else except himself; that if the door to development is locked, it is locked from the inside. Finally, they must assume that the objective of executive development is to help the executive become more aware and accepting of himself and others.

Healthy human beings realize that the objectives for which corporations are created require cooperative effort. They are willing to give of themselves in order to maintain the organization, so as to achieve its (and their) goals.

The over-all objective of the personnel program of the future will be to enhance the "human" effectiveness of the organization so that it can solve any problem over which it has control.

The first step in this process is to diagnose the "human health" of the organization. We are learning that the diagnosis must go beyond the morale survey with its compilation of columns of figures representing how employees feel and what their attitudes are toward various aspects of the organization. The diagnostic methods, if they are to be of help, must capture the complexity of the organization's makeup, indicate the major and the minor factors and at least hypothesize the probable causal connections among them. The diagnostic and research skills involved are complex and difficult, but they can be learned. And they represent one area in which personnel teams will have to be competent.

Another kind of competence that will be needed is the ability to help an organization unfreeze itself and to grow and improve. Implicit in this are the security, confidence and courage to experiment with new ideas.

Flexibility, endurance and a high degree of cohesiveness are necessary if the organization is to cope with the confusion, tension, pressure and pain that usually accompany organizational changes. And by cohesiveness, I do not mean that people must like one another. The deepest and most lasting cohesiveness among individuals is based upon human relationships that permit and encourage each individual to express and realize his potential. Cohesiveness is based more on shared responsibilities than on the compulsion to like and be liked.

Not for outsiders

These factors cannot be manufactured, delegated, ordered, bought or issued to the organization. They must be developed from within. For an outside consultant usually "operates" on a corporation. Through his own skill and techniques he is able to get the company to improve itself without the necessity for top management to understand fully or control the processes of organizational change. And so the company is left increasingly dependent upon the consultant for further change.

Effective organizational development cannot be evaluated or justified by determining whether the desired goal has been reached. The processes by which a change is made must also increase the organization's effectiveness to solve problems through its own internal commitment and administrative competence.

Questions

1. What does the author feel will be the major area of emphasis in the "new era"? How may this emphasis affect personnel policies and practices?
2. What conflict does he feel exists between the requirements of an organization and the behavior of the personnel within it?
3. In what ways does Argyris feel that present day communication programs may tend to increase employee mistrust of management practices? Do you agree or disagree with his position?
4. How does the author feel that cooperative effort and cohesiveness within an organization can best be achieved?
5. To what extent do you agree and/or disagree with this article?

5. PERSONNEL MANAGEMENT— ITS ASSETS AND LIABILITIES *

Peter F. Drucker

THE LIMITATIONS OF PERSONNEL ADMINISTRATION ARE NOT HARD TO PERCEIVE. THEY ARE INDEED ADMITTED BY MOST OF THE PEOPLE IN THE FIELD—AT LEAST BY IMPLICATION.

The constant worry of all Personnel Administrators is their inability to prove that they make any contribution to the enterprise. Their preoccupation is with the search for a "gimmick" that will impress their management associates. Their constant complaint is that they lack status. For Personnel Administration (using the term in its common usage) is largely a collection of incidental techniques without much internal cohesion. Some wit once said maliciously that it puts together and calls "personnel management" all those things that do not deal with the work of people and that are not management.

There is, unfortunately, some justice to the gibe. As Personnel Administration conceives the job of managing worker and work, it is partly a file clerk's job, partly a housekeeping job, partly a social worker's job, and partly "fire-fighting" to head off union trouble or to settle it. The things the Personnel Administrator is typically responsibile for—safety and pension plans, the suggestion system, the employment office and union grievances—are necessary chores. They are mostly unpleasant chores. I doubt, though, that they should be put together in one department. For they are a hodgepodge, as becomes apparent with one look at the organization chart of the typical Personnel Department or at the table of contents of the typical textbook on Personnel Management. The chores are not one function by kinship of skills required to carry the activities. Nor are they one function by being linked together in the work process, by forming together a distinct stage in the work of the manager or in the process of the business.

* Part V of the Practice of Management. Reprinted by permission from the *Dun's Review and Modern Industry*, Vol. 63, No. 2314 (June, 1954), pp. 42-43, 80-94. Copyright, 1954, Dun & Bradstreet Publications Corp.

None of these activities is itself of such a nature or importance as to call for more than moderate capacity in its management. None by itself has major impact upon the business. By putting a great many of these activities together in one function we do not thereby obtain a major function entitled to representation in top management or requiring the services of a top executive for its management. For it is quality (the kind of work and its impact . . .) that alone makes a major function or defines the orbit of a senior executive.

Even if these things are best done by being put together into one department, they do not add up to managing people. They truly have little to do with the job to be done in this area. That the Personnel Department as a rule stays away from the management of the enterprise's most important human resource, managers, has been mentioned (DUN'S REVIEW AND MODERN INDUSTRY, May, 1954, page 41). It also studiously avoids, as a rule, the two most important areas in the management of workers: the organization of the work, and the organization of people to do the work. It accepts both as it finds them. It usually does not concern itself with the motivations, incentives, and satisfactions offered, except to put into orderly symmetry whatever system is in use. Its main concern is with things outside and next to the job. That these side lines are sometimes called "treating the worker as an individual" is a grim joke; for where else in the work-relationship should the worker be treated as an individual if not in his work and job, which Personnel Departments tend to exclude from their purview?

THE REASON FOR THE STERILITY OF PERSONNEL ADMINISTRATION LIES IN ITS THREE BASIC MISCONCEPTIONS.

First, Personnel Administration assumes that people do not want to work. As Douglas McGregor ("Line Management's Responsibility for Human Relations") points out, it views "work as a kind of punishment that people must undergo in order to get satisfaction elsewhere." And it tends therefore to put emphasis on satisfactions outside and beyond the work. Secondly, Personnel Administration looks upon the management of worker and work as the job of an expert specialist rather than as part of the manager's job. It is the classical example of a "staff" department and of the mischief and confusion the "staff" concept causes. To be sure, there is constant talk in all personnel departments of the need to educate operating managers in managing people. But 90 per cent of the budget, manpower, and efforts of every personnel department I know is devoted to "personnel programs," thought up, established, and operated by the personnel department.

This means in effect, however, either that Personnel Administration has to usurp the functions and responsibilities of the operating managers, or that operating managers, in self-defense, have to confine Personnel Administration to the management of the incidental chores; that is, to managing those things that are not essential to the management of worker and work. It is not surprising that the latter has been the all but universal trend.

Finally, Personnel Administration tends to be "firefighting." It tends to see "personnel" as concerned with "problems" and "headaches" that threaten the otherwise smooth and unruffled course of production. It was born with this tendency. The unionization drives of the 1930's have made it dominant. It is not too much to say that many Personnel Administrators . . . have a stake in "trouble."

But worker and work simply cannot be managed if "trouble" is the focus. It is not even enough to make "fire prevention" rather than "fire-fighting" the focus. Managing worker and work must focus on the positive and must build on underlying strength and harmony.

HUMAN RELATIONS, THE SECOND PREVAILING CONCEPT OF THE MANAGEMENT OF WORKER AND WORK, STARTS OUT WITH THE RIGHT BASIC CONCEPTS: PEOPLE WANT TO WORK: AND MANAGING PEOPLE IS THE MANAGER'S JOB, NOT THAT OF A SPECIALIST.

It is, therefore, not just a collection of unrelated activities. It also rests on a profound insight, which is summarized in the expression "one cannot hire a hand."

Human Relations does, therefore, recognize that the human resource is a specific resource. It emphasized this against mechanistic concepts of the human being, against the belief in the "slot-machine man" who responds only and automatically to monetary stimulus. It made American management aware of the fact that the human resource requires a definite attitude, definite methods, and definite concern, which is a tremendous contribution. Human Relations, when first developed, was one of the great liberating forces, knocking off blinders management had been wearing for a century, blinders that completely prevented it from seeing reality. That Human Relations is today stressed in Europe and Latin America as one of the most important things to be learned from the United States is fully justified.

Yet Human Relations is, at least in the form in which it exists thus far, primarily a negative contribution. It freed management from the domination of viciously wrong ideas, but it did not give management new positive concepts that can be applied. It tells us what the human being is not and, from that, it tells us how not to manage. It does not tell us how to manage.

One reason is the belief in "spontaneous motivation." "Remove fear," the Human Relations people seem to say, "and people will work." This was a tremendous contribution at a time when management still felt that people could be motivated only through fear. Even more important was the implied attack on the assumption that men do not want to work. However, absence of wrong motivation, we have learned, is not enough. And on positive motivations Human Relations offers little but generalities.

Human Relations also lacks an adequate focus on work. Yet positive motivations must have their center in work and job, and especially in the relationship between a man and his work. Human Relations puts all the stress on interpersonal relations and on the "informal group." Its starting point was in individual psychology, rather than in an analysis of worker and work. As a result, it assumes that it is immaterial what kind of work a man does since it is only his relation to his fellow men that determines his attitude, his behavior, and his effectiveness.

Its favorite saying, that "the happy worker is an efficient and a productive worker," though a neat epigram, is at best a half-truth. The business of the enterprise is not the creation of happiness, but the selling and making of shoes. Moreover, the worker cannot be happy in the abstract.

Despite its emphasis on the social nature of man, Human Relations refuses to accept the fact that organized groups are not just the extension of individuals, but have their own relationships, have a real and healthy problem of power, have conflicts which are not conflicts of personalities but objective conflicts of vision and interests—all of which are of a political sphere. This shows in the almost panicky fear of the labor union that runs through the entire work of the original Human Relations school at Harvard University.

Human Relations, moreover, lacks any awareness of the economic dimension of the problem.

As a result there is a tendency for Human Relations to degenerate into mere slogans, which become an alibi for having no management policy in respect to the human organization. Worse still, because

Human Relations started out from the attempt to "adjust the maladjusted" individual to the "reality" (which is always assumed to be rational and real) there is a strong manipulative tendency in the whole concept. With it there is the serious danger of Human Relations degenerating into a new Freudian paternalism, into a mere tool for justifying management's action, into a device to "sell" whatever management is doing.

It is no accident that there is so much talk in Human Relations about "giving workers a sense of responsibility" and so very little about their responsibility; so much emphasis on their "feeling of importance" and so little on making them and their work important. Whenever we start out with the assumption that the individual has to be "adjusted," we start out on a search for controlling, manipulating, "selling" him. And we deny by implication that there may be anything in our own actions that needs adjustment.

In fact, the very popularity of Human Relations in this country today may reflect above all the ease with which it can be mistaken for a soothing sirup for fractious children, and misused to explain away resistance to management and to its policies as "irrational" and "emotional."

This does not mean that we have to discard Human Relations. On the contrary, its insights are a major foundation in managing the human organization. But it is not the building. Really, it is only one of the foundations. The building has still to be built. It will rest on more than Human Relations. It will also have to rise well above it. I say this with full respect for the achievement of the Human-Relations pioneers (indeed, I am sometimes counted one of their disciples). But though their achievement is great, it is not adequate, certainly not if left standing by itself.

Let us for the moment, then, have done with both Personnel Administration and Human Relations.

The concept that actually underlies the management of worker and work in American industry is Scientific Management. The most effective, often the only effective, "personnel manager" (at least in manufacturing industry) is usually the industrial engineer.

Scientific Management focuses on the work. Its core is the organized study of work, the analysis of work into its simplest elements and the systematic improvement of the worker's performance of every one of these elements of his work. Scientific Management, therefore, does focus on the *performance* of work. It has both basic concepts and easily applicable tools and techniques. And it has no difficulty proving the contribution it makes; its results in the form of higher output are highly visible and readily measurable.

At bottom, Scientific Management is all but a systematic philosophy of worker and work. Altogether it may well be the most powerful as well as the most lasting contribution America has made to Western thought since the Federalist Papers.

Continuing Study

As long as industrial society endures we shall never lose again the insight that human work can be studied systematically, can be analyzed, can be improved by work on its elemental parts. Like all great insights, it was simplicity itself. People had worked for thousands of years. They had talked about improving work all that time. But nobody had ever thought of looking at human work systematically until Frederick W. Taylor did so around 1885. Work was completely taken for granted; and it is an axiom that one never sees what one takes for granted. Scientific Management was thus one of the great liberating, one of the great pioneering insights. Without it a real study of human beings at work would be impossible. Without it we could never, in managing worker and work, go beyond good intentions, exhortations, for the "speed-up." However dubious the actual conclusions of Scientific Management may be, its basic insight is a necessary foundation for thought and work in the field.

It is also the one American concept that has penetrated the entire world. When we started, after World War II, to give assistance to Western Europe's attempt to improve productivity, we, as well as the Western Europeans, thought that such assistance meant primarily the exportation of Scientific Management techniques.

We preached that "productivity is an attitude." We stressed the importance of mass distribution, of capital investment, of research. But what we actually did was to send over industrial engineers equipped with Scientific Management tools and imbued with its philosophy. And where the European industrialist, on the whole, turned a deaf ear to our recommendations of mass distribution, capital investment, or research, he took to Scientific Management techniques with alacrity. For . . . he has come to believe—wrongly—that Scientific Management is the essence of America's industrial achievement.

No New Advances

From 1890 to 1920, Scientific Management produced one brilliant new insight after the other and one creative new thinker after the other: Taylor, Fayol, Gantt, the Gilbreths. During the last 30 years, it has given us little but pedestrian and wearisome tomes on the techniques, if not on the gadgets, of narrower and narrower specialties. There have been oceans of paper but few, if any, new discoveries or new insight. There has been a great deal of refinement; yet the most mature and most cogent statement on Scientific Management is still the testimony Taylor gave before a Special Committee of the House of Representatives in 1912.

The reason for all this is that Scientific Management, despite all its wordly success, did not succeed in solving the problem of managing worker and work. As so often happens in the history of ideas, its insight was only half an insight. It has two blind spots, an engineering blind spot and a philosophical blind spot. What it does not see is as important as what it sees; indeed if we do not learn to see where Scientific Management has been blind, we may lose even the benefit of its genuine vision.

The first of Scientific Management's blind spots is the belief that because we must analyze work into its simplest constituent motions we must also organize it as a series of individual motions, each if possible carried out by an individual worker.

This is, in the first place, false logic. It confuses a principle of analysis with a principle of action. To take apart and to put together are different things—or else the surgeons had long since succeeded in making grow new legs or new eyes. To confuse the two is grossly unscientific. It mistakes classification for essential knowledge; and the beginning of science is the realization that classification, while absolutely necessary, does not tell us one thing about the nature of the thing classified. All it does is to enable us to know what thing we are looking at.

The belief that work is best performed as it is analyzed is also wretched engineering of the work.

The best proof of this is given by the greatest and most successful achievement resulting from the application of the concepts that underlie what we call Scientific Management: the alphabet.

Chaos into ABC

Its inventor, an anonymous clerk in a long-forgotten Semitic trading town, 3,500 years ago, will never be awarded the Gold Medal of the International Management Congress. But his analysis of the basic, simple, and standardized elements that underlay the thousands of pictograms, ideograms, logograms, syllable signs and phonetic marks of the writing of his day, and their replacement by two dozen signs capable of expressing all sounds and of conveying all words and thoughts, was straight "Scientific Management" of the very highest order. Yet, the alphabet would not only be totally useless, it would be a complete barrier to communication, were we expected to say "Cee-Ay-Tee," when we want to say "cat," just because we spell the word with these three letters.

The job of integrating letters into words is not a simple one. A moron child can usually learn the letters. But even a very bright child usually has great difficulties making the jump from "Cee-Ay-Tee" to "cat." Indeed, practically all reading difficulties of children (the biggest problem of elementary education) are problems of integrating letters into words. And yet the alphabet not only triumphed despite the difficulty of integration. It is the integration that is its triumph and its real achievement.

Be that as it may, Scientific Management's confusion between analysis of work and action in work is a complete misunderstanding of the properties of the human resource. Scientific Management purports to organize human work. But it assumes, without any attempt to test or to verify the assumption, that the human being is something of a machine tool.

It is perfectly true that we have to analyze the work into its constituent motions. It is perfectly true that we can best improve work by improving the way the individual motions are being performed. But it is simply not true that the closer the work comes to confining itself to the individual motion the better the human being will perform it. This is not even true of a machine tool. To assert it of human beings is simply nonsense. It is complete disregard for their actual properties. Individual motions the human being does very poorly; viewed as a machine tool he is indeed very badly designed. But, whether Scientific Management likes it or not, the fact is that man was not designed as a self-propelled and procreative machine tool.

Look Objectively

Let us leave aside all such considerations as man's will, his personality, emotions, appetites, and soul. Let us view man only as a productive resource, and only in engineering terms of input and output. We have no choice but to accept the fact that man's specific contribution is always to perform many motions, to integrate, to control, to judge. The individual motions must indeed be analyzed, studied, and improved. But the human resource will only be utilized productively if *a job* is being formed out of the motions, a job that puts to work man's specific qualities.

The second blind spot of Scientific Management is the "divorce of planning from doing"—one of its cardinal tenets.

Again a sound analytical principle is being mistaken for a principle of action. But, in addition, the "divorce of planning from doing" reflects a very dubious and very dangerous philosophical concept of an "elite" that has a monopoly on esoteric knowledge and thereby manipulates the unwashed peasantry.

To have discovered that "planning" is different from "doing" was one of Taylor's most valuable insights. To emphasize that the work will become the easier, the more effective, and the more productive the more we plan it before we do it, may well have been his greatest contribution to America's industrial rise. On it rests the entire structure of modern management. That we are able today to speak seriously and with meaning of "management by objectives" is a direct result of Taylor's discovery of planning as a separate part of the job, and of his emphasis on its importance. Without it management would always remain based on "hunch" and "folk wisdom," and could not be analyzed, described, learned, or taught.

Only One Job

But it does not follow from the separation of "planning" and "doing" in the analysis of work that the "planner" and the "doer" should be two different people. It does not follow, as Scientific Management teaches, that the industrial world should be divided into two classes of people: first, the few who decide what is to be done, design the job, set the pace, rhythm and motions, order others what to do and how to do it; and, two, the many who do what and as they are being told.

"Planning" and "doing" are separate *parts* of the job; they are not separate jobs. There is no work that can be performed effectively unless it contains elements of both. One cannot "plan" exclusively all the time. There must be at least a trace of "doing" in one's job. Otherwise, one dreams rather than performs. One cannot, above all, "do" exclusively. Without a trace of "planning" for his job, the worker does not have the control he needs even for the most mechanical and repetitive routine chore.

The "divorce of planning from doing" deprives us of the full benefit of the insights of Scientific Management. It sharply cuts down the yield to be obtained from the analysis of work, and especially the yield to be obtained from planning. There is sufficient evidence in industry to show that productivity greatly increases when the workers are given responsibility for planning their work. The same increase in productivity (not to mention the increase in worker attitude and pride) has been obtained wherever we have combined the "divorce of planning from doing" with the "marriage of planner to doer."

The two blind spots of Scientific Management together explain why its application . . . increases the worker's resistance to change.

Because he is being taught individual motions rather than given a job, his ability to unlearn is stifled rather than developed. He acquires experience and habit rather than knowledge and understanding. Because the worker is supposed to "do" rather than to know, let alone to "plan," every change represents the threat of the incomprehensible and therefore threatens his psychological security.

Short Term Outlook

It is an old criticism of Scientific Management that it can set up a job so as to get the most output per hour, but perhaps not so as to get the most output over 500 hours. It may be a much more serious and much better-founded criticism that it may know how to organize the present job for maximum output, but only be seriously impairing output in the worker's next job. Of course, if the job were considered unchangeable this would not matter.

But we know that change is inevitable and that it is, indeed, a major function of the enterprise to bring it about. We also know that the next few decades will bring tremendous changes—and nowhere more than in the worker's job.

The coming of the new technology converts what may have been considered limitations on the full effectiveness of Scientific Management into crippling diseases.

The new technology simply cannot operate under Scientific Management. Any country that fails to overcome its basic misconceptions will inevitably stifle its economic development and fall behind in its productivity. In reality, the major problems of managing worker and work under the new technology will be to enable the worker to do a complete and integrated job and to do responsible "planning."

The worker under automation will no longer do the repetitive, routine chores of machine-feeding and materials-handling. Instead he will build, maintain, and control machines that do the repetitive, routine work. To do this he must be able to do many operations, must have the largest rather than the smallest content of his job, must be able to co-ordinate. This does not mean that he must be again a manually skilled worker like the worker of yore. On the contrary, every one of the operations should be analyzed by means of Scientific Management to the point where they can be done by unskilled people. But the operations must be integrated again into a job. Otherwise, the work needed under automation cannot be done.

Basic Needs

A telephone maintenance man in an automatic-dialing exchange shows what the work will be like. He is not a skilled mechanic. Every one of the things he has to do has been reduced to simple elements that can be learned in a very short time. He "goes by the book," rather than by manual skill acquired in years of experience. But his job comprises a great variety of different operations. It requires a good deal of judgment. It requires muscular and intellectual co-ordination.

Likewise, the new technology demands that the least production worker be capable of a good deal of planning. The more planning he can do, the more he can take responsibility for what he does, the more productive a worker he will be. If he just does what he is being told, he can do only harm. To maintain the equipment, to set it, and to control it, all demand responsibility and decision-making; that is, Taylor's "planning." Our problem will not be that "planning" and "doing" are not divorced enough; the problem will be that many workers of tomorrow may have to be able to do more "planning" than a good many people today are capable of.

We must preserve the fundamental insights of Scientific Management, just as we must preserve those of Human Relations. But we must go beyond the application of Scientific Management, must learn to see where it has been blind. And the coming of the new technology makes this task doubly urgent.

Is personnel management bankrupt? We can now give the answer: No, it is not bankrupt. Its liabilities do not exceed its assets. But it is certainly insolvent.

It is certainly unable to honor, with the ready cash of performance, the promises of managing worker and work it so liberally makes. Its assets are great: the fundamental insights of Human Relations, the equally fundamental insights of Scientific Management. But these assets are frozen. There is also a lot of small stuff lying around in the form of Personnel Administration techniques and gadgets. But all this does not help us too much in the big job of unfreezing the frozen assets, though it may produce enough salable merchandise to pay the petty bills. Perhaps the biggest working capital are the things we have learned not to do. But what banker ever lent on such collateral.

The facts permit, however, a more optimistic interpretation. The last 20 years were indeed years of minor refinements rather than of basic thinking. But everything points to a different picture for the next 20 years. Technological changes will force new thinking, new experimentation, new methods. And there are signs that the process has already begun.

The relationship between a man and the kind of work he does, which traditional Human-Relations thinking pushes aside as almost irrelevant, is now being studied by men close to the Human-Relations school (one significant example is *The Man on the Assembly Line*, by Walker and Guest). The problem of the organization of the job according to the properties of the human resource, rather than on the assumption of man as a badly designed machine tool, is given serious attention by men of standing (including Professor Joseph M. Juran) in Scientific Management.

These are only beginnings, to be sure. But they give grounds for real hope that, 20 years from now, we shall be able to spell out basic principles, proven policies, and tested techniques for the management of worker and work. And the right basic approaches we can by and large already spell out today.

Questions

1. What criticisms does the author make regarding the objectives being pursued by many company personnel programs?
2. Would the author's criticisms apply more closely to a company with a separate personnel department or to one without such a department?
3. Do you feel that those personnel programs that have achieved favorable acclaim are concerned primarily with overcoming "problems and headaches" that threaten production? How can such a tendency be avoided?
4. What does the author consider to be the fallacy of Taylor's proposal to:
   (a) Separate the planning functions from the doing functions?
   (b) Divide a job into its simplest activities?
5. What improvement does the human relations approach offer over the personnel administration approach? What improvements are still needed in the former approach?

6. THE FUNCTIONAL CONCEPT IN ORGANIZATION *

E. H. Anderson

The functional concept in organization has been the subject of much discussion, much difference of opinion, and apparently, much misunderstanding. It is the purpose of this paper to bring the concept into sharper focus in the light of modern conditions and modern usage. In order to do this it is necessary first to re-examine the concept as it was developed originally, second to distinguish it from other concepts in organization, and finally to examine its present application with respect to several situations and types of activity.

The functional concept became the subject of critical study after it was developed into a plan or structure of relationships, usually known as a type of organization, by F. W. Taylor and called by him functional foremanship.[1] This so-called type of organization was adopted generally as an important feature of scientific management by Gilbreth, Gantt and other exponents of the scientific management movement during the early part of the present century. An important exception, however, was Harrington Emerson, who rejected the idea as being unworkable and offered in its stead the line-staff type. From a survey of current management literature, Emerson's plan has won out both in theory and in practice. In so doing, however, the line-staff concept has been so broadened and loosened that it has come to include many features of the functional concept. As a consequence, many writers and practitioners in describing their organization as line-staff fail to recognize the mixture of concepts with the result that their plans of organization are confusing to those who are trying to make them work. As they say, "why do they call this man a staff officer when everybody knows that he makes the decisions and that it is his word that counts? It seems at times that management almost abhors the concept but proceeds nevertheless to make use of it surreptitiously.

* From *Advanced Management*, Vol. 25, No. 10 (October, 1960), pp. 16-19. Reprinted with permission.
[1] F. W. Taylor, "Shop Management." *Scientific Management* (New York: Harper & Bros. Publishers, 1957), p. 99 ff.

Functionalization

Organizing according to functions usually leads to the division of a company's total activity into groups of activities having to do with production, sales, accounting, finance and possible others. These functions known usually as major functions may then be further divided into minor functions, such as purchasing, personnel, production control, plant maintenance, advertising, sales promotion, collecting, market analysis, auditing, costing, and so on. This basis of division is distinguished from other bases, such as product, process, equipment, location, shift, and certain characteristics of the personnel, e.g., age, sex, race, nationality, etc.

When these various functions are thus recognized and their activities separated from one another, they are usually organized to constitute departments and sub-departments and placed each under the control of a supervisor or departmental manager. The supervisor or manager is then customarily given full authority over the personnel of his department and held responsible for the accomplishment of the work and the objectives of his function for the benefit of the whole enterprise. This process of dividing the work of the enterprise into functions, sub-functions, and so on, is what is known as functionalization.

Functionalization means, therefore, functional division; it does not necessarily mean or imply the functional type of relationship established for purposes of supervision and control which is characteristic of the so-called functional type of organization. Both of these functional concepts, functional division and functional control, were contained in the plan developed by Taylor and known as functional foremanship. In this plan, the duties of the first or lowest rank of supervisors were differentiated according to what were recognized as the functions of the shop. Taylor applied the principle of functionalization in dividing up and delimiting the duties and responsibilities of his foreman (more appropriately, his assistant foreman). This step, however, is only half of what Taylor did and it is only half of what constitutes the functional type of relationship in organization.

Functional control

The other half of functional foremanship is contained in the peculiar relationship of supervisors or assistant foreman (called functional foreman) to the workers, and vice versa. This relationship is one in which each supervisor to whom a certain function is assigned has some authority over all subordinates who may be involved even partially with the execution of his function and, accordingly, one in which all such subordinates may be under the authority and control of more than one of these supervisors at the same time. This idea of giving two or more supervisors, each controlling a different function of the enterprise, concurrent jurisdiction over the same persons is the peculiar feature that has characterized and distinguished the functional relationship in organization. The true functional type of organization is, therefore, one containing both functionalization, or functional division, and functional control, or control by special functional supervisors who are given authority for such a purpose over all subordinates in the organization.

Functional control consisting of supervisory authority limited to a certain function but not limited to persons and the concomitant responsibility of persons being made subordinate to two or more such supervisors at the same time has been hard to comprehend and often still harder to defend as a practical plan of organization. As is usually said, it violates the principle of unity of command, it causes a person to have to serve two masters, and it leads to conflicting loyalties and jurisdictional squabbles. Much of this criticism is indeed true especially when the plan is not thoroughly understood by all parties concerned and when it is not adequately implemented by appropriate procedures, regulations and systems. These conditions, it may be noted, are to some extent true with respect to all types of organization, but they are an absolute necessity for functional authority and control to operate successfully.[2]

Functional vs. line authority

The application of the functional relationship in supervision and control throughout all ranks in an organization, as Taylor applied it to foremanship, has been one of the most perplexing problems in organizing. The essence of the problem lies in either doing away with the line supervisors entirely or in somehow integrating functional officers, those with functional authority, with line officers, those having full authority. It is usually felt that the line officer

---

[2] E. H. Anderson and G. T. Schwenning, *The Science of Production Organization* (New York: John Wiley & Sons, Inc., 1947), pp. 133-137, and 172-181.

with full authority to act in all matters concerning his unit is necessary to cope with personal, local and emergency problems as they arise. Promptness is more to be desired than correctness in some instances, and Gordian Knots do have to be cut sometimes. This being true there is the paradox of reconciling the full authority of one officer with the yet additional authority of another, a functional officer.

The way out of this paradox is much simpler than it may at first appear. This is because there is actually little place in modern industry for "full" authority as the word implies. The authority of the line officer, even the chief executive, is limited by law, by company policy laid down by the board of directors, by resources available, by labor unions, and at all times by custom and accepted standards of conduct. Furthermore, below the level of the chief executive, as soon as the first step is taken toward dividing up the work of the enterprise into operating units, there must be initiated some method of getting the divided parts or units back together again into an integral whole. This is usually best accomplished by establishing policies, procedures, systems and other devices for co-ordinating and controlling certain aspects or elements of activities common to the operations of the various line units. Unless this is done the enterprise is a mere aggregation of distinct operating units, not a single managerial entity.

To the extent that unified control over the various departments or divisions is established by the control of the separate aspects of their activities, the managers or supervisors of such units find accordingly their spheres of activity diminished and their independence curtailed and since the chief executive, due to the limitation of his span of attention and control, cannot personally supervise all the activities necessary for co-ordination and control, his only recourse is to appoint special assistants for the task. In dividing up this work and assigning it to assistants, it is usually most logical to do so on the basis of functions, i.e., activities having each a specific purpose essential to the successful operation and control of the whole enterprise. Such responsibility and authority as may be delegated to these various supervisors of functions must be accordingly withheld or reserved from that delegated to line or operating unit managers because they now have full authority only within limits or with reservations, or, as is said, with strings tied to it. It is thus by a method of reservation, or failure to delegate line officers, that full authority is often restricted and diluted to such an extent that it may not differ greatly from functional authority. In such cases the only distinction may be that the line officer always has residual authority (that not specifically delegated to others) and full authority to act in order to adjust conflicts, eliminate confusion, and meet emergencies. The functional officer, on the other hand, may be said to have only specially delegated authority only over the proper performance of his particular function.[3] As to terminology, therefore, the term "functional organization" is a misnomer; in practice it is always a "line-functional" organization.

The staff concept

The staff officer in an organization is one who, as it is said, wields no authority but merely advises. Actually, however, advising should be the duty of every officer in an organization. No person should be exempt from the responsibility of giving advice as to his particular sphere of responsibility. Whenever there is close and effective cooperation among the officers of the organization the advisory relationships existing—often mutual—are usually too numerous and varied to be classified or represented adequately on an organization chart. They compose what is commonly known as the informal organization. The staff officer is merely one who deals only with information and advice as his major activity. The particular responsibility of the staff officer is to supply authoritative information to all those members who are entitled to receive it; his authority is the authority to get information, within his special field, from all those who may have it. He usually also has the duty of interpreting this information, transcribing it into useful form, and assisting and advising in its use.

In the line-staff organization the members holding line positions ordinarily perform all operations necessary for carrying on the main work of the enterprise and perhaps for short periods of time. The duty of the staff is to assist in such activities as assembling information, planning for the future, improving present procedures, evaluating past performance, and especially in recent years, helping establish and maintain communication with outside agencies. Such activities, though not always needed for usual day-to-day operations,

---

[3] Elmore Peterson and E. G. Plowman, *Business Organization and Management* (4th ed.; Homewood: Richard D. Irwin, Inc., 1958), p. 353.

may be indispensable in enabling the enterprise to operate with efficiency and to reach its stated objectives. In a small organization or simple operation, these activities are usually performed by the chief executive himself, but in a large or complex operation they must be delegated to others, and when so, they should be formally recognized and distinguished in the organization structure.

Functional vs. staff authority

The difference between functional and staff authority is often hard to distinguish, for in some cases it is more nearly a difference in degree than a difference in kind. Functional authority, as often differentiated, is that degree of authority standing somewhere between the so-called full or command authority of the line officer and the advisory or informational authority of the staff officer. It is frequently called "instructional authority" since the relationship between supervisor and subordinate resembles more nearly that between instructor and pupil than that between master and servant.

Functional authority, in practice, is generally exercised and transmitted in the form of instructions, routines and regulations, and pertains more often to methods of procedure than to personal commands or orders for action that may be issued by line officers. The functional officer is neither an impersonal advisor nor a personal boss; he takes motivation and discipline to some extent for granted. In Taylor's plan, it will be remembered, motivation was taken care of by an incentive wage system and discipline was the responsibility of a special foreman.

The several types of officers are perhaps hardest to distinguish when all three are found in the same organization. In general, the functional officer is concerned with activities of a routine nature requiring a high degree of specialized skill, and exercises control over other members of the organization by obtaining their compliance with certain programs and procedures. As is often said, he is a program or procedural supervisor, or a supervisor of procedures, as distinguished from the line officer who is a supervisor of operations and operators, and the staff officer who is a supervisor of knowledge.

It is only when all routine activities and all those requiring a high degree of specialized skill are thus assigned to functional officers that the staff of any organization is left free to perform its true function. The staff was developed as a prop or an aide for the line executive to lean upon and call upon for help; to its officers could be assigned special tasks that relieved the executive of some of his burdens. These officers became known as the eyes, the ears, the brain, and sometimes the tongue of the office of the line executive. The relationship of the staff officer to his superior line executive must be, therefore, intimate and to some extent personal. The staff officer cannot become so engrossed in the performance and perfection of his specialty that he fails to perform as a member of the line team or loses sight of the over-all operation of the line unit. He should not have the specially delegated authority or responsibility for control of only a particular function such as that possessed by the functional officer.

The evolution of organization relationship

The differences in the three types of organization relationships usually come about as stages in the growth of an enterprise and its adaptation to a greater degree of specialization of functions. There should be, in fact, an evolutionary process of organizing, adapting, and re-organizing that leads to the blending of one type into another with expedient mutations and combinations.

The failure to recognize the problems and the processes of a growing and evolving organization structure in a dynamic society is one of the greatest faults of organizers. Furthermore, the tendency to describe new situations and relationships with inadequate concepts and obsolete terminology is one of the greatest obstacles to developing an organization structure that can be understood by its members. In this field, it is hard to say which is the greater obstacle to understanding, using the same words to express different concepts or using different words to mean the same thing.

Functionalism

Finally, it should be noted that functionalism, the application of the concept generally, is one of the major characteristics of modern society. Functionalism is essentially an advanced stage of the division of labor applied to social, industrial and even political organization. Our government, for example, is divided among federal, state, and local authorities; these are again divided among legislative, judicial and executive branches; and the executive branch is again divided among various departments, bureaus, and commissions, each exercising functional control in a particular field. Furthermore, a dominant characteristic of our society is its multiplicity of institutions, associations, and professions each rendering a particular service and each exercising authority within the law over the performance of its respective function. Private industry is also characterized by a vast complex of trade associations, unions, institutes and professional societies each controlling to some extent the performance of its particular function.

The democratic society of America, it may be noted, did not develop according to the principles of line organization, nor of line and staff. Unity of command, the hierarchy, full authority, the subservience of staff, etc., were adapted from military organization. Totalitarianism was anathema to both Thomas Jefferson and Adam Smith.

The concept of the functional officer began with the first Druid, medicine man or priest and it has developed until it has become the professional specialist characteristic of our present-day civilization. These professional specialists began early in our history to associate themselves for the purpose of exchanging experience, increasing their skill, and exercising some degree of control over the practice of their professions. The early guilds, secret orders, and societies formed for such purposes often played a dominant role in the control of social and economic activity. Later, schools and universities were established to train professional practitioners and to certify by appropriate degrees to their competence. More recently associations and institutes have been established to control certain aspects of professional practice, such as entrance requirements, the dissemination of knowledge, standards of performance, codes of ethics, mutual support of members, promotion of the profession, and sometimes scales of charges and remuneration.

These professional associations, through their various programs and agencies, provide modern industry with one of its most essential services. Each association specializing in its particular area or function usually has within its ranks the leaders and the super-experts in each aspect of its field. To them management can go for obtaining competent recruits, advanced technical information, and sometimes specific answers to its problems. They serve industry in the same way to some extent that the various technical corps headquarters serve the combat branches of the Army. General management, therefore, since it cannot hope to have knowledge superior to that of all the functional specialists in its own organization, is provided a source of assistance in supervising, evaluating and controlling its own experts.

By using these associations, general management can delegate authority to its functional experts with some degree of confidence since it now has an agency for evaluating the performance of their various functional responsibilities.

Thus, the functional concept begins with the concept of specialization, it proceeds upward to the lower ranks of management to become functional foremanship, then to the higher ranks as functionalization and functional control, and, finally, to society at large as functionalism. And, last but by no means least, the concept applies not only to the division of activities, but also to both their immediate and their ultimate control.

Questions

1. What criticism does the author raise concerning current use of the term line and staff organization?
2. What is the distinction between the concept of functional division and functional control?
3. What differences are there, if any, between staff authority and functional authority?
4. How does functional authority relate to specialization and to the division of work?
5. What need is there, if any, for functional authority?

7. GROUND RULES FOR USING COMMITTEES *

Cyril O'Donnell

A camel, someone has said, is a horse designed by a committee—and this is fairly typical of the current attitude toward this form of group activity. The use of committees has been criticized as a way of avoiding individual executive action, as a means of covering up managerial inadequacies, as a form of inefficient corporate "togetherness," and as a device for legitimizing procrastination and indecisiveness. What's more, every one of these accusations is justified, at least in many cases.

What is frequently overlooked, however, is that these are not valid criticisms of committees, but rather of the *misuse* of committees. For a committee that can be charged with any of these faults is not being employed as a committee should be used. Committees do have legitimate functions and, properly used, they constitute an invaluable management tool. The question is, how should they be properly used?

One common error is the confusion of committees with other kinds of joint action. Many people apply the term "committee" to any meeting of two or more people, but this definition is obviously too flexible and imprecise. It would necessarily include such diverse activities as business conferences, staff meetings, meetings of department heads, executive committee meetings, and even luncheon engagements, all of which are designed to serve quite different purposes. Conferences and typical staff meetings are primarily communication devices, utilized for economic purposes; a meeting of department heads may be called to clear up snags or overcome delays in some area that concerns all of them; meetings of an executive committee on which the president sits are held primarily for communication purposes. In none of these instances does a true committee exist.

The true committee

What, then, is a committee? We might define it as *two or more persons appointed by their immediate superior for the purpose of*

* From *Management Review*, Vol. 50, No. 10 (October, 1961), pp. 63-67. Reprinted with permission.

acting or advising their superior about a subject that is not clearly within the competence of any of them.

This implies that the superior does not sit in on the committee meetings; that the membership is confined to two or more of his immediate subordinates; and that the subject matter to be considered is not within the assigned duties of any individual member. Such a committee is properly considered an organizational device because it is performing an activity that, for various reasons, is not otherwise assigned. It may or may not have authority to take action, and it may be either an *ad hoc* group or a permanent committee.

Basic requirements

The proper use of committees is based on two fundamental assumptions. In the first place, it assumes that the structure of the enterprise and the association of activities in this structure conform to the principles of good organization. Experienced business managers recognize that it is not possible, even in a well-organized company, to cover all types of activities or to assign all duties to specific individuals. Even when it is possible to make such assignments, they sometimes prefer not to do so. The important point is that the committee device is not a crutch for poor organization structure—it supplements good structure.

The second basic assumption is that the enterprise has effective managers. Too often the committee device is used to supplement and buttress inefficient men. The use of a committee to support mediocrity in management is an extremely poor and even dangerous device. True, it may sometimes be necessary in the short run. But this situation should be clearly recognized, and vigorous efforts should be made to achieve good organization and employ effective managers as quickly as possible.

The one time when a committee can be legitimately used—and the only circumstance in which its use can be justified—is when it can do a job better than a single manager. This means that the net effect must be superior in the light of such factors as cost, time, decisiveness, justice, and sound judgment.

Pooled experience

There are three situations in which a committee may meet this criterion. To begin with, a committee is a sound organizational device when it is used to obtain the considered views of subordinates about a subject beyond the experience of their superior. If the superior has the breadth and depth of experience represented by the members of a committee, it is obvious that he has no need of group action. Lacking this experience, the superior might conceivably ask for the advice of individual subordinates without organizing a committee. This is quite often done—as, for example, when an executive calls on a department or division manager for his views on a particular subject. Quite often, however, such an informal approach will result in the subordinate's giving views that are narrow in conception and not fully considered. As a member of a committee, the same subordinate would frame his views with an eye to potential questions or criticism of his fellow members, and he would thus be likely to be less extreme and insular in his viewpoint.

A good example of this kind of committee is the typical policy committee, whose purpose is to formulate policy to best fit the needs of the enterprise. For example, the question in the mind of the president may be, "Do we need a policy on pricing, and, if so, how should it be framed?" If he has come up through engineering or production, the president may lack the technical knowledge and experience required to decide a matter of this type. Consequently, he would find it advisable to refer the matter to his policy committee. The members of the committee would develop their views, not only with respect to special interests of the division or function they represent, but also from the viewpoint of the welfare of the company as a whole. Their considered views would result in a consensus, which they would report in the form of a recommendation to the president. In this instance, the committee would be acting in a staff capacity, and it would probably be a standing committee.

Too much power

A second appropriate use of a committee as an organizational device is to exercise authority that is too great for any one man. The authority may be considered too great because it requires broader knowledge than any one man can be expected to have, because there is too much risk of bias or prejudice, or because it is difficult to find a person willing to exercise the authority. Good examples of such committees are investment committees, wage-and-salary committees, and boards of directors. It would be unusual to find a treasurer or a chairman of a board of directors who would be willing to take it on himself to decide how the surplus funds of a firm should be invested— and, indeed, it is likely to be too risky for the firm to rely on the judgment of any one man. Similar considerations are involved with respect to the wage-and-salary committee and the board of directors, which is a committee representing the stockholders. Committees of these types are standing committees that are delegated line authority. They make decisions on a majority basis and are true "plural executives."

Spreading responsibility

A third appropriate reason to use a committee as an organizational device is to diffuse responsibility among several executives. Very often it is undesirable to pinpoint responsibility for action on one person. A good example of this type of committee is the bonus committee, which determines the exact distribution of a fund among the qualified members or recipients. Although the total amount of a bonus fund may be expressed in terms of a percentage of profits before taxes, the method of distributing the bonus is not always directly related to the salaries of the potential recipients; distribution is frequently made on the basis of an evaluation of their contributions to the company in the past year. One manager might well find the assignment of making this evaluation very uncomfortable, and he would be the target of complaints and accusations from those who felt that they were unfairly treated. When a committee is used for this purpose, responsibility is spread among the members, and disappointed recipients are less disposed to complain; they are more likely to be satisfied that no bias or prejudice was involved in the decision of a group.

A committee of this type is likely to be an *ad hoc* group, and it normally has a staff position with respect to the chief executive officer. However, at the option of their superior, the committee may be delegated line authority to act in the situation.

Committee operation

Three important elements are necessary to make committees truly and effectively operational. First, the purpose for which the committee is being established must be distinctly defined. A written statement will help to achieve clarity, and it will eliminate the need for committee members to spend time deciding exactly what they are supposed to be doing.

Second, the authority of the committee must be clearly specified. This is an easy matter, but it should be given careful attention. The committee may perform a staff function, having authority only to investigate and recommend to their superior, or it may be given authority to make decisions. Which is the case must be clearly determined and communicated.

Finally, the chairman of a committee should at all times be appointed on the basis of his ability to conduct an efficient meeting. Efficiency requires that the chairman prepare an agenda in advance so the members will have time to study the subject and consider their views. It means that the chairman must insure that all members are heard from, encouraging the reticent and keeping the loquacious in check. When all the contributions of the members are in, he should state the consensus of the meeting to be sure that he has properly understood it, and he should see that minutes of the meeting are distributed in rough form for correction and review prior to their final distribution.

If these points are given adequate consideration, management can be sure that its committees will operate effectively.

An annual checkup

It is an efficient practice for a company to make an annual audit of its committees, evaluating each one to determine whether it can be justified as an organizational device. If any existing group fails to meet one of the three basic purposes of committees, there is a serious question of its legitimacy.

As this audit is conducted from year to year, managers will gain a thorough understanding of the appropriate use of committees. They will shy away from using committees as crutches for inadequacies, as excuses for delay, or as devices to shift decision-making responsibility, and they will learn to use them to do the jobs for which they are uniquely suited.

When this has been accomplished, the committee will have attained its proper and respected place in the organization structure of the enterprise.

Questions

1. What is a *true* committee and how does it differ from a group of individuals in an organization who may meet at intervals to discuss problems of mutual interest?
2. Under what conditions may a committee perform a task more effectively than an individual manager? less effectively?
3. Is it ever desirable to use a committee for the purpose of dividing the responsibility for making a decision among several individuals rather than to have this responsibility exercised by only one individual?
4. Can you think of any other uses of a committee in addition to those mentioned in this article?
5. How may the use of committees contribute to the more effective management of personnel?

Additional Readings for Chapter I

Allen, Louis A. "The Line-Staff Relationship," *Management Record*. Vol. 17, No. 9 (September, 1955), pp. 346-349, 374-376.

Anderson, E. H. "The Complex Problem of Organization," *Advanced Management*. Vol. 20, No. 3 (March, 1955), pp. 13-16.

Boddewyn, J. "Frederick Winslow Taylor Revisited," *The Journal of the Academy of Management*. Vol. 4, No. 2 (August, 1961), pp. 100-107.

Brown, Alvin. "Some Reflections on Organization: Truths, Half-Truths, and Delusions," *Personnel*. Vol. 31, No. 1 (July, 1954), pp. 31-42.

Buchanan, Paul C., and Walter R. Mahler. "The Personnel Executive as a Specialist in Change," *Personnel Administration*. Vol. 24, No. 5 (September-October, 1961), pp. 4-10.

Chapple, Eliot D., and Leonard R. Sayles. "The Man, the Job, and the Organization," *Personnel*. Vol. 34, No. 5 (March-April, 1958), pp. 8-20.

Davis, Ralph C. "What the Staff Function Actually Is," *Advanced Management*. Vol. 19, No. 5 (May, 1954), pp. 13-16.

Eilbert, Henry. "The Development of Personnel Management in the United States," *Business History Review*. Vol. 33, No. 3 (Autumn, 1959), pp. 345-364.

Filley, Alan C. "Common Misconceptions in Business Management," *Business Horizons*. Vol. 7, No. 3 (Fall, 1964), pp. 87-96.

Fox, William M. "Personnel Administration: Past and Present," *Personnel Administration*. Vol. 19, No. 4 (July-August, 1956), pp. 5-10.

—————————. "Fred Taylor: Foreman," *Supervisory Management*. Vol. 1, No. 12 (November, 1956), pp. 24-29.

Knudsen, Harry R. "Enter the Personnel Generalist," *Personnel*. Vol. 37, No. 2 (March-April, 1960), pp. 33-41.

Koontz, Harold. "The Management Theory Jungle," *Journal of the Academy of Management*. Vol. 4, No. 3 (December, 1961), pp. 174-188.

McFarland, Dalton E. "Dilemma of the Industrial Relations Director," *Harvard Business Review*. Vol. 32, No. 4 (July-August, 1954), pp. 123-132.

Mee, John F. "Pioneers of Management," *Advanced Management—Office Executive*. Vol. 1, No. 10 (October, 1962), pp. 26-29.

Odiorne, George S. "Gearing Personnel Plans and Programs to Organization Needs," *Personnel Administration*. Vol. 24, No. 5 (September-October, 1961), pp. 11-17.

Saltonstall, Robert. "Evaluating Personnel Administration," *Harvard Business Review*. Vol. 30, No. 6 (November-December, 1952), pp. 93-104.

Schleh, Edward C. "Make Your Staff Pay Its Way," *Harvard Business Review*. Vol. 35, No. 2 (March-April, 1957), pp. 115-122.

—————. "Securing Acceptance of the Personnel Program," *Personnel*. Vol. 33, No. 2 (September, 1956), pp. 136-140.

Seybold, John W. "How Personal Can a Personnel Policy Be?" *Personnel Journal*. Vol. 37, No. 8 (January, 1959), pp. 285-287.

Strother, George B. "Personnel Management in Theory and Practice," *Personnel*. Vol. 36, No. 3 (May-June, 1959), pp. 63-71.

Urwick, Lyndall. "The Manager's Span of Control," *Harvard Business Review*. Vol. 34, No. 3 (May-June, 1956), pp. 39-47.

—————. "The Tactics of Jungle Warfare," *Academy of Management Journal*. Vol. 6, No. 4 (December, 1963), pp. 316-329.

CHAPTER 2

Developing Human Resources

One of the primary reasons why greater attention is being given to the management of personnel is that the importance of human resources in the fulfillment of the objectives of the organization and the rising costs of these resources have become well recognized. While the success of a business organization depends upon having the proper equipment, procuring adequate raw materials, and other factors, the personnel who comprise the organization represent the most important variable in the total operation. These human resources must be selected and developed carefully if the organization is to function efficiently.

The functions relating to the development of an effective work force, including the recruiting and screening of personnel, were among the first ones to be performed by personnel departments when they came into being a few decades ago. As time passed, the personnel department assumed additional responsibilities related to the development of human resources, such as training and other functions. Thus, in most companies the department now provides for the staff supervision of these functions and cooperates with those managers and supervisors within the organization who are responsible for the personnel functions in their respective departments.

Special personnel programs were instituted in many companies in the period following World War II for the purpose of developing managers. Such programs, commonly referred to as management development programs, are concerned with the recruiting, selecting, and training of personnel who are expected to be qualified to fill vacancies as they occur in managerial jobs. While companies have always had to develop executives, the formal programs covering this function have given recognition to the fact that the careful selection and cultivation of executive personnel is as important, if not more so, as is the selection and cultivation of personnel hired to fill the jobs at lower levels in the organizational hierarchy. While the nature of these management development programs has changed in various ways, the basic objectives have remained the same.

Regardless of whether one is concerned with the developing of managers or employees, there are important factors to be considered in the development of human resources. The articles that were selected for this chapter focus on several of the personnel functions that are performed in order that the organization may obtain individuals with high potential and develop them to the maximum levels of performance.

Many of the articles found in the various business and psychological journals are devoted to the various techniques used in the selection process. While there are some articles dealing with such procedures as reference checks and physical examinations, the bulk of the literature concerns employment interviewing and testing. Many articles point out the inadequacies of most employment interviews with the result that many persons performing this function are taking a new look at their procedures and are trying different approaches.

The first article by N. A. Moyer gives a careful analysis of the nondirective interview technique as it may be used in employment interviewing. Not all of the experts would agree on using the nondirective approach, but many employment managers and interviewers have found it particularly useful in eliciting information that may not be furnished through a more structured interview. While both nondirective and structured interviews are used in employment interviewing, more has been written about the structured type of interview with the result that many persons do not obtain a thorough understanding of the nondirective approach. It is believed that this article represents one of the clearest descriptions of the approach and the rationale for it.

Employment interviewing—a face-to-face relationship that requires personal judgment and evaluation—often fails to accomplish the desired goal. Companies fail to obtain the personnel with the abilities and potentialities needed because the interviewer's own personality causes him to rely on information and clues that may be either misleading or irrelevant. McKay's article describes a phenomenon called "selective perception" that results in looking for evidence that supports one's original judgment. McKay's article tells the story of how Mr. Cheney saw qualities in a Mr. Rigtrip that were only a figment of his highly motivated imagination. While the story concerns the selection of executive personnel, the principles apply to the selection of personnel at all levels in the organization, as well as to appraisal interviews and disciplinary action.

In recent years there has been an increasing number of articles concerning the use of psychological tests in personnel selection. In many of them the authors blame the tests for the misuses of them rather than the persons who use them improperly. The article by Herbert H. Meyer and Joseph M. Bertotti represents a sound approach to the problem of testing and makes it clear that where tests are used properly a company can raise its batting average and achieve a better qualified work team.

Harold Mayfield continues the discussion of testing job applicants in his article. He provides a careful analysis of the difficulties that disadvantaged persons often encounter with typical intelligence tests and concludes by suggesting steps that employers can take to overcome the "cultural bias" in tests and to eliminate discrimination without lowering meaningful requirements.

In the last two articles in this chapter the training of employees and managers is discussed. Filley and Jesse survey the research on leadership styles in training and conclude with some practical solutions to the problem of the best approach to use in a particular training situation. The article by the late Irving Weschler is as timely as when it was written in 1955. It comes from the pen of one of those who helped to pioneer sensitivity training for managerial personnel.

8. NONDIRECTIVE INTERVIEWING: A TECHNIQUE FOR GETTING THE APPLICANT TO DO MORE OF THE TALKING *

N. A. Moyer

A nondirective interview, as its name implies, is an interview in which little or no attempt is made to direct the applicant's conversation. In most cases, when a supervisor is interviewing an applicant for a job, ordinary employment-interview techniques will provide the information he needs. But the nondirective approach can be very helpful when the interview does not seem to be yielding enough facts.

This kind of interview is conducted in a conversational manner—pretty much like any other. The chief difference is that the interviewer listens and occasionally comments in certain ways that encourage the applicant to talk freely, about any subject that interests him. The candidate may wish to talk about his scholastic background, for instance. The interviewer will listen interestedly to what he has to say, even though at the time he may be more concerned with the applicant's work experience. Some direction may be necessary to bring out all the information required or to resolve apparent inconsistencies. However, experience has shown that if an applicant is permitted to talk about matters that seem important to him, he is likely to cover most of the topics in which an interviewer is interested, except that the coverage will vary from applicant to applicant.

This approach offers several advantages. It tends to put the applicant at ease because he does not have to be alert to respond to a series of questions. It permits him to talk about the thing that interests him at the moment and, in his experience, seems appropriate. It is thus likely to reveal the applicant's true interests and emotional background. The information obtained tends to be more reliable in this type of interview because the applicant has no way of knowing what appraisal is being made of his comments.

A favorable relationship, once established, creates an atmosphere in which the applicant feels that the interviewer accepts and understands him. In such an atmosphere, a candidate is likely to say

* From *Supervisory Management*, Vol. 2, No. 7 (June, 1957), pp. 28-39. Reprinted with permission.

things to a perfect stranger that he might hesitate to say to his closest friends. Further, if he is trying to create an impression, the more he talks, the more readily contradictions will appear in his story.

Preparing for the interview

The more an interviewer knows about an applicant beforehand, the better he will be able to listen for the things he needs to know. This knowledge facilitates an accurate appraisal of the applicant's qualifications. In some instances, applicants are referred by company employees who know a great deal about the applicants. This knowledge can obviously be useful to the interviewer. In other cases, it is possible to obtain information from former employers or the schools that the applicants attended.

In addition to this outside information, the interviewer of course reviews the information on the application blank before talking to a candidate. He then formulates a plan for conducting the interview. He considers possible topics to start the applicant talking, and reviews the over-all pattern of the applicant's background, and his qualifications for the job.

Conducting the Interview

In conducting the interview, there are two basic problems:

1. To get the complete story about the applicant's background.

2. To determine what it means in terms of the job under consideration.

Starting the applicant talking

After the interviewer has introduced himself and put the applicant at ease, he tries to get him talking about his personal history. This is done as promptly as the natural course of the conversation permits. There are many ways to get the applicant started, each of which may be appropriate under given circumstances. A natural opening may spring from the reason the applicant applied or from the kind of work he is interested in doing. The latter is usually related to his previous work experience or school history, or both. Either of these subjects, therefore, provides a fertile field for conversation.

The applicant is given to understand that he is expected to say whatever he wishes without waiting for questions. In many instances, it is unnecessary to tell him this specifically, since his thoughts flow naturally from the opening remarks. If the applicant does not take the cue, the interviewer may say something like this: "We are interested, as we assume you are, in finding the job for which you are best suited. Instead of my asking you a lot of questions, why don't you tell me the story of your background and experience in your own words?"

If the applicant still hesitates, the interviewer may make an opening statement based upon information in the application; for example:

> I-1　I notice you have applied for a clerical position.
> A-1　Yes. I have a friend who is employed by the company, and he told me to apply here for a job.
> I-2　Judging from your previous employment, I thought perhaps you would be interested in teaching physical education after you finished school.
> A-2　Definitely not. I would like to do secretarial work. Playground work was all right, but I got tired of sitting around. I would like to do clerical work.

Keeping the applicant talking

Getting the applicant to tell about himself and appraising what is heard and seen is a simultaneous process from the opening to the close of the interview. For the purpose of discussion, these processes will, however, be treated separately.

Here are some suggestions that have been found useful in getting the applicant to tell his story, to give the interviewer adequate opportunity for appraisal.

1. *Give your entire attention to the applicant.* The interviewer should observe both what the applicant says and how he expresses it. He should show his interest and attention by his manner and response. Interest and attention can be reflected not just by what is said, but by facial expression, the movement and expression of the eyes, or a nod of the head. Since the interviewer cannot give his entire attention to the applicant if he writes during the interview, no notes should be made except for corrections or modifications on the application blank.

2. *Listen.* Besides being attentive and interested in what the applicant has to say, the interviewer must resist the temptation to do too much talking. Restraint is necessary if the applicant is to talk freely.

3. *Never argue.* Arguing may antagonize the applicant and spoil all chances of getting the information essential for a complete

appraisal. Nothing does more to divert or to stifle the natural expression of the applicant's thoughts.

4. *Do not interrupt or change the subject abruptly.* As we have indicated, the applicant should be permitted to talk about what seems important to him. He should not be compelled to observe a preconceived order that the interviewer has in mind. If the latter does not respond to the interests of the applicant, the interview may shift to a subject that will stop the conversation. Notice what happened in the following case:

> A-1 I'm the type that didn't want to go to school. I wanted to make money so I went to work. Besides. . . .
> I-1 Did you like school?
> A-2 Yes, but I had to go out and work.
> I-2 What course were you taking?
> A-3 Commercial.

It seems reasonable that the applicant would have answered many of the questions in the interviewer's mind if she had been permitted to tell her story in her own words. The first question was definitely an interruption of the applicant's story. Notice how this put the candidate on the defensive with a "Yes, but—" answer. From here on, the interview became nothing more than a series of questions and short answers.

Now, let's take a look at another case, where the interviewer keeps in step with the applicant:

> I-1 I notice you were employed at the ——— Corporation.
> A-1 Yes. They called me a finisher, but what I really did was inspect the work. I made good money there for the work I did. The reason I moved from ——— was on account of my husband. He was an auto mechanic and had a business of his own. Then the depression came along and his business went into bankruptcy.
> I-2 That's too bad.
> A-2 Well, after that my husband came to ——— and tried to get a state job. I got a job in a garment factory. I worked there a short time, pressing pajamas. The reason I left was on account of transportation. We moved some distance out of town.
> I-3 I suppose that would present a problem.
> A-3 Yes. I decided to start working for myself. I did a lot of home-made baking—cakes, bread, and doughnuts. I did not have a license because I did this at home. My mother-in-law helped me until her death a short time ago.

5. *Use questions sparingly.* Some proper uses of questions are:

a. *To start and keep the applicant talking*—by linking a transitional question to a statement of response, such as: "That must have made you feel proud, didn't it?" or: "That's interesting, will you tell me more?"

b. *To fill a gap in the story.* In relating his experiences, the applicant may have unintentionally omitted a point of interest that can be cleared up by an appropriate question.

c. *To obtain more specific information.* The applicant may think the interviewer is not interested in details of his story and may, therefore, treat the subject too generally. A question about some detail may encourage him to elaborate, and reveal the whole story.

d. *To check conclusions.* The applicant's statement may be rephrased in a question. Questions should be tactful and sympathetic and obviously intended to help the interviewer understand the applicant's remarks.

Generally speaking, leading questions should be avoided; so should those that can be answered by "Yes" or "No." Also, the interviewer should not embarrass the applicant by asking him "Why?" The "why" usually becomes apparent if the interviewer gets the complete story.

6. *Allow pauses in the conversation.* Pauses usually occur for one of the following reasons: applicant's lapse of memory, failure to understand the interviewer's remarks, inability to express himself, or thinking of something he wants to avoid saying. These pauses may indicate that the interviewer has failed to observe one or more of the suggestions for listening. If the interviewer recognizes the reason for the lull, he can often interject a remark to get the applicant started again. Frequently, the interviewer is tempted during a lull to start asking questions, when all that may be necessary is to "sit it out" while the applicant collects his thoughts. If the applicant is interrupted, he may fail to reveal important information.

Lengthy pauses, of course, should not be permitted, for they tend to make the applicant tense and uncomfortable. But reasonable pauses may be profitable, for they create an atmosphere of composure and unhurriedness that encourages conversation.

Following is an example of an applicant who seemed to have difficulty in expressing herself. This situation was further aggravated by the interviewer's eagerness to get her talking. The applicant had stated that she left school because her father had been ill.

I-11 Was he seriously ill?
A-11 Yes.
I-12 What was the trouble?
A-12 (No answer.)
I-13 Would you like to tell me about school? What subjects you had, and which were your best subjects? Do you remember? You're not nervous, are you? It is important that we have this information, and if you are nervous you won't be able to think. **Try to remember.**
A-13 I can't seem to remember.

I-14 Were you like this at the XYZ Company when you were interviewed?

A-14 We took tests.

I-15 What kinds of tests?

A-15 Some of them were hard.

I-16 What kinds of tests were they? Can you remember that? What
method did they use?

This is an unfortunate example of what can happen to an in-
experienced interviewer when he loses his composure and patience.
He violated virtually every principle of nondirective interviewing.
No applicant could possibly have answered the multiple questions in
I-13 and I-16. This case emphasizes the fact that the interviewer
must be composed and at ease if he expects the candidate to be at ease.

7. *Phrase responses briefly.* Responses should be brief and should
refer to the applicant's interests or feelings. It is often helpful to
repeat the last few words of the applicant's statement, make a short
comment, or ask a brief question, such as:

"Tell me more."

"That's interesting."

"What were the circumstances?"

"What happened then?"

"That must have been exciting."

". . . until 11:00 p.m.?"

"You say, 'it's not worth the effort'?"

"I see."

8. *Keep conversation at a level suited to the applicant.* This may
require the interviewer to vary his style somewhat; however, almost
everyone understands plain, simple language. This applies especially
to discussing the job, which involves not only telling the applicant
about it, but getting his reactions to it. Telling a telephone-operator
candidate that she will have to work a "divided trick," for example,
may have little meaning for her.

9. *Try to understand the applicant.* If the applicant feels he is
talking to someone who really understands him, he may volunteer
information about himself that he may never before have revealed to
anyone. To establish such confidence in the interviewer, two things
are necessary:

a. The interviewer must appreciate the applicant's *underlying feelings*
about the situation being discussed, as well as the content of the
applicant's remarks. The interviewer is successful only if he can
place himself sympathetically in the candidate's role.

b. The interviewer must demonstrate this understanding so that it can
be recognized by the applicant. He must respond by his words and

manner to what the applicant *feels* rather than to the content of his remarks.

Following is a case that illustrates this:

In discussing his family background, the applicant stated that he was living with his grandparents and had done so since he was about three years old, because his parents were divorced. He implied that he had not enjoyed the advantages of some youths or the same happy life. The interviewer responded that apparently he had encountered considerable trouble in his lifetime. The applicant's retort was that life is nothing but trouble; he then proceeded to explain how he had suffered at the hands of fate. The story that followed gave the interviewer considerable insight into the man's emotional stability and outlook on life.

10. *What to do if the applicant seems to be withholding information.* If the foregoing suggestions are followed, there should be little difficulty in getting the applicant to discuss his background and experience. However, an occasional applicant will deliberately or unknowingly withhold information that is needed for proper selection and placement.

There may be obvious gaps in the applicant's story. These may conceal some phase of his experience that would not be particularly creditable. For example, a period not covered by his employment record may be passed over because he was dismissed from his job. In such case, the applicant may be requested to account for the time involved.

In other instances, the applicant's story may be inconsistent with information in the application or data from other sources. It may be necessary to point out these inconsistencies to give the applicant an opportunity to clear them up.

Sometimes, when an applicant is faced with conflicts in his story, he will falsify the facts. However, if he is encouraged to talk freely, he is likely to contradict himself and reveal the true story.

Still other applicants, confronted with something they do not wish to disclose, will simply remain uncommunicative. When questions are directed to them, they may become indignant and refuse to cooperate further. When the interviewer notices these tendencies, he should drop the subject immediately and talk about something else. If the candidate is urged to talk about some matter of interest to him, he may return to the subject that he had previously shied away **from.**

If the interviewer has used every means at his disposal to get the applicant talking about a particular subject, and the applicant still avoids it, it may be necessary to adopt a more direct approach. The interviewer explains that this kind of information is requested from all candidates in order to make a fair appraisal of their qualifications. If the applicant then fails to disclose the information, the interviewer must appraise this behavior in relation to his acceptability for employment.

The following illustration is an example of successful handling of an applicant who was withholding information.

On the application blank of a young man, a period of about five years was unaccounted for in terms of school or work experience. From the start, this fact naturally aroused the interviewer's interest. He did not show his interest, however, until later in the interview. In time, the applicant got around to the subject, evidently feeling that he should explain. He stated that he had held a number of odd jobs during this interval, which he did not feel worth mentioning on the application form. By that time, the interviewer sensed something in this person's background that he preferred not to discuss.

After further conversation on other subjects, during which the interviewer made a special effort to gain his confidence, the subject arose again. The interviewer said, "You find some things rather difficult to talk about, don't you?" The applicant replied that he did, and that some experiences had made him cautious. He went on to say that he had been rudely treated when he told another employment interviewer that he had spent some time in a reformatory. He followed this statement by saying he would not discuss the subject further because he was sure that he would be misundertood again. The interviewer replied that he could appreciate how he felt, but that the applicant could feel sure that no matter what was said, the interviewer would try to understand it from the applicant's point of view. Before long, the whole story was frankly told.

Sources of information

The material that follows is intended partly to aid in getting the complete story about an applicant, and partly to show the significance of specific kinds of data. In addition to the impressions gained from face-to-face contact with the applicant, there are five general background areas that provide useful information for evaluating applicants: work and military history, schooling, spare-time activities, home and family background, and health.

It is assumed, of course, that before interviewing an applicant for a particular job, the interviewer is familiar with the exact qualifications needed. Without this knowledge, he would fail to recognize the pertinence of the information obtained.

Getting the complete story depends largely on how thoroughly the various phases of an applicant's background are covered.

1. VOICE, MANNER, AND APPEARANCE.

This area of observation is treated first because it forms the first impression the interviewer gets after he meets the applicant. This initial impression may affect the interviewer's conduct in the interview as well as his appraisal of the data. To interpret his observations impartially, the interviewer must be on guard against his personal likes and dislikes in people. This is not always easy, because there are many popular misconceptions and stereotypes. For example, if an applicant is well groomed, handsome, fluent, and pleasing in manner, he may be rated above average in intelligence. Conversely, an applicant who suffers from severe skin blemishes or whose general appearance is untidy may be rated lower in intelligence.

2. WORK AND MILITARY HISTORY.

A person's work history obviously represents an important portion of his life's experience. It may consist of full- or part-time work or merely home duties. Work history often provides information about an applicant's ability to do a specific job; it may also provide clues to his employment stability, cooperativeness, dependability, industry, integrity, attendance, health, emotional stability, sociability, temperament, interests, attitude, motivation, and leadership capacity.

The applicant should be encouraged to give an exhaustive account of his work background, telling what he did and how he did it. The interviewer should note similarity in the work or working conditions to the job under consideration.

The degree of supervision is important. Did the applicant lay out his own work and make many of the decisions required for job performance?

If there is an indication of friction with his supervisor, it is important to note the manner in which the applicant describes the situation. Does he admit that he might have been partially at fault, or does he take the attitude that the supervisor "had it in for him," "always picked on him for some reason or other," and discriminated against him? Such an attitude may betoken personality maladjustment which would make the applicant a poor employment risk.

The details of male applicants' military experience can provide valuable information. If the candidate is permitted to tell his story freely, such items as the following can be covered without difficulty: branch of the service entered, and why he chose it (if he made the choice); kind of training and experience received; whether he chose his particular assignment; and why, and to what extent, his vocational interests were satisfied and his abilities utilized. Places of assignment, advancement, promotions and how they were earned, recognition received (e.g., awards and citations), and health history should be explored. The interviewer should encourage the applicant to express his feelings and opinions, to get information on the candidate's reaction to his assignments in terms of interest, motivation, adaptability, and skills acquired, as well as his degree of adjustment to men at his level and to his superior officers.

3. SCHOOLING.

This area includes formal schooling, military training, night school, and correspondence or vocational courses. For applicants who lack work experience, this is the most important source of information. Like the work history, it provides information that indicates not only ability for a particular job but also personal characteristics. Some valuable data would be:

Grades completed (graduated or not?).
Age of leaving school.
Date of leaving school.
Class standing.
Subjects liked and disliked.
Reasons for selecting major course.
Reasons for selecting special courses since leaving school. (Were they completed? If not, why not?)
Does applicant have mechanical, electrical, mathematical, or other specialized training required for the job?

Much can be learned from the applicant's participation in student activities—athletic organizations, clubs, fraternities, publication staffs, class organizations—also offices held or active committee work in class or club.

The real reason for leaving school may be even more revealing than the reason for leaving a job. It may indicate that the applicant did not have sufficient intelligence to pass school subjects, or that his family needed financial assistance, or that he preferred to work with his hands rather than with academic subjects. The reason for leaving school may indicate his degree of stability, which, in turn, may affect job success.

4. Spare-Time Activities.

Spare-time activities, perhaps more than any other, indicate an applicant's interests, because in these he is free to choose what he likes. Subjects worth investigating are hobbies, church activities, community activities, studies continued, quantity and type of reading. One measure of an applicant's social adjustment may be found in whether he likes to be alone or with people, what kinds of people he likes, and in what social activities he participates.

5. Home and Family Background.

An applicant's home or family background is likely to have a far-reaching effect upon his performance as an employee, because character and personality are largely molded in the home. The shape an individual's personality takes depends upon the conditions to which he was exposed during his childhood and adult life, as well as the adjustments he made to these conditions. They therefore provide a source from which the interviewer can learn much about a candidate's dependability, cooperation, industry, integrity, conduct, motivation, and the likelihood of his remaining a permanent employee.

6. Health.

The interviewer is not expected to pass judgment on the applicant's physical fitness unless he appears obviously unqualified. However, an applicant will sometimes discuss with an interviewer health conditions that he might hesitate to mention to an examining physician.

Interpreting the Interview

The interpretative process consists of four steps:

Determine the meaning of the findings.

Check the reliability of these facts and impressions.

Evaluate the findings and determine the favorable and unfavorable indications of fitness for the job.

Consider the over-all findings and decide upon the acceptability of the candidate.

Determining meaning of findings

In order for the interviewer fully to understand the significance of the information obtained, he should consider everything the applicant says as evidence of the kind of person he is. The candidate's hopes and expectations, as well as his degree of adjustment to present and past situations, should be weighed.

For example, if the applicant says that he left his former job because he "couldn't get anywhere," the interviewer should ask himself such questions as: What does the applicant mean by "getting anywhere"? Advancement in salary or promotion in position?

If the applicant has salary in mind, how often does he expect to get an increase, and how much? How much does he expect to make ultimately? In other words: How great is the need and how strong the desire for more money?

The interviewer should realize that an applicant seeks a job because his previous situation has changed or because there is something about it that he desires to change. He may be seeking work for the first time because he has completed his formal school training, or he may be seeking employment because he is dissatisfied with his present job. Whatever the reasons, the interviewer should try to discover the applicant's desires and expectations, and to determine what there was about his previous situation that fostered or threatened the achievement of these goals.

The interviewer should consider whether the interviewee gives evidence of a satisfactory or unsatisfactory relationship to the situation he is talking about. For instance, if the applicant says his former boss doesn't treat employees right, the interviewer should consider what this means. If the applicant is well adjusted, it is probable that his fellow employees would make the same statement. If, however, it is just the applicant who feels that his boss doesn't treat employees right, this may indicate that the candidate has difficulty in adjusting to supervision, and would, consequently, be a poor employment risk.

The interviewer should also ask himself whether he is listening to someone who has never made satisfactory adjustments to his previous situations—his former job, his school, or his home life. If an applicant's school record shows that he lacked the perseverance necessary to graduate; if, though he has been out of school for over a year, he still depends upon his parents for support, and he does not know what kind of work he would like to do—then he may become a problem employee.

Other evaluation

The interviewer can use three checks to test the reliability of the applicant's statements:

1. The reliability of statements can be *partially* judged from the tone and inflection of the applicant's voice, his gestures, hesitations,

and general demeanor. Great care must be exercised here, however, since the inferences drawn from these observations are subject to serious error. Nervousness may be a contributing factor.

2. The consistency of impressions and information obtained during the interview can be determined by checking the extent to which an act is out of line with previous behavior, or the degree to which a statement conflicts with a previous statement. However, apparent contradictions may not be real but may be due to error in observation or interpretation.

3. An external check of selected statements can be made by comparing them with information obtained from the application blank, former employers, schools, and other references; also from results of tests and physical examinations where these are available at the interview.

Before deciding on the acceptability of a candidate, the interviewer should consider to what extent he meets the job requirements. The interviewer should keep in mind the minimum traits or qualifications needed for satisfactory job performance. If the applicant meets this minimum requirement, the particular traits need not be considered further.

Some qualifications obviously cannot be appraised adequately through the interview, but must be determined from test results or physical examination. In addition, the interviewer may wish to confirm interview findings by investigating references or visiting the home. In this case, final judgment about the applicant's acceptability must be withheld, but this need not delay his being tested and undergoing his physical examination, since the matters in question are obviously not serious enough to warrant rejection.

If the interviewer has considered the extent to which the applicant meets each job qualification, he should then be ready to make the over-all decision.

Making this decision involves weighing the individual against the job as a whole and deciding whether he is qualified or not. It is at this point that the interviewer's efforts culminate. The accuracy of his decision depends on how fully he has drawn out the applicant and how objectively he has appraised the findings. It also depends on his knowledge and understanding of people and of jobs.

Is it worth the time?

While it takes considerable time to conduct this type of interview, experience indicates that it is worth it. Obviously, it is not necessary to cover an applicant's background entirely if the interviewer finds evidence that the applicant is not qualified. This may occur early in the process. Perhaps even the information contained on the application blank is enough to show that he lacks the essential qualifications.

Once the interviewer obtains conclusive evidence that the applicant is unqualified, he will bring the interview to a close as rapidly as can be done tactfully. Frequently, interviews in which the applicant is not offered a job are completed in 5 to 10 minutes, while it may take 30 to 45 minutes to interview an applicant who appears suitable for employment. If this results in the selection of an applicant who becomes a satisfied and satisfactory employee, the time is well spent from the viewpoint of both the applicant and the company.

Questions

1. The author believes that the nondirective employment interview has many advantages. Can you think of some of the disadvantages of this type of interview?
2. What is the fundamental difference between listening to the words and phrases an applicant uses and trying to understand his feelings?
3. Is a nondirective employment interview actually without interviewer direction?
4. Do you believe that understanding an applicant's feelings would have any public relations value to the company?
5. What skills would the typical student have to acquire in order to be an effective nondirective interviewer?

9. RED FLAGS MISSED—
WRONG MAN HIRED *

Quinn G. McKay

Paul Cheney, president of Space Chemicals, Inc., had just left the Seattle-Tacoma Airport on a jetliner for a business trip to Boston. The purpose of his trip was not to recruit management personnel and yet, as the plane sped eastward, his mind was preoccupied with a staffing problem.

During the past few weeks company officers had concentrated considerable thought and conversation on the critical need for a vice-president to handle production. Space Chemicals, a firm engaged primarily in developing and producing fuels and chemicals for space exploration, had been incorporated for less than a year. Demands from government and private industry had accelerated the company's growth at an unusual rate. Obtaining experienced top managers with the essential technical background was always a critical problem; the industry as a whole had expanded so rapidly that most companies were continually bidding for managers already well established in other firms as well as for those openly seeking new employment.

After changing planes in Chicago, Cheney found himself seated next to a Mr. Rigtrip. Introductions revealed that both were working in the area of space chemicals. During the conversation that followed, Cheney became more and more impressed by Rigtrip's technical knowledge of space fuels and related problems, and by his apparent personal friendship with a great many key men of the industry, both in government and private corporations.

Cheney asked Rigtrip if he would consider an employment offer with another firm. His new acquaintance replied that he was being promoted to the head office in Boston, and, while he much preferred managing the plant in Illinois and did not want to move, he felt that he must accept the promotion.

* From *Business Horizons*, Vol. 6, No. 2 (Summer, 1963), pp. 47-52. Reprinted with permission.

"Wouldn't you at least make a trip to Seattle and look over our setup?" pressed Cheney.

"No," Rigtrip insisted. "I just couldn't consider employment with another firm at this time."

Cheney prevailed on the man until, at the Logan Airport in Boston, Rigtrip reluctantly said, "Well, give me a call in about two weeks when I've had a chance to evaluate my new situation, and we'll discuss it then."

Cheney's call two weeks later resulted in Rigtrip's agreeing to make a trip to Seattle and a three-day visit at Space Chemicals, Inc. During his visit Rigtrip was interviewed privately by each of the top executives. Some of these interviews lasted three hours. He was taken golfing, to dinner, to a cocktail party, and to other activities; during this time, company executives had ample opportunity to observe his actions and reactions in a variety of social and business situations. Finally, Space Chemicals officers agreed unanimously that here was an ideal vice-president for production if only he could be lured from his present employer. Not one negative comment was made about the man's qualifications. In fact, most of the conversation focused on the problem of making an offer that would induce him to come to Seattle.

Finally, just before Rigtrip left to return to Boston, President Cheney made him a salary and stock option offer that was significantly better than his current earnings. Rigtrip said he would consider it, talk it over with his wife, and telephone his answer in the next few days. Four days later the phone rang at Space Chemicals in Seattle, and the president informed the operator that he would accept the charges.

"I've given serious thought to your offer," Rigtrip stated, "and I've called to tell you that I will accept the position of vice-president with your company."

Three weeks later, the new vice-president was on the job in Seattle and, as agreed, was given a comparatively free rein on production matters. The company officers and directors were relieved to have a competent man handling this important aspect of the business. Within a few weeks, however, things began going wrong in production. Finally the situation degenerated to such a state that Rigtrip was asked to resign from the company. As one officer put it, "He turned out to be a complete dud." Shortly after the vice-president's services had been terminated, Cheney found out from the man's former employer that Rigtrip was not really being promoted to the head office in Boston after all. Actually he had made such a mess of things at the plant in Illinois that he was being kicked upstairs to get him out of the way.

In a postmortem of this expensive and disappointing experience, Space Chemicals officers asked themselves, "What went wrong?" Each recalled numerous red flags that had been thrown out during the three-day visit. Certain of Rigtrip's actions and statements, if investigated, would have exposed his deficiencies before he was hired. For example, when asked to describe the responsibilities of his new job in Boston, Rigtrip replied, "I think they'll involve expert advising on critical matters. However, they really haven't been completely outlined yet. That's why I had time to come out here and am now willing to consider this opportunity. I'm an operating man. I must always have a challenge or I'm not satisfied."

When talking about the plant in Illinois, Rigtrip commented, "The plant had shown a good record under my leadership until a little over a year ago when employee turnover started to rise. The real cause of this problem was that the head office insisted on implementing certain policies I knew wouldn't be effective. And they weren't, as evidenced by the way the employees became upset. I was just in the process of getting one of the policies changed to get things straightened out when this promotion came to go to the head office."

Reflecting later on the first statement, Cheney could see that a man who really was the caliber Rigtrip claimed to be would have fully understood his new mission before the transfer occurred. As for the second, it seemed more than a coincidence that a promotion came when performance in the plant was down for a suspect reason.

Why weren't these experienced, mature business executives more astute and objective in their selection process? Why were they oblivious to all of the red flags? These men were and are competent executives, and Space Chemicals has continued as a profitable concern. The problem was not that they were unable to obtain information on the candidate, but that they ignored what was available and at times apparently obvious.

A phenomenon called *selective perception* seems to be a major cause of the difficulty at Space Chemicals and also at many other organizations.

What Is Selective Perception?

Most people find it significantly easier to recall pleasant and satisfying experiences than mildly disturbing or mildly unpleasant experiences. This psychological characteristic, which enables man to ignore or block out certain experiences while recognizing and retaining a consciousness of others, is called selective perception. In human behavior, "monotonous events that seem to bear little *threat* or *promise* are largely ignored." [1] Stated another way, experiences that receive recognition must appear to be either significantly rewarding or significantly dangerous. "Lukewarm" or mildly disturbing experiences go by practically unnoticed and are usually all but forgotten.

Harold J. Leavitt has described selective perception in this way: "People perceive what they think will help satisfy needs; ignore what is disturbing; and again perceive disturbances that persist and increase." [2]

Such human behavior is frequently upsetting to executives who often find that young managers are prone to avoid or even forget unpleasant little tasks such as writing difficult letters or disciplining. On the other hand, this same phenomenon permits a division head to complete a production report even though men and machines are making considerable noise in the background.

A particular aspect of selective perception referred to by the psychologists as hypothesis-theory [3] is of more than casual importance in selecting executives. This natural human characteristic tends to make first impressions unduly important. Most of us at one time or another have used the phrase, "First impressions are the most important." This truism has a psychological basis; humans do not accept all experiences at random.

Managers, like other people, tend to make quick judgments about a person at the first meeting. It is usually an over-all or general evaluation on the order of "I like him" or "I don't like him." After this first evaluation, managers tend to select from subsequent experiences with that man evidence that supports the original judgment and to ignore evidence that suggests the inaccuracy of the judgment.

---

[1] George A. W. Boehm, "That Wonderful Machine, The Brain," *Fortune*, LXVII (February, 1963), 125.

[2] Harold J. Leavitt, *Managerial Psychology* (Chicago: University of Chicago Press, 1960), p. 32.

[3] Theoretical and empirical support for this idea is found in Bruner and Postman's writings. For a review of these works, *see* F. H. Allport, *Theories of Perception and the Concept of Structure* (New York: John Wiley & Sons, Inc., 1955), Chapter 15, particularly pp. 380-83.

In other words, an executive's first impression of a potential employee will usually color reactions to subsequent experiences with that man. For instance, when involved in conversation with a person who has favorably impressed him, or when reading his application forms or letters of recommendation, the manager will tend to pay attention to evidence of high motivation, neatness, alertness, and intelligence while ignoring indications of laziness, unkempt appearance, and/or slowness at learning. Ordinarily, a glaring weakness is required to bring about a change in the original judgment. How obvious the weakness would have to be depends upon the intensity of the first impression, which is, in large measure, determined by the needs of the selector. If a manager's first impression of an applicant is negative, subsequent indications of laziness or ineptitude will tend to make him even more critical of the candidate.

Because this human characteristic may have resulted in the selection of some incompetent personnel and the exclusion of some competent candidates, one must conclude that first impressions are not only important for the applicant but have serious implications for the executive who is doing the selecting.

Implications For Management

At least three closely related areas of the management function are directly affected by selective perception: selecting managers "in" (hiring) or "out" (firing), appraisal interviews, and disciplining. Awareness of the influence of selective perception is more important in selecting managers than in selecting nonmanagement personnel. Interest, aptitude, and personality tests are useful in selecting for lesser jobs. As more and more weight is placed on these test results, the influence of selective perception will be diminished. However, in the case of management positions, objective tests will provide at best only a guide or aid to selection. Most managers are still selected on personal evaluations, judgments, and impressions formed by the executive or executives in charge.

Whenever personal judgment and evaluation are used, selective perception may exercise a significant influence on the final choice. The term "may" must be used because the degree of distortion resulting from selective perception will vary in direct proportion to the intensity of the need or danger for the selector. Cheney and his fellow officers at Space Chemicals had a critical need for a vice-president of production. For some months the intensity of this need had been building up as a result of company growth and of the frustrating results of the search for a qualified man. It is easy to understand how selective perception so completely distorted the personal evaluation of Rigtrip. On hearing Rigtrip use the industry terminology and drop the names of important people, Cheney formed a strong judgment, which he carried to his fellow officers. From each subsequent experience with Rigtrip, Cheney saw and paid attention to evidence which indicated that the candidate would make a good vice-president, because this appeared to satisfy a critical need. In each experience, Cheney literally ignored or blocked out those facts that suggested Rigtrip was less than competent, because to recognize them would be mildly disturbing. Finally, when the situation degenerated to a point of danger, all the officers saw and paid attention to Rigtrip's inadequacies and he was "selected out."

Appraisal interviews are affected much the same way by selective perception. While working with another person, we usually form a total judgment of him on the order of "He is a good worker" or "He is a poor worker." As time passes, this judgment is reinforced through selective perception until sometimes, in extreme instances, it becomes unalterable. This prompts a subordinate to observe honestly that "The boss just can't see anything wrong with that lazy, conniving Joe." If a superior has prejudged a worker to be "good," he literally tends to ignore or is unable to see his weaknesses during the appraisal. When and only when the weakness becomes so glaring as to be dangerous is the threshold reached and a change in judgment forced. An original judgment of a worker as "poor" results in the opposite conclusion.

Appraisal interview forms that require factor-by-factor evaluation are attempts to reduce the distortion of selective perception. These help except where the judgment or set has become so intense as to block out contrary information entirely.

Selective perception can result in unfair disciplinary action. Over the years, President Cheney has had a pleasant, satisfying working relationship with Sterling, the vice-president. Time has created a situation wherein it is difficult for the president to see faulty behavior that warrants disciplinary action. Sterling's misbehavior must reach the point of being dangerous before it will be seen by the president. Other subordinates may feel that Sterling tends to "get away with murder," that Ray, a division manager, on the other hand, has never been fully trusted by the president. Because Ray's

misdeeds tend to confirm or satisfy the president's original evaluation, he tends to see all of Ray's missteps and to ignore those acts
that suggest Ray is as competent as Sterling. Hence, the urge to
discipline Ray is more frequent and more intense than the desire to
discipline Sterling, even though their performance may be comparable. Not infrequently a situation of this kind becomes the
basis for subordinates' accusations that "The boss is unfair and plays
favorites." In such situations, the president may honestly think
he is being perfectly objective, because selective perception literally
blocks out the good performance of Ray and the bad performance
of Sterling.[4] He is probably being objective with the information
he sees, but he isn't seeing all the information.

Suggested Action

Few indeed are so naïve as to think the problems connected with
selective perception can be completely eradicated. Until we learn
more about how the brain gathers and stores experiences, we will
have to live with this condition. However, I would urge that steps
be taken to minimize the undesirable effects of this human trait
in the organizational setting.

Be aware that this influence exists. Most of us readily admit and
recognize it in the judgment of others but are prone to deny that it
has any bearing on our judgments and our evaluations. Be willing
to admit that the phenomenon is at work, whether we can immediately observe it in our own behavior or not. Usually, in a few
moments of honest reflection, managers can cite specific incidents of
the characteristic at work in their own experience. Be willing to
admit that strong personal needs exist and that, in a given situation, it
is natural to see those aspects which appear to satisfy the need and
to ignore those aspects which mildly suggest this will not satisfy
the needs. Recognize that the stronger the need and the more
urgent the problem, the stronger and more complete will be the
influence of selective perception.

Develop a critical attitude. A totally critical attitude about everything is dangerous, but an appropriately critical attitude may avoid

---

[4] Actually the perceiver must "see" each aspect in order to decide that he
wants to reject or ignore. This awareness followed by instant rejection occurs
so rapidly that it apparently takes place at the subconscious level.

unpleasantness like that experienced at Space Chemicals. Management should be critical, particularly when a man or a situation appears to have practically no negative aspects. With a man who is "perfect" for the job, it would be wise to say, "No man is perfect. Let me now enumerate all of his drawbacks." Or if a man is "poorly suited," say to yourself, "No man is completely bad. Let me concentrate on his good points." Cultivating the capacity to ask critical questions of one's judgment will help avoid the blind spots created by selective perception.

Closely related to the previous measure is the *development of tough mindedness in answering the questions raised.* When the need to obtain an executive is great and the first judgment of the candidate has been positive, there is a strong tendency to discount the inadequacies of a "good" man even after questioning has revealed them. The greater the necessity to fill a certain management position, the greater will be the desire to dismiss discovered shortcomings as unimportant. Tough mindedness in investigating and evaluating both apparent weaknesses and apparent strengths will minimize the distortion occasioned by selective perception.

When considering a candidate, *ask for an evaluation from another person* who is not likely to be so emotionally involved in the situation as to be preconditioned. A consultant or a fellow businessman outside the company are good sources of objective evaluations. Granted, these outsiders cannot and would not be expected to make a final decision; they would not be adequately acquainted with the needs of the company. But the fact that they are not intimately acquainted with these needs would tend to make them more objective in observing and evaluating strengths and weaknesses overlooked by those in the company.

The judgment of several officers within the company is essential. Their needs, however, may all be identical since they have been conditioned together about the situation. The perception of each would be distorted in the same direction and hence would fail to provide the much needed different perspective. Cheney no doubt discussed Rigtrip with the other company officers when he returned from his trip to Boston. His description of the man was probably a glowing one, which preconditioned the executives who subsequently interviewed him.

When taking a candidate to another person in the company or outside, a more objective evaluation can be obtained if the executive will not bias the evaluator with the introduction. The company president is creating a bias if he walks into the vice-president's office and says, "This is John Downs. I've talked with him and he looks like a very good prospect for the job of division manager. Would you have a talk with him?" Knowing that the boss apparently approves of this man will establish in the vice-president a first impression that will cause him to notice particularly Downs's strengths. If a weakness does appear, the vice-president will tend to ignore it, because recognition of it would mean going against his superior's judgment. Ordinarily the vice-president would need to observe glaring inadequacies before he would be armed with enough confidence to suggest that the boss was wrong. Of course, the relationship between the president and the vice-president is another factor that will either exaggerate or minimize the degree of this influence.

Selective perception is a phenomenon that must be dealt with in executive selection. This human trait biases judgments in selecting as well as evaluating for appraisals and disciplinary actions. The negative effects of selective perception can be minimized if, when selecting executives, a manager will recognize and admit the characteristics, ask critical questions, be tough minded when answering these questions, and, when possible and appropriate, ask an outsider for his evaluation of the candidate.

Questions

1. Would you conclude that Mr. Rigtrip was untruthful in his statements about his employment with the Boston company? Explain.
2. We note that Mr. Cheney reacted favorably to Mr. Rigtrip's use of space chemical terminology and to his familiarity with "big names" in the field. What implication does this have for the interview as a method of assessing qualifications of a prospective employee?
3. Several studies have shown the tendency to rate "old timers" in a company much higher than those individuals who have less service. How does this fact relate to the concept of selective perception?
4. If an executive desires to obtain the frank opinions of his subordinates, how should he proceed?
5. Other than the "red flags" that were missed, what sources of information were available to Mr. Cheney and his fellow officers concerning Mr. Rigtrip's qualifications?

10. TESTS: THEIR USE AND MISUSE IN SELECTION *

Herbert H. Meyer and Joseph M. Bertotti

Psychological tests and other formal screening methods offer no short cut to the problem of finding the right man for the job—nor are they tools for the amateur. But if they're properly and cautiously used, they can be a great help in selection and placement decisions.

Managers are beginning to place increasing emphasis on "scientific" methods of screening, such as, (1) special interviewing procedures, (2) more thorough reference checks and investigations, and (3) psychological tests designed to measure certain abilities and interests.

However, there has been a good deal of misunderstanding about these new selection methods, on both sides of the interviewing desk. For example, although test results are only a small part of a systematic appraisal, the candidate may regard them as the most critical, decisive part.

Most of us, in fact, tend to be apprehensive about taking tests, because we associate them with our school days, where they were a "pass-or-fail" matter. We tend to feel that our futures depend on the test results, even when we've been assured otherwise.

Tests as a selection tool

Because of the possible misunderstandings, certain facts about psychological tests should be made clear.

1. *What is a test?* A psychological test may be defined as *a sample of performance taken under standardized conditions.* Usually, this sample is carefully selected to *represent a broad area of performance.* This point is particularly important, for the criticism often leveled at the tests is that they don't measure practical performance. We sometimes hear the complaint, "What difference does it make whether or not a man can solve some simple paper-and-pencil problems? He doesn't have to do anything like that on the job." True enough; but

* From *Supervisory Management,* Vol. 2, No. 6 (May, 1957), pp. 20-27. Reprinted with permission.

years of experimentation have shown that the ability to solve these paper-and-pencil problems is definitely related to the ability to perform certain practical tasks.

The word "standardized" in our definition deserves special attention. An important way in which a psychological test differs from other placement measures is that it can be given under standard conditions, such as time and place. In this way, the candidates' performances can be more directly and accurately compared.

2. *What can tests measure?* Research studies indicate that tests are most valuable for measuring certain *abilities* or *aptitudes*. The most widely used tests are those designed to measure "general intelligence" or general learning ability. Studies have shown that it is difficult to judge this ability on the basis of an interview—or even on the basis of observation on the job. Yet it is an important factor in job performance.

Years of experimentation confirm that the intellectual tasks in a "general-ability" test predict certain aspects of practical performance. In other words, people who score high on these tests usually have the *capacity* to use good judgment, to think ahead, and to make wise decisions quickly in various situations—all the activities that are generally thought to require intelligence.

Tests are also a fairly accurate measure of abilities for specific jobs, such as the ability to grasp mechanical concepts, to visualize objects in space, or to work with facts or figures. These skills would be difficult to measure by other selection methods, like the interview.

3. *Personality and interest tests.* Tests are used also to measure interests and personality traits. But interpreting the results of such tests requires considerable caution. While interests and personality are important factors in determining job success, they are extremely difficult to measure accurately.

The diagram on the opposite page shows the degree of accuracy possible in measuring different human characteristics. Accuracy goes down as the characteristics become less tangible, and therefore harder to measure. Physical characteristics like height and weight, for instance, can be measured with the highest degree of accuracy, and a personality trait like emotional stability, with the lowest.

One reason that personality tests often fail to predict accurately is probably that personality traits are not always consistent. Our personalities vary somewhat with the situations we are in. We are all "retiring" in some situations and "aggressive" in others. We may show great perseverance in one kind of activity and very little in another.

MEASURES OF HUMAN CHARACTERISTICS

Physical Characteristics

Height
Weight

Visual Acuity
Hearing

Abilities & Skills

Dexterity
Mathematical Ability
Verbal Ability
"Intelligence"
Clerical Skills
Mechanical Aptitudes

Interests

Mechanical Interest
Scientific Interest
Economic Interests
Cultural Interests

Personality Traits

Sociability
Dominance
Cooperativeness
Tolerance

Emotional Stability

High degree of accuracy

Low degree of accuracy

ACCURACY OF OBJECTIVE MEASURES

Another shortcoming of these tests is that most of them in use today are rather transparent to any reasonably intelligent applicant. A job candidate eager to make a good impression can usually see through the test—at least to some extent. He can indicate certain interests or personality traits that he thinks will put him in the most favorable light, whether or not he actually possesses them.

Although a trained psychologist can pick up some valuable clues from interest and personality tests, he also knows that he cannot place too much faith in the validity of the scores he gets. For this reason, the tests must be administered only by well-trained, highly qualified psychologists and personnel specialists. An untrained person's literal interpretation of personality-test scores could be highly damaging to the person tested.

Other limitations

There are other limitations in using these tests for selection and placement, such as the following:

1. *Tests are designed to supplement other screening methods, not to replace them.* Tests cannot measure all the factors that must be considered in a selection or placement decision. There are many important qualifications that can be evaluated only on the basis of other factors, such as past performance, education, special training, or demonstrated interests.

Even in the matter of abilities, tests indicate only what a man should be able to do—they cannot measure what he *will* do. This point cannot be emphasized too strongly. However much ability a person has, it is of little value to him if, for some reason, he cannot apply it to his job. Even a top score on an "intelligence" test, for instance, will not compensate for lack of drive.

2. *Test scores have a relatively high margin of error.* A further limitation of tests is the natural tendency to accept the numerical scores as exact measures. We are all accustomed to dealing with physical measures where the margin of error is insignificant. If a table measures, say, 36 inches in length, for all practical purposes we can accept its length as 36 inches. In a psychological test, on the other hand, there is a far greater margin of error. A score of 36 may mean a true score of something between 30 and 40. Hence, small differences in scores between candidates are relatively meaningless.

3. *Tests alone are inaccurate predictors of job success.* Even more important is the fact that test results are still less accurate in *predicting* the behavior they are designed to sample. A test may provide

a reasonably accurate measure of mechanical aptitude, for **example**, but it may be relatively inaccurate in predicting success in a mechanical job.

It is much like the problem of predicting weather from a barometric reading. The barometer may provide an accurate measure of air pressure, but a prediction of future weather conditions based solely on this measure may be relatively unreliable.

Let's carry this analogy a step further. While the barometer is not a highly accurate predictor of weather, we can do a better job of weather forecasting with it than without it. The same principle applies in the use of tests for predicting job success, *provided the characteristics tested are required in the job.*

This warning deserves special emphasis. Obvious though this principle may seem, tests are often used without sufficient attention to specific job requirements. Unless we have an accurate "man specification" for the position to be filled, even the most reliable appraisal tools will be of little value in predicting success on the job.

A common error along this line is to assume that the higher the score on any test, the better the chances for success on any job. In some jobs, precisely the opposite holds true. Thus, people who score high on intelligence tests often make a poor adjustment to relatively routine work. A very high intelligence-test score accompanied by a mediocre record of achievement, for example, may indicate that the applicant is lazy, has poor work habits, or has personality problems that interfere with his efficiency. We would try to verify this clue, of course, in the interview or through reference checks.

In one study of tests for selecting supervisors, the applicants who scored either very low *or* very high on a test of "supervisory judgment" were found to be the poorer performers in supervisory jobs. In this case, the research study showed that applicants scoring in the middle range on this test were the best bets, even though the test seemed to be measuring desirable supervisory knowledge—or at least the "right" supervisory attitudes.

Making tests work

If the manager is to use tests properly, he should consider other information and observe certain cautions, such as the following:

1. *Accurate "man specifications."* We can't hit the bull's eye if we have not defined the target clearly. Appraisal information cannot be used for every situation; it is valuable only in predicting success

in specific situations. The same ability or trait may be an asset in one position and a liability in another.

Therefore, the specific requirements for success on the job should be spelled out; and test results should be interpreted in the light of these requirements.

2. *Past-performance records and other background information.* Test results should be presented as a *supplement* to these other appraisal sources. They should not overbalance the placement decision.

3. *Strictly confidential handling of test results and other evaluative information.* If findings were passed on indiscriminately, they could easily be misinterpreted or misused, and they could be highly damaging to the candidate's reputation. All such information should be strictly confidential.

Particular care should be used in passing on an evaluation for a specific job opening, when the same man later becomes a candidate for another job. A man might not have qualified for a highly technical position, . . . but might be well suited for a managerial job.

4. *Cautious interpretation of personality-test findings.* As we have said, personality tests are generally less valid than tests of abilities or aptitudes. On the other hand, *if we accept "testimonial" evidence, personality tests seem to be very valid.* This is because personality traits are so nebulous that almost any pattern of findings will seem to fit a candidate. In other words, we tend to see in a candidate the traits which the test results say he has. If results inaccurately point up personal liabilities, they could unjustly damage the candidate's reputation.

In any case, even if we could measure personality traits accurately we do not know what constitutes the ideal personality for an accountant, a salesman, a lawyer, a manager, or even a company president. Research studies have shown that men with entirely different personalities have often been successful in the same positions.

5. *Avoiding emergency evaluations.* All too often, an employee has little or no experience with tests until some emergency arises, and a personnel change that would affect him must be made. Perhaps his department is being reorganized, or a specific promotional opportunity arises. If, at this time, he is asked to undergo a formal evaluation procedure, it may be difficult to convince him that his future status will not be decided on the basis of the test results alone. Such emergency evaluations often give rise to complaints, especially by long-service employees. They may feel that more weight will be given to the test results than to their performance record.

6. *Careful explanation of the program.* Each person to be tested or appraised should be given a thorough explanation of the evaluation program, the part that the tests or evaluation will play in personnel decisions, and the potential value of the program to him.

In fact, when formal appraisal procedures are used to any extent within a department, it is well to *explain the program to everyone who might be involved.* This is the best way to prevent misunderstandings.

The manager should stress the fact that tests are not the only source of appraisal information—that other sources may be equally important. Nothing can damage the reputation of the testing program as much as a manager's using it as a scapegoat when he has the undesirable task of explaining to a candidate why he did not qualify for an assignment.

7. *Feedback of evaluation findings.* The results of an evaluation should be communicated to the candidate. Failure to report back often causes unnecessary apprehension about the meaning of the findings.

Though every person who takes tests can *benefit from the findings* if they are presented to him properly, it is well to recognize that this feedback is not easy. If poorly handled, it can do more harm than good.

Raising our batting average

Though tests may appear to offer an easier and quicker way of making selection and placement decisions, unfortunately this is not the case. Properly used, tests do not provide a short cut. In fact, with more thorough and systematic methods in the evaluation program, the manager may find that he spends *more* time on personnel decisions.

Furthermore, using tests does not necessarily make selection decisions any more clear cut or automatic. *Tests cannot be used as a substitute for good judgment.* Actually, the additional information they provide may make the decision more difficult. However, though using tests may require more discerning judgment, the information they provide should help make our judgments more accurate and more reliable.

Finally, it should be emphasized that the use of these evaluation procedures will not result in perfect predictions of performance. Even if our measures were perfect—which they are not—human behavior is not consistent enough for perfect predictions. Despite the most advanced procedures, we shall continue to make some mistakes. The important point is: Do we make fewer mistakes when we use objective and systematic techniques?

The research study mentioned earlier indicated that supervisors selected on the basis of systematic testing methods have shown up far better in performance ratings than supervisors selected without expert evaluation.

We may conclude, then, that if we use more thorough, objective methods, we can raise our batting average and achieve a better-qualified team.

Questions

1. Why are businessmen likely to expect "too much" from tests that are used in a selection program?
2. The authors mention the need for cautious interpretation of personality-test findings. Do you feel that applicants should be given their test results? Why?
3. One of the big shortcomings of personality tests is the fact that the job applicant can "see through" the test. In your reading have you learned of any ways that this limitation can be minimized?
4. The authors point out the fact that one's behavior (personality) is dependent in part upon the situation. How does this notion vary with the typical layman's view of personality?
5. A test is defined as a sample of performances taken under standardized conditions. If decisions are to be made concerning the qualifications of applicants for a particular job, what types of samples must be taken?

11. EQUAL EMPLOYMENT OPPORTUNITY: SHOULD HIRING STANDARDS BE RELAXED? *

Harold Mayfield

Never before has there been so much interest in helping people of minority groups, especially Negroes, to get jobs and equal opportunity for advancement. As a result, many of us have begun to realize for the first time that a good deal of what looks like unfairness is built into our traditional employment practices.

Psychological tests in particular have been criticized on the grounds that they place those who have suffered from discrimination at a marked disadvantage. Therefore, say zealous workers on behalf of the underprivileged, we should stop using tests in hiring these people.

This issue was recently brought into the hot light of national publicity when a state FEPC examiner ordered the Motorola Company, of Chicago, to cease using an employment test he considered "unfair to disadvantaged groups." In a similar vein was an announcement somewhat earlier by Pitney-Bowes that it was reviewing its testing procedures in an attempt to give special consideration to Negroes.

At about the same time, the opponents of testing were also receiving support from other quarters. Some educators were questioning whether tests used in schools, particularly for young children, might not be increasing the disadvantage of those from underprivileged families. On February 6, 1964, columnist Ralph McGill chose as his topic, "IQ Tests Unfair." And on the next day the *New York Herald Tribune* reported that the New York City school system planned to abandon traditional written IQ tests.

Thus, an observer on the sidelines might hastily infer that the use of tests for the employment of minority groups has generally been discredited—indeed, that tests and any other means of judging applicants in which underprivileged people show up to a disadvantage are unfair per se and should be discontinued.

* From *Personnel*, Vol. 41, No. 5 (September-October, 1964), pp. 8-17. Reprinted with permission.

This assumption I dispute. It rests, I believe, on an oversimplified view of the realities of the employment process and it ignores the values, to the company and the individual, of a penetrating, multi-pronged evaluation of the abilities and attitudes of a person being fitted to a job. True, any diagnostic tool can be misused. But is this a condemnation of the tool? Or a reason to cease diagnosis?

There are two important realities here that are not understood by many people who are not actually engaged in the process of selecting people for employment. First, many individuals who have grown up under unfortunate circumstances are not merely at a disadvantage in the employment office; they are also at a disadvantage on the shop floor. Their disadvantage is *real*, not imaginary, not easily remedied by short training courses or just by putting them to work.

Second, in every underprivileged group there are many able people, fully up to the actual requirements of most starting jobs in industry. These people are much more likely to be *identified* than to be *excluded* by any valid selection tool—and, when properly applied, psychological tests are still more valid than any other step in the selection process.

People who were reared in homes without books, magazines, and newspapers, without the stimulating influence of educated associates, without the example of quiet study, are clearly at a disadvantage in many aspects of modern life. This disadvantage may be almost overwhelming if it is intensified by poverty, crowded living conditions, inability to speak English well, and the pressures of racial discrimination.

These are indeed the "culturally deprived." They tend to do poorly in school, to read poorly, to express themselves poorly, to handle numbers poorly, and to have an outlook on life markedly different from that of the middle-class people who hold most of the positions of responsibility in business, education, and government. Consequently, they have special difficulty getting jobs and rising to better ones. If there is any unemployment, these are the people who feel it first and most severely.

A Self-Perpetuating Problem

Thus, we have a self-perpetuating problem. In our society, people cannot rise from a second-class status without (1) jobs and

(2) hope of advancement. But the culturally deprived cannot get jobs, let alone rise higher, because of their second-class background.

In the nature of things, every employer tries to get the "best" people he can find. Obviously, a company is at a disadvantage if its employees are of lower caliber than its competitors'. No businessman can overlook this consideration.

Normally, then, the person responsible for filling a job will try to hire as "high type" an employee as the job will attract. Naturally, his concept of what is meant by a "high type" will be affected by his personal feelings in the matter. In fact, the process of picking someone "who will fit in around here" is often somewhat on a par with asking oneself if one would like the applicant to be a guest in one's home. Judged by such intangible criteria, a member of a minority group will often fail to appear to good advantage.

Likewise, when it comes to the seemingly more precise business of appraising education and experience, the applicant from a culturally deprived background may not measure up to the standards the employment man considers desirable. He may well be short on schooling, specific experience for the job, and evidence of stability in employment.

More sophisticated employment procedures do not, of course, rely on personal judgment alone. They usually include tests of skills needed on the job, such as typing and shorthand, or the more generalized tests that explore the applicant's verbal, numerical, and abstract reasoning abilities. It's now generally conceded that where such tests have been validated on a given job they do increase the probability of picking the right man for it. Unfortunately, people from culturally deprived backgrounds usually do not do so well on employment tests as people from more favored environments. Thus, the culturally deprived often do not fare well at any of the hurdles in the employment office—the interview, appraisal of education and experience, and tests.

The Argument Against Tests

Many of the criteria on which job applicants are judged can be explained away as superficial or irrelevant and not truly indicative of underlying capabilities. But some psychological tests cannot be dismissed so easily, because they are believed to get at many of the qualities basic to successful performance in a particular job.

If people from poor background score badly on tests, as so many do, is it to be concluded that it is because they are lacking in these qualities? Those who would dispense with tests for the culturally deprived say *No*. They argue that the tests themselves are not fair to people from poor environments for two main reasons:

1. The questions in tests (particularly in "intelligence" or "mental ability" tests) revolve around subject matter, vocabulary, and modes of thought that are characteristic of middle-class homes.

Thus, whereas most middle-class applicants are likely to have heard, "Remington is the name of a typewriter," people brought up in poverty may simply never have been exposed to this fact. Again, some of the items used in tests of reasoning ability may be expressed in the following form: "The sky is to blue as the grass is to ————." That phrase, "is to," is familiar enough to people from literate homes, but may be totally outside the experience of the less fortunate. If so, such a question is simply an indicator of the *environment* rather than the *ability* of the person being tested. In fact, it has been found that the difference in performance of the two groups on this question diminishes if the sentence is reworded to read, "The sky *goes with* blue as the grass goes with ————." The meaning is the same in both versions, but it is the unfamiliar mode of expression in the first that causes some people of deprived backgrounds to score poorly on questions expressed in this form. (In all fairness, though, it should be added that fewer than 10 per cent of the items in most general ability tests are of this type. Many more items take such forms as cube counting or immediate memory recall, where poor performance is not so easily attributable to cultural bias.)

As for the vocabulary of intelligence tests, whereas words like fireplace, chandelier, wallpaper, salad fork, and dining room are likely to represent everyday items to the middle-class child, a child from a poor home may never have heard of them. On the other hand, such items familiar to the deprived child as pump, coal stove, kerosene lamp, and rain barrel are seldom used.[1]

2. People from deprived backgrounds are handicapped not only by what they do not know but also by the attitudes they bring to the examination. Often they see the whole testing situation as hostile and threatening, and the test administrator as a figure from an unfriendly segment of society. This state of mind can impair

---

[1] F. Riessman, *The Culturally Deprived Child* (New York: Harper & Row, 1962), p. 52.

performance on a test, to the point where the testee makes ridiculous answers or even hands in a blank sheet of paper.

In short, we are confronted with the suspicious circumstance that people who are *like us* do well on *our* tests, while people from markedly different backgrounds—such as American Indians, Negroes, and backwoods whites—tend to do poorly. However, it is significant that when the backgrounds of these same people are improved, their test scores improve also. One classic series of studies showed that Negro children who moved from the South to New York had progressively higher intelligence scores the longer they were in New York. The same series also showed that children from the country started out behind city children but caught up within a few years in city schools.[2]

A recent study has also shown that Negro students in integrated colleges have done better academically than their College Board examinations predicted and have had a lower drop-out rate than that of college students generally.[3] This finding suggests that an underprivileged group may be powerfully motivated to succeed under the right circumstances.

Can the Cultural Bias Be Overcome?

All this warns us that it is easy to underestimate deprived people on the basis of their test scores and that there is a "cultural bias" in tests that may keep us from seeing their true abilities. Is there any way of overcoming this difficulty, short of abandoning altogether the testing of underprivileged groups, as their sympathizers claim?

One remedy that has been suggested is to lower passing standards for those handicapped by a poor environment. Thus, the members of underprivileged groups might be given bonus points on tests to compensate for the inequity, in much the same way as veterans of the armed forces receive additional points on some civil service exams.

Such a system would certainly give a temporary compensatory advantage to the members of the group in question. But it is highly

---

[2] Summarized in P. F. Lazarsfeld and M. Rosenberg, *The Language of Social Research* (New York: The Free Press of Glencoe, 1955), pp. 175-183.
[3] K. B. Clark and L. Plotkin, *The Negro Student at Integrated Colleges* (New York: National Scholarship Service and Fund for Negro Students, 6 E. 82 St., 1963).

questionable whether it would be beneficial to the employer, or even, in the long run, to the underprivileged themselves.

With all their weaknesses, properly validated psychological tests are the *best* predictors of job success we have. Moreover, they are free from personal bias. They can undoubtedly be helpful in identifying latent talent that is not apparent in the applicant's appearance or previous experience. In any case, not all underprivileged people do poorly on employment tests. Despite their handicaps, the more capable usually do quite well enough to qualify for most industrial jobs, and those who do poorly are actually difficult to fit in anywhere.

The job applicant comes to the employment office as an adult, with his patterns of thought and behavior well established. The complex bundle of abilities that tests identify as "intelligence" is, in fact, a set of developed skills that the applicant possesses at that point in time and hence can bring to the performance of a job. These qualities are the product of native potential, plus motivation, plus opportunity. Where they are lacking, the deficiency cannot be quickly or perhaps ever completely remedied—just as a person may suffer for life from the consequences of a poor diet and an unhealthful environment in childhood.

While tests can reveal some gross deficiencies, such as illiteracy or inability to do arithmetic, that would be disqualifying on many jobs, they are also more likely to draw attention to a capable person than to disqualify him unfairly. At Owens-Illinois late in 1963 we found that Negroes then presenting themselves for factory work at widely scattered locations were fully equal in test scores to white applicants at the same plants. In other words, about the same proportion of each group met or failed to meet our standards.

Opinion vs. Fact

Tests, in short, reveal hard *facts* that need to be considered along with the many *opinions* that go into the employment decision. To junk this advantage for uncertain benefits would seem to be throwing out the baby with the bath water.

Of course, there should always be a place in the employment process for the exercise of judgment. Tests are just one phase of the process. In every good employment system, the person in charge is expected to override test results when other considerations are exceptionally favorable or compelling. But he should do so with open eyes, not blindly. He needs more facts, not fewer, in making such a decision.

Some well-meaning people are so intent on getting jobs for underprivileged people that they tend to overlook the other side of the coin. Placing a man on a job he cannot really handle is no favor to him or to the cause.

It's true that some apparently unqualified people perform beyond all expectations, but this phenomenon is not peculiar to underprivileged groups. To assume that a person will succeed merely because he is underprivileged is a sentimental fallacy. To follow a general practice of hiring people who by valid standards are unqualified is to abandon good sense.

Some Difficulties in the Way

In any case, some practical difficulties stand in the way of any attempt to adjust tests and other selection standards to the benefit of the underprivileged. How are we to decide who is culturally deprived? All Negroes are not culturally deprived. Some Anglo-Saxons are. Some dwellers in slums have educated parents. Not all people with foreign accents or with shabby clothes are at a disadvantage in intellectual tasks.

And conversely, not everyone who performs poorly on tests can be assumed to be the product of a poor environment. With no handicaps to bar their way, there are always some people who sink in the social scale and end up in conditions we might associate with cultural deprivation.

Broadly speaking, an employer has to sort out four classes of applicants: (a) people of good endowment and good environment; (b) people of good endowment and poor environment; (c) people of poor endowment and good environment; and (d) people of poor endowment and poor environment. The first group gets ample attention because of its evident merit and a special watch must be kept for the second. But the third and fourth groups are acceptable only if placed with care. In the attempt to single out people of genuine promise, the conscientious employment manager will use every selection tool at his disposal. No one, of course, can do it infallibly, but someone must try.

If lowering passing standards or dispensing with tests altogether seems to offer no acceptable solution, isn't it at least possible to construct "culture free" tests? The idea is attractive—but the hard fact is that for the purpose of predicting success in the complex setting of most business jobs, tests that are free of cultural factors do not seem likely within this decade—if they are possible at all.

There are two strong reasons for not holding out much hope in this direction:

1. The test materials that are most useful today are a product of at least a half century of exploring and disproving alternative approaches. This process has been so laborious that any radically different approach probably has ahead of it a long and rocky path of development—if, indeed, mental ability can conceivably be tested independently of experience.

2. Jobs in business are set within the cultural framework of the predominant group in our society—not within the cultural framework of the city slums, the rural backwoods, or an Indian tribe. People from these other cultures are *truly* handicapped in performing business jobs and not all of them can or will make the transition. It is difficult to imagine a business situation where someone lacking the ability to read, to express himself in speaking and writing, to comprehend the thinking of his associates, or to use numbers readily will not be at a disadvantage.

There are also more subtle qualities of attitude, mostly learned in early life, that are characteristic of our culture and basic to our business system. These include acceptance of personal competition, respect for authority, concern for the distant future, admiration of thrift, industriousness, subordination of the personal good to the group welfare under certain circumstances, willingness to settle most personal disagreements peaceably, a complex code of ethics governing relations of one person to another, and so on. These attitudes are a part of our cultural heritage. Anyone who was brought up to think differently on such matters will have difficulties in working with others—and most jobs in business call for some degree of cooperative effort. Moreover, we have to face the melancholy fact that some people have been deeply scarred by their unfortunate backgrounds and have developed antisocial attitudes that call for rescue work not many business enterprises are willing or able to undertake.

Ultimately, of course, all men of good will hope that better attitudes and with them better opportunities will spread to a great many people who do not now possess them. But this goal is most readily attainable by those who are closest to it already. For others, progress in this generation will be slow. Not all members of underprivileged groups are fitted by ability or temperament for industrial work. In fact, only about 25 per cent of all jobs in America are now in manufacturing industry, and many people must expect to earn their living in other fields, some of which, unfortunately—the rapidly growing service occupations, for example—also offer scant opportunity to the culturally deprived.

Other Steps Employers Can Take

If, on closer examination, the argument for abolishing tests in hiring the underprivileged does not seem to stand up very well, there are nevertheless other steps employers can take to insure that applicants with poor backgrounds are given a fair deal:

Re-examine job requirements

Usually the requirements for a particular job are set up by the supervisor of that job. If he says he needs a high school graduate with three years' experience in a particular field, and such a person can be found, the standards he sets are not likely to be seriously challenged. Invariably, the supervisor can give convincing reasons for having set them. But how valid are they?

The fact is, very few employment standards have been validated scientifically. Often they are little more than the supervisor's personal notion of the kind of employee needed. Sometimes they are motivated by a desire to raise the "tone" of the business. In other words, they represent a standard of *social acceptability* instead of capability to do the job. Many times, though, people of lower intelligence, lower aspirations, and less privileged backgrounds are better suited to certain jobs than those of higher caliber. But since there is seldom any factual evidence on this point, the supervisor may be hard to convince. And at higher levels, it may smack of disloyalty to advocate "lowering employment standards," because this seems to violate the business tradition that everything should move steadily upward.

Employers should re-examine all *arbitrary* employment standards —and remember that nearly all employment standards are arbitrary. There is good reason to believe that "overhiring" is one of the greatest errors in present employment practice, especially where selection is done conscientiously. Overhiring may be justified when there are plans for the rapid upgrading of new hires. But more often than not, the number of upgradings is very small in proportion to total hires and the result is painful frustration and turnover.

To require specialized experience from an applicant may virtually bar deprived groups from occupations. Thus, in some areas, Negroes may find it nearly impossible to get the experience demanded to qualify for sales and some other white-collar jobs. Yet the evidence that such experience is necessary is usually lacking. A realistic adjustment of employment standards would certainly open up more jobs to capable people from underprivileged groups.

Re-examine other phases of the selection process

Assuming that the company is using tests that have been properly validated, it can safely be said that the other phases of its selection process, namely, the employment interview and the appraisal of the applicant's background and experience, will rest on shakier ground than the testing procedure, with all its drawbacks. (Of course, if tests are used without validation, they will probably be unfair to all applicants and to the employer as well.)

Contrary to popular belief, it is not the employment office, but the supervisor who makes the final selection decision. Typically, the personnel people will send the supervisor several candidates, all of whom are believed to be fully qualified for the job. Then the supervisor makes his choice and nobody worries much about his thought processes in doing so. As long as no principle is being violated and suitable people are available, the personnel man will try to adjust his practices to the supervisor's quirks, without necessarily endorsing them. But underlying the supervisor's decision may be all kinds of curious prejudices that never come out into the open.

A partial remedy for this state of affairs is indoctrination of the whole managerial group, not simply the personnel interviewers. Thus, in weighing an applicant's personal history, managers should be alerted to the need to make allowances for obvious differences in opportunities. For example, in the case of an applicant from an underprivileged group, a record of job changes and some financial difficulties may not signal the same degree of personal irresponsibility that it might indicate in a person from a more favorable environment.

In other words, the company must be willing to look for extenuating circumstances. Rigid standards based on middle-class ideas of propriety may exclude many potentially good workers from deprived groups.

Intensify recruiting efforts

The company that exerts special effort to extend job opportunities to the less fortunate segments of the population is looking beyond the convenience of the moment to certain long-range goals and to the good of society in general. At the same time management will normally wish to accomplish these long-range aims without weakening itself competitively.

While many members of disadvantaged groups become superior employees, the fact must be faced that some of these people are difficult to place anywhere in industry. Moreover, it is to the interest of the company and of the people themselves not to place them in jobs where they are not likely to succeed.

Thus, there are strong reasons to use extra care in the selection and placement of the underprivileged. The first step in this direction is energetic recruiting.

Experience has shown that worthy members of a deprived group often have to be sought out. Perhaps because of discouraging experiences in the past, they are much less enterprising about applying for jobs than are people from more favored groups. Many of them are already employed but at jobs far below their capabilities.

Extra Effort Is Justified

There is some debate at the moment about "discrimination *in favor* of Negroes," but few will dispute its desirability in this sense. The importance of the cause justifies some extra effort, and to spend this effort in recruiting is beneficial to the company without being detrimental to any other group.

At present there is a great reservoir of good will (call it a twinge of conscience if you will) toward the Negro in most groups of working people, and it would be unfortunate to turn this good will to resentment by preferential treatment of the wrong kind. For the time being, the greatest benefaction we can bestow on the underprivileged members of our society is to make a conscious effort to place them in the jobs for which they are best fitted. The worst thing, surely, is for us to abandon tried-and-tested selection procedures simply in order to place as many on the payroll as possible.

Questions

1. What does the author mean by the term "overhiring"? What are the dangers of "overhiring"?

2. Name some of the common prejudices about people that may be found among supervisory personnel. What type of training programs for supervisors could a company establish in order to minimize their prejudices?

3. Government agencies that require applicants to qualify on civil service tests are likely to have more persons from minority groups. How do you account for this?

4. The article focuses on the problems of using selection tests with persons from minority groups. Are there other selection devices that may also have elements of unfairness about them?

5. Analyze your own prejudices. With what "types" of persons would you prefer to work? Why? Submit your responses (anonymously) to this question in writing to the instructor for analysis and discussion.

12. TRAINING LEADERSHIP STYLE: A SURVEY OF RESEARCH *

Alan C. Filley and Franklin C. Jesse

The training function has become an established and important part of the personnel program in private and public enterprise. Personnel managers and training directors have gradually improved and refined training techniques and content in order to increase the probability of meeting training objectives. A variable of paramount importance in achieving training program effectiveness is the leadership style used by the trainer, and it is to this role that the present article addresses itself. We are interested in suggesting, insofar as possible, the proper balance which the trainer should maintain between what is often called the *leader-centered* training approach on the one hand, and the *group-centered* training method on the other.

With the leader-centered approach the trainer assumes an active control of training-group activities and topics for discussion. He alone answers individual questions. Communication and attention of group members is directed to him. The emphasis of the training session is upon the training leader's presentation of information rather than upon group discussion. The behavior of the trainer described here as leader-centered is essentially the same as behavior described in other studies as authoritarian, supervisory, directive, or instructor-centered.

In contrast, the group-centered style of training leadership places emphasis upon group discussion and interaction. This style utilizes much less direction and comment from the training leader than the leader-centered style. The substance of the training session tends to be generated through group discussion instead of originating from the training leader. The training leader is involved only for occasional stimulation and channeling of discussion, or for redirection of individual problems or questions to the group for its consideration.[1] The group-centered style is essentially the same as the training

* From *Personnel Administration*, Vol. 28, No. 3 (May-June, 1965), pp. 14-21. Reprinted with permission.

[1] Numbers in parentheses refer to articles listed in the bibliography at the end of the article.

leadership approach described in various studies as democratic, participatory, permissive, non-directive, student-centered, or discussion-leadership.

Training Leadership Style versus Group Structure

Before discussing determinants of proper training leadership style under varying needs or conditions it is well to note the difference between trainer style and the presence or absence of structure within the training group. The role of the training leader should be well defined even though the degree of direction by the trainer will vary importantly between the leader- and the group-centered methods. Should the training leader abdicate his leadership responsibility, leaving the group with no structure, the performance of the group toward training goals is likely to be blocked until the group can establish its own new structure. Such group-defined structure may be expected to be less effective in meeting training goals than the purposive structure of the training leader. The question is not whether structure should be present or absent in the training group, for evidence clearly suggests the need for group structure; [1, 7, 37] rather it is the balance or type of training leader involvement within the structure which is important.

Training Goals as Determinants of Training Leader Style

A review of research related to training leadership style suggests some meaningful patterns which may be used by the trainer to select the leadership style which is most likely to be effective for prescribed needs. The primary basis for selecting training style appears to be the objective of the training session itself. The objectives for which meaningful research results may be summarized are (a) to present new information, (b) to change behavior or attitudes, and (c) to create satisfaction among group members. In addition, certain secondary factors influence the leadership role which should be used to attain one or more of the major goals.

Before exploring the pattern of research findings a word of caution is in order. The studies reported here were selected with no predetermined bias toward one form of leadership or another, and conflicting evidence is reported when it appears. Yet one should view our conclusions concerning proper style with a healthy amount of tentativeness for some degree of interpretation is always necessary when one synthesizes the results of individual studies. **Reliance upon** this interpretation by the reader must be tempered with the knowledge that studies are sometimes limited in number and often differ in definitions, experimental procedure, measuring tools, and degrees of significance. Given these limitations, however, some rewarding and practical suggestions may be induced from the mass of experimental evidence which relates to the training leadership problem.

Goal #1: Presentation of new information

If the major purpose of a training program is to provide new information, the leader-centered method is to be favored as a training leadership style.[3, 4, 13, 17, 20, 46, 49, 55] However, where one is concerned with retention of knowledge, where the group is known to be above average in intelligence, or where the material taught is not precise or explicit, then the advantage of the leader-centered over the group-centered method is more often not significant or reversed.[4, 15, 20, 23, 54]

From the standpoint of affecting initial learning, the literature sampled suggests that the leader-centered method is generally superior in communicating the kind of factual or technical material taught in most under-graduate college courses, as measured by objective-type examinations or other measures of recall. Training programs in government and business with analogous training content might range from those informing employees of the scope of a company's operations to those which instruct the employee in the operation of machines or the performance of office procedures.

The chief advantage of the group-centered method in encouraging retention seems to be the reinforcement gained in the exchange of ideas between group members and the stimulation of idea association with other concepts not specifically course related.[4, 54] This advantage would appear to be less real if one notes that much stimulation and association in industrial training takes place once the trainee has returned to the job. Assuming some reinforcement in the job situation, the advantage of leader-centered training in learning new information might well be realized for retention as well, for measures of effectiveness frequently precede rather than follow job practice.

The effect of course content and group intelligence on desirable training methods will be discussed later in this article.

Goal #2: Behavior and attitude adjustment

A second and very important goal of a training program might be to encourage behavior or attitude adjustment on the part of individual participants. The possible uses of training programs with this goal would range from increasing understanding of individual problems among employees to promoting employee acceptance of policies or programs judged by management as desirable. The development of leadership skills might be another application but the limited evidence on this particular subject is inconclusive.[17]

Present evidence clearly suggests the superiority of the participatory or group-centered approach over the leader-centered method for promoting self-adjustment and insight into personal problems or problems of interpersonal relations.[3, 8, 9, 20, 24, 37] When using college students in an experimental situation, directive teaching elicited defense mechanisms of hostility, withdrawal, apathy, and aggressiveness while a more group-centered type of teaching method elicited emotional readjustment and decreased anxiety.[20]

When the purpose of training is to cause attitude change of group members, the group-centered method is also clearly superior to the leader-centered method.[3, 10, 11, 17, 28, 34] Group members change their attitudes toward the group norm or toward values provided to the group in a training situation to a greater extent when they are members of a participatory group. Similarly, there is evidence that the participatory leader has a greater influence on the attitudes of the group than a more directive type of training leader.[28, 35] This difference was suggested when the participatory style was more effective in changing attitudes of foremen to a personnel appraisal program.[34]

Goal #3: Satisfaction of group members

A third goal of a training program is to promote general satisfaction of participants. This particular goal can be misused as the sole criterion of effectiveness for training programs, as when trainers judge program effectiveness on the appearance of friendliness among group members or upon member expression of enjoyment in attending training sessions. Positive values to be gained in meeting the satisfaction goal relate to the promotion of group cohesiveness, individual satisfaction with the others in the group, and individual satisfaction with training leadership and programs.

While satisfaction alone is seldom sufficient to warrant the cost of public or private training, there are conditions under which it might be defensible. For example, an important purpose of a management training program for new employees might well be to develop solidarity among these new employees and to enhance their loyalty to the company.

There is strong support for the notion that cohesiveness among group members is facilitated to a greater extent when the group leader uses the participatory style.[10, 11, 20, 29, 46] For example, members of a participatory group were shown to know more names of other members and to develop intensive acquaintances with more members than members of a leader-directed group.[46]

Individual feelings of satisfaction or enjoyment in belonging to a group are stronger in permissive than in leader-centered groups.[10, 11, 17, 33, 35, 43, 47, 55] For example, members of a group led by group-centered methods rated each other and the group higher on a scale measuring emotional attachment (affect scale) than members of a leader-centered group.[10, 11]

Satisfaction in this context is principally the individual's preference for other group members and the group as a whole. It does not necessarily refer to member satisfaction with the value of the program for the purpose of meeting job-related goals. This difference is illustrated in an experiment in which group members (students) enjoyed their permissive sessions more than the directive sessions, but did not consider them as valuable in helping them to prepare for exams.[55]

Thus, if one considers the satisfaction of participants in meeting training goals rather than with group members, the preference is for a more directive, lecture type of training.[7, 18, 19, 32, 42, 46, 55] Lecture leaders themselves are considered more interesting, frank, satisfying, purposeful, enlightening, industrious, and persuasive than participatory leaders.[42] Group members feel that the directive training leader is better able to promote learning on their part and are more satisfied with his general leadership ability.[18, 42] When members rate the participatory training leader higher than the directive leader, it is generally for qualities of permissiveness and ability to stimulate independent judgment.[3, 18, 42]

Satisfaction with leader-centered training methods of training participants in industrial organizations was demonstrated in a change of training style in an in-house executive development program which had had little acceptance or enthusiasm by managers. When standards were elevated, teaching methods made more leader-centered, and scheduling was improved, the result was marked acceptance and participation by company management.[30] The same pattern may be seen in survey research of industrial managers who had attended management development programs in the year preceding the survey. Given a choice of two methods, managers showed a significant preference for "a method . . . centered around authoritative discussion by a lecturer or conference leader," rather than "a method . . . centered around discussion by the group attending the conference, led by a qualified discussion leader." [19]

While individual satisfaction with the group and its members is promoted by group-centered training methods, it appears clear that leader-centered methods engender greater satisfaction with the attainment of training goals.

Other Determinants of Training Leader Style

While the goal of training is a major determinant of training style, characteristics of the group, its members, and the training content also affect the role of the leader. While the evidence is limited, one may infer the following from available research.

1. The larger the group, the less possible group-centered methods become. The opportunity for group members to communicate and interact decreases exponentially as group size increases limiting the ideal size of a group requiring member interaction to about five persons.[27] Attempts have sometimes been made to offset this limitation with the use of "buzz groups" or other sub-groups within a larger group.

2. The particular orientation of the group toward task or social values also appears to be an important determinant. Task-centered groups such as those containing managers from private or public enterprise seem to prefer more leader-centered methods while socially-oriented groups like those from church or civil organizations desire more group-centered methods.[2] Such a distinction is consistent with research on individual orientation which shows a posture toward affiliation, achievement, or power, or some combination of these.[36] Membership needs which are strongly affiliation-oriented might be expected to prescribe a group-centered method, while strong power-oriented needs would suggest a leader-centered method.[7, 18, 55]

3. The average intelligence of the group will affect the training leader style which is most effective. While occasionally conflicting present evidence suggests that groups with above average intelligence learn

more with group-centered methods, while groups of lower intelligence learn more with leader-centered methods.[14, 23, 39, 55] For example, in playing a game based on "Twenty Questions" in an experimental setting, the "Brights" did best under group-centered direction while the "Dulls" did best under a leader-centered style.[14] Similarly, poorer college students were shown to do better on examinations when taught by group-centered methods.[55] Finally, since lower intelligence persons are often authoritarian and since authoritarian personalities prefer authoritarian direction, it is further suggested that lower intelligence persons would prefer a leader-centered type of training direction.[39]

4. The group judgment of the leader's authority and expertise may help to determine the ideal training leadership style. Group members appear to accept a group-centered approach to the extent that the authority of the training leader is confirmed. Thus, if his authority is not clear, the leader would do well to use a more leader-centered approach, at least initially, in the training session.[29, 30, 56]

5. The length of the training period may also affect the suitable training leadership style. Since group participants need confirmation of group roles,[7, 29, 45] and particularly of the leadership role, it seems logical to suggest that shorter training periods would require a more leader-centered approach than longer training periods. Thus, a study of decision-making conferences lasting from 16 to 191 minutes in 72 business and government groups, found that except for urgent problems the group decreased in satisfaction and cohesion when the chairman did not control the group process or allowed sharing of his leadership role.[7] Where training progresses over weeks or months member roles become defined and perception of leadership competence and authority are confirmed without such an emphasis on leader direction. Perhaps the best solution for longer training periods would be initial leader-centered techniques followed by group-centered methods.

6. Finally, while seldom explicitly stated in studies reviewed, it may be observed that the content of training seems to have an important effect upon the ideal training method to be used. To the extent that material communicated is well defined, specific, and requires little interpretation or confirmation, then the leader-centered approach is suggested.[54] To the extent that material requires clarification or group problem-solving the group-centered method seems to be better, particularly where the intelligence of group members is above average. Thus, it was observed, for example, that more favorable, though nonsignificant results were experienced with group-centered methods on examinations in two philosophy courses taught with group-centered methods and leader-centered methods respectively, while significantly more favorable results on examinations were experienced with a leader-centered method in a similar study of two psychology courses.[46] Apparently, the more explicit material of the psychology courses, in contrast to the courses in philosophy, favored the leader-centered method.

Selection of a Proper Leadership Method

The next logical step in dealing with training leadership style would seem to be a research project in which the variables believed to be important would be varied singly and severally in order to fix the importance, direction, and weight of each. Hopefully one might eventually develop a normative scale which would give the training leader a rather precise statement of the right style to be used under various conditions.

Until a precise scale prescribing leader methods can be developed, some general observations concerning priority of determinants would seem to be worthwhile. It appears that the goal of the training session should be weighted heavily in determining ideal, training style. Thus, where the management training program is designed to give background information about the company and its products, the leader-centered method is suggested. Where the program is designed to encourage employee solidarity and loyalty, or where the program seeks to establish member agreement with general company objectives, then the group-centered method would seem to be more effective.

Given the major training objective, the general style may then be mediated according to group size, orientation, intelligence, and judgment of leader authority; the time allotted for training; and the subject matter to be covered. Thus a training leader with the task of training group members in methods of economic forecasting, where the group is assured of the trainer's authority, is small in size, is intelligent, and is not rushed for time, should probably temper his leader-centered approach with more group discussion than where these conditions are reversed. The training leader would do well to consider each of the determinants of training style before deciding on the proper method to be used.

Summary

To summarize, research suggests the following hypotheses regarding training leadership style:

The leader-centered method of training is more effective:

1. when the training objective is to facilitate initial learning by participants.
2. in promoting member satisfaction with the achievement of training goals.

3. in promoting general satisfaction with the leader's ability.
4. in larger groups.
5. in task-centered groups.
6. in groups with lower than average intelligence.
7. in authoritarian groups.
8. in confirming the expertise and authority of the training leader.
9. where time for training is relatively short.
10. where training content is explicit and contains little confirmation or interpretation.

The group-centered training method is more effective:

1. if the objective of training is to insure retention of new information (assuming no review or practice if a leader-centered alternative is considered).
2. if the objective of training is to promote self-adjustment and insight into personal problems, and problems of interpersonal relations.
3. when the objective of training is to change specific attitudes of group members.
4. when the objective of training is to promote group cohesiveness and satisfaction of membership with the group.
5. in small groups.
6. in socially-oriented groups.
7. in groups with higher than average intelligence, particularly when high authoritarian members are omitted.
8. in groups which are assured of the authority and expertise of the leader.
9. where time for training is relatively longer.
10. where training content is less explicit requiring interpretation and value acceptance.

References

1. Adams, S. "Social Climate and Productivity in Small Military Groups," *Amer. Soc. Rev.* 1954, 19, 421-425.
2. Anderson, R. C. "Learning in Discussions: A Resumé of the Authoritarian-Democratic Studies," *Harvard Educ. Rev.* 1959, 29, 201-214.
3. Asch, M. J. "Non-directive Teaching in Psychology—An Experimental Study." *Psychol. Monogr.* 1951, 65:4 (Whole No. 321).
4. Bane, C. L. "The Lecture vs. the Class Discussion Method of College Teaching," *School and Society.* 1925, 21, 300-302.
5. Bavelas, A., L. Festinger, P. Woodward, and A. Zander. "The Relative Effectiveness of a Lecture Method and a Method of Group Decision for Changing Food Habits," *Bulletin of the Committee on Food Habits.* National Research Council. (Mimeographed)
6. Bennett, E. B. "Discussion, Decision, and Consensus in Group Decision," *Hu. Relat.* 1955, 8, 251-273.
7. Berkowitz, L. "Sharing Leadership in Small Decision-Making Groups," *J. Abnorm. Soc. Psychol.* 1953, 48, 231-238.
8. Bills, R. E. "Personality Changes During Student-Centered Teaching," *J. Educ. Res.* 1957, 50, 121-126.

9. Bovard, E. W., Jr. "Clinical Insight as a Function of Group Process," *J. Abnorm. Soc. Psychol.* 1952, 47, 534-539.

10. ——————. "Experimental Production of Interpersonal Affect," *J. Abnorm. Soc. Psychol.* 1951, 46, 521-528.

11. ——————. "Group Structure and Perception," *J. Abnorm. Soc. Psychol.* 1951, 46, 398-405.

12. Brinkley, S. G. "Mental Ability in College Classes: Student Estimates of Relative Value of Ten Learning Situations," *J. Exp. Educ.* 1952, 20, 373-378.

13. Burke, H. R. "An Experimental Study of Teaching Methods in a College Freshman Orientation Course," *Dissertation Abstr.* 1956, 16, 77-78.

14. Calvin, A. D., F. K. Hoffman, and E. L. Harden. "The Effect of Intelligence and Social Atmosphere on Group Problem-Solving Behavior," *J. Soc. Psychol.* 1957, 45, 61-74.

15. Carlson, C. R. "A Study of the Relative Effectiveness of Lecture and Directed Discussion Methods of Teaching Tests and Measurements to Prospective Air Force Instructors," *Dissertation Abstr.* 1953, 13, 1112-1113.

16. Deignan, F. J. "A Comparison of the Effectiveness of Two Group Discussion Methods," *Dissertation Abstr.* 1956, 16, 1111-1110.

17. DiVesta, F. J. "Instructor Centered vs. Group Centered Approaches in Teaching a Course in Human Relations." *J. Applied Psychol.* 1954, 38, 329-336.

18. Eglash, A. "A Group Discussion of Teaching Psychology." *J. Educ. Psychol.* 1954, 45, 257-267.

19. Filley, A. C., and F. H. Reighard. "A Preliminary Survey of Training Attitudes and Needs Among Actual and Potential Attendees at Management Institute Programs." Commerce Extension Division, University of Wisconsin, Mimeographed report, 1962.

20. Flanders, N. A. "Personal-Social Anxiety as a Factor in Experimental Learning Situations," *J. Educ. Res.* 1951, 45, 100-110.

21. Fouriezos, N. T., M. L. Hutt, and H. Guetzkow. "Measurement of Self-Oriented Needs in Discussion Groups," *J. Abnorm. Soc. Psychol.* 1950, 45, 682-690.

22. Farquhar, W. H. "An Investigation of the Relationship of Three Teaching Methods to Student Behavior in a How-to-Study Course," *Dissertation Abstr.* 1955, 15, 1550.

23. Gerberich, J. R., and K. O. Warner. "Relative Instructional Efficiencies of the Lecture and Discussion Methods in a University Course in American National Government," *J. Educ. Res.* 1936, 29, 574-579.

24. Gross, L. "An Experimental Study of the Validity of the Nondirective Method of Teaching," *J. Psychol.* 1948, 26, 243-248.

25. Guetzkow, H., E. L. Kelley, and W. J. McKeachie. "An Experimental Comparison of Recitation, Discussion, and Tutorial Methods in College Teaching," *J. Educ. Psychol.* 1954, 45, 193-207.

26. Haigh, C. V., and W. Schmidt. "The Learning of Subject Matter in Teacher-Centered and Group-Centered Classes," *J. Educ. Psychol.* 1956, 47, 295-301.

27. Hare, A. P. *Handbook of Small Group Research,* Chapter 8. New York: Free Press, 1962.

28. —————. "Small Group Discussion with Participatory and Supervisory Leadership," *J. Abnorm. Soc. Psychol.* 1953, 48, 273-275.

29. Heyns, R. W. "The Effects of Variation in Leadership on Participant Behavior in Discussion Groups," *Microfilm Abstr.* 1949, 9, 161-163.

30. House, R. J. "An Experiment in the Use of Management Training Standards," *J. Acad. Management.* 1962, 5, 76-81.

31. Husband, R. "A Statistical Comparison of the Efficacy of Large Lecture vs. Smaller Recitation Sections Upon Achievement in General Psychology," *Amer. Psychologist.* 1949, 4, 216.

32. Krumboltz, J. D. "An Investigation of the Effect of Three Teaching Methods on Motivational Outcomes in a How-to-Study Course," *Dissertation Abstr.* 1955, 15, 2470.

33. Leavitt, H. J. "Some Effects of Certain Communication Patterns on Group Performance," *J. Abnorm. Soc. Psychol.* 1951, 46, 38-50.

34. Levin, J., and J. Butler. "Lecture vs. Group Decision in Changing Behavior," *J. Appl. Psychol.* 1952, 36, 29-33.

35. Maier, N. "An Experimental Test of the Effect of Training on Discussion Leadership," *Hum. Relat.* 1953, 6, 161-173.

36. McClelland, D. C. "Business Drive and National Achievement," *Harvard Bus. Rev.* 1962, 40, 99-112.

37. McKeachie, W. J. "Anxiety in the College Classroom," *J. Educ. Res.* 1951, 45, 153-160.

38. —————. "Student Centered vs. Instructor Centered Instruction," *J. Educ. Psychol.* 1954, 45, 143-150.

39. Medalia, N. Z. "Authoritarianism, Leader Acceptance, and Group Cohesion," *J. Abnorm. Soc. Psychol.* 1955, 51, 207-213.

40. Neuman, S. E. "Student vs. Instructor Design of Study Method," *J. Educ. Psychol.* 1957, 48, 328-333.

41. Ostlund, L. A. "An Experimental Study of Case-Discussion Learning," *J. Exp. Educ.* 1956, 25, 81-89.

42. Page, R., and E. McGinnies. "Comparison of Two Styles of Leadership in Small Group Discussion," *J. Appl. Psychol.* 1959, 43, 240-245.

43. Porter, R. M. "Relationship of Participation to Satisfaction in Small Group Discussions," *Dissertation Abstr.* 1955, 15, 2493.

44. Preston, M. G., and R. K. Heintz. "Effects of Participatory vs. Supervisory Leadership on Group Judgment," *J. Abnorm. Soc. Psychol.* 1949, 44, 345-355.

45. Roseborough, M. E. "Experimental Studies of Small Groups," *Psychol. Bull.* 1953, 50, 275-303.

46. Ruja, H. "Outcomes of Lecture and Discussion Procedures in Three College Courses," *J. Exp. Educ.* 1954, 22, 385-394.

47. Shaw, M. E. "A Comparison of Two Types of Leadership in Various Communication Nets," *J. Abnorm. Soc. Psychol.* 1955, 50, 127-134.

48. Slomowitz, M. "A Comparison of Personality Changes and Content Achievement Gains Occurring in Two Modes of Instruction," *Dissertation Abstr.* 1955, 15, 1790.

49. Spence, R. B. "Lecture and Class Discussion in Teaching Educational Psychology," *J. Exp. Psychol.* 1928, 19, 454-462.

50. Stovall, T. F. "Lecture vs. Discussion," *Phi Delta Kappan.* 1958, 39, 255-258.

51. Thelen, H. A., and Withall. "Three Frames of Reference: The Description of Climate," *Hum. Relat.* 1949, 2, 159-176.
52. Thompson, O., and F. Tom. "Comparison of the Effectiveness of a Pupil-Centered vs. a Teacher-Centered Pattern for Teaching Vocational Agriculture," *J. Educ. Res.* 1957, 50, 667-678.
53. Turnapal, L. "Evaluate Your Training Programs," *Amer. Soc. Training Directors.* 1957, 2, 11.
54. Ward, J. N. "Group-Study vs. Lecture-Demonstration Method in Physical Science Instruction for General Education College Students," *J. Exp. Educ.* 1956, 24, 197-210.
55. Wispe, L. G. "Evaluating Section Teaching Methods in the Introductory Course," *J. Educ. Res.* 1951, 45, 161-186.
56. Zander, A., and J. Cyr. "Changing Attitudes Toward a Merit Rating System," *Personnel Psychol.* 1955, 8, 429-448.

Questions

1. Why should the leader of a training group give primary consideration to the objectives of the training when selecting a training style?
2. Some managers and supervisors seldom, if ever, use a group-centered training approach. Why? What can be done to overcome this?
3. It has been found that when the purpose of training is to cause a change of attitude on the part of the participants, the group-centered method is clearly superior to the leader-centered method. How do you account for this?
4. Of what value would the material in this article be to a training department manager and his staff?

13. A NEW FOCUS IN EXECUTIVE TRAINING *

Irving R. Weschler

It happened at the fifth meeting. For four weeks, thirty executives had been coming to the campus of the University to attend a workshop in supervision. At each meeting they had sought to clarify their aims, and had continually tried to get the "professors" to lay down a set of rules. "You're the experts here," they said; "you tell us what we can do to become more effective!"

At the fifth meeting, the group's feeling about its own progress became the initial focus of discussion. The "talkers" participated as usual, conversation shifting rapidly from one point to another. Dissatisfaction was mounting, expressed through loud, snide remarks by some, and through apathy by others.

George Franklin appeared particularly disturbed. Finally, pounding the table, he exclaimed, "I don't know what is going on here! I should be paid for listening to this drivel. I'm getting just a bit sick of wasting my time around here. If the 'profs' don't put me out—I quit!" George was pleased. He was angry and he had said so. As he sat back in his chair, he felt he had the group behind him. He felt he'd had the guts to say what most of the others were thinking! Some members of the group applauded loudly, but many others showed obvious disapproval. They wondered why George was excited over so trivial an issue; why he hadn't done something constructive rather than just sounding off, as usual. Why, they wondered, did he say their comments were "drivel"?

George Franklin became the focus of discussion. "What do you mean, George, by saying this is nonsense?" "What are you really mad at, George?" "What do you expect—a neat set of rules to meet all of your problems?" George was getting uncomfortable. These were questions difficult for him to answer. Gradually, he began to realize that a large part of the group disagreed with him; then he began to wonder why. He was learning something about people he hadn't known before. New questions were raised—some relating to

* From *Advanced Management*, Vol. 20, No. 5 (May, 1955), pp. 19-22. Reprinted with permission. *The names of persons mentioned in this article are fictitious.*

the job: "How does it feel, George, to have people disagree with you when you thought you had them behind you?" "Is it important for you to know who is really with you and who isn't?" "How does this apply to the plant?" "What can we do to find out how our employees really feel about us?"

Bob White was first annoyed with George and now with the discussion. He was getting tense, a bit shaky perhaps. Bob didn't like anybody to get a raw deal—and he felt that George was getting it. At first, Bob tried to minimize George's outburst; then he suggested that the group get on to the real issues, but the group continued to focus on George. Finally, Bob said, "Why don't you leave George alone and stop picking on him? We're not getting anywhere this way."

With the help of the leaders, the group focused on Bob. "What do you mean, 'picking' on him?" "Why, Bob, have you tried to change the discussion?" "Why are you so protective of George?" Bob began to realize that the group *wanted* to focus on George; he also saw that George didn't think that he was being picked on, but felt that he was learning something about himself and about how others reacted to him. "Why do I always get 'upset,'" Bob began to wonder, "when people start to look at each other? Why do I feel sort of sick when people get angry at each other? Why don't my people ever talk back to me—do I let them get it off their chests, or do I cut them off?" Now Bob was learning something about how people saw him, while gaining some insight into his own behavior. Not much yet. but just enough to work on—perhaps. Some other time he would feel free to explore this a bit further.

Most executives, as illustrated above, can talk the "human relations" language, but fewer are able to put into practice some of the ideas to which they so readily subscribe. It is often interesting, for example, to watch some of the proponents of the "open-door" policy of communications violate the very spirit of the practice to which administratively they are so loudly committed. A recent hit play makes the same point dramatically when a commanding officer of an occupation unit in the Far East threatens to "teach the natives democracy if I have to shoot every one of them." Sensitivity training [1]

---

[1] For related philosophies and methods of training, *see* Robert Tannenbaum, Verne Kalleiian. and Irving R. Weschler. "Training Managers for Leadership," *Personnel*, Vol. 30, No. 4 (January, 1954), pp. 254-260; *also* Herbert A. Thelen, *Dynamics of Groups at Work* (Chicago, Ill.: The University of Chicago Press. 1954), 379 pp., and National Training Laboratory in Group Development, *Explorations in Human Relations Training: An Assessment of Experience, 1947-1953* (Washington, D. C.: National Education Association, 1953), 87 pp.

attempts therefore, to close the gap between knowing and doing by exposing the participants to both the intellectual and the emotional understanding needed for effective performance.

The aims of sensitivity training

There are several specific aims in this type of training. First, each trainee should get a better picture of the kind of person he is, of the impact he has on others, and of the characteristic behaviors he employs to protect himself against real or imagined threats. As a result of the training process, he is likely to discover some of his "blind spots"—those problem areas in his personality which he is unable to perceive without gross distortion and which frequently operate to his detriment in relating to others.

Second, the participants should check the accuracy of their perceptions as to what other people are like. Many trainees tend to think in stereotypes, which if strong may drastically color their perceptions. Participants learn to recognize individual differences, to accept them for what they are, and to understand better how their own needs and desires distort their perceptions of others.

Third, the participants should obtain more factual information, useful and pertinent in this area. This may include some theory and research data on individual differences, personality, leadership, communication, and group dynamics.

Fourth, each trainee should develop new "human relations" skills, including ways of dealing with conflicts and tensions. As the participants put into practice their understanding of themselves and others, they learn how to communicate effectively, how to interview and listen, how to inform and evaluate, how to praise and discipline, and how to motivate. These specific skills can usually not be acquired until some of the insights mentioned above have first been attained.

Finally, the participants should be helped to become more aware of "group process," those forces unique to a group which ultimately may result in its success or failure. They should learn to recognize functional and blocking member roles; they should become aware of, and learn to deal with, "hidden agenda," those personal or situational pressures which simmer underneath a surface of good manners and friendly interchange; they should become acquainted with the procedural skills which allow a group to get its work done in the most expeditious manner.

The nature of the training process

Sensitivity training is still experimental. As carried out in university workshops, group development laboratories, and plant settings, no single formula for conducting this type of training has been developed. In general, however, certain essential elements have emerged.

First, the training is "feeling-oriented" as well as "content-oriented." The participants learn to deal not only with specific cases and examples from their "on-the-job" situations, but also to analyze their own reactions and feelings toward one another and toward the situations in which they become involved at the training session.

Second, a certain amount of frustration appears to be essential to the success of the training. Each person attempts to keep his concept of himself intact, and little training impact can be expected unless the trainee is able to examine his "self-concept," to re-evaluate it, and to instigate those changes which he feels would benefit him. The process is not an easy one; we must experience frustration and anxiety in order to gain some insight into our "inner selves." These insights cannot be learned by reading a book; they arise most easily in the "give and take" of interpersonal relations.

Trainees decide what to talk about

Third, the training design is partly unstructured. Opportunities are provided for the trainees to decide what they want to talk about, what kinds of problems they desire to deal with, and what means to use in reaching their goals. As the trainees deal with these problems, they begin to act in characteristic ways—some participate freely, some remain silent, some dominate the discussion, and some become angry. These and other modes of dealing with problems become "grist for the mill"—they provide jumping-off points for discussion and analysis.

Fourth, auxiliary training devices and techniques are utilized to facilitate the interaction process among the participants. Included are the use of case studies, role-playing, buzz groups, film forums, and the like. At present, we think that these training devices should be introduced rather early in the training experience in order to place trainees in the kinds of situations to which they are more accustomed. As training progresses, artificial stimuli will be less frequently needed to produce the "raw material" of the training process.

Fifth, a permissive atmosphere is maintained. When people know that their attitudes are respected and their feelings accepted, full participation is facilitated. Since the expression of attitudes and feelings is essential to the training process, even when people feel they might appear unkind, impolite or perhaps ridiculous, the group atmosphere must remain friendly enough so that these sentiments can be elicited.

A permissive atmosphere is not easy to describe. We know it does not exist when the discussion leader insists on imposing his own goals, ideas and methods. We must not be fooled by the "let's all join in the fun" appeal of some service organizations, the "let's be a happy family" flavor of some industrial concerns or college campuses, or the phony "hi, Joe!" variety of "hearty atmosphere." It is only when discussions are characterized by a lack of moralistic or judgmental attitudes toward almost anything that might be said, when people feel free to speak frankly and to listen with understanding that true "permissiveness" can be said to exist.

Expressions of resistance to the training process

In the training situation, no attempt is made to tell participants whether to change or how to change. They are helped to see themselves more objectively; if, then, *they* are dissatisfied with certain aspects of their behavior, the decision to change and the direction of change is up to them.

Paradoxically, many of those who really want to profit find themselves blocked by feelings, fears, and anxieties from experiencing the deeper impact of the training process. These "defenses" keep them from making the kind of progress which they so earnestly desire.

Every one of us utilizes defenses, usually those with which we feel most comfortable. We use different ones at different times, and in various combinations and proportions, some more effectively and appropriately than others. Each person's particular pattern of defenses largely characterizes his personality.

It is rather easy to see some of the more familiar defenses in others, but very difficult to recognize them in ourselves: the "sour grapes" attitude ("we didn't want this contract, anyhow"); the displacement of hostility on an inappropriate person (arguing with one's wife when really feeling angry at the boss); the blaming of equipment for poor personal performance; the flight into fantasy ("when I am in charge of this department, things will be different!"). Some of us are great rationalizers; some of us take our troubles out on our subordinates; some of us see no faults in ourselves, but only in others; some of us develop bodily symptoms which have no organic basis. In any event, it is important to realize that we are not always conscious of the true motivation of all of our actions; too often, we are blissfully ignorant of the needs and fears which make us act as we do.

The training process focuses, in part, on the identification of those defenses that interfere with effective personal functioning in the work setting. But while some participants are able to achieve insight into how they act and react, others markedly resist this process and rigidly adhere to their original views of themselves and the world around them.

In the course of our experience, we have learned to identify some expressions which we think reflect typical resistances to this type of training.[2] Although any or all of these feelings may have some rational basis, the participants commonly fail to examine their validity and prefer to hold to their notions of what they are and how they are seen by others. Among the common phrases through which these feelings of resistance are expressed are:

1. "You can't change human nature." This assumes that our personalities are fixed, that we are born to be stubborn, talkative, honest, treacherous, late for work, or leaders of men. If we believe this, then training can accomplish nothing. There is no point in getting involved in something which is bound to have little, if any, impact.

2. "I know myself better than anyone else ever will!" This person cannot accept the idea that hidden or unconscious drives and motives do exist. His best defenses for dealing with this unknown self— his proven tactics for avoiding possible exposure—are denial and rationalization.

3. "If there is one thing I know, it's how to deal with people." This person may readily admit lack of knowledge about the technical aspects of his job, but his self-picture does not permit weakness in the human relations department. His may believe strongly in himself and come to the training to be approved "as is." He often claims knowledge of how to handle a situation, and doesn't hesitate to tell someone else what to do. Prevented from getting evidence which might be contradictory to his expressed feelings of adequacy, he

---

[2] Jack R. Gibb, who conducts leadership training programs at the University of Colorado, has described a similar set of expressions which serve his trainees as defenses against real or imagined threats to their self-concepts. *See* J. R. Gibb and Lorraine M. Gibb, *Applied Group Dynamics: A Laboratory Manual for Group Training in Human Relations Skill* (1953), 121 pp. (mimeo).

avoids testing the reality of whatever fears he has with reference to his abilities to relate to people.

4. "We are here to learn about human relations. You are the expert—so give us the answers." Behind this attitude lies the more customary school experience which utilizes lectures, case materials, tests, and the like. Most people have learned to expect this type of activity whenever they take a course; moreover, experience with books and newspaper columns has taught them to look for specific answers, for rules and gimmicks to solve their human relations problems. Thus, they wish to submit to the trainer's authority, yet at the same time refuse to accept his caution that they will find answers only by participating in a dynamic group process.

5. "Let's stop getting personal—let's be mature and look at the facts!" The person who holds this belief does not like to deal with emotions, feelings, and perceptions. He thinks it unnecessary, if not outright dangerous. To him, every situation calls for a rational principle—the problem is to find the principle that applies. Demanding "the facts" in each instance, he refuses to accept emotions, feelings, and perceptions as facts.

6. "What do you expect us to do—psychoanalyze everybody?" This question reflects a major misunderstanding about the training process. At no time is it recommended that the "open thyself" atmosphere of the training process be transferred into day-to-day business operations. On the contrary, it is the unique motive of the training process which permits people to "see more and better" so that they can then react more effectively to the demands of their daily interpersonal contacts.

7. "I think this is great—I'm learning a lot by sitting back and *watching* all the others." This individual is convinced that there is something to the training process, but does not wish to get involved. By not participating, he avoids exposing himself. Thus he decreases his potential learning experience.

8. "We run a business, not a nursery school." This attitude implies that the training encourages impractical, time consuming, and unrealistic supervisory practices. The trainee assumes that knowing the technical and administrative features of a job are sufficient; he believes that the way to solve problems in human relations is either to avoid them or to discipline those with whom he has difficulties. He fails to admit the possibility that his poor record in interpersonal relations may have its roots in his own behavior and is likely to cite

the ample supply of labor as his main reason for not fooling with "employees who won't do their jobs."

9. "I don't know what you are doing to us, but I don't like it." Behind this expression is a fear that the person's individuality will be lost, that his initiative will disappear, and that his abilities will be attacked and his weaknesses magnified. He thinks that sensitivity training is an attempt at indoctrination over which he has no control. He does not realize that the training process is largely of the group's own making—that what is done is largely a function of what the group wants to do and how it wants to do it. The possibility that individuality is encouraged and enhanced by this type of experience through increasing realistic understanding is not admitted.

Evaluating the training results

Sensitivity training must be evaluated in terms of aims, methods, and achievements. Ideally, this process should consist of three phases. First, a potential trainee should be appraised by his superiors, peers, subordinates, and himself prior to training. Second, his performance in training should be assessed by the trainers, the group members, and himself. Finally, he should be evaluated again by his superiors, peers, subordinates, and himself, some time after the training is completed.

The criteria of evaluation are likely to vary for each evaluator and for each situation. On the job, the trainee's superiors may stress the productivity of his work-groups, their morale, turnover, and similar factors. His peers may look for cooperation and friendliness. His subordinates may be more interested in understanding, acceptance of their frailities, or involvement in decision-making. He, himself, may be most concerned with his ability to handle day-to-day tasks, to keep production up, to deal with arguments and "hurt" feelings when they occur, and to avoid being "called-down" by his superiors.

In the training situation, the trainers may value greater insights into defenses, more realistic perception of others, understanding of communication processes, or newly-found awareness of the forces operating in a group. Fellow participants may stress willingness to understand and listen to others, effectiveness in role-playing, recognition of the impact on a discussion or efforts to help the progress of his group to achieve its goals. He, himself, may most wish to develop feelings of confidence and security, to improve his ability to handle tough situations, to gain skills in interviewing and listening, and to experience relief from some of the tensions and anxieties with which he feels himself saddled.

Self-assessment first result of training

After the training, each group is apt to look for changes in the trainee's behavior related to the criteria first discussed above. The trainee himself, however, is likely to alter some of his criteria in terms of the experiences he has had in the training situation. Experience shows that if participation in the training process has been effective, the first impact will probably occur in the trainee's own perception about himself and others. His new self-assessment may lead to more confidence and security, and to less anxiety in his day-to-day relations on the job. Next, the repercussions of such insights will probably be felt by those with whom he deals. He may "blow up" less often, turn an attentive rather than a deaf ear to suggestions, or play a more constructive role in staff meetings. As he begins to feel his way and explores new behavior patterns, he must be supported by his co-workers to utilize the understanding and skills which he has learned. He needs an environment where human relations practices are part of the total organizational philosophy, where "gimmicks" and manipulative devices are recognized and deprecated for what they are.

As yet, the results of sensitivity training have not been subjected to a rigorous scientific analysis to ascertain the specific type and direction of changes which have undoubtedly taken place. However, reports from both trainees and co-workers indicate that this method of training does lead to greater "human relations" know-how, which in turn often seems to be followed by higher productivity, better morale, and lower turnover. Sensitivity training, of course, is not a "cure-all" for every organizational problem; there are too many other technical and administrative aspects to effective management. We do see it, however, as an exciting development in executive training—with a future rich in promise and in potential rewards.

Questions

1. What are the aims of sensitivity training and how do these aims compare with those for a subject-matter course in human relations?
2. Why must sensitivity training, to some extent at least, be unstructured?
3. Are there any elements of similarity between nondirective counseling and sensitivity training?

4. Will sensitivity training be of any value to a manager who must return to an organization where his boss continually violates good principles of human relations?

Additional Readings for Chapter 2

Allen, Louis A. "What Makes for Successful Executive Development," *Management Record.* Vol. 16, No. 6 (June, 1954), pp. 218-220.

Argyris, Chris. "Organizational Health and Executive Development," *Advanced Management.* Vol. 24, No. 12 (December, 1959), pp. 8-11.

Auvil, Carl E. "The Trickle-Down Theory of Management," *Personnel Administration.* Vol. 25, No. 5 (September-October, 1962), pp. 51-55.

Bailes, Stephen M. "Fundamental Aspects of Establishing a Skills Inventory," *Personnel Journal.* Vol. 41, No. 5 (May, 1962), pp. 226-230.

Bass, Bernard M. "The Management Training Laboratory," *Advanced Management.* Vol. 25, No. 7 (July, 1960), pp. 11-15.

Bellows, Roger. "The Management of Learning: I. Theory and Practice," *Personnel Administration.* Vol. 23, No. 1 (January, 1960), pp. 21-28.

——————. "The Management of Learning: II. Efficiency and Economy," *Personnel Administration.* Vol. 23, No. 2 (March-April, 1960), pp. 4-10.

Bird, Caroline. "More Room at the Top: Company Experiences in Employing Negroes in Professional and Management Jobs," *Management Review.* Vol. 52, No. 3 (March, 1963), pp. 4-16.

Cohen, Kalman J., and Eric Rhenman. "The Role of Management Games in Education and Research," *Management Science.* Vol. 7, No. 2 (January, 1961), pp. 131-166.

Dill, William R. "What Management Games Do Best," *Business Horizons.* Vol. 4, No. 3 (Fall, 1961), pp. 55-64.

Dukes, Carlton W. "Effective Measurement of a Professional Recruiting Effort—A Systems Approach," *Personnel Journal.* Vol. 44, No. 1 (January, 1965), pp. 12-17.

Efferson, C. A. "Organization Planning for Management Growth," *Management Record.* Vol. 20, No. 4 (April, 1958), pp. 134-137.

Flanagan, John C. "Use and Abuse of Intelligence Tests," *Public Personnel Review.* Vol. 22, No. 1 (January, 1961), pp. 24-28.

——————. "What They Say About Testing—And What To Do About It," *Public Personnel Review.* Vol. 25, No. 3 (July, 1964), pp. 174-179.

French, Seward H., Jr., and Harold Guetzkow. "Birth of a Training Organization," *Personnel Journal.* Vol. 34, No. 6 (November, 1955), pp. 212-218.

French, Wendell L. "What Every Executive Should Know About Psychological Testing," *Personnel Journal.* Vol. 39, No. 9 (February, 1961), pp. 351-355, 377.

Garton, Robert D. "Assimilating the College Graduate: Challenge to Industry," *Personnel Administration.* Vol. 24, No. 1 (January-February, 1961), pp. 10-17.

Gellerman, Saul W. "A Hard Look at Testing," *Personnel.* Vol. 38, No. 3 (May-June, 1961), pp. 8-15.

——————. "Personnel Testing: What the Critics Overlook," *Personnel*. Vol. 40, No. 3 (May-June, 1963), pp. 18-26.

Gibson, George W. "A New Dimension for 'In-Basket' Training," *Personnel*. Vol. 38, No. 4 (July-August, 1961), pp. 76-79.

Gillen, Ralph L., and Herbert Hubben. "Motivating the Boss; The Key to Executive Development," *Business Horizons*. Vol. 3, No. 3 (Fall, 1960), pp. 49-61.

——————. "How Good Are Personality Tests, Anyway?" *Administrative Management*. Vol. XXIII, No. 10 (October, 1962), pp. 26-28, 30; Part II, Vol. XXIII, No. 11 (November, 1962), pp. 38-39.

Jenks, James M. "The Development of Middle Management," *Advanced Management*. Vol. 25, No. 3 (March, 1960), pp. 23-25.

Kruger, Daniel H. "The United States Employment Service," *Business Topics*. Vol. 12, No. 3 (Summer, 1964), pp. 19-29.

Levinson, Harry. "A Psychologist Looks at Executive Development," *Harvard Business Review*. Vol. 40, No. 5 (September-October, 1962), pp. 69-75.

Mandell, Milton M. "Checking References: How to Get the Facts," *Supervisory Management*. Vol. 3, No. 3 (March, 1958), pp. 10-16.

Mayfield, Eugene C. "The Selection Interview—A Re-Evaluation of Published Research," *Personnel Psychology*. Vol. 17, No. 3 (Autumn, 1964), pp. 239-260.

Murphy, John R., and Irving A. Goldberg. "Strategies for Using Programmed Instruction," *Harvard Business Review*. Vol. 42, No. 3 (May-June, 1964), pp. 115-132.

Newton, T. G. "How Training Needs Are Determined," *Journal of the American Society of Training Directors*. Vol. 8, No. 5 (September-October, 1956), pp. 13-16, 52-63.

Schein, Edgar H. "Forces Which Undermine Management Development," *California Management Review*. Vol. 5, No. 4 (Summer, 1963), pp. 23-34.

Souerwine, Andrew H. "More Value from Personnel Testing," *Harvard Business Review*. Vol. 39, No. 2 (March-April, 1961), pp. 123-130.

Stolz, Robert K. "Getting Back to Fundamentals in Executive Development," *Personnel*. Vol. 30, No. 6 (May, 1954), pp. 434-444.

Tannenbaum, Robert, Verne Kallejian, and Irving R. Weschler. "Training Managers for Leadership," *Personnel*. Vol. 30, No. 4 (January, 1954), pp. 254-260.

Trull, Samuel G. "Strategies of Effective Interviewing," *Harvard Business Review*. Vol. 42, No. 1 (January-February, 1964), pp. 89-94.

Ward, Lewis B. "Putting Executives to the Test," *Harvard Business Review*. Vol. 38, No. 4 (July-August, 1960), pp. 6-15, 164-180.

Whistler, Thomas L. "Performance Appraisal and the Organizational Man," *Journal of Business*. Vol. 31, No. 1 (February, 1958), pp. 19-27.

Wilson, J. Watson. "Toward Better Use of Psychological Testing," *Personnel*. Vol. 39, No. 3 (May-June, 1962), pp. 55-62.

CHAPTER 3

Achieving Efficient Performance

While the careful selection and proper training of personnel is essential to the development of an effective work force, it is vital that a continuing effort be exerted by managers and supervisors to create conditions that will result in efficient performance of all employees. It is not enough just to hire individuals with good potential, provide training for them, and then wait for results. Successful managers are found to be those who establish conditions that will motivate employees toward individual and organizational goals and who learn effective ways of communicating with employees about the quality of their performance.

The creation of motivating conditions and the communication with employees about their performance constitute the most difficult tasks that any manager faces. Fortunately, however, there are many journal articles as well as books that provide a background for understanding the complex nature of the problem and that offer practical suggestions which may be utilized.

Regardless of the extent of one's knowledge about human motivation and the evaluation of job performance, there is still the gap between knowing what to do and being able to do it, which confronts every manager at one time or another. Fortunately, many management and supervisory training programs provide opportunities for role playing or for trying out new skills in a laboratory environment. After developing some degree of competency and confidence in a training situation, the manager is likely to feel more adequate in the real-life situation.

While one must learn to bridge the gap between knowing and doing, an understanding of human needs and the incentives that may be used to motivate employees to perform at high levels is an important step in achieving efficiency among employees. Similarly, a knowledge of approaches that have been used in evaluating the performance of employees and in communicating with them about their performance is essential.

In recent years it has been recognized that the most effective part of the evaluation procedure, if properly conducted, is the interview between the supervisor and the subordinate. In most instances it has been recommended that these interviews follow an approach that will provide the employee with an opportunity to see his own strengths and weaknesses and to develop a plan for personal improvement that appears necessary and realistic to him. This approach to evaluation is consistent with modern views of employee motivation.

It is likely that from the beginnings of time managers have been concerned about motivation and have raised the question: How can I get better performance from my people? We do know for a certainty that they are asking this question today. The answer, unfortunately, is rather complex; but if one is willing to study and examine the process of human motivation and to modify the working conditions, the likelihood of obtaining an answer is favorable. It should be recognized at the outset, however, that an abiding and sincere interest in the employees and their welfare is a fundamental requirement.

The articles that have been selected for this chapter contain important concepts in evaluation and motivation. Some of the concepts are well established. Others are based on theories which are still being examined in the light of experimental evidence; and until more evidence to support them is available, one can only examine them, try them out in a practical situation, and then analyze the results. Unless one has attained a sophisticated understanding of the theories, he should not reject them but continue to explore their possibilities.

The first article was written by the dean of personnel managers—Whiting Williams. It presents his philosophy of employee motivation which grew out of firsthand experiences with workers as long as a half century ago. His four key words, which the reader will find in the article, might well be placed on the desk of every personnel worker, as well as every manager and supervisor. These words are simple in nature but strike at the heart of human needs.

The second article by the late Douglas M. McGregor presents a theory of motivation commonly referred to as Theory Y. A few years after this article was published, McGregor's book, *The Human Side of Enterprise* (McGraw-Hill, 1960), appeared with a more complete discussion of the theory.

In his article Lippitt stresses the importance of improving the functioning of organizations so that the individual employee can obtain optimum growth while the objectives of the organization are being met. The reader will note that his philosophy coincides with that of McGregor in that both recognize the importance of creating conditions that will enable the individual to reach his full potential. Lippitt believes that supervisors should develop a collaborative relationship with subordinates in order that the needs of individual employees can be understood better and action taken to provide opportunities that will contribute to their fulfillment.

It was mentioned earlier that one of the "headaches" that many managers report having is the periodic chore of appraising employee performance and then attempting to tell the employees about it. Robert K. Stolz provides us with some suggestions on how appraisal discussions can be made constructive rather than destructive. One of the most valuable contributions of the article is the statement concerning the laying of a solid foundation for effective appraisal discussions. The appraisal of executive performance has received increased emphasis with the growth of executive development programs in the period following World War II. The article by Arch Patton contains suggestions that are applicable not only to executives but also to supervisors and employees.

14. WHAT EVERY WORKER WANTS *

Whiting Williams

The first of my rather unusual efforts to understand the worker started when the president of the steel company for whom I was working called me in one day and said that he and his associates didn't think I was doing a good job of bridging the gap between the mind of management and the minds of the workers. Like anyone else under similar circumstances, I went home and proceeded to walk the floor for a few nights. As a result, I went in and asked him if he would give me a leave of absence for six months for the purpose of living the life of our workers. He gave me permission, but asked the same question that has been asked me ever since by people when they hear of my experiences. Said he: "How will you disguise yourself sufficiently to gain the confidence of the workers?"

I have always had to explain that in the rough labor gangs where I proceeded to live the life of my fellow workmen, all of them accepted me so completely as the ordinary laborer I pretended to be, that it actually hurt my feelings! Only one man pierced my disguise—and he was very intoxicated at the time! He said, "There's something wrong with you, stranger. Either you have been convicted of a serious crime, or you are a victim of some secret sin, or you wouldn't come to work in this God-forsaken town!"

I have to report that what really worried me was the danger of getting too close to the whole situation, especially in various countries abroad. In Russia I was really scared when being interviewed by my fellow coal miners and was suddenly arrested by the secret police who gave me a good work-out before they finally released me.

In 1922, Collier's Weekly asked me to find out the causes of the great railway shopman's strike. That meant I had to go through the picket lines. I will never forget my reception there. We were being taken in under protection of a policeman, and one picket

* From *Connecticut Industry* (May, 1951). An edited version of an address given by Mr. Williams in November, 1950, before the annual convention of the NTDMA. Reprinted with permission.

said, "Hey, has anybody told you about the dynamite that goes off in there? We guys on the outside don't know how many of you dirty scabs get knocked off in there, because the company buries them at night, but it sure does make one hell of a noise!"

During the depression I ran again into unexpected danger. I had been accepted as a bum in Chicago until I made the mistake of drinking out of a milk bottle a harmless looking concoction that looked like milk and water. It goes by the name of "smoke," also by the name of "jungle juice." It was a combination of gasoline and denatured alcohol!

What did I learn that helps explain why it is that today our miracle of production here in America means that we are the sole protection of all the other free nations of the world against Russia? How have we gotten this amazing will to work which now stands us in such good stead? What has made us the protector of the free world?

Fear, Hope and Pride—Important Words

I believe it is our particular idea of what makes us humans tick. I can best give you that idea by telling you of my experience. I took a train in January, 1919, to go to Pittsburgh to get a job in the steel works. I changed my name, put on old clothes, and $25 in my pocket, with the expectation that it was up to me to live the life of a jobless man if my $25 gave out. In four hours I ran onto a very important word. That word is "fear," the fear of the loss of the job. As long as I live, I will never get over the impression made on me of the universality of that particular fear.

Shortly afterward I learned the importance of a second word in the workman's mind. That word is "hope," hope for promotion.

I wish I could claim I pondered why that fear was so intense and that hope so unquenchable. But I thought I knew. All the professors and psychologists said they knew all about it. They said the only value in the worker's mind was money, that that fear was only fear for the loss of income, that that hope was only the hope for a larger income.

I had plenty of time to ponder that question, and the longer I pondered the less adequate that explanation appeared to be. To make a long story short, there is a third word that goes with "fear" and "hope" in the workman's mind. That word is "pride." I believe that pride represents the satisfaction of the two deepest, strongest, most useful of hankerings. Hankering Number One is for our own self-respect—the right to believe that we individually represent certain values in the scheme of things—that we are worth while, important, "somebody." If you think that is an easy satisfaction to enjoy, let me say, on the contrary, the enjoyment of that particular satisfaction represents just about the hardest job that you or I or anyone knows about, for the reason that I have yet to see a human being of any sort who is as sure of his or her right to believe in his or her importance as he or she would like to be.

When I say that, I will gamble that half of you will say "You are right" but half of you will say "You are wrong." But *none* of us are all the time as sure of ourselves as we would like to be. Whether we are drunk or sober, young or old, male or female, sane or insane, all of us are everlastingly trying to fight off the feeling of having to think of ourselves as a human zero of insignificance and unimportance.

That leads to hankering Number Two, the hankering we all have for the confirmation of our right to enjoy our self-respect which comes to us from sources outside ourselves, in the form of recognition, esteem, honor.

I recommend, therefore, as most helpful to understanding the worker's mind, these fundamentals:

First, that today the saving of our physical skin has become infinitely less important as a factor in our human relations than the saving of our social "face." This is so dependent upon our right to think well of ourselves . . ., that our "face" is very easily hurt by some slur, some look of the eye or other small slight.

Secondly, that whereas today at least two-thirds of the human race are bothered by hunger, here in America our hunger for food has become infinitely less important than hunger for attention, recognition, understanding.

As an example of that, I was at a cocktail party not long ago when a friend nudged me and said, "Look at the way that handsome man is annoying that beautiful blonde over there." I looked, and said, "Why, he isn't even looking at her!" My friend said, "Hell, that's what I'm trying to tell you!"

If you want to annoy any human being, beautiful blonde or whatnot, all you have to do is ignore him!

Third, that our hunger finds its chief and surest satisfaction in connection with our jobs, our work. I think I can claim rather varied contacts. To learn about people, I have associated with bums and with workers here and abroad, and I have sat with captains of industry in London, Paris, Berlin, Chicago, and New York. I give you my word, whether they were bums, board chairmen or in betweens, they were all just about equally less sure of themselves than they would *like* to be, all about equally as hungry to maintain "face," to have a word of approval.

But here is the point. Whether they were at the bottom or the top of the ladder, every blessed one of them gave me as final, incontrovertible, proof of certificate: "This is my job; this is the kind of service I give my fellow men; this is the kind of equipment I make useful to my fellow citizens. On the basis of that I demand a certain amount of attention."

The Job—A Measurement of Usefulness

I found, therefore, that the job serves as an amazingly useful scale for measuring the distance we have achieved up from the useless zero. Thus, I finally got a job as a laborer in the cinder-pit of a steel plant. Three weeks later the boss asked me about going into the millwright gang. I supposed only the money would be of interest to the ordinary worker. So when he told me I would get only two cents more an hour I thought it wasn't important. An hour later I had the new tools in my hand, and when I came by old companions I made a sensation. Every blessed one of them greeted me: "Hey, boodie, where you catch-em job? Millwright gang? No more pick and shovel for you! My God, you are one lucky son-of-gun!"

That was the first of a series of experiences that taught me that to every worker his job represents a rung upon a ladder indicating his comparative importance, establishing his position as a man among his fellow citizens outside the job. Every rung represents a distance, partly established by the amount of money but also by the skill and the training required. Thousands of details are involved. A tool designer has a right to consider himself a more important person and citizen than the tool operator, because of his job. Likewise the tool operator considers himself more important than the sweeper-up. Everywhere it's like that.

We have today a serious problem just because the whole trend of these modern times, with which I don't agree, is to lessen the differential between the skilled man and the unskilled by raising the unskilled.

The point is that when we give honor and recognition to the man at the top of the ladder, anyone from the bottom up has the right to consider himself worth while because his job makes him essential to the man at the top.

When I became an assistant repairman in a mine in Wales, I was way down below the lowest level. A thousand feet down there in the darkness, Evan Pugh, the repairman, and I would be hoping for a message to do our stuff. Then one of the miners would come in and say, "Evan, you better come quick before the pit falls in!" Half an hour afterward we would realize that only after we had done that repair job could the whole mine start working again. Then Evan would say to me, "It's very plain to see they can't run their bloody old mine without you and me!"

There is nothing that can compare with a man's job for helping him believe in himself. Everywhere I have gone, I have found the same thing. The reason we have such a grand responsible bunch of locomotive engineers is because they get the kowtowing of all their associates and companions because they have gone from the bottom of the ladder up to the top. What we overlook is that the fireman is likely to say, as one of them once said to me as I rode with him: "You see, the engineer takes himself very serious. I ain't saying nothin', but let me tell you, Mr. Engineer don't get his engine very far unless he gets his power from me!"

Everybody's Job Important to Him

You can't think of anybody whose job doesn't seem to him important. One time I unintentionally insulted the International Secretary of the Hobo Union because I thought he was a tramp. He said, "We 'boes are migratory workers, itinerant laborers; if we don't go to the right part of the country at the right time, millions of dollars worth of crops go to hell. So we *have* to take the train. A tramp only walks for a job. A bum is a guy that neither rides nor walks nor works. He's no good."

But the bum considers himself more worth while than, we will say, the Jungle-Buzzard, because that guy expects to eat mulligan stew without contributing anything to it. But you would hurt the Jungle-Buzzard's feelings if you didn't realize that he is better than a Mission Stiff. The Mission Stiff gets free food and clothes and a clean bed because he fools the keeper of the mission into thinking he has saved another soul. But you would hurt the feelings of the Mission Stiff if you didn't realize that he is better than a Lush Diver, who makes his living robbing drunks. But all these consider themselves superior to the lowest of them all. He is a Scissor Bill:

he will do anything provided he has something in his stomach. If somebody comes along and puts a couple of squares under his belt, he will say, "To hell with the revolution; let's wait a while!"

All these say, "My job is the thing that makes me worth while. It proves that I'm important, that the world needs me!"

Nobody can be sure of the loyalty of his workers unless he understands this absolutely fundamental fact. His job of course puts money in a man's pocket, but most important it also puts self-respect and self-belief in the bottom of his heart. If you miss that, you miss everything!

It is this tie-up of soul and body represented by the job that explains that fear. That fear, in turn, explains many of the peculiarities of workers. It "justifies" unions, limitation of output and so on. It also explains their hope for promotion. Besides an increase in income, this means a larger distance away from that dreadful zero at the bottom.

This tie-up also means that every single one of us would like to take pride in our work. If we can't take pride in our jobs, we can't take pride in ourselves, and then you might as well seek our body at the bottom of the river.

That tie-up also explains why your feelings, my feelings, every worker's feelings, can be hurt more easily during the hours of our job than any other of the twenty-four. Your wives may say you are touchy enough when you come home, but it doesn't compare with your touchiness during the hours of your job. It also explains why big issues come from management's failure to take care of some little annoyance that hurts men's feelings.

Importance of Little Things

In my opinion, many labor leaders understand these fundamentals better than employers, particularly the wish of their members to feel important, if not in their work, then in a strike. They also realize the importance of little things. For instance, while I was working in the mines in Wales I got into a "strike of folded arms." We went to work but we knew if we set hands to tools we would be beaten up by the committee of Reds or Bolshies. They were trying to make us feel important as strikers and they had us sing about the blood red flag of revolution and how it could be pinned to the top of the Houses of Parliament. They did a bang-up job of it.

But they also understood the importance of little things. I said to one of them, "You call yourself a leader. Why don't you have the employers put down gravel so we won't have to walk in mud?" And he said, "When we ask the masters, they tell us 'You are troublemakers; out with you!' If only the masters some years back had seen fit to think of us not so much as troublemakers as trouble-finders, 'twould be a better mine here!"

Those employers made a great mistake in thinking those fellows had gone radical. Because my miner friends explained, "These Bolshies do go too far. We must have law and order. But, after all, these Bolshies do be the mouthpiece of us all for all of us been fair unhappy!" They were made unhappy by all sorts of little annoyances.

Today one reason why the big unions have done as much as they have is because they first send out investigators who bring back all the gripes, big and little. Then they send out their organizers to tell every member of that industry, "If you sign on the dotted line, you will never again be bothered by any of these troubles."

I have found this importance of the job everywhere. But nowhere to the same extent as here in the United States. Here, above everywhere else in the world, a man's respectability is based upon his job. The biggest reason, therefore, why we have become the world's protector, is that we, as nowhere else, have made a man's respectability, a man's right to consider himself worthy in the eyes of his companions, dependent on his job.

We have out-produced the rest of the world, for the reason that we have harnessed the performance of useful service to those two hankerings. We have said to our youngsters, "If you would like to grow up into a worthy citizen with the confirmation and esteem of your fellows, all you need to do is climb that ladder of the job!" The biggest difference between Europe and ourselves is this. When you ask, over there, "Who is John Smith?" they assume you mean, "What is the class where he was born? Who is his father? Here we all know, we mean one thing, "What is his *job?* What is the nature of his skill, his equipment, his usefulness as shown by his work?"

Today I am worried because that system of respectability and honor based upon work which has made us great is now under serious threat. That threat gets fairly deep into politics.

You have the greatest of all opportunities to help save our system of making respectability and honor depend upon work. For if I am right about the importance of fear, hope, and pride, then as employers, you have a greater opportunity than anybody else, first, to lessen fear; secondly, to justify hope; and most important and difficult, to build pride in your workers—pride of their skill, pride of their craft, pride of their company, pride of their industry. Pride is the key to their performance.

Value of Personal Contacts

Here are a few of the tools which you can use for building pride. The simplest and one of the most effective tools is making sure that you are utilizing to the full your opportunity for personal contacts. I have been a fan about what can be done by personal contact ever since I got a job in the mines in Germany's Saar Valley. I was told the German miners were going to murder the French engineers who were put over them by the League of Nations. But to my surprise they spoke well of these officers. In explanation, the engineers said, "We are taught in our mining schools always to keep in close touch with our miners. Every day we talk to a few of them face to face till, in a month we contact all of them." Sure enough, I'd be loading coal and along would come the French engineer-manager. He would ask us, "How are you getting along? Have you got good tools? Is the ventilation all right?" Then after talking with us about the cost of living, and so on, he would say, "We will see you again next month."

Most amazed, the Germans would exclaim, "We have been taught to hate every Frenchman, yet they treat us better than we have ever been treated before."

So I say today, American industry is in danger of depending too much on mass arrangements, mass programs. But if you leave out personal contacts, those programs won't work. Our heavy dependence on these big mass plans in industry isn't much more silly than if some husband were to say that he and his wife, in order to avoid divorce, were going to sign a contract that would cover every problem. So if he was blown up by his wife on a Tuesday morning he could point to page so-and-so and say, "See, this clause proves you're wrong!" There is no substitute for personal contact for learning the worker's fears, hopes, prides.

Answering the Why's

The second tool is better communications, fuller explanation of the new machine or new method, why, why, why, all over the place. You can't overdo it. Whether you are a mother in the home or a boss in the factory, when you ask me to do so-and-so "because I tell you" you are destroying my face, my belief in myself. I wish I could put upon the desk of every executive and manager a sign saying, "Explain. If you can't, explain *why* you can't explain."

The next tool I recommend is the freer use of the pat on the back, when deserved. Mind you, I underline the word "deserved" because if you want to lose the respect of a good craftsman, you need only praise as good a job which he as a craftsman knows is lousy. I have had vice-presidents of some of the biggest corporations in America almost weep on my shoulder because they couldn't get from their president one single word to enable them to know where they stood. They would give their right arm to have a report back from the president with two words, "Very good," instead of just two initials.

A manager told me one time in a plant in Cleveland that he called in a foreman and told him that the Vice-President had asked if he could lend him for a couple of weeks to another plant. "I told him I couldn't spare him because he was too useful to me." Result? Big Jim, the foreman, said with tears in his eyes, "I have wondered all these years if you thought I was any damn good. That's the best news ever!"

And there was the mine superintendent who called in a Polish workman one day and said, "Steve, that was a good suggestion you made. Here's a ten-dollar bill." Twenty-four hours later Steve came in and said, "Please, boss, write me a letter; say that you called me good man and gave me ten-dollar bill because I make good suggestion." The boss said, "Steve, I am very busy. Why do you want me to take the trouble to write you a letter? I gave you a ten-dollar bill; what more do you want?" And Steve said, "Because last night I go home and tell my woman you give me ten-dollar bill because I make good suggestion. My woman she say me lousy liar!"

Mrs. Lindbergh tells in her book about how she and Lindy once had a terrible time getting their plane off the water in Africa. Chapter after chapter goes on, and they haven't got the plane up in the air. Finally the time comes, and they take off. Then Mrs. Lindbergh writes a note to her husband, because of the noise in the cockpit. "Was it the gas?" Lindbergh shakes his head. Another note: "Do you think we can make it?" Lindbergh nods his head, "Yes." Then she rather apologizes for the next message. Evidently she felt so pleased and relieved that she wrote him this note: "I think you are wonderful!" and handed it over to him.

Millions of wives today would give their right arms to get that kind of a note from their husbands. The paradox is, though, that most of those wives assume it isn't necessary to write that kind of note to husbands. Why? Because he has a job and they have no such certificate of their worth.

That is a dangerous idea, because when even the best of husbands gets that kind of note from his secretary or from the handsome blonde down the street—"I think you are wonderful"—if the best of husbands gets such a note from anybody who is appreciative, the chances are he will say, "What an intelligent—what a *charming* woman!" This is because you can put it down in the book that nobody, whatever his condition, is as sure of his value as he would *like* to be.

When you give a man a job in your plant you give him something infinitely more important than a chance to make a living. You determine the conditions of his whole life. If he can feel, with your help, the right to consider himself worth while, as playing a worthy part in the protection and maintenance of America, then you have built that man into a happy human being in the way that no other human being of any sort can do as well as you, his employer.

All this has a more important bearing today than ever before, because we are in a war of "isms"—different ideas of human nature and motivation. The best statement I have seen of our American idea was given by Fosdick. He says, "The essence of Americanism and of democracy is to attribute to ordinary human beings extra-ordinary possibilities."

I believe, after I have observed things in Europe, the reason why Socialism and Communism fail to produce things is just because they attribute extraordinary possibilities only to a few carefully chosen officials. They assume that all of the rest of us are nothing but scissor bills. In other words, all the government has to do is fill our bellies and clothe our backs and then we will be so thankful we will keep them everlastingly in power.

But if there is anything we Americans are not—we are not scissor bills. We don't follow the line of least resistance. We have no respect for a leader who asks so little of us that we can't think better of ourselves than we could before. We hate a leader who takes to himself all the credit and the glory and gives us nothing but the money. But we gladly go through hell for the leader who asks the impossible of us—provided that, when we give it, he shares with us the right to think better of ourselves in the measure of our effort!

All this means, finally, that you can't do your best for yourself, for your workers or for your country, unless you have in mind the limitless possibilities that are placed inside of us by those two hankerings. Rather than fall down and be considered unworthy, we are glad to pay the price of life itself! . . .

Today we are faced in America with what I believe is a tragic paradox. We are being taught that of course nobody works except for money. Nobody should be so silly as to assume that he can get cooperation without paying so much per. At the same time, the fathers, the sons, and the brothers of these workers over in the mountains of Korea are today walking willingly to meet the possibility of death! Why? Because of the money we pay them? No! The only reason they walk willingly to meet death is that as they walk they feel the certainty of your recognition and mine and of all mankind, of the nobility that makes them do it! They would rather die with honor than live without it!

We all know that if we were to withhold that honor, were to take off from their place of honor the names of our honored dead, and were to pay no recognition to our Gold Star mothers, then in time of war, we would stand naked and defenseless before our enemies.

You cannot be a good American unless you understand that. Also in time of peace, what has made us great and what will continue to make us great is our willingness to give honor, recognition to a man in proportion to the usefulness of his service.

Old Evan Pugh used to tell me about an undermanager that he worked for who was very hard-boiled—until he studied human nature as captain of a company on the Western Front during World War I. There he learned about the possibilities of human nature. So when he came back to his old job he put into operation a different way of handling men. One night Old Evan reported: "Yesterday the undermanager down in the pit said to me, 'That do be a first-class job ye've done.' And I do say to him, 'Mr. undermanager, in forty-three years of workin' in this pit—in forty-three years, that do be the first time that any company man do say to me a kindly word about my job.'" Then he continued: "Every man do know that for a kindly word, he'll work his guts out—that no dog behave well for the man with a whip. And every man of sensibility do know that for him, the whip of the tongue and the lash of the lip be worse nor any whip on any dog! Every man must have a chance here on the job to show himself the man!"

My belief, therefore, is that we may come through just because, as I have gone among the other nations, I have found this one thing is true of you and me as Americans—namely, that every one of us would love to have it said of us what the old writer in Ecclesiastes said of the ancient artisans and craftsmen:

> All these have put their trust in their hands,
> And each becometh wise in his own works.
> Yea, though they be not sought for in the council of the people
> Nor be exalted in the assembly;
> And be not found amongst them that utter dark sayings;
> Yet without these shall not a city be inhabited,
> Nor shall men sojourn or walk up and down therein.
> For these maintain the fabric of the world
> And in the handiwork of their craft is their prayer.

As long as you employers help make sure that our prayer remains there in the work of our hands and our hearts and our heads, so long the future of America is safe; but with the utmost seriousness may I say, only so long.

I give you four words as helpful to this understanding of the worker and the gaining of his cooperation. Those four words are: Listen, Explain, Respect, Appreciate!

Questions

1. Mr. Williams reports that the professors and psychologists with whom he talked in 1919 said that the only value in the worker's mind was money and the only fear was for the loss of income. Do you believe that most managers would feel this way? Why?
2. Do you agree with Williams that the trend to lessen the differential between the skilled and the unskilled workers by raising the wages of the unskilled is undesirable? Why?
3. How can the executives of a large company maintain the personal contact with subordinates that Williams feels is important? Are there any dangers in this procedure?
4. This article was written about fifteen years ago. Do you believe that Americans exhibit any tendency toward becoming "scissor bills"? What evidence do you have for your belief?
5. Can you think of current industrial personnel problems that might be better understood by having observers "live the life of the workers," as Williams did over 45 years ago? Are there any ethical considerations in such an approach?

15. THE HUMAN SIDE OF ENTERPRISE *

Douglas M. McGregor

It has become trite to say that industry has the fundamental know-how to utilize physical science and technology for the material benefit of mankind, and that we must now learn how to utilize the social sciences to make our human organizations truly effective.

To a degree, the social sciences today are in a position like that of the physical sciences with respect to atomic energy in the thirties. We know that past conceptions of the nature of man are inadequate and, in many ways, incorrect. We are becoming quite certain that, under proper conditions, unimagined resources of creative human energy could become available within the organizational setting.

We cannot tell industrial management how to apply this new knowledge in simple, economic ways. We know it will require years of exploration, much costly development research, and a substantial amount of creative imagination on the part of management to discover how to apply this growing knowledge to the organization of human effort in industry.

Management's Task: The Conventional View

The conventional conception of management's task in harnessing human energy to organizational requirements can be stated broadly in terms of three propositions. In order to avoid the complications introduced by a label, let us call this set of propositions "Theory X":

1. Management is responsible for organizing the elements of productive enterprise—money, materials, equipment, people—in the interest of economic ends.

2. With respect to people, this is a process of directing their efforts, motivating them, controlling their actions, modifying their behavior to fit the needs of the organization.

* From *The Management Review*, Vol. 46, No. 11 (November, 1957), pp. 22-28, 88-92. Reprinted with permission. This article is based on an address by the late Dr. McGregor before the Fifth Anniversary Convocation of the M.I.T. School of Industrial Management.

3. Without this active intervention by management, people would be passive—even resistant—to organizational needs. They must therefore be persuaded, rewarded, punished, controlled—their activities must be directed. This is management's task. We often sum it up by saying that management consists of getting things done through other people.

Behind this conventional theory there are several additional beliefs—less explicit, but widespread:

4. The average man is by nature indolent—he works as little as possible.

5. He lacks ambition, dislikes responsibility, prefers to be led.

6. He is inherently self-centered, indifferent to organizational needs.

7. He is by nature resistant to change.

8. He is gullible, not very bright, the ready dupe of the charlatan and the demagogue.

The human side of economic enterprise today is fashioned from propositions and beliefs such as these. Conventional organization structures and managerial policies, practices, and programs reflect these assumptions.

In accomplishing its task—with these assumptions as guides—management has conceived of a range of possibilities.

At one extreme, management can be "hard" or "strong." The methods for directing behavior involve coercion and threat (usually disguised), close supervision, tight controls over behavior. At the other extreme, management can be "soft" or "weak." The methods for directing behavior involve being permissive, satisfying people's demands, achieving harmony. Then they will be tractable, accept direction.

This range has been fairly completely explored during the past half century, and management has learned some things from the exploration. There are difficulties in the "hard" approach. Force breeds counter-forces: restriction of output, antagonism, militant unionism, subtle but effective sabotage of management objectives. This "hard" approach is especially difficult during times of full employment.

There are also difficulties in the "soft" approach. It leads frequently to the abdication of management—to harmony, perhaps, but to indifferent performance. People take advantage of the soft approach. They continually expect more, but they give less and less.

Currently, the popular theme is "firm but fair." This is an attempt to gain the advantages of both the hard and the soft approaches. It is reminiscent of Teddy Roosevelt's "speak softly and carry a big stick."

Is the Conventional View Correct?

The findings which are beginning to emerge from the social sciences challenge this whole set of beliefs about man and human nature and about the task of management. The evidence is far from conclusive, certainly, but it is suggestive. It comes from the laboratory, the clinic, the schoolroom, the home, and even to a limited extent from industry itself.

The social scientist does not deny that human behavior in industrial organization today is approximately what management perceives it to be. He has, in fact, observed it and studied it fairly extensively. But he is pretty sure that this behavior is *not* a consequence of man's inherent nature. It is a consequence rather of the nature of industrial organizations, of management philosophy, policy, and practice. The conventional approach of Theory X is based on mistaken notions of what is cause and what is effect.

Perhaps the best way to indicate why the conventional approach of management is inadequate is to consider the subject of motivation.

Physiological Needs

Man is a wanting animal—as soon as one of his needs is satisfied, another appears in its place. This process is unending. It continues from birth to death.

Man's needs are organized in a series of levels—a hierarchy of importance. At the lowest level, but pre-eminent in importance when they are thwarted, are his *physiological needs*. Man lives for bread alone, when there is no bread. Unless the circumstances are unusual, his needs for love, for status, for recognition are inoperative when his stomach has been empty for a while. But when he eats regularly and adequately, hunger ceases to be an important motivation. The same is true of the other physiological needs of man—for rest, exercise, shelter, protection from the elements.

A *satisfied need is not a motivator of behavior!* This is a fact of profound significance that is regularly ignored in the conventional approach to the management of people. Consider your own need for air: Except as you are deprived of it, it has no appreciable motivating effect upon your behavior.

Safety Needs

When the physiological needs are reasonably satisfied, needs at the next higher level begin to dominate man's behavior—to motivate him. These are called *safety needs*. They are needs for protection against danger, threat, deprivation. Some people mistakenly refer to these as needs for security. However, unless man is in a dependent relationship where he fears arbitrary deprivation, he does not demand security. The need is for the "fairest possible break." When he is confident of this, he is more than willing to take risks. But when he feels threatened or dependent, his greatest need is for guarantees, for protection, for security.

The fact needs little emphasis that, since every industrial employee is in a dependent relationship, safety needs may assume considerable importance. Arbitrary management actions, behavior which arouses uncertainty with respect to continued employment or which reflects favoritism or discrimination, unpredictable administration of policy—these can be powerful motivators of the safety needs in the employment relationship *at every level*, from worker to vice-president.

Social Needs

When man's physiological needs are satisfied and he is no longer fearful about his physical welfare, his *social needs* become important motivators of his behavior—needs for belonging, for association, for acceptance by his fellows, for giving and receiving friendship and love.

Management knows today of the existence of these needs, but it often assumes quite wrongly that they represent a threat to the organization. Many studies have demonstrated that the tightly knit, cohesive work group may, under proper conditions, be far more effective than an equal number of separate individuals in achieving organizational goals.

Yet management, fearing group hostility to its own objectives, often goes to considerable lengths to control and direct human efforts in ways that are inimical to the natural "groupiness" of human beings. When man's social needs—and perhaps his safety needs, too —are thus thwarted, he behaves in ways which tend to defeat organizational objectives. He becomes resistant, antagonistic, uncooperative. But this behavior is a consequence, not a cause.

Ego Needs

Above the social needs—in the sense that they do not become motivators until lower needs are reasonably satisfied—are the needs of greatest significance to management and to man himself. They are the *egoistic needs,* and they are of two kinds:

1. Those needs that relate to one's self-esteem—needs for self-confidence, for independence, for achievement, for competence, for knowledge.

2. Those needs that relate to one's reputation—needs for status, for recognition, for appreciation, for the deserved respect of one's fellows.

Unlike the lower needs, these are rarely satisfied; man seeks indefinitely for more satisfaction of these needs once they have become important to him. But they do not appear in any significant way until physiological, safety, and social needs are all reasonably satisfied.

The typical industrial organization offers few opportunities for the satisfaction of these egoistic needs to people at lower levels in the hierarchy. The conventional methods of organizing work, particularly in mass production industries, give little heed to these aspects of human motivation. If the practices of scientific management were deliberately calculated to thwart these needs, they could hardly accomplish this purpose better than they do.

Self-Fulfillment Needs

Finally—a capstone, as it were, on the hierarchy of man's needs—there are what we may call the *needs for self-fulfillment.* These are the needs for realizing one's own potentialities, for continued self-development, for being creative in the broadest sense of that term.

It is clear that the conditions of modern life give only limited opportunity for these relatively weak needs to obtain expression. The deprivation most people experience with respect to other lower-level needs diverts their energies into the struggle to satisfy *those* needs, and the needs for self-fulfillment remain dormant.

Management and Motivation

We recognize readily enough that a man suffering from a severe dietary deficiency is sick. The deprivation of physiological needs has behavioral consequences. The same is true—although less well recognized—of deprivation of higher-level needs. The man whose needs for safety, association, independence, or status are thwarted is sick just as surely as the man who has rickets. And his sickness will have behavioral consequences. We will be mistaken if we attribute his resultant passivity, his hostility, his refusal to accept responsibility to his inherent "human nature." These forms of behavior are *symptoms* of illness—of deprivation of his social and egoistic needs.

The man whose lower-level needs are satisfied is not motivated to satisfy those needs any longer. For practical purposes they exist no longer. Management often asks, "Why aren't people more productive? We pay good wages, provide good working conditions, have excellent fringe benefits and steady employment. Yet people do not seem to be willing to put forth more than minimum effort."

The fact that management has provided for these physiological and safety needs has shifted the motivational emphasis to the social and perhaps to the egoistic needs. Unless there are opportunities *at work* to satisfy these higher-level needs, people will be deprived; and their behavior will reflect this deprivation. Under such conditions, if management continues to focus its attention on physiological needs, its efforts are bound to be ineffective.

People *will* make insistent demands for more money under these conditions. It becomes more important than ever to buy the material goods and services which can provide limited satisfaction of the thwarted needs. Although money has only limited value in satisfying many higher-level needs, it can become the focus of interest if it is the *only* means available.

The Carrot-and-Stick Approach

The carrot-and-stick theory of motivation (like Newtonian physical theory) works reasonably well under certain circumstances. The *means* for satisfying man's physiological and (within limits) his safety needs can be provided or withheld by management. Employment itself is such a means, and so are wages, working conditions, and benefits. By these means the individual can be controlled so long as he is struggling for subsistence.

But the carrot-and-stick theory does not work at all once man has reached an adequate subsistence level and is motivated primarily by higher needs. Management cannot provide a man with self-respect, or with the respect of his fellows, or with the satisfaction of needs for self-fulfillment. It can create such conditions that he is encouraged and enabled to seek such satisfactions for *himself,* or it can thwart him by failing to create those conditions.

But this creation of conditions is not "control." It is not a good device for directing behavior. And so management finds itself in an odd position. The high standard of living created by our modern technological know-how provides quite adequately for the satisfaction of physiological and safety needs. The only significant exception is where management practices have not created confidence in a "fair break"—and thus where safety needs are thwarted. But by making possible the satisfaction of low-level needs, management has deprived itself of the ability to use as motivators the devices on which conventional theory has taught it to rely—rewards, promises, incentives, or threats and other coercive devices.

The philosophy of management by direction and control—*regardless of whether it is hard or soft*—is inadequate to motivate because the human needs on which this approach relies are today unimportant motivators of behavior. Direction and control are essentially useless in motivating people whose important needs are social and egoistic. Both the hard and the soft approach fail today because they are simply irrelevant to the situation.

People, deprived of opportunities to satisfy at work the needs which are now important to them, behave exactly as we might predict—with indolence, passivity, resistance to change, lack of responsibility, willingness to follow the demagogue, unreasonable demands for economic benefits. It would seem that we are caught in a web of our own weaving.

A New Theory of Management

For these and many other reasons, we require a different theory of the task of managing people based on more adequate assumptions about human nature and human motivation. I am going to be so bold as to suggest the broad dimensions of such a theory. Call it "Theory Y," if you will.

1. Management is responsible for organizing the elements of productive enterprise—money, materials, equipment, people—in the interest of economic ends.

2. People are *not* by nature passive or resistant to organizational needs. They have become so as a result of experience in organizations.

3. The motivation, the potential for development, the capacity for assuming responsibility, the readiness to direct behavior toward organizational goals are all present in people. Management does not put them there. It is a responsibility of management to make

it possible for people to recognize and develop these human characteristics for themselves.

4. The essential task of management is to arrange organizational conditions and methods of operation so that people can achieve their own goals *best* by directing *their own* efforts toward organizational objectives.

This is a process primarily of creating opportunities, releasing potential, removing obstacles, encouraging growth, providing guidance. It is what Peter Drucker has called "management by objectives" in contrast to "management by control." It does *not* involve the abdication of management, the absence of leadership, the lowering of standards, or the other characteristics usually associated with the "soft" approach under Theory X.

Some Difficulties

It is no more possible to create an organization today which will be a full, effective application of this theory than it was to build an atomic power plant in 1945. There are many formidable obstacles to overcome.

The conditions imposed by conventional organization theory and by the approach to scientific management for the past half century have tied men to limited jobs which do not utilize their capabilities, have discouraged the acceptance of responsibility, have encouraged passivity, have eliminated meaning from work. Man's habits, attitudes, expectations—his whole conception of membership in an industrial organization—have been conditioned by his experience under these circumstances.

People today are accustomed to being directed, manipulated, controlled in industrial organizations and to finding satisfaction for their social, egoistic, and self-fulfillment needs away from the job. This is true of much of management as well as of workers. Genuine "industrial citizenship"—to borrow again a term from Drucker—is a remote and unrealistic idea, the meaning of which has not even been considered by most members of industrial organizations.

Another way of saying this is that Theory X places exclusive reliance upon external control of human behavior, while Theory Y relies heavily on self-control and self-direction. It is worth noting that this difference is the difference between treating people as children and treating them as mature adults. After generations of the former, we cannot expect to shift to the latter over night.

Steps in the Right Direction

Before we are overwhelmed by the obstacles, let us remember that the application of theory is always slow. Progress is usually achieved in small steps. Some innovative ideas which are entirely consistent with Theory Y are today being applied with some success.

Decentralization and delegation

These are ways of freeing people from the too-close control of conventional organization, giving them a degree of freedom to direct their own activities, to assume responsibility, and, importantly, to satisfy their egoistic needs. In this connection, the flat organization of Sears, Roebuck and Company provides an interesting example. It forces "management by objectives," since it enlarges the number of people reporting to a manager until he cannot direct and control them in the conventional manner.

Job enlargement

This concept, pioneered by I.B.M. and Detroit Edison, is quite consistent with Theory Y. It encourages the acceptance of responsibility at the bottom of the organization; it provides opportunities for satisfying social and egoistic needs. In fact, the reorganization of work at the factory level offers one of the more challenging opportunities for innovation consistent with Theory Y.

Participation and consultative management

Under proper conditions, participation and consultative management provide encouragement to people to direct their creative energies toward organizational objectives, give them some voice in decisions that affect them, provide significant opportunities for the satisfaction of social and egoistic needs. The Scanlon Plan is the outstanding embodiment of these ideas in practice.

Performance appraisal

Even a cursory examination of conventional programs of performance appraisal within the ranks of management will reveal how completely consistent they are with Theory X. In fact, most such programs tend to treat the individual as though he were a product under inspection on the assembly line.

A few companies—among them General Mills, Ansul Chemical, and General Electric—have been experimenting with approaches which involve the individual in setting "targets" or objectives *for himself* and in a *self*-evaluation of performance semiannually or annually. Of course, the superior plays an important leadership role in this process—one, in fact, which demands substantially more competence than the conventional approach. The role is, however, considerably more congenial to many managers than the role of "judge" or "inspector" which is usually forced upon them. Above all, the individual is encouraged to take a greater responsibility for planning and appraising his own contribution to organizational objectives; and the accompanying effects on egoistic and self-fulfillment needs are substantial.

Applying the Ideas

The not infrequent failure of such ideas as these to work as well as expected is often attributable to the fact that a management has "bought the idea" but applied it within the framework of Theory X and its assumptions.

Delegation is not an effective way of exercising management by control. Participation becomes a farce when it is applied as a sales gimmick or device for kidding people into thinking they are important. Only the management that has confidence in human capacities and is itself directed toward organizational objectives rather than toward the preservation of personal power can grasp the implications of this emerging theory. Such management will find and apply successfully other innovative ideas as we move slowly toward the full implementation of a theory like Y.

The Human Side of Enterprise

It is quite possible for us to realize substantial improvements in the effectiveness of industrial organizations during the next decade or two. The social sciences can contribute much to such developments; we are only beginning to grasp the implications of the growing body of knowledge in these fields. But if this conviction is to become a reality instead of a pious hope, we will need to view the process much as we view the process of releasing the energy of the atom for constructive human ends—as a slow, costly, sometimes discouraging approach toward a goal which would seem to many to be quite unrealistic.

The ingenuity and the perseverance of industrial management in the pursuit of economic ends have changed many scientific and technological dreams into commonplace realities. It is now becoming clear that the application of these same talents to the human side of enterprise will not only enhance substantially these materialistic achievements, but will bring us one step closer to "the good society."

Questions

1. In what ways can management assist subordinates in obtaining greater satisfaction of the needs for self-fulfillment?
2. What are the basic differences between Theory X and Theory Y? Why are managers often reluctant to accept the assumptions upon which Theory Y is based?
3. How does "management by objectives" differ from "management by control"? Is there any wisdom in having an employee set objectives for himself?
4. What significance does the statement "a satisfied need is not a motivator of behavior" have for the manager or supervisor in his relationship with subordinates?
5. McGregor cites decentralization and delegation, job enlargement, participation and consultative management, and performance appraisal as steps in the right direction toward applying Theory Y. Can you think of any other ways in which Theory Y may be implemented?

16. ORGANIZATIONAL CLIMATE AND INDIVIDUAL GROWTH *
The Consultative Process at Work

Gordon L. Lippitt

Mankind's continual search for compatability between his organized relationships and individual growth is being constantly explored by social scientists and practitioners. That kind of organizational system which manifested itself early in history frequently exhibited a high degree of control by managerial coercion that is no longer meeting the needs of today's organized society or the needs of the individuals in it. The rapid changes in society have brought with them changes in organizational system, and need for even greater change. One of the most apparent changes has been that of control through benevolence and persuasion. Whether viewed from the paternalism of large organizations in the thirties in the United States, or the "sell-the-other-fellow" approach used by sales and pseudo-human relations advocates, such an approach has been very much in evidence in the leadership of industrial, governmental, social, and welfare organizations. In fact, some writers give a great deal of credence to this approach to leadership.[1]

There is, however, a third way by which influence can be manifested in organizational life. This has been referred to as the "helping" approach in work relations, and finds itself in existence where one finds the consultative organizational system at work. This kind of influence on others, as expressed by McGregor [2] as "typified by the exceptionally sophisticated and sensitive individual in any professional field, does not consist in playing God with the client, but in placing the professional's knowledge and skill at the client's disposal. It is a particularly important form of social influence which is not at all well understood." The effects of the coercive, benevolent, or consultative ways of influencing others are measured by the degree

* From *Personnel Administration*, Vol. 23, No. 5 (September-October, 1960), pp. 12-19, 43. Reprinted with permission.

[1] R. N. McMurry, "Case for the Benevolent Autocrat," *Harvard Business Review* (January-February, 1958).

[2] D. McGregor, *The Human Side of Enterprise* (New York: McGraw-Hill Book Company, 1960), p. 19.

to which they help change the ability of persons to achieve goals and meet evident needs. In an organization, the ability of others to help me meet my needs is a very important dimension in the acceptance of the method of influence.

Man's needs differ, collectively or individually, at any particular time. Nevertheless, certain levels of needs have been determined as common to man's life experience. Maslow [3] organizes man's needs into a "hierarchy of needs." At the fundamental level of man's existence one finds the *physical needs.* Food, water, and air form the basic elements of life itself. One does not search for much else in life when these elements are not provided. Historically, even the earliest coercive examples of industrialized civilization helped man to meet these basic life needs.

At the next level of need, however, we have the basic *social needs* of man. Needs for affection, belonging, achievement, and recognition are part of the motivational system of each individual. The historical shift in organizational influence patterns from autocratic (coercive) systems to benevolent (paternalistic) systems was brought to the fore by the increasing standard of living in which man's physical needs were being met, and he was now wanting and expecting more from his work relations. The provision for workers, employees, and clients of swimming-pools, retirement benefits, annual picnics, and similar activities has been a "reaching-out" by the organization to meet the "needs" of the workers. Such endeavors were motivated by multiple causes—desire by management for higher production, to combat increased unionization, to help the workers enjoy life more adequately, to meet the requirements of government regulations, and to help the increasing size of organizations to be able to function effectively.

These endeavors to meet some of the social needs of individuals through benevolent patterns of activity and leadership have been partially successful. Certain improved working conditions, closer relationships with the workers, more effective controls, and less frustration have resulted from the benevolent system. On the other hand, the paternalism implicit in this approach to relations with others creates dependence, does not account for man's change and growth, and creates a tension between the highest level of man's needs and the organization at work.

---

[3] A. H. Maslow, *Motivation and Personality* (New York: Harpers, 1954).

Argyris [4] points out some significant incompatabilities between individual personality growth and the organizational system. As he states it:

> If the principles of formal organization are used as ideally defined, then the employees will tend to work in an environment where (1) they are provided minimal control over their work-a-day world, (2) they are expected to be passive, dependent, subordinate, (3) they are expected to have a short-time perspective, (4) they are induced to perfect and value the frequent use of a few superficial abilities, and (5) they are expected to produce under conditions leading to psychological failure.

Argyris, in describing his maturation of personality, refers to the fact that as an individual grows from childhood to adulthood he moves from passivity to a more active social role, from dependence on his environment to independence, from specialized functioning to flexibility, and from a subordinate to a supraordinate position in life.

The concept and practices in many organizations are such as to delimit the opportunity for individual growth. Even organizations with lofty ideals and purposes—such as church, health, welfare, and educational systems—while giving "lip service" to the practice of something they refer to as "democratic administration," actually execute only the rather obvious, good-intentioned kind of concern for others that may develop dependency and warmth but limits the individual's growth to achieve his highest needs.

Let us examine these needs at the top of man's "hierarchy of needs."

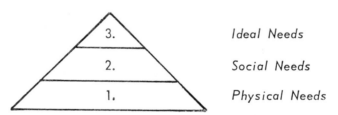

A number of social scientists have listed the concept of self-actualization as one of man's highest needs. In the writings of Jung, Rogers, Maslow,[5] and Allport we find this concept discussed. Maslow,[6] in his interviews of selected subjects, found self-actualizing persons to be characterized by the following:

---

[4] C. Argyris, "The Individual and Organization: Some Problems of Mutual Adjustment," *Administrative Science Quarterly*, Vol. 2, #1, 1957.
[5] Maslow, *op. cit.*, p. 2.
[6] A. H. Maslow, "Self-Actualizing People: A Study of Psychological Health." Reprinted from Personality Symposium No. 1, 1950.

1. Efficient perception of reality and comfortable with reality
2. Acceptance of self, others, and nature
3. Spontaneity (spontaneous competence) [7]
4. Problem-centered
5. Quality of detachment
6. Autonomy, independence from culture and environment
7. Continual freshness of appreciation
8. Effective in interpersonal relations
9. "Gemeinschaftsgefühl" (empathy for mankind)

Such persons are idiosyncratic in the expression of themselves, "for self-actualization is actualization of a self, and no two selves are altogether alike." Other writers have referred to the concept of self-fulfillment as one of the highest goals of man. These two concepts would seem to be closely linked.

An additional concept to which much attention has been given is the *creative ability* of man. In today's organization we need persons who will create new methods, new products, new ideas, and new solutions. Studies of originality have been undertaken in the past few years. It shows that "originality results from divergent thinking; it means getting out of a mental rut and looking at things in a new and different way. This kind of thinking occurs at the discovery phase, the insight phase, the inventive phase." [8] Such creativity is essential for social growth and problem-solving. Most organizations have more creative talent than they are using effectively. In many organizations the need and ability for creativity are stifled by the size of the organization, control factors in organization programs, and the pattern of leadership being manifested in the leadership of others.

The third of man's highest needs is his *sense of values*. The need for man to find meaning out of existence, to develop a philosophy of life, to see the world as something of and beyond himself, and to give an expression of faith in something meaningful, is one of the great potentials of man.

If an individual is primarily concerned with his physical needs, it is difficult for him to reach for this "higher" man. It would seem, however, that in most organizations, to meet the challenge of a changing society will require the organization's functioning in such a way as to encourage the individual to achieve his highest goals and in so doing contribute to the goals of the organization.

---

[7] Referred to as "spontaneous competence" by G. Lippitt and Ross Snyder in an Unpublished manuscript for National Training Laboratories Church Leadership Laboratory, 1956.

[8] "Creativity and Conformity: A Problem for Organizations," *The Foundation for Research on Human Behavior*, 1958, p. 11.

This does not mean that individuals shall function in a completely "free" way, unfrustrated, and non-conforming. All of life requires the mutual adjustment amongst law, order, and freedom. The concept of an organizational climate to provide growth opportunities for the individual does not imply that *all* of man's needs shall or can be met in the life of work. It does imply, however, that organizational leaders and members need to search and work diligently for those kinds of human relationships that will provide the best possible opportunities for an individual to reach his full potential.

Consultative system defined

What is meant by this concept of the consultative relationship in the organization? A number of scholars have contributed to the concept. Bennis [9] has dealt with some of the characteristics, and in a recent program [10] of the National Training Laboratories the staff further conceptualized some of the differences between the consultative versus the authoritarian systems.

In the consultative system—

1. *The organization is viewed as an organism—not as a machine.* Implicit in this characteristic is the reality that an organism, whether singular or multiple, must adapt to exist. It must change its functioning to meet new needs. In this context, the organization is seen not just as a formal structure, but as a living, flexible, changing, and complex network of relationships among people to achieve both individual and organizational goals.

2. *Provision is made in the organization for relevant decision-making by the members of the organization as over against centralized decision-making.* The process of involving persons in the decisions which they will implement is an important aspect of a consultative process. Obviously, all persons will not be involved in every decision, even though effective communication is one level of involvement. The degree of participation will depend on forces in the situation, forces in the leader, and forces in the subordinate, or member, groups. Those forces will provide guidelines for the degree to which an

---

[9] W. G. Bennis, "Leadership Theory and Administrative Behavior: The Problem of Authority," *Administrative Science Quarterly*, Vol. 4, No. 3 (December, 1959).
[10] Take-Home Packet, Management Work Conference, National Training Laboratories, January, 1960.

organization leader involves members in decision-making that is relevant to their competency, experience, and meets the leader pattern of response to a particular situation.[11]

3. *Mutual confidence as the basis for cooperation rather than authority-obedience basis.* A consultative relationship is built upon the confidence persons have in one another's integrity, goal orientation, and commitment to a problem-solving process. Such confidence does not need to depend upon authority or status in the organization for its success.

4. *Face-to-face groups as the unit of organization rather than persons seen as individuals in assigned "places" in the organization.* Recent research has given a great deal of recognition to the importance of the group as a functional unit in the organization. This has been made particularly evident from the productivity and morale studies research. Likert,[12] comments thus on the importance of organizational work units:

> Each of us seeks to satisfy our desire for a sense of personal worth and importance primarily by the response we get from people we are close to, in whom we are interested, and whose approval and support we are eager to have. The face-to-face groups with whom we spend the bulk of our time are, consequently, the most important to us. Our work group is one of the most important of our face-to-face groups and one from which we are particularly eager to derive a sense of personal worth.

Studies in the field of psychology, sociology, and psychiatry reinforce this statement. It clearly indicates than if an organization is to make the maximum use of the human resources and meet the highest level of man's needs it will best come to function in situations where the individual relates effectively in those organizational groups in which he is a member and those in which he is a leader. Such well-knit and effective face-to-face work units will develop out of conditions which provide the consultative relationship between leader and members.

Such emphasis on the group is an aid to individual growth and development. "Social science, by discovering what happens in group

---

[11] R. Tannenbaum and W. Schmidt, "Choosing a Leadership Pattern," *Harvard Business Review*, 1958.
[12] R. Likert, "Developing Patterns of Management," *American Management Association*, No. 182, 1956, p. 7.

situations and what causes different individual behavior, and by contributing to the recent growing movement of leadership and membership training, has aided materially in freeing and developing the individual, rather than submerging him in the group." [13]

To develop such group relations is one of the goals in the consultative organizational process.

5. *Person-centered leadership as over against task-centered leadership.* Many factors in the traditional organizational pattern cause the persons in an organization to be seen as the "doers of work." The task is the important concern of the supervisor. In the consultative approach, the supervisor sees his major responsibility as the development of others to adult patterns of self-control, developing effective work-group functioning, and to focus on the "person-centered" needs so as to "release" the potential of others. Fortunately, this kind of supervision fits the job to the person, rather than fitting a person to a job description.

In the area of performance improvement, the supervisor will make possible opportunities for the person to set his own "targets" for good achievement, work standards, and personal growth. Through the "target-setting" [14] type of experience the individual meets his task goals in terms of his own drives, standards, and needs.

6. *A two-way flow of communication with appropriate "feedback" opportunities as over against a one-way pattern of communication.* In the assumptions underlying the consultative system is the importance of the two-way process of communication which is found in both the formal and informal aspect of organization life. Opportunities to see oneself and the effect of one's supervision are a prime necessity of effective organizational accomplishment. The need for a "feedback" communication system is essential.

> Engineers have built into guided missiles a mechanism that enables the missile to guide or steer itself. This mechanism, called a feedback mechanism, collects information showing how far the missile is off the target. This information then enables the feedback mechanism automatically to change or correct the flight of the missile so that it gets back on the target. . . .
> . . . Each individual and group needs a feedback process. Each individual needs to get accurate information about the difference between

[13] L. P. Bradford and G. Lippitt, "The Individual Counts in Effective Group Relations," *NEA Journal*, November, 1954.
[14] McGregor, *op. cit.*, p. 1.

what he is trying to do and how well he is doing it. He needs to be able to use this information to correct or change his action. Then, basically, he is steering himself." [15]

An organization, through its policies, philosophy, and practice of its management, can develop the climate of acceptance of the appropriate skills to permit this level of interpersonal communication.

Implications for the organization

The implications of the consultative system are as follows:

1. *To develop clearly the objectives of the organization so that standards of work relations can be relevant to these objectives.* A number of organizational theorists have written recently in the literature about "management by objective." [16] Such clear goals for the organization make it possible for supervisor-subordinate relationships to develop in such a way that the goals of the individual may be seen in terms of the organizational goals. The degree of incompatability between these two sets of goals will be mainly affected by the kinds of relationships between supervisor and subordinate.

2. *Supervisory training at all levels of management that focuses on the ability of supervisors to develop a collaborative relationship with their supervisors, peers, and subordinates.* In the multiple roles in which the supervisor finds himself, he will recognize the necessity not only to take into account factors of interdependence, but the reality of the task considerations. The supervisor is a "helper, trainer, consultant, and coordinator; and . . . the arm of reality, a person with power over a subordinate." [17] To make meaningful the power-and-growth role, the supervisor must exercise his many roles in a sensitive, insightful, and diagnostic manner. Such skills should be in the focus of an enlightened supervisory-training program.

3. *To develop a performance-improvement process along with appraisal and manpower inventory procedures that are consistent with the organization's philosophy and training program.* In many instances, performance appraisal is combined or confused with performance improvement. The concept of continued growth by the

---

[15] L. P. Bradford, "A Fundamental of Education," *Adult Education*, Vol. 11, No. 4 (April, 1952).
[16] McGregor, *op. cit.*, p. 1.
[17] Bennis, *op. cit.*, p. 6.

individual on the job is the responsibility of each individual and of the supervisor. If a consultative organizational system is to work, there must be present opportunities for individuals in the organization to set their performance standards and, in relationship with others, to try to achieve, revise, and secure "feedback" on the objectives so set. This two-person continued growth is separate from the process of appraisal by superiors and the need for organizational management to have an inventory of persons to fill positions from within the organization.

The goals of an organization, the personnel (rewards system) policy, and training programs of the organization must have common understanding and commitment to the consultative organizational process if it is to work effectively and be the direction in which an organization is developing.

Implications for the individual

The concept of the consultative organizational system has the following implications for the individual in the organization:

1. *To further an increased awareness of one's own behavior and one's effect on others.* In whatever way the individual finds possible, he should, through training, through additional educational opportunities, and through opportunities to assess himself, increase his own self-insight. In this way, the individual is more capable of relating himself effectively with others.

2. *To examine one's attitudes and assumptions as they affect one's job performance and relationships.* Part of one's personal growth is the need to "test" the assumptions we make about other individuals. Our behavior is determined by these assumptions. If we assume that a person is lazy and "cutting corners," we will behave accordingly in our relationship with that person. If, on the other hand, our assumption about another person is conditioned by our perception of him as "eager, makes mistakes but learns from them, and is willing to listen" then our relationship will be so conditioned. These assumptions about others are closely related to one's own value system.

3. *To increase one's knowledge of persons, work groups, and industrial organizations.* The "knowledge lag" between what is

known about human behavior and the practioner's application is considerable. New research has confirmed some old truths of human behavior, as well as indicated new approaches to effective resolution of conflict and decision-making. The new research in the behavioral sciences related to the individual, groups, organizational life, and community dynamics, as now reported and written in readily available resources, indicates that today's individual can improve his understanding of this knowledge through a variety of learning opportunities.

4. *To increase one's skill in diagnosing human situations.* The ability of an individual to diagnose the causes of situations rather than to deal only at the symptomatic level, is an area of growth for an individual to perform in a helping role with others. The ability to look "beneath the surface" and probe for underlying causes in the work situation is essential to effective relationships with others. One of the skills explicit in this regard is the skill to *listen* to other persons. "The biggest block to personal communication is man's inability to listen intelligently, understandingly, and skillfully to another person. This deficiency in the modern world is widespread and appalling." [18] This skill of listening is but one of several ways by which the individual becomes more diagnostic in his relationship with others.

5. *To envision one's understanding and skill relative to continuing social change and the process of change.* While it is necessary for all leaders to understand the phenomena of change which are inevitable and universal, it is also important that leaders who are to function in a "helping" fashion with others understand the phenomena of *planned change.* "That is, change which derives from a purposeful decision to effect improvement in a personality system or social system and which is achieved with the help of professional guidance." [19]

Such change, if it is not to be manipulative, results in A moving toward A's goals, and, in so doing, helping B to move toward B's goals. Such a cooperative relationship situation is one in which effective understanding of resistance to change is taken into account

---

[18] C. Rogers and F. Roethlisberger, "Barriers and Gateways to Communication," *Harvard Business Review*, July-August, 1952.
[19] R. Lippitt, J. Watson, and Bruce Westley, *The Dynamics of Planned Change* (New York: Harcourt, Brace, & Co., 1958), p. vii.

through proper goal-setting, involvement, alternative-testing, participative decision-making, and attention to reassessment of the change by the persons initiating the change and receiving it. Such skills are a part of the helping relationship.

Summary

The author does not intend to indicate that the authoritative system and consultative system are in reality "alternatives." "The consultative system works only so long as a combination of self-control, member responsibility, and scientific method are ingredients of decision-making. When and if these break down, the authority structure is brought into action." [20] As implied earlier in this article, man's physical and social needs must be met before we can reach those levels of functioning that will release the fullest of man's potential. In a society where we have reached the highest standard of living in history, it seems appropriate that this higher level of organizational functioning is realistic and possible. If we affirm that "the strength of democracy is directly proportioned to the practice of it by its citizen leaders," [21] then we must search for those kinds of leadership behavior and organizational climate that can provide for this optimum of individual growth while attaining the objectives of organized man.

Questions

1. In what ways can their participation in decision-making facilitate the individual growth of employees? Is there likely to be a relationship between individual growth and efficient job performance?
2. The author believes that management by objective is essential for a successful consultative relationship between superior and subordinate. Do you agree? Why?
3. What skills must a manager have in order to make two-way communication a reality?
4. How do you account for the "knowledge lag" between what is known about human behavior and the application of this knowledge in work situations?
5. Explain what is meant by the statement "The consultative system works only so long as a combination of self-control, member responsibility, and scientific method are ingredients of decision-making."

[20] Management Work Conference Take-Home Packet, Arden House, National Training Laboratories, 1960, Session II.
[21] G. Lippitt, "What Do We Know About Leadership?", *NEA Journal*, December, 1955.

17. CAN APPRAISAL INTERVIEWS BE MADE EFFECTIVE? *

Robert K. Stolz

Why is it that the appraisal interview continues to present a gigantic headache to just about everyone concerned—top management, personnel men, the appraisers, and the appraised? Certainly, the theory behind the interview is clear enough: the line manager, after appraising the performance of a subordinate, should discuss the results with him to help him see his strengths and weaknesses more clearly; this discussion and clarification will motivate the subordinate to build on his strengths and eliminate his weaknesses. It must be conceded that there is nothing wrong with this theory—provided it works.

Many people, in fact, claim that it does—but there is a growing and articulate school of thought that holds that in practice the core of the discussion is the manager's review of his subordinate's weaknesses and that for this reason the interview tends to undermine the subordinate's self-confidence. These skeptics also say that the interview places the superior in the uncomfortable position of being a judge over his subordinate and thus injures the superior-subordinate relationship.

The truth of the matter, it seems to me, lies somewhere between these extremes. Experience tells us that the typical manager does *not* fall apart at the first breath of criticism from his superior and that the appraisal interview, therefore, cannot be so destructive as its opponents maintain. The arguments of the "nonbelievers," then, seem to involve a considerable amount of distortion. At the same time, even the staunchest "believers" have begun to see that appraisal discussions frequently don't bring a fraction of the benefits originally anticipated. And it has become clear that many managers do resist holding appraisal discussions.

* From *Personnel*, Vol. 38, No. 2 (March-April, 1961), pp. 32-37. Reprinted with permission.

Two pertinent observations

In recent years, I have audited a great number of management development programs in various industries and have thus had a chance to interview several hundred managers who had participated in appraisal discussions either as superior or as subordinate. From these interviews on how the appraisal discussions were handled and what, if anything, they accomplished I have drawn two observations relevant here:

1. In companies where people are judged on the basis of the results of their work and where an attempt is made to orient the appraisal discussion to the job, rarely if ever is a healthy relationship between superior and subordinate destroyed. I *have* found one or two cases in which a basically poor relationship was brought to a head by the discussion, but I don't consider this an unhealthy move.

On the other hand, in companies whose rating forms focus on personality traits, appraisal interviews are usually carried out half-heartedly, in an atmosphere of mutual embarrassment, and with little success. But such appraisal programs are probably in the minority today.

2. Every company has some managers—perhaps many, perhaps a few—who are really skillful in communicating appraisal results to their subordinates. The interviews these men hold, I am convinced, do have a positive effect on the subordinates' development. The effect is not usually a dramatic one, but I have run into a few cases in which the interview brought about a pronounced improvement in performance.

Trouble is, of course, that these men represent the exception rather than the rule. Most appraisal discussions are conducted in a perfunctory manner, and therefore prove sterile.

Let me illustrate this point with an anecdote. A senior executive once told me how pleased he was about an appraisal interview he had just held. What made it so worthwhile, he explained, was that it had enabled him to get across an important criticism of the subordinate in question—that he was a poor delegator and, as a result, was constantly creating bottlenecks as well as frustrating his own subordinates.

Later on, I discussed the appraisal interview with the subordinate and was amazed to discover how he had interpreted his boss's words. "The boss told me he hoped there would be more delegation around here in the future," he said. After a moment's reflection, he added, "It's about time the boss started delegating more himself!"

So the message was lost. And it has been lost in many thousands of instances.

These discussions are not destructive, but neither are they constructive. Though the subordinate usually thinks he got something out of his appraisal interview, he isn't quite sure what. And though the manager agrees that it was a worthwhile discussion, he can't offer very much evidence that anything important was accomplished. But then, who knows? It may be, as the believers maintain, that the discussion represented a beginning, the opening of a door, or that it accomplished more than is yet evident on the surface. These are possibilities, of course, and I willingly concede them. But I am still convinced that the majority of appraisal discussions have little or no effect.

Where and why communication breaks down

If this is so, the key question becomes: Why does so little real communication take place in a situation that fairly screams out for an honest and frank exchange of views?

Goodness knows, it isn't because companies haven't tried. They have tried just about everything. First they tried the "personnel sandwich" approach—telling the subordinate his strong points, then slipping in a few remarks about his weaknesses, and finally ending up with a review of his strengths. But this didn't work. Too often, the superior failed to put the meat in the sandwich, or the subordinate resented what he recognized as a technique.

So the "call it by another name" approach was invented. Under this plan, the superior would introduce the appraisal interview by saying to the subordinate, "Now I don't want you to consider this an appraisal interview. This is something different—a self-development planning conference!" Trouble was, what usually followed wasn't "something different," and everyone knew it. So this didn't work too well, either.

Then industry tried the "self-appraisal" approach. Some personnel men seem convinced that this is the answer, but self-appraisal has run into difficulty, too, and, in my experience there is not much lasting enthusiasm for it among line managers. One company calls it the "cat and mouse" approach. Under this method, though it is obvious that the boss has already appraised the subordinate, he refuses to tell him the results. Instead, he sits back and says, "Now suppose you tell me how you appraise your own performance." And the subordinate thinks to himself, "What are you trying to do—play cat and mouse with me? I know you've appraised my performance. If you've got something to say, say it. If not, let's get back to work."

I don't mean to debunk techniques, for we do, of course, need them. It seems to me, however, that we have relied on them too much and have unwittingly allowed insincerity and evasiveness to creep into our approaches.

Needless to say, we cannot explain this simply by accusing management, or individual managers, of being gimmick-happy or prone to hypocrisy and equivocation. There are many reasons why a manager may try to skirt the real issues in an appraisal discussion—with or without the aid of these techniques.

It may be that he has never developed an atmosphere of mutual confidence and trust with his subordinate, and is now finding that without such an atmosphere it's pretty difficult to have a frank exchange of views. Or he may feel that a frank discussion would injure his personal relationship with the subordinate. Or he may lack confidence in his appraisal findings, or in his ability to deal with questions that the subordinate might raise in a more open discussion—questions like: "What's the real reason I didn't get a raise last January?"

So there are a lot of reasons why superior and subordinate don't get down to cases in appraisal discussions.

In view of all this, what can be done to stimulate a franker and more honest discussion? No one knows the complete answer to this, but here are a few suggestions.

Laying a solid foundation

First, companies must recognize more clearly that they can have effective appraisal discussions only if they lay a sound foundation for them long before the interviews are held. Among the elements of a sound foundation are these:

- The superior must have nurtured an atmosphere of understanding and trust. This sounds terribly elementary—but the battle can be won or lost right here.
- The superior must have put enough time and effort into his appraisal to have confidence in it. Only then can he feel comfortable about discussing it.

• The appraisal discussion must fit naturally into the way the business is run and the normal relationship of the superior and the subordinate. This means that everyone must understand that appraisal and the communication of appraisal results are part of the basic management job. To further this understanding, the superior and subordinate should get together some months ahead of appraisal time and agree on the critical requirements of the latter's job. At the same time, they should decide on the elements of performance that should be examined continuously as evidence of how well the requirements are being met. (Managers will recognize this as simply a part of the management job.) The appraisal discussion then becomes something normal and expected.

A job-centered "mutual confession of sin"

Second, most managers need help on the conduct of the interview itself. It should be pointed out to them that when major job problems have to be faced one effective technique is what might be called the "mutual confession of sin." The superior who starts out by saying, "Joe, I've been giving considerable thought to your performance recently and have concluded that you are a poor planner" is not likely to get an honest exchange of views. But he might get at the issue quite effectively by saying, "Joe, one problem that's been bothering us both is that production of your department has been consistently behind schedule for a number of months. I don't really know what the trouble is. Maybe it's my fault. Maybe I haven't given you the support or the budget that you need. But in all honesty I would like to question, too, whether or not you have been planning your production properly. Let's talk about it."

This lays the foundation for effective discussion. It gets at the problem. It assures the subordinate that he isn't being made the fall guy and that he's going to have his day in court. This saves face, but it goes far beyond that and it isn't devious or evasive. What it involves is a realistic acknowledgment that failure to achieve the desired results is rarely attributable to the subordinate alone. This mutual-confession-of-sin approach says to the subordinate: "We've got a problem. We're in this together. Let's discuss it."

Tackling the real issues

My third suggestion on how to stimulate a franker and more honest exchange of views is preceded by a lot of *ifs*. *If* a manager has developed a climate of respect and trust, and *if* he and his

FUNDAMENTALS OF SUCCESSFUL
APPRAISAL INTERVIEWS

EFFECTIVE COMMUNICATION of appraisals, says the author, is not easy
and can never be guaranteed. But it *is* possible if the following points,
derived from hundreds of interviews with both the appraisers and the
appraised, are constantly borne in mind:

1. Successful communication of appraisal results depends more on
   mutual respect and trust than on technique.
2. The problem of appraisal discussion cannot really be separated
   from the problem of appraisal. A sound appraisal system—one
   that both the superior and the subordinate have confidence in—
   is a foundation-stone of the appraisal discussion.
3. The line manager must be willing to take the time at the outset
   to identify the really critical requirements of the subordinate's
   job so that his performance appraisal can be focused on these
   requirements.
4. The appraisal discussion should center on results achieved on
   the job and not on the subordinate's personality.
5. Subordinates distrust evasive techniques and beating around the
   bush. If a sound foundation for the appraisal discussion has
   been laid, the supervisor should strive for frankness and candor,
   rather than worrying about whether he is being sufficiently
   tactful.

subordinate are agreed on the critical requirements of the subordinate's job, and *if* he has given sufficient time and attention to his
appraisal, then he should be forthright in the appraisal discussion.
In studying the approaches of men known in their companies as
skillful in communicating appraisal results, I have been struck by
one point above all others—their willingness to be direct and to get
at the basic issues. This is done tactfully, of course. No one is arguing for a "get tough" policy.

But many companies have leaned too far in the other direction.
They haven't trusted their managers to have a normal sense of tact—
and have devised endless ways of sugar-coating the pill. This sugar-
coating has simply encouraged the managers to duck the real issues
and avoid discussing what is really on their minds.

The single complaint most common among subordinates, I have
found in interviewing them after appraisal discussions, is not that
the appraisal wasn't fair—an occasional response—or that the superior was callous and undiplomatic—a very rare one. It was that the

boss obviously had something on his mind but wouldn't come out with it honestly and straightforwardly.

It seems clear that the men being appraised do not, for the most part, share their bosses' reluctance to talk about the appraisal results—that they are in fact eager for fuller and freer discussion in the appraisal interview. If the company and its individual managers recognize that the interview is a difficult and demanding situation and try to fulfill its requirements as outlined here, they can, I believe, achieve greater success than they have so far in communicating appraisal results.

Questions

1. How can the appraisal interview contribute to the achievement of efficient employee performance?
2. Stolz believes that managers have relied too much on communication techniques and have unwittingly allowed insincerity and evasiveness to creep into performance interviews. Do you believe that the method which he recommends assures success in communicating performance appraisal to the employee?
3. The article refers mainly to appraisal interviews between executives and their subordinates. Would the suggestions contained in the article be applicable to first-line supervisors in their appraisal of subordinates?
4. The author states that the appraisal discussion should center on results achieved and on the job and not on the subordinate's personality? Do you agree? Why?
5. What is involved in the "mutual confession of sin" approach that is likely to make for success in appraisal situations? Are there other situations, other than the job, where it may be applied to good advantage?

18. HOW TO APPRAISE
EXECUTIVE PERFORMANCE *

Arch Patton

What makes an executive successful? Why does one man forge his way to the top, while another, equally trained, fails to live up to company expectations? How can we better understand the process by which executives develop?

In hopes of finding answers to these important questions, one of the country's largest corporations made a survey, a few years ago, of the educational, economic, and social backgrounds of more than 100 top-echelon executives. The objective of the study was to discover if the early life experiences of this demonstrably successful group of men had common elements that could be used to improve the corporation's executive selection and development process.

As Diverse as America

The research team carefully studied the early family life of each top-management executive, including his family's financial and social status, the extent of his formal education, subjects studied, marks received, and his early work experience. When the results of the survey were reviewed, it was found that the environment of the company's key executives during their formative years tended to be as diverse as America itself. These highly successful executives came from poor as well as wealthy families, some had Master's degrees while others failed to finish high school, and outstanding and average students were found in equal numbers.

Only one common historic relationship was discovered: *within two years after joining the company, the compensation of each executive topped the average for his age group, and this pay differential above the average widened at an accelerating rate throughout his career.*

The results of this study underscore the dangers inherent in a recruiting process that slavishly follows preconceived ideas of what

---

* From *Harvard Business Review*, Vol. 38, No. 1 (January-February, 1960), pp. 63-70. Reprinted with permission.

it takes to make an outstanding executive. The results indicate, furthermore, that intelligence, courage, aggressiveness, and other qualities making for business success are incubated in virtually every conceivable early environment.

The most significant contribution of the survey may turn out to be a better understanding of the executive development process. For if we cannot prejudge the *capacity* of the individual with any certainty, it follows that we must assign critical importance to the ability to judge on-the-job *performance*. This performance appraisal is a never-ending process, for individuals reach the peak of their ability, or willingness, to accept responsibility at different stages in their careers. As every top executive knows, many apparently well-endowed individuals reach "plateaus" of arrested development early in their careers, while others seem able to draw indefinitely on hidden reserves of strength to take on ever larger responsibilities.

In effect, this means that the soundest basis for judging an individual's ability to handle a higher-level job is how well he is dealing with similar problems in his present job. Or, to put it another way, an executive's past and present performance is the most reliable key to his future performance. This being the case, the ability of management to judge an individual's performance is basic to the continuing success of the enterprise.

Early Appraisal Efforts

The need for sound appraisals of executive performance has been recognized in industry for many years. The first efforts in this direction tended to have psychological overtones and usually consisted of appraisals of traits that were deemed important to a successful executive. Thus, these early approaches did not appraise performance in terms of the results stemming from decisions made or influenced by an individual, but rather in terms of preconceived characteristics that management personnel were presumed to have. Particularly in the years following World War II, performance appraisal was often looked on as an integral part of an executive development program.

Subjective approach

Unfortunately, the executive characteristics appraised in development programs—leadership, initiative, dependability, judgment, getting along with people, ambition, and so on—do not necessarily measure a man's *effectiveness* on the job. Indeed, all too often judgments of performance under such plans reflect what is *thought* of the man rather than what he *does*.

The great weakness in this approach has proved to be the lack of performance criteria that are related to job responsibilities. Such concentration on personality traits ignores the more objective measures of on-the-job performance that are developed from budgets and accounting reports. This highly subjective approach, in turn, has made it difficult for management to communicate its judgment of an executive's performance to the man who has been evaluated. It is the rare individual who will concede that he does not display executive characteristics, and an even rarer boss who can comfortably explain shortcomings of so personal a nature to his subordinate. By contrast, the more objective criteria—rising or falling sales, profit margins, scrap losses, employee turnover, absenteeism, machine down time, and the like—are more readily understood by the subordinate and easier to explain because they are in quantitative terms which are part of the operating language of the business.

Another factor that tends to obsolete trait-oriented appraisals in recent years has been the increasing use of executive incentive plans in industry. More and more companies have found their bonus plans "in trouble" because eligible executives do not believe that incentive payments based on subjective appraisals reflect their individual efforts. This belief apparently results from an instinctive revulsion among executives to having their compensation largely dependent on what senior executives *think* of them. First, they suspect favoritism, and second, they exhibit a subconscious desire to have their performance measured by yardsticks that are based on more tangible, quantitative targets they have learned to understand and trust.

Mathematical approach

Some companies have taken steps to overcome the "popularity contest" aspects of subjective appraisals and to meet the growing need for judging performance in terms of individual targets. Often, however, such procedures have swung to the other extreme in bonus plan administration: setting individual goals for the year in quantitative terms (e.g., increase sales 10% or cut scrap losses 7%) and paying off on "performance" directly keyed to those goals.

This approach has the great advantage of eliminating subjective judgment as the determinant of an individual's bonus. Furthermore, it does measure performance, and in terms that are understandable to the individual.

But the experience of many companies which have adopted this mathematical approach indicates that it, too, has serious shortcomings. The most important weakness revolves around the fact that once the individual targets have been established, mathematics takes over the basic responsibility of management to manage. If the individual goals set at the beginning of the year are consistent between divisions, or between functions within divisions, the mathematically derived payoff at the year's end, undoubtedly, will be unfair. Some executives will be overpaid and others underpaid as a result of forces beyond the control of the individual. An unexpected price war, for instance, may seriously reduce profit margins in one division, while margins in another division benefit from the liquidation of a competitor. With mathematics deciding who gets what bonus, such basic economic shifts go unrecognized.

Then, too, the mathematically derived payoff that results from preset goals merits no adjustment in rewards for the *difficulty* of accomplishment. A manufacturing department, for example, may have surmounted major problems in fulfilling commitments that were easily attained by the sales department, or vice versa. But unless the program permits the *judgment* of management to reflect the difficulty of accomplishment, great incentive values are lost to the inflexibility of mathematics.

Because unfavorable results frequently stem from these relatively extreme approaches to performance appraisal—the wholly subjective and the mathematically determined evaluations—a number of leading companies have blended the best of the two into what appears destined to become a formidable management tool. The remainder of this article will examine in some detail the philosophy underlying the new concept, the administrative problems encountered, and the benefits derived from its use.

Planned Performance

Essentially, this composite approach to appraisal is aimed at providing a sound basis for judging the relative performance of executives, expressed in terms of their individual responsibilities. It establishes annual targets for the individual that are implicit in the job he holds. And it provides for *judging* performance in terms of these targets rather than a purely mathematical measurement. In addition, it relates these individual targets to the short- and long-term goals of the enterprise. This means that each member of the management team is working toward the same agreed-on objectives of the company or division and will be judged by how well he performs these tasks.

Company goals

This approach is called by a variety of names: programed management, management by objective, or planned performance programing. But whatever the title, its users have a common objective: that individual performance be judged in terms of agreed-on tasks reflecting the goals of the business. The first step, therefore, involves the development of long- and short-range company goals. The longer-term objectives are useful in "stretching" executive thinking—in making managers think "bigger"—but are also valuable as a guide to the practicability of the forecast targets:

> Let us assume, for instance, that a single-product manufacturer, after considerable study, sets a five-year goal of doubling his unit volume. As a result, he has decided how much must be added to current sales in the first, second, and later years to attain this goal. The practicability of these estimates, of course, needs to be checked against the ability of the company to manufacture, sell, and finance such increases in volume. It makes no sense, for example, to set goals beyond the company's ability to provide funds at reasonable cost, or to agree to sell more of a product than facilities can be expected to turn out.
>
> Once it is decided that a 15% increase in company volume is a realistic target for the first year, the next step is to determine what must be accomplished by each functional group in order to attain such a goal. To do so necessitates a careful assessment of interfunctional relationships. For instance, perhaps it is possible for the sales department to develop 15% more business by a greater utilization of salesmen's time; but if this is accomplished, new facilities might be needed by manufacturing in order to meet this goal. (These new facilities, in turn, would obviously have to be considered in relation to the forecast needs of future years as well.)
>
> On the other hand, production facilities might be adequate to attain the necessary volume, but the sales department might have to introduce a new line of products in order to reach this figure. If this occurs, of course, other functional areas are likely to be involved. In addition to changes that a new line might necessitate in the sales department, i.e., the introduction of a specialized sales force, the engineering department would be expected to design the new line, credit standards might have to be tightened or loosened, transportation costs or lead times might need alteration, and so on.

Functional tasks

Experience has shown that translating short-term company objectives into 12-month goals for individual functional executives is best done by setting up both quantitative and qualitative tasks to be accomplished during the period. In other words, executive responsibilities include (a) those that can be *measured*, such as sales, behind-schedule production, or credit losses, and (b) those that must be *judged*, made up of the intangibles that arise when an executive develops a new process, establishes a training program, improves the quality of engineering candidates, and the like.

The advantage of separating qualitative and quantitative tasks lies in the very human tendency among executives to "let the numbers decide." It appears to be much easier for a superior to point out shortcomings to a subordinate when he can blame such an unpleasant conclusion on the results of a quantitative evaluation. Explaining weaknesses that must be *judged* impressionistically, while frequently more important to the training process, causes greater discomfort to the superior. The separation of the two induces a deeper awareness of the importance of both elements.

Further, these tasks need to be set up for both line and staff positions—a process that has proved to be a serious stumbling block to performance appraisal programs. Trouble results largely from line-oriented senior executives finding it difficult to visualize the possibility of setting realistic targets for staff jobs. There appears to be an unfortunate tendency among some senior executives to write off the entire approach because of this blind spot where staff is concerned. Thus:

> Dislike of this approach frequently occurs when the responsibilities of staff functions are vague, and their contribution to the management process has not been adequately developed. The senior executive subconsciously questions the value of the staff function, yet has come to believe that "staff is a hallmark of modern management." He remembers the time, a few years ago, when his company had two vice presidents—sales and manufacturing. Today, there may be vice presidents for finance, engineering, personnel, administration, and so on, but the senior executive does not have the same "feel" for these jobs that he has for the line sales or manufacturing jobs with which he grew up.

This problem has been reduced, however, as top management more and more recognizes the need for spending as much *time* in establishing company and functional goals at the outset as it spends

in appraising performance at the end of the year. This more thoughtful approach to task setting results in a better understanding of
staff activities, as well as a more practical evaluation of the contributions that can be made in this area.

A number of techniques have been found helpful in cutting the
problem down to size. If the tasks of the line organization are
worked out first, for example, the process of thinking through the
supporting goals of the staff functions is simplified. Similarly, there
appears to be an advantage in setting up quantitative goals first
and, subsequently, building the qualitative tasks on this foundation.
One company has developed a master list of general goals for each
functional area, some quantitative and some qualitative. While individual tasks will vary, of course, from year to year, these general
goals have been found to be worth keeping in mind.

Examples of annual tasks developed as a basis for appraising the
performance of a division head, a personnel executive, and a manufacturing executive are shown in EXHIBITS I, II, and III. The tasks
in these examples are obviously fewer than would be the case in
real life, but they are adequate to show the kind of tasks that can
be used as a basis for appraising the performance of top line and
staff executives.

Lower-level tempo

The annual tasks established for the key functions naturally set
the tempo for executives below the top functional level. The goals
of subordinates are necessarily tied in with the targets set up for the
boss. However, some confusion has crept into the picture at this
point. There are those who regard goal setting as the job of the
subordinate, with the supervisor merely helping the subordinate
relate his own tasks "to the realities of the organization," as one
commentator put it. The great advantage of this method, in the
eyes of its supporters, is psychological. The executive sets his own
tasks, hence paces his own development.

My experience indicates that it is unrealistic to expect middle-
management executives to be broad-gauged enough to set their own
tasks. They do not fully comprehend the goals that have been
established for their boss by top management in order to maintain
integration between functions. Further, there is little evidence that
lower-echelon executives (those without full functional responsibility)

EXHIBIT I. PLANNED PERFORMANCE TARGETS FOR DIVISION MANAGER

Annual target plans

List of major accomplishments needed this year to meet corporation, division, or department goals.

Quantitative targets

Objectives for the year ahead that can be appraised in terms of *how much;* for example, "increase return on investment from 12% to 15%."

1. Increase billings by 17%, maintaining a 50%-30%-20% product mix in Departments A, B, and C.
2. Increase over-all profits (BT) by 35%.
3. Increase asset turnover from 1.3 times a year to 1.5 times.
4. Increase return on total assets from 18% to 21%.
5. Increase inventory turnover from 6.1 to 5.8 months.
6. Expand market share from 21% to 24%.

Qualitative targets

Objectives that can best be appraised in terms of *how well;* for example, "improve technical appraisal program," or "make more effective use of budgetary control."

1. Develop a new line of motors for introduction in 1961. Complete engineering phase, start production engineering.
2. Develop a more effective basis for testing candidates for supervisory positions, with particular reference to individual aptitudes for specific positions.
3. Increase the number of promotable executives by better training methods, including the introduction of job rotation and the establishment of a special assignment program designed to broaden the skills of outstanding men.
4. Start weekly department head meetings as a training and information medium.

---

are likely to set personal targets that fully "stretch" their capabilities. The political environment in most companies is such that it is very important for executives to "hit the target" they have agreed on. Since "stretched" goals are more difficult to attain, the incentive to play it safe is frequently overwhelming.

This does not mean that lower-level executives should not have an important voice in their job targets. The record indicates they should. But since their tasks are keyed directly to the goals of the functional executive, the latter must determine the targets of a subordinate, virtually in self-protection. Indeed, many of the tasks of the top functional executive are delegated directly to the subordinate:

EXHIBIT II. PLANNED PERFORMANCE TARGETS FOR DIRECTOR OF
PERSONNEL

Annual target plans

List of major accomplishments needed this year to meet corporation, division, or department goals.

Quantitative targets

Objectives for the year ahead that can be appraised in terms of *how much;* for example, "increase return on investment from 12% to 15%."

1. Reduce clerical costs of operating the employment function (recruiting and screening applicants) 60%.
2. Reduce cafeteria operating loss 3%.
3. Increase the typing pool from 25 to 30 employees.
4. Reduce the number of secretaries in headquarters staff by 15.

Qualitative targets

Objectives that can best be appraised in terms of *how well;* for example, "improve technical appraisal program," or "make more effective use of budgetary control."

1. Develop a safety training program for the operating divisions.
2. Simplify and reduce the number of clerical salary classifications.
3. Complete the management inventory.
4. Develop an approach to executive performance appraisal that will improve bonus plan administration.
5. Speed up new employee indoctrination procedure (estimated target—one hour).
6. Develop a program to provide the negotiating group with information that anticipates union demands more accurately.
7. Work with the manufacturing function to eliminate "assistants to" general foremen and plant superintendents within five years.

● For example, when a chief engineer has responsibility for reducing the number of motor frames in the product line, he almost certainly delegates this particular chore to someone on his staff.

● When the top manufacturing executive is charged with cutting 20% off the lead time in component purchases, this too will be passed along if he is a good executive.

Thus, the tasks of this lower-level group are much like those of their superiors. The main difference is in the number of special, short-term assignments that do not appear in any job description because they change so rapidly.

Judging performance

With job targets set up for top and middle-management executives, the next step involves determining where each executive's

EXHIBIT III. PLANNED PERFORMANCE TARGETS FOR DIRECTOR OF
MANUFACTURING

Annual target plans

List of major accomplishments needed this year to meet corporation, division, or department goals.

Quantitative targets

Objectives for the year ahead that can be appraised in terms of *how much;* for example, "increase return on investment from 12% to 15%."
1. Cut lead time on component purchases from 120 to 100 days.
2. Reduce WDC to 70% in terms of present prices.
3. Manufacturing's phase of the cost reduction program for the division is one third of the $1,500,000 excess saving over last year.
4. Improve delivery schedule performance by 5 percentage points (to 83%).
5. Reduce spoilage ratio by 2% net from 1959 figure.
6. Improve net allowed hours ratio by 3%.

Qualitative targets

Objectives that can best be appraised in terms of *how well;* for example "improve technical appraisal program," or "make more effective use of budgetary control."
1. Speed up the recognition and utilization of suggestions developed in the suggestion system.
2. Improve production planning on the assembly floor to reduce the need for stand-by stocks of subassemblies.
3. Restudy the manufacturing process now used for product "X" to reduce the direct labor needs.

performance of agreed-on tasks falls in the spectrum from outstanding to poor.

Companies doing the best job of appraising the performance of their executives appear to have a number of points in common. For one thing, most of them have incentive bonus plans. The existence of this constant prod to developing better appraisal techniques seems to pay off in good results. Perhaps this reflects top management's willingness to spend more time on something involving a lot of money.

Another common attribute of such companies is top management's recognition that the most important aspect of the entire appraisal process lies in the identification of outstanding and poor performers. Many appraisal programs bog down because of the time spent trying to identify minuscule differences in performance among the middle

60% to 70% of the executive group whose performance approximates the average! As a result of the effort spent in this direction, the 30% to 40% of the executives who are either outstanding or poor performers receive inadequate attention. Naturally, this becomes a critically important roadblock to success if the appraisal program includes an unwieldy number of executives.

In this connection, a technique so simple that it hardly seems worth mentioning has proved of considerable value. The outstanding performer and the poorest performer are first identified; then, in pairs, the second most outstanding and the second poorest are determined; and so on in pairs until it becomes difficult to distinguish between the performance of individual executives. Thus, a sense of proportion and reality is built into what otherwise tends to be a swampy morass.

One of the most difficult problems in judging performance lies in the values to be assigned line versus staff contributions. A few companies have developed an approach that appears helpful and sounds practical. While its use seems to be limited to those with incentive plans, there is no apparent need for such a limitation. This approach involves appraising the performance of fully profit-responsible executives (such as division managers) first, line executives (sales and manufacturing) second, and staff executives only after tentative values have been set for the profit-responsible and line executives. In other words, the performance of staff executives is "slotted" around already established relationships among the line executives.

This technique makes sense. The performance of the fully profit-responsible executive can be measured with a good deal of accuracy, by means of share-of-market, return-on-investment comparisons, and the like. Yardsticks for appraising sales and manufacturing executives are also good. However, measures of the staff executive's performance still leave much to be desired, and the evaluation of his performance should benefit from being tied in to the more tangible landmarks used for line executives.

The risk, of course, is that staff executives will be "slotted" on a position-in-the-hierarchy basis, or, in other words, judged by their position on the organization chart rather than by their performance. But a hardheaded judgment of the relative value of the tasks agreed upon, as well as a careful assessment of performance will go a long way toward protecting against this risk.

Action needed

Having determined where individual performance falls in the continuum from outstanding to poor, it is necessary to do something about these findings. One of the recurring problems in appraisal programs is that lower-echelon executives come to believe "nothing happens" as a result of the admittedly time-consuming appraisal effort.

An obvious first step is to see that the individual knows what is thought of his performance, and why. Since management's judgment of his performance is based on results racked up in the attainment of specific tasks, the individual's weaknesses and strengths are clearly delineated, and the supervising executive can discuss reasonably concrete "hits and misses" with the subordinate. This overcomes the natural reluctance among executives to criticize purely personal traits in their subordinates. Further, it focuses attention on specific opportunities for improvement. The planned performance approach, therefore, provides a basis for self-development on the part of the individual, as well as an assessment of "how he is doing."

For performance appraisal to be firmly rooted in a company's way of life it should play a key role in promotions, merit increases, and bonus payments. The outsider reviewing corporate administration practices all too frequently finds top performers, as measured by the appraisal program, doing no better than the average performer where bonuses, merit increases, and promotions are concerned. It may not make sense, but the rationalizations are plentiful. For instance, a top performer will be passed over for a merit increase "because his bonus was boosted this year"; or his bonus will be held unchanged despite outstanding performance "because he recently received a merit increase."

The point is this: if performance appraisal is worthwhile, it should provide the backbone for executive personnel administration.

Early problems

To date at least, only a handful of companies have seriously attempted to set up such a programed approach to performance appraisal. Because most of these pioneering efforts were started in the past few years, it is too early to look for success stories. However, the top executives of companies that have tackled task planning are almost uniformly enthusiastic with results achieved so far. The principal accomplishment, in their view, is the establishment of a task-oriented way of life. Job objectives are more clearly defined and, therefore, better coordinated. Individual executives know what is expected of them and can target their activities more effectively. Last but certainly not least, the annual review of "hits and misses" between superior and subordinate becomes more realistic and more productive of improved future performance.

Needless to say, there have been problems. It is significant, however, that the major problem areas follow a reasonably consistent pattern from company to company. For example:

- The detailed probing of individual job responsibilities essential to this approach takes a great deal of time and necessitates some highly creative thinking. Since executives are human, many of them tend to resist both the effort and the thought processes that are involved. For this reason, it is essential that the chief executive be solidly behind the project. If, for instance, executives come to suspect that their own bonuses may suffer from any neglect of the necessary time and thought requirements, so much the better.

- Another common problem of successful performance programing is the need for a competent and creative "control function." Executives who are to be rewarded or penalized, in part at least, on results developed by the budgeting and accounting function should have great confidence in the control techniques used, as well as the skill and honesty of this group. It is relatively simple to devise yardsticks, but the objectivity and courage of the top control executives must be respected at all levels if these measures are to be effective. Executives need to have faith that tasks set for the various functions are equally difficult, and that figures are not going to be juggled to protect someone's favorite.

The judgment of individual performance in terms of agreed-on tasks (such as those in Exhibits I, II, and III) requires maturity of a high order at the top level. One of the great advantages of the approach is the coordination of effort that results from its thoughtful, orderly task-setting process. If top management is overly arbitrary in its judgments, understandable problems develop. The chief executive who looks only to the results, without a careful weighing of the difficulties encountered in the accomplishments, is storing up future trouble.

- The planned performance approach also necessitates a personnel staff of unusual competence. This group necessarily plays a key role in advising top management when an imbalance occurs between functions. Several appraisal programs have suffered because the top personnel executives were unwilling or unable to convince top management of developing problem areas. In one instance, the personnel executive knew that the annual tasks set for one functional group were consistently more difficult to attain than were those of other groups. As a result this group had lost about 25% in bonus income over a four-year period. Top management became aware of the problem only after several promising young executives quit, and a subsequent study disclosed the source of the trouble.

Since this approach to performance appraisal is most effective when confined to executives who importantly influence company profits, many personnel executives find themselves dealing with new and complex problems when an executive appraisal program is adopted. As one personnel vice president put it, "I used to spend 95% of my time on problems dealing directly or indirectly with moves having union overtones. Now, more than half my time is spent on the recruitment, development, organization, and motivation of executives!"

Many personnel executives have found it difficult to effect a change-over. Thus, top management faces a serious handicap, since a strong, capable personnel group is a major ingredient in a successful appraisal program.

• The "cutoff point" of executives to be included in the appraisal program has proved to be another problem area. If too many are included, the programing task becomes monumental. The most effective course appears to involve starting off with a relatively limited group of key executives whose profit impact is unmistakable, and adding levels of executives to the program as its usefulness "proves out." The temptation to include too many, however, is almost overwhelming and needs to be consciously restrained.

Results to date indicate that the programed approach to performance appraisal is not for the laissez-faire management. It is a new way of life—and as difficult as it is rewarding.

Conclusion

The planned performance approach provides several important advantages over earlier attempts at executive appraisal:

1. The long- and short-term objectives of the enterprise become an integral part of the performance appraisal process.
2. The job responsibilities of executives provide the basis for setting individual targets. As a result of the necessity for thinking through the interrelationships between job activities, there is a more effective targeting of individual effort.
3. The outstanding and poor performers receive primary attention, spotlighting those eligible for promotion or merit increases and those requiring training or elimination.
4. Personality plays a less important part in the final evaluation of performance, for the focus is on what a man does rather than what is thought of him. Thus, subjective criteria are replaced by objective ones.
5. Mathematics is put in its proper role, providing guidelines rather than final decisions.

Companies using this appraisal approach believe its greatest contribution stems from the disciplines it imposes on the management process. Planned performance forces a company:

- To think hard about its objectives and review them constantly.

- To study the responsibilities involved in individual positions and determine their relative importance to the business.

- To set practical work tasks for individuals and hold them accountable for their attainment.

- To take whatever action is called for by the information presented to it, in order to build a more effective management team.

In a sense, therefore, such a program involves a down-to-earth executive development program. Since people learn by doing, on-the-job training has great advantages over the more formal executive development programs that bloomed in profusion after the war.

The planned performance approach requires an enormous invest-ment of top management's time in its early years. Since it usually involves a more disciplined way of life in the management process, it needs strong support from the chief executive and those directly under him. Because of the great time demands involved, companies have found it advantageous to limit the number of positions included in the program to those having a clearly recognizable impact on profits.

The approach also requires unusually skilled and resourceful con-trol, market, and economic research functions. Because quantitative yardsticks play a major role in establishing targets and judging per-formance, they must be demonstrably good or executive belief in the fairness of the process will be undermined. It should be recorded, however, that the performance of executives is subject to constant scrutiny, for decisions bearing on promotions, merit increases, and bonuses are being made by top management almost daily. The ques-tion is whether the planned performance approach is worth the time and the effort that are needed to make it effective.

Companies that have worked hardest to develop their skill in this area believe it to be a major improvement over earlier efforts. And the fact that these concerns are pacesetters in industry implies that the competitive pressure exerted by their success with this new management tool will force an ever-widening circle of companies to think in similar terms about executive performance appraisal.

Questions

1. The author states that the programed approach to performance ap-praisal is not for the laissez-faire type of management. Do you agree? Why?

2. Operative employees have traditionally bcen evaluated in terms of their productivity or the extent to which they met the specific performance standards of their jobs. How do you account for the delay in using this approach in evaluating executive personnel?
3. What effect would the programed approach to performance appraisal be likely to have on communications among executives?
4. A strong, capable personnel department is said to be a major ingredient in a successful appraisal program. How would you describe a strong, capable personnel department?

Additional Readings for Chapter 3

Adams, Harold F. "Problems in Appraisal Programs," *Journal of the American Society of Training Directors.* Vol. 13, No. 9 (September, 1959), pp. 3-11.

Barrett, Richard S. "Explorations in Job Satisfaction and Performance Rating," *Personnel Administration.* Vol. 27, No. 5 (September-October, 1964), pp. 14-21.

Buel, William D. "Items, Scales and Raters: Some Suggestions and Comments," *Personnel Administration.* Vol. 25, No. 5 (September-October, 1962), pp. 15-20.

Daniels, John, and Richard J. Comiskey. "The Unproductive Employee—Cause, Effect and Remedy," *Personnel Administration.* Vol. 27, No. 2 (March-April, 1964), pp. 30-39.

Farson, Richard E. "Praise Reappraised," *Harvard Business Review.* Vol. 41, No. 5 (September-October, 1963), pp. 61-66.

Feinberg, Mortimer R. "Performance Appraisal and Executive Morale," *Management Review.* Vol. 50, No. 6 (June, 1961), pp. 25-31.

Friedlander, Frank. "Comparative Work Value Systems," *Personnel Psychology.* Vol. 18, No. 1 (Spring, 1965), pp. 1-20.

Glickman, Albert S. "Is Performance Appraisal Practical?" *Personnel Administration.* Vol. 27, No. 5 (September-October, 1964), pp. 28-32.

Herzberg, Frederick. "The Motivation-Hygiene Concept and Problems of Manpower," *Personnel Administration.* Vol. 27, No. 1 (January-February, 1964), pp. 3-7.

Katz, Robert L. "Toward a More *Effective* Enterprise," *Harvard Business Review.* Vol. 38, No. 5 (September-October, 1960), pp. 80-102.

Kilbridge, Maurice D. "Reduced Costs Through Job Enlargement: A Case," *The Journal of Business.* Vol. XXXIII, No. 4 (October, 1960), pp. 357-362.

Kindall, Alva F., and James Gatza. "Positive Program for Performance Appraisal," *Harvard Business Review.* Vol. 41, No. 6 (November-December, 1963), pp. 153-159, 162-166.

Kuriloff, Arthur H. "An Experiment in Management—Putting Theory Y to the Test," *Personnel.* Vol. 40, No. 6 (November-December, 1963), pp. 8-17.

Kyte, Aileen L. "Motivating and Appraising Scientific Personnel," *Management Record.* Vol. XXIII, No. 6 (June, 1961), pp. 2-10.

Mayfield, Harold. "In Defense of Performance Appraisal," *Harvard Business Review.* Vol. 38, No. 2 (March-April, 1960), pp. 81-87.

Meyer, Herbert H., Emanuel Kay, and John R. P. French, Jr. "Split Roles in Performance Appraisal," *Harvard Business Review.* Vol. 43, No. 1 (January-February, 1965), pp. 123-129.

Moore, Leo B. "Too Much Management, Too Little Change," *Harvard Business Review.* Vol. 34, No. 1 (January-February, 1956), pp. 41-48.

Mosel, James N. "Incentives, Supervision and Probability," *Personnel Administration.* Vol. 25, No. 1 (January-February, 1962), pp. 9-14.

Pepinsky, Harold B., and Karl W. Weick. "The Simulation of Productivity in Organizations," *Personnel Administration.* Vol. 24, No. 6 (November-December, 1961), pp. 18-24.

Porter, Lyman W. "A Study of Perceived Need Satisfactions in Bottom and Middle Management Jobs," *Journal of Applied Psychology.* Vol. 45, No. 1 (February, 1961), pp. 1-10.

Purcell, Theodore V. "Observing People," *Harvard Business Review.* Vol. 33, No. 2 (March-April, 1955), pp. 90-100.

Solem, Allen R. "Some Supervisory Problems in Appraisal Interviewing," *Personnel Administration.* Vol. 23, No. 3 (May-June, 1960), pp. 27-35.

Speroff, B. J. "Experimental Procedures and Techniques for Evaluating Supervisory Performance," *Personnel Administration.* Vol. 24, No. 3 (May-June, 1961), pp. 4-10.

Stolz, Robert E. "Assessing Research Productivity," *Personnel Administration.* Vol. 25, No. 1 (January-February, 1962), pp. 44-49.

Terry, Herbert. "Comparative Evaluation of Performance Using Multiple Criteria," *Management Science.* Vol. 9, No. 3 (April, 1963), pp. 431-442.

——————. "Whatever Became of Merit Rating?", *Personnel.* Vol. 34, No. 4 (January-February, 1958), pp. 8-18.

CHAPTER 4

Providing Effective Leadership

The success of an organization is contingent upon the effective performance of each of its members. Their ability to realize their full potential and to contribute maximally to the accomplishment of the organizational objectives is dependent upon many factors. Most of these factors are under the purview of the leaders who control the destiny of the organization. In the small organization where the owner is the active manager, the effectiveness of leadership is not likely to receive much attention. In the larger organization, however, where there are many managerial positions to be filled, increasing attention has been given to the development of quality leadership. It is recognized that the productive efficiency, adjustment, and morale of personnel at all levels in the organization are affected by the characteristics of its managers and supervisors.

It is known today, largely as a result of studies in industrial leadership in the last quarter century, that the leadership function is more complex than was once realized. Earlier notions of leadership focused heavily upon the personal qualities of leaders with an implicit assumption that leaders were born, not made. More recently, however, with careful study of leadership in various contexts or situations, it has become apparent that leadership involves more than the possession of certain personal traits. The situation in which a person is assigned to lead coupled with his own behavior in relation to that situation can have a vital effect upon his success or failure as a leader.

Studies in human motivation have also made their contribution to leadership theory. They have revealed the motivational effects of employee participation in job activities, with the result that many experts in this area are enthusiastic in proposing that employees be permitted to participate in decision making as well as in other significant areas of the work. Other dimensions of the leadership process such as how much the leader structures the work and how considerate he is of employee feelings add further refinement to this complicated role.

A survey of the literature in the journals will reveal a substantial number of articles devoted to this important topic. It is believed that the following articles, however, provide a representative coverage of the intricacies of the various facets of leadership encountered by everyone from the chief executive in the organization to the first-line supervisors.

The first article by Robert L. Katz is particularly valuable in describing three basic skills—technical, human, and conceptual—and in showing their relative importance to successful leadership at different levels in the organizational hierarchy. At all levels in the organization the leader's success in carrying out the organizational objectives is dependent to some degree on the type of skill that Katz labels "human." He achieves results through the efforts of others who are subordinate to him. Very little has been written, however, about the problems of subordination. As Dale S. Beach says, "There is need to systematically examine work relationships from the perspective of the subordinate." We agree with his statement and, therefore, have included his interesting article. Beach has an interesting plan for a judicial system for nonunion employees that is designed to reduce the anxiety and frustration of employees.

The third article by Stanley Young includes a provocative discussion of the manager's authority in the employment relationship. He hypothesizes that no authority relationship exists between the manager and employee. If his hypothesis is supported, it then becomes readily apparent that in order to be effective as a leader one must develop effective skills.

One of the most significant and useful articles ever written about leadership skills is that by Robert Tannenbaum and Warren H. Schmidt. It provides useful guidance on the forces to be considered by the manager in determining the extent to which he desires to have employees participate in the decision-making process. Their stress on the manager's need to be insightful and flexible is characteristic of the sensitivity training programs with which they have been closely identified.

The article by our colleague, James R. Bell, focuses on the suggestion system which has long been used as an example of an activity which provides for employee participation. Bell explodes some of the myths concerning the role of the suggestion system as well as illustrating the adverse effects that the suggestion system, as typically established, can have on the morale of supervisory personnel. His critical analysis of the typical suggestion system represents the approach that all personnel workers should take toward the various personnel management programs.

Effective leadership requires, among other things, a genuine concern for the emotional adjustment of employees. Management can no longer have a short-sighted view of adjustment and must bear some of the responsibility for what happens to the individual. Although the extent to which supervisors and managers should attempt to provide assistance in this area may be subject to question, it is generally assumed that the company should try to provide some degree of help to emotionally disturbed employees or at least try to direct them to a competent professional source of assistance. Suggestions on the type of help to give and how to make referrals are given in the article by Harry Levinson.

19. EXECUTIVE SKILLS: WHAT MAKES A GOOD ADMINISTRATOR? *

Robert L. Katz

Ever since World War II, leaders in industry, government, labor, the armed forces, and in education have increasingly proclaimed the need for "good administrators." Recently, L. L. Colbert, President of Chrysler Corporation, called the need for better men in management the most critical need of our times. Gwilym A. Price, President of Westinghouse Corporation, has said: "the problem of choosing and training personnel so as to insure effective and orderly succession to the top levels of management is the most engrossing problem that faces corporate management. . . . Every company is constantly seeking ways to assess human abilities, and so to eliminate the risks of accident and haphazard choice in the selection of its leaders." *Fortune* magazine reported: "If any one management problem dominated executives' thinking in 1953, it was the executive himself, or, more accurately, how to find the right kind of people to be executives. . . . Over the long pull, . . . the basic management problem that will probably get the most sustained attention is that of executive development." And a host of similar comments could be added.

Clearly, the problem of finding and developing good administrators (leaders, managers, or executives) is receiving enormous attention. Yet there is very little agreement as to what a good administrator is.

Some executives have placed central importance on a single characteristic. For example, Clarence B. Randall, President of Inland Steel Corporation, has said: "The outstanding characteristic of the good executive is his capacity for reaching decisions—for making up his mind and then translating thought into action."

Charles P. McCormick, President of McCormick & Company, has said: "A real leader (is one who) has the ability to get others to work willingly through his influence and example."

* From a pamphlet published by the Amos Tuck School of Business (1954), 16 pp. Reprinted with permission.

Crawford H. Greenewalt, President of E. I. DuPont de Nemours & Company, has suggested: ". . . an executive is good when he can make a smoothly functioning team out of people with the many different skills required in the operation of a modern business. His most important function is to reconcile, to coordinate, to compromise, and to appraise the various viewpoints and talents under his direction to the end that each individual contributes his full measure to the business at hand."

Still others, mostly educators and consultants, have attempted to set down lists of characteristics which typify the good administrator. For example, Dean G. L. Bach of Carnegie Institute of Technology cites five qualities which "distinguish really first-rate managers from the much larger number of solid and reliable but not outstanding businessmen." These include (1) orderly ability to size up problems and reach action decisions on the best facts available; (2) ability to deal effectively with people; (3) instinctive acceptance of responsibility; (4) thorough understanding of the interrelations between the specific business and the economic, social, and political forces of the entire environment; (5) imagination and adaptation to change.

Burleigh B. Gardner, Executive Director of Social Research, Inc., designates eleven traits which characterize the successful executive. These are: (1) motivation by achievement; (2) an accepting attitude toward authority of superiors; (3) strong mobility drives; (4) organizational ability; (5) decisiveness; (6) firmness of conviction; (7) activity and aggression; (8) the need to overcome a sense of frustration; (9) realism; (10) responsive attitude toward superiors; sympathetic, but impersonal attitude toward subordinates; (11) mature attitude toward parents.

It would not be difficult to add a hundred more definitions from equally distinguished sources, for every practicing executive has his own approach to "what makes a good administrator." Each of these has some elements in common, yet disagrees on certain characteristics or on emphasis.

It is the purpose of this paper to suggest that effective administration rests on *three developable skills* which synthesize many of these definitions and which may provide a useful way of looking at, and understanding, the administrative process. This approach is based on the first-hand observation of executives at work, coupled with the study of current field research in administration. It is certainly not the only acceptable approach, nor is it necessarily all-inclusive. Nevertheless, it is offered in the hope that, although tentative, it may afford a helpful guide to the selection and training of administrators.

In the sections which follow, an attempt will be made to define and demonstrate what these three skills are; to suggest that the relative importance of the three skills varies with the level of responsibility; to present some of the implications of this variation for selection, training, and promotion of executives; and to propose ways in which these skills can be developed.

A three-skill approach

In this paper, it is assumed that an administrator is one who: (a) directs the activities of other people, and (b) assumes the responsibility for achieving certain objectives through these efforts. Within this definition, successful administration appears to rest upon three basic skills, which we will call *technical, human,* and *conceptual.* It would be unrealistic to assert that these skills are not interrelated; yet there may be real merit in examining each one separately (and in developing them independently).

Technical skill, as used here, implies an understanding of, and proficiency in, a specific kind of activity, particularly one involving methods, processes, procedures or techniques. It is easy for us to visualize the technical skill of the surgeon, the musician, the accountant, or the engineer when each is performing his specialized functions. It involves specialized knowledge, analytical ability within that specialty, and facility in the use of the tools and techniques of the specific discipline.

Of the three skills described in this paper, *technical skill* is perhaps the most familiar because it is the most concrete, and because, in our age of specialization, it is the skill required of the greatest number of people. Most of our vocational and on-the-job training programs are largely concerned with developing this specialized technical skill.

Human skill is defined here as the executive's ability to work effectively as a group member and to build cooperative effort within the team he leads. As *technical skill* is primarily concerned with working with "things" (processes or physical objects), so *human skill* is primarily concerned with working with people. This skill is demonstrated in the way the individual perceives (and recognizes the perceptions of) his superiors, equals, and subordinates, and in the way he behaves subsequently.

The person with highly developed *human skill* is aware of his own attitudes, assumptions and beliefs about other individuals and groups, and is able to see the usefulness and limitations of these feelings. By accepting the existence of viewpoints, perceptions, and beliefs which are different from his own, he is skillful in understanding what others really mean by their words and behavior. He is equally skillful in communicating to others, in their own contexts, what he means by *his* behavior. He works to create an atmosphere of approval and security in which subordinates feel free to express themselves without fear of censure or ridicule, by encouraging them to participate in the planning and carrying out of those things which directly affect them. He is sufficiently sensitive to the needs and motivations of others in his organization that he can judge the possible reactions to, and outcomes of, various courses of action he may undertake. Having this sensitivity, he is able and willing to *take action* in a way which takes these perceptions by others into account.

Real skill in working with others must become a natural, continuous activity, since it involves not only sensitivity at times of decision-making, but also in the day-by-day behavior of the individual. *Human skill* cannot be a "sometime thing." Techniques cannot be randomly applied, nor can "personality traits" be put on or removed like an overcoat. Because everything which an executive says and does (or leaves unsaid or undone) has an effect upon his associates, his true self will, in time, show through. Thus, to be effective, this skill must be naturally developed and unconsciously (and consistently) demonstrated in the individual's every action. . . .

Because *human skill* is so vital a part of everything the administrator does, examples of inadequate human skill are easier to describe than are highly skillful performances. Perhaps consideration of an actual situation would be helpful: [1]

When a new conveyor unit was installed in a shoe factory where workers had previously been free to determine their own work rate, the production manager asked the industrial engineer who had designed the conveyor to serve as foreman (even though a qualified foreman was available). The engineer (who reported directly to the production manager) objected, but under pressure agreed to take the job "until a suitable foreman could be found," even though this was a job of lower status than his present one. Then the following conversation took place:

---

[1] Auburn Shoe Mfg. Co. (EA-A101). Copyrighted by President and Fellows of Harvard College. Reprinted by permission.

PRODUCTION MANAGER: "I've had a lot of experience with conveyors. I want you to keep this conveyor going at all times except for rest periods, and I want it going at top speed. Get these people thinking in terms of two pairs of shoes per minute, 70 dozen pairs a day, 350 dozen pairs a week. They are all experienced operators on their individual jobs, and it's just a matter of getting them to do their jobs in a little different way. I want you to make that base rate of 250 dozen pair a week work!" (Base rate was established at 75% of the maximum designed capacity. This base rate was 50% higher than under the old system.)

ENGINEER: "If I'm going to be foreman of the conveyor unit, I want to do things my way. I've worked on conveyors, and I don't agree with you on first getting people used to a conveyor going at top speed. These people have never seen a conveyor. You'll scare them. I'd like to run the conveyor at one-third speed for a couple of weeks and then gradually increase the speed.

"I think we should discuss setting the base rate (production quota before incentive bonus) on a daily basis instead of a weekly basis. (Workers had previously been paid on a daily straight piece-work basis.)

"I'd also suggest setting a daily base rate at 45 or even 40 dozen pair. You have to set a base rate low enough for them to make. Once they know they can make the base rate, they will go after the bonus."

PRODUCTION MANAGER: "You do it your way on the speed; but remember it's the results that count. On the base rate, I'm not discussing it with you; I'm *telling* you to make the 250 dozen pair a week work. I don't want a daily base rate."

Here is a situation in which the production manager was so preoccupied with getting the physical output that he paid no attention to the people through whom that output must be achieved. Notice, first, that he made the engineer who designed the unit serve as foreman, apparently hoping to force the engineer to justify his design by producing the maximum output. However, the production manager was oblivious to (1) the way the engineer perceived this appointment (as a demotion) and (2) the need for the engineer to be able to control the variables if he was to be held responsible for output. Instead, the production manager imposed a production standard and refused any changes in the work situation.

Moreover, although this was a radically new situation for the operators, the production manager expected them to immediately produce at well above their previous output—even though the workers had an unfamiliar production system to cope with, the operators had never worked together as a team before, the operators and their new foreman had never worked together before, and the foreman was not in agreement with the production goals or standards. By ignoring all these human factors, the production manager not only placed the engineer in an extremely difficult operating situation, but also, by refusing to allow the engineer to "run his own show," discouraged the very assumption of responsibility he'd hoped for in making the appointment.

Under these circumstances, it is easy to understand how the relationship between these two men rapidly deteriorated, and how production, after two months' operation, was at only 125 dozen pairs per week (only 75 per cent of what it had been under the old system) !

Conceptual skill, as used here, involves the ability to see the enterprise as a whole; it includes recognizing how the various functions of the organization depend on one another, and how changes in any one part affect all the others; and it extends to visualizing the relationship of the individual business to the industry, the community, and the political, social and economic forces of the nation as a whole. Recognizing these relationships, and perceiving the significant elements in any situation, the administrator should then be able to act in a way which advances the over-all welfare of the organization.

Hence, the success of any decision depends upon the *conceptual skill* of the people who make the decision and those who put it into action. When, for example, an important change in marketing policy is made, it is critical that the effects upon production, control, finance, research, and the people involved be considered. And it remains critical right down to the last executive who must implement the new policy. If each executive recognizes the over-all relationships and significances of the change, he is almost certain to be more effective in administering it. Consequently its chances for succeeding are greatly increased.

Not only does the effective coordination of the various parts of the business depend on the *conceptual skill* of the administrators involved, but so also does the whole future direction and tone of the organization. The attitudes of the top executives color the whole character of the organization's response and determine the "corporate personality" which distinguishes one company's ways of doing business from another. These attitudes are a reflection of the administrator's *conceptual skill* (referred to by some as his "creative ability")—the way he perceives and responds to the direction in which the business should grow, company objectives and policies, stockholders' and employees' interests, etc.

Conceptual skill, as defined above, is what Chester I. Barnard, former President of the New Jersey Bell Telephone Co., implies in ". . . the essential aspect of the (executive) process is the sensing of the organization as a whole and the total situation relevant to it." Examples of inadequate *conceptual skill* are all around us. For instance:

In a large manufacturing concern which had a long tradition of job-shop type operations, primary responsibility for production control had been left to the foremen and other low-level supervisors. "Village" type operations with small working groups and informal organizations were the rule. A heavy influx of orders following World War II tripled the normal production requirements and severely taxed the whole manufacturing organization. At this point, a new production manager was brought in from outside the company, and he established a wide range of controls and formalized the entire operating structure. As long as the boom demand lasted, the employees made every effort to conform with the new procedures and environment. But when demand subsided to pre-war levels, serious labor relations problems developed, friction was high among department heads, and the company found itself saddled with a heavy indirect labor cost. Management sought to reinstate its old procedures; it fired the production manager, and attempted to give greater authority to the foremen once again. However, during the four years of formalized control, the foremen had grown away from their old practices, many had left the company, and adequate replacements had not been developed. Without strong foreman leadership, the traditional job-shop operations proved costly and inefficient.

In this instance, when the new production controls and formalized organization were introduced, management did not foresee the consequences of this action in the event of a future contraction of business. Later, when conditions changed and it was necessary to pare down operations, they were again unable to recognize the implications of their action and reverted to the old procedures which, under existing circumstances, were no longer appropriate. This compounded *conceptual* inadequacy left the company at a serious competitive disadvantage.

Because a company's over-all success is dependent upon its executives' *conceptual skill* in establishing and carrying out policy decisions, this skill is the unifying, coordinating ingredient of the administrative process, and of undeniable over-all importance.

We may notice that, in a very real sense, *conceptual skill,* as here defined, embodies both the technical and human aspects of the organization. This may seem to point up the artificiality of attempting to separate *technical, human,* and *conceptual skills.* Each example cited in this paper appears to contain elements of all three. Yet it appears that the concept of *skill,* as an ability to translate knowledge into action, enables one to distinguish between the three skills of performing the technical activities (*technical skill*), understanding and motivating individuals and groups (*human skill*), and coordinating and integrating all of the organization's activities and interests toward a common objectve (*conceptual skill*).

A comparison of this skill approach with others

Before pursuing the implications of this three-skill approach, it may be useful to pause to consider the definitions of "what makes a good administrator" cited in the opening pages of this paper. How does this skill approach stack up against these definitions?

Clarence Randall's criterion of decisiveness must be based on a highly developed *conceptual skill,* plus the sensitivity in carrying out the decision which is implied in *human skill.*

Charles McCormick's definition of getting others to work willingly is almost straight *human skill.*

Crawford Greenewalt's standard of "reconciling, coordinating, compromising and appraising various viewpoints and talents" is a mixture of *conceptual* and *human skills,* as is Dean Bach's five-point approach.

Burleigh Gardner's eleven traits seem to be common to men with highly developed *human* and *conceptual skills.*

Perhaps there are other definitions, other criteria which may be suggested that will not lend themselves to this three-skill approach. Nevertheless, because it seems useful and consistent, this approach is offered here in the hope that it may be of some value to the business community.

Implications of this approach

The separation of effective administration into three basic skills is primarily an analytical distinction. In practice, these skills are so closely interrelated that it is difficult to determine where one ends and another begins. However, just because the skills are interrelated does not imply that we cannot get some value from looking at them separately, or by varying their emphasis. In playing golf, the action of the hands, wrists, hips, shoulders, arms, and head are all interrelated; yet in improving one's swing, it is often valuable to work on one of these elements separately. Also, under different playing conditions, the relative importance of these elements varies. Similarly, although all three are important at every level of administration, the *technical, human* and *conceptual skills* of the administrator vary in importance at different levels of responsibility.

Technical skill is responsible for many of the great advances of modern industry. It is indispensable to efficient operation. Yet it has greatest importance at the lower levels of administration. As the administrator moves further and further from the actual physical doing, this need for *technical skill* becomes less important, provided he has skilled subordinates and can help them solve their own problems. At the top, technical skill may be almost nonexistent, and the executive may still be able to perform effectively if his *human* and *conceptual skills* are highly developed.

For example: in one large capital-goods producing company, the controller was called upon to replace the manufacturing vice-president who had been stricken suddenly with a severe illness. The controller had no previous production experience, but he had been with the company for more than 20 years and knew many of the key production personnel intimately. By setting up an advisory staff, and by delegating an unusual amount of authority to his department heads, he was able to devote himself to coordination of the various functions. By so doing, he produced a highly efficient team. The results were lower costs, greater productivity, and higher morale than the production division had ever before experienced. Management had gambled that his ability to work with people was more important than his lack of a technical production background, and the gamble more than paid off.

Other examples are evident all around us. We are all familiar with those "professional managers" who are becoming the prototypes of our modern executive world. These men shift with great ease, and with no apparent loss in effectiveness, from one industry to another. Their *human* and *conceptual skills* seem to make up for their unfamiliarity with the new job's technical aspects.

Human skill, the ability to work with others, is essential to effective administration at every level. One recent research study has shown that *human skill* is of paramount importance at the foreman level pointing out that the chief function of the foreman as an administrator is to attain collaboration of people in the work group. Another study reinforces this finding and extends it to the middle management group, adding that the administrator should be primarily concerned with facilitating communication in the organization. While another study, concerned primarily with top management, underscores the need for self-awareness and sensitivity to human relationships by executives at that level. These findings would tend to indicate that *human skill* is of great importance at every administrative level (but notice the difference in emphasis).

Human skill seems to be most important at lower levels, where the number of direct contacts between administrators and subordinates is greatest. As we go higher and higher in the administrative echelons, the number and frequency of these personal contacts decrease, and the need for *human skill* becomes proportionately (although probably not absolutely) less. At the same time, *conceptual skill* becomes increasingly more important with the need for policy decisions and broad scale action. The *human skill* of dealing with individuals then becomes subordinate to the *conceptual skill* of integrating group interests and activities into a coordinated whole.

In fact, a recent research study by Professor Argyris of Yale University has given us the example of an extremely effective plant manager, who, although possessing little *human skill* as defined here, was nonetheless very successful. This manager, a largely autonomous division head, made his supervisors, through the effects of his strong personality and the "pressure" he applied, highly dependent upon him for most of their "rewards, penalties, authority, perpetuation, communication and identification." As a result, the supervisors spent much of their time competing with one another for the manager's favor. They told him only the things they thought he wanted to hear, and spent much time trying to find out his desires. They depended on him to set their objectives and to show them how to reach them. Because the manager was inconsistent and unpredictable in his behavior, the supervisors were insecure and continually engaged in interdepartmental squabbles which they tried to keep hidden from the manager. Clearly, *human skill* . . . was lacking.

Yet, by the evaluation of his superiors and by his results in increasing efficiency and raising profits and morale (!), this manager was exceedingly effective. Professor Argyris suggests that employees in modern industrial organizations tend to have a "built-in" sense of dependence on superiors which capable and alert men can turn to advantage. In the context of the three-skill approach, it seems that this manager was able to capitalize on this dependence because he recognized the interrelationships of all the activities under his control, identified himself with the organization and sublimated the individual interests of his subordinates to *his* (the organization's) interest, set his goals realistically, and showed his subordinates how to reach these goals. This would seem to be an excellent example of a situation in which strong *conceptual skill* more than compensated for a lack of *human skill*.

Conceptual skill, as indicated in the preceding sections, becomes increasingly critical in more responsible executive positions where its effects are maximized and most easily observed. In fact, recent research findings lead to the conclusion that at the top level of administration, this *conceptual skill* becomes the most important ability of all. Herman W. Steinkraus, President of Bridgeport Brass Company, seems to confirm this: "One of the most important lessons which I learned on this job (the presidency) is the importance of coordinating the various departments into an effective team, and, secondly, to recognize the shifting emphasis from time to time of the relative importance of various departments to the business."

Conceptual skill is unquestionably valuable at any administrative level. However, while at lower levels this ability may be useful and may mark a man for advancement, recent studies would seem to indicate that *human skill* is much more important than *conceptual skill* in effectively accomplishing the administrative objectives of low-level positions.

If these conclusions are valid, then selection and training of candidates for administrative positions might well be based on the extent to which the individual possesses the requisite skills most important to the level of responsibility for which he is being considered.

Developing these skills

For years many people have contended that leadership ability is inherent in certain chosen individuals. We talk of "born leaders," "born executives," "born salesmen." It is undoubtedly true that certain people, naturally or innately, possess greater aptitude or ability in certain skills. But research in psychology and physiology would also indicate, first, that those having strong aptitudes and abilities can improve their skill through practice and training, and, second, that even those lacking the "natural ability" can improve their performance and effectiveness.

The *skill* conception of administration suggests that we may hope to improve our administrative effectiveness and to develop better administrators for the future. This skill conception implies *learning by doing*. Different people learn in different ways, but skills are developed through practice and through relating learning to one's own personal experience and background. What then, are the implications of the skill approach to administration, described here, for executive development?

Development of *technical skill* has received great attention for many years by industry and educational institutions alike, and much progress has been made. Sound grounding in the principles, structures, and processes of the individual specialty, coupled with actual practice and experience during which the individual is watched and helped by a superior, appear to be most effective. In view of the vast amount of work which has been done in training people in technical skills, it would seem unnecessary . . . to suggest more.

Human skill, however, has been much less understood, and only recently has systematic progress in developing it been made. Many approaches to the development of *human skill* are being pursued by various universities and professional men today. These are rooted in such disciplines as psychology, sociology, and anthropology.

Some of these approaches find their application in "applied psychology," "scientific management," and a host of other manifestations requiring technical specialists to help the businessman with his human problems. As a practical matter, however, the executive must develop his own *human skill*, rather than lean on the advice of others. To be effective, he must develop his own personal point of view toward human activity, so that he will: (1) know his own limitations; (2) have an attitude about his own experiences which will enable him to re-evaluate and learn from them; (3) develop ability in understanding what others by their actions and words (explicit or implicit) are trying to communicate to him; and (4) develop skill in successfully communicating his ideas and attitude to others.

This *human skill* can be developed by some individuals without formal training. Others can be individually aided by their immediate superiors, as an integral part of the "coaching" process to be described later. (This aid depends for effectiveness, obviously, upon the extent to which the superior possesses the *human skill*.) For larger groups, the use of case problems, coupled with impromptu role playing can be very effective. This training can be established on a formal or informal basis, but requires a skilled instructor and an organized sequence of activities. It affords as good an approximation to reality as can be provided on a continuing classroom basis, and offers an opportunity for critical reflection not often found in actual practice. An important part of the procedure is the self-examination of the student's own concepts and values, which may enable him to develop more useful attitudes about himself and about others. With the change in attitude, hopefully, there may also come some active skill in dealing with human problems.

Conceptual skill, like *human skill*, has not been universally understood. A number of methods have been tried to aid in developing this ability, with varying success. Some of the best results have always been achieved through the "coaching" of subordinates by superiors. This is no new idea. It implies that one of the key responsibilities of the executive is to help his subordinates to develop their administrative potentials. One way a superior can help "coach" his subordinate is by assigning a particular responsibility, and then responding with searching questions or opinions, rather than giving answers, when the subordinate seeks help. When Benjamin F. Fairless, now Chairman of the Board of the United States Steel Corporation, was president of the corporation he described his coaching activities as follows: "When one of my vice-presidents or the head of one of our operating companies comes to me for instructions, I generally counter by asking him questions. First thing I know, he has told me how to solve the problem himself."

Obviously, this is an ideal and wholly natural procedure for administrative training, and applies to *technical* and *human* skill development, as well as to *conceptual*. However, its success must necessarily rest on the abilities and willingness of the superior to help the subordinate.

Another excellent way to develop *conceptual skill* is through trading jobs, that is, by moving promising young men through different functions of the business, but retaining the same level of responsibility. This gives the man the chance literally to "be in the other fellow's shoes."

Other possibilities include: special assignments, particularly those which involve interdepartmental problems; and management boards, such as the McCormick Multiple Management plan, in which junior executives serve as advisors to top management on policy matters.

For larger groups, the kind of case problems course described above, only employing cases involving broad management policy and interdepartmental coordination, may be useful. Courses of this kind, often called "General Management" or "Business Policy" are becoming more prevalent.

Like *human skill, conceptual skill,* too, must become a natural part of the executive's make-up. Different methods may be indicated for developing different people, by virtue of their backgrounds, attitudes, and experience. But in every case, that method should be chosen which will enable the executive to develop his own personal skill in visualizing the enterprise as a whole and in coordinating and integrating its various parts.

The purpose of this paper has been to show that effective administration depends on three basic personal skills, which have been called *technical, human,* and *conceptual.* The administrator needs: (1) sufficient *technical skill* to accomplish the mechanics of the particular job for which he is responsible; (2) sufficient *human skill* in working with others to be an effective group member and to be able to build cooperative effort within the team he leads; (3) sufficient *conceptual skill* to recognize the interrelationships of the various factors involved in his situation, leading to that action which achieves the maximum good for the total organization.

The relative importance of these three skills seems to vary with the level of administrative responsibility. At low levels, the principal need is for *technical* and *human skills.* At higher levels, administrative effectiveness depends largely on *human* and *conceptual skills.* At the top, *conceptual skill* becomes the most important of all for successful administration.

This three-skill approach emphasizes that good administrators are not necessarily born: they may be developed. It synthesizes many isolated traits considered common to successful administrators in an effort to provide a useful way of looking at the administrative process. By helping to identify the skills most needed at various levels of responsibility, it may prove useful in the selection, training and promotion of executives.

Questions

1. Would you agree with the author when he says that human skill seems to be most important at the lower levels and less important at the higher levels in an organization? Why?
2. It has been said that leaders are born that way. Does Katz agree with this type of thinking?
3. Katz quotes Professor Argyris who suggests that employees in modern industrial organizations tend to have a "built-in" sense of dependence on superiors. How would you account for this dependence?
4. Can you think of other skills that a manager should have that are not included in the three skills described in this article?
5. Katz describes the leader with highly developed human skill as being sensitive to the needs and motivations of others in his organization. How does this statement conform to commonly held notions about effective leadership?

20. AN ORGANIZATIONAL PROBLEM— SUBORDINATE-SUPERIOR RELATIONS *

Dale S. Beach

As evidenced by the content of the abundant literature in the management field and the expansion and prospering of supervisory training and executive development programs in industry, it is apparent that increasing attention in recent years has been devoted to the problems of the human relations of administration, of leadership, supervision, and personnel management. However, inadequate attention is being given to the problems of subordination.

Supervision and subordination are closely related. By improving the caliber of management, by giving the practicing manager greater insights and understanding of the supervisory process, we expect that some of the problems of superior-subordinate will be alleviated. However, the emphasis has been that of management looking downward to determine how to motivate people to increase their effectiveness, and how to raise morale in order to reduce turnover and grievances and minimize disciplinary problems. There is need to systematically examine work relationships from the perspective of the subordinate. Practically everyone, except the independent proprietor, has a boss. Certainly the myriad supervisors and executives in the large corporation all have their superiors. Even the president has the board of directors that he must satisfy.

Since a manager is unable to do everything himself he has the power to assign certain duties and responsibilities to his subordinates. The prevailing structure in nearly all organizations in our society which are devoted to work and the production of goods and services (purely social organizations, for example, would be excluded from this analysis) is primarily authoritarian. There is a formal chain of command; everyone has his own boss and he is expected to comply with the orders transmitted to him from above. Force, in one form or another, frequently dwells in the background where it may be called upon to insure compliance with the wishes and directives of those in command. The superior dispenses rewards and punishments to gain

* From *Advanced Management*, Vol. 25, No. 12 (December, 1960), pp. 12-15. Reprinted with permission.

the necessary adherence to his orders. Under such a system the subordinate, whether he be a rank and file worker or a general manager, must constantly focus his attention upward. He must comply. He must please.

Organizational nature of the superior-subordinate relationship

To go back to ancient times and earlier in the history of our world, domination of one individual over another occurred because one had greater strength, cunning, and agility so that he could subjugate another. Of course, when whole tribes were vanquished in battle by other tribes, the former often became slaves to their conquerors.

When a group of people endeavored to work together to accomplish a common goal it was necessary to make the master-subordinate or leader-follower arrangements more formal and lasting. Instead of the chief or leader maintaining his position through brute force or through persuasion, groups have evolved through the centuries to the point where it is the position or office and not the person, himself, that determines who is boss and who is the follower. Formal organization structures have been established such that a subordinate respects the office of president, for example, and obeys the orders of whomever happens to occupy that post. This institutionalized arrangement does not deny, of course, that some leaders by their nature and methods are able to win greater loyalty and effort from their followers than others.

Modern leadership theory advocates positive motivation—the holding out of the prospect of rewards to the subordinates so that they will want to conform to the wishes of the leader. The leader seeks to provide satisfaction for the wants and needs of his people while at the same time they are working effectively for the goals of the enterprise. Nevertheless, if the positive approach does not succeed, rule through compulsion and fear is always lurking in the background. Threat of unpleasant work assignments, loss of status, denial of a wage increase, and loss of job are possible courses of action which the superior can take to insure compliance with his orders.

The superior-subordinate relationship

The superior, whether he be a foreman, superintendent, or general manager, delegates duties and authority to his subordinates and in turn holds them accountable for the proper carrying out of the assigned work. The performance of his work unit is determined to a great extent by the caliber of his employees and by the work which they do. Their success is his success and their failure is likewise his.

He may wish he had better men. He may re-train and try to mold their attitudes and behavior. He may cajole, encourage, or threaten. For a supervisor knows that his superiors are continually evaluating his effectiveness in guiding his work unit toward the accomplishment of its goals. He feels that he must present as favorable a picture as possible to his boss in order to maintain his own position.

The relationship between a leader and an employee is an adaptive one. If the relationship is to be enduring and successful each must adjust and modify his behavior to fit the attitudes, demands, and reactions of the other. Because of individual differences among subordinates they may react in a variety of ways to a particular act or pronouncement. One's life history and system of values will influence the way in which he interprets and responds to the behavior of his boss.

How often have we noticed that some individuals who are rising up the executive ladder, while they have a personality of their own and a certain set of beliefs and ideals, seem to take on or adopt as their own many of the values and attitudes of the executive to whom they report presently. And when these same men are in time transferred to other units such that they are now subordinate to different executives possessing somewhat different viewpoints and personalities, we find that they gradually express these new sentiments as their own. These men, if questioned, would not admit to changing their colors to suit their environment. But whether the change is achieved consciously or unconsciously the position in which a subordinate finds himself practically demands a measure of this behavior.

When a new superior takes over

The problems of adjustment and change are highlighted when a new supervisor or manager takes over. The incumbent employees have already made the necessary adjustments in their attitudes, expectations, and behavior in order to get along successfully with the previous boss. They must go through the same process again for the new man. The problems are especially great if the new superior has come from another company or organization. His methods of operation, values, and expectations will in all likelihood be different.

He expects personal loyalty and acquiescence to his orders. If the supervisor is authoritarian he expects "yes" men; if a participative-type leader he expects intelligent contributions and suggestions. So, very often we see that subordinates leave a company, are transferred or discharged because of disagreements and clashes of personality with the new manager. This phenomenon is particularly prevalent at the middle and upper levels of management where people are particularly likely to be "all wrapped up" in their jobs and take them very seriously. There may be fundamental clashes over policy and operating procedures especially if past practice has been solidified and stable over the years.

Some illustrations

Let us highlight our discussion of the problems of subordination by looking at some specific examples.

In the installation and maintenance department of one public utility one foreman made such a profound impression upon two of the ten men who worked for him over a period of several years that they actually changed their religious beliefs and denominational affiliation to conform to his. In this same company in another work unit, a tee-totaling foreman persuaded all of his subordinates to give up drinking and smoking. They did this and apparently the change was permanent. However, later when this foreman was transferred to another unit he was replaced by one who definitely did not share his views. The employees noted this change in leadership climate and many reverted to their former ways.

Take the case of a group of professional employees in a particular research organization. The director of this unit had been a popular, highly respected, permissive type of leader who had managed to develop a high level of esprit de corps and of motivation in the group. His work unit was effectively accomplishing its goals. This man was especially gifted in the art of developing enthusiasm among his men. Because of his accomplishments this individual was promoted to a position of greater responsibility in another department of the company. His successor has proved to be a martinet. He will not allow any participation by his subordinates in decision making. He refuses to accept suggestions. He disciplines subordinates in front of the group. Work loads and dead-lines are unreasonable. Down-ward communications are often conflicting and seldom put in writing. Upward communication is discouraged. The group as a whole is completely demoralized and frustrated. Yet this autocrat operates within the letter of the organizational personnel policies while con-stantly violating the spirit. To relieve their frustration and to protect themselves the men are all searching for a means of escape. All are actively seeking other positions either within the company or with other firms. They feel that appeal to higher authority within the company (over their immediate superior's head) would lead to further repressive measures from their boss.

If there are disagreements over practices, procedures, methods, and treatment the subordinate can discuss these with his boss to seek an adjustment. He may even appeal over the head of his superior to the next higher level of management. But the subordinate knows that regardless of the answer obtained, he must still live with his boss in their day-to-day relationships.

Need for the establishment of a judicial system

To solve this dilemma work organizations, which include business and industrial establishments, must take steps to insure that the judicial function be adequately provided for. At the present time it is almost universally a standard practice for the supervisors, managers and executives to perform both the executive and judicial functions. Top management executives may perform the legislative function as well. There is no separation of powers as in civil government. The manager is not only the initiator of action but he is also the judge, jury, and prosecutor. This anomaly is particularly striking in employee discipline and grievance cases.

In democratically oriented governments the judicial, executive, and legislative divisions are elected by the governed (the people). The judiciary is not subservient to nor a part of the executive branch. Of course work organizations are not democratic governments; they are to a great extent authoritarian. Therefore, it would be impractical to attempt to superimpose the governmental system upon work estab-lishments. But this fact does not obviate the conclusion that they should make better provision for the judicial function than they now do. Any methods selected would have to be designed to fit the par-ticular goals and structure of the organization.

Some possible solutions

There are a number of organizational arrangements which might be adopted to meet this need for a judicial system. Because of differences in objectives, structure, and the environment in which they operate it is unlikely that any one solution will be suitable to all organizations. Some experimentation is desirable.

Unionization of employees almost always brings about the installation of a formal grievance procedure having arbitration by an independent third party (the judicial function) as a final step of appeal. This approach to the problem works well especially where the parties (both union and employer) have honestly endeavored to make it succeed and where they have acquired experience with the procedure. Essentially, under this system, the union represents the employee, presents the grievance to management, and if a satisfactory solution is not reached, the union appeals the case to successively higher levels of management. An independent arbitrator serving in the role of a judge may receive the grievance on appeal and render a decision with which both parties generally agree to abide.

Management, itself, then must take the initiative in establishing a formalized appeal and judicial procedure to provide a means of airing disagreements and complaints, evaluating them, testing them against established personnel policies and practices, and implementing the decisions. Such a procedure or organizational arrangement would be suitable for settling many problems in addition to those occasioned by the superior-subordinate relationship. However, it would seem that these would predominate. Indeed, the typical procedure in industry provides that an employee must first discuss his problems related to the work environment with his boss before going elsewhere.

A grievance procedure for non-union employees (supervisors and managers are employees too and could also use the procedure) may use an impartial outside arbitrator or panel of arbitrators as the final step. Usually where companies have set up a grievance procedure for non-union employees no provision is made for arbitration. The chief executive officer constitutes the court of final appeal. Employers often feel that it would be unwise to have their authority over people and operations within the organization diluted by some outside agency. From the subordinate's viewpoint it would certainly be advantageous to gain the benefit of an outside impartial judicial agency after exhausting the steps within the organization.

Another approach that could be used would be to set up a joint committee composed of management and employee representatives, perhaps with rotating membership, that would serve as a final appeal step within the establishment. This committee could be endowed with the authority to hear testimony, conduct investigations, and render binding decisions which would presumably be enforced by operating or line management. If this committee or board of review were to be established for the purpose of adjusting and deciding cases involving supervisors and managers themselves it could simply be composed of a group of executives, perhaps from different levels in the structure.

Labor unions, as organizations, also have an authority structure, problems of internal union discipline, and grievances by members in relation to actions of their own leaders. Recognizing the need for providing members with an opportunity for judicial review the Labor-Management Reporting and Disclosure Act of 1959 contains a "Bill of Rights" for individual union members.

Two and one-half years before passage of this law the United Automobile Workers Union, as a specific example, established a public review board composed of independent and eminent citizens to which members could appeal their grievances against the union. The constitution of the union was amended at that time to set up this appeal

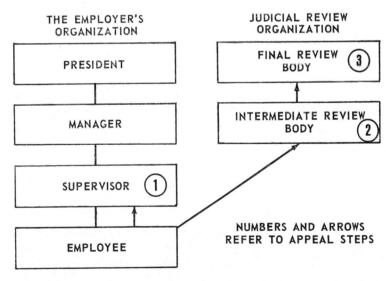

A schematic chart showing a procedure for judicial review of problems and disputes arising during the course of work relationships. The structure must be adapted to meet needs of particular organizations. There should, however, always be some measure of independence between employer and judicial review organizations.

board and to give it the authority and duty to make final and binding decisions in all cases placed before it by aggrieved members or subordinate bodies of the U.A.W.[1]

Many organizations (probably most of them) have not become sufficiently aware of the problem to feel that any new organizational arrangement is necessary. Many executives believe that by creating management training programs which give predominant emphasis to the human relations of administration they can so improve the understanding and leadership performance of their subordinate managers, department heads, and supervisors that most of these problems of superior-subordinate will be solved or essentially alleviated. Indeed, training courses can certainly improve mutual understanding and the caliber of leadership. But they cannot be expected to solve what is, to a large extent, an organizational problem created by the essentially authoritarian nature of most work groups.

Summary

All organizations devoted to the accomplishment of work whether they be private business, educational, military, or governmental must of necessity have a well-defined authority structure in order to survive and in order to accomplish their goals. They must contain the leader and the led and in large establishments they contain several levels of leaders. The leader or superior must be in a position to allocate rewards and penalties to his subordinates in order to insure a unified, cooperative effort directed toward the accomplishment of a goal. A certain amount of power and force seems to be essential for the system to function effectively. This coercion, of course, must be controlled and carefully channeled.

The power of the superior over the lives of his subordinates causes them to continually seek his approval and support. Their survival, security, and progress are determined primarily by the strength and nature of this relationship. Excessive upward orientation toward the boss is a prevalent phenomenon. The subordinate becomes dependent rather than independent. He must conform to the expectations of his boss. In a great many situations the relationships work out entirely satisfactorily, but if perchance things go sour, if there is a divergence

---

[1] Booklet published by the United Automobile Workers Union entitled *A More Perfect Union . . . The U.A.W. Public Review Board—Why, What, How.*

of attitudes, values, and methods, if they do not see eye-to-eye, the subordinate is often placed in a dilemma. His alternatives usually are few in number and many of them involve great personal accommodation (often sacrifice) and some involve considerable risk.

It is specifically proposed that top management must become fully cognizant of the problem and all its ramifications and that it make the necessary organizational and procedural modifications to correct this problem. Provision for an effective and workable judicial system must be made. The potential benefits in terms of reduced anxiety and frustration on the part of employees are great. They can become more highly motivated to work toward the goals of the organization. The way can then be opened for a more complete utilization of the creative and productive energies of employees.

Questions

1. How do you account for the fact that employees often seek to adopt new modes of personal behavior to conform to the foreman's desires? Is this type of influence healthy? Discuss.
2. The author suggests a grievance procedure for nonunion employees. Is such a procedure likely to serve its intended purpose? Why?
3. There have been hundreds of journal articles concerning effective leadership skills of managers and supervisors. Little is written, however, on what employees can do to make themselves more effective as subordinates. Would articles written for employees be of any value? Explain.
4. What are the advantages and disadvantages of having a panel of arbitrators composed of individuals selected from groups outside the organization to review employee grievances?
5. What types of grievances might union members have against the union that could be handled by an appeal board?

21. MANAGERIAL AUTHORITY IN THE EMPLOYMENT RELATIONSHIP *[1]

Stanley Young

A certain degree of controversy surrounds the issue of managerial authority vis-à-vis the employee.[2] Many of the differences concerning the authority issue seem to emanate from a misunderstanding of the nature of the legal and economic relationship between the manager and non-manager. Although the nature of this relationship is determined by other factors such as psychological, technological, ethical and sociological ones, the scope of this study will be restricted to reviewing briefly the legal and economic aspects of the employment relationship insofar as they relate to the authority issue. It is hoped that such an analysis will help to resolve some of the incongruities which apparently exist.

As a working hypothesis, it is here suggested that there exists no authority relationship between manager and employee, only a relationship of exchange between a buyer and a seller.[3] And unless the definition of authority is expanded to include all exchange relationships, the issue of managerial authority is extraneous in a study of the employment relationship.

Legal Characteristics

What are the assumed legal origins of managerial authority and of what validity are they? One assumption found in the formal or classical authority model of the organization has the following elements.[4] Insofar as the employee is concerned, a superior-subordinate

---

* From the *Journal of the Academy of Management*, Vol. 5, No. 3 (December, 1962), pp. 207-213. Reprinted with permission.

[1] The author is indebted to Henry Manne, LL.D., Associate Professor of Law, George Washington University, Washington, D.C., for his review of the legal aspects of this study.

[2] For a brief discussion of the various approaches to managerial authority, see Robert Guest, *Organizational Change* (Homewood, Ill.: The Dorsey Press, Inc., 1962), pp. 118-133; M. J. Mandeville, "Organizational Authority," *Journal of the Academy of Management*, August, 1960, pp. 107-111.

[3] This study is limited to the employer-employee relationship. The non-employment relationship, as for example found in the family or the military, falls outside the scope of this analysis.

[4] Discussions of the formal authority of management generally include these described characteristics. *See*: Robert Tannenbaum, Irving R. Weschler, and

relationship exists in which authority is defined as the legal right of the superior (the manager) to command the employee (the subordinate) to behave in a certain manner within the organization. Presumably, the employee has a legal obligation to obey.

It is further assumed that the origin of this authority derives from the property rights of ownership which have been delegated to the manager. Authority is viewed as a downward flow through a chain of command from the stockholders, Board of Directors, to the first line of supervision. This is the familiar pyramidal or hierarchical organization.

The shortcoming of this model is that it assumes a non-existent legal right. There is no property right in which the employee is legally obligated to obey the instructions of the owner. The confusion arises over the definition of property. Property relates to the assets of the firm: materials, equipment, buildings and good will; but it does not include employees. Property rights are concerned with the freedom to use and exchange such assets.[5]

Some managers erroneously assume that they have the same right to determine how the services of employees will be used as they do the machines or materials of the firm. Clearly the stockholders cannot delegate a right to managers which they as stockholders do not have.

Management's right to command frequently is asserted to originate in the employment contract. It is postulated that when the employee enters into an employment agreement, in exchange for a wage or salary he agrees to accept the authority of the firm. For example, Herbert Simon notes that the entrepreneur gains the right to dispose of the employee's time by entering into an employment contract with him.[6] Koontz and O'Donnell allege that the employment contract provides that the employer will give orders and the employee will obey them.[7]

According to this point of view, the purchase of labor is no different than the purchase of equipment or material. Once a firm pays the vendor for material, the determination of how that material will be

Fred Massarik, *Leadership and Organization* (New York: McGraw-Hill, 1961), pp. 256-276; George Terry, *Principles of Management* (Homewood, Ill.: Richard Irwin, 1956), pp. 268-270; Dalton E. McFarland, *Management Principles and Practices* (New York: Macmillan Co., 1958), pp. 190-207; Harold Koontz and Cyril O'Donnell, *Principles of Management* (New York: McGraw-Hill, 1955), pp. 48-52 and pp. 399-402.

[5] For a discussion concerning the nature of property rights, *see*: John Commons, *Legal Foundations of Capitalism* (New York: Macmillan Co., 1939).

[6] Herbert Simon, *Administrative Behavior* (2d Edition; New York: Macmillan Co., 1957), p. 7.

[7] Koontz and O'Donnell, *op. cit.*, p. 402.

used passes from the vendor to the buyer. In similar fashion, it is thought that once the employee agrees to accept a wage, the firm gains the right to determine how his time will be utilized. The assumption that the employment contract is analogous to the exchange of physical goods is not correct.

What are the legal characteristics of the employment agreement? The manager is delegated the legal right or authority to act as a buyer for the firm and use the organization's assets to purchase personal services from the employee, or the seller. The willingness of the employee to render service would in turn be the property which he is exchanging for a consideration from the firm. The employee has the same property rights as respects his person, as the employer does, his assets. Thus an exchange or buyer-seller relationship exists that is comparable to any commercial one.

The employment contract has certain unique characteristics. In the customary verbal, terminal, individual employment contract one finds that initially the parties have only agreed to continue their relationship as long as it remains mutually beneficial.

A manager's orders to an employee can be legally viewed as a buyer's proposal to change the obligations of the seller. The employee has a legal right to reject, accept or make a counter-offer to such demands. He is under no legal obligation to accept the instructions of a manager as is generally assumed. Neither is obligated to accept the proposals of the other; each party must perform only those conditions to which it has mutually agreed.[8] Because the parties do not usually bind themselves to a specific future performance, either one can suggest changes in any aspect of the relationship at will.[9]

The parties are free to negotiate at any time and in any manner. They can agree to any terms that are mutually acceptable so long as the contract is legally bona fide; that is, the contract must not be fraudulent, mutual consideration should exist, and no law should be violated. The employee can thus propose terms as respects how the property of the firm will be utilized in the same way the manager can suggest how the property of the employee will be used.

---

[8] As respects what constitute an agreement, *see* Richard Eells and Clarence Walton, *Conceptual Foundations of Business* (Homewood, Ill.: Richard Irwin, 1961), p. 201.

[9] In the terminal agreement, the employer cannot sue for damages concerning violation of contract, because the employee did commit himself to perform services over a given period in the future. When a (non) terminal agreement exists, although the employer cannot legally enforce personal performance, he may be able to collect financial damages for lack of performance.

Either party can terminate the contract at will, without cause. The employer can discharge the employee; or the employee can quit. Either party can demand the acceptance of certain proposals as a condition for a continued contractual relationship.

John Commons has said, "The contract at the beginning of his (the employee) employment is therefore not a contract. It is a usage, a custom, a habit—it is an understanding between the two, that at each point in the continuous flow of impliedly renewing the contract, the terms of renewal shall conform to what was understood, but without any duty on either side to renew or conform. The laborer is thus continuously on the labor market—even while he is working at his job he is both producing and bargaining and the two are inseparable." [10]

Economic Characteristics

Unfortunately much confusion regarding managerial authority derives from the inability to distinguish the difference between legal rights and economic power.[11] At times it is postulated that the origin of managerial authority derives from the employee's fear of job loss; and rather than face this possibility, the employee accepts the buyer's proposals.

However, this concept of authority is based on the buyer's bargaining capability, rather than his legal rights. If the buyer's bargaining power were of such a nature that the employee followed all instructions, then operationally, it would appear to make little difference whether or not the manager had the right or power to command, because the end result essentially would be the same. But if the concept of managerial authority is restricted to the use of economic sanctions, then the extent to which the employee will conform to managerial instructions would depend upon the relative bargaining power of each party. One cannot assume *a priori* that acceptance of managerial demands is always preferable to the loss of job; or that the bargaining power of the buyer will under all conditions be superior to that of the seller; or that the buyer's bargaining power will be sufficient to gain acceptance of all his orders. There may be many proposals which the seller will not accept.

---

[10] Commons, *op. cit.*, p. 286.

[11] Cyril O'Donnell would seem to confuse legal and economic sanctions in his article, "The Source of Managerial Authority," *Political Science Quarterly*, Vol. 67, No. 4 (December, 1952), pp. 573-588.

The employee can also use economic sanctions in the form of a threat to quit unless his demands are met. At times the bargaining power of the employee will be greater than that of the manager, as in the case of the highly gifted scientist or the productive salesman.

In both instances the parties can threaten not to consummate the contract in order to achieve more favorable terms of exchange. The employment agreement is not unique in this regard, since this is the usual action in any buyer-seller relationship.

The effectiveness of economic coercion depends in large measure on the characteristics of the labor market. As respects what the employer will pay, or what the employee will do, it is generally assumed that given the imperfections of the market place, such conditions will be determined by the familiar supply and demand for labor.[12]

Although it is accepted that the market determines what the employer has to pay for employee services, it is not equally recognized that the market also determines how much or what type of service the manager will receive from his labor expenditure. Most managers know that they must pay the going rate, but they are not equally aware of the fact that they will receive in turn, a "going performance." [13]

If the demand for a particular occupation is increasing and the supply is decreasing presumably the manager will not only have to pay a higher rate, but he may also receive less service from the seller. The employee may make such demands as shorter hours, longer coffee breaks and greater personal discretion on the job. Hence, the manager's economic power, in terms of the extent of cooperation he can purchase, is decreasing. However, if extensive unemployment should exist, then the manager's economic power would increase.

Thus the effectiveness of economic power depends on the availability to each party of alternative economic opportunities. Managerial authority, viewed as though it were resting on an economic base, would be conditioned by the following factors. First, the manager and the employee would each have the authority to exercise this kind of power. Second, it is not unique to the employment exchange but obtains in all exchange relationships. Third, the degree of bargaining power is limited, dynamic and relative to that of the other party; and

---

[12] For a recent analysis of the extent to which market forces determine the terms of employment, *see:* Allen Carter, *Theory of Wages and Employment* (Homewood, Ill.: Richard Irwin, 1959).

[13] Simon Rottenberg, "On Choice in Labor Markets," *Labor and Trade Unionism,* ed. Walter Galenson and Seymour Lipset (New York: John Wiley, 1960), pp. 40-52.

finally, economic power is circumscribed by market or competitive factors.

Consequently, if by managerial authority it is meant the right to command, then the conclusion must be that no such right exists and that economic ability is affected by those factors noted herein.

Implications of the Analysis

What inferences can be deduced from the foregoing analysis? In reference to the nature of the employment relationship, the question of managerial authority is extraneous to its analysis. An exchange relationship rather than an authority one exists and both relationships can be distinguished in terms of their institutional properties.

Authority versus the exchange relationship

An authority relationship is usually thought to originate in a higher legal framework (legislation or the common law) which establishes superior-subordinate relationships in which specific legal rights and obligations are fixed and upheld via legal sanctions.

The military may be characterized as having established authority relationships. Legislation (the Articles of War) has stipulated the relationship between officer and soldier; the officer holds the right to command and the soldier has the legal obligation to obey. Violation of orders can lead to the use of legal sanctions such as prison or in the case of dire circumstances, the loss of life. Even though there is, perhaps, a limit to the effectiveness of such legal sanctions, nevertheless the military establishment can legally compel a man to perform services against his will; but in the economic organization, this would be unlawful.

On the other hand, in exchange relationships (which are the existent ones), there are no superior-subordinate relationships, instead there are legal co-equals who voluntarily enter into a contractual relationship which specifies their respective rights and obligations. The parties themselves determine these rights and obligations rather than some external authority. Neither assumes any obligations which are not freely agreed to, nor can one specify an obligation which the other does not accept. The sanctions are economic and contractual terms are dynamic and ever changing.

The characteristics of an authority and exchange relationship are for the most part clear and distinguishable. If all the determinates in an exchange relationship are included in the definition of authority, both the economic and the non-economic ones, then as Professor Mandeville [14] suggests, the term authority becomes fairly meaningless. In addition, the term is contrary to accepted usage and provides little in the way of analytical guides.

In buyer-seller relationships (other than employer-employee ones) such as found in the purchase of goods, one does not usually think in terms of an authority relationship. The fact that an individual as a buyer purchases an automobile in no way confers upon him the authority to direct the activities of automobile companies or sellers. Moreover, if one uses the term authority to include the use of economic coercion, then one would have to regard all buyer-seller relationships as authority relationships.

On the other hand, if one initially assumes that the manager-employee relationship is one of exchange rather than one of authority, then the question of managerial authority becomes moot. Although the construction of a theory of organizational negotiations falls outside the scope of this analysis, it is suggested that the exchange construct rather than the authority one provides a more realistic and effective model with which to analyze the determinants of the manager-employee relationship.

For example, insofar as the legal aspects are concerned, the terms of exchange tend to remain relatively stable. These terms represent the parties' mutual obligations and might be viewed as being quasi-legal in nature, or constituting the law of organization.

The conflict between the "classical" and the "human relations" approach can be resolved in terms of the rights and power of the parties' buyer and seller roles. The so-called "zone of acceptance" in the human relations approach can be interpreted as a range of terms of employment that sellers find acceptable. The dynamic quality of such a zone would reflect changing bargaining factors. Leadership characteristics can be subsumed in terms of either personality variables or negotiating style of either the buyer or seller. Agreement concerning terms of exchange would represent integration of the parties' objectives. The interaction process is the search for such agreement.

---

[14] M. J. Mandeville, "The Nature of Authority," Comment and Reply by Mandeville to an article by Edward C. Weber in *Journal of the Academy of Management*, April, 1961, pp. 62-66.

Role conception

Of what practical significance is it to draw a distinction between an authority relationship and one of exchange? Many managers assume that they do as a matter of fact have authority over the employee. Apart from holding a serious misconception as respects the nature of his role in the relationship, this assumption can prevent him from reaching an effective exchange.

The character of the relationship between the manager and employee is determined largely by legal and economic factors, which neither the manager nor the employee can determine. If the manager desires greater cooperation from the employee, he must negotiate for it. Both our legal and economic systems have already predetermined that this is the manner in which cooperation between the two parties will be established.

The manager has assumed the traditionally entrepreneurial economic functions of both buying and selling. The manager can decide how he will negotiate, but not whether or not he will. In his daily interaction with the employee, he attempts to achieve greater employee cooperation. And whether or not he realizes it implicitly or explicitly, he is continually in a process of negotiating an ever-changing employment contract.

To assume that an authority relationship prevails tends to oversimplify the problem of gaining employee cooperation. It supposes that there is an existing state of cooperation or obedience on the part of subordinates and that the primary task of the superior is to determine the subordinates' functions. It further implies that there is no necessity to gain the cooperation of subordinates. The manager becomes analogous to the army officer who commands and leads his men.

If the manager clearly recognizes and accepts his role as a buyer of labor, he knows that a mutual working together of the buyer and seller must be sought constantly and negotiated. The manager ever faces the difficult task not only of determining what he wants from the employee, but also of negotiating with the seller in order to obtain his acceptance of the buyer's proposals. Gaining cooperation via negotiations requires considerable skill and is a complex process. It is a process that requires flexibility and compromise. The principle of quid pro quo is its essence and the skills needed are those of a pioneer trader.

The manager is legally free to adopt any negotiating style he desires; participating or non-participating, democratic or autocratic, rigid or flexible. Given the many factors, economic and non-economic, that affect the bargaining outcome, it is difficult to assess how significant the negotiating style of the buyer is in any given situation, because it would represent only one of the variables.

Another source of confusion concerning the authority issue is that managers frequently choose an authoritarian negotiating strategy. Here again there would be little reason to confuse bargaining behavior with the institutional bases of power and authority.

The manager's assumption that he has some form of authority over the employee not only makes the negotiating process difficult, but it may well reduce his effectiveness as a purchaser of labor services. If the objective of the manager is to maximize the return on labor dollar expenditures, then the use of a command strategy is less effective than if alternative strategies were considered by the manager.

Questions

1. Why do managers persist in believing that they have authority over employees as they do over equipment and materials?
2. In what way does the relationship between superior and subordinate in business institutions differ from that in military establishments?
3. What effect has the growth of labor unions had on the traditional concept of managerial authority?
4. Can you see any relationship between the human relations movement and the author's thesis?

22. HOW TO CHOOSE A LEADERSHIP PATTERN *

Robert Tannenbaum and Warren H. Schmidt

- "I put most problems into my group's hands and leave it to them to carry the ball from there. I serve merely as a catalyst, mirroring back the people's thoughts and feelings so that they can better understand them."
- "It's foolish to make decisions oneself on matters that affect people. I always talk things over with my subordinates, but I make it clear to them that I'm the one who has to have the final say."
- "Once I have decided on a course of action, I do my best to sell my ideas to my employees."
- "I'm being paid to lead. If I let a lot of other people make the decisions I should be making, then I'm not worth my salt."
- "I believe in getting things done. I can't waste time calling meetings. Someone has to call the shots around here, and I think it should be me."

Each of these statements represents a point of view about "good leadership." Considerable experience, factual data, and theoretical principles could be cited to support each statement, even though they seem to be inconsistent when placed together. Such contradictions point up the dilemma in which the modern manager frequently finds himself.

New Problem

The problem of how the modern manager can be "democratic" in his relations with subordinates and at the same time maintain the necessary authority and control in the organization for which he is responsible has come into focus increasingly in recent years.

Earlier in the century this problem was not so acutely felt. The successful executive was generally pictured as possessing intelligence, imagination, initiative, the capacity to make rapid (and generally wise) decisions, and the ability to inspire subordinates. People tended to think of the world as being divided into "leaders" and "followers."

* From *Harvard Business Review*, Vol. 36, No. 2 (March-April, 1958), pp. 95-101. Reprinted with permission.

New focus

Gradually, however, from the social sciences emerged the concept of "group dynamics" with its focus on *members* of the group rather than solely on the leader. Research efforts of social scientists underscored the importance of employee involvement and participation in decision making. Evidence began to challenge the efficiency of highly directive leadership, and increasing attention was paid to problems of motivation and human relations.

Through training laboratories in group development that sprang up across the country, many of the newer notions of leadership began to exert an impact. These training laboratories were carefully designed to give people a first-hand experience in full participation and decision making. The designated "leaders" deliberately attempted to reduce their own power and to make group members as responsible as possible for setting their own goals and methods within the laboratory experience.

It was perhaps inevitable that some of the people who attended the training laboratories regarded this kind of leadership as being truly "democratic" and went home with the determination to build fully participative decision making into their own organizations. Whenever their bosses made a decision without convening a staff meeting, they tended to perceive this as authoritarian behavior. The true symbol of democratic leadership to some was the meeting—and the less directed from the top, the more democratic it was.

Some of the more enthusiastic alumni of these training laboratories began to get the habit of categorizing leader behavior as "democratic" *or* "authoritarian." The boss who made too many decisions himself was thought of as an authoritarian, and his directive behavior was often attributed solely to his personality.

New need

The net result of the research findings and of the human relations training based upon them has been to call into question the stereotype of an effective leader. Consequently, the modern manager often finds himself in an uncomfortable state of mind.

Often he is not quite sure how to behave; there are times when he is torn between exerting "strong" leadership and "permissive" leadership. Sometimes new knowledge pushes him in one direction ("I should really get the group to help make this decision"), but at the same time his experience pushes him in another direction ("I really understand the problem better than the group and therefore I should make the decision"). He is not sure when a group decision is really appropriate or when holding a staff meeting serves merely as a device for avoiding his own decision-making responsibility.

The purpose of our article is to suggest a framework which managers may find useful in grappling with this dilemma. First we shall look at the different patterns of leadership behavior that the manager can choose from in relating himself to his subordinates. Then we shall turn to some of the questions suggested by this range of patterns. For instance, how important is it for a manager's subordinates to know what type of leadership he is using in a situation? What factors should he consider in deciding on a leadership pattern? What difference do his long-run objectives make as compared to his immediate objectives?

Range of Behavior

EXHIBIT I presents the continuum or range of possible leadership behavior available to a manager. Each type of action is related to the degree of authority used by the boss and to the amount of freedom available to his subordinates in reaching decisions. The actions seen on the extreme left characterize the manager who maintains a high degree of control while those seen on the extreme right characterize the manager who releases a high degree of control. Neither extreme is absolute; authority and freedom are never without their limitations.

EXHIBIT I. CONTINUUM OF LEADERSHIP BEHAVIOR

Boss-centered leadership						Subordinate-centered leadership
Use of authority by the manager				Area of freedom for subordinates		
↑ Manager makes decision and announces it.	↑ Manager "sells" decision.	↑ Manager presents ideas and invites questions.	↑ Manager presents tentative decision subject to change.	↑ Manager presents problem, gets suggestions, makes decision.	↑ Manager defines limits; asks group to make decision.	↑ Manager permits subordinates to function within limits defined by superior.

Now let us look more closely at each of the behavior points occurring along this continuum:

The manager makes the decision and announces it.

In this case the boss identifies a problem, considers alternative solutions, chooses one of them, and then reports this decision to his subordinates for implementation. He may or may not give consideration to what he believes his subordinates will think or feel about his decision; in any case, he provides no opportunity for them to participate directly in the decision-making process. Coercion may or may not be used or implied.

The manager "sells" his decision.

Here the manager, as before, takes responsibility for identifying the problem and arriving at a decision. However, rather than simply announcing it, he takes the additional step of persuading his subordinates to accept it. In doing so, he recognizes the possibility of some resistance among those who will be faced with the decision, and seeks to reduce this resistance by indicating, for example, what the employees have to gain from his decision.

The manager presents his ideas, invites questions.

Here the boss who has arrived at a decision and who seeks acceptance of his ideas provides an opportunity for his subordinates to get a fuller explanation of his thinking and his intentions. After presenting the ideas, he invites questions so that his associates can better understand what he is trying to accomplish. This "give and take" also enables the manager and the subordinates to explore more fully the implications of his decision.

The manager presents a tentative decision subject to change.

This kind of behavior permits the subordinates to exert some influence on the decision. The initiative for identifying and diagnosing the problem remains with the boss. Before meeting with his staff, he has thought the problem through and arrived at a decision—but only a tentative one. Before finalizing it, he presents his proposed solution for the reaction of those who will be affected by it. He says in effect, "I'd like to hear what you have to say about this plan that I have developed. I'll appreciate your frank reactions, but will reserve for myself the final decision."

The manager presents the problem, gets suggestions, and then makes his decision.

Up to this point the boss has come before the group with a solution of his own. Not so in this case. The subordinates now get the first chance to suggest solutions. The manager's initial role involves identifying the problem. He might, for example, say something of this sort: "We are faced with a number of complaints from newspapers and the general public on our service policy. What is wrong here? What ideas do you have for coming to grips with this problem?"

The function of the group becomes one of increasing the manager's repertory of possible solutions to the problem. The purpose is to capitalize on the knowledge and experience of those who are on the "firing line." From the expanded list of alternatives developed by the manager and his subordinates, the manager then selects the solution that he regards as most promising.[1]

---

[1] For a fuller explanation of this approach, *see* Leo Moore, "Too Much Management, Too Little Change," HBR (January-February, 1956), p. 41.

The manager defines the limits and requests the group to make a decision.

At this point the manager passes to the group (possibly including himself as a member) the right to make decisions. Before doing so, however, he defines the problem to be solved and the boundaries within which the decision must be made.

An example might be the handling of a parking problem at a plant. The boss decides that this is something that should be worked on by the people involved, so he calls them together and points up the existence of the problem. Then he tells them:

> "There is the open field just north of the main plant which has been designated for additional employee parking. We can build underground or surface multilevel facilities as long as the cost does not exceed $100,000. Within these limits we are free to work out whatever solution makes sense to us. After we decide on a specific plan, the company will spend the available money in whatever way we indicate."

The manager permits the group to make decisions within prescribed limits.

This represents an extreme degree of group freedom only occasionally encountered in formal organizations, as, for example, in many research groups. Here the team of managers or engineers undertakes the identification and diagnosis of the problem, develops alternative procedures for solving it, and decides on one or more of these alternative solutions. The only limits directly imposed on the group by the organization are those specified by the superior of the team's boss. If the boss participates in the decision-making process, he attempts to do so with no more authority than any other member of the group. He commits himself in advance to assist in implementing whatever decision the group makes.

Key Questions

As the continuum in Exhibit I demonstrates, there are a number of alternative ways in which a manager can relate himself to the group or individuals he is supervising. At the extreme left of the range, the emphasis is on the manager—on what *he* is interested in, how *he* sees things, how *he* feels about them. As we move toward the subordinate-centered end of the continuum, however, the focus is increasingly on the subordinates—on what *they* are interested in, how *they* look at things, how *they* feel about them.

When business leadership is regarded in this way, a number of questions arise. Let us take four of especial importance:

Can a boss ever relinquish his responsibility by delegating it to someone else?

Our view is that the manager must expect to be held responsible by his superior for the quality of the decisions made, even though operationally these decisions may have been made on a group basis. He should, therefore, be ready to accept whatever risk is involved whenever he delegates decision-making power to his subordinates. Delegation is not a way of "passing the buck." Also, it should be emphasized that the amount of freedom the boss gives to his subordinates cannot be greater than the freedom which he himself has been given by his own superior.

Should the manager participate with his subordinates once he has delegated responsibility to them?

The manager should carefully think over this question and decide on his role prior to involving the subordinate group. He should ask if his presence will inhibit or facilitate the problem-solving process. There may be some instances when he should leave the group to let it solve the problem for itself. Typically, however, the boss has useful ideas to contribute, and should function as an additional member of the group. In the latter instance, it is important that he indicate clearly to the group that he sees himself in a *member* role rather than in an authority role.

How important is it for the group to recognize what kind of leadership behavior the boss is using?

It makes a great deal of difference. Many relationship problems between boss and subordinate occur because the boss fails to make clear how he plans to use his authority. If, for example, he actually intends to make a certain decision himself, but the subordinate group gets the impression that he has delegated this authority, considerable confusion and resentment are likely to follow. Problems may also occur when the boss uses a "democratic" facade to conceal the fact that he has already made a decision which he hopes the group will accept as its own. The attempt to "make them think it was their idea in the first place" is a risky one. We believe that it is highly important for the manager to be honest and clear in describing what authority he is keeping and what role he is asking his subordinates to assume in solving a particular problem.

Can you tell how "democratic" a manager is by the number of decisions his subordinates make?

The sheer *number* of decisions is not an accurate index of the amount of freedom that a subordinate group enjoys. More important is the *significance* of the decisions which the boss entrusts to his subordinates. Obviously a decision on how to arrange desks is of an entirely different order from a decision involving the introduction of new electronic data-processing equipment. Even though the widest possible limits are given in dealing with the first issue, the group will sense no particular degree of responsibility. For a boss to permit the group to decide equipment policy, even within rather narrow limits, would reflect a greater degree of confidence in them on his part.

Deciding How to Lead

Now let us turn from the types of leadership that are possible in a company situation to the question of what types are *practical* and *desirable*. What factors or forces should a manager consider in deciding how to manage? Three are of particular importance:

- Forces in the manager.
- Forces in the subordinates.
- Forces in the situation.

We should like briefly to describe these elements and indicate how they might influence a manager's action in a decision-making situation.[2] The strength of each of them will, of course, vary from instance to instance, but the manager who is sensitive to them can better assess the problems which face him and determine which mode of leadership behavior is most appropriate for him.

Forces in the manager

The manager's behavior in any given instance will be influenced greatly by the many forces operating within his own personality. He will, of course, perceive his leadership problems in a unique way on the basis of his background, knowledge, and experience. Among the important internal forces affecting him will be the following:

(1) *His value system.* How strongly does he feel that individuals should have a share in making the decisions which affect them? Or, how convinced is he that the official who is paid to assume responsibility should personally carry the burden of decision making? The strength of his convictions on questions like these will tend to move the manager to one end or the other of the continuum shown in EXHIBIT I. His behavior will also be influenced by the relative importance that he attaches to organizational efficiency, personal growth of subordinates, and company profits.[3]

(2) *His confidence in his subordinates.* Managers differ greatly in the amount of trust they have in other people generally, and this carries over to the particular employees they supervise at a given time. In viewing his particular group of subordinates, the manager is likely to consider their knowledge and competence with respect to the problem. A central question he might ask himself is: "Who is best qualified to deal with this problem?" Often he may, justifiably or not, have more confidence in his own capabilities than in those of his subordinates.

(3) *His own leadership inclinations.* There are some managers who seem to function more comfortably and naturally as highly directive leaders. Resolving problems and issuing orders come easily to them. Other managers seem to operate more comfortably in a team role, where they are continually sharing many of their functions with their subordinates.

(4) *His feelings of security in an uncertain situation.* The manager who releases control over the decision-making process thereby reduces the predictability of the outcome. Some managers have a greater need than others for predictability and stability in their environment. This "tolerance for ambiguity" is being viewed increasingly by psychologists as a key variable in a person's manner of dealing with problems.

The manager brings these and other highly personal variables to each situation he faces. If he can see them as forces which, consciously or unconsciously, influence his behavior, he can better

---

[2] *See also* Robert Tannenbaum and Massarik, "Participation by Subordinates in the Managerial Decision-Making Process," *Canadian Journal of Economics and Political Science* (August, 1950), pp. 413-418.

[3] *See* Chris Argyris, "Top Management Dilemma: Company Needs vs. Individual Development," *Personnel* (September, 1955), pp. 123-134.

understand what makes him prefer to act in a given way. And understanding this, he can often make himself more effective.

Forces in the subordinate

Before deciding how to lead a certain group, the manager will also want to consider a number of forces affecting his subordinates' behavior. He will want to remember that each employee, like himself, is influenced by many personality variables. In addition, each subordinate has a set of expectations about how the boss should act in relation to him (the phrase "expected behavior" is one we hear more and more often these days at discussions of leadership and teaching). The better the manager understands these factors, the more accurately he can determine what kind of behavior on his part will enable his subordinates to act most effectively.

Generally speaking, the manager can permit his subordinates greater freedom if the following essential conditions exist:

- If the subordinates have relatively high needs for independence. (As we all know, people differ greatly in the amount of direction that they desire.)
- If the subordinates have a readiness to assume responsibility for decision making. (Some see additional responsibility as a tribute to their ability; others see it as "passing the buck.")
- If they have a relatively high tolerance for ambiguity. (Some employees prefer to have clear-cut directives given to them; others prefer a wider area of freedom.)
- If they are interested in the problem and feel that it is important.
- If they understand and identify with the goals of the organization.
- If they have the necessary knowledge and experience to deal with the problem.
- If they have learned to expect to share in decision making. (Persons who have come to expect strong leadership and are then suddenly confronted with the request to share more fully in decision making are often upset by this new experience. On the other hand, persons who have enjoyed a considerable amount of freedom resent the boss who begins to make all the decisions himself.)

The manager will probably tend to make fuller use of his own authority if the above conditions do *not* exist; at times there may be no realistic alternative to running a "one-man show."

The restrictive effect of many of the forces will, of course, be greatly modified by the general feeling of confidence which subordinates have in the boss. Where they have learned to respect and trust him, he is free to vary his behavior. He will feel certain that he will not be perceived as an authoritarian boss on those occasions when he makes decisions by himself. Similarly, he will not be seen as using staff meetings to avoid his decision-making responsibility. In a climate of mutual confidence and respect, people tend to feel less threatened by deviations from a normal practice, which in turn makes possible a higher degree of flexibility in the whole relationship.

Forces in the situation

In addition to the forces which exist in the manager himself and in his subordinates, certain characteristics of the general situation will also affect the manager's behavior. Among the more critical environmental pressures that surround him are those which stem from the organization, the work group, the nature of the problem, and the pressures of time. Let us look briefly at each of these:

Type of Organization. Like individuals, organizations have values and traditions which inevitably influence the behavior of the people who work in them. The manager who is a newcomer to a company quickly discovers that certain kinds of behavior are approved while others are not. He also discovers that to deviate radically from what is generally accepted is likely to create problems for him.

These values and traditions are communicated in many ways—through job descriptions, policy pronouncements, and public statements by top executives. Some organizations, for example, hold to the notion that the desirable executive is one who is dynamic, imaginative, decisive, and persuasive. Other organizations put more emphasis upon the importance of the executive's ability to work effectively with people—his human relations skills. The fact that his superiors have a defined concept of what the good executive should be will very likely push the manager toward one end or the other of the behavioral range.

In addition to the above, the amount of employee participation is influenced by such variables as the size of the working units, their geographical distribution, and the degree of inter- and intra-organizational security required to attain company goals. For example, the wide geographical dispersion of an organization may preclude a practical system of participative decision making, even though this would otherwise be desirable. Similarly, the size of the working units or the need for keeping plans confidential may make it necessary for the boss to exercise more control than would otherwise be the case. Factors like these may limit considerably the manager's ability to function flexibly on the continuum.

Group Effectiveness. Before turning decision-making responsibility over to a subordinate group, the boss should consider how effectively its members work together as a unit.

One of the relevant factors here is the experience the group has had in working together. It can generally be expected that a group which has functioned for some time will have developed habits of cooperation and thus be able to tackle a problem more effectively than a new group. It can also be expected that a group of people with similar backgrounds and interests will work more quickly and easily than people with dissimilar backgrounds, because the communication problems are likely to be less complex.

The degree of confidence that the members have in their ability to solve problems as a group is also a key consideration. Finally, such group variables as cohesiveness, permissiveness, mutual acceptance, and commonality of purpose will exert subtle but powerful influence on the group's functioning.

The Problem Itself. The nature of the problem may determine what degree of authority should be delegated by the manager to his subordinates. Obviously he will ask himself whether they have the kind of knowledge which is needed. It is possible to do them a real disservice by assigning a problem that their experience does not equip them to handle.

Since the problems faced in large or growing industries increasingly require knowledge of specialists from many different fields, it might be inferred that the more complex a problem, the more anxious a manager will be to get some assistance in solving it. However, this is not always the case. There will be times when the very complexity of the problem calls for one person to work it out. For example, if the manager has most of the background and factual data relevant to a given issue, it may be easier for him to think it through himself than to take the time to fill in his staff on all the pertinent background information.

The key question to ask, of course, is: "Have I heard the ideas of everyone who has the necessary knowledge to make a significant contribution to the solution of this problem?"

The Pressure of Time. This is perhaps the most clearly felt pressure on the manager (in spite of the fact that it may sometimes be imagined). The more that he feels the need for an immediate decision, the more difficult it is to involve other people. In organizations which are in a constant state of "crisis" and "crash programing" one is likely to find managers personally using a high degree of authority with relatively little delegation to subordinates. When the time pressure is less intense, however, it becomes much more possible to bring subordinates in on the decision-making process.

These, then, are the principal forces that impinge on the manager in any given instance and that tend to determine his tactical behavior in relation to his subordinates. In each case his behavior ideally will be that which makes possible the most effective attainment of his immediate goal within the limits facing him.

Long-Run Strategy

As the manager works with his organization on the problems that come up day by day, his choice of a leadership pattern is usually limited. He must take account of the forces just described and, within the restrictions they impose on him, do the best that he can. But as he looks ahead months or even years, he can shift his thinking from tactics to large-scale strategy. No longer need he be fettered by all of the forces mentioned, for he can view many of them as variables over which he has some control. He can, for example, gain new insights or skills for himself, supply training for individual sub-ordinates, and provide participative experiences for his employee group.

In trying to bring about a change in these variables, however, he is faced with a challenging question: At which point along the continuum *should* he act?

Attaining objectives

The answer depends largely on what he wants to accomplish. Let us suppose that he is interested in the same objectives that most modern managers seek to attain when they can shift their attention from the pressure of immediate assignments:

1. To raise the level of employee motivation.
2. To increase the readiness of subordinates to accept change.
3. To improve the quality of all managerial decisions.
4. To develop teamwork and morale.
5. To further the individual development of employees.

In recent years the manager has been deluged with a flow of advice on how best to achieve these longer-run objectives. It is little wonder that he is often both bewildered and annoyed. However, there are some guidelines which he can usefully follow in making a decision.

Most research and much of the experience of recent years give a strong factual basis to the theory that a fairly high degree of subordinate-centered behavior is associated with the accomplishment of the five purposes mentioned.[4] This does not mean that a manager should always leave all decisions to his assistants. To provide the individual or the group with greater freedom than they are ready for at any given time may very well tend to generate anxieties and therefore inhibit rather than facilitate the attainment of desired objectives. But this should not keep the manager from making a continuing effort to confront his subordinates with the challenge of freedom.

Conclusion

In summary, there are two implications in the basic thesis that we have been developing. The first is that the successful leader is

---

[4] For example, *see* Warren H. Schmidt and Paul C. Buchanan, *Techniques that Produce Teamwork* (New London, Arthur C. Croft Publications, 1954); and Morris S. Viteles, *Motivation and Morale in Industry* (New York, W. W. Norton & Company, Inc., 1953).

one who is keenly aware of those forces which are most relevant to his behavior at any given time. He accurately understands himself, the individuals and group he is dealing with, and the company and broader social environment in which he operates. And certainly he is able to assess the present readiness for growth of his subordinates.

But this sensitivity or understanding is not enough, which brings us to the second implication. The successful leader is one who is able to behave appropriately in the light of these perceptions. If direction is in order, he is able to direct; if considerable participative freedom is called for, he is able to provide such freedom.

Thus, the successful manager of men can be primarily characterized neither as a strong leader nor as a permissive one. Rather, he is one who maintains a high batting average in accurately assessing the forces that determine what his most appropriate behavior at any given time should be and in actually being able to behave accordingly. Being both insightful and flexible, he is less likely to see the problems of leadership as a dilemma.

Questions

1. Why should the manager make it clear to his subordinates just what authority he is keeping and what role he is asking his subordinates to assume in solving a particular problem?
2. What risks are involved when a manager delegates decision-making power to his subordinates? Is this type of delegation a form of buck passing?
3. If you as a manager were somewhat skeptical of using the most extreme type of subordinate-centered leadership, what types of problems might you try to solve by this approach?
4. Do you feel that the pressure of time is usually a valid reason for a manager not using more democratic (subordinate-centered) leadership approaches?
5. The authors characterize the successful leader as one who is both insightful and flexible. What is meant by these characteristics and can they be learned?

23. A RE-EXAMINATION OF SUGGESTION SYSTEM PHILOSOPHY *

James R. Bell

In a rapidly changing technological society where social values are constantly being modified we need frequently to re-examine and restate the basic assumptions or philosophy underlying our personnel management programs. We need to follow this re-examination with appropriate revisions of our personnel practices and procedures. This paper is an attempt to examine the validity of suggestion system philosophy to see how well it accords with suggestion system practice and to propose changes in both to accord with the realities and needs of the work place.

The following propositions regarding suggestion systems are those regularly encountered in the literature of personnel. They have been drawn at random from current texts on personnel management. The evaluation of them will disclose that certain familiar postulates relating to suggestion systems are either lacking in factual support or are actually contradictory to the assumptions which underline other well-established personnel practices. The conclusion recommends a single guiding postulate for suggestion systems and proposes some changes in suggestion system practices.

Proposition no. I

Employees have a vast reservoir of good ideas for improving their work and need only the encouragement of management and systematic procedures to release a flood of beneficial suggestions.

The basis for this assumption is hard to identify. Extended observation of almost any ordinary work group will reveal just the contrary. Most employees are trained to do their jobs in certain ways; they accept this training and their work methods uncritically and most of them go about their work for years on end without giving very much thought to change. Most of us like the status quo. Well-formed habits and routines are comfortable and reassuring.

* From *National Association of Suggestion Systems Quarterly*, Summer, 1965, pp. 15-20. Reprinted with permission.

Change is upsetting. Some contemporary research causes us to doubt that creativity is characteristic of the average American adult male. Many employees sincerely believe that management has worked out how it wants the work done and has devised the best ways for doing it.

There are additional reasons for doubting that suggestion systems will really unleash employee creativity. Because of the routine character of much of today's work in business and government, the employee's time-saving idea of today may put him out of a job tomorrow. It is unlikely that employees, in great numbers, are going to come forward enthusiastically to present ideas which may one day result in their own unemployment. Some unions resist suggestion systems for this reason.

Suggestion system statistics belie the proposition. Thirty-three suggestions per 100 employees per year is considered a good rate of submission. One hundred ninety-seven National Association of Suggestion Systems members reported for 1963 that among each 100 eligible employees 25 submitted suggestions. Adopted suggestions, the better ideas, number about one-fourth to one-third of those submitted. This means that the pool of ideas is to be found among only four or five per cent of the employees. Some large governmental merit award programs have submission rates as low as five to ten per cent which means that only one to three per cent of the employees are submitting acceptable suggestions. These data hardly support proposition No. 1 that there is a good pool of untapped worthwhile ideas among employees.

Finally, if employees have a genuine "need" for creative expression, why is it that suggestion system managers must devote so much time and money to promotion, publicity, urging, coercing, pleading to get so few good suggestions from so few employees?

Proposition no. 2

With a good suggestion system, employees will have a "sense of participation" and this is good for employee relations generally.

This proposition is one of those bits of folklore which has been responsible for the uncritical establishment of not only idea award programs, but numerous "employee relations" gimmicks. No one has determined just what constitutes a "sense of participation"; how you determine its presence; and if it is present (which no one can establish) what contribution it may be making to the attainment of the goals of the organization.

Brushing aside these substantial questions however, it is clear from the statistics that so few employees submit suggestions that the sense of participation can hardly extend widely within the work force. A recent Air Force study revealed that 73 per cent of the employees had never submitted a suggestion. NASS members with a total of over one-half million employees reported for 1963 that less than 10 per cent of the eligible employees submitted suggestions. Only eight per cent of the eligible employees received awards for adopted suggestions. Where and how does this sense of participation arise and who feels it? Put directly: how, under these circumstances, can an idea award program make a substantial contribution to the improvement of general employee relations?

Proposition no. 3

Suggestion systems are a means of communication between employees and management. Employees will feel that they are closer to and in a sense participating in management.

An obvious first question: who is management? In training courses we tell first-line supervisors and middle management that they are the foundations of the management structure: "on the management team" is the way it goes. The foreman and supervisor are exhorted to make the "vital shift" from worker to manager. Job descriptions spell out in detail the managerial responsibilities. Yet in spite of all this, suggestion systems are designed to by-pass, and to obviate communication with this "key" level of management. How can employees communicate with management under these circumstances?

It is doubtful that the suggester is really communicating with line management at any level. He is provided a channel for, in effect, saying to a non-line management agency (award board, suggestion monitor or whatever it may be called), "I don't trust the management here so I'm sending my idea to you. I think you will both protect my identity (until it has to be revealed) and see that my suggestion gets fair consideration."

The general literature on organization communication stresses the need and the means of maintaining two-way free communication between employees and management, not excluding lower and middle management. The mechanics of many suggestion systems are clearly counter to this philosophy. The consideration of employee ideas as they are forced back down the management chain from the impersonal suggestion office can hardly be claimed either to give employees a sense of participating in management or to improve employee-management communications. Discussions with many supervisors have convinced the author that the established procedures more often antagonize supervisors than improve their communication with employees. The suggestion system procedure as generally established assumes that the formalized systematic by-passing of management is better than using management channels for the discussion by employees and managers of problems of work which should be of mutual concern.

Proposition no. 4

Even though there may be serious flaws in the suggestion system philosophy as now expressed, it cannot be denied that the good suggestions, although comparatively few in number, do result in tremendous savings.

This assertion can neither be proved nor disproved. No comparative studies have been made (so far as the author can determine) which reveal how many employee suggestions were made before an idea award system was established, how much was saved thereby, and how that compares with the results after a system has been installed.

No responsible personnel man or manager would deny however that over the last 50 years a great deal of our progress in technology and in operating practices and mechanics in government and business has been due to employee ideas freely contributed without expectation of payment or other award. Did employees have no ideas before the advent of suggestion systems? And did they hold their ideas back because no pay was offered for them? Even the most ardent supporter of suggestion systems would not contend this. We will never know how much clear gain in operational savings arises from idea award plans.

Once a system is established a valid criticism is that the savings are overstated. What factors should go into estimating them? First, there should be the amount of the award; second, the costs of operating the systems; third, the full costs of investigating the idea; fourth, the full costs of experimentation and installation of the idea; and fifth, the full costs of developing the suggestion initially to the extent that it is done on time taken from the job. The first and second items are easily identified and no doubt are fully stated. The full costs of investigation are rarely charged and in many cases not at all. One company calculated that an average of two hours time was given to considering each suggestion submitted. At ten dollars per hour each submitted suggestion would cost twenty dollars to investigate. The fourth item, costs of experimentation and installation, are usually included but how fully is unknown. It may be that managerial resistance to suggestion systems and to the notion of paying for employee ideas results in these costs often being overstated. The last cost, time taken from the job by the suggester and his collaborators in developing the idea, is rarely, if ever, stated.

One other reservation regarding purported savings must be expressed. It has to do with long-run savings. Many awards are based on the first year savings. Some systems arbitrarily assume that the saving will continue undiminished for a given period of time, say five to ten years and the system is entitled therefore to claim savings of five to ten times the first year's savings. Some long-run savings can legitimately be claimed. Exactly how much could only be determined by a laborious and costly follow-up to determine how much each suggestion did in reality save. Because of the rapid changes in modern technology and procedures and considering the minor nature of most of the suggestions, there is good reason to suspect that long-run savings may be overstated. In any case there is no doubt that costs are not fully stated and that suggestion system initial savings may well be overstated.

The foregoing evaluation of suggestion system philosophy and practice does not argue for the abandonment of such systems. It does argue for a reappraisal of philosophy and practice and an attempt to bring both into conformity with the reality of modern organization life. There are inconsistencies between claims for and performance of such programs. Far too much has been assumed for too long without critical analysis simply because spectacular savings could be claimed as against awards made.

It is proposed that a single principle, namely monetary gain to the organization, be the basis for establishing employee suggestion plans: that they be viewed purely and simply as a method for buying employee ideas—for that is what they are. Drop all pretense that they "give a sense of participation," "improve communication," "stimulate employee creativity," and so on. If such by-products result, so much the better, but the system should not be founded on such unprovable and in some cases, unlikely propositions.

If the suggestion system is an organized way of buying employee ideas to improve productivity and to save money, then the whole matter of procedures can be faced up to squarely. New attitudes toward management participation and communication will emerge and the hypocrisy in the present systems can be swept away. But here, we encounter perhaps the most serious contradiction and obstacle of all—the matter of supervisory participation.

We shall have to reconcile basic conflicting ideas regarding supervisors and their functions. On the one hand we claim that a supervisor is paid to improve methods—he is among other things an innovator. That is why he cannot receive awards for suggestions affecting his own unit. On the other hand many supervisors are actually controllers, inspectors, expeditors, stabilizers if you will, guardians of the status quo. Most supervisors are neither paid to nor especially encouraged to innovate. Simple proof that the supervisor is not really viewed as an innovator is seen in the deliberate building of the suggestion system channel around him because it is believed that he fears new ideas and will suppress them. This conflict regarding supervisory attitudes and performance must be resolved before suggestion system procedures can be reconstructed within a new philosophy.

It is proposed that lower and middle managers be brought into full partnership in award plans and that they share equitably in suggestion awards applicable to their work and which originate in their units. Supervisors must be given an incentive to promote new ideas. Various schemes can be developed and different bases of compensation can be established. Perhaps supervisory awards can begin with a 15 per cent sharing at the first level and scale down to 10 and 5 per cent for the next two levels above. Fuller participation by the supervisor in idea development will result in more good suggestions, result in higher awards, and reduce the large number of poor suggestions. Supervisory payments must be over and above, not taken from, the employee's award.

The proposed procedure means that all suggestions must be initiated and perfected in the line as a part of normal work activity. They will be routed around management and back down as at present. Line management must have the last word in the matter of work improvements which are essential to the management function. What is offered is a kind of profit sharing plan based on operational savings. In larger organizations a high-level committee may be desirable to review accepted suggestions, to examine the basis for estimated savings, and to maintain reasonable uniformity of standards. With this different philosophy the suggestion system coordinator's function should change. He can become a man whose duty is to help management identify "problem areas" and to stimulate employees and supervisors to develop solutions to them.

In summary, what is proposed here is a clarification and simplification of suggestion system objectives and the creation of a simple line system for stimulating, perfecting, and installing money-saving operational improvements. It is a plan for buying the good ideas and the creativity of all employees: non-supervisors and managers alike.

Questions

1. What effects, if any, is the typical suggestion system likely to have on the supervisor's promotion of new ideas? Does the system usually provide for his participation?
2. Bell concludes that even a good suggestion system does not give employees a sense of participation. Do you agree? Why?
3. What are some of the problems encountered in estimating the financial savings that accrue from a suggestion submitted by an employee?
4. Do you believe that employees should be financially rewarded for suggestions concerning the improvement of their own job procedures? Why?
5. The author reexamines the basic assumptions of philosophy which he believes underlie the typical suggestion program. Would this be a desirable procedure to follow in other areas of personnel management? Why?

24. EMOTIONAL FIRST AID ON THE JOB *

Harry Levinson

Few situations are more delicate than suddenly being faced by a deeply troubled friend or associate. Because of the complexities of business relationships, an executive confronted with an emotionally upset colleague or subordinate often finds himself in an even more difficult position. Executives who have experienced such situations have repeatedly asked, "What can I do? What should I do? To whom can I turn for help?"

An understanding of the nature of emotional disturbances is an important preparation for such emergencies. Emotional disturbances are the most common of illnesses. Everyone frequently suffers from them. Just as a cold is a mild form of upper respiratory disorder, so a temporary fit of anger or a daylong feeling of the "blues" is a mild form of emotional disorder.

The effects of even temporary emotional upsets are universally recognized in such common phrases as, "He was so mad he didn't know what he was doing," or "He got up on the wrong side of the bed." We may say about something that upsets us, "It made me sick," and actually have felt physically sick. Or, "I was so scared I shook like a leaf for 15 minutes afterwards." It is our daily experience that our emotions do affect our judgment, our physical health, and the degree of control which we can exercise over ourselves.

Emotional disturbances always involve impairment of our relationships with others. When we are angry or sad, by definition we cannot be cordial. If we become highly excited, it is difficult for others to understand us or to keep pace with us. If we develop "nervous headaches" or some other physical symptom and take to our bed, we are out of touch with others for at least a short time.

Since impairment of relations with others is so central in emotional disturbances, we frequently gain the psychological strength to cope more adequately with whatever problem we face by experiencing

* From *Menninger Quarterly*, September, 1957. Reprinted with permission.

more constructive relationships. The most important instrument, therefore, which anyone has with which to help a person who is emotionally distressed is himself—his own personality and the way in which he relates himself to the disturbed person.

Recognition

Emotional disturbance is seen in the manifestations of prolonged or excessive anxiety.

All of us strive to keep our personalities in balance. We commonly speak of being "on an even keel" or having "ups and downs," of being "up in the clouds" or "down in the dumps." When we become temporarily upset emotionally, automatic mechanisms try to bring us back into balance. Just as disease or infection is quickly reacted to with fever, so is anger reacted to with shouting, striking, making greater efforts at self-control, or showing physical symptoms like hypertension. We return to our previous equilibrium once the feeling is successfully met.

Anxiety triggers this psychological balancing action when our equilibrium is threatened. If we violate a rule of conscience, anxiety motivates us to make atonement so that we may once again be psychologically comfortable or in balance. If we have made part of ourselves certain goals and aspirations, such as a college education or a successful business career, we are not fully comfortable unless we are striving to achieve these goals. Anxiety is at work. Anxiety, therefore, is a most important and useful mechanism for self-protection, adaptation, and motivation.

We see manifestations of anxiety when we are worried or upset. We become tense, restless, or even tremble in agitation. We may perspire freely or have little appetite. Perhaps we cannot concentrate very well on matters other than those which are upsetting us. Thus, if severe enough, anxiety can disrupt the ordinary, ongoing activities of the personality. We then speak of an emotional disorder.

Because anxiety has this disruptive potential, the personality cannot tolerate too much of it too long. It must have ways of coping with anxiety. In the process of growing up, therefore, all of us have learned characteristic ways of coping with those situations which tend to arouse anxiety in us. These ways of coping become predominant characteristics of our personalities. The shy person is most comfortable when away from others; the hail-fellow-well-met is most comfortable when with others.

There are three major signs of emotional disturbance when our ordinary means of warding off excessive or prolonged anxiety are not adequate. First, we may try to use to a greater degree the same methods which previously had protected us. Under the pressure of increasing anxiety the shy person may withdraw even further from people, or the hail-fellow-well-met may increase his social activities to a fever pitch. Second, if these increased efforts are not adequate, we may see direct signs of anxiety—panic, extreme tension and agitation, "jitteriness", excessive perspiring, flushing, inability to concentrate. Third, if we are still unable to cope with the anxiety we may break down altogether and no longer be able to exercise adequate control over our thoughts, feelings, and actions. Our thinking may become irrational and our emotions inappropriate. The tidy person may become slovenly, the quiet person noisy.

Relief

The executive usually faces either of two situations when he is confronted by an associate who is emotionally distressed.

One, he may, as a supervisor, observe that a subordinate is showing less and less ability to perform his work, or that the fellow is causing increasing friction with others, or that there is some other interference with the job. Recognizing emotional distress, the executive may be reluctant to add further burdens through criticism or evaluation. However, while it is always painful for one to be told his job performance is unsatisfactory, and it may be even more painful when one is already emotionally distressed, it is neither helpful nor fair to permit the subordinate's performance to depreciate. In fact, it is often quite helpful to the troubled person to be apprised of the way his distress is affecting his job and of the tolerance limits of the organization. It may be just this kind of frank discussion which motivates him to seek professional help. In addition, he is acutely aware of his distress and may feel desperately in need of someone to open an avenue of help—to make a first move which he finds impossible to make. Thus the executive should state the job situation and its consequences factually and clearly.

In the second situation, the executive, as a responsible and respected person in the organization, may be approached by a person spontaneously seeking help. Sometimes the problem may be directly specified, at other times it may be alluded to indirectly, and at still other times the distressed person may be able to talk only of a vague generalized feeling of distress.

In either of these two situations, when the distress has been made the concern of the executive, either because it interferes with someone's work or because someone seeks his help, he can offer immediate help in the form of being a "friend in need." The troubled person can feel, in effect, "It's all right to talk here. He will help me." Mere willingness to act as a friend in need quickly leads to three objectives: 1) the troubled person tends to get some relief from his anxiety by having temporarily at his disposal someone else's resources in addition to his own; 2) getting his problem out from within himself creates a freer atmosphere in which he can make decisions or choices about what he must do next; 3) the first two objectives lead to a greater readiness for seeking whatever additional help may be necessary.

At this point, however, difficulties begin to arise for the person in the helping role. Most frequently his own anxiety is aroused—the behavior of the troubled person may frighten him; the problem at hand may touch on his own inner conflicts; he may be asked or required to take some action which may be burdensome or unpleasant.

Such difficulties may become apparent in implementing two basic principles: listening and limiting. The executive must learn what the problem is and the limits both of what he can do and what he ought to do in terms of his particular business situation.

Listening

This is perhaps the most talked about, least understood, and least practiced principle of human relations. It is the key to emergency relief. Listening to a person express his feelings implies a willingness to help. This, in turn conveys to the troubled person that he is respected as a human being. It is also recognition of the fact that every person *has* to feel as he does.

Listening requires that the troubled person be permitted to tell his story in his own way with only occasional questions for clarification of something not quite clear or for an example of a particularly important feeling.

To fail to listen is to indicate to the troubled person that he turned to the wrong person for help.

The listening process is also disrupted when the listener's own anxiety leads him to blame, criticize, pity, or offer logic as a response to feelings. All of us have said to another, "You don't need to feel that way." Yet to tell this to a troubled person or to make light of his problem indicates only that we do not really feel what is going on within him.

Most of our behavior is motivated by thoughts and feelings which are unconscious. Unconscious feelings are like microbes—they cannot be seen without special techniques or skills, and they cannot be washed away with water or sweet words. People cannot readily control their feelings. Often, when they are anxious, they do not know why they feel that way. To "tell" them why they feel as they do is of no help. Not only does it disrupt the listening process but, in fact, it also is dangerous psychologizing of the worst kind because, without long formal training, the listener cannot possibly know the causes. He can only create even greater anxiety. Furthermore, clinical experience has repeatedly demonstrated the futility of "telling" people. They can use such knowledge only when they discover it for themselves and to discover it usually requires professional help.

People do not *want* to be upset and worried. If they could only "snap out of it," they would. When they seek help, they expect consideration of their problems, not summary dismissal of them. Often we unwittingly dismiss people and thereby fail to listen.

Sometimes the problem may seem so trivial or so easy to solve that the listener becomes resentful for having his time taken up with it: "He thinks *he* has problems!" Such a feeling can only be a handicap to a listening relationship because it conveys to the troubled person the communication that his troubles are insignificant. If they are important enough to trouble him, then they are significant as far as he is concerned.

A good example occurred during a major flood in Topeka. An emergency first aid station was set up for several thousand refugees. A line of them waited at the first aid station for medical help. The physician asked one middle-aged man his complaint. "Athlete's foot," said the man. Both startled and bothered that the man should trouble him with such a minor symptom in the midst of a major emergency, the physician nonetheless contained himself. "How long have you had athlete's foot?" he asked. "Four years," the man replied. Now the physician had to strain to suppress an urgent impulse to give vent to his ire. With a little patience and a few more questions he discovered that the man was all alone in the world and that the flood had swept away the only stablizing point in his life, his small home. He had come to the physician not because he had athlete's foot but because he desperately needed someone to talk to, some way of reaching out to another human being and of getting attention and love in return. The few moments the physician spent with that man were as valuable to him as surgery might have been to another.

Another abrupt interference with listening is impatience. There are times when it is extremely difficult to ascertain the problem. However, it is important to recognize that we have difficulty enough expressing our feelings when we are not troubled. That difficulty is compounded when we are experiencing strong emotion. Often the troubled person may go around in verbal circles. The listener must, therefore, be willing to tolerate some repetition or vagueness until the feelings involved can be expressed.

Periods of silence seem particularly to make the listener impatient. Usually he rushes in with a comment to fill the gap. But periods of silence are important to a troubled person who is trying to pull his thoughts together under the stress of strong emotion. The listener should wait them out.

Another disruption of the listening process is the flight of the listener. Escape takes many different forms. Suddenly there is no longer any time to listen, or perhaps some sage wisdom urgently needs to be transmitted to the troubled person. Advice, prescriptions, and remedies all have the singular merit of being "solutions" which do not require the presence or participation of the listener.

Finally, listening is defeated by pontification. Unless the troubled person is too ill to do so, he must come in to his own decisions about his course of action. The role of the listener is seldom to act for the troubled person or to direct his action. Most often it is either to serve as a sounding board for the expression of feelings, to help clarify the problem, or to help bring into relief possible alternative actions. The only exception is guided by this rule of thumb: the more serious the disturbance and the less control the troubled person has over himself, the greater control someone else will have to assume. An excited secretary seeing visions in the outer office obviously requires that someone get her to a doctor immediately.

Limiting

As important as the action which can be taken is the recognition of those limits which circumscribe emotional first aid, some of which are especially imperative in a business situation.

Neither time nor the function of an executive permits frequently repeated interviews. A person who cannot be helped in one or two interviews should be referred.

Obviously the professional skills of the executive do not include psychotherapy. He therefore can only perform a relief function. As a colleague, Dr. Bernard Hall, has put it, the executive cannot expect to go beyond the ordinary means and channels of supervision available to him. He cannot expect to alleviate problems for which these means are not adequate. Occasionally executives criticize themselves for failing to help people with whom even the most skilled clinicians would have difficulty. Such expectations are unrealistic, to say the least, and such recriminations are unwarranted.

This is not to say that relief efforts are unimportant. Emotional first aid often enables people to obtain a new perspective on their problems and to deal with them more effectively. In effect, such "relief counseling" is to psychiatric treatment as first aid is to medical treatment. There is a critically important place for first aid efforts. They are neither unimportant nor are they to be minimized. It is to say, however, that no one can be all things to all people. There are limits to what one as a human being in his particular position can do.

The troubled person himself and the nature of his problem both pose certain limitations. Emotional first aid will not be of much help to people who are particularly inflexible, those who have little awareness of their more obvious problems, or those who have little sensitivity to their own feelings. For example, a man who cannot admit to himself that he is angry when it is appropriate to be angry is insensitive to his own feelings.

Troubled people who are in an acute panic—trembling, easily agitated, frightened—and those who are so upset as to be a danger to themselves or others require help beyond first aid. If the problem is chronic and if the person customarily has been unable to cope successfully with life's problems, first aid will not be of much help. First aid is of greatest help if the problem relates to external stress, or to immediate and acute family or job difficulties.

The person who seeks help for emotional distress bares himself to the view of another. In effect he removes some of the protective layers of his personality to let the other person see what is troubling him. He may burst into an angry tirade or into tears because he feels it is safe to do so in the presence of the other person. This should not cause embarrassment or anger in return because it is an act of confidence. He does this because he assumes that by expressing his feelings he will obtain help, and furthermore that the listener will protect him by not communicating to other people what he has learned. If this trust is violated, the listener not only debases the human dignity of the troubled person but also discredits his own reputation for integrity. If he cannot keep confidential what he hears, both he and the troubled person will be much better off if he does not try to offer first aid.

Referral

Every person in a position of responsibility such that others may turn to him for help with emotional problems should have ready access to a specialized professional person to whom he can turn or to whom he can refer. Insecurity about how to deal with particularly difficult and pressing problems beyond our competence is relieved by knowing that we need only to pick up a telephone to have competent advice. If the company does not employ an industrial physician, it behooves the executive to become acquainted with a competent psychiatrist, clinical psychologist, or psychiatric social worker to whom he can turn in an emergency. He will find it invaluable to know the community resources which are available for help and how to use them. In any sizable community there are literally dozens of sources of help. One needs only to know the proper telephone numbers to mobilize them. One important potential source of help, and often a valuable support, is the troubled person's own family physician.

Serious problems will have to be referred. Such a referral must indicate always honestly and sincerely to the troubled person that another door is being opened for additional help. Neither action nor word must suggest a feeling that the troubled person is "crazy," hopeless, or unworthy of attention. If the listener is not honest in his referral, if he does not himself believe that the referral will be of help, this feeling will be communicated to the person being referred and he will not use the referral source.

When people are troubled, they may misunderstand or become confused. One way to avoid misunderstanding in referral is to make a practice of summarizing with the troubled person what has gone on and where the matter now seems to stand. Referral does not mean the listener's door should be closed; he might specifically indicate that he is standing by to help further in any way he can.

People who should be referred to professional sources of help include those who show psychotic symptoms, that is they act in such a way that their behavior appears to be irrational and uncontrolled.

Most obvious examples of this are people who hear voices, talk to themselves consistently, or believe things are happening about them which in reality are not so. People who speak of suicide or make suicidal attempts, those who threaten others with physical violence, those who have repeated offenses against the law or the rules of the organization, those who are paralyzed into inactivity by their inability to make decisions, those who have constant physical symptoms or mannerisms which they cannot control—all should be referred. In addition, people whose needs are better and more directly served by an outside agency should be quickly referred. Occasionally people seeking help are friends of the executive or have with him a relationship which is too close to permit him to be objective or to permit them to be comfortable in bringing their troubles to him. Such people should also be referred.

A final word of caution. People frequently are somewhat embarrassed after having sought counsel for emotional distress. Some may feel they have said too much, others that to have admitted a need for help is somehow not acceptable adult behavior. As a result they may afterwards avoid or ignore the person to whom they turned for help. The listener should anticipate such behavior and not be offended by it. Sometimes it can be avoided if he indicates that he knows the troubled person probably will have such feelings because most people do.

Questions

1. What type of first aid does the author recommend be given to the subordinate who needs help? In what way is the recommended action comparable to medical first aid? Discuss.
2. Why is it of little value to tell a person who is emotionally disturbed to "snap out of it"? Discuss.
3. The man with the complaint of "athlete's foot" was not as troubled by that as something else. What implications does his case have for understanding a person's problems? What did the physician do that apparently helped the man?
4. The author emphasizes the importance of listening to another person's feelings and realizing that he has to feel as he does. What implications does this have for trying to change a person's feelings?
5. Why is it advisable to make fairly specific referrals in cases where an employee needs professional assistance? Why is it not advisable to just tell the person that he should get some help?

Additional Readings for Chapter 4

Balma, M. J., J. C. Maloney, and C. H. Lawshe. "The Role of the Foreman in Modern Industry," *Advanced Management*. Vol. 25, No. 8 (August, 1960), pp. 16-20.

Bennis, Warren G. "Revisionist Theory of Leadership," *Harvard Business Review*. Vol. 39, No. 1 (January-February, 1961), pp. 26-28, 31, 34-36, 146-150.

Black, James M. "Don't Make Your Boss a Problem," *Supervisory Management*. Vol. 7, No. 5 (May, 1962), pp. 3-5.

Boedecker, Ray F. "Why Delegation Goes Wrong," *Supervisory Management*. Vol. 9, No. 2 (February, 1964), pp. 4-8.

Braceland, Francis J. "Living With Executive Pressures," *Advanced Management Journal*. Vol. 29, No. 4 (October, 1964), pp. 42-48.

Burtt, Harold C. "Why Most Supervisory Training Drops Dead," *Management Methods*. Vol. 13, No. 4 (January, 1958), pp. 28-34.

Cooper, Alfred M. "Self-Multiplication," *Supervision*. Vol. 16, No. 9 (September, 1954), pp. 18-20.

Ewing, David W. "Tension Can Be An Asset," *Harvard Business Review*. Vol. 42, No. 5 (September-October, 1954), pp. 71-78.

Fleishman, Edwin A., and Edwin F. Harris. "Patterns of Leadership Behavior Related to Employee Grievances and Turnover," *Personnel Psychology*. Vol. 15, No. 1 (Spring, 1962), pp. 43-56.

Gibbons, Charles C. "Letter to an Ambitious Supervisor," *Supervisory Management*. Vol. 8, No. 9 (September, 1963), pp. 4-9.

Given, William B. "Reaching Out in Management," *Harvard Business Review*. Vol. 30, No. 2 (March-April, 1952), pp. 33-45.

Harris, Philip. "Affirmation of the Foreman's Role," *Business Topics*. Vol. 13, No. 1 (Winter, 1965), pp. 42-50.

Huberman, John. "Discipline Without Punishment," *Harvard Business Review*. Vol. 42, No. 4 (July-August, 1964), pp. 62-68.

Kutash, Samuel B. "Problem Workers or Workers With Problems," *Supervisory Management*. Vol. 6, No. 2 (February, 1961), pp. 2-13.

Levinson, Harry. "Industrial Mental Health: Progress and Prospects," *Personnel*. Vol. 38, No. 3 (May-June, 1961), pp. 35-42.

——————. "What Killed Bob Lyons?" *Harvard Business Review*. Vol. 41, No. 1 (January-February, 1963), pp. 127-143.

Mann, Floyd C., and James K. Dent. "The Supervisor: Member of Two Organizational Families," *Harvard Business Review*. Vol. 32, No. 6 (November-December, 1954), pp. 103-112.

McMurry, Robert N. "Mental Illness: Society's and Industry's Six Billion Dollar Burden," *Personnel Administration*. Vol. 25, No. 4 (July-August, 1962), pp. 4-18.

Menninger, William C. "A Prescription for Executive Mental Health," *Advanced Management*. Vol. 25, No. 8 (September, 1960), pp. 16-17.

Menninger, William C., and Harry Levinson. "Psychiatry in Industry: Some Trends and Perspectives," *Personnel*. Vol. 32, No. 2 (September, 1955), pp. 90-99.

Odiorne, George. "Management's Motivation Muddle," *Michigan Business Review*. Vol. 17, No. 2 (March, 1965), pp. 27-32.

Pfiffner, John M. "The Effective Supervisor: An Organization Research Study," *Personnel*. Vol. 31, No. 6 (May, 1955), pp. 530-540.

Porterfield, John D. "Stress and the Manager," *Personnel Administration*. Vol. 25, No. 4 (July-August, 1962), pp. 29-37.

Schell, Edwin H. "Dealing with Difficult Personalities," *Advanced Management Journal*. (September, 1963), pp. 113-118.

Schmidt, Warren H., and Robert Tannenbaum. "Management of Differences," *Harvard Business Review*. Vol. 38, No. 6 (November-December, 1960), pp. 107-115.

Seligson, Harry. "Rethinking the Foreman's Job," *Personnel Journal*. Vol. 35, No. 10 (March, 1957), pp. 372-373, 378.

Slater, Philip E., and Warren G. Bennis. "Democracy Is Inevitable," *Harvard Business Review*. Vol. 42, No. 2 (March-April, 1964), pp. 51-59.

Tannenbaum, Robert, and Fred Massarik. "Leadership: A Frame of Reference," *Management Science*. Vol. 4, No. 1 (October, 1957), pp. 1-19.

Tear, Daniel G. "How to Look At People," *Advanced Management*. Vol. 26, No. 4 (April, 1961), pp. 16-19.

Trice, Harrison M. "New Light on Identifying the Alcoholic Employee," *Personnel*. Vol. 41, No. 5 (September-October, 1964), pp. 18-25.

Turner, Arthur N. "Foremen—Key to Worker Morale," *Harvard Business Review*. Vol. 32, No. 1 (January-February, 1954), pp. 76-86.

Wallen, Richard W. "The 3 Types of Executive Personality," *Dun's Review and Modern Industry*. Vol. 81, No. 2 (February, 1963), pp. 54-56, 106.

Zaleznik, Abraham. "The Human Dilemmas of Leadership," *Harvard Business Review*. Vol. 41, No. 4 (July-August, 1963), pp. 49-55.

CHAPTER 5

Organizational Behavior

In a study of personnel management, consideration must be given not only to the face-to-face relationships between superiors and subordinates but also to the organizational framework in which they carry on their daily activities. Organizations are formally characterized by authority and responsibility that are assigned to job holders who, according to the organizational chart, have a fixed relationship to each other for the performance of their duties. In reality, however, the organization never functions in quite the manner outlined on paper. There are a variety of individual and group forces that will have a modifying effect upon that which has been so neatly arranged by the experts in organizational and manpower planning. This disparity between what is planned and what actually happens is not necessarily the result of poor planning. It is explained better by the fact that an organization is comprised of people; and where there are people, one is likely to find complexities that are not easily understood or explained.

Traditional organizational theory, which is still a governing influence in modern management, is predicated primarily upon what people *should* do rather than upon what they *actually* do. It uses a logical approach to human activities rather than a behavioral science approach. While organizations must have certain objectives and principles to guide their activities if successful results are to be achieved, a greater recognition of the true nature of human beings in the organizational environment is necessary if the organization is to meet these objectives and if human talents and values within the organization are to be conserved.

In recent years students of organizational theory and of the behavioral sciences have attempted to approach the nature of the organization more realistically. Much has been written on the subject, but as yet there is no body of principles based on experimental findings that can be cited as definitive. The study of individual behavior has required many years and many questions are as yet unanswered. In building a thorough understanding of organizational behavior, the road will be long and difficult. Nevertheless, the student of personnel management should become acquainted with studies that are made and examine the concepts that are emerging from the experts in the behavioral sciences.

One of the more traditional areas of organizational behavior that have received considerable emphasis is that of communication. Its importance in the effective management of personnel has long been recognized, although until behavioral science concepts were related to analyses of the communication process, discussion of the topic did not include many of the essential factors. The first article by Leonard Sayles is one of those that examines communication from the psychological point of view and concludes with practical recommendations for the superior who desires to communicate with subordinates. Sayles wisely points out, however, that good communication does not result merely from having the techniques but also requires the existence of a healthy cooperative relationship between the superior and his subordinates.

In the next article, Carl R. Rogers and Fritz Roethlisberger propose that communication may be improved if we all learn how to become better listeners and to really understand what the other person is trying to say to us. Rogers' concept of nonevaluative listening has attracted considerable attention among thoughtful persons who view communication as a way to achieve understanding rather than as a device for manipulating the other fellow.

The communication skills discussed by Sayles and by Rogers and Roethlisberger in the first two articles are essential to the success of group participation—the subject of the article by Keith Davis. Davis cites classical experiments in participative management and discusses the prerequisites for participation. He discusses the problems of pseudo-participation and excessive participation which are often overlooked by enthusiasts of this approach.

One of the criticisms that have been leveled against the large business organization in the United States is that big business demands conformity by its employees. In the article by George Strauss we find an analysis of the various kinds of conformity and a discussion of forces that make it occur. His conclusion is based on a close evaluation of the forces that most authors have not provided in their articles.

The last article in this chapter is by Arthur N. Turner. It focuses on the human problems of large assembly-line plants where a technological environment that fails to provide the necessary satisfaction and meaning in work has been created. The excellent description of relationships between man and machines and among managers, foremen, and employees provides the basis for a provocative study of organizational behavior in this type of environment.

25. ON-THE-JOB COMMUNICATION *

Leonard Sayles

Part I—Why Isn't It Easier?

Watch two old friends talking to each other. Do they have difficulty communicating? Probably not. They might not even have to use complete sentences—often a single word or a raised eyebrow conveys all the meaning necessary. Since the friends know each other thoroughly, key words or signs are all they need to exchange their ideas.

For the supervisor at work, communicating isn't that easy. In giving a simple order to a subordinate, asking why an assignment wasn't completed on time, or listening to a suggestion from an employee, the supervisor is faced with many communication barriers that almost never exist between close friends.

Let's look at these barriers, along with some specific examples of how they can impede communication between a supervisor and his subordinates.

The speaker and listener differ in experience and background

A supervisor tells one of his key men that the company may have to cut back production because some important orders were lost. But the employee hears: "You can expect to be laid off soon."

Why? In other companies where he's worked, lost orders always meant he was out of a job.

Our understanding of what we hear depends largely on our own experience and background. Instead of hearing what people tell us, we may hear what our mind tells us has been said. There is often a vast difference.

Differences in experience often influence the way workers respond to incentive plans. A company offers to give merit increases and higher-paying jobs to superior employees. Some workers fail to

---

* From *Supervisory Management*, Vol. 7, No. 7 (July, 1962), pp. 2-6; and Vol. 7, No. 8 (August, 1962), pp. 12-15. Reprinted with permission.

respond with enthusiasm—even though they want to earn additional money. Why? It may be that they have never gained anything from being good workers. Perhaps they belong to an ethnic group that is often ignored when better jobs are filled. Perhaps they've worked in companies that "cut the rate" when employees made more money by working harder. Whatever the reason, they hear the company's announcement this way:

"Certain workers whom we choose will get benefits by working harder; others will get nothing."

We fail to convey the information the listener needs and can understand

For example, a supervisor may fill a trainee's mind with information he is not ready to grasp. In one survey, cashier-trainees in department stores reported that much of their induction training was meaningless to them. The reason: Without any experience on the job, they didn't understand how they could apply the information. It was only after they were on the job handling sales slips that they could have absorbed the knowledge. For this reason, training is more effective when the supervisor can simulate actual on-the-job problems to which the new information can be applied.

It is the supervisor's job, too, to make sure that the information he *gets* from subordinates is what he needs. Often, a subordinate is in the dark about what information his boss wants from him. The boss then complains that the subordinate is failing to keep him informed in vital areas or that he is deluging him with information he doesn't need.

Our stereotypes and beliefs influence what we hear

A man with a strong prejudice is often confronted by information that contradicts it. But the prejudice may be so powerful that he will twist the information to support it.

For example, let's say a supervisor is convinced that because one worker in his department belongs to a certain ethnic group, he is, therefore, always looking for the easy way out. One day, the worker comes up with a carefully worked out, practical shortcut on his job. Instead of praising him for his initiative, the supervisor thinks to himself: "Just proves they're all alike—always trying to get away with less work."

Look at how a supervisor can come to three different conclusions about the same situation, depending on his preconceptions. The situation: He sees a group of employees laughing together.

1. If he believes that hard work has to be unpleasant, he decides the employees are wasting time and should be given tougher assignments.
2. If he believes that good work and cheerful attitudes go together, he will congratulate himself for being a good manager.
3. If he is personally insecure, he may assume that the laughing employees are making jokes about him.

Our emotional state of mind colors what we hear

The worried, fearful employee finds threats in everything he hears. Let's say new equipment is being introduced in a department. The employees fear the worst. As a result, everthing seen and heard is interpreted as confirmation that they will suffer:

> I saw the supervisor looking at the seniority list— it looks as though they're going to lay off half the department after that new machinery comes in.

We're dead set against a speaker's message because we suspect his motivation

The classic example of this particular barrier is to be found in labor-management relations. Many union members are convinced that management is out to weaken their union, and they refuse to believe anything management tells them. Similarly, management may regard all grievances as political maneuvers designed to win union votes. Both sides are sometimes right, of course. But too often this closed-mind attitude makes it impossible for the two sides to reach each other.

The same suspicion can impede communication between supervisors, too. Often one supervisor may reject worthwhile ideas from an associate simply because he's convinced that the man is trying to show him up.

In dealing with subordinates, the supervisor can be at the receiving end of such disbelief. If an employee is convinced that his boss is trying to manipulate him, all the human-relations techniques in the book—no matter how sincerely they are used—will be unsuccessful.

Let's say an employee makes a cost-cutting suggestion to his supervisor. The supervisor says, "Thanks, I'll think about it." If the subordinate believes that the supervisor isn't really interested in developing people, he'll hear this as, "Stick to your own job and let me take care of the thinking around here."

On the other hand, if he thinks the supervisor genuinely wants to encourage initiative, he'll hear: "I'm pleased that you came up with this suggestion—I'll see if there is some way we can use it."

We fail to evaluate the meaning behind what we hear

Sometimes we go to the opposite extreme—instead of judging what we hear entirely by the speaker's imagined motivation, we completely ignore the possible latent meaning of his words. We forget that most statements are a combination of fact *and* feeling.

An employee comes over to his supervisor and says disgustedly, "This lousy machine is broken again." An alert supervisor will wonder if there isn't more in this complaint than just a maintenance problem. Could the employee be saying, "I don't like this job" or, "I think I'm getting a raw deal"? These possibilities deserve investigation.

We fail to realize that what we're saying has symbolic meaning for our listeners

What we say often has a far greater meaning than it appears to on the surface. That's why we sometimes get a surprisingly strong reaction to what we consider a rather mild statement.

Recently, for example, a production supervisor told his men, "We're going to start using plastic for these parts instead of chrome steel." He reassured them that no one would lose his job, and there would be no changes in earnings or working conditions. It was simply an economy move to reduce the cost of this particular component.

Yet the morale of the whole department was shaken. The supervisor didn't realize that the men were proud of the superior appearance and durability of the chrome-steel component. The phrase "chrome steel" was loaded with symbolic meaning: product prestige, a feeling of superiority, a determination to be the best even if it cost more.

We forget that words mean different things to different people

Words and phrases often lead to trouble because the speaker and listener interpret them differently. (See "Words to Manage By," October, 1961, page 2.) For example:

> A supervisor spots a dangerous pool of oil on the shop floor near a machinist. As he passes, he says, "Get that oil wiped up as soon as you can—it's a real safety hazard." The machinist nods.
>
> Ten minutes later, the supervisor is called back—an inspector has just taken a bad spill on the oil. The supervisor bawls out the machinist for failing to follow his instructions. But the machinist says:
>
> "You told me to get it wiped up as soon as I could. I thought you could see that I was working on a delicate cut and had to finish that first."

To the supervisor, "as soon as you can" meant immediately. To the machinist, it meant as soon as he had finished the piece on which he was working.

Our reference group often dictates the way we hear a message

The group we identify ourselves with—psychologists call it the reference group—tends to shape our opinions on many matters. The result is often another block to true communication. Here's an example:

> A night-shift operator finds a note left for him by the day man who runs the same machine: "Don't expect to get any good work from this —I didn't. It needs cleaning and some decent maintenance for a change."
>
> The day man was just trying to be helpful, even though he didn't know the night man. But the night man read the note this way: "Your sloppy maintenance is to blame for my difficulty."

How come? Based mostly on imagined slights, the night man's reference group—the rest of the night shift—had developed a resentful attitude toward the day shift. Influenced by this attitude, the night man interpreted the note as a slap at him.

Part II—It's Easier When You Know How!

A large group of supervisory trainees listened intently as their instructor gave them elaborate directions on how to arrange five dominoes in a certain pattern. They were not allowed to ask any questions of the instructor.

In another room, the same directions were being given, but here the trainees were allowed to ask as many questions as they wanted of the instructor.

The results were startingly different. In the first room, only three trainees were able to arrange the dominoes correctly. In the second room, only four trainees did *not* arrange them correctly.

This experiment in communication points up what is perhaps the single most important technique in better communicating: feedback. There are other weapons in the supervisor's communications arsenal —and we'll get to these later—but feedback is probably packed with more potential than any of them.

That's because feedback can tell the supervisor *if* he is communicating and *what* he is communicating to his listener. It turns communication from a shot-in-the-dark that may or may not be hitting the target to a two-way process that leaves both speaker and listener better informed.

Let's look at what feedback is. Actually most of us use this principle constantly without recognizing it. Put simply, it means modifying what we say and how we say it according to the response we get from our listener. This is the same way a thermostat regulates the amount of furnace heat on the basis of feedback, which in this case is the temperature of the room.

When a supervisor uses this method deliberately, he can develop better ways of learning what is being understood by the subordinate to whom he's talking. Various experiments have revealed that the accuracy of communication increases with the amount of feedback. Limiting the listener to "Yes" or "No" responses (asking him, for example, "Do you understand that?") is less effective than encouraging him to ask his own questions.

Face-to-face communication

The first essential for maximum feedback is face-to-face communication. Only then can the communicator find out if the receiver understands, if he agrees, if he's sympathetic, indifferent, hostile, or just confused. The feedback comes not only through the listener's words, but through his nonverbal behavior, too.

We can watch for expressions of puzzlement, anger, or comprehension that may flicker across his face. Gestures and other physical actions can reveal impatience, animosity, or agreement.

With the set of his lips, the movement of an eyebrow, a listener can often tell us more than he does in hours of talk, because these expressions may indicate attitudes that he is reluctant or unable to express in words. For example, a subordinate is understandably unwilling to challenge the orders of his boss. Even when he has information that makes him skeptical of the success of a proposed plan, he may still want to keep his misgivings to himself. But in the course of an informal, face-to-face discussion, an alert supervisor can detect a lack of enthusiasm in his tone of voice and his facial expressions.

While a supervisor should not—and probably doesn't want to—think of himself as a psychiatrist, he should learn to "listen with a third ear" to what a subordinate is saying. What is the employee really trying to say? Is the problem deeper than he's letting on? What isn't he saying? What subjects is he avoiding, and why?

Interpreting feedback is not always easy. What we say may symbolize something to our listeners that is not apparent to us. One such case occurred recently in a large merchandising company. To help him in the preparation of market analysis, a new district sales manager asked his salesmen to compute certain correlation coefficients on the basis of their sales records. The task was not difficult—they simply had to use an easy formula. But they failed to do it. One excuse followed another: The computations were too complicated, it was clerk's work, it wasn't in their job description, the coefficients were really useless anyhow, and so on. Their distaste for this task seemed to be out of all proportion to the difficulty involved.

Solving the mystery

Why was the modest request greeted with such stubborn resistance? The sales manager came up with the answer after much investigation and interviewing. Three years before, the salesmen had had an authoritarian supervisor whom they thoroughly disliked. He had tried to introduce this same statistical technique. When the new manager brought it up, they immediately rejected it, because to them it had become a symbol of oppressive supervision.

Once the mystery had been solved, the sales manager decided to withdraw his request temporarily. After giving his men time to develop confidence in him, he reintroduced the request and had no trouble getting their cooperation.

Other communication aids

Vital as it is, feedback is only one of a number of aids the supervisor can use to improve his communicating. Here are some others:

1. *Projection.* Before you communicate something, put yourself in your listener's shoes. How is he likely to react to your message, and what should you do to make sure he understands it the way you mean it? For example, you tell an employee he is wanted in the front office. His silent reaction may be, "I'm in for a dressing-down from the big boss." If this isn't the case, you should make it clear to him.

   Often there may be a wide gap between the supervisor's experience and that of his listener. The supervisor must try to bridge that gap.

2. *Timing.* Once an erroneous belief has been established in employees' minds through rumor and misunderstanding, it is very difficult to dislodge—even with the facts. The answer is to get the facts across *before* misconceptions have a chance to gain a foothold.

3. *Believability.* Your words won't mean anything to employees if they're skeptical of your sincerity. Anything you tell them must be supported by your actions. And when something happens that contradicts what you've told them, you should give them a full explanation.

4. *Simplicity.* This is an especially important ingredient of your written communications. Every manager should put his bulletin-board announcements, policy statements, and directives in simple, direct language.

5. *Repetition.* Saying something over again often helps to make it stick. This is particularly true when you're giving an employee complicated instructions. If he misunderstands what you said the first time, he'll have a chance to catch it the next time around.

6. *Freshness.* There are times when you should avoid repetition and find new ways of saying things. Timeworn, overfamiliar phrases will be ignored by your subordinates—they'll figure they've heard it all before. Discussing this problem recently, one worker said, "I know just what the boss is going to say the minute he starts with that line about all of us being one big happy team—so I don't listen."

   It's a good idea to review your favorite phrases once in a while and replace them with fresh variations. You'll have a much better chance of gaining the attention of your listeners.

Good communication does not, of course, depend only on these techniques. It must be based as well on a healthy, cooperative relationship between the supervisor and his subordinates. The supervisor who has the confidence of his subordinates will find it much easier to explain, for example, why air conditioning must be postponed till next year than will the supervisor who hasn't. And using the techniques outlined here will help him get the message across to them.

Questions

1. What are some of the common barriers that are likely to exist in a superior-subordinate relationship that are not usually present between friends? What can be done to overcome these barriers?

2. Labor-management relations often contain barriers to communication. Why? Do you feel that any improvements are being made in this area? What evidence do you have to support your opinion?

3. Why is it important for a supervisor to listen with a "third ear" in face-to-face communication with subordinates? What precautions should one use in using his "third ear"?

4. The author advises the use of repetition but warns of some of the dangers. What are the dangers and how can they be minimized?

26. BARRIERS AND GATEWAYS TO COMMUNICATION *

Carl R. Rogers and F. J. Roethlisberger

Part I

It may seem curious that a person like myself, whose whole professional effort is devoted to psychotherapy, should be interested in problems of communication. What relationship is there between obstacles to communication and providing therapeutic help to individuals with emotional maladjustments?

Actually the relationship is very close indeed. The whole task of psychotherapy is the task of dealing with a failure in communication. The emotionally maladjusted person, the "neurotic," is in difficulty, first, because communication within himself has broken down and, secondly, because as a result of this his communication with others has been damaged. To put it another way, in the "neurotic" individual parts of himself which have been termed unconscious, or repressed, or denied to awareness, become blocked off so that they no longer communicate themselves to the conscious or managing part of himself; as long as this is true, there are distortions in the way he communicates himself to others, and so he suffers both within himself and in his interpersonal relations.

The task of psychotherapy is to help the person achieve, through a special relationship with a therapist, good communication within himself. Once this is achieved, he can communicate more freely and more effectively with others. We may say then that psychotherapy is good communication, within and between men. We may also turn that statement around and it will still be true. Good communication, free communication, within or between men, is always therapeutic.

It is, then, from a background of experience with communication in counseling and psychotherapy that I want to present two ideas: (1) I wish to state what I believe is one of the major factors in blocking or impeding communication, and then (2) I wish to present what in our experience has proved to be a very important way of improving or facilitating communication.

* From *Harvard Business Review*, Vol. 30, No. 4 (July-August, 1952), pp. 46-52. Reprinted with permission.

Barrier: the tendency to evaluate

I should like to propose, as a hypothesis for consideration, that the major barrier to mutual interpersonal communication is our very natural tendency to judge, to evaluate, to approve (or disapprove) the statement of the other person or the other group. Let me illustrate my meaning with some very simple examples. Suppose someone, commenting on this discussion, makes the statement, "I didn't like what that man said." What will you respond? Almost invariably your reply will be either approval or disapproval of the attitude expressed. Either you respond, "I didn't either; I thought it was terrible," or else you tend to reply, "Oh, I thought it was really good." In other words, your primary reaction is to evaluate it from *your* point of view, your own frame of reference.

Or take another example. Suppose I say with some feeling, "I think the Republicans are behaving in ways that show a lot of good sound sense these days." What is the response that arises in your mind? The overwhelming likelihood is that it will be evaluative. In other words, you will find yourself agreeing, or disagreeing, or making some judgment about me such as "He must be a conservative," or "He seems solid in his thinking." Or let us take an illustration from the international scene. Russia says vehemently, "The treaty with Japan is a war plot on the part of the United States." We rise as one person to say, "That's a lie!"

This last illustration brings in another element connected with my hypothesis. Although the tendency to make evaluations is common in almost all interchange of language, it is very much heightened in those situations where feelings and emotions are deeply involved. So the stronger our feelings, the more likely it is that there will be no mutual element in the communication. There will be just two ideas, two feelings, two judgments, missing each other in psychological space.

I am sure you recognize this from your own experience. When you have not been emotionally involved yourself and have listened to a heated discussion, you often go away thinking, "Well, they actually weren't talking about the same thing." And they were not. Each was making a judgment, an evaluation, from his own frame of reference. There was really nothing which could be called communication in any genuine sense. This tendency to react to any emotionally meaningful statement by forming an evaluation of it from our own point of view is, I repeat, the major barrier to interpersonal communication.

Gateway: listening with understanding

Is there any way of solving this problem, of avoiding this barrier? I feel that we are making exciting progress toward this goal, and I should like to present it as simply as I can. Real communication occurs, and this evaluative tendency is avoided, when we listen with understanding. What does that mean? It means to see the expressed idea and attitude from the other person's point of view, to sense how it feels to him, to achieve his frame of reference in regard to the thing he is talking about.

Stated so briefly, this may sound absurdly simple, but it is not. It is an approach which we have found extremely potent in the field of psychotherapy. It is the most effective agent we know for altering the basic personality structure of an individual and for improving his relationships and his communications with others. If I can listen to what he can tell me, if I can understand how it seems to him, if I can see its personal meaning for him, if I can sense the emotional flavor which it has for him, then I will be releasing potent forces of change in him.

Again, if I can really understand how he hates his father, or hates the company, or hates Communists—if I can catch the flavor of his fear of insanity, or his fear of atom bombs, or of Russia—it will be of the greatest help to him in altering those hatreds and fears and in establishing realistic and harmonious relationships with the very people and situations toward which he has felt hatred and fear. We know from our research that such empathic understanding—understanding *with* a person, not *about* him—is such an effective approach that it can bring about major changes in personality.

Some of you may be feeling that you listen well to people and yet you have never seen such results. The chances are great indeed that your listening has not been of the type I have described. Fortunately, I can suggest a little laboratory experiment which you can try to test the quality of your understanding. The next time you get into an argument with your wife, or your friend, or with a small group of friends, just stop the discussion for a moment and, for an experiment, institute this rule: "Each person can speak up for himself only *after* he has first restated the ideas and feelings of the previous speaker accurately and to that speaker's satisfaction."

You see what this would mean. It would simply mean that before presenting your own point of view, it would be necessary for you to achieve the other speaker's frame of reference—to understand his thoughts and feelings so well that you could summarize them for him.

Sounds simple, doesn't it? But if you try it, you will discover that it is one of the most difficult things you have ever tried to do. However, once you have been able to see the other's point of view, your own comments will have to be drastically revised. You will also find the emotion going out of the discussion, the differences being reduced, and those differences which remain being of a rational and understandable sort.

Can you imagine what this kind of an approach would mean if it were projected into larger areas? What would happen to a labor-management dispute if it were conducted in such a way that labor, without necessarily agreeing, could accurately state management's point of view in a way that management could accept; and management, without approving labor's stand, could state labor's case in a way that labor agreed was accurate? It would mean that real communication was established, and one could practically guarantee that some reasonable solution would be reached.

If, then, this way of approach is an effective avenue to good communication and good relationships, as I am quite sure you will agree if you try the experiment I have mentioned, why is it not more widely tried and used? I will try to list the difficulties which keep it from being utilized.

Need for Courage. In the first place it takes courage, a quality which is not too widespread. I am indebted to Dr. S. I. Hayakawa, the semanticist, for pointing out that to carry on psychotherapy in this fashion is to take a very real risk, and that courage is required. If you really understand another person in this way, if you are willing to enter his private world and see the way life appears to him, without any attempt to make evaluative judgments, you run the risk of being changed yourself. You might see it his way; you might find yourself influenced in your attitudes or your personality.

This risk of being changed is one of the most frightening prospects many of us can face. If I enter, as fully as I am able, into the private world of a neurotic or psychotic individual, isn't there a risk that I might become lost in that world? Most of us are afraid to take that risk. Or if we were listening to a Russian Communist, or Senator Joe McCarthy, how many of us would dare to try to see the world from each of their points of view? The great majority of us could not *listen*; we would find ourselves compelled to *evaluate*, because listening would seem too dangerous. So the first requirement is courage, and we do not always have it.

Heightened Emotions. But there is a second obstacle. It is just when emotions are strongest that it is most difficult to achieve the frame of reference of the other person or group. Yet it is then that the attitude is most needed if communication is to be established. We have not found this to be an insuperable obstacle in our experience in psychotherapy. A third party, who is able to lay aside his own feelings and evaluations, can assist greatly by listening with understanding to each person or group and clarifying the views and attitudes each holds.

We have found this effective in small groups in which contradictory or antagonistic attitudes exist. When the parties to a dispute realize that they are being understood, that someone sees how the situation seems to them, the statements grow less exaggerated and less defensive, and it is no longer necessary to maintain the attitude, "I am 100% right and you are 100% wrong." The influence of such an understanding catalyst in the group permits the members to come closer and closer to the objective truth involved in the relationship. In this way mutual communication is established, and some type of agreement becomes much more possible.

So we may say that though heightened emotions make it much more difficult to understand *with* an opponent, our experience makes it clear that a neutral, understanding, catalyst type of leader or therapist can overcome this obstacle in a small group.

Size of Group. That last phrase, however, suggests another obstacle to utilizing the approach I have described. Thus far all our experience has been with small face-to-face groups—groups exhibiting industrial tensions, religious tensions, racial tensions, and therapy groups in which many personal tensions are present. In these small groups our experience, confirmed by a limited amount of research, shows that this basic approach leads to improved communication, to greater acceptance of others and by others, and to attitudes which are more positive and more problem-solving in nature. There is a decrease in defensiveness, in exaggerated statements, in evaluative and critical behavior.

But these findings are from small groups. What about trying to achieve understanding between larger groups that are geographically remote, or between face-to-face groups that are not speaking for themselves but simply as representatives of others, like the delegates at Kaesong? Frankly we do not know the answers to these questions. I believe the situation might be put this way: As social scientists we have a tentative test-tube solution of the problem of breakdown in communication. But to confirm the validity of this test-tube solution and to adapt it to the enormous problems of communication breakdown between classes, groups, and nations would involve additional funds, much more research, and creative thinking of a high order.

Yet with our present limited knowledge we can see some steps which might be taken even in large groups to increase the amount of listening *with* and decrease the amount of evaluation *about*. To be imaginative for a moment, let us suppose that a therapeutically oriented international group went to the Russian leaders and said, "We want to achieve a genuine understanding of your views and, even more important, of your attitudes and feelings toward the United States. We will summarize and resummarize these views and feelings if necessary, until you agree that our description represents the situation as it seems to you."

Then suppose they did the same thing with the leaders in our own country. If they then gave the widest possible distribution to these two views, with the feelings clearly described but not expressed in name-calling, might not the effect be very great? It would not guarantee the type of understanding I have been describing, but it would make it much more possible. We can understand the feelings of a person who hates us much more readily when his attitudes are accurately described to us by a neutral third party than we can when he is shaking his fist at us.

Faith in Social Sciences. But even to describe such a first step is to suggest another obstacle to this approach of understanding. Our civilization does not yet have enough faith in the social sciences to utilize their findings. The opposite is true of the physical sciences. During the war when a test-tube solution was found to the problem of synthetic rubber, millions of dollars and an army of talent were turned loose on the problem of using that finding. If synthetic rubber could be made in milligrams, it could and would be made in the thousands of tons. And it was. But in the social science realm, if a way is found of facilitating communication and mutual understanding in small groups, there is no guarantee that the finding will be utilized. It may be a generation or more before the money and the brains will be turned loose to exploit that finding.

Summary

In closing, I should like to summarize this small-scale solution to the problem of barriers in communication, and to point out certain of its characteristics.

I have said that our research and experience to date would make it appear that breakdowns in communication, and the evaluative tendency which is the major barrier to communication, can be avoided. The solution is provided by creating a situation in which each of the different parties comes to understand the other from the *other's* point of view. This has been achieved, in practice, even when feelings run high, by the influence of a person who is willing to understand each point of view empathically, and who thus acts as a catalyst to precipitate further understanding.

This procedure has important characteristics. It can be initiated by one party, without waiting for the other to be ready. It can even be initiated by a neutral third person, provided he can gain a minimum of cooperation from one of the parties.

This procedure can deal with the insincerities, the defensive exaggerations, and lies, the "false fronts" which characterize almost every failure in communication. These defensive distortions drop away with astonishing speed as people find that the only intent is to understand, not to judge.

This approach leads steadily and rapidly toward the discovery of the truth, toward a realistic appraisal of the objective barriers to communication. The dropping of some defensiveness by one party leads to further dropping of defensiveness by the other party, and truth is thus approached.

This procedure gradually achieves mutual communication. Mutual communication tends to be pointed toward solving a problem rather than toward attacking a person or group. It leads to a situation in which I see how the problem appears to you as well as to me, and you see how it appears to me as well as to you. Thus accurately and realistically defined, the problem is almost certain to yield to intelligent attack; or if it is in part insoluble, it will be comfortably accepted as such.

This then appears to be a test-tube solution to the breakdown of communication as it occurs in small groups. Can we take this small-scale answer, investigate it further, refine it, develop it, and apply it to the tragic and well-nigh fatal failures of communication which threaten the very existence of our modern world? It seems to me that this is a possibility and a challenge which we should explore.

Part II

In thinking about the many barriers to personal communication, particularly those that are due to differences of background, experience, and motivation, it seems to me extraordinary that any two persons can ever understand each other. Such reflections provoke the question of how communication is possible when people do not see and assume the same things and share the same values.

On this question there are two schools of thought. One school assumes that communication between A and B, for example, has failed when B does not accept what A has to say as being fact, true, or valid; and that the goal of communication is to get B to agree with A's opinions, ideas, facts, or information.

The position of the other school of thought is quite different. It assumes that communication has failed when B does not feel free to express his feelings to A because B fears they will not be accepted by A. Communication is facilitated when on the part of A or B or both there is a willingness to express and accept differences.

As these are quite divergent conceptions, let us explore them further with an example. Bill, an employee, is talking with his boss in the boss's office. The boss says, "I think, Bill, that this is the best way to do your job." Bill says, "Oh yeah!" According to the first school of thought, this reply would be a sign of poor communication. Bill does not understand the best way of doing his work. To improve communication, therefore, it is up to the boss to explain to Bill why his way is the best.

From the point of view of the second school of thought, Bill's reply is a sign neither of good nor of bad communication. Bill's response is indeterminate. But the boss has an opportunity to find out what Bill means if he so desires. Let us assume that this is what he chooses to do, i.e., find out what Bill means. So this boss tries to get Bill to talk more about his job while he (the boss) listens.

For purposes of simplification, I shall call the boss representing the first school of thought *"Smith"* and the boss representing the second school of thought *"Jones."* In the presence of the so-called same stimulus each behaves differently. Smith chooses to *explain*; Jones chooses to *listen*. In my experience Jones's response works better than Smith's. It works better because Jones is making a more proper evaluation of what is taking place between him and Bill than Smith is. Let us test this hypothesis by continuing with our example.

What Smith assumes, sees, and feels

Smith assumes that he understands what Bill means when Bill says, "Oh yeah!" so there is no need to find out. Smith is sure that Bill does not understand why this is the best way to do his job, so Smith has to tell him. In this process let us assume Smith is logical, lucid, and clear. He presents his facts and evidence well. But, alas, Bill remains unconvinced. What does Smith do? Operating under the assumption that what is taking place between him and Bill is something essentially logical, Smith can draw only one of two conclusions: either (1) he has not been clear enough, or (2) Bill is too damned stupid to understand. So he either has to "spell out" his case in words of fewer and fewer syllables or give up. Smith is reluctant to do the latter, so he continues to explain. What happens?

If Bill still does not accept Smith's explanation of why this is the best way for him to do his job, a pattern of interacting feelings is produced of which Smith is often unaware. The more Smith cannot get Bill to understand him, the more frustrated Smith becomes and the more Bill becomes a threat to his logical capacity. Since Smith sees himself as a fairly reasonable and logical chap, this is a difficult feeling to accept. It is much easier for him to perceive Bill as uncooperative or stupid. This perception, however, will affect what Smith says and does. Under these pressures Bill comes to be evaluated more and more in terms of Smith's values. By this process Smith tends to treat Bill's values as unimportant. He tends to deny Bill's uniqueness and difference. He treats Bill as if he had little capacity for self-direction.

Let us be clear. Smith does not see that he is doing these things. When he is feverishly scratching hieroglyphics on the back of an envelope, trying to explain to Bill why this is the best way to do his job, Smith is trying to be helpful. He is a man of goodwill, and he wants to set Bill straight. This is the way Smith sees himself and his behavior. But it is for this very reason that Bill's "Oh yeah!" is getting under Smith's skin.

"How dumb can a guy be?" is Smith's attitude, and unfortunately Bill will hear that more than Smith's good intentions. Bill will feel misunderstood. He will not see Smith as a man of goodwill trying to be helpful. Rather he will perceive him as a threat to his self-esteem and personal integrity. Against this threat Bill will feel the need to defend himself at all cost. Not being so logically articulate as Smith, Bill expresses this need, again, by saying, "Oh yeah!"

What Jones assumes, sees, and feels

Let us leave this sad scene between Smith and Bill, which I fear is going to terminate by Bill's either leaving in a huff or being kicked out of Smith's office. Let us turn for a moment to Jones and see what he is assuming, seeing, hearing, feeling, doing, and saying when he interacts with Bill.

Jones, it will be remembered, does not assume that he knows what Bill means when he says, "Oh yeah!" so he has to find out. Moreover, he assumes that when Bill said this, he had not exhausted his vocabulary or his feelings. Bill may not necessarily mean one thing; he may mean several different things. So Jones decides to listen.

In this process Jones is not under any illusion that what will take place will be eventually logical. Rather he is assuming that what will take place will be primarily an interaction of feelings. Therefore, he cannot ignore the feelings of Bill, the effect of Bill's feelings on him, or the effect of his feelings on Bill. In other words, he cannot ignore his relationship to Bill; he cannot assume that it will make no difference to what Bill will hear or accept.

Therefore, Jones will be paying strict attention to all of the things Smith has ignored. He will be addressing himself to Bill's feelings, his own, and the interactions between them.

Jones will therefore realize that he has ruffled Bill's feelings with his comment, "I think, Bill, this is the best way to do your job." So instead of trying to get Bill to understand him, he decides to try to understand Bill. He does this by encouraging Bill to speak. Instead of telling Bill how he should feel or think, he asks Bill such questions as, "Is this what you feel?" "Is this what you see?" "Is this what you assume?" Instead of ignoring Bill's evaluations as irrelevant, not valid, inconsequential, or false, he tries to understand Bill's reality as he feels it, perceives it, and assumes it to be. As Bill begins to open up, Jones's curiosity is piqued by this process.

"Bill isn't so dumb; he's quite an interesting guy" becomes Jones's attitude. And that is what Bill hears. Therefore Bill feels understood and accepted as a person. He becomes less defensive. He is in a better frame of mind to explore and re-examine his own perceptions, feelings, and assumptions. In this process he perceives Jones as a source of help. Bill feels free to express his differences. He feels that Jones has some respect for his capacity for self-direction. These positive feelings toward Jones make Bill more inclined to say, "Well,

Jones, I don't quite agree with you that this is the best way to do my job, but I'll tell you what I'll do. I'll try to do it that way for a few days, and then I'll tell you what I think."

Conclusion

I grant that my two orientations do not work themselves out in practice in quite so simple or neat a fashion as I have been able to work them out on paper. There are many other ways in which Bill could have responded to Smith in the first place. He might even have said, "O.K., boss, I agree that your way of doing my job is better." But Smith still would not have known how Bill felt when he made this statement or whether Bill was actually going to do his job differently. Likewise, Bill could have responded to Jones in a way different from my example. In spite of Jones's attitude, Bill might still be reluctant to express himself freely to his boss.

The purpose of my examples has not been to demonstrate the right or wrong way of communicating. My purpose has been simply to provide something concrete to point to when I make the following generalizations:

(1) Smith represents to me a very common pattern of misunderstanding. The misunderstanding does not arise because Smith is not clear enough in expressing himself. It arises because of Smith's misevaluation of what is taking place when two people are talking together.

(2) Smith's misevaluation of the process of personal communication consists of certain very common assumptions, e.g., (a) that what is taking place is something essentially logical; (b) that words in themselves apart from the people involved mean something; and (c) that the purpose of the interaction is to get Bill to see things from Smith's point of view.

(3) Because of these assumptions, a chain reaction of perceptions and negative feelings is engendered which blocks communication. By ignoring Bill's feelings and by rationalizing his own, Smith ignores his relationship to Bill as one of the most important determinants of the communication. As a result, Bill hears Smith's attitude more clearly than the logical content of Smith's words. Bill feels that his individual uniqueness is being denied. His personal integrity being at stake, he becomes defensive and belligerent. As a result, Smith

feels frustrated. He perceives Bill as stupid. So he says and does things which only provoke more defensiveness on the part of Bill.

(4) In the case of Jones, I have tried to show what might possibly happen if we made a different evaluation of what is taking place when two people are talking together. Jones makes a different set of assumptions. He assumes (a) that what is taking place between him and Bill is an interaction of sentiments; (b) that Bill—not his words in themselves—means something; (c) that the object of the interaction is to give Bill an opportunity to express freely his differences.

(5) Because of these assumptions, a psychological chain reaction of reinforcing feelings and perceptions is set up which facilitates communication between Bill and him. When Jones addresses himself to Bill's feelings and perceptions from Bill's point of view, Bill feels understood and accepted as a person; he feels free to express his differences. Bill sees Jones as a source of help; Jones sees Bill as an interesting person. Bill in turn becomes more cooperative.

(6) If I have identified correctly these very common patterns of personal communication, then some interesting hypotheses can be stated:

> (a) Jones's method works better than Smith's, not because of any magic, but because Jones has a better map than Smith of the process of personal communication.
>
> (b) The practice of Jones's method, however, is not merely an intellectual exercise. It depends on Jones's capacity and willingness to see and accept points of view different from his own, and to practice this orientation in a face-to-face relationship. This practice involves an emotional as well as an intellectual achievement. It depends in part on Jones's awareness of himself, in part on the practice of a skill.
>
> (c) Although our colleges and universities try to get students to appreciate intellectually points of view different from their own, very little is done to help them to implement this general intellectual appreciation in a simple face-to-face relationship—at the level of a skill. Most educational institutions train their students to be logical, lucid, and clear. Very little is done to help them to listen more skillfully. As a result, our educated world contains too many Smiths and too few Joneses.
>
> (d) The biggest block to personal communication is man's inability to listen intelligently, understandingly, and skillfully to another person. This deficiency in the modern world is widespread and appalling. In our universities as well as elsewhere, too little is being done about it.

(7) In conclusion, let me apologize for acting toward you the way Smith did. But who am I to violate a long-standing academic tradition!

Questions

1. What does Rogers mean by the statement "good communication, free communication, with or between men, is always therapeutic"? Discuss.
2. Is any evaluation of what another person says undesirable? Why?
3. What is the fundamental difference between Smith and Jones? Would you classify the majority of managers and supervisors as Smiths or Joneses? Why?
4. The authors mention that if we are to understand others we cannot use only a logical approach. What is meant by this?
5. Some executives are likely to feel that it is a sign of weakness to listen when their job is to direct the activities of others. Is there any incompatibility between listening and carrying out the directive functions of leadership? Discuss.
6. Why are we slow to have faith in the social sciences yet readily accept the research findings of the physical sciences?

27. THE CASE FOR PARTICIPATIVE MANAGEMENT *

Keith Davis

Participation is an overworked word in business and government, but an underworked activity. The idea sounds good to most managers, but they are frequently unsure of what to do with it. Some grossly misinterpret what it is, so that when they say, "Participation is great," they are really talking about something else; others are not sure when to apply it or how far to go with it.

One reason for the slow growth of participation is that it is a difficult philosophy to understand, and even more difficult to develop in a group. Genuine social science skill is required to make participation work. Many supervisors get in over their heads in a burst of enthusiasm and, after experiencing a rebuff, tend to withdraw from further efforts at participation. It appears that improperly applied participation may be worse for productivity and morale than simply doing nothing. Ineffective attempts to secure participation may make a group feel manipulated, resentful, confused, or lacking in objectives.

In spite of the difficulty of developing participation, it does have enormous potential for raising productivity, bettering morale, and improving creative thinking. The need of people to participate is not a passing fancy. It is rooted deep in the culture of free men around the world, and it is probably a basic drive in man.[1] Because of its significance and permanence, participation is a method to which leaders need to devote long-range efforts. Means of tapping this source of creativity and of using its cohesive power for teamwork need to be developed. Participation affords a means of building some of the human values needed in a group. It can create an asset in morale so that when necessary orders are given, people will respond more cooperatively because they are participating in their group, although they did not participate in determining the instruction they

---

* From *Business Horizons*, Vol. 6, No. 3 (Fall, 1963), pp. 55-60. Reprinted with permission.

[1] Comparative studies in England and the United States suggest that participation is a basic human drive rather than a cultural acquisition. *See* N. R. F. Maier and L. R. Hoffman, "Group Decision in England and the United States," *Personnel Psychology*, XV (Spring, 1962), p. 86.

have most recently received. The importance of participation has been described as follows:

> Two thousand years ago we put participation in the religion which has come to dominate the Western world. Two hundred years ago we put this essential element in our political and social structure. We are just beginning to realize that we ought to put participation in business as well.[2]

Classical experiments

Classical experiments by Roethlisberger, Bavelas, and Coch and French confirm our belief that participation is extremely valuable. Roethlisberger and his associates originally sought to show the relationship of physical change in environment and output. In the course of their experiments, new relationships, many of them involving participation, developed between workers and supervisors, and workers and experimenters. The results convincingly showed that these social changes improved both productivity and morale. Although participation was not the whole cause of these improvements, it seemed to be a significant cause.[3]

Bavelas worked with a group of women performing a sewing operation on a group incentive basis. For his experiment, he chose a superior group whose production averaged about 74 units hourly, with a range of 70 to 78. He asked them to set their own production goal. After considerable discussion they agreed unanimously on a goal of 84 units hourly, which they exceeded within five days. A goal of 95, set at a later meeting, could not be met. The goal was then reduced to the relatively permanent level of 90 units. During the next several months, the group's output averaged about 87 units with a range of 80 to 93. The net increase after participation was about 13 units hourly.[4] Coch and French achieved similar results in experiments with sewing machine operators.[5]

---

[2] Ralph M. Besse, "Business Statesmanship," *Personnel Administration,* XX (January-February, 1957), p. 12.

[3] F. J. Roethlisberger, *Management and Morale* (Cambridge: Harvard University Press, 1941), p. 14.

[4] Norman R. F. Maier, *Psychology in Industry* (Boston: Houghton Mifflin Company, 1946), pp. 264-66. Lawrence and Smith have since repeated Bavelas' experiments with similar results. *See* Lois C. Lawrence and Patricia Cain Smith, "Group Decision and Employee Participation," *The Journal of Applied Psychology,* XXXIX (October, 1955), pp. 334-37.

[5] Lester Coch and John R. P. French, Jr., "Overcoming Resistance to Change," *Human Relations,* I (No. 4, 1948), pp. 512-32 and John R. P. French, Jr. and Alvin Zander, "The Group Dynamics Approach," in Arthur Kornhauser, ed., *Psychology of Labor-Management Relations* (Champaign, Ill.: Industrial Relations Research Association, 1949), pp. 73-75.

The benefits of participation are evident in the experience of a large aircraft manufacturer, who employed from 5,000 to 20,000 shopworkers during the decade following World War II. The company used a safety committee system in which each department was represented by one worker. During these ten years, not one person suffered a disabling injury while serving as safety committeeman. This record was made despite the facts that hundreds of workers served on the committee during the decade, and accident-prone workers sometimes were appointed to the post in order to make them safety conscious. Although some committeemen probably returned to work earlier than they should have after an accident in order to preserve their record, the facts still show a significant difference between committeemen and other workers. Part of the difference was surely due to the fact that the committeemen were participating in a safety program.

Participation is especially important in encouraging people to accept change, a persistent pressure on all of us in our dynamic society. Participation is helpful both in planning and installing change, because when employees understand the objectives and content of a change, they are confident that management is not trying to "pull a fast one" on them. Participation may actually improve carefully devised management plans, because it elicits the ideas of the persons who are most thoroughly acquainted with the working effects of those plans. It may cancel a poor plan and thus save management many headaches. In any case, it broadens the outlook of those involved and helps them feel that they have an active part in what is taking place.

When a change is within management's control, such as the determination of a new work method, best results are realized when the group participates in the recognition of the need for change. Participation is less effective if it begins only after management has decided that a change is necessary.

Key ideas in participation

Participation is defined as an individual's mental and emotional involvement in a group situation that encourages him to contribute to group goals and to share responsibility for them. This definition contains three important ideas.

First, participation means mental and emotional involvement rather than mere muscular activity. The involvement of a person's *self*, rather than just his skill, is the product of his mind and his emotions. The person who participates is ego-involved instead of merely task-involved.[6] Some managers mistake task-involvement for true participation. They go through the motions of participation, but it is clear to employees that their manager is an autocrat who does not really want their ideas. Employees cannot become involved in this kind of situation.

A *second* important characteristic of participation is that it motivates contribution. Individuals are given an opportunity to direct their initiative and creativity toward the objectives of the group. In this way, participation differs from consent,[7] which uses only the creativity and ideas of the leader who brings his idea to the group for their approval. Participation requires more than mere approval of something already decided. It is a two-way psychological and social relationship among people rather than a procedure imposing ideas from above.

A *third* characteristic of participation is that it encourages people to accept responsibility for an activity. Because they are self-involved in the group, they want to see it work successfully. Participation helps them become responsible citizens rather than non-responsible automatons. As individuals begin to accept responsibility for group activities, they become interested in and receptive to teamwork, because they see in it a means of accomplishing a job for which they feel responsible. A person who is actively involved in something is naturally more committed to carrying it out. Of his own free will, he creates responsibility rather than having it forced upon him by delegation. By making himself responsible, he gains a measure of independence and dignity as an individual making his own decisions, even though these decisions are heavily influenced by his group environment.

Managers often ask, "If I share decisions with my personnel, don't I lose authority? I can't afford to give up authority because I'm responsible." This is a perfectly normal worry of an executive who is considering the values of participation for the first time, but it is hardly a justifiable worry. The participative manager still retains his authority to decide. He shares his problems with the group by means of a process that may be called social delegation. Social

[6] Gordon W. Allport, "The Psychology of Participation," *The Psychological Review*, LIII (May, 1945), p. 22.

[7] Mary P. Follett, "The Psychology of Consent and Participation," in *Dynamic Administration: The Collected Papers of Mary Parker Follett*, eds. Henry C. Metcalf and L. Urwick (New York: Harper and Brothers, 1941), pp. 210-12.

delegation in the human relations domain is comparable to formal delegation in the organizational domain. Neither type of delegation weakens a manager's organizational authority. No manager of the future—say twenty years hence—will object to a certain amount of social delegation through participation under normal conditions. It will be as much his stock in trade as formal delegation is today.

Practice limitations

These experiments (and the conclusions drawn from them) have a number of limitations that managers cannot ignore. Their success is no guarantee that all similar practices will be successful. The experiments described were performed by professional men skilled in human relations; similar efforts by ordinary supervisors undoubtedly would not produce such consistent results. The step from experimentation to practice is a long one indeed. The experiments were mostly one-shot efforts in a narrow work situation, using small groups who were doing repetitive work and undergoing changes. Participation in large work groups may be more difficult. In any case, managers should not go overboard for participation as they once did for scientific management. The latter was a worthwhile development, but managers' failure to recognize its uses and limitations in particular situations nearly ruined it.

In developing participation, we must be able to strike a precarious balance between counterfeit participation, which would arouse distrust, and excessive participation, which would consume valuable work time and destroy unified direction. Many issues are involved. Counterfeit participation may be tinsel and ribbon to make people happy, or it may be a more insidious tool handled by skilled social scientists, the engineers of consent.

Another danger of participation—as was true of scientific management—is that practitioners will get lost in the procedures of participation and overlook its philosophy. The substance of participation does not automatically flow from its procedures; there is no such mechanistic connection. Rather, when procedures are used at the right time and in the right circumstances, they enable it to develop.

Another issue concerns a person's right not to participate. There is no evidence that advanced participation is required for everybody; there is evidence that many persons do not want to be bothered with participation. Shall we force them into a mold merely because we think it is good for them? Some persons want a minimum of inter-action with their supervisor and associates. The role expectation of many employees is to work for an autocratic supervisor, and con-sequently they produce effectively with this type of leadership. Research shows that the more authoritarian personality derives less benefit from participative methods, while the more equalitarian per-sonality is more favorably affected.[8] Sometimes a group can be kept participating only by pressure from above. When that pressure is released, the group reverts to patterns of less participation.[9]

Prerequisites for participation

Finally, it should be emphasized that the success of participation is directly related to how well certain prerequisites are satisfied. Some of these conditions occur in the participants; some exist in the environment. Taken together, they mean that participation works better in some situations than others—and that in certain situations, it works not at all.[10]

The first prerequisite is that ample time must be allowed to participate before action is required. Participation may not be appro-priate in emergency situations. Second, the financial cost of par-ticipation should not exceed the values, economic and otherwise, that it produces. Third, the subject of participation must be relevant to the participant's organization, something in which he is interested, or he will regard it as mere busy work. Fourth, the participant should have the abilities, intelligence, and knowledge to participate effectively.

Fifth, the participants must be able to communicate in order to be able to exchange ideas. Sixth, no one (employee or manager) should feel that his position is threatened by participation. Seventh, par-ticipation for deciding a course of action in an organization can take place only within the group's area of job freedom. Some degree of restriction on subunits is necessary in any organization in order to maintain internal stability; subunits cannot make decisions that

[8] Victor H. Vroom, "Some Personality Determinants of the Effects of Par-ticipation," *Journal of Abnormal and Social Psychology*, LIX (November, 1959), pp. 322-27.

[9] Robert N. McMurry, "The Case for Benevolent Autocracy," *Harvard Busi-ness Review*, XXXVI (January-February, 1958), pp. 82-90.

[10] For further explanation, *see* Robert Tannenbaum, Irving R. Weschler, and Fred Massarik, *Leadership and Organization: A Behavioral Science Approach* (New York: McGraw-Hill Book Company, Inc., 1961), pp. 88-100.

violate company policy, collective bargaining agreements, or similar restraints.

Since participation is a deep-seated need of man, it is worth trying: (1) if the manager understands what he is doing; (2) if he has developed some social science skill; (3) if he will meet the prerequisites; (4) if he will respect the role expectations of his people; and (5) if he will begin in a small way, rather than shooting for the moon in the first few months. Managers should proceed with caution, building each improvement upon past successes—but by all means, they should proceed.

Questions

1. How does Davis define "participation"? In what way does it relate to the continuum of leadership by Tannenbaum and Schmidt (Article 22)?
2. Will the composition of the work group affect the extent to which its members will accept responsibility for group activities? Explain.
3. Is there a relationship between participation and employee motivation? Explain.
4. Why do managers sometimes resist sharing decision making with subordinates? How can this resistance be overcome?

28. ORGANIZATION MAN— PROSPECT FOR THE FUTURE *

George Strauss

Should the primary qualifications of a manager be skill in human relations or the ability to make good decisions?[1] Should he be an individualist or a conformist, a specialist, or a generalist? Should he dedicate himself, body and soul, to the company's service or should he keep a significant part of his life "private"? At what point should he think of his personal off-the-job satisfactions and tell the company to go hang? These related questions—according to such varied novelists and essayists as Ayn Rand, Ernest Dale, J. P. Marquand, David Riesman, Sloan Wilson, Malcolm McNair, Philip Wylie, and Herman Wouk—are among the central dilemmas of our society.[2] William H. Whyte's indictment of *The Organization Man* has become a classic.

The various authors seem to make two basic charges against Organization Man: first, that he is too much of a conformist, and second, that he pays too much attention to human relations and not enough to decision-making. As I shall suggest, these two charges are in general interrelated. The man who emphasizes human relations is likely to be a conformist, but there are exceptional cases where this does not hold and the two charges must be considered separately.

Conformity

The first charge against Organization Man is that he is too conformist, too unimaginative, too afraid to make bold decisions.

* Reprinted from the *California Management Review*, Vol. VI, No. 3, Spring, 1964. Copyright 1964 by The Regents of the University of California.

[1] The author is indebted for helpful suggestions in the preparation of this paper to Professors Vaughn Blankenship, Edward Feigenbaum, and Lyman Porter, all of the University of California, Berkeley.

[2] Conformity seems to have been a major issue throughout American intellectual history. De Tocqueville commented on it in the 1830's. George F. Babbitt was the Organization Man of the 1920's. But there is a significant change: the big-city corporation rather than the small-town main street is now the villain. Some of these questions are discussed by Seymour M. Lipset in his "A Changing American Character?" in *Culture and Social Character*, eds. Seymour M. Lipset and Leo Lowenthal (Glencoe: The Free Press, 1961).

Instead, in his behavior, his leisure, his social activities, his opinions, even his private values, he tries to conform to safe, accepted middle-class standards. And so his performance is also safely mediocre. (Some suggest that Organization Man conforms by not being overly ambitious; by keeping his personal ambition in check and by disavowing strong urges to get to the top, he serves the company better than if he were highly competitive.)

Kinds of conformity

I should like to suggest that the concept of conformity may be oversimplified, and that at least three kinds of conformity may be involved:

1. Conformity to accepted middle-class standards.
2. Organizational loyalty or conformity to organizational objectives.
3. Group cohesion, or conformity to the values of one's own work group.

As we shall see, it is sometimes impossible to practice all three forms of conformity at once. For the most part, I shall be concerned with the second form of conformity, organizational loyalty.

Human Relations

The second charge is that Organization Man is primarily a human relations expert rather than a decision-maker; back slapping is more important to him than creative thinking. In a recent article, Ernest Dale observes:

> The new manager is above all an expert on human relations. Some even equate management entirely with human relations. Like the teacher who teaches children, not subjects, these managers declare that management *is* the direction of people. What the people should be doing and how they should be doing it are, again, the problems of the specialist.[3]

Whyte's book would not have been as popular as it was if it hadn't reached home, if it hadn't drawn blood.[4] His caricature of

---

[3] "Executives Who Can't Manage," *Atlantic*, July, 1962.

[4] Ironically, for a while a new wave of conformity swept industry: a near-unanimous denunciation of conformity—and the wolf-pack was led by top executives and personnel directors of some of America's most conformity-requiring companies. Elsewhere I have suggested that the antihuman relations aspects of this crusade are related to management's recent be-tough-to-unions policy. *See* George Strauss, "The Shifting Power Balance in the Plant," *Industrial Relations*, Vol. I, No. 3 (1962), pp. 65-96.

management has raised serious moral and organizational problems. But the indictment is overdrawn and the issues oversimplified.

I will try to evaluate the pressures which lead to greater or less emphasis on conformity and human relations. I shall first consider the pressures which arise out of three new organizational trends: functionalization, decentralization, and computerization. Then I will look at the pressures arising out of management development. Finally, I will attempt a new evaluation of where Organization Man stands today.

My first thesis is that, far from dominating the scene, Organization Man is subject to strong competition from three other organizational trends. These are:

1. *Functionalization*—the growth of a sense of professional and departmental identification among functional specialists.
2. *Decentralization.*
3. *Computerization*—the impact of "information technology" and the computer.

The first two trends facilitate and reward individual and departmental diversity. The impact of the computer is less clear, but on balance it seems to favor greater emphasis on analytical skills and individualistic thinking at higher levels of management and on human relations and possibly organizational loyalty at lower levels.

Functionalism and professionalism

Not too long ago the vast majority of employees in most companies belonged to line—were engaged in the firm's primary function —production in a factory, sales in a store, etc. But the picture is changing fairly rapidly in many organizations today: staff or functional groups—accounting, personnel, quality control, research, development, and the like—are growing in size and status, so at times staff seems to be the tail that wags the dog.

Staff dealings. In large firms today, staff tends to deal not with line, but with other staff departments. Take a routine activity: sales lands a big order; sales liaison passes it on to the production scheduling, which in turn asks engineering for blueprints and specifications; engineering writes specifications, on the basis of which production scheduling writes requisitions; with these requisitions in hand, purchasing places orders for components. A dozen functional departments may be concerned before the "work flow" involves a single production worker or a single member of what is normally known as line management.

Normally interdepartmental "work flow" relations run smoothly, but even in the best-run organizations there is considerable pulling and hauling among departments. Naturally each function seeks to advance its own point of view; design engineering, for example, looks for technical perfection, industrial engineering for manufacturing ease, and marketing for sales appeal. In addition to differences in point of view, there are status conflicts: each function feels that its importance is under-recognized by other functions and by top management.

To complicate matters further, there is evidence to suggest that many functional fields are turning to professionalism as a means of bolstering their own self-esteem, of raising their status, and of strengthening their position against other departments.[5] Engineering and accounting have already achieved professional status; purchasing and, to a lesser extent personnel, among others, are striving in that direction. Hopefully, once a department is accepted as a profession, other departments will be less likely to dispute its professional judgment. Further, as a profession it will be able to keep nonprofessionals from poaching on its preserves and will be able to disregard orders from higher management which would require it to engage in what it considers to be unprofessional acts.

Thus, the picture which we get when we look at functional and professional departments is not that of a highly co-ordinated organization, tightly controlled by top management. Rather it is of a mass of competing functional power groups, each seeking to influence company decisions in terms of its own interests, or, at least, in terms of its own distorted image of the company's interests.

Consequently, functional loyalties develop which tend to exclude those of the organization as a whole. Each function has its own discipline of analysis (that of the accountant is very different from that of the engineer); though bargaining and human relations skills may be very important in interdepartmental disputes, within the function analytical skills are valued above all.

Functionalism creates severe problems for higher management. As more and more people *think* of themselves as professionals (or at least develop functional loyalty), it becomes increasingly difficult to

---

[5] *See* George Strauss, "Work Flow Frictions, Interfunctional Rivalry, and Professionalism," *Human Organization* (in press).

maintain any sense of identification with the central organization. And, since top management has time to umpire only a few of the interdepartmental conflicts, individuals must be encouraged to resolve these by themselves, and this suggests the value of training in human relations.[6] Thus, the very emphasis on functional expertise requires an organization-man counterbalance.

Decentralization

Decentralization presents another dilemma. On the one hand, a primary reason for decentralization is to encourage diversity and experimentation. On the other hand, effective decentralization is not possible without a strong sense of organizational loyalty.

Much of what passes as decentralization is just ritual, and there is no commonly accepted meaning of the term. Still the main thrust of decentralization is clear: it means giving divisional managers full control over all functional areas necessary for the completion of their tasks, thus cutting back the power of top management and of staff functional groups in central headquarters. In effect, each divisional manager is given his own company to run.

The success of a decentralization program depends, to a large extent, on whether divisional managers can be motivated to behave in the interests of the organization as a whole. Normally managers are rewarded on the basis of results. Thus, in decentralized management, the process of measuring results becomes critical. But often, the very fact that results are measured causes side effects which harm the organization.

1. Since the emphasis is placed on measurable results, relatively little attention is given to those things which are hard to measure (scrap losses can be measured to the nearest cent; customer goodwill cannot be).
2. Since measurements are made at relatively short intervals, managements are motivated to look good now, and to play down activities which pay off only in the long run. Thus, productivity may be emphasized over employee morale.
3. Since each department is measured on the basis of its own performance, interdepartmental conflict is encouraged and departmental

---

[6] One study suggests that staff men (functional men) are more likely than line men to see their jobs as requiring traits such as being "cooperative," "adaptable," "tactful," or "agreeable" rather than being "forceful," "decisive," or "self-confident." Lyman W. Porter and Mildred M. Henry, *Job Attitudes in Management: VI. Perceptions of the Importance of Certain Personality Traits as A Function of Line vs. Staff Type of Job* (in press). In other words, staff men seem to be more human-relations oriented than line men.

managers often make decisions on a "suboptimal" basis in the
interest of their own department but not of the organization as
a whole.

As with functionalism, the net impact of decentralization is to
encourage departmental rather than organization-wide loyalty.
Though the department manager must possess sufficient human
relations skills not to produce an immediate crisis, his payoff is in
terms of short-run profit. (This is particularly true in companies
which rotate their managers from plant to plant so that no manager
stays in one place long enough to reap the fruits of the long-range
program.)

Computerization

There seems little doubt that the computer will have a substantial effect on management. It will "automate" many routine
(and even some not-so-routine) decisions; it will sharply cut back
on the number and status of middle managers; and, it will reverse
the trend towards decentralization. All three tendencies are
already evident; the question is, how far will they go and how will
they affect the behavior of managers at various levels of the corporate hierarchy. Will the impact of the computer make the manager
more or less human-relations oriented? Will he display more or
less conformity? To answer these questions it is necessary to look
at what a computer can and cannot do.

The computer can perform three sets of functions (among others).

1. It can process large amounts of data rapidly, thus making it possible
   to disseminate information quickly and accurately through the
   organization. As a consequence, top management can exercise increasingly tight control over subordinate units.[7]
2. It can easily solve routine problems which once took a great deal of
   managerial time.
3. With the aid of new mathematical techniques such as linear programming, the computer can handle problems which previously were
   too complex for any one individual to solve on a corporation-wide
   basis.

In the past, such complex decisions were often made on a decentralized basis or by committees, and often represented a compromise
among the interests of functional subgroups (in technical terms, they
were suboptimal solutions). Now, computers are increasingly able to

---

[7] Much work remains to be done before such information and control systems
are made really effective.

make decisions which are optimal from the point of view of the organization as a whole.

But for some time to come, there will still be many areas in which computers will be relatively ineffective. In terms of *decision-making processes,* the computer is strongest in selecting among given alternatives, according to a *preset* method of analysis; it is weakest in the creative areas of suggesting new alternatives and of developing new methods for evaluating these alternatives [8] as well as in the human-relations areas of implementing decisions. In terms of *subject matter,* the computer is relatively inefficient (if efficient at all) in dealing with problems which are difficult to quantify, such as sales and industrial relations. Thus, computers promise to be most effective in making routine or fairly routine decisions in areas such as production scheduling and inventory control where the relevant variables can be expressed in quantitative or symbolic terms.

What does computerization mean for various levels of management? It seems likely that jobs in top management will become more creative and demanding.[9] Once freed of details of routine analysis, top managers will be free to engage in long-range planning and human development.[10] Functional specialization (in particular analytic thinking-ahead on specialized problems) will become more important at the top, and relations among top managers will become increasingly collegial rather than hierarchical. Particularly among the functional groups, analytical skills will become all-important and there will be a premium upon being an innovator and a nonconformist.

The picture for middle and lower management is less clear. Leavitt and Whisler predict that as computers permit top management to make more and more decisions on a company-wide basis, "jobs at today's middle-management levels will become increasingly structured. Much of the work will be programmed, i.e., covered by sets of operating rules governing the day-to-day decisions that are made." [11] Consequently, there will emerge an increasingly distinct and impenetrable line between top management, which makes

---

[8] So-called "heuristic" problem-solving techniques are now available which permit the computer to engage in highly creative "thought." But these are not likely to have much practical value for management in the near future.

[9] Some managers have become so adjusted to filling their days with routine decisions that they will find it impossible to adapt to the new regime. Instead they will occupy their hours with new forms of busy-work.

[10] *See,* for example, Harold J. Leavitt and Thomas L. Whisler, "Management in the 1980's," *Harvard Business Review,* Vol. 36, No. 6 (1958), p. 47.

[11] *Ibid.,* p. 41. Herbert Simon makes roughly the same point, "The kinds of activities which now characterize middle management will become more completely

the decisions, and middle and lower management, which to an increasing extent will just carry them out.

Others suggest just the opposite, that computerization may actually lead to further decentralization. The computer can send information down the levels of hierarchy just as easily as it can send it up, and lower level managers may use techniques such as linear programming to solve problems at their level. Personally, I am inclined to agree with Leavitt and Whisler that decentralization of this sort is unlikely. In most instances, top management originally agreed to decentralization reluctantly and because, in the pre-computer era, this seemed to be the only possible way to run a large corporation. Further, the decentralized use of the computer would require sacrificing its advantages as a tool in making decisions on an optimal, organization-wide basis.

Management Control

My own opinion is that, given the opportunity, top management will recapture control but only in those areas in which the computer is relatively effective. Routine, programmable decision-making will gravitate to the computer at all levels of management. Creative, unprogrammed decisions will be made by top management to a greater extent than now. Subordinate managers will be concerned not only with implementing decisions, but also with human-relations areas, such as sales and industrial relations. Indeed, to the extent that other areas are automated, these human-relations areas may take up an increasing proportion of the remaining management time.

All this will have an impact on management development. Leavitt and Whisler predict very substantial changes.

> The stereotype of the conforming junior executive, more interested in being well liked than in working, should become far less significant in a highly depersonalized, highly programmed, and more machine-like middle management world. Of course, the pressures to conform will in one sense become more intense, for the individual will be required to stay within the limits of routines that are set for him. But the constant behavioral pressures to be a "good guy," to get along, will have less reason for existence.[12]

---

automated than the others, and hence will have a smaller part in the whole management picture." "Management by Machine," in *Management and the Corporation in 1985*, eds. Melvin Anshen and George L. Bach (New York: McGraw-Hill, 1960), p. 50).

[12] Leavitt and Whisler, *op. cit.*, p. 46.

Working one's way up through the ranks may be abandoned as a means of training and evaluating top managers. New channels of mobility may have to be worked out. New skills, such as those of systems analysis, which require viewing the organization as a functioning whole, may in part supplement the specialized skills which are learned in the few (or even a large number of) subordinate departments. These new skills can perhaps be better learned in college than on the job.

In my opinion, Leavitt and Whisler's conclusions may be a little strong. It is probably true that the line between top and middle management may grow sharper in the future. But the critical difference may not be in terms of the degree to which their work is programmed, but in terms of the nature of the work. Top management's work will be analytical; middle management's more in the area of human relations. (On the other hand, since the computer can quickly disseminate *quantifiable* performance data, even greater emphasis may be placed on achieving measurable results in the short run. If so, human relations may be viewed, even at middle-management levels, as an overexpensive luxury.)

The foregoing discussion should cast cold water on the prevalent notion that conformity and human relations will sweep the field. The processes of functionalization and decentralization create diversity rather than conformity. The impact of the computer is less clear, but the evidence suggests that more than conformity will be required for success in the top management of the future.

Then what is the debate all about? Is Organization Man a myth? Quite the contrary is true. I should like to suggest that much of what we call management development represents a conscious or unconscious attempt by certain groups within the organization to indoctrinate junior management with a sense of organizational loyalty, and thus to counterbalance the diversive forces already mentioned. Similarly, the emphasis on social skills of getting along with people is a means of offsetting the natural tendency of each individual and department to put its own objectives first. Indeed, management development is often the battlefield over which many of the ethical and practical issues relating to conformity and human relations are fought. Selection, training, and promotional procedures can be devised to produce the human-relations oriented, organizational conformist that Whyte depicts, or they may be used to create an atmosphere in which individuals will come to the foreground who are analytically oriented and who are individualistic (or perhaps professionally or functionally oriented) in their approach to problems.

Most large corporations have some sort of management development program which is planned and directed on an organizationwide basis, and many of these programs are controlled either by a personnel or a special management development department. These departments are for the most part biased in favor of promoting organizational identification and human-relations skills. Yet, as we shall see, policies which are made by staff departments are often sabotaged by operating executives.

Management development, broadly conceived, can be divided into four processes: selection; learning on the job; performance evaluation and coaching; and formal training. Let us look at each of these in turn.

Selection

The managerial selection process is critical in molding organizational character, for the individuals selected today will be the top managers of tomorrow. Company practices in this area are confused and contradictory. But many of the most difficult problems bristle with Organization-Man implications.

What kind of executives should the organization seek to attract, those with a liberal arts background or those who have specialized in practical subjects, such as accounting or marketing? This question has given rise to a host of articles and internal management debate. It was dealt with at length in the influential Ford and Carnegie evaluations of business schools.[13] With few exceptions those who have written about the subject, including many top managers, firmly agree that the potential executive should get a broad "liberal" education, with a considerable, if not primary, emphasis on the liberal arts. Until recently, the British went even further: they insisted that classics and philosophy provided the ideal background for the civil service. (Or are both American and British management really

---

[13] Robert Aaron Gordon and James Edwin Howell, *Higher Education for Business* (New York: Columbia University Press, 1959) and Frank C. Pierson and others, *The Education of American Businessmen* (New York: McGraw-Hill, 1959). Professor Vaughn Blankenship argues that these reports miss the main point: the main purpose of a business school is (and probably should be) to teach not analytic skills but social skills, what to wear and to drink, how to talk, what views are safe, and so forth. Recent studies have suggested that one of the chief purposes of the medical school is to teach medical students how to feel, act, and look like doctors. *See,* for example, Howard S. Becker *et al., Boys in White: Student Culture in Medical School* (Chicago: University of Chicago Press, 1961).

saying they want "gentlemen," properly indoctrinated with upper- or upper-middle-class manners and values?)

Yet, when company recruiters make their offers to the June graduates, it is the specialized men who still get the best offers. How can one explain this? Is it because the recruiters are looking primarily for men to fill bottom-rung jobs, while the requirements of top management are very different? Or is it because the verbalized ideology of management tends towards the all-purpose organization man, while the real forces tend towards specialization?

The question of personality testing dramatizes several issues. A number of large companies now use tests such as TAT, Rorschach, and MMPI, as aids both in selecting new managers and determining whom to promote. But it can be argued that such tests give over-emphasis to conformity and ability to get along with people. They are useful chiefly in a negative sense, in eliminating those with abnormalities. However, in doing this they also run the risk of eliminating the exceptional individual that management most needs to attract to high-level jobs (although they may possibly be misfits in subordinate jobs).[14] Some of the greatest and most creative people in history have had emotional troubles of one sort or another and were great in spite of them or even because of them; in fact, the driving force behind many executives' ambitions often originates in psychic imbalance. Some of these tests delve too deeply; they tell you about a man's basic drives, but not how well he handles them. We all have a whole range of primitive, uncivilized desires; the real question is how well we keep them under control.

In addition, it is argued that such testing is morally wrong and invades privacy. Companies which would gladly admit that a man's sexual *behavior* with his wife is his own private business, have no hesitancy in probing into his private, even unconscious sexual *thoughts*. Further, these tests can be grievously misused. I still recoil from a discussion with an airplane seat partner, a regional sales manager who had just given his salesmen the MMPI, a highly sophisticated test which includes among other scales, one purporting to masculinity-feminity. "Boy," he said, "you should see the number of fairies we got rid of this way." Others argue that, properly used, such tests are of considerable value and that the company should get every possible bit of information about a man whom it is thinking of hiring or promoting. After all, executives who seem to do well at lower levels may easily break under the greater pressure that higher level positions entail.

---

[14] It is also argued that, since the validity of these tests is hard to prove, they do neither harm nor good.

Therein lies the central question: how much of a man's life is legitimately within the company's domain? Are there areas of privacy which, for practical or ethical grounds, it should not enter? What, for example, about the practice which some companies follow of examining the wives and even fiancées of potential executives to make sure that they are not too domineering or too insistent that their husbands spend their evenings at home, and that they make good hostesses and will agree cheerfully to move their homes from coast to coast on a few days' notice?

Learning on the job

What sort of experience is most useful for the junior executive who is being groomed for a possible top management job? Should it be one which impresses over-all organization values, particularly those of human relations? Or should it emphasize the development of technical, analytical skills?

It is axiomatic in many personnel circles that experience-getting should not be left to chance, and that the experience should be as broad, as organization-oriented as possible. A man should be moved up a carefully defined ladder and tested every step of the way. Some companies have worked out automated, highly-programmed schemes of development which resemble the assembly line. Individual experience and ability are reduced to an IBM card and in some cases a man's future is worked out many years in advance (facetiously, one might suggest that there is very little he can do to change it one way or another). Picked "crown princes" are given special attention, force fed, and, of course, become good managers because everyone expects them to be.

Rotation is the traditional method of impressing an organizational point of view on an executive. In many companies he must spend the first twenty or so years of his career moving from job to job. Not only does such treatment tend to make the executive a generalist, but it also makes it possible to compare one man against another and to keep individual departments from becoming stagnant. It permits greater flexibility too; in case of sudden expansion of one line of work, there will always be a number of people around who have had some experience in it.

But many of the implications have not been adequately considered, especially where rotation involves moving from one community to another. For example, rotation is particularly hard on children who must constantly readjust to new schools and new friends: after a while they learn to withdraw into themselves. It is also hard on parents. A man is not likely to pour much love into fixing a house or developing a garden, if he doesn't expect to stay around for long. Like their children, parents learn not to develop close ties to friends or relatives, to the community, or to a single portion of the company.[15] By ruthlessly rooting out all other ties, rotation develops the Organization Man who identifies only with the company for which he works.[16] Of course, this company-centered organization man is not the all-around well-adjusted individual some companies purport to desire. But dedicated individuals are rarely "well-rounded."

Not everyone is willing to accept rotation. Some good men refuse to move around, and as a consequence, people are selected for higher management not on the basis of innate ability alone, but also because of their willingness to move. Thus, rotation serves the purpose of screening out those who refuse to put loyalty to company over loyalty to community and friends.

Musical chairs. Rotation, as practiced in many companies, is like a game of musical chairs. The trick is not to get left out. As long as you do adequately, you stay on into the next round. You avoid taking risks, because an outstanding performance won't help you very much, while a mistake can knock you out of the running for good. Thus rotation encourages men to play it safe.

Though rotation encourages conformity and organizational identification, it also has impacts which are dysfunctional to the organization as a whole:

- Just as moving around discourages a man from planting a tree in his garden or starting long-term projects at home, so it also discourages him from starting long-term projects at work. If a project doesn't have a payoff in a year or so, there is no point in starting it when one's successor will reap the advantages. Thus rotation may actually cause suboptimal behavior.
- Rotation means that a man spends a large part of his time learning the job. It may be a long time before he can contribute anything,

---

[15] Ironically, some of the companies which practice rotation most assiduously also have implicit requirement for promotion that a man should "be active in the community." But newcomers to a community are rarely accepted quickly into the really important community organizations. In one community this problem was solved by establishing a complete new set of "service clubs" which catered just to the transient. Turnover in these organizations was very fast, and it was easy for a man to move up quickly to a top position.

[16] W. Lloyd Warner and John Abegglen talk of the upwardly mobile executive as a man who is "always arriving." *See* their *Big Business Leaders in America* (New York: Harpers, 1955).

particularly before he learns the technical and social geography of his department. At first, all he knows are the formal rules, so he enforces these even when they are not appropriate.

- Also rotation leads to subtle class distinctions. The men who are not rotated tend to develop defensive reactions and identify with their own departments against the "carpetbaggers" from outside. This cleavage leads to misunderstanding and poor communications, with top management exerting pressure to get the local "stick-in-the-muds" to accept change and with local management strongly resisting every effort in this direction. But just as a first sergeant can often make or break his commanding officer, so the rotatee becomes dependent, at least during the first months of his tenure, on the "permanent party." Very often the permanent party decides to run its own show and through subtle and indirect methods keeps the rotatee from finding out what is happening in his own organization. As we know, informal communications play an important part in any organization and the rotatee tends to be isolated.

Fortunately, management today seems to be becoming less enchanted with rotation as an end in itself. (I say fortunately because I am very much disturbed by the large number of rootless people in management who have no real ties, no real life except their own company.) Some companies are beginning to realize that rotation imposes too high a price for what is often but a superficial form of organization identification. While rotation gives trainees a broad experience, this experience is all at a relatively low level. Yet even before the advent of the computer, different kinds of skills were required at various levels of management. At lower levels, technical ability, a willingness to obey orders, and skill in dealing with people are the chief requirements. At higher levels, the ability to innovate and make bold decisions becomes more important. The men who do outstanding jobs in the middle management may be totally ineffective at the top. On the other hand, the brilliant innovator might seem quite inadequate in a subordinate post. In other words, rotation fosters the organization-man characteristics of conformity and human relations; more than this is required at higher levels.

Instead of rotation, some companies are experimenting with providing junior managers with "sample" top-management experiences. The nature of these assignments varies greatly. Normally they are on a temporary or part-time basis. Some organizations have "junior boards of directors" or "management cabinets" to which senior boards of directors may refer special problems. More frequently, trainees are assigned to capital budgeting, product development, or long-range planning committees where they work in the company of more senior executives. At times a trainee may be assigned to study a problem area, prepare recommendations, and present and defend them in person before a top-management committee. Or he may work as an "assistant-to" a member of top management.

In general, programs of this sort permit the junior manager to be observed and evaluated by a group of top executives and reduce his dependence on a single boss. The junior is judged on his ability to handle the top-level job, not just on his ability to deal with lower-level jobs. The crown-prince problem is minimized, since the trainee performs his special assignments in the presence of higher management rather than in the presence of subordinates.

Programs of this sort place a premium on analytical ability rather than human relations or just plain conformity. For this reason they may become increasingly prevalent as the computer era unfolds.

Performance evaluation

The principal objective of most managers is to win salary increases and promotions. Most "progressive" companies have elaborate performance evaluation schemes which represent the *formal* machinery by which such rewards are distributed. Thus performance evaluation can play a critical role in motivating managers and in determining what sorts of managerial behavior will pay off. (Though, as I shall suggest, in some companies performance evaluation is but an often disregarded ritual, and the important decisions are made by other means.)

Perhaps in no other area has there been more controversy and have the fundamental issues been so obscured as in regards to performance evaluation. Many of these disputes involve highly technical questions, such as the use of forced choice or critical incidents. But here I will consider two sets of questions relating to Organization Man.

The first set relates to the criteria by which performance is measured. Specifically, should the rating be primarily concerned with the subordinate's *traits*, such as "co-operation" and "leadership," or with his objectively measurable *performance*, such as production rate and cost control? Ratings based on traits motivate managers to display skills and not deviate too far from the organizationally accepted patterns of behavior. Ratings based on measurable performance encourage the manager to be concerned primarily with his own department.

Trait rating may be useful if the purpose of the evaluation is to determine eligibility for promotion, particularly if the requirements of the higher level job are somewhat different from those of the job the subordinate currently occupies. Performance rating of men who now hold different jobs is something like comparing apples and nuts, since many special situational factors may be involved.

Trait rating, however, emphasizes personality, whether an individual is a good organization man; while, as we have suggested previously, many people in industry turn out good performances in spite of apparent personality defects. Trait rating is also poorly designed for training purposes. Tell a man that he is unimaginative or shy and there is little that he can do about it; further, he interprets this as a personal attack. But show him that his scrap figures are out of line and you have an opening for an objective, fruitful discussion which may lead to improved performance.

The second set of questions may relate to Organization Man more peripherally. Basically, they are concerned with the *objective* of evaluation. Should the purpose of evaluation be *tough*—to identify outstanding performers and to determine who will get promotions or wage increases, or should it be *soft*—to help executives develop themselves?

Soft approach. Personnel men, on the whole, have taken the soft approach. Though most agree that a man should be told where he stands, one of the primary objectives of the human relations movement has been to play down status differences, to make superior-subordinate relations more palatable, and to create the feeling of everyone being on the same team. Many efforts have been made to sugar-coat the evaluation interview: (1) to change its name to "counseling interview"; (2) to use the "sandwich technique" (tell the subordinate his strong points, gently tell him his weak points, and end up positively with his strong points again); or (3) to ask the subordinate to evaluate himself first. But whatever is done, the boss is obviously still the boss, and the subordinate has to sit and take it. The serpent has entered the human relations Garden of Eden.

In many cases, these interviews accomplish little except cause pain and tension for rater and ratee. Subordinates tend to react to the interview with defensiveness, suspicion, and hostility. Since many are primarily concerned with defending themselves, they resist the bosses' criticism and suggestions. Superiors, for their part, recognize that any sort of negative rating may be difficult to defend and may lead to "unpleasantness with the subordinate." Sometimes all parties conspire to ignore the process, in spite of the personnel department's proddings. Further, many human-relations-oriented executives "are uncomfortable when they are placed in the position of 'playing God.' The respect we hold for the inherent value of the individual leaves us distressed when we must take responsibility for judging the personal worth of a fellow man." [17] One wonders whether the tough, inner-directed boss who was the standard of yesteryear would have equally loathed to "play God."

McGregor suggests an approach which deemphasizes status differences even more and bases ratings on objective results. He proposes that managers should set their own performance goals, say at the beginning of the year, and that at the end of the year, evaluation should be concerned with the problems he has faced in reaching them. The focus should be on job performance and not on the individual.

Yet I fear that formal evaluation schemes will never be particularly successful, if for no other reason than that these systems are promulgated by staff groups in central headquarters, but administered by a busy operating executive who has a different set of values and who often gives relatively low priority to management development. As McGregor suggests, there are strong social inhibitions against counting off a man's inadequacies to his face. On the other hand, few executives have the time, patience, or ability to use McGregor's nondirective approach. Instead executives tend to use a host of indirect but effective (and possibly more humane) methods of letting subordinates know where they stand.[18] In most instances, but far from all, control over promotions and salary increases remains firmly in the hands of operating executives.

Formal training

Training can be used to create specialists as well as organization men. But control over formal training is normally vested in the personnel department and the emphasis has generally been on indoctrinating executives with a broad, general company point of view, and on developing greater sensitivity in dealing with human relations.

---

[17] Douglas McGregor, "An Uneasy Look at Performance Appraisal," *Harvard Business Review*, Vol. 35, No. 3 (1957), p. 90.

[18] For example, Editors of Fortune, "How to Fire an Executive," in *Executive Life* (New York: Doubleday, 1956). Erwin Goffman has written on the process of "cooling out," that is, of "letting a man down gently." This process occurs in business as elsewhere.

Sometimes training is frankly a form of indoctrination, as in the case of a company that asked the author to conduct a training program because supervisors were not showing enough loyalty. Many training programs are little more than exhortations to work harder and develop team spirit.

More sophisticated training programs often have a strong "participative" flavor. Participants are taught to be "group centered," to engage in nondirective listening and to be permissive conference leaders. S. M. Lipset points out how these "democratic" techniques foster company-wide identification and provide motivation to work for the objectives of the organization as a whole:

> The shift from the family-owned company to the management-run corporation, as Whyte pointed out, has made group activities and adjustment to group norms seem more important than individual responsibilities within corporate bureaucracies. But whatever else group dynamics in industry may be concerned with, it certainly provides an excellent way of getting men to work hard for the company. . . . By extending the control of work to committees at different levels in the corporation, and by incorporating democratic values into the internal operation of bureaucracy, contemporary American business has found a means of inculcating into a large number of people a sense of responsibility for the whole organization. "Non-owners" now feel responsible, and the number of hard-working "entrepreneurs" who never watch the clock, and who take work home with them, has been enormously enlarged.[19]

Interestingly, the two most stylish forms of management training today, the T group and the business game, involve radically different concepts as to the nature of the manager's job. The T group [20] is designed to help executives develop greater sensitivity to their own behavior in groups and to the perceptions of others. T groups seek to promote values such as "trust," "openness," and "authentic relations." They also seek to create an atmosphere in which nonconformity can be expressed. However, many T group practitioners seem to assume that after initial nonconformity has been expressed and accepted, eventually a unanimous group decision will be reached. A group in which the parties learn to understand each other and still disagree is usually considered to be a failure.

Business games, particularly those which involve a computer, generally require analytical ability and little or no human-relations skills. They assume that all the relevant problems of decision-making can be

---

[19] Lipset, *op. cit.*, p. 169.
[20] Executive action, sensitivity training, and laboratory training are all variations of the T group approach.

reduced to statistical measures. Once a decision has been reached, there is no problem of implementation; [21] all the participant need do is write his answer on the answer sheet and the computer obeys without question. Business games are still very much of a fad. But just possibly their popularity may reflect the fact that the advent of the computer lessens the need for human relations and organizational indoctrination, at least at some levels.[22]

Waves of enthusiasm. In spite of periodic waves of enthusiasm for formal training programs on the part of higher management, the results of such programs are often disappointing. One reason is that training is often considered a staff function and line may give it but token support. Attitudes of this sort are quickly discerned by the trainees themselves who begin to feel that training is a waste of time and resent being held in class as a captive audience.

In addition, what trainees learn in class is often in direct conflict with the day-to-day practices of line management. The class room instructor emphasizes good human relations; the boss wants tight control and high productivity at all costs. Subject to such conflicting pressures, some trainees vacillate between toughness and human relations, and appear to subordinates as inconsistent and insincere. Under the circumstances, it may be a blessing that so many supervisors leave their training in the classroom and never let it interfere with daily behavior. In any case training programs are often a fairly ineffective means of developing organizational loyalty or human relations skills.

My purpose here has been to summarize arguments regarding the two related questions of analytical versus human-relations skills and of individualism versus organizational loyalty. My analysis has been oversimple: I have been guilty of distorting complex issues to a Procrustean framework and perhaps also of conjuring up questions of high principle where less subtle matters are involved.

The first question relates to the nature of executive skills. Two sorts of skills are required by the successful executive, though these skills are not distributed among executives in an equal manner. The

---

[21] True, if teams are involved in the game, then there is a human-relations problem of getting team members to agree to a decision. Interestingly, advocates of T groups and business games both claim their techniques improve decision-making abilities, but they use the term "decision-making" in very different ways. *See*, for example, Robert R. Blake and Jane S. Mouton, *Group Dynamics—Key to Decision-Making* (Houston, Texas: Gulf Publishing Company, 1961).

[22] It might make a useful study to compare the companies and groups within management which have promoted each of these types of training.

executive must have the ability to analyze often complex problems and make decisions. At lower levels the problems are often technical, so technical training and background are required; at higher levels the problems involve broad social, economic, and technological trends. But since a corporation is too complex for one man to make all the decisions, the executive must also co-ordinate the efforts of other decision-makers and insure that decisions are carried out. So he requires human-relations skills, which are very different from those of analysis.

The second question relates to conformity and organizational loyalty. Ideally every top manager seeks to induce his subordinates to work in a *co-ordinated* fashion toward the objectives of the organization as a whole, and to do so with *enthusiasm* and *imagination*. The trouble is that enthusiasm and imagination conflict with co-ordination; individualism conflicts with conformity. If the executive permits too much individualism, subordinate efforts will be unco-ordinated and directed toward individual and sub-group goals. And functional, professional, and departmental loyalties are engendered which conflict with loyalty to the organization as a whole.

Tight controls

Conformity to organizational objectives can be obtained through tight central controls, but conformity of this sort comes at the cost of enthusiasm and imagination. Conformity can also be obtained through subtle manipulation of the rewards system in a manner which leads to organizational loyalty through indoctrination. Indoctrination is a process by which individuals internalize the organization's hierarchy of goals. Indoctrination, to a large extent, explains the strength of organizations like the Communist Party, the Catholic Church, and the Marine Corps, and, to a lesser extent, the strength of most successful armies and large companies. Large corporations develop characteristic methods of operation, and a General Motors man may approach problems in a very different fashion than one from Jersey Standard.

Indoctrination makes delegation of authority easier. It reduces the need for rigid sets of rules, since highly indoctrinated individuals all think in roughly the same terms and make their decisions on the same premises as their superiors. They are willing to subordinate their own personal interests and the interests of their own departments to the higher interests of the large organization. Ideally, then, the organization can permit innovative flexibility as to *means*, knowing there will be uniformity as to *ends*. Thus, in the heyday of the British Empire, it was possible to send a colonial administrator to the wilds of Africa with only the most minimal instructions and with the fullest confidence that, regardless of contingencies, he would always do credit to England.

The truly indoctrinated individual is not a conformist in small things. He is willing to break rules when he feels they conflict with the organization's basic values. Indeed many of the Catholic Church's greatest saints got into trouble with their ecclesiastical superiors. Within the confines of the organization's basic values, many indoctrinated individuals engage in highly innovative thinking.

Because of competing claims for individual loyalty, family, community, department, and so forth, few business firms will win the complete organizational loyalty of their managers. After all, effective indoctrination requires a man to devote his entire life to the organization. In effect this is what many management development programs seek to encourage. But the company will never be as successful as religious groups in winning such complete dedication. Religious zealots may be willing to sacrifice their personal ambitions to advance the "True Faith." But the typical corporate executive seeks to advance *himself*; his objective is personal success, not higher corporate profits. Thus indoctrination runs the danger of making corporate Organization Man a conformist only as to means; as to ends he remains basically selfish. Still, indoctrination can be an effective tool to counterbalance the divisive forces in a corporation without imposing strict controls.

These two issues—decision-making versus analytical skills and individualism versus organizational loyalty—are closely related. Those who view management's primary job as that of human relations naturally look upon indoctrination as a useful means of co-ordinating activities and implementing policies. Those who claim that management's job is chiefly to make decisions see implementation as less of a problem, and at lower levels their specialized skills and viewpoints may conflict with loyalty to the organization as a whole.

Management development is a battleground on which many of these issues are fought. Those who support the decision-making approach, particularly at lower levels, also feel that the company should recruit specialists, that rotation for its own sake is not desirable, that rewards should be given for concrete performance rather than personality traits, that authority should not be sugar-coated and that broad, organization-oriented training is relatively worthless. Since the human-relations party occupies the staff personnel positions where formal statements of company policy are made and since it frequently writes the speeches made by company executives, one often gets the picture that human relations and conformity are the order of the day. But the picture gets less clear as one gets to operating levels.

To what extent, then, does the typical executive fit the caricature of Organization Man? W. H. Whyte, for example, depicts the businessman of today as an organizational conformist in sharp contrast to the rough and ruthless go-getter of the past. But I think this contrast may be too strong. The less successful executive may perhaps conform to the stereotype of Organization Man. But it may well be that the really successful rising young executive is a man who can be either conformist or nonconformist as the situation demands.[23] He conforms in little things and avoids unnecessarily antagonizing his peers and bosses. In terms of social behavior and attitudes, he conforms; but in his own area of job competence, he takes the initiative *at the proper time.* Perhaps the sense of "when is the proper time" is among the necessary requirements for a good executive. To be sure, he knows how to deal with people—to manipulate them, if you like—but human relations, for him, is a tool, not an end in itself. In other words, the successful executive is sensitive to his environment, but like the good sailor, he does not float aimlessly with the tide, but takes advantage of every eddy and current to help him toward his long-run objective.

Questions

1. Strauss points out that as the functional fields achieve more professional status there are likely to be interdepartmental conflicts that can best be solved if the persons concerned have had training in human relations skills. What skills are suggested in the article by Davis that would be useful in handling interdepartmental conflicts?
2. The author believes that with the development of computerization there will be a premium upon innovation and nonconformity at the top levels

[23] For a pioneering study in this area, *see* William R. Dill, Thomas L. Hilton, and Walter R. Reitman, *The New Managers* (Englewood Cliffs: Prentice-Hall, 1962). W. H. Whyte, himself, points out that Organization Man rarely gets to the top.

of management. However, the picture for middle and lower management is less clear. What do you predict will be required of middle and lower managers as far as innovation and nonconformity are concerned? Why?

3. Do you agree with the author's criticism of rotation as a method of training managerial personnel? Why?

4. The word "conformity" is used frequently by critics of the modern corporation. How does Strauss use the word? What value does his approach have for the student of organizational behavior?

5. The findings from one study (cited in footnote 6) suggest that staff men seem to be more human-relations oriented than line men. Why is this likely to occur? Is it desirable that there be a difference?

6. In conclusion, would you agree with the author that the Organization Man should be defined differently today than when originally described by Whyte?

29. MANAGEMENT AND THE ASSEMBLY LINE *

Arthur N. Turner

Is top management in mass production industry caught in a web of its own making? There is evidence that unfortunately this may be the case. Using the automobile assembly plant as an example, I shall show that management has created a technological environment which fails to provide necessary satisfaction and meaning in work, and which thereby militates against the company's own objectives.

It is true that in recent years much has been done to make life on the job less tiring and more enjoyable. Many devices and tools have been designed and installed in order to relieve workers of unnecessary physical effort. Steps are constantly being taken to make working conditions more pleasant. Much money and thought have been invested in safety measures and medical facilities. Nowhere is all of this more true than in automobile manufacturing, and there is no doubt that all these steps have contributed in important ways to worker morale.

The fact remains that a considerable number of mass production workers dislike their work and feel suspicious or hostile toward management. Business leaders need to understand why this is so, in order to experiment with methods of changing the nature of the production process in humanly desirable ways, or at least to encourage those tendencies which counteract its undesirable human and social effects.

The difficulty in so doing is that management itself is part of the process. Not only its behavior but also its basic way of thinking about people and things may be shaped by the technological process of which management is a part. In particular, the method of production and type of work environment epitomized by the automobile assembly line influence the basic assumptions about human motivation and capacity which are held at all levels of the management organization. The danger is that behavior resulting from such assumptions may reinforce the undesirable human and social effects

---

* From *Harvard Business Review*, Vol. 33, No. 5 (September-October, 1955), pp. 40-48. Reprinted with permission.

which seem inherent in this type of technology unless consciously counteracted.

If this is true, it is important for top managers to understand the danger and their own involvement in the process, because the only way such a "vicious circle" can be broken is when those with responsibility and opportunity to do something about it understand what is happening. Here, briefly, are some of the main propositions which I think need to be considered:

- The two most important characteristics of automobile assembly work, mechanical pacing and repetitive job patterns, are important sources of worker dissatisfaction because they cause feelings of too much "pressure" and "impersonality." The latter feeling in particular is reinforced by certain company policies with respect to production scheduling, illness, promotion, and old age.
- The foremen who are the most successful leaders use a variety of methods to counteract feelings of "pressure" and "impersonality." In so doing, they often have to violate both the engineering rationale and the formal thinking of the organization about appropriate management behavior.
- "It's the people on top that make the difference." One of the most effective things that can be done from above to help foremen is to relieve unnecessary pressure and avoid too much emphasis on short-run, obvious costs in appraising performance.
- The foremen alone cannot cope with worker dissatisfaction. Management must support them with its production and personnel policies. There is a significant relationship between workers' attitudes toward the foremen and their attitudes toward the company.
- Experiments should be undertaken to introduce more individual and group participation in assembly line work and more variety and interest in assembly jobs.
- The assumptions that workers like repetitive work and need to be paced, even if invalid (as the evidence indeed indicates), tend to justify themselves by the results they produce. This disguises the fact that they set off a vicious circle of negative attitudes, which in the end runs counter to management's own interest.

Most of the evidence on which this article is based is drawn from a long-term program of research into the human and social implications of technological progress, headed by Charles R. Walker, Director of Research and Technology and Industrial Relations, Yale University. . . . The article is not intended as a report on the findings, but rather as an indication of their meaning to businessmen.[1]

---

[1] A more complete account of the research will appear in a forthcoming book: Charles R. Walker, Robert H. Guest, and Arthur N. Turner, *The Foreman on the Assembly Line*, to be published by the Harvard University Press. This book is designed as a sequel to Charles R. Walker and Robert H. Guest, *The Man on the Assembly Line* (Cambridge: Harvard University Press, 1952); *see* the article of the same title, HBR (May-June, 1952), p. 71.

Impact of the Line

What is the relationship between the nature of mass production work and the worker and foreman on the assembly line? What are the jobs of worker and foreman like under mass production? How do they react to these jobs and to the technological environment in which they work? What are the effects of these jobs and this environment on human relationships at the worker and foreman level?

The two most prominent characteristics of automobile assembly line work are *mechanical pacing* and *repetitiveness*. Each of these characteristics can be thought of as a technologically determined fact; for most workers they are the two most important facts about their immediate jobs. Each of them is associated with an important feeling which showed itself through most of our interviews—mechanical pacing with a feeling of pressure, repetitiveness with a feeling of impersonality.

Interviews with workers and with foremen make clear that it is very important for management from the top down to appreciate the strength and the prevalence of these feelings of pressure and impersonality, and the importance of mitigating or counteracting them insofar as this is possible.

Mechanical pacing—pressure

It is difficult for an outsider to appreciate the pervasiveness of the moving line and its associated sense of pressure. A recently promoted foreman said: "There are always pressures, whether you are a worker or a foreman. The line itself is a pressure, that continual movement." As workers describing it often say: "Everything moves; that line is coming at you all the time."

Not only the main line which weaves its way throughout the whole plant, but also a host of subassembly lines, "merry-go-rounds," and overhead conveyors are in constant motion while the plant is operating, carrying the work from one man to the next, and (at least at first sight) regulating the pace at which most of the men have to work. After an initial period of more or less difficult adjustment, most workers get used to being surrounded by this constantly moving "iron monster," as many of them refer to the line; but it is impossible for them to ignore it because it is everywhere, and their activities always seem to be regulated by its demands.

For most workers, mechanical pacing is an important source of dissatisfaction with the job. Men get used to it, but they seldom learn to like it. In both plants where our research has been conducted, over 30% of the workers interviewed indicated that the most strongly disliked feature of their total work experience was being paced by the moving line, feeling unable to do the required work in the time allowed. Apparently one of the hardest things for them to do is to learn to live with the line and not let it get them down. According to our findings, this is as true (or more so) for long-service workers with up to 15 years' seniority as for relative newcomers to assembly work.

It is striking how frequently the word "pressure" occurred. Some workers used it to refer to the immediate compulsion of having to keep up in their work with the pace of the line. For other men there was a less obvious relation with the nature of the job. They seemed to feel pressure from "the company," or from local management, or simply in the general atmosphere without any definite idea of where it came from. Significantly, "pressure" was frequently mentioned not only by workers but also by members of management at all levels.

Counteracting Pressure. Of course, some kind of pressure exists in any purposeful human activity. The point here is that many men on the assembly line feel a degree of pressure which is too great, not just for their own happiness, but for the accomplishment of the larger purposes of the organization. As many foremen and others recognize, it is not enough to "learn to live with pressure"; it is also necessary, on the assembly line, to know how to counteract it.

Indeed, the foreman's success as a leader depends on his ability and willingness to understand and take into consideration the psychological importance of assembly line technology on the attitudes and actions of his men. The foreman, *with management's help*, needs to lessen, not reinforce, the pressures associated with the moving line. This is what the successful foreman does, a remarkable achievement considering the influences that surround him and the constant pressures he is under himself.

There are at least three methods by which some foremen succeed in counteracting the pressures on their men associated with the mechanical pacing of the moving line:

    1. *Recognizing individual differences in capacity and pace of working*—Many foremen, contrary to the engineering assumptions according to which assembly line jobs are designed, recognize in assigning work that two or more men do not necessarily work at the same pace on a given job all the time, and so they make allowances for variations be-

tween individuals and for differences in the pace worked by the same man from day to day or hour to hour.

2. *Trusting workers' willingness to work*—Many other foremen, also contrary to the apparent rationale for the moving line, believe that most men want to do their share of the work and want to do it well. For example, such foremen feel free to leave their section, confident that the work will continue to be well done while they are away.

3. *Refraining from using unnecessary pressure themselves and absorbing pressure from above*—Significantly, a number of the most experienced and most successful foremen consciously refrain from adding to the pressure of the line. They do not push their men constantly to keep up with it, and they purposely absorb a large part of the pressure placed on them to get the work out instead of passing all of it on to their men. In fact, our studies have convinced us that the ability "to act as a shock absorber" is one of the most necessary supervisory requirements in an assembly plant.

All of the foregoing practices are recognized implicitly by many management people as important parts of the successful foreman's job, but they are seldom made explicit or given formal recognition or reward. Yet it makes the foreman's job (or any other supervisor's job) far easier and far more satisfying to perform well when his superiors show they understand the nature of the problems he has to deal with.

Repetitiveness—impersonality

Many assembly line workers would agree with the man who said:

> I object to doing the same thing every day. I don't like it. After a while you become like one of the tools down there. You cease to function mentally. If you've got a specific job on a fender, you do it mechanically. After a while you're a robot.

Next to mechanical pacing the most important mass production characteristic of assembly line work is its repetitiveness. Under the principle of breaking down operations into their simplest component parts, and in view of the short time cycle for most jobs when the line is running at a rate of 30 or more cars per hour, the average job requires frequent repetition of a rapid sequence of relatively simple motions throughout the day. Our studies indicated that repetitiveness is likely to be a less prominent cause for dissatisfaction among longer service men than newcomers, but even a majority of the veterans complained of it.

The minimum skill required, the monotony, and the lack of intrinsic interest in the work are basic to the general feeling of impersonality and anonymity which is typical among assembly line workers. However, it would be a mistake to attribute this feeling only to the assembly line. When workers in the two plants studied discussed "the company" as a place to work, a majority exhibited clearly unfavorable attitudes toward the company's treatment of them or said specifically that the company did not do much of anything for the men.

The most important reasons for this negative verdict were the feeling that "to the company you're just a number; they're not interested in the men, just production"; alleged impersonal treatment of the individual worker, especially as he gets too old to keep up with the line or when he becomes sick or injured on the job; restricted opportunity for advancement; fluctuating employment; lack of interest in the immediate job.

One of the most difficult problems is that for the average assembly worker there is little in the way of a group to which he can belong in a meaningful way. Perhaps the most important counterweight to anonymity and lack of belonging or purpose, if they exist in a factory, is the sense of belonging to a small work group. Research and experience have shown repeatedly that workers, like anyone else, tend to derive satisfaction from association with a group of their fellows who perform the task together and share experiences on the job from day to day.[2]

But the development of groups requires frequent and easy interaction (i.e., some form of verbal or nonverbal communication) between the members, and this is not found on the assembly line. For one thing, the noise in many sections of the plant interferes with interaction; so does the fact that most jobs, while simple, cannot be performed automatically, requiring constant attention as they do if the operator is to keep up with the line. In addition, and perhaps more important, the nature of the work in most cases does not *require* interaction. With a few exceptions there is little teamwork in the literal sense. Most jobs are performed singly, or with only occasional help from one "partner" performing similar work on the other side of the line. Also, the distribution of work stations along the line and the organization of the work from one foreman's section to the next make for no obvious boundaries between potential groups.

---

[2] *See*, for example, Elton Mayo and George F. Lombard, *Teamwork and Labor Turnover in the Aircraft Industry of Southern California* (Boston: Harvard Business School, Division of Research, Business Research Studies, No. 32, 1944). For a discussion of the relevance of social science research on small group behavior, *see* Donld R. Schoen, "Looking Around: Group Meetings," HBR (May-June, 1955), p. 131.

Naturally, under these circumstances, it is difficult for real work groups to develop. It should be pointed out, however, that the causes of this situation are not completely technological. The importance of group experience is seldom recognized by those who organize and manage the work.

Harmful Policies. There are a number of other circumstances and company policies which contribute to a sense of anonymity or are used by workers as evidence of the company's lack of personal interest in them. Most important are the harmful results, on workers and foremen, of frequent fluctuations in production schedule.

The foreman who has to spend much of his time adjusting his work assignments to changes in line speed and instructing his men in new combinations of operations, and whose section is forever having new men added to it and old ones taken away, finds it difficult to establish the kind of group relationship which is required to counteract anonymity. And to the workers, layoffs or short work weeks at one time of the year and then long overtime hours day after day at another time of the year often seem like unnecessarily impersonal treatment, whatever the average number of hours worked per week may turn out to be when the year is over. All this amounts to a strong argument for smoother, more stable production schedules (no matter what one thinks of the other features of the guaranteed annual wage, with which such schedules are frequently associated).

Impersonal treatment also shows up in such specific form as the practice of sending plant guards to the homes of absent workers to investigate their reasons for being absent, or the alleged difficulty of obtaining relief to go to the plant hospital when ill or injured on the job. In all these problems there is no simple cause-and-effect relationship. For instance, the plant guards are sent to workers' homes *because* it has been found that some absent workers claim to be sick when they are not; yet, in turn, some workers stay away from work and give false excuses *because* they have found that management expects them to behave in this fashion and they do not feel they are trusted.

Countermeasures by Foremen. Accordingly, it is not only because of the nature of the work on the assembly line but also because of a number of other circumstances which workers perceive as impersonal treatment that management faces the need to reduce as far as possible a rather widespread sense of anonymity and lack of purpose. To a large extent impersonality, like pressure, can only be successfully counteracted by the foreman with management's help.

There are four principal methods by which the foreman on the assembly line counteracts impersonality:

1. *Permitting job rotation and in other ways introducing more variety and interest in the work*—For example, some foremen in their interviews told in detail how they allowed some of their men informally to exchange jobs so as to "break the monotony," or pulled some operations off the line so that workers in rotation could be assigned to building a bank of subassemblies, which increased the variety of their work and their sense of responsibility, at the same time improving the foreman's flexibility in job assignment in case of absenteeism.

2. *Delegating to his men a share of responsibility for the performance of the job*—Some foremen, especially the more experienced and successful ones, manage to give their men considerably more responsibility for determining how to do the work than would be called for by a strict adherence to the engineering principles according to which the jobs are designed. For instance, some foremen rely on their men to keep the stockman informed so that they do not run short of parts, to shut the line down in case of emergency and start it up again, to decide when to change from one subassembly job to another, to check on numerous quality items, and to tell the repairman what points need special attention from time to time.

We also observed that many foremen constantly received signals from their operators concerning the quality of work coming to them from previous operations, a particularly valuable form of assistance. Finally, a few foremen go so far as to give their key operators or utility men a degree of responsibility which would not be formally sanctioned by either management or union: having them take care of minor paper work or even look after part or all of the foreman's section of the line.

3. *Paying attention to his men as individuals and establishing with each one a personal relationship apart from the job relationship*—Most foremen emphasize the importance of "treating your men as individuals, since no two are alike." To the best foremen this is not merely an abstract principle of "human relations"; it is a practical method of establishing with each man the kind of personal relationship which effectively counteracts the impersonality of the job. Management generally recognizes the importance of this practice.

4. *Dealing with his men as a group and acting as their leader, responsible for strengthening their group bonds and encouraging their group objectives*—The better foremen talk of their men as a group with common objectives which they as leaders share to a large extent. They approach such problems as dealing with a minor disciplinary case, improving quality, or coping with absenteeism as matters which involve all the men in the section collectively, rather than any one man separately. They recognize informal patterns of leadership and loyalty within the group, and utilize them when appropriate. They are careful not to violate unnecessarily the customs and habits which any group fosters. In every way possible they encourage the growth of a group feeling by participating in the group's informal customs and jokes and even occasionally by encouraging outside group activities.

In so doing these foremen violate both the engineering rationale and the formal thinking of the organization about appropriate management behavior, for management does not generally recognize the importance of the group concept. But at the same time they manage to counteract more successfully than would otherwise be possible the feeling of impersonality which tends to develop among men on the assembly line.

Attitude of Management

In our research we have been reminded again and again that "it's the people on top that make the difference." Workers, foremen, and members of higher management repeatedly emphasize the extent to which the behavior of anyone in the management hierarchy toward those below him depends on how he in turn is treated by his superiors.

The members of management who most directly influence the foremen's behavior are clearly their immediate superiors, general foremen, and department superintendents. But their behavior in turn is influenced by the degree of help and understanding they receive from upper plant management. And, as any plant manager will acknowledge, the kind of actions and attitudes he feels free to take toward his own people depend to a large extent on the behavior of top management of the parent organization. Like everyone else, he is in need of his superiors understanding his position if he is to do his job well.

Accordingly, we can discuss what management's policies should be without being specific as to the level of management we are talking about; a policy can only succeed at *any* level if it is also practiced at a higher level—and thus ultimately at the very top level.

Toward foremen

What should management's policies be in order to improve human relations at the foreman-worker level and to help counteract the negative human and social effects on workers and foremen of mass production technology?

A number of possibilities are worth considering. In the first place, there is the matter of promotion and training in supervision —and, even more important, management's own day-to-day example. Lip service to principles and ideals is not enough and can easily do more harm than good. What counts more than lofty phrases or pious exhortations are such practical matters as:

  • Who in fact is promoted to greater responsibility—the superior who in some surface way makes a good impression on his boss, or the superior who really has his men as a group behind him?

• Is whatever training that is given obviously and realistically related to the felt needs and daily experiences of those being trained? [3]

• Do those on top show by their daily behavior (not merely by a sudden burst of conscience) that they believe in listening to what others have to say, in taking account of human needs and hopes, in rewarding success with people as generously as success with things?

The most important way by which management at all levels can learn to help the foreman is, I believe, by being familiar with the nature of the foreman's job. Foremen who are interviewed or observed at work often welcome such research because, they are likely to say, "Now at last those on top will find out what a foreman's job is like." When management understands the foreman's role and appreciates the pressures and conflicts of the foreman's position, there can develop within the organization a pattern of administrative behavior and a point of view which will in time make the foreman's job much easier.

More specifically, management can do a great deal to help foremen establish constructive relations with their men simply by avoiding unnecessary pressure and by not putting too much emphasis on competition between plants and between departments based *solely* on short-run, obvious costs.

At all levels in management a subordinate does a better job when his superior shows some trust in his ability and tries to help, not merely condemn, when something goes wrong. Foremen and plant managers alike find it difficult to think constructively about their jobs when they are constantly prodded with comparative cost figures which tell only part of the story. (Examples of facts which are often left out of such comparisons are: costs of turnover and absenteeism; repair costs, including overtime; and difficulties caused by schedule fluctuations.) Neither foreman nor plant manager objects to being compared with others in similar positions, provided that such comparisons are made intelligently, that the inevitable shortcomings in the data are acknowledged, and that the superiors making the comparisons show an attitude of understanding and helpfulness.

Toward workers

The worker, as well as the foreman, influences the climate of the foreman-worker relationship. No matter how strongly the fore-

---

[3] *See* F. J. Roethlisberger, "Training Supervisors in Human Relations," HBR (September, 1951), p. 47.

man may wish to alter his behavior and attitude toward his men, he may find it difficult or impossible to make such headway unless the men's attitude and behavior change. When workers are long accustomed to their foreman behaving in a certain way, they may resent a sudden change in their foreman's behavior, hold it suspect, or fail to perceive that the behavior has changed at all. In any case the foreman is likely to conclude that his effort was impractical, and so abandon further attempts. This is why management efforts to improve foreman-worker relationships solely through changing *foremen* often fail.

The point is that management can help foremen in their worker relationships by adopting policies and practices toward workers which encourage them to interpret their foremen's behavior constructively. Our studies show a statistically significant relationship between workers' attitudes toward the foremen and their attitudes toward the company; workers who dislike their foreman tend also to dislike the company's policies, and vice versa. (One exception to this generalization, apparently, is the Chicago plant of Swift & Company.)[4] As a foreman who acts in ways which make his men like and respect him thereby improves their attitudes toward the company as a whole, so the management which adopts policies that improve worker attitudes toward the company thereby makes it easier for the men to like their supervisors.

One management policy which could be very important in improving workers' over-all attitudes would be to do everything possible to avoid unnecessary fluctuations in production schedules. Another would be to cope with the opinion of many workers that there is no provision for them as they get older and find it difficult to keep up with the line.

The problem of aging on the assembly line is a very difficult one, especially in nonintegrated final assembly plans where few off-line jobs are available. In such plants a pension plan, no matter how generous, does not solve the problem, because it only provides relief at age 65. What workers are looking for is evidence that management (the union, too) is interested in their future and concerned with finding other work for them as they approach retirement. Without such evidence they feel that management is not concerned with them as human beings.

[4] *See* Theodore V. Purcell, *The Worker Speaks His Mind on Company and Union* (Cambridge: Harvard University Press, 1953), p. 123; and "Observing People," HBR (March-April, 1955), p. 90.

It is important also for management to recognize the role that the union *can* (but does not always) play in counteracting workers' feelings of anonymity and lack of purpose in their work experience. Thus, in the plant studied in *The Man on the Assembly Line* it was found that:

> The union met in part the psychological and social needs that work in the plant had created. . . . In other words, for a considerable number of Plant X workers the union appeared as a kind of psychological bulwark against pace and boredom and against the bigness and impersonality of management.[5]

But in the second plant, studied subsequently, the union did not appear to be fulfilling this role. Attitudes toward the union were similar to attitudes toward the company; for most workers the union was a distant impersonal force which was not identified in their minds with their individual interests. The union's failure added to management's problem instead of (as some might suppose) relieving it. As union relations mature, there is a need for management to accept fully the fact that a strong, active union can be more helpful to it than one which is weak or divided.

Finally, I believe that the potentials of the small informal group should be recognized. There is an unfortunate tendency for some members of management to oppose as harmful what in fact could be of major assistance in improving morale. If the values of meaningful group life in counteracting impersonality were recognized, work could be designed and procedures adopted which would enable groups to further the objectives of management and the well-being of the organization as a whole.

Toward the technology

How can management's policies in relation to technology help the development of constructive human relations at the foreman and worker level? Experiments should be undertaken to introduce more individual and group participation in assembly line work, more variety and interest into assembly jobs. Tentative steps in this direction taken informally by some foremen show that much can be done without in any way sacrificing the technical efficiency of progressive assembly.[6]

---

[5] Charles R. Walker and Robert H. Guest, *op. cit.*, p. 133.
[6] *See* Charles R. Walker and Robert H. Guest, *op. cit.*, pp. 141-161. *See also* Charles R. Walker, "The Problem of the Repetitive Job," HBR (May, 1950), p. 54.

There is a real question whether work standardization and simplification, coupled with a uniform, mechanically determined pace throughout the plant, have not been pushed too far for maximum effectiveness, especially when such factors as decline in quality, repair costs, absenteeism, turnover, worker disinterest in the job, and loss of loyalty to the company are fully taken into account. Has there been perhaps a too automatic acceptance of a rather narrow engineering approach to what is after all a human as well as a mechanical problem? As one authority says:

> We should remember that we can never wholly separate the human and the mechanical problem. . . . [Inevitably] the study of human relations in business and the study of the technique of operating are bound up together.[7]

There is no *inevitable* conflict between technical progress and work satisfaction. What we need are production methods which fully utilize human and social potentialities without sacrificing technical efficiency. This calls for basic rethinking and careful research on how to combine human and engineering considerations in the design of production processes. Both the system of thought of the social scientist or administrator interested in improving human relations practice and the thinking of the engineer or administrator interested in improving technical efficiency are needed, not separately and in opposition to each other, but working together on the same problem, since each depends on the other for success.[8]

Dangerous Assumptions

The policies and practices which management adopts necessarily grow out of a certain way of thinking about technology and human relations. For example, whether management tries to help foremen counteract some of the pressure and impersonality associated with the assembly line will depend on its interpretation of the cause of these problems and its judgment as to whether they are undesirable and need to be counteracted. When management itself is thoroughly involved with a particular technology, and committed to its basic concepts, it is difficult to see what the human implications of that

---

[7] *Dynamic Administration: The Collected Papers of Mary Parker Follett,* edited by Henry C. Metcalf and L. Urwick (New York: Harper & Brothers, 1941), p. 124.

[8] E. R. Walker, "Adjustment, Individual and Social, to Technological Change," in Industrial Relations Research Association, *Industrial Productivity* (Madison, Wisconsin, 1951), pp. 210-211.

technology may be. There is a natural temptation for managers to carry over into their thinking about human motivation the assumptions that seem to underlie the assembly line technology.

Work simplification

Consider, for example, the assumptions which underlie the traditional principles of work simplification. If it is true that work gets done most efficiently when every job is made as simple as possible and motions are highly repetitive, does it not follow that workers in general are content with uninteresting work and actually shun the additional responsibility of more complex jobs? Some members of management, in order to rationalize to themselves the nature of mass production work, go so far as to believe sincerely that this is the case.

The trouble with such assumptions is that, *even if true* (which is extremely doubtful in view of all the evidence), they are not useful guides to action. What about the worker who is not "average"? Even more important, what are the *results* of such assumptions in supervisory behavior and company policy?

The management which believes that workers dislike responsibility does not try to give it to them. And if management assumes that workers like repetitive jobs, it is not likely to support experiments to make the work more interesting or challenging. Consequently, workers tend to feel that management does not *want* them to take responsibility and does not *expect* them to have an interest in their work; for workers, like everyone else, often behave according to how they think other people want and expect them to behave. The very fact that they feel this way creates a problem, whether they would in fact have responded to more interesting jobs or not. The vicious circle of attitudes can only be broken, I am convinced, when management boldly acts on new, positive assumptions about workers' capacity and willingness to take a real interest in their jobs.

Power of coercion

Much the same basic problem exists in relation to mechanical pacing and pressure. The assembly line is primarily an efficient method of moving work in process. But in management's thinking it frequently becomes much more than this. It becomes the agency that gets the work done in the time allowed. Now, if this is assumed, some important further assumptions follow. For example, in order to justify the coercion of the line it is difficult not to assume that by and large people fail to work well unless they *are* coerced. Perhaps no manager would endorse this assumption stated so baldly, but is there not an inevitable danger that it will follow in his thinking, at least subconsciously, if he holds to the first belief?

Admittedly, the moving line has something to do with compelling the completion of each job in a predetermined time. And sometimes certain people *do* have to be coerced in order to do good work, just as under certain (exceptional) circumstances some people prefer repetitive jobs. But basically the cause-and-effect relationship is the other way around. As one manager said:

> People say, "The men start working as soon as the line starts." It should be the other way around. It should be, "The line starts when the people start to work." It's some sort of reverse thinking that everyone gets into, that motivation is mechanical and not human. You don't carry that kind of thinking over when you talk about your car. There you realize that the car won't go unless the human wants it to go. *But on the assembly line people get their thinking mixed up.*

Perhaps this executive was overstating the case. However, he clearly recognized the danger that assembly line technology may tempt management to make certain questionable assumptions about human motivations and capacities. Even if one believes that these assumptions are statistically verifiable, morally right, or socially acceptable, he should still look askance at them. What about the *consequences* of them? If he holds them, how is he likely to act, and how will his actions affect other people? In short, how do they work out in practice?

Let us look at the matter from a pragmatic point of view. These negative assumptions can lead to a serious loss of potential. A management that justifies minute subdivision of the task into its simplest component parts, on the ground that many men prefer repetitive and relatively meaningless jobs, will not benefit from a release of creative interest in the job. Similarly, a management that emphasizes the coercive element in the moving line, on the ground that no one works effectively without externally imposed pressure, will not find the improved productivity that comes from people working hard because they want to and because they participate in setting the goals which are to be reached.

The foreman who gives his men the benefit of the doubt, who is willing to assume that his men want to and are able to do well and that their interest can be stimulated, gets the best results in the long run. But to do so he requires a great deal of support from his superiors and from the total management organization. That is why it is so important for the influence of assembly line technology to be consciously, purposefully counteracted. Otherwise negative assumptions about human ability and motivation may become unthinkingly accepted by managers down the line.

Conclusion

Managers often fail to practice what they preach. Yet sometimes this is very fortunate, because some of management's theories, especially concerning "how to get people to do things," would never work if uniformly put into practice! Many an organization seems to hold together and to succeed largely because certain principles about human behavior are successfully ignored or counteracted—in spite of the fact that the formal structure of the organization and the method of organizing the work process seem to be based on these very principles.

In some cases, if management followed too literally its own ideology, it would in practice defeat its own purposes. As Chester Barnard has pointed out:

> Disturbances of the equilibrium of cooperative systems have come from false ideologies, particularly on the part of those who are leaders or executives in formal organizations. The effect of these false notions is to vitiate the sense of experience when consciously dealing with problems of the theory of organization, and to reinforce personal predictions, prejudices, and interests, as destructive factors, in the guidance of organization practice.[9]

In other words, the ideology of engineering may be so destructive in terms of morale that the organization slows down despite the technical achievement.

There are many ways in which "false ideologies" can arise and be reinforced. This article has stressed the effects of mass production technology upon management's way of thinking and behaving—the relationship between the technology of the assembly line and certain unfruitful assumptions about human motivation. In other industries the points made here might be less striking and obvious, but I believe that an understanding of them is important to administrators of *any* large-scale enterprise.

---

[9] Chester I. Barnard, *The Functions of the Executive* (Cambridge: Harvard University Press, 1938), p. 286.

Our studies have repeatedly shown that the foremen judged most successful by both management and men are those who somehow counteract the technological influences toward a sense of pressure and impersonality. Does this not mean that the rationale behind extreme routinization and rigid mechanical pacing of work may be based on inadequate assumptions about why people behave as they do?

Admittedly these assumptions are hard to break because they tend to justify themselves. Action based upon them produces results which seem to confirm them. Perhaps this is only to be expected. The question is whether *other* action would not produce other and *better* results—and there is no easy answer. But it has been frequently demonstrated that top management has the peculiar and unpleasant duty to ask itself difficult questions, to re-examine fundamental values and beliefs, to compare means with ends and practice with theory, even when it hurts. Fortunately, this is exactly what many business leaders are doing.

Questions

1. Do you think that supervisors should absorb pressure from above rather than pass it on to employees? Why?
2. The author cites several instances where the foremen do not adhere to good engineering principles in order to make jobs more interesting and less monotonous. Is this action justifiable? What are some of the dangers?
3. Why do managers often believe that workers dislike responsibility?
4. Do you see any contradictions between formal principles of management and what is reported in this article about behavior of employees on the assembly line?
5. Would you conclude that the foreman on the assembly line has a more difficult job than the foreman or supervisor in other types of work situations?
6. From your reading of this article can you list some characteristics of employees who are likely to find assembly line work reasonably satisfying?

Additional Readings for Chapter 5

Argyris, Chris. "Organizational Effectiveness Under Stress," *Harvard Business Review*. Vol. 38, No. 3 (May-June, 1960), pp. 137-146.

Bellows, Roger. "Communication and Conformity," *Personnel Administration*. Vol. 23, No. 5 (September-October, 1960), pp. 20-28.

Berrien, F. K. "The Cybernetics of Management," *Personnel Administration*. Vol. 24, No. 4 (July-August, 1961), pp. 6-13.

Black, James M. "Employee Communication: All Dressed Up and No Place to Go?" *Management Review*. Vol. 48, No. 7 (July, 1959), pp. 4-8.

Buchanan, Paul C. "How Can *We* Gain *Their* Commitment?" *Personnel*. Vol. 42, No. 1 (January-February, 1965), pp. 21-26.

Chase, Stuart. "Executive Communications: Breaking the Semantic Barrier," *Management Review*. Vol. 46, No. 4 (April, 1957), pp. 58-66.

Clark, James J. "A Healthy Organization," *California Management Review*. Vol. 6, No. 4 (Summer, 1962), pp. 16-29.

Cohen, Arthur M. "Communication Networks: In Research and Training," *Personnel Administration*. Vol. 27, No. 3 (May-June, 1964), pp. 18-25.

Davis, Keith. "Group Behavior and the Organization Chart," *Advanced Management-Office Executive*. Vol. 1, No. 6 (June, 1962), pp. 14-16, 18.

Dunnette, Marvin D. "Are Meetings Any Good for Solving Problems?" *Personnel Administration*. Vol. 27, No. 2 (March-April, 1964), pp. 12-16.

Gibb, Jack R. "Communication and Productivity," *Personnel Administration*. Vol. 27, No. 1 (January-February, 1964), pp. 8-13.

Goode, Cecil E. "Greater Productivity Through the Organization of Work," *Personnel Administration*. Vol. 27, No. 1 (January-February, 1964), pp. 34-38.

Hayakawa, S. I. "Success and Failure In Communications," *Journal of the American Society of Training Directors*. Vol. 12, No. 7 (July, 1958), pp. 11-18.

Kahn, Robert L., and Charles F. Cannell. "Nobody Tells Me Anything," *Dun's Review and Modern Industry*. Vol. 70, No. 5 (November, 1957), pp. 36-38.

Kay, Brian R. "Rolecentrism: Potential Source of Conflict and Communication Failure," *Personnel Administration*. Vol. 28, No. 1 (January-February, 1965), pp. 20-24.

Korman, Abraham K. "A Cause of Communication Failure," *Personnel Administration*. Vol. 23, No. 3 (May-June, 1960), pp. 17-21.

Leavitt, Harold J. "Unhuman Organizations," *Harvard Business Review*. Vol. 40, No. 4 (July-August, 1962), pp. 90-98.

Levinson, Harry. "Reciprocation: The Relationship Between Man and Organization," *Administrative Science Quarterly*. Vol. 9, No. 4 (March, 1965), pp. 370-390.

Likert, Rensis, and Stanley E. Seashore. "Employee Attitudes and Output," *Monthly Labor Review*. Vol. 77, No. 6 (June, 1954), pp. 641-648.

MacKinney, A. C., *et al.* "Has Specialization Reduced Job Satisfaction?" *Personnel*. Vol. 39, No. 1 (January-February, 1962), pp. 8-17.

Maier, N. R. F., and L. R. Hoffman. "Group Decision in England and the United States," *Personnel Psychology*. Vol. 15, No. 1 (Spring, 1962), pp. 75-87.

Moore, David G., and Robert K. Burns. "How Good Is Good Morale," *Factory Management and Maintenance*. Vol. 114, No. 2 (February, 1956), pp. 130-136.

Patchen, Martin. "Participation in Decision-Making and Motivation," *Personnel Administration*. Vol. 27, No. 6 (November-December, 1964), pp. 24-31.

Porter, Lyman W. "Where is the Organization Man?" *Harvard Business Review*. Vol. 41, No. 6 (November-December, 1963), pp. 53-61.

Randall, Clarence B. "The Myth of Communications," *Dun's Review and Modern Industry*. Vol. 75, No. 1 (January, 1960), pp. 37-39.

Shelton, Henry W. "Mutual Ratings: Group Dynamics in Action," *Advanced Management Journal*. Vol. 30, No. 1 (January, 1965), pp. 55-58.

Stieglitz, Harold. "Barriers to Communications," *Management Record*. Vol. 20, No. 1 (January, 1958), pp. 2-5.

Viteles, Morris S. "What Raises a Man's Morale," *Personnel*. Vol. 30, No. 4 (January, 1954), pp. 302-313.

Walton, Eugene. "Motivation to Communicate," *Personnel Administration*. Vol. 25, No. 2 (March-April, 1962), pp. 17-19, 39.

Wilton, Frank. "Communications: What Do We Mean?" *Advanced Management*. Vol. 25, No. 8 (August, 1960), p. 12.

Worthy, James G. "Management Attitude and Employee Morale," *Management Review*. Vol. 43, No. 12 (December, 1954), pp. 789-790.

CHAPTER 6

Economic Incentives and Security

A major concern of every organization is that of keeping costs under control. One of the largest, if not the largest, costs of operation in any organization is that of labor. Both companies and government organizations, therefore, are confronted continually with the problem of trying to relate the wages and fringe benefits that are paid to their employees to the contributions that each person is rendering. Since the nature of the job being performed and effort being exerted tends to differ from employee to employee, the problem of administering a remuneration and fringe benefit program is an exceedingly difficult and complicated one. The problem is complicated still further by the fact that remuneration should serve not only to reward an individual for his past performance but also to motivate him to improve his future performance. The fact that the motivational value to be derived by an individual from his remuneration is dependent upon the way in which it is administered and upon the particular needs of each individual does not make the process of remuneration any simpler. In recent years the motivational value of wages has been questioned by some writers. Recent research in the behavioral sciences, as well the growth of fringe benefits, is cited as evidence to support the position that remuneration provides only minimum motivational value.

In this chapter the article by David W. Belcher defends the importance of money as a motivator and suggests why some contemporary wage and salary programs may be failing to achieve their intended objectives. In the next article Frances M. Torbert provides an excellent comparative analysis of the more widely known financial incentive systems and offers some useful suggestions for making financial incentives work. Costello and Zalkin, in their article, discuss a plan for making merit raises have greater incentive value.

Since fringe benefits have grown to the point where they constitute nearly 25 percent of the labor cost in many companies, the article by J. H. Foegen is a very timely one. This article discusses some of the detrimental features of fringe benefits and the growing problems that these benefits may create for companies in the future. In recent years increased attention has been focused upon the employment of the older worker. As the result of legislation, social pressures, labor shortages, and the tendency of employees to be held to a company by its pension plan, companies in the future are likely to have a larger proportion of older workers employed. The article by Daniel H. Kruger analyzes some of the problems of managing the older workers and suggests how they may be handled more effectively. Since more employees are remaining with an organization until their retirement, more attention must be given to retirement programs for these individuals. Growing recognition is being given to the fact that even though an adequate pension may minimize problems of financial adjustment, there are other areas of adjustment in which an employee who is approaching retirement may require assistance. The final article of the chapter by Herman K. Murphey presents a forceful case against compulsory retirement.

30. OMINOUS TRENDS IN WAGE AND SALARY ADMINISTRATION *

David W. Belcher

Lately, the field of wage and salary administration has been attacked with increasing frequency. It has been variously charged with erroneous assumptions, stereotyped thinking, and misunderstanding of the nature of motivation.[1] This, therefore, would seem to be an appropriate time to try to assess where wage and salary administration now stands—and where it is going.

Actually, it has even been prophesied that the wage system itself will disappear; but this seems to be a question we need not concern ourselves with just yet. If advancing technology does lead to the demise of the wage system, this is a change that will undoubtedly take some time. Meanwhile, employees will continue to be paid for their work.

But though we may continue to believe in the viability of the wage system, this does not mean that we can view the future of the function of wage and salary administration in an equally positive light. It is not beyond the realm of possibility that this function could either disappear altogether, decrease greatly in importance, or become sufficiently routine to be taken over by one of the smaller computers. In fact, a number of trends, if not reversed in the near future, appear to point in this direction.

The first of these trends is the growing acceptance of Herzberg's satisfiers-dissatisfiers theory of motivation. This theory, which appears to destroy the concept of pay as a motivator, derives from a study of professional employees that found pay to be one of a group of factors that Herzberg classifies as dissatisfiers or maintenance factors. These are the factors that, if lacking or deficient, can reduce employee motivation; on the other hand, regardless of how much

* From *Personnel*, Vol. 41, No. 5 (September-October, 1964), pp. 42-50. Reprinted with permission.

[1] *See*, for example, F. Munson, "Four Fallacies for Wage and Salary Administrators," *Personnel*, July-August, 1963, pp. 57-64; R. T. Golembiewski, "A Behavioral Approach to Wage Administration: Work Flow and Structural Design," *Academy of Management Journal*, December, 1963, pp. 267-277; and A. B. Campbell, "Salary Administration: Fundamentals, Fallacies, Predictions," *Advanced Management-Office Executive*, February, 1963, pp. 11-14.

they are improved, they don't seem to improve job performance beyond the neutral point. Along with pay, such factors as supervision, interpersonal relations, working conditions, company policy, benefits, and job security were found to fall into this group.[2]

Among the employees Herzberg studied, the motivators were what he calls satisfiers or achievement factors. These are the factors related to success in work and individual growth—the nature of the work itself, responsibility, and advancement.

It is not difficult to understand the readiness of the average manager to accept this theory. Not only does it deal with factors he is familiar with and deals with every day; it also corresponds quite closely to his experience that employees often react somewhat tepidly to such inducements as better working conditions, greater job security, and higher benefits.

The behavioral scientists have also hailed Herzberg's findings as further substantiating Maslow's well-known theory that human needs ascend in a hierarchy, each level of which must be satisfied before the next level of needs appears.[3] Since satisfied needs no longer motivate, it is necessary, according to Maslow, to find out what level of needs an individual has reached in order to spur him to greater effort. In this country most people are no longer concerned about satisfying the basic needs for food, shelter, and safety, and are now at least at the third level in the hierarchy—the social needs. (Herzberg's theory seems to indicate, however, that present-day employees have progressed beyond this stage and are operating at the level of esteem and self-fulfillment.)

Pay still the most important

Though Maslow's theory has led some behavioral scientists to conclude that money has lost its power to motivate because people are now moved by needs that money can't satisfy,[4] it's still pretty generally assumed that money is what we primarily work for. If motivation is now recognized as being much more complex than we

---

[2] F. Herzberg *et al.*, *The Motivation to Work* (2d ed.; New York: John Wiley & Sons, Inc., 1959). Though the methodology of this study and over-generalization of its findings have recently been criticized, acceptance of the theory has been encouraged by its agreement with Maslow's needs hierarchy and by managers' common-sense interpretation of employee reaction to Herzberg's maintenance factors.

[3] A. H. Maslow, *Motivation and Personality* (New York: Harper & Brothers, 1954).

[4] C. D. McDermid, "How Money Motivates Men," *Business Horizons*, Winter, 1960, pp. 93-100.

used to assume, pay still constitutes the most important single motivator used in our society.[5]

To regard Herzberg's theory as disproving pay as a motivator may be something of a misrepresentation of the theory itself. Rather, it can be argued that whether pay is an achievement or a maintenance factor depends on how pay is determined. If pay is geared to achievement and serves as recognition of achievement it would seem to be an achievement factor and thus a motivator. It is when pay is unrelated to performance that it serves purely as a maintenance factor.

The moribund merit philosophy

Unfortunately, it appears that the field of wage and salary administration is determined to make pay a maintenance factor—and thus to rob it of its motivation value. While almost every pay plan makes provision for what are called merit increases, in practice few increases granted fall into this category. Thus, a three-year study by the Brookings Institution of the effects of collective bargaining on management policy and practice in 150 U.S. companies found that while there was a great deal of management conviction about the merit philosophy, there was very little evidence that it was actually being followed.[6]

Corporate wage and salary administrators have been no less guilty than the unions in destroying the merit philosophy. Their insistence on "other bases for increases" and concern for consistency has led them to bury merit among such a myriad of other considerations that the recipient of a raise is fortunate if he can find where merit comes into the picture. Assuming that a man does get a raise for successful performance, if his previous raises have included "other bases for increases" he is likely to perceive his latest hike as being due to a tight labor market in his field, and any motivating value the increase might have had is lost.

Part of the difficulty, of course, is to convince management that money for economic adjustments serves a different purpose and must be separated from merit increases if the latter are to have any positive effect. Part is due also to the assumption that money in any form is an incentive. At the very least Herzberg's findings cast

---

[5] M. Haire *et al.*, "Psychological Research on Pay: An Overview," *Industrial Relations*, October, 1963, pp. 3-8.

[6] S. H. Slichter *et al.*, *The Impact of Collective Bargaining on Management* (Washington, D.C.: The Brookings Institution, 1960), p. 606.

serious doubt on the latter point. (A recent study found, though, that some overpaid people when placed on an hourly basis worked harder to redress the balance.[7])

Logically, at least, the wage and salary administrator who agrees to a program of increases on "an individual basis" instead of convincing management of the need to separate economic and merit adjustments is helping to destroy the motivating value of pay. The use of maturity curves in the administration of salaries for professional employees appears to be another sign of the death rattle of the merit philosophy. As with other systems, lip service is paid to merit but in practice the result is simply increases based upon seniority.

Thus, an apparent trend toward downgrading pay as a motivation tool is being reinforced by the people charged with seeing that payroll dollars accomplish the purposes of the organization. This seems to be the time for wage and salary administration to redesign pay plans to insure that pay operates as a motivator and to spend time educating managers in how pay can be designed to motivate.

The emphasis on techniques

Another trend in the field, which has lasted longer but shows no sign of changing course, is the emphasis on techniques rather than objectives. Wage and salary administrators seem to cling to methods of dealing with pay problems merely because things have been done this way for so long. Practices have grown into universal use simply on the basis of precedent, but few of the underlying assumptions of these practices have ever been tested or even questioned.

In fact, the basic assumptions of wage and salary administration have not been made explicit. They must be inferred from the policies and practices in common use. As a result, some of the recent criticism of the field has missed the point by attacking it as being based on certain assumptions that are not assumptions at all. Munson, for example, takes the position that wage and salary administration assumes that wages and salaries are determined by the market when, in fact, the failure of the market to answer most compensation questions is the basic reason for the existence of wage and salary administration.[8]

---

[7] J. S. Adams, "Wage Inequities, Productivity and Work Quality," *Industrial Relations*, October, 1963, pp. 9-16.

[8] Munson, *loc. cit.*

Another assumption, according to Munson, is that "the function of wage and salary administration is to relate (a) individual performance to (b) job worth to (c) market forces and, by juggling these three balls, arrive at a proper wage or salary." Actually, this is not an assumption of wage and salary administration but a description of attempts to measure contribution on three different scales. The basic assumptions are: (1) that contribution is a proper basis for wage and salary administration, (2) that contribution can be measured on these scales, and (3) a number of premises about motivation and employee satisfaction.

Typically, the practice of wage and salary administration appears to be based upon assumptions such as these:

1. Pay is an incentive to job performance.
2. Pay in the form of money has more incentive value than pay in the form of benefits.
3. Employee satisfaction with pay is evidence of its incentive value.
4. Consistent treatment of employees in the matter of pay is a prerequisite to obtaining incentive value from pay.
5. Incentive value is lost when employees are overpaid.
6. Employees react negatively to pay inequities.
7. Pay inequities are similarly defined by all types and levels of employees.
8. Employees regard internal pay inequities as more serious than external inequities.
9. Employees react only to gross external inequities.
10. Employee comparisons of pay are made first in terms of job, and second in terms of performance on jobs.
11. Employees compare their pay with that of people in similar jobs.
12. Employee comparisons of pay are uninfluenced by levels of aspiration and pay history.
13. Managers make pay comparisons that are essentially similar to those of rank-and-file employees.
14. Professional employees make external rather than internal comparisons.
15. Employees accept the concept of a hierarchy of jobs and pay.
16. Employees' determinants of the job hierarchy are similar to management's determinants.
17. Employees agree with management on what they are paid for and weigh the factors (performance, seniority, job knowledge and skill, labor market, and so on) the same.

In fact, little is known about the accuracy of these and other assumptions on which wage and salary administration is based. What is more serious, wage and salary administrators appear neither to question these assumptions nor to show any inclination to test them, despite the excellent position they are in to gather data and even to experiment. In fact, some even seem to be opposed to testing any assumptions at all.

Fortunately, a few studies are being made—chiefly by the psychologists.[9] The findings to date suggest that careful re-examination of current practice is overdue.

For example, as has already been pointed out, current motivation theory implies that, in the matter of the incentive value of pay, practice is pointing in precisely the wrong direction. The theory suggests that pay serves as an incentive only when it is designed to do so—when it is clearly seen as a form of recognition or evidence of achievement.

A recent study found that managers at the same level in different companies manifested a remarkable unanimity of opinion as to the relative pay they felt they should receive, whether they received it or not. At each level the managers also agreed that their pay differed from the level of compensation they deemed appropriate, and the lower the level, the greater was their perceived difference.[10]

This finding raises the question whether there is a positive or a negative relation between dissatisfaction and performance. Is there an incentive here that grows stronger with dissatisfaction with pay? If so, should not wage and salary administrators spend more time devising methods of channeling this incentive toward the achievement of organizational goals and less time trying merely to remove dissatisfaction? In fact, shouldn't wage and salary administrators see their job as *creating* dissatisfaction with present pay?

It would seem that the wage and salary administrator must decide whether pay is to be designed to satisfy employees or to motivate them. And, if motivation is the aim, he must then decide what kind—motivation to come and stay with the organization, motivation to produce, motivation to develop, and so on.

As for the problem of pay inequities, effective techniques for removing these depend upon the accuracy of the assumptions about how employees define inequities. Patchen, for example, found that an employee defines equity not only in terms of the absolute amount of his salary but also in terms of how his salary matches that of other people he compares himself with. If the difference between his salary and that received by these people seems to be appropriate in terms of the other differences between them (e.g., age, education,

[9] "A Symposium: Psychological Research on Pay," *Industrial Relations*, October, 1963, pp. 3-49.

[10] E. E. Lawler III and L. W. Porter, "Perceptions Regarding Management Compensation," *Industrial Relations*, October, 1963, pp. 41-49.

skill, and so on), then the comparison increases his satisfaction. If, however, the salary difference seems greater than these differences, his pay satisfaction is diminished.[11]

Another recent study found that first-line managers and higher middle managers (department heads, for example) tended to make intracompany comparisons, while middle managers closely compared themselves with groups outside the organization.[12] Further, those managers with more education were more likely to compare with groups outside the company.

These findings hold strong suggestions for both executive and professional compensation. With the growing professionalism in many positions, pay equity is more often defined by outside rather than by inside groups. The same study also found a strong relation between a manager's satisfaction with his pay and his belief that it was equitable in comparison with that of his subordinates—a finding that suggests a method of determining the points where internal or external comparison takes precedence.

Money vs. benefits

The typical assumption that money carries a higher value to employees than benefits has also been tested recently by Nealey. His study found that there are large differences in the value of a particular benefit from group to group, depending upon age, sex, marital status, number of children, type of job held, and yearly income.[13] That this should be so is not surprising, but it is at least possible that the common observation that benefit plans carry a low incentive value is merely the result of providing the same benefits to all employees.

A few companies are now permitting their executives to choose the components of their pay package with the aim of maximizing the motivation value of each pay and benefit dollar. While it might be troublesome administratively to extend the same practice to wage earners, the question whether wage earners should be permitted to choose among equal cost items in the light of their individual situations or be provided with an identical package whether they want it

---

[11] M. Patchen, *The Choice of Wage Comparisons* (Englewood Cliffs, N. J.: Prentice-Hall, Inc., 1961).

[12] I. R. Andrews and M. M. Henry, "Management Attitudes Toward Pay," *Industrial Relations*, October, 1963, pp. 29-39.

[13] S. M. Nealey, "Pay and Benefit Preference," *Industrial Relations*, October, 1963, pp. 17-28.

or not may well repay consideration. Actually, it may make more sense to allow rank-and-file employees to make such choices than to allow managers to do so. According to a recent study by Mahoney, managers want only a very small proportion of their compensation in the form of benefits.[14]

In the Nealey study, the pay and benefit choices of employees were compared with their attitudes toward company policy and practices on promotion, employment security, wages, and supervision. Dissatisfied employees preferred pay to benefits, Nealey found. He also found that preferences for pay increases over benefits declined as employee income increased. The Mahoney study, which was confined to managers, did not bear out this finding. It thus appears that managers and nonmanagers view compensation quite differently.

A more logical approach

The fact that it is possible to determine employee preferences on pay and benefits means that it is equally possible to ascertain their preferences as regards the weight to be attached to performance, seniority, job factors, and the labor market in determining pay. Wouldn't it make more sense to base wages and salaries on these actual preferences rather than unsupported assumptions about what they are?

The emphasis of wage and salary administration on techniques has obscured its objectives and made it possible to ignore the assumptions on which the techniques are based. When the field is defined as wage surveys, job evaluation, and merit rating, the internal logic is that equity and contribution are measured and the former is achieved by paying for the latter.

It is only when questions are raised about the ability of the techniques to measure and achieve equity and contribution that the underlying assumptions become apparent. Equity implies numerous assumptions concerning employee comparisons and perceived satisfactions or dissatisfactions with the results of these comparisons. Contribution implies assumptions concerning what measures of contribution are perceived as appropriate and, if more than one measure is to be employed, which should bear the heavier weight. Achieving motivation from wage and salary programs logically depends upon creating differentials that (1) are perceived as appropriate and

---

[14] T. A. Mahoney, "Compensation Preferences of Managers," *Industrial Relations*, May, 1964, pp. 135-144.

(2) motivate contribution to organizational goals. If the assumptions underlying programs designed to achieve equity or measure contribution are unrealistic, neither can be achieved.

"Specialist sclerosis"

Another trend worth noting is the fact that wage and salary administration is now in the advanced stages of "specialist sclerosis," or hardening of the administrative arteries. While the field is probably no more prone to this disease than other staff specialties, the adverse effects on the balance of the organization may be more severe.

The first symptom of specialist sclerosis is the forcing of old solutions on new problems instead of a search for new solutions. Thus, the past 50 years have been spent on improving the old techniques rather than on innovating. It has taken a little time, but the traditionalists have finally swallowed the maturity curve approach. (Not that the maturity curve represents any great improvement, but at any rate it is a new approach based upon at least one valid assumption—that professionals compare salaries with outsiders.)

The second symptom of specialist sclerosis is the tendency to make the job easier even at the cost of sacrificing organizational goals in the process. Thus the growing use of (1) global surveys, with their gross statistical instead of job comparisons, and maturity curves; (2) ready-made job evaluation plans; (3) other considerations (besides merit) in granting pay increases; and (4) methods that water down incentive plans instead of either eliminating them or designing new ones. The fact that the first tendency may turn out to be as good in terms of organizational objectives as the last two are bad does not alter the fact that all were probably adopted to make the job easier.

The third symptom is the tendency of the wage and salary administrator to become a policeman. Instead of perceiving his function as one of helping managers to accomplish the purposes of the organization, he sees himself as a man with his back to the wall of the corporate treasury with a single weapon to protect it—a baseball bat. Instead of perceiving himself as a trainer and innovator, he acquires police power and exercises control by approval. Apparently, he views his role as a bureaucrat in the worst sense of the word.

Last comes the reverence for techniques rather than ideas. Evidence of this symptom is the tendency to force programs upon managers instead of functioning as a source of ideas on how to get the most out of payroll dollars. Actually, the wage and salary administrator is in an excellent position to generate ideas for solutions to organizational problems.

From his knowledge of the labor market, the wage and salary man should be able to suggest: (1) job categories where it would be profitable to raise or lower hiring standards and pay, (2) job categories where further recruitment efforts should be broadened or curtailed, and (3) skills in long supply that could fill shortage areas with a minimum of retraining. From his knowledge of jobs in the organization, he should be able to offer suggestions for redesigning jobs, organization planning, and manpower budgeting. And from his knowledge of employees, he should be able to contribute to such problems as employee development and shifts in personnel beyond departmental lines.

In defense of the wage and salary administrator, it must be admitted that the ominous trends examined here did not entirely originate with him or even with his predecessors. The prevalent notion that pay has ceased to be a motivator is due at least in part to neglect of the motivation problem by economists, as well as to the emphasis by behavioral scientists on other factors in the work situation. But it must also be admitted that wage and salary administration policies and practices have reinforced rather than countered this viewpoint.

Of course, wage and salary administrators are not alone in failing to question or test the assumptions behind their practices, nor are they any more prone to specialist sclerosis than any other breed of specialists. But such excuses will not save the field from the destruction these trends portend. The only hope of reversing these trends lies in the encouragement of empirical research and a much greater willingness to innovate than wage and salary practitioners have manifested thus far.

Questions

1. What effect, if any, have the theories of Herzberg and Maslow had upon attitudes of some behavioral scientists toward the value of wages as an effective motivator?

2. What does the author consider to be the key factor in determining whether or not money will serve as an effective motivator?

3. In what ways have company wage and salary administration practices tended to reduce the motivational value of wages?

4. In this article the question "Shouldn't wage and salary administrators see their job as creating dissatisfaction with present pay?" is raised. What is this question getting at? What is your response to the question?

5. What major criticism does this article raise concerning the role of the wage and salary administrator? What suggestions does it offer regarding the improvement of this role?

31. MAKING INCENTIVES WORK *

Frances Torbert

- Are there incentive plans which increase acceptance of the goals of business, reduce resistance to change, and maintain high productivity?
- How many companies overrate the effectiveness of their piecework incentive programs?
- Do most incentive plans distort earnings in relation to employee skill and effort?
- What is automation doing to the concept of piecework?
- Can we study pay practices without examining management, worker, and union attitudes and behavior?

"If you read the surveys and listen to some industrial engineers, you think piecework is still *the* answer," said a plant manager recently, "but I'm betting that in less than five years 60% of piecework plans will be dead and buried." The speaker, who used to be enthusiastic about individual incentives, is sure that in two years management in his firm will have shifted to some other program.

Interviews with many executives, especially in smaller companies, suggest that stability in incentive programs may be more apparent than real. Predictions on the two- to five-year picture in automation tend to confirm the forecast, without regard to company size.

Piece rates and similar *individual* incentives may continue in more than 40% of present applications; in a few aspects of semi-automated work, there may be areas of usefulness for them. But in a period of rapid technological change and shifts in labor-management relations, perhaps we should take another look at piecework and the advantages of some of its possible alternatives—particularly *group* incentive plans. Once heralded as the solution to all labor-management problems, group plans still have their enthusiasts as well as their skeptics. What progress have these programs made?

Piecework Problems

Even without automation, which in its advanced forms makes individual piece rates absurd, many things are happening which

* From the *Harvard Business Review*, Vol 37, No. 5 (September-October, 1959), pp. 81-92. Reprinted with permission.

reduce the usefulness of individual incentives. The increased percentage of indirect labor, the variety of tasks performed by indirect workers, and the blurring of the distinction between direct and indirect work have presented a major problem. Much time and money have gone into attempts to set standards for indirect work, and a few large companies claim success in this venture. But attempts to use individual incentives for these employees have not often succeeded in smaller firms. Most attempts at piece-rate and similar programs for indirect workers have had poor results.

Even in direct labor areas the amount of trouble appears to be greater than many managers admit. Loose rates, maintenance costs for standards revision and clerical work, grievances, worker resistance to change, whipsawing union pressures of rates and base pay, and related problems are causing some employers to pay more to get work done under incentives than competitors are paying under daywork. Further, companies which pay time wages more often have retained proper relationships between pay and skill. Maintenance men and other skilled workers are particularly likely to find their pay "out of whack" when semiskilled workers have been able to maintain high earnings under incentives.

Restriction of output

And what about the worker who does not respond—who does not *want* to respond—to incentives? Researchers have not neglected him, either.

Whiting Williams and others described restrictive behavior in the early part of this century, and the Hawthorne studies, made at Western Electric Company in the 1920's, documented output restriction unforgettably. A flood of information on restrictions comes every year from workers and ex-workers; yet claims regarding the power of incentives continue.

Perhaps the most interesting recent report of incentive responses is from Melville Dalton:

> He studied a group of 84 experienced machine-shop workers. Output figures for these men were kept for two years. Only 9 men—less than 11%—made an all-out response to the piece-rate incentive, and 25% did not respond at all. The rest responded unevenly, but kept a ceiling on their efforts at all times. Many of the men in this group showed feelings of distress about the incentives. The other two groups of workers had resolved their conflicts. According to Dalton, "the rate busters renounced the group; the bottom producers renounced the incentives."

The rate busters were "lone wolves," who were highly money-conscious. They not only were anxious to earn as much as possible; they also saved their money and were reluctant and niggardly contributors to charity drives. The all-out restricters, with the lowest incomes, led active social lives inside and outside the shop.

The men in the middle included 9 with ulcers or incipient ulcers—an illness often associated with tension. None of the other men were thus afflicted. Said one of the men in the middle group:

> Nobody gets any good out of an incentive system. It makes bad feeling among the workers, between the workers and the checkers, and between workers and the bosses. Now you take that son-of-a-bitch over there [nodding toward a rate buster], the incentive system made him what he is. He's got a bad principle and the system brought it out. . . .
>
> The thing that's so damn aggravating is that one job pays twice as much as it should and the next only one fourth what it should. What you make you lose. . . .[1]

Dalton and Whyte agree that these men may not be typical of experienced incentive workers. Yet the study yields results which resemble those in other analyses. Indeed, as a whole this group appears to have responded to incentives with somewhat *more* effort than groups described in other studies.

Worker connivance

All of this raises some very practical questions for management. How many firms want to settle for adriot fooling of time-study men by cynical workers, large numbers of grievances (20% or more) growing out of rate complaints, and divisive feelings between workers and the company? How many want to encourage featherbedding? Pressure by workers for more service from tool cribs, more runners, shop clerks, and other accessory employees "so we won't have to do nonincentive work" is exerted even when direct workers are actually holding a ceiling on effort.

Herbert R. Northrup, who reports such practices, gives interesting evidence of a production increase to suit a special purpose:

> Success in converting the incentive system into a featherbedding device is revealed annually during the first two weeks in May. Earnings during this period determine vacations [in a certain company]. Curiously enough, earnings generally spurt about 30 per cent above the average for the previous six weeks.[2]

---

[1] *See* William F. Whyte and others, *Money and Motivation* (New York, Harper & Brothers, 1955), pp. 39-49.

[2] "The Other Side of Incentives," *Personnel* (January-February, 1959), pp. 32-41.

One foreman told me that, harried by workers, industrial engineers, and cost accounting people, he often connives with his men to
get and keep loose rates. He commented:

> Piecework brings out the worst in men. They decide that the
> company plays dirty, so they play dirty, too. And these managers who
> think workers are so dumb are actually being out-smarted every day
> of the year. They brought it on themselves.

In perspective

But all is not black with piecework. It has worked fairly well,
especially in firms with records of outstanding fairness and competence. Moreover, piecework has certain advantages to workers
besides possible monetary gains. Incentive systems may free men
from supervision: "I've made my quota; now I can loaf or talk."
Again, the operative on a repetitious job may find that time passes
less slowly when he is thinking about making his quota—if he
decides to make the effort. Also, there are the amusements of organized goldbricking, of "deals" with tool-crib men, of figuring out
improved hiding places for "kitties," of working out a slow timing
for a fast job, and so on.

On balance, however, it is difficult to recommend piecework for
many companies. If it solves problems, it tends to solve them in the
short run only to multiply them in the long run. And in a dynamic
society in which productivity *and* cooperation are needed, piecework
tends to destroy the will to cooperate. Group incentive programs—
which stimulate both effort and cooperation—may be better (though
not, of course, perfect) alternatives.

Group Incentives

In "Life in the Automatic Factory," Charles R. Walker has
reported that conventional individual incentives are inappropriate
for automated work.[3] In a pipe mill he studied:

> The operators of highly automatic machinery complained that in-
> centive coverage was too narrow. They wanted maintenance men in-
> cluded, even if the result were a reduction in their own pay. Down
> time is a major problem under automation; hence the relationship of
> maintenance to production is an intrinsic one.
>
> When asked for comments about their new work, the men requested
> "a chance to help solve mill problems." They also observed that unless
> the work performed by each man was properly related to that of every-
> one else costly troubles developed.

---

[3] HBR (January-February, 1958), pp. 111-119.

This suggests the advisability of group incentives, combined with production committees or employee meetings to aid in solving scheduling and operating difficulties under automation. Some managements report that group incentives have got them out of serious economic difficulties even with conventional technology.

One California company with departmental and subdepartmental group incentive plans found that production almost doubled when a deteriorated piece-rate system was discarded in favor of the group bonuses. Base rates in this firm are kept carefully in line with area wage rates. Transferability of workers between departments now is readily accepted. Average bonuses have ranged from 15% to 20% of base pay. Self-policing by group members is excellent, and low production workers have been discharged because of pressure from other employees for their elimination.

Employee-initiated action

Group incentives do not always work so well, but chances for success usually increase when a management adds the ingredient of interaction. To illustrate how a group bonus can fail to motivate until changes of this kind are introduced, let us take another illustration from Whyte:

In the paint room of a company which manufactured wooden toys, women spray-painted the toys, then hung them on hooks which carried them into a drying oven. The girls were on a group learners' bonus for six months. Industrial engineers had estimated that workers would reach standard performance at the end of this time.

But things went badly. Absenteeism, turnover, and complaints were serious. Many hooks went into the oven empty. The girls said that time-study men expected the impossible, and complained of heat from the oven, of fumes, and of the messy nature of the work.

A consultant was brought in. The foreman decided, after having a talk with him, to meet with the girls to discuss their work. At the meeting, the girls complained that the room was poorly ventilated and hot. The foreman volunteered to seek a solution to this problem, and suggested a later meeting to report results. At the second meeting the girls asked for some large fans. Management agreed to this, and three fans were installed.

The employees' attitude seemed enough improved so that the foreman ventured another meeting. It had barely started when the girls complained that time-study men had set the conveyor speed too fast. Then they asked to be allowed to control its speed themselves. They said they could keep up with the conveyor part of the time, but not all day long.

This heretical request was at first turned down. But after meetings between standards men and the foreman, there finally came an admission that some latitude on conveyor speed was possible. The decision was made to try the girls' idea.

A dial marked "low, medium, fast" was installed. (The medium speed was a little above the constant speed at which the engineers had previously set the belt.) After experimenting with the speeds, the girls settled on a definite pattern. For the first half hour of the day the dial was set at a point slightly above "medium." The next two-and-a-half hours were run at high speed. The half hour before lunch and the half hour after lunch were run at low. Then the speed was changed to high, and left there until the last forty-five minutes, which were worked at the medium setting.

The girls now reported that they were working at a comfortable pace; scarcely a hook went by empty; and rejects did not increase. It is not hard to surmise what happened to productivity. Two months before the learners' bonus was to end, production was 30% to 50% above the expected level. The girls were now collecting their base pay, learners' bonus, and regular bonus.

Thus, management was on the spot in the matter of pay relationships. The girls were earning more money than many skilled workers, and the latter knew it. Whyte reports:

> . . . Without consultation, the superintendent revoked the learning bonus, and returned the painting operation to its original status: the hooks moved again at their constant, time-studied speed, production dropped again, and within a month all but two of the girls had quit. The foreman stayed on for several months, but, feeling aggrieved, then left for another job.[4]

Tapping the potentials

There are a number of observations to be made about this case. One is that human beings are not comfortable always working at the same speed. (A handful of industrial engineers have, on their own, proposed varying speeds for machine-paced work.) Another lesson is that basic changes should not be made in one part of an organization if management does not understand the changes and is not prepared to try them throughout the firm. Another problem is that of intergroup pay discrepancies.

But the central question here is: *Do we really tap the interest and capacity of work groups and hence improve productivity and morale unless we give workers some chance to have a say in their work?* Neither group nor individual bonuses do this automatically.

One of the deepest needs of psychologically healthy people is to be able to initiate action in some of the matters which are important to them. Rank-and-file workers who take part in decisions affecting their work nearly always change their attitudes favorably. Under such conditions, higher production and work standards are maintained, contrary to "old-line" management expectations.[5]

---

[4] William F. Whyte, *op. cit.*, pp. 90-96.

[5] For a few examples of desirable outcomes in cases where workers have a hand in decisions involving their work assignments, *see* Chapters 8 and 9 of

If we can generalize from the paint room case, we may conclude that when employees are allowed to take the initiative in a few matters of direct concern to them, they can take production "through the ceiling." Could not the same principle apply with equal force to workers in the quality control, inventory, selling, and other areas? The possibilities of company-wide improvement seem great. Suppose, for instance, that in the foregoing case the other departments of the company had been given a comparable chance to initiate action— might not the company have captured a larger share of its market and increased its profits?

Some companies actually have used, on an organization-wide basis, a combination of group incentives and opportunities for employees to share in the task of thinking about their work:

> ● Such an approach is followed in principle by firms which use the Scanlon plan or some adaptation of it.
> ● In a plan devised by Allen Rucker of The Eddy-Rucker-Nickels Company, employee committees and meetings are a basic ingredient of the incentive operation.
> ● The Lincoln Electric Company does not use group bonuses, but does use a vigorous employee committee, which has met with top management on all problems affecting work and workers since 1913.
> ● The Nunn-Bush Shoe Company has involved workers and union in some aspects of decision making, at the same time that it has given employees 52 paychecks a year based on labor's percentage share in value added by manufacture.

I could cite a number of other companies that have created similar successful combinations of group incentives and employee productivity improvement committees.

Elements of Cooperation

The concepts of participative and consultative management have frequently come under attack.[6] The validity of such challenges cannot be denied. Even in companies where executives sincerely want the values of participation, there are forces at work which push toward conventional (e.g., highly authoritarian) leadership. Often a major force of this kind is the pre-existing relationship between company and union. Furthermore, many executives are incredulous and cynical in their attitudes toward the whole concept.

Norman R. F. Maier, *Principles of Human Relations* (New York, John Wiley & Sons, Inc., 1952); Lester Coch and John French, Jr., "Overcoming Resistance to Change," *Human Relations*, Vol. I, No. 4 (1948), pp. 512-532; and F. J. Roethlisberger, *Management and Morale* (Cambridge, Harvard University Press, 1941), p. 14.

[6] Robert N. McMurry, "The Case for Benevolent Autocracy," HBR (January-February, 1958), pp. 82-90.

But a few companies *have* successfully employed these concepts, and their experience is a revealing one. It points up the vital importance of creating an appropriate philosophy and framework. Unless both a framework *and* a point of view prevail, "participation" tends to be one of the shortest-lived of management fads.

Employee reaction

Experience with Rucker and Scanlon plan companies, the behavior of the paint room girls, and records of other situations in which workers have responded well to group incentives and to the chance to initiate action regarding their work offer proof to the cynics that good results are obtained with such programs. There is testimony from many managements of conventionally run companies that *their* workers are apathetic and alienated. Researchers have substantiated this claim. They describe employees who regard their work only as a means to a paycheck. Also, they often describe the work assignments of these workers, and the management controls which surround them, as conducive to indifference or alienation.

The president of a small company which has successfully installed and maintained a Rucker plan says that his employees were chiefly listless or anticompany before the plan installation, and that in the first few months after the program started many remained that way. Then, week by week, the change in the way people felt and acted became more noticeable. He told me:

> I learned for the first time how much people can change when they have a reason to. A factory full of 'don't care' employees is not inevitable. . . . The company and the union may make Rucker's plan fail. But if employees believe you're honest, *and you are*, you can stop worrying about *them*. Don't try to tell me that the main trouble isn't with us. Up till a few years ago I was reaping what I'd sowed, but I was blaming it on the other fellow.

This executive's experience may have made him overly optimistic, but interviews with top-management people in over 20 Rucker and Scanlon plan companies and with H. L. Nunn seem to bear him out. Every single employee does not "catch fire" as a result of these programs. Some employees dislike or ignore them. But the failures in using the plans seem to be management or union leadership failures. Employee response is good when leadership is good. Most employees not only respond to the well-run plan; they carry their apathetic colleagues along with them—or pressure the company to eliminate them, as in the California example described above.

Hampered by habit

Management habits are so hard to break that most companies do not want to make the effort if they are "getting by" as is. Also, we have not cultivated much patience in matters involving worker-management cooperation. A few misunderstandings, delays, and instances of immature or hostile behavior on either side will lead the other to resort to the clichés with which each has castigated the other for so many years. Leaders, instead of trying again, triumphantly announce, "I told you it wouldn't work! Those so-and-so's [in management *or* working groups] can't be trusted."

Basic self-confidence on both sides of the fence is a prerequisite to cooperation. The less secure the leaders, the greater the problem of getting started on a cooperative relationship. Both management and leaders of organized labor are influenced by ways of thinking and repetitions of slogans about themselves and each other. They are often timid about what counterparts in labor or management will say of them if they try anything unfamiliar to less courageous colleagues. The gibes of conformists on both sides of the fence have sometimes frightened company presidents and union leaders into maintaining a wary stance, even after they have glimpsed a more productive relationship.

Many managers also fail to recognize the contributions which employees can make if given the opportunity. They are unaware of the barriers which they, their staff departments, and their foremen unconsciously set up to stall off workers' ideas, despite conventional suggestion systems and "open door" policies. According to one authority:

> The worker has a highly detailed knowledge of the particular operations that are taking place around him. He knows from experience throughout the shift what causes bottlenecks and why. He can explain how raw materials differ from day to day. . . . He knows, too, where teamwork is falling down . . . why the best methods are not being utilized. . . . On technical matters the worker often has ideas for improvement but he needs help to develop them. Where this help is readily available . . . the worker can [avoid] the embarrassment of being told that his was a 'stupid idea.' [7]

Unless management and workers—organized or not—undertake to create a built-in structure for listening to each other and working together, old habits of thought and attitudes of mutual doubt and fear are bound to continue. They do not disappear quickly or completely

---

[7] Robert Saltonstall, *Human Relations in Administration* (New York, McGraw-Hill Book Company, Inc., 1959), p. 260.

even under a structured program for cooperation. However, if in addition to a framework for product and method improvement, there is a group monetary incentive—departmental or company-wide —the drive to improve cooperation *and* performance is obviously enhanced. A few companies use structured improvement committees with time wages or piecework, but the records of their successes are not as well documented as in the cases which combine group incentives and a ladder of production committees.

The Scanlon Plan

I should like to turn now from general concepts and principles to some of the specific plans already mentioned. A logical place to begin is with the program named after the late Joseph Scanlon.

How it works

What actually happens when a company and its work force agree to adopt the Scanlon plan?

First of all they usually study the program at length. Then they set up an incentive plan which generally includes everyone in the company. In Scanlon plan companies, a formula is developed to measure and distribute gains made through resultant improvements in productivity. This formula is developed in different ways, depending on the nature of the company's work, labor cost experience, and other factors. A common method is to find a historically normal labor cost and then divide among covered employees the difference between the established "norm" and what is achieved under the plan.[8]

Once the relationship between total payroll and the sales value produced by it is established, a bonus pool is created for any month when labor costs are below the norm. To protect against deficit months, a reserve of 25% is set aside from the pool. If anything is left in this reserve at the end of the year, an extra payment is made. After the reserve has been taken out for a given month, the balance of the bonus is split, with 25% usually going to the company and the remaining 75% to employees. Take the following example:

> A plant finds that its labor cost is normally 40% of the sales value of production, plus or minus inventory change. If shipments plus in-

---

[8] *See* Chapters 3, 6, and 10 of *The Scanlon Plan,* edited by Fred Lesieur (Cambridge, The Technology Press, and New York, John Wiley & Sons, Inc., 1958).

ventory increase in a given month are $1,000,000 and labor costs are $370,000, there would then be a bonus pool of $30,000.

Since the company gets 25% of the pool, after reserves have been set aside, the ratio does not have to be adjusted for minor changes that would affect the norm. It *is* essential, however, that the norm be changed when price or wage changes, major purchases of labor- or time-saving machinery, or anything else materially affects the ratio of costs to the sales value of production. A "memorandum of understanding" lists the bases for ratio changes.

This concept of changes in the ratio alarms company and union leaders when there has been a history of union-management warfare over every issue involving pay. They cannot believe that realistic ratio changes can be made which will be regarded as fair by both sides. In Scanlon companies ratio changes *are* made, and the process of change becomes one of the elements of recognizing the mutual, though not identical, interests of workers and company.

There is no form of economic education in industry which compares in effectiveness with group incentives and group interaction based on facts about sales and costs. Because these matters come to be understood and are important to all, adjustments can be worked out.

Cooperation steps

Companies with effective Scanlon installations point out that the money incentive, while essential, is not the heart of the plan. At Scanlon plan conferences held annually at the Massachusetts Institute of Technology, it is always observed that people sent to learn about the plan are much concerned about ratios and employee earnings. Firms using the plan are convinced that successful results depend on fundamental changes in concepts about working together.

We would do well to consider the procedure typically followed by companies adopting the Scanlon plan:

(1) A basic structural step in cooperation is the elimination of the conventional suggestion system if there is one (many are already half-dead). In each department or other significant work group, employees elect by secret ballot a representative to meet with the supervisor to study better work methods. Meetings are held once or twice a month, and are attended not only by foremen and production committee members, but also by any other employees in the group who have suggestions about methods, materials, machines, scrap control, or other pertinent matters. Minutes are kept of each meeting.

(2) If the suggestions are valid and do not involve other departments, significant money outlays, or other major changes outside the foreman's "area of freedom," they can be adopted as soon as perfected. If the foreman or another supervisor can show the employees that there are reasons why the idea will not work, it is either abandoned or reworked to make it usable.

(3) If the idea seems good to employees, even though it is not reacted to favorably by the foreman, it can be referred to a screening committee. It must go to the screening committee if it requires interdepartmental action, or higher-level study or approval. The screening committee is composed of elected employee members and representatives of top management, usually the company president or executive vice-president, the controller, and top production executives.

(4) In this and the department committee there is no voting on suggestions. Top management has unqualified veto power on ideas. Worker representatives may act as advocates for suggestions, but in practice often are divided among themselves on the merits of a specific idea. Guests from department-level committees are often present to discuss ideas originating with them.

(5) The screening committee also announces production and costs for the previous month, and the resulting bonus, if any. In addition, it studies ideas which come from its own membership, plus other problems of company-wide interest. What production and screening committees do and how they do it are a far cry from the operation of a conventional suggestion plan. An observer reports:

> Sometimes the workers throw the book at management; sometimes management points out where the shop has fallen down. Engineers argue against machine-tool operators; foremen attack the engineers for unrealistic blueprints.[9]

This sort of approach links incentives with technological change. It stands in marked contrast to the situation that exists, for example, in companies which combine suggestion systems and piecework—the effect being that the two are often directly opposed in employees' minds. If workers under piece rates submit suggestions for better work methods, industrial engineering departments usually restudy jobs. The result may be a new rate which makes it harder for employees to "make out." If a bright idea can be kept from the motion-and-time-study men, earnings will increase under existing piece rates, or former earnings will be maintained with less output of time and effort.

Changed attitudes

A number of advantages usually result from the changed climate of a group program:

---

[9] *Ibid.*, p. 26.

- The free and *continuous* opportunity for employees to initiate action in and of itself tends to create a production-centered climate. Arguments and conflicts of interest will take place as always, but the reason will be more because employees are *concerned* over their work than because they resent management or are out to "beat the company."

- Introduction of new methods and machines by management is regarded differently. One company executive says that resistance to change has disappeared within his firm.

- Because it is advantageous to do so, workers develop an interest in training new employees.

- Workers also tend to bear down on employees who are not responding to the program.

- Workers discipline themselves more. Hence in many companies with participative programs the foreman is freed almost completely from discipline problems. He can concentrate on better scheduling and other profitable activities.

- An observer can spend weeks in a Scanlon plan company without observing anything that suggests a "speed up." Employees do not look or act rushed, their work pace is comfortable, there are pauses for conversation but less time is wasted.

- Not only do employees show new interest in company success by doing more careful work, but they exert pressures on management to manage better.

If there is any trouble with the Scanlon plan, it may be that it is sometimes *too* successful. For example, after the program has been in operation for a while it may become startlingly clear that the piece-work rates formerly used were extremely ineffective in motivating workers. Such a revelation is not calculated to please any supervisors who supported the piecework system. Again, the new program may lead to the discovery of waste in clerical departments, unrealistic activities in engineering, and absurdities in accounting practice— all of which can be corrected through the use of Scanlon plan principles, but which might be interpreted to reflect poorly on some managers' past performance.

Such danger lies in any major improvement, of course. I do not want to overestimate it, but only to note that, as always, tact and courage can do much to make the Scanlon machinery effective.

Other Incentive Plans

Two other group incentive programs deserve attention here. One of them is a widely used plan devised by Allen W. Rucker, a management consultant. The other was developed by a businessman, H. L. Nunn.

Share of production

The Rucker plan is most applied to hourly rated factory workers and to executives, but in some cases is developed to cover all employees in a company. It is based on sophisticated and extensive figure analysis. A historical relationship is established between total earning (including fringe benefits) of hourly rated employees and the net production values created by the company. If major changes in products or processes occur, the plan is re-engineered.

Under this plan, company and workers share any increases in "value added by manufacture" which grows out of their joint efforts. This principle, of course, eliminates the cost of raw materials purchased and related costs such as supplies and power. For every 1% increase in production value the plan provides for an increase of 1% in total payroll credit for eligible workers. Thus an integrated incentive is provided for:

1. Reduction in material and supply costs.
2. Reduction in scrap and returns by customers.
3. Improvement in product quality.
4. Less labor cost for the same values, or the same cost for greater values.

Since the plan is based on realized production value income, the company's ability to increase sales volume and provide stable employment is increased, as is its ability to lower prices to meet competition.

Rucker has shown that, for the United States as a whole, factory workers' pay has been proportionate to production values for 50 years. The relationship has prevailed to within 1.663%. Labor's average share has been 39.395%; management's, 60.605%. (For individual industries and companies similar stable relationships have been established.) Booms, depressions, wars, changes in political leadership in the nation, and the introduction of increasing amounts of labor- and time-saving machinery have scarcely affected the ratios. Labor *time*, says Rucker, has been cut about 70% since 1914, but wages have made up almost precisely the same percentage of value added by manufacture.

In installations of Rucker incentives, employee committees are used, although they are often set up somewhat differently from those used in Scanlon plans. In most companies a "share of production" committee is established, consisting of worker representatives from every major department, plus one third to one half as many shop supervisors. There are usually two co-chairmen, a top executive, and the current union president. If there is no union, an employee representative is cochairman. Members may serve on the committee for as little as three months, with other members replacing them to bring in new ideas. In some companies worker representatives serve for a year.

Discussions with union and management personnel in Rucker plan companies show that in the most successful installations, employee committee members are as aggressive as in the Scanlon companies. However, they do not get to be this way automatically. Management must give them a free hand to criticize, suggest, and gather information if the program is to fully develop its potential.

Labor & management

The Nunn-Bush Shoe Company plan started as a percentage-of-sales program. H. L. Nunn discovered that from 1926 through 1934 wages as a percentage of Nunn-Bush sales had varied within a narrow range—18.2% to 21.7%. He set 20% of sales as the ratio for a program involving 52 paychecks a year.

After learning of Rucker's work on value added to raw materials, Nunn felt that it was an economically sounder approach, but he did not persuade his employees and management to change to the new basis until sharp postwar increases in the price of leather got the original plan into trouble. Workers, after much discussion, voted in 1948 to switch to 36% of value added instead of 20% of sales. The percentage is reviewed and changed as conditions warrant.[10]

Long before the incentive plan was established in 1935, the company had developed an unusual relationship with its employees and an intramural union. The substance of the program, in addition to solicitation of employee ideas on production, is presented in the following statement, agreed to by company and workers in 1915:

> Management will forego all customary prerogatives of arbitrary discharge and discipline of members and will share the privilege of selecting new employees. Management will forego all arbitrary right to name conditions of employment and proposes to sit down with the elected representatives of this society [union] and come to mutual agreements on all these matters.
> From the members of this working force we will ask in return their solemn pledge to forego any action by force through power of strike or otherwise.[11]

---

[10] H. L. Nunn, *The Whole Man Goes to Work* (New York, Harper & Brothers, 1953), Chapters 12 and 13.
[11] *Ibid.*, p. 61.

Not only has this company never had a strike; it has never had to take a dispute to arbitration. A reading of the minutes of Nunn-Bush union meetings suggests a new concept of union-management cooperation. Here, in practice, is evidence of responsible industrial self-government.

Conditions of Success

From a technological point of view there seem to be few bars to greater use of programs that combine group incentives and structured opportunities for cooperation. The record shows that quite large companies and firms with complex production and marketing operations can use Scanlon or Rucker programs, or plans of their own devising. Such plans do, however, exact certain conditions from management and the union. Four in particular strike me as being very important.

(1) *Management must be reasonably competent, and willing to become more so.* Competence, of course, involves the ability to make decisions:

> Many organizations have developed the habit of postponing decisions wherever that is possible. Rather than decide the issue and risk being proved wrong, management may decide not to decide, to await further developments. But by the time these developments have occurred there is no decision left to make: there is only one alternative. This implicit type of decision making, more widespread than we might care to admit, is not consistent with the successful operation of the plan.[12]

(2) *Management must be as honest as it is competent.* Petty attitudes and conscious or unconscious attempts to "pull just a few fast ones" will wreck a group program overnight. Nor do the moral lapses need to be major ones to destroy the possibility of success.

(3) *Union leadership should also be above average in competence and integrity, for identical reasons.* Of course, much depends here on the attitude of the rank and file. Men with experience in interaction plans have observed that once company and workers truly commit themselves to making a plan work, the necessary leaders usually appear, in both groups, and assume responsibility.

(4) *Ideally, firms should already have a management-training program which includes realistic consideration of problems of human relations.* As Chris Argyris has said, many such programs are concerned with "pseudo-human relations" techniques which usually do

---

[12] Lesieur, *op. cit.*, p. 62.

more harm than good.[13] And even if they are sound, they often have not included top executives!

There are several reasons why solid human relations training is needed. To quote from *The Scanlon Plan* again:

> [Decisions on production problems] must now be made after consultation with the employees. In many cases, such consultation shows up previous practices as ill-considered at best and just plain stupid at worst. That kind of dramatic exposition, often not put too diplomatically by the employee, may undermine the personal security of line management people. Initially, many of them try to suppress the efforts of the production committees, and only forceful and prompt action by top management makes the continuance of committee efforts possible. Others react with lengthy rationalization, explaining why none of the employees' suggestions can be carried out, or asserting that the ideas have been in their minds a long time, but that the employees would not cooperate in carrying them out.[14]

If supervisors and managers come to understand themselves and their own problems better, the difficulties just described will be lessened. Training also should include an attempt to help the managers see worker attitudes and problems more imaginatively. If the training has included a practical program in conference leadership and in helping groups arrive at decisions, supervisors will be better able to handle participative programs. Frustration, time wasting, and unproductive conflict will be reduced, although never eliminated completely.

Pressures & conflicts

If a group incentive program really works, if it really stirs up company-wide interest in productivity, it should not be surprising that management finds itself receiving unaccustomed attention from the union. Union committees may bear down hard on management inefficiency. They may even be critical of entirely defensible company practices. It takes a strong, patient management to work through this kind of situation. Indignation and anger are often spontaneous reactions. Executives would do well to recognize that group incentives can also make life more difficult at times for labor officials, too.

In some situations the union may develop an internal split. Prestige may gravitate to production committee and screening committee members at the expense of men holding other union jobs. Leadership

---

[13] "The Organization: What Makes It Healthy?" HBR (November-December, 1958), p. 110.

[14] Lesieur, *op. cit.*, p. 61.

in the union may become so involved in the plan that valid member grievances are neglected.

It is no surprise that maintaining union and program goals simultaneously creates conflicts for unions. Even in conventional situations the unions may be under great tension because of clashing interests within their own membership groups. The cause of internal peace may not be served by the addition of new problems and issues. However, I have encountered no union locals which wanted to drop the kind of plan discussed here.

Monetary Payoffs

Peter Drucker has said that the major incentives to productivity and efficiency are social and moral rather than financial.[15] Certainly bonuses are not the most important thing about Scanlon- and Rucker-type plans, but their importance should not be underestimated.

Productivity increases

Figures on productivity gains under the Scanlon plan are given by Elbridge S. Puckett in a report entitled "Productivity Achievements."[16] Some of his averages are listed in EXHIBIT I.

EXHIBIT I. PERCENTAGE INCREASES IN PRODUCTIVITY

Company	First-year relative efficiency	Second-year relative efficiency	Two-year average relative efficiency (Unweighted)
	(1)	(2)	(3)
A	14.9%	10.9%	12.9%
B	21.9	12.7	17.3
C	16.7	13.2	15.0
D	36.7	29.3	33.0
E	28.9	49.4	39.2
F	32.9	42.9	37.9
G	38.7	25.1	31.9
H	14.1	16.5	15.3
I	12.9	23.2	18.1
J	6.8	13.7	10.3
Average (unweighted)	22.5%	23.7%	23.1%

---

[15] *The New Society* (New York, Harper & Brothers, 1949).
[16] Lesieur, *op. cit.*, pp. 112-113.

Efficiency in each case is expressed as a percentage of efficiency in the base period. The average relative efficiency for the two-year period is unweighted. Puckett defends the unweighted average on the ground that it yields a more conservative result than would be developed by a weighted figure.

It will be seen that the poorest productivity gain in the first year was 6.8%, the best 38.7%. During the second year the range was 10.9% to 49.4%. Puckett notes that of the four firms which achieved gains of 30% or better, only one had had previous financial difficulties. This suggests that the company which is already relatively efficient and profitable may have the greatest capacity for improvement under a Scanlon program.

It is also interesting to see that the two largest firms in the group studied made gains equal to the average for all firms. The smallest of the ten plants had 30 employees, the largest 1,200. One company was nonunion, one had an independent union, and the rest were covered by locals of various international unions.

Three of the companies which attained the largest gain in productivity had a labor content of less than 35% of sales production value. The firm with the lowest labor content—under 20%—increased productivity as much as the ten-firm average. A job shop firm did as well as companies using mass production methods.

Employee earnings

In the firms studied by Puckett, bonuses in the two-year period averaged 17.4% of gross pay. In the plant with a productivity increase of 39.2%, the bonus averaged about 29.4%. (All firms split labor-cost savings 75% to participants and 25% to the company.)

In other companies which use programs of a similar type, excellent over-all gains have been amassed. For instance.

> A small tool company in Texas installed a "break-even point control bonus" which evolved from a suggestion made at an employee committee meeting. In 1948, plant volume was under $1 million; return on investment was 28%. In 1956, volume was above $2.5 million; income on investment, 177%.[17] Employees in 1957 were receiving 13.9% of gross sales made after passing the break-even point or date—a sizeable amount for distribution among some 135 employees.

Rucker plan companies report bonuses with ranges similar to those found in Scanlon plan companies (the bonuses being in addition

---

[17] Ruel McDaniel, "Profit Sharing for a Small Business," *American Business* (June, 1957).

to hourly rates competitive with other industries). **During the reces-sion** of 1958, some of these firms dropped their programs (as did some Scanlon companies), but typical bonuses over the last eight years have been in the 17% to 20% range. In some companies much higher percentages have been maintained.

Profit Sharing

Many companies have used profit sharing as a group incentive. It is, of course, broader and looser than plans of the Scanlon and Rucker kind. Joseph Scanlon, however, installed profit sharing, plus production committees, in a few companies where he could not find a more specific accounting handle for the program. Any company with profit sharing can replace its conventional suggestion system with Scanlon-style production committees if it wishes. Pitney-Bowes is an example of a company combining profit sharing with a committee structure:

> The company, which is nonunion, has four levels of committees. There are sectional, departmental, and divisional "councils," and a main council. Every two years employees elect deputies to represent them in these councils. The main council has a suggestion committee composed of both worker and management members. An exceptionally large number of suggestions per employee are submitted, and of these a large per cent are usable.

A few other companies combine profit sharing and employee-initiated action, but in most cases relationships between company and workers remain conventional. If the thesis is that participation, despite its imperfections, works better than nonparticipation, many profit-sharing companies may not be obtaining all the benefits which their programs could yield. They are not creating a "managerial" attitude among their workers.

Some weaknesses

Can profit sharing be a substitute for Scanlon- and Rucker-type programs? In my opinion it rarely can, unless a program like that of Pitney-Bowes is established.

For one thing, there are some weaknesses in profit sharing as an incentive. Profits may result from successful inventory speculations, auspicious patents, and a dozen other situations in which employees are not involved. Similarly, losses may be experienced when worker effort and ingenuity are at a maximum. If it becomes clear to employees in a bad year that nothing they can do will bring about a

profit to the company, they may not be as aggressive in helping to
reduce losses as they would be under a Scanlon or Rucker program
where some bonus might be earned even in a bad year.

Also, the fact that most profit-sharing plans pay only once a year,
or are taken as retirement compensation, tends to make the return
seem remote to workers. Scanlon, Rucker, and similar programs
usually pay off monthly. A few, with very uneven production, pay
quarterly.

Barriers & Gateways

In the extremely large manufacturing firms in the United States,
there are many reasons—especially size and complexity—why company-wide programs of group incentives combined with employee
participation in job problems may be extraordinarily difficult to
develop. In most of our largest companies, the programs described
in these pages are also not likely to get serious consideration because
most of these firms are unionized and their bargaining is "pattern-
setting" for the nation. For both unions and managements the impact
of their relationships is highly political, and is so considered by the
public as well as the parties involved. This creates an atmosphere
which is not conducive to active cooperation. Only a few very large
companies seem to be moving toward genuinely greater opportunity
for presentation of workers' ideas in structured relationships.

The great majority of companies are not, of course, in the size
range of the General Motors Corporation or the United States Steel
Corporation. Yet in smaller companies, too, only a small percentage
have adopted labor-cost saving, share-of-sales, or share-of-production
bonuses coupled with employee involvement in methods of improving
productivity.

Why so few? The character of the industry is sometimes significant. Worthwhile productivity increases might not materialize, for
example, in the cement industry, because of the character of its manufacturing processes. In a greater number of cases, areas of difficulty
already covered and often based on distrust (including management's
unconscious tendency to think of employees as an anonymous rabble
and the unions' "vested interest in conflict") are the central problems.
Many small company managers and union leaders do not even know
about these plans. Or they know a little, but see only threats to
their prerogatives.

"The world of industry," William F. Whyte has said, "is full of
executives who will sacrifice almost anything to maintain their

'power' to give orders that will not be effectively carried out." [18]
Likewise, there are employees who devote much of their energy and
ingenuity to outwitting managers, and union heads who use their
power irresponsibly.

What can be done to modify this picture? In companies where
managers and workers are in opposition on matters vital to our
society's progress, and even its safety, the questions might well be
raised:

> • Should new efforts be made to essay methods of leadership that
> involve "an aggressive willingness to share" the tasks of improving
> performance in the factory?
> • Are companies and unions ready for a new look at methods of
> payment?

Obviously, profound changes in the labor-management pattern of
a firm are not made overnight. But there is always hope for progress
when long-run mutual interests exist. The process of creating more
responsible opportunities for workers can go hand in hand with improvement in product quality and with cost reduction. This we know
from the experience of many companies.

Past and present relations between workers and managers may
not justify much expectation of rapid change in interaction patterns,
even though pay incentive plans may change. Possibly we shall continue indefinitely with a handful of companies which give real
industrial citizenship to employees (together with good results for
stockholders), a large group of "benevolent autocracies," an indeterminate number of autocracies not so benevolent, and a few firms
where the air is full of suspicion and of divisive motives. But the
present and the future are never the same. Perhaps a weapon in the
leadership struggle we are all engaged in is, in Alexander Heron's
words, opportunity for rank-and-file workers to have a larger "share
in the task of thinking" about the tasks they perform. [19]

Questions

1. What does the author consider that the trend will be with regard to
   financial incentive plans? Why?
2. Is it the mechanics of a particular incentive system or the conditions
   relating to its administration and use that make it a success or failure?
3. Why do group incentives rather than individual incentives often tend to
   become the ones that are more feasible to use with the development of
   increased automation?

[18] Whyte, *op. cit.*, p. 259.
[19] Alexander Heron, *Why Men Work* (Stanford, California, Stanford University Press, 1948), p. 172.

4. Which do you feel would be likely to have the greatest motivational effect upon a particular group of employees, providing them with increased earnings or greater participation in the administration of the plan? Discuss.
5. What is the relationship between employee economic education and the administration of a financial incentive plan? Can the two factors contribute to each other? How?
6. Is the monetary payoff the most important factor governing the success of a financial incentive system?
7. What possible effects might the installation of a financial incentive system have upon union-management relations and vice versa?

32. MERIT RAISE OR MERIT BONUS: A PSYCHOLOGICAL APPROACH *

Timothy W. Costello and Sheldon S. Zalkind

Despite widespread use, merit raises are currently being subjected to much criticism for failure to achieve their goals in the salary programs of many companies. An important reason for this failure may very well be that such plans do not allow for the operation of several basic psychological principles in the areas of motivation and learning.

Can the well-established principles of psychological reinforcement theory be blended with the practical requirements of a large organization, to produce an incentive pay system for white collar employees? We believe they can—if personnel administrators are willing to make innovations and then subject these to research validation. We describe both a suggested innovation in merit pay and a design for research on its effectiveness.

We first examine some problems of currently-used merit raise systems, then consider some relevant psychological principles, and go on to propose a new approach to merit pay. Some readers will find it a radically different approach and therefore unacceptable; others may complain of some practical difficulties. We would like to present the case for providing a more effective and motivating reward system than those currently in use.

Current systems

Merit raise systems, with minor variations, are standardized and rather well known. Usually a value is assigned to each job in the organization on the basis of a job evaluation program. This value is then converted to the dollars and cents that the company will pay for that job. This is almost always done in terms of a range or bracket, which may be about 30% of the minimum figure. Theoretically, movement through the range occurs on the basis of meritorious performance, which is frequently assessed through some formal program of performance appraisal or merit-rating. Merit raises are made on an

---

* From *Personnel Administration*, Vol. 25, No. 6 (November-December, 1962), pp. 10-17. Reprinted with permission.

annual basis at salary review time. Some companies, in addition, review salaries semi-annually for new employees; some consider senior employees only biennially.

Criticisms of present approaches

Although the usual system, on its face, seems to have much to recommend it, and is as a result widely used for salaried employees at middle management levels and below, personnel people who use a system of merit raises have many criticisms of it. The criticisms suggest that many companies feel they are saddled with a system that they know doesn't work.

A major criticism, and this must be considered basic in any wage and salary program, is that the program does not serve to motivate better performance. The principal difficulty is that an annual merit increase (or for young employees, even a semi-annual one) is too remote in time from the good performance the supervisor wants to reward.[1] As a result no connection is seen between the increased money and specific examples of good performance. The best attempts of supervisors to spell out such a connection by talking to the employees seem not to work. Even when the raise is tied in with merit rating, the end result is not better performance. Too often either a high merit rating is given to justify a raise awarded on some other basis or a low rating is given to justify inability to provide a salary increase.

A second criticism is that the "merit" raise has, as a matter of fact, become in many cases an automatic increment, rotated among the members of a department. This criticism is not directed against the intent of the system so much as it is against the framework in which department heads administer it. But, then, any system is only as good as those who use it allow it to be. So we must consider the system as it is used, not as it exists in policy manuals.

For both these reasons, its lack of perceived relation to particular performance and its confused relationship with automatic increments, the present system often leads to false expectations and inevitable

---

[1] For typical psychological principles and research bearing on this point *see* B. F. Skinner, "Reinforcement Today," *American Psychologist*, 1958, 13, pp. 94-99; C. B. Ferster and B. F. Skinner, *Schedules of Reinforcement* (New York: Appleton-Century-Crofts, Inc., 1957); R. B. Ammons, "Effects of Knowledge of Performance: A Survey and Tentative Theoretical Formulation," *Journal of General Psychology*, 1956, 54, pp. 279-299.

disappointment for many.[2] Failure to get a raise under these conditions may lead to reductions in levels of performance. In the absence of any clear cue system or gauges which an employee can use to assess his own performance in relation to a merit increase, and because the increase so often is used covertly to recognize another year of service, the average employee expectantly awaits salary review time with no realistic basis for his expectations of an increase or the amount of the increase. When he is rewarded with a salary increase, it often cannot match the amount of his expectations.

More subtle difficulties also develop with a merit raise system. Because the system as it now functions tends to pit one employee against another (a fixed budget to be divided in "your favor" this year and in "his favor" next year) rather than each person's own good or bad performance, it can undermine team spirit and prevent the development of cohesive work groups. Largely because of an absence of knowledge about the basis for a merit raise, particular merit raises given out covertly are described as unfair (the news almost always seems to get out). "Unfair," as is well known, is an even more condemnatory term for a salary system than "not enough." [3] Finally, the system tends to play into the need many employees have to complain about something. The particular pattern of merit raises is often griped about as a kind of scapegoat for other job factors that are either not so easily identified (e.g, factors in the nature of the work) or are too ego-deflating to be named (e.g., failure to develop on the job).[4] As a result the supervisor is confronted with gripes that are unrelated to the real cause of maladjustment. He can hardly handle the real problems effectively unless he knows what they are.

The end product of currently used merit raise programs would seem to be that not getting a raise is a major source of frustration; but getting one is not perceived as recognition for work well done. The merit increase neither motivates better performance in those who receive it, nor sets a motivating example for the others who do not. Both the money spent and the opportunity to meet the recognition needs of employees are lost.

---

[2] A study examining the effect of expectations on attitude and performance is A. J. Spector, "Expectations, Fulfillment, and Morale," *Journal of Abnormal and Social Psychology*, 1956, 52, pp. 51-56.

[3] For a full discussion of this point, *see* Paul Pigors and Charles A. Myers, *Personnel Administration* (New York: McGraw-Hill Book Company, 1956), p. 276 and pp. 284-285.

[4] F. Herzberg, B. Mausner and B. B. Snyderman, *The Motivation to Work* (2d ed.; New York: John Wiley & Sons, Inc., 1959), p. 82.

Some basic principles

Drawing from the abundant psychological research on learning and motivation we should like first to suggest some principles that must underlie any merit raise program. Then we describe a program which we believe uses these principles and, at the same time, meets the objections to merit raises that we have previously identified.

1. To effect a change in behavior—or in personnel language to motivate an employee to better performance—the desired response (higher productivity, learning a new job, a better attitude) must first be allowed (encouraged) to occur and then be reinforced by an appropriate satisfier *as soon as possible* after the behavior is displayed.[5]
2. The employee must be apprised of his performance (or, in psychological terms, given knowledge of results) as soon after performance and in as specific a fashion as possible. He must get to see the relationship between the goal set for him and what he is actually doing.[6]
3. The most lasting type of reinforcement (or the reward which is likely to keep an employee's performance at a high level for the longest time) is one that is given irregularly (but nevertheless in a fashion clearly related to specific performance) rather than after every example of good performance.[7] The latter condition is, as a matter of fact, impossible to maintain in the business organization.

It would seem that these principles, clearly established by a wide variety of research, are violated by present day merit systems. Such systems may be relatively easy to administer, but they don't seem to do what is intended.

What alternative might fit our knowledge of psychological principles and still be usable administratively?

For one thing, a *raise and a bonus need to be distinguished*. Obviously good performance, of the sort the administrator wishes to encourage, or reinforce, cannot be rewarded continually with raises, which then become part of the fixed salary of the individual. Raises cannot easily be given frequently, nor can they be easily linked to desired performance. But a flexible use of *bonuses* may help meet the criticisms of merit raises and still take advantage of the principles of reinforcement.

---

[5] Skinner, *op. cit.*
[6] Ammons, *op. cit.*
[7] In a recent article, Aldis has related schedules of reinforcement to varieties of wage and salary payments, with suggestions for some modifications. Owen Aldis, "Of Pigeons and Men," *Harvard Business Review*, July-August, 1961, pp. 59-63.

A merit bonus system

Suppose each department head were given a budget for labor costs, only *part* of which was to meet regular salaries, determined as now within the job evaluation framework, the other part to be used for merit bonus payments administered on a *monthly* basis. Such monthly bonus payments would be made to a number of employees after their supervisor had observed evidence of superior performance on their part. The possibilities for using such a device to meet the principles we have described can readily be seen. There are, of course, some hazards as well.

Let us first describe the specific procedures we believe must be followed if our suggested program is to work out practically and effectively from various points of view. Encouraging superior performance is only one, although an important one, of the many functions a salary program must serve. Meeting cost of living changes and providing additional salary for increased seniority are two other important functions. We take account of these, we believe, in the procedure outlined below.

1. Satisfactory lower salary levels have to be set for the various jobs through a job evaluation program, and, in relation to company policy and prevailing standards in the community.

2. The upper end of each bracket is also determined in the same fashion but with two other considerations in mind: (a) that progress in the bracket will be determined by years of service, providing certain minimum performance standards are met; and (b) that opportunity for earning additional income on the job will be provided through a monthly bonus system.

3. Over and above the salary budget needed for each department to meet its commitments described above, an allocation is made for merit bonuses to be administered by the first supervisory level in consultation with the next higher level. The specific sum can be determined as a percentage of the base salary budget and in relationship to particular company or departmental considerations. In any case, the bonus, if given, should be large enough to provide a noticable *month-end* increment for the rewarded employees. The question of how many employees receive bonuses any month is again a matter of company determination, depending on actual performance, general salary level, etc. What is most important is that the bonus not be "frozen" into the salary of the rewarded employees.

4. When the supervisor administers the program, certain conditions have to be met: (a) Standards of performance to be considered for bonus awards must be clearly spelled out and made known to all employees. In addition, of course, the new system must be discussed in staff meetings with employee groups; (b) As soon as the supervisor decides that a particular employee will receive an award, he

should inform the employee of that fact, the amount, and the reason for it. In doing so, the important point is to indicate that it is given as recognition of superior performance. The supervisor will also have to explain that the award is for this month only and will be awarded again as other improvements are observed. The system demands that not every improvement in performance be so awarded, from a practical company point of view, to keep labor costs within reasonable limits, and from a psychological point of view, to provide a periodic or irregular reinforcement. Bonuses should be awarded relatively frequently but neither consistently, nor whimsically unrelated to performance. Psychological research over the years (referred to above) demonstrates the superior effectiveness of irregularly given reinforcements for the maintenance of desired behavior over long periods of time. The point is a critical one in the plan we are proposing.

5. The initiative for helping non-rewarded employees to achieve a bonus award should come from the supervisor. An appraisal interview focused on coaching and counselling relationships to help the individual employee improve his performance might well meet this need. Appraisal interviews would in addition continue to be used to help all qualified employees to develop themselves for promotion opportunities.

Advantages and disadvantages

Let's first consider what such a program might hope to accomplish, then consider some of its hazards and limitations.

1. It meets the requirements of our three principles—good performance is rewarded soon after it occurs, specific knowledge of results is provided, reinforcement occurs on an irregular basis but clearly in relation to good performance, thus helping to maintain the desired performance over a longer period of time.

2. Merit awards are clearly separated from automatic increments. A good case can be made out for the position that an employee who has acquired another year's experience is worth more than one who has not. But particular meritorious service should also be rewarded apart from seniority. We believe our system meets both requirements of a salary program, but clearly distinguishes to the employee his salary potential and his merit bonus. Through automatic increments, and upgrading, basic salary can increase, while the added bonuses vary in relation to specific and recent performance.

3. The system provides opportunity for making use of recognition for work well done—a strong motive force in its own right.[8] In this way the money award serves two purposes: it is an economic reward and a psychologically satisfying symbol of a job well done.

4. The system provides specific focus for the appraisal interview for all employee levels. As a consequence it is more likely that such

_____

[8] Herzberg, _op. cit._, p. 60.

interviews will actually be undertaken and, when they are, they are more likely to do some good.

The system has some hazards and definite limitations, as all personnel administrators will quickly recognize.

Actually it is a modified type of incentive system for white collar workers, for whose work precise production measurements are not always possible. "Measurement" for the incentive award is the supervisor's judgment. If he is unfair, biased, or uninformed, the system will backfire—the present system, of course, now frequently backfires. Since he holds important sanctions over his employees, his own level of supervisory performance is crucial for the system. This, of course, is not necessarily all bad. Two things come to mind: evidence indicates that effective supervisors are seen as having more influence;[9] poor supervision is more likely to be made quickly apparent by ineffectiveness in administering the new bonus system and thus remedial measures can be adopted by those in higher echelons.

Payroll sections will surely complain about the additional work. But a little additional paper work should not be the basis for an administrative decision which should have major impact on employee performance. As a matter of fact payroll sections do effectively cope with comparable, more complicated piece-rate calculations.

Of a much more serious nature is the possible reaction of employees who are accustomed to fixed weekly, bi-weekly or monthly incomes, and who (perhaps we should add quickly) provide fixed, not always satisfactory, levels of performance.

In any case, our suggestion would be to try the system out under the controls and limits of the research design we describe in our concluding section. If employee attitudes are likely to be extreme and negative, the effect will be contained within a small section of the company and a change can quickly be made. If research suggests that the effects are good, a considerable bonus for both management and the employees is in the offing.

Research required

Obviously, we are not suggesting that all companies rush in and install this "New Plan" throughout their entire organization. The

---

[9] D. C. Pelz, "Influence: A Key to Effective Leadership in the First-Line Supervisor," *Personnel*, 1952, 29, pp. 209-217.

installation and implementation of any new plan usually is accompanied by much argument, debate and discussion, and we assume that the same would be the case here. What we are suggesting is that the potential effectiveness of this plan be tested carefully with adequate concern to obtain data, permitting it to be compared to present systems. The plan's potential utility should *not* be decided on the basis of mere impressions.

While a "let's try it out" approach would undoubtedly give some interesting results, the more fruitful test of the plan would come through a research approach. Let us sketch in some of the conditions for this research. Specific tailoring to particular organizational situations might be needed and could readily be provided.

The reader has possibly already anticipated the need to try the new system out with some units (as experimental groups) while *not* using it with other comparable units (or control groups) which continue with whatever present plan is operating. Administratively this would require that the organization be one with similar units, so located that communication between the groups would be quite unlikely to occur. Offices or plants in separate cities might meet this requirement. (The word "group" is used here to mean the experimental condition being used. In practice, many existing sections or work groups might be part of each "Group" discussed below).

The introduction of *any* plan or change can bring about two sorts of reaction which can affect the behavior of those involved, without the plan or change *itself* being responsible for the results. A more elaborate research attempt, beyond just an Experimental-Control Group comparison, might thus become necessary. The well-known Hawthorne studies dramatized the possible increments in attitude or performance that can occur by paying attention to people and by their awareness of being a part of an experiment. Thus our Control condition (of "no change" in plan) requires that one Control Group have no new plan, no change in emphasis on the present way of doing things, and no awareness of being part of a study. But another Control Group should be set up, *not* changing the present system, but making people conscious of merit-salary links. A "public relations" emphasis, with talks of a "new revitalized" program of merit raises, and of increased concern for evaluation (without actually changing—presumably—the merit or award system itself either in performance or in reward) would help control for the "Hawthorne effect." Obviously, while we would predict that the Experimental Groups would do better, in the long run, than this "Merit Conscious" Control Group, we can't be sure until the proper comparisons are made.

In addition to the "Hawthorne effect," the opposite effect—resistance to or suspicion of any change—could occur. Thus, our experimental conditions have to be subdivided. One Group would need to have the plan introduced with a minimum of fanfare, perhaps even with an arbitrary implication that there is reason to believe that it won't work but "we're trying it anyway." Another Experimental Group should have the plan introduced as the company "normally" might, with some publicity, explanation of the company's faith in it, etc., and indicating that it is being used experimentally with this Group. A third Experimental Group should take advantage of some of the concepts of "participation," with small discussion groups indicating their reactions to the plan, asking questions, etc., and seeking to minimize resistance. (They cannot "participate" in the fuller sense of helping to work out, or modify the plan or else, there go your controlled conditions for research).

We recognize that using two Control and three Experimental conditions poses additional administrative problems, beyond the simpler single Experimental—and single Control Group approach, but personnel administration is beginning to face up to the need for research validation of its techniques, even though the research, at times, might initially seem cumbersome.

What of the *measures* which would be used with various groups? Many of the standard criteria of organizational effectiveness should be obtained. Primary, of course, would be performance (or production) data. Absenteeism, turnover, costs, number of suggestions, grievances, dispensary visits, and similar objective data could be gathered. Performance ratings, both for those awarded and those not, could be compiled.

How people feel, both about the plan and other aspects of the job and the company, would be an important source of information on the plan. Surveys (before the experiment as well as later on) should cover the usual range of attitude and morale areas, and not just the pay question. Information should be gathered on the attitudes towards other members of their group, how they interact, feelings about those receiving bonuses, etc. The impact of the system on the entire group, the way in which it ties into a feeling of accomplishment and of recognition would be important to measure.

These measures, taken comparably for the Experimental and Control Groups, would provide the administrator with evidence as to whether the system has potential compared to the presently-used system. Whether or not the new system can be judged more effective depends, of course, on the over-all group performance, not merely on the performance of the rewarded individuals.[10]

We don't think the proposed Merit Bonus System (or any system) will solve all of management's incentive problems. But present systems of merit raises, though traditional, are not necessarily influencing people to perform well in their work. Separating bonuses from raises, providing much more frequent and irregularly spaced use of bonuses, and linking them closely to performance may be a way of taking advantage of the leads provided by research on motivation and learning.

Questions

1. What do the authors consider to be the principal limitations of most remuneration systems that they hope will be overcome by the system that they propose?
2. Upon what psychological principles is the system that they propose based?
3. What are some of the difficulties that are inherent in any bonus system which might be encountered in the one proposed by the authors?
4. Does the proposed plan resemble any of those that are discussed by Frances Torbert in Article No. 31; for example, the Scanlon Plan?
5. What are some of the conditions that would have to be achieved in a company before it may be possible to embark upon the experiment suggested by the authors?

---

[10] There is evidence to suggest that, at times, awards given to some members of a unit help to improve the entire group's morale. S. A. Stouffer *et al.*, *The American Soldier* (Princeton: Princeton University Press, 1949), Vol. I, pp. 309-310.

33. FRINGE DETRIMENTS *

J. H. Foegen

As fringe benefits—non-wage, supplementary payments made to employees—continue to increase from year to year, it becomes increasingly important to recognize the existence of, and to take a good look at, the bad as well as the good side of those benefits. For purposes of this discussion, the negative side will be called "detriments." After a brief look at some of the reasons why the present fringe situation developed, attention will be given first to the prospect of the possible detrimental aspects of fringe as it presently exists, and then to the possibility that present benefits may well turn into detriments at some time in the future.

Perhaps the most important thing to note in talking about the background of fringe benefits is that fringe was never designed or intended to become what it has in fact become. As the term "fringe" itself implies, these benefits were to be clearly marginal items, incidentals intended to supplement the money wage payment, but no more than that. Obviously, as a result of continuous growth both in scope and in depth, fringe is much more important than this today.

The big reason for this is that growth was seldom consciously planned.[1] From time to time, different benefits were added, more or less opportunistically, until the present-day hodgepodge resulted. Since few if any controls were developed, it was only natural that such would be the case, given a number of important operating factors.

Causes of fringe

One of these factors was simply the conscientiousness of some individual employers. Some company managements, from the early days of industrialization to the present, have been firmly convinced that workers should be considered human beings, not just inanimate factors of production, and should therefore be treated as well as possible.

---

* From *Personnel Administration*, Vol. 25, No. 3 (May-June, 1962), pp. 13-18. Reprinted with permission.

[1] This idea is discussed more fully in the author's article, "Product Mix for Fringe Benefits," *Harvard Business Review*, July-August, 1961, p. 64.

Not only should the wage paid be a "just" wage, in the sense of adequacy and equity, but working conditions and job security should be the best that management could provide while still looking out for the legitimate, reasonable interests of capital and customers. Under the pressure of competition and the profit motive, unfortunately, these circumstances occurred in fairly isolated cases. Nevertheless, *some* employers did have a sense of responsibility toward their workers, as evidenced by a few unilaterally-initiated pension plans that antedate the turn of the century.[2]

Another of the causes of the birth of fringe, one that the previously-discussed employer conscientiousness often shaded into, was paternalism. Although remnants of both of these factors still remain today, the former usually evokes the picture of the pre-World War I period in industrial history, while the heyday of paternalism is considered by most to have been in the 1920's. The basis of this philosophy of course was the idea that the worker had to be looked after, and taken care of as well as possible, usually for one of two reasons, and possibly for both.

On the one hand, paternalism bolstered the ego-satisfaction of the employer. Employees were seen as essentially inferior, and unequal to management in ability and status. This was no fault of their own, however, and so, being utterly dependent upon the employer for their livelihood, it was the duty of that employer to watch out for them, much as a father looks out for his minor children. Psychologically, it made the employer feel superior if he could voluntarily provide certain benefits for his workers.

It is entirely possible, of course, that the resentment in the ranks caused by this management attitude contributed to the rise of unionism. It is also interesting to compare this situation with that of the present, when gains for the workers are claimed by the union in many cases, and when the union likes to give the impression that the worker would get absolutely nothing were it not for that union's efforts; this certainly does little for the employer's ego-satisfaction.

In addition to the bolstering of the employer's ego, paternalistic handouts of benefits or fringe also occurred in an attempt to keep unionism from getting a foothold in the plant. The theory was that if the employees got enough wages and benefits from the employers, they would see no need for a union. It is somewhat ironic that in

---

[2] Credit for the first U. S. private pension plan is usually given to the American Express Co., 1875. For additional discussion, *see* Robert Tilove, "Pension Funds and Economic Freedom" (New York: The Fund for the Republic, 1959).

paternalistically passing out favors to the workers in order to forestall the rise of unionism, management actually was bringing about more rapidly the very situation it was trying to prevent. Such was the case, however, and paternalism gave impetus to the rise of fringe both directly, in the case of employer handouts, and also indirectly, to the extent that it fostered the growth of unions, which in turn put on pressure for still more benefits.

This union pressure was and is a third major cause of fringe growth. It began to make itself felt in the 1930's and 1940's, as unions, coming into a more favorable political climate first, followed by a more favorable economic one as well, became progressively stronger. It continues today in unrelenting fashion. As unions became stronger economically, they naturally demanded increasingly better wages and working conditions, and, by threatening strikes or by actually carrying them out, they often got what they asked for.

A final cause of fringe growth, one that many feel is the most important one, was the imposition of wage controls by the government during World War II. Wages were frozen during much of this period as an anti-inflationary measure. Fringe benefits, however, since they were of a non-monetary nature or would not require immediate money payments, were allowed to increase. Unions, taking their cue from Washington, used them as a way to get around the static wage situation. In 4 wartime years, the habit of asking for and getting fringe benefits became ingrained enough so that later, when wage controls were lifted, unions continued to ask for increases in fringe as well as in wages and other working conditions.

In all times except the very recent past, however, regardless of whether it resulted from employer conscientiousness, paternalism, union pressure or wartime wage controls, fringe was still a marginal, supplementary payment. Today, however, with fringe running between 20% and 25% of a company's payroll,[3] and with no letup in sight, a second look is being taken at the whole concept to see whether perhaps the benefits are not all that they seem to be. In the present discussion, consideration will be given first to some detriments already present in the fringe situation, and then to some possible future problems.

---

[3] According to "Fringe Benefits—1959," in which the U. S. Chamber of Commerce reports on a survey of 1064 reporting companies, "The average payment in 1959 was 22.8% of payroll, 54.8¢ per payroll hour, or $1132 per year per employee" (p. 5).

Before proceeding further, however, it should be admitted that fringe benefits do not constitute a detriment directly either to the individual or the economy in the short run. The individual worker will not refuse more paid vacations, sick leave, group insurance and the like. But from the standpoint of the economy as a whole, and even from that of the individual in the long run, there is ample reason for serious reflection.

With that important qualification out of the way, let us consider a few of the bad points or detriments in the present fringe situation.

Fringe detriments

Perhaps most obvious of the three to be considered here is that most fringe contributes to inflation, if inflation is currently a problem, and puts an immediate additional squeeze on profit margins regardless. The reason, of course, is that most benefits cost the employer money, and this money has to come from somewhere. It will not come from sacrificed profits if management can at all avoid it. It might come from increased productivity, although conditions are not always favorable. It might even come from intended or possible wage increases that have gone by the board in order to provide for added fringe, although this is difficult to prove. The most likely source will be in prices, and, if prices are raised to cover the increased cost of added fringe, inflation receives that much more impetus.

Somewhat less obvious is the fact that fringe has a tendency to freeze labor mobility. Most benefits are as yet not vested, that is, their receipt is contingent upon continued employment by the granting company. To the extent that this is so, a considerable number of employees can be expected to remain with the firm even if they might otherwise like to leave, and even if it might be a good thing for the economy as a whole, if they *did* leave. If a family man has built up considerable seniority rights with a company that is also contributing every month to a fund that will provide him with a pension when he retires, but only if he continues to work for the company, it is very unlikely that the employee will leave that employer for any but the most drastic of reasons.

As another example, the "fringe benefits" of having lived in a community for a long time are not vested, i.e., if you leave the community, friends, relatives, and a familiar situation will of necessity be left behind. This keeps many people today from moving out of chronically depressed areas. While this is an understandable human reaction, it nevertheless inhibits the mobility of the work force. The hold that company-granted fringe benefits have on workers in a sense artificially reinforces this natural tendency.

This is not to say of course that mobility is all bad. Employee turnover remains a costly problem to most employers. A stable group of workers with the security of various fringe benefits may have high morale and be an advantage in many ways to the employer. But again from the standpoint of the whole economy, efficiency and prosperity demand at least a reasonable minimum of labor force mobility, and non-vested fringe is here an inhibiting factor.

Perhaps least obvious of present day fringe detriments is that fringe inhibits the worker's freedom of choice in spending his money. In other words, the worker might not want what he is getting; he might well want something else in the way of benefits, or even cash, instead.[4] He might well prefer more pay instead of more holidays or insurance; he could then spend that pay for the goods and services that he individually chooses. To the extent that the union bargains or the employer gives a certain fringe benefit, however, his freedom of choice in spending his money is to that extent effectively curtailed.

In this way, fringe bears some similarity to taxes. Under the present Federal income tax laws, the government takes part of an employee's wages in taxes, and theoretically at least pays him back in the form of various "fringe benefits" i.e., roads, defense, aids to education and so forth, whether the individual wants these things or not. In similar fashion, under a regular fringe benefit setup, the employer withholds part of what the employee at least *might* otherwise get in wages, and pays it to him as fringe that the collective body, the union, has bargained for him, whether he as an individual wants it or not. In both cases, either the government or the employer is spending the employee's money for him, and his freedom of choice in spending it is decreased.

Regardless of the benefits to be found in fringe, detriments in the present situation can also be seen in the areas of inflation, labor mobility, and individual free choice in the spending of income.

---

[4] The assumption is that if the fringe benefit were not received, then its equivalent value in cash would be added to the worker's pay check. This is not necessarily true.

Future problems

The biggest problem, however, is not to be found in the present, but in the future. If fringe as it exists today is still on balance good—and this, it seems, can at least be effectively argued—then given the continued increase in its depth and scope, will fringe turn into a detriment at some point in the future? Or can it continue to increase as at present with no untoward consequences, as some say wages can? Is "creeping fringe" of no danger, as some say "creeping inflation" is no danger? Nobody really knows, of course, but the problem gives rise to a number of questions that are worth considering.

For example, what happens when fringe approaches, reaches, or even passes 100% of payroll? Obviously, it started out at zero per cent. It is now in the range 20-25% and continues to increase. What happens when money wages becomes less important than fringe, or even equally so?

This is somewhat similar to a problem found in the area of unemployment compensation. A perennial argument here is what would happen if unemployment compensation benefits were to approach 100% of regular earnings. Unemployment compensation as originally intended was supposed to be "fringe" or marginal, or subsistence-type income. But with supplementary unemployment benefits, some workers can already collect 65% of their previous take-home pay, and the auto workers' union wants to raise this to 80%.[5] If and when the union is successful, this will begin to approach 100%. If unemployment compensation becomes as great as normal wages, will people prefer not to work? In similar fashion, if fringe becomes increasingly more important, will money wages lose all significance and/or disappear, and will workers' pay be entirely in fringe, with all the ghosts of "welfare statism" that possibility conjures up?

Another question: What will happen to the wage structure as more and more fringe is added? This structure, the result of job evaluation and subsequent pricing, has in the past been based on skill, responsibility, working conditions, and training as well as on experience. But much fringe is granted either across the board, or is related only to seniority, for example such things as holidays and vacations. As fringe grows absolutely and relative to wages, will this tend to make the wage structure obsolete? If so, perhaps a "fringe

---

[5] *Wall Street Journal*, June 28, 1961.

structure" might be a helpful or necessary supplement, to show who gets how much fringe and why.

Along another line of thought, can a company grant too much in the way of fringe benefits, the emphasis here being on the word "benefit" rather than on the word "fringe"? There is some criticism already heard of a growing "private welfare state" that supplements whatever similar trend exists in the public area. In other words, can employees absorb an unlimited amount of benefits without danger to their own self-reliance? The idea of being taken care of either by the social programs of the state or by the fringe programs of large corporations or both seems to be not unpopular even today. The joke about the new employee asking an employment interviewer what kind of pension plan the company has is all too familiar. But is this really a joke?

Finally, since large firms can usually pay the most benefits, as fringe levels increase and as prospective entrants into the labor force become increasingly fringe-conscious, what effect might this have on the ability of small firms, of necessity relatively poor in fringe, to compete in the market and to continue to exist? Business and government continue to pay lip service to the need for small firms and for competition, but if large concerns are able to offer not only lower prices to the customer but also more and better fringe benefits to employees increasingly sensitive to such things, what chance will small-firm competition have?

Conclusions

In conclusion then, the following points can be made: (1) The concept of fringe is undeniably well established. Employers, unions and workers have all become accustomed to it and it is not likely to fade from the scene in the foreseeable future. Whether viewed as non-money wages, or as something entirely separate from wages, it has at any rate been accepted as a part of working conditions, and union philosophy is pledged to continued improvement in this area. (2) Fringe continues to look good to the individual and in the short run, regardless of its real or imagined long-run consequences for the economy. (3) Serious misgivings do arise, however, in the areas of inflation, labor mobility, spending choices, wage structures, self-reliance, competition, and the relative importance of fringe as against payroll.

Questions

1. In what ways have fringe benefits departed from the purpose for which they were established originally? What are the reasons for this departure?

2. What reasons did employers have originally for establishing fringe benefits? How do these reasons differ from those upon which fringe benefits are being installed today?

3. In what respects does the author feel that some fringe benefits possibly have worked to the detriment of both the employer and employee?

4. Do you agree or disagree with the criticism that fringe benefit programs are creating a "private welfare state"?

5. How serious do you feel is the effect that fringe benefits have upon an employee's freedom of choice?

6. To what extent, if any, should a company be expected to provide for the welfare of its employees beyond providing good wages and working conditions?

34. EMPLOYMENT PROBLEMS OF THE OLDER WORKER *

Daniel H. Kruger

The problem of aging is as old as recorded history. The Psalmist tells us: "Cast me not off in time of old age; when my strength fails, forsake me not." Some 2,000 years later, in a modern dynamic industrial society, we hear the same plea from persons who cannot find suitable employment because of age. There is, however, one important difference between the entreaty of the Psalmist and the plight of the older worker. The latter frequently has strength, ability and experience which are eroding away because they are not being put to good use.

We indeed live in a marvelous age of technology. Striking examples of our scientific and technical know-how dazzles us on all sides. While the engineering genius of the nation can put a complicated satellite into orbit, the same nation, as a whole, cannot place the older worker in an orbit of meaningful and useful employment. The nation has yet to learn how to utilize its human resources adequately. If would almost seem that the well-worn statement—people are our most precious asset—has an empty ring when one considers the number of older workers who cannot find suitable employment.

In order to understand the employment problems of older workers one must consider the importance of employment. Having a job, earning a livelihood is, for most people, more than a utilitarian device for obtaining income in order to provide the necessities of life for themselves and their dependents. It is the basis for social standing. Self-respect, a feeling of worth, a sense of well being are all related to having a job. In the words of Professor Wilma Donahue, "we measure our success in terms of what we accomplish in the work-a-day world." [1] For people past the middle of life, making a living in the United States is a time-absorbing function in the pursuit of which the individual becomes accustomed to spending the best part of his

* From *Business Topics*, Vol. 7, No. 4 (Autumn, 1959), pp. 29-39. Reprinted with permission.

[1] *Proceedings of a Conference on Problems of Older Workers*, June 1 and 2, 1951 (University of Wisconsin: Industrial Relations Center), p. 135.

day. People, by and large, not only want to work; they are in the habit of working. According to Professor Otto Pollak, blocking behavior patterns which are the result of long-time conditioning creates, in many instances, serious psychological discomforts.[2]

This observation brings into sharp focus the fact that the interest in the older worker has more than an economic dimension. The loss of opportunity to make a living is more than a loss of income or the loss of a productive citizen in the community. We are concerned not only with the economic problem but with the capacities and opportunities of our older citizens to maintain a worthwhile existence, socially, psychologically and physiologically. Useful employment, therefore, is a human need which cannot be satisfied by the assurance of income alone.

Who is an older worker? Is he a person who has reached a certain chronological age or one whose capacities have declined specifically because of his advancing years? One definition of an older worker is one who wants to work and is able to work but is denied employment or finds his employment opportunities restricted because of his age. This chronological barrier varies widely. For example, it may be 30 for airline stewardesses, or 45 for telephone linemen. These are age restrictions which companies apply arbitrarily. Another definition of the older worker is one who has reached the chronological age of 45 years. The two definitions are not poles apart: persons 45 and over are the ones who experience the greatest difficulties in finding suitable employment.

Relative to the employment problems of the older workers, interest is in those who are *able, willing and looking for work*. This definition understates the magnitude of the problem because it does not include those who have withdrawn from the labor force because of their inability to find a job. One can easily get discouraged after having been told many times that there is no employment available and then see younger persons successful in their bid for employment at the same place of business.

Size of Problem

Much is heard these days about the population growth of the United States. In 1900, the population of the country was nearly 76

---

[2] Otto Pollak, "The Older Worker in the Labor Market," *The Aged and Society*, A Symposium on the Problems of an Aging Population, Publication No. 5 (Champaign, Illinois: Industrial Relations Research Association, 1950), p. 56.

million; in 1950 it was 150 million. It was estimated that the total population in 1958 was 175 million. Between 1900 and 1950 the population almost doubled. Since 1950 the population has increased by 16 percent. While the population has been growing, it also has been aging. According to the Bureau of Census data, during the period 1900-55 the number in the 45 to 64 age group tripled and the 65-and-over age group quadrupled.[3] The marked decline in the birth rate between the two World Wars and the increased life expectancy help to explain these significant changes in the structure of the population.

It is estimated that the older and the younger age groups will continue to grow at a faster rate than those of the intermediate age groups for some years to come.[4] In the census projections of population for 1955 to 1975, the age group 45 and over will increase 34 percent and the group under 25 years of age will increase by 58 percent. The age group 25-44 will increase by 13 percent. The impressive growth in the number and proportion of younger persons in the population will present serious problems for older workers. The entrance of such large numbers of younger persons into the labor force will create stresses and strains in the labor market which will affect the employment opportunities for the older workers.

The magnitude of the problem is brought into sharp focus by the Bureau of Census labor force projection for 1975. It is estimated that jobs must be provided for at least 7.2 million persons age 45 and over in addition to those in that age group now in the work force.[5] Viewed another way, there will be on the average 360,000 additional workers age 45 and over in the labor force each year from 1955 to 1975.

The major difficulties

The older person who is seeking employment encounters major difficulties and roadblocks. The first of these may be lumped together as real difficulties while the second can be classified as imagined. While the latter are imagined they are real in the sense that both workers and employers are influenced by them. They are imagined in that they have little or no basis in fact. All too frequently employment opportunities for older workers are denied because of prejudices on part of employers.

---

[3] U.S. Bureau of Employment Security, *Older Worker Adjustment to Labor Market Practices*, An Analysis of Experience in Seven Major Labor Markets, BES No. R151 (Washington: Government Printing Office, 1956), pp. 7, 221.

[4] *Ibid.*, p. 7.

[5] *Ibid.*, pp. 7-9.

The first real difficulty, then, is the arbitrary age restrictions themselves which employers have established. Moreover, the policies of the unions also have created situations which have affected the employment of older workers. Thirdly, the individual older worker has contributed to the magnitude of the problem.

The role of the unions

Regarding the unions' role, the unions have sought to protect the job rights of the older workers through seniority rules and contract provisions against arbitrary discharge. Such provisions, it should be noted, are of greater benefit to the employed older worker than to the unemployed one. The seniority clauses have hindered the employment of older workers. Persons with long seniority, when unemployed, are at times reluctant to accept employment at another company because it means that all seniority will be lost. If they accept employment they will be placed at the bottom of the seniority list. By the same token, employers are reluctant to hire older workers with long seniority at another firm because they know that employees will leave when recalled by their former employers.

The individual employee has the problem of finding a job appropriate to his skills and experience. A person may be the best buggy repairman in the country but who rides in a buggy these days? In other words, the changing nature of employment opportunities has brought about a change in the kinds of skills needed in today's labor market. Change is all about us, and older workers must recognize the adjustments they must make to compete successfully in the labor market.

Employers' misconceptions

Employers hold certain attitudes towards hiring older workers. Their hiring practices reflect these attitudes which in turn restrict the availability of job opportunities for older workers. What are the prevailing attitudes of employers for not hiring older workers? A Department of Labor study examined the hiring and retention policies and practices of employers regarding older workers in seven major labor markets. Among the reasons cited most frequently by employers which adversely affect the hiring of older workers are: [6]

---

[6] For a more exhaustive list of reasons given by employers for not hiring older workers, *see* U.S. Bureau of Employment Security, *Counseling and Placement Services for Older Workers*, BES No. E152 (Washington: Government Printing Office, 1956), pp. 39-40.

- Older job seekers cannot maintain normal production standards.
- Older job seekers cannot meet company physical requirements.
- Older workers are inflexible; they are too set in their ways; they resist change.
- Hiring older job seekers must necessarily increase pension and insurance costs.
- Older workers are excessively absent from work.

There are other reasons but these five will suffice to indicate the scope of employer attitudes toward hiring older persons. It is apparent that employment practices have failed to accommodate themselves to significant population changes, i.e., the aging of the labor force. Restrictive hiring practices bar older job seekers from employment principally because of age. There are a number of studies conducted by government, industry and educational institutions which reveal that employers resort to "conventional wisdom in restricting job opportunities for older workers. Let us examine the findings of some of these studies to determine the factual basis for such widespread employer views.

One of the major reasons most frequently cited by employers for limiting the hiring of older workers was their inability to maintain normal production standards.[7] Since this view is so widespread, the U. S. Department of Labor set out to examine the relationship between age and work performance.[8] Output data were obtained for about 2,200 production workers in eight manufacturing establishments in two industries: footwear and men's clothing. Because of the difficulties involved in such a study, only limited conclusions can be made.[9] The data show that output per man-hour remained fairly stable through age 54 and declined slightly for the 55-64 age group. When individual performance records were examined it was found that variations in the output of persons in the same age group were very large. These variations, in fact, were greater than the differences in average output among age groups. Many workers in the older age group, (55-64) had a higher output than younger persons doing comparable work.[10] These data emphasize the point that an

----

[7] U.S. Bureau of Employment Security, *Older Worker Adjustment to Labor Market Practices, op. cit.,* p. 7.

[8] U.S. Bureau of Labor Statistics, *Job Performance and Age: A Study in Measurement,* Bulletin No. 1203 (Washington: Government Printing Office, 1956).

[9] *Ibid.,* p. iii, cites difficulties involved in making such a study.

[10] *Ibid.,* pp. 1-2 and pp. 25-36.

employer should evaluate the potentialities of each individual applicant rather than draw conclusions from his chronological age. There are older workers who can and do maintain production standards.

Many employers have established pre-employment physical examinations as a part of their hiring practices. These examinations, in essence, define the physical standards of employment. As would be expected, older workers usually find it more difficult to meet the physical requirements. In the seven labor market survey the Department of Labor found that one in every ten workers under age 45 reported physical handicaps.[11] The proportion increases with age. Among the job seekers 45-55 years of age, it was one out of seven. For workers in the 65-and-over age group, it is one out of four. This should not be surprising. Relatively more older workers are apt to have physical handicaps than younger workers because they have been exposed to hazards both occupational and otherwise for a longer period of time.

Not all older workers are physically unfit. There are those who can meet company physical standards. Others could probably do so if employers would relax their high physical standards somewhat. All jobs are not standardized; all jobs do not make the same physical demands on all workers. Thus it would seem that high inflexible standards are not actually required of all workers for all jobs.

The handicapped

Those older job seekers who are physically handicapped present a different type of employment problem. There are other federal and state programs designed to help such persons. There is a tendency to lump together both the physically handicapped older worker and those older workers in good health, which distorts the employment prospects of the latter. Persuading an employer to hire physically able older workers is a difficult task.[12] It is even more difficult if the older job seeker is physically handicapped. Thus some differentiation should be made between the two groups of older workers. While both the physically fit older worker and the physically handi-

---

[11] U.S. Bureau of Employment Security, *Older Worker Adjustment to Labor Market Practices*, p. 18.

[12] *See* U.S. Bureau of Employment Security, *Counseling and Placement Services for Older Workers*, BES No. E152. Apparently the problem of placing older workers is such that the Bureau of Employment Security prepared a special bulletin on the subject. *See also* BES No. E169 entitled *Services to Older Workers by the Public Employment Service.*

capped older worker seek employment, there are two sets of problems which require different approaches. To treat them as one and the same kind of employment problem complicates the hiring of those physically able.

New tricks

"You can't teach an old dog new tricks" is a common expression, but does this apply to older workers? Unfortunately there are employers who view the older worker and old Fido both as being too set in their ways. Employers restrict employment opportunities to older workers on the grounds that they lack flexibility, are hard to train, lack versatility, resist change and are unwilling to accept new ideas.[13] Such generalizations are essentially subjective. Only by individual evaluation can their validity be determined. There are studies which indicate that there are significant differences among individuals at any given age.[14]

Older persons can and do learn new techniques. In a rote performance task by age groups, it was found that some persons in their fifties and sixties required more trials, made more errors and required more time to complete the task than did persons in their twenties.[15] There were, however, significant variations between individuals in the higher age groups. Some of the persons in the fifties and sixties *were learning as readily as the majority in the younger age ranges.*

The notion that all olders workers are reluctant to make considerable adjustment in their work patterns does not stand up when the facts are examined. Studies made by state employment security agencies indicate that a significant number of workers age 45 and over who have been placed on new jobs "are willing to accept changes once they face realities of their employment problems." [16] Approximately 57 percent of the workers changed industrial division while almost 40 percent made occupational changes.[17] In both instances men tended to change more often than women.

[13] U.S. Bureau of Employment Security, *Counseling and Placement Services for Older Workers*, p. 39.

[14] U.S. Bureau of Employment Security, *Older Worker Adjustment to Labor Market Practices*, p. 18.

[15] A. T. Welford and D. Speakman, "The Employability of Older People," *The Aged And Society, op. cit.*, pp. 190-191.

[16] U.S. Bureau of Employment Security, *Counseling and Placement Services for Older Workers*, p. 60.

[17] *Ibid.*, pp. 61-62.

Change in pay

In addition to the above changes, there were pay changes among these older workers.[18] Thirty percent received the same pay as they had previously. Another 18 percent were placed in jobs at a higher pay than they had been receiving in their previous employment. Forty-five percent accepted jobs at a lower pay than in their previous employment.

The significance of these studies is that those older workers placed by the employment service did accept changes in industry, occupation and pay. Thus it would seem that the ability of older workers to obtain new employment depends in some measure on their willingness to accept change.[19] Older workers, by and large, recognize that changes must be made if they are to compete successfully in the labor market.

Pension and insurance costs

Employers often cite pension and insurance costs as a barrier to the employment of older workers. Their arguments are generally of two kinds:

1. Hiring older job seekers increases pension costs. Providing adequate pension rights is held to be more costly for an older new employee than for a younger one.
2. Permitting older new employees to waive pension rights or to earn less than "adequate" rights would create an unfavorable public reaction toward the employer.[20]

To examine these arguments frequently cited by employers the Secretary of Labor in 1956 invited a group of experts from the pension and insurance fields to participate in a series of discussions to clarify the issue of pension and insurance costs on hiring policy and practice. In its report the committee states that:

> It is abundantly clear that pension and insurance costs need not stand in the way of the traditionally sound personnel policy of hiring on the ability to do the job, regardless of age or other nonperformance specifications.[21]

---

18 *Ibid.*, p. 62.
19 *Ibid.*, p. 63.
20 U.S. Bureau of Employment Security, *Pension Costs in Relation to the Hiring of Older Workers*, BES No. E150 (Washington: Government Printing Office, 1956), p. 4.
21 *Ibid.*, p. ii.

The report states the real and ultimate costs of pensions are the amounts finally paid out to the employee during his period of retirement, not the current contribution.[22] The ultimate cost depends on the terms of the pension plan and on future developments which are more likely to affect the costs for the younger men over his longer period of working life than those for the older man over his shorter period.[23] It is true that the contributions to the pension fund for younger employees are lower because the employer can spread the costs over a longer period of time. The funds invested accumulate and earn compound interest over a longer period. There are, however, countervailing factors which tend to reduce the age-cost differentials and may even balance them out. The impact of these factors which tend to be cumulative increase pension costs more than proportionately over time.[24]

Life expectancy

One of the factors tending to lower the relative costs of pensions for older workers is the extension of life expectancy. As persons live longer, the period of retirement will be lengthened, increasing the total amount of pension. An employee 35 years of age today will live more years after reaching age 65 than will the employee who is 50 years old today. As a result the employee of 35 will collect his pension for a greater number of years than will the employee of 50. Of course, if the normal age of retirement is raised, e.g., from 65 to 70, the period of benefit payments is shortened and the costs of pensions will be reduced.[25]

The terms of the plan

The second factor affecting pension costs is the terms of the plan. Most private plans in operation today provide benefit payments which are related to length of service, to the levels of current or future earnings or both. If benefits are related to length of service, the current cost of providing pensions for older workers will not be substantially higher, since the benefit formulas generally result in lower benefit payments for the older worker because of his shorter period of service. If, on the other hand, benefits are related to future earnings, such as the last five years, last ten years, or highest five

---

[22] *Ibid.,* p. 23.
[23] *Ibid.,* p. 24.
[24] *Ibid.*
[25] *Ibid.,* p. 25.

years of earnings, there is a probable cost advantage in having older workers.[26] An employee of 30 or 35 has a much greater chance to increase his future earnings than does an employee of 45 or 50. The younger employee has a longer time in which to increase his individual earnings (on which the pension will be based) through experience, added skills and knowledge and seniority. Experience has shown that pension plans have been revised from time to time to keep benefit payments in some reasonable relationship to levels of terminal earnings.[27] In all probability such revisions will continue to be made as the general levels of earnings increase. Thus pension benefits paid to the younger new employee on retirement will be higher than would appear from his current earnings. Higher benefit payments will increase the costs of pensions.

The cost of private pension plans should not be a real obstacle to the employment of older workers. The notion that pension costs are higher for older workers does not stand up when the facts are considered. There is, however, another aspect to the pension argument which employers use in denying employment opportunities to older workers. They are fearful of creating an unfavorable impression by retiring older workers with few years of service with little or no pension.[28] The basis for such fears has been removed or greatly reduced by the broadened coverage and increased benefits under the Social Security Act (OASI). It has been estimated that single men age 45 to 64 working steadily, at present day wages, will have earnings sufficient to qualify them for monthly social security benefits averaging $100.[29] Furthermore, an increasing number of older workers are acquiring vested rights to some private pension benefits in previous employment. Thus with social security benefits plus vested pension rights, a modest supplementary pension such as could be earned in ten years or less under most pension formulas ought not to subject the employer to unfavorable criticism.[30]

Compensation rates

Employers also claim that the costs of insurance, such as workmen's compensation, sickness, and accident and group life insurance, greatly increase when older persons are hired. Since there is wide-

---

[26] *Ibid.*, p. 24.
[27] *Ibid.*
[28] *Ibid.*, p. 23.
[29] *Ibid.*
[30] *Ibid.*

spread belief that older workers are more accident prone, it is assumed that insurance rates to cover job-connected injuries are higher for the older workers.[31] There is little evidence available to indicate that age is a significant factor in determining workmen's compensation rates. Corson and McConnell point out that there is no clear evidence that the employment of older workers raises workmen's compensation rates.[32]

The rates charged by insurance companies for ordinary health and accident insurance are not generally affected by the age of the employee. Since the risk is so widely diffused this kind of protection is relatively inexpensive. The costs of such insurance depend largely on type of coverage and number of dependents. Thus the costs may be lower for older age groups where dependents are usually fewer and maternity is no longer a significant hazard.[33]

The cost of life insurance increases with age. Premiums for group life insurance are normally based on the age structure of all covered employees as a group. One distinctive feature of group life insurance is that it is written without medical examinations. The amount of insurance for each employee is definitely fixed by some rule or pre-determined schedule, e.g., broad wage groups. Under the contributory plan in which employer and employee share the cost, each employee, without regard to age, pays a fixed level rate, usually about 60 cents or so a month for each $1,000 of insurance. The premium rates, however, are affected by changes in the age composition of the group. As the average age of the group increases, adjustments are made in the premium rate. The cost of such protection is not significantly higher for older workers because normal labor turnover tends to produce a relatively stable age group.[34] If these benefits are continued in retirement, costs can be of some importance because the incidence of the risk becomes high. Although life insurance is often carried over into retirement, the benefits payable are usually reduced, e.g., half or less of the amount in force during active employment. Costs for sickness and accident insurance, if also continued into retirement, may be substantially increased unless the benefits payable are limited to particular amounts and duration.

---

[31] *Ibid.*, p. 19.

[32] John J. Corson and John W. McConnell, *Economic Needs of Older People* (New York: The Twentieth Century Fund, 1956), p. 64.

[33] U.S. Bureau of Employment Security, *Pension Cost in Relation to the Hiring of Older Workers*, p. 21.

[34] For a good discussion of industrial group life insurance, *see* Malvin E. Davis, *Industrial Life Insurance in the United States* (New York: McGraw-Hill, 1944), Appendix B.

The total package

The pension and insurance experts who prepared the Labor Department report suggested that employers lump together all insurance (workmen's compensation, sickness and accident, and group life) and pension costs into a benefit package and examine the costs of each in terms of the total package.[35] By so doing employers may get a more rational view of pensions as one element in the cost of doing business. Furthermore, if maternity costs for dependents are included, employers may find that the cost of benefits other than pensions may be less for the man of 55 than for the man of 35.[36] The insurance experts concluded that selective hiring of new older workers can hardly add a fraction of a percent to the current annual charges for the total benefit package.[37]

Employers also claim that older workers are excessively absent from work because of illness and for other reasons. The U. S. Department of Labor studied the attendance records of 4,000 production workers in footwear and clothing plants. The data show that there is no appreciable relationship between attendance rates and age.[38] In a study of office executives in New York, *only one* respondent out of 118 indicated that the turnover and absenteeism record of older office workers is worse than that of younger people.[39] In another Department of Labor study, employers in seven cities reported that their older workers have consistently *less* absenteeism and are more apt to stay on the job.[40] From these studies it appears that older workers in both production and office have good attendance records.

Waste of resources

There are many other available studies which refute the misconceptions held by employers relative to the hiring of older workers. Despite these studies the attitudes of employers erect formidable obstacles in the path of older workers in their bid for employment. This is done by the simple method of setting arbitrary age limits.

---

[35] U.S. Bureau of Employment Security, *Pension Cost in Relation to the Hiring of Older Workers*, p. 62.

[36] *Ibid.*

[37] *Ibid.*

[38] U.S. Bureau of Employment Security, *Job Performance and Age*, pp. 36-38.

[39] Office Executives Association of New York, *Survey of Hiring Practices and Opinions Relating to Office Workers* by Age (New York: National Office Management Association, 1958), p. 5.

[40] U.S. Bureau of Employment Security, *Counseling and Placement Service for Older Workers*, p. 48.

Steps must be taken to minimize this deplorable waste of the human resources of the nation. There is no single solution. Constructive action in ameliorating the employment problems of older workers requires a whole series of solutions. The nature of the problem is such that the solutions of 1959 might not work in 1965 or 1970. As Evan Clague has pointed out, "It behooves the community to take continuous stock of this unfolding problem."

Included among the possible solutions for improving the employment prospects of older workers are:

1. The creation of a considerable number of new jobs would certainly help the situation, but this is no panacea. Older workers must possess the necessary skills required for such jobs if they are to compete successfully in the job market.

2. A revision of employers' hiring policies and practices is needed. If employers would hire on the basis of individual merit rather than on chronological age many qualified older workers could obtain suitable employment.

3. Through job engineering programs, engineers could redesign jobs to make them fit older people. Such a step would compensate for the decline in the abilities of those older workers who are still productive employees.

4. The whole area of retirement needs critical examination. Retirement on a mass scale is a relatively new phenomenon in American life. It is a by-product of an industrial society with social insurance and industrial pensions. Proper and well-conceived preparation for retirement programs may help employees to understand and more readily accept their retirement. Another possibility is the inauguration of selective retirement programs recognizing that all persons do not decline at the same rate. There are other aspects of retirement programs which affect the employment of older workers.

5. Before constructive action can be taken, the community must recognize the existence of the employment problems of older workers. Once they are recognized and identified, efforts must be expended in developing workable solutions.[41]

The above are only a few of the many remedial steps which can be taken in improving the employment prospects of older workers. These are briefly presented to indicate that there are solutions avail-

---

[41] *Proceedings of a Conference on Problems of Older Workers, op. cit.,* p. 74.

able. The situation is grave but not hopeless: the community does have alternative courses of action. Either every effort must be made to find suitable employment for those older workers who are willing and able to work or the community will face the prospects of an increasing number of unemployed older workers dependent upon public support.

Questions

1. What importance does a job have for the individual beyond that of providing him with a livelihood?
2. Have the unions in general tended to help or to hinder employment for older workers?
3. What are the principal reasons behind employer reluctance to hire older workers?
4. What effect, if any, will the hiring of older workers have upon the cost of fringe benefits for an employer?
5. What labor costs, if any, may be lower among companies utilizing workers from the older age groups?
6. In what ways does discrimination against the hiring of the older worker constitute a significant cost to society? Is the nation's present conflict with international communism affected in any way by this problem?

35. AGAINST COMPULSORY RETIREMENT *

Herman K. Murphey

Compulsory retirement is socially undesirable, economically unsound, and ethically wrong.

The imposition of arbitrary age limits on the right to work is incompatible with the principles of individual freedom and free enterprise upon which our society is based. Age discrimination is in the same category as class or race discrimination. Society should not deprive older workers of equality of opportunity in the competitive struggle to make a living.

Compulsory retirement is based on the theory that there is only so much work to be done or so many jobs to be shared and that, consequently, older workers must be shoved aside to make way for others. This make-work theory is economically unsound. Arbitrary curtailment of earning power because of age is as economically wasteful as plowing under crops. Unwillingness to utilize the productive capacities of everyone regardless of age shows a lack of sound economic principles.

Unnecessary retirement of older workers means a loss of the contribution those workers might make to national income and to tax collections, and at the same time adds to the burden of the social security system. The harmful effects of that policy will increase in the future as a result of the expected larger proportion of older persons in the total population. Ultimately, the burden of supporting that group may compel a return to the sound principle of full ulitization of human effort to achieve the greatest possible output.

Forced retirement of persons able and willing to work is ethically wrong. It deprives such individuals of the satisfactions resulting from productive achievement. It substitutes a dole for earnings. It destroys self-confidence. It places a stigma on the individual by implying that his productive capacity has become of no value. Forced retirement means fixed income. There is no assurance that such

* From *Personnel Journal*, Vol. 35, No. 3 (July-August, 1956), pp. 100-102. Reprinted with permission.

income will remain fixed in terms of purchasing power. The employer
who follows the practice of compulsory retirement may be condemn-
ing persons able and willing to work to a life of semi-privation as
well as mental stagnation.

The reasons advanced in support of compulsory retirement are
numerous but unsubstantial. It is sometimes advocated as an easy
way of getting rid of superannuated employees. But the employer
who lets his employees reach that stage is negligent. A slowing down
in performance resulting from age or any other cause requires a
reappraisal of the abilities of the person with a view to possible
changes in the job or a transfer to other work. In some cases retirement may be the only solution, but there is no evidence that decline
in work performance necessitating retirement occurs at the precise
age of sixty-five.

Treat Older Workers Individually

The uniform practice of arbitrarily retiring employees is an
example of an unfortunate tendency in personnel administration to
adopt fixed rules and follow established patterns. In dealing with
individuals some consideration must be given to the conditions and
circumstances in each case. This is recognized in promotions and to
some extent in determining salaries. An employer must evaluate jobs
and establish rates of pay. He must pick and choose his supervisors
and executives. Why then should he shirk his responsibilities in picking and choosing aging workers capable of continued employment?

Compulsory retirement is also advocated as a means of creating
more opportunities for the advancement of younger workers. This
make-work idea is not only unsound but it is also unfair to the older
workers. Why should youth be given special favor? Death, voluntary
retirement, the continuing job changes resulting from expansion of
activities, or resignations will always create job opportunities for
the younger people. Moreover, whenever a subordinate could do a
better job than his superior he should be given the opportunity
regardless of the age of that superior. All that age asks is the
opportunity to compete with youth.

It may be argued that the employer who has provided what seems
to be an adequate pension has fulfilled his obligations, since the
retired employee still has the right to seek work elsewhere. It should
be pointed out that forced retirement may deprive the retired worker
of earnings greater than the contribution of the employer. His
chances of finding other employment depend largely upon the type

of work he was doing. Most jobs today are specialized, and the average retired employee will have difficulty in finding work suited to his experience and ability. Odd jobs are not a satisfactory solution. Also, forced retirement is practically the same as discharge and suggests to prospective employers that the individual in question is incapable of work.

Make Pension Requirements Plain

The notion that retirement policy is a procedural matter entirely disassociated from a pension plan is false. The pension agreement is a contract and acceptance by the employee of the retirement policy set up by the employer is one of the considerations of the contract. Failure on the part of the employer to disclose the nature of that policy at the time the contract is made constitutes fraud. Even if it is clearly understood between the parties that compulsory retirement at a given age is part of the agreement, it can still be argued that a person entering a pension plan has no way of evaluating what he is giving up or how he will feel about retirement when he reaches sixty-five.

There are equally false notions about the determination of earnings where pensioners are retained as employees. The pension has no bearing on the amount a person should be paid. Earnings should be determined by ability to produce. It is as unfair to reduce the wage or salary of a pensioner by the amount of his pension, providing that he is as productive as his fellow nonpensioners, as it would be to deduct the investment income of an executive from his compensation.

The fallacy of compulsory retirement rests on its disregard of differences in men and jobs. Some workers are eager to retire at sixty-five or earlier. Some are forced to do so because of physical conditions. But there are many who would prefer to continue working either because they enjoy their work, because they want to keep occupied, or because of financial obligations or other reasons. Jobs differ as well as individuals. The retirement age for a baseball player or a boxer obviously comes earlier than in other occupations. Retirement from physical work is not in the same category as retirement from mental activity. Imposing an arbitrary age limit on the right to work without regard to the human factor or the job is fundamentally wrong.

Questions

1. Do you agree with the author when he says that compulsory retirement is socially undesirable, economically unsound, and ethically wrong? Why?
2. This article was written by a retired executive. Do you as a student agree with his viewpoint? Discuss.
3. Why has compulsory retirement become almost a standard procedure in American business? Do you think that there will be any changes toward removing maximum age limits or raising them? Discuss.
4. What effect has social security legislation had on compulsory retirement?
5. Are you familiar with retirement plans in other countries? What is the attitude in these countries toward the older person and his employment capabilities?

Additional Readings for Chapter 6

Aldis, Owen. "Of Pigeons and Men," *Harvard Business Review*. Vol. 39, No. 4 (July-August, 1961), pp. 59-63.

Aldridge, Gordon J. "Aging and Retirement: A Union Responsibility," *Business Topics*. Vol. 9, No. 4 (Autumn, 1961), pp. 71-77.

Austin, C. Henry, and William J. Carroll. "Essentials of Successful Pension Planning," *Management Review*. Vol. 43, No. 7 (July, 1954), pp. 466-480.

Belcher, David W. "Toward a Behavioral Science Theory of Wages," *Journal of the Academy of Management*. Vol. 5, No. 2 (August, 1962), pp. 102-116.

Brown, Kenneth D. "Personnel Management and an Aging Work Force," *Personnel Administration*. Vol. 23, No. 1 (January-February, 1960), pp. 14-19.

Cohen, Arthur M., and Wilbur R. Meredith. "Management and Employee Needs," *Advanced Management—Office Executive*. Vol. 1, No. 8 (August, 1962), pp. 28-30, 32.

Diebold, John. "Automation Needs a Human Policy," *Challenge*. Vol. 7, No. 8 (May, 1959), pp. 42-46.

Doberstein, Robert R. "Money and the Whole Man," *Personnel*. Vol. 38, No. 3 (May-June, 1961), pp. 16-24.

Fogel, Walter. "Wage Administration and Job Rate Ranges," *California Management Review*. Vol. 7, No. 3 (Spring, 1965), pp. 77-84.

—————————. "Fringe Benefits: Some Neglected Considerations," *Personnel*. Vol. 33, No. 4 (January, 1957), pp. 337-346.

Gitlow, A. L. " 'Fringe' Benefits: A Review," *Personnel Journal*. Vol. 34, No. 4 (September, 1955), pp. 126-130.

Jaques, Elliott. "Objective Measures of Pay Differentials," *Harvard Business Review*. Vol. 40, No. 1 (January-February, 1962), pp. 133-138.

Kaponya, Paul G. "Salaries for *All* Workers," *Harvard Business Review*. Vol. 40, No. 3 (May-June, 1962), pp. 49-57.

Lasser, David. "Labor Looks at Industrial Engineering," *Advanced Management*. Vol. 21, No. 1 (January, 1956), pp. 14-17.

McCarthy, Russel C. "Automation and Unemployment: A Second Look," *Management Review*. Vol. 51, No. 5 (May, 1962), pp. 34-43.

Northrup, Herbert R. "The Other Side of Incentives," *Personnel*. Vol. 36, No. 1 (January-February, 1959), pp. 32-41.

Otis, Jay L. "A Psychologist Looks at Salary Administration," *Management of Personnel Quarterly*. Vol. 2, No. 2 (Summer, 1963), pp. 22-27.

Owen, W. V. "Some Observations on Wages and Salaries," *Personnel Administration*. Vol. 19, No. 3 (May-June, 1956), pp. 19-25.

Perrow, Charles. "Are Retirement Adjustment Programs Necessary?" *Harvard Business Review*. Vol. 35, No. 4 (July-August, 1957), pp. 109-115.

Rhode, Jack F. "Fixed or Variable Retirement Ages?" *Personnel Administration*. Vol. 24, No. 1 (January-February, 1961), pp. 18-22.

Scheer, Wilbert E. "Do Fringe Benefits Pay Their Way?" *Administrative Management*. Vol. XXIV, No. 5 (May, 1963), pp. 48-50.

Shaw, Reid L. "A Grievance Procedure for Non-Unionized Employees," *Personnel*. Vol. 36, No. 4 (July-August, 1959), pp. 66-70.

Sherwin, Douglas S. "The Job of Job Evaluation," *Harvard Business Review*. Vol. 35, No. 3 (May-June, 1957), pp. 63-71.

Smith, Leonard J., and Charles H. Weiss. "Executive Compensation Programs," *Personnel Journal*. Vol. 37, No. 4 (November, 1958), pp. 126-130.

Stallcup, Evan. "A Fresh Look at the Safety Program: When Enough Is Too Much," *Personnel*. Vol. 38, No. 6 (November-December, 1961), pp. 26-37.

Stanley, John D., and Marjorie T. "Fringe Benefit Policy: Orientation and Objectives," *Personnel Administration*. Vol. 25, No. 3 (May-June, 1962), pp. 19-28.

Torrence, George W. "Phantom Stock Plans," *Management Record*. Vol. 22, No. 4 (April, 1960), pp. 2-5.

Winstanley, N. B. "How Much Is He Worth?" *Mill & Factory*. Vol. 58, No. 1 (January, 1956), pp. 80-82.

CHAPTER 7

Union Relations

The right of employees to organize and to bargain collectively with employers over the conditions of their employment is not only accepted by our society but is also guaranteed by legislation. Although only approximately a quarter of this nation's work force is unionized, the influence of the portion that is organized and the labor agreements negotiated by it exert a very significant effect upon personnel management. The bargaining agreements that a union negotiates with an employer establish the pattern of employment relations and conditions for those employees who are its members. The bargaining agreements also establish the pattern for any of the company's personnel who are not unionized, if they are to be given comparable treatment. Companies that are not unionized must also provide treatment and employment conditions that are comparable to those provided for in union agreements if they are to recruit and to retain competent employees and not become the subject of a union organizing campaign.

In spite of the significant impact that unions have had upon our industrial society and upon personnel management policies and practices, they have had their share of internal problems. Unions are confronted not only with the threat of automation upon the jobs of members but also with a condition of apathy and lethargy among these members. The article by Bernard Karsh discusses this apathy and the problems which it creates for the local union and for organized labor in general.

In addition to facing the threat of automation and the apathy of its members, many unions are also encountering stronger bargaining resistance from employers. The nature of these problems and of the changes that are taking place in union-management relations are discussed by Dallas L. Jones. The article by Neil W. Chamberlain, on the other hand, points up some of the problems confronting the employer as the result of union challenges to what management once considered to be its exclusive prerogative. The expansion of seniority provisions in the labor agreement by the union constitutes one of the greatest challenges to management control. The nature and complexity of these seniority provisions and the effect that they can exert upon personnel decisions is discussed in this chapter by Walter L. Daykin.

The extent to which an employer is able to achieve a labor agreement under which he can manage his business effectively is dependent, among other things, upon his negotiating ability. The article by Thomas G. Downing discusses the strategy and tactics that can be used in achieving collective bargaining objects. In administering the agreement that has been negotiated, it can be expected that some differences may arise between the employer and the union over the interpretation of certain provisions of this agreement. Those differences that cannot be resolved by the two parties generally must be settled by an arbitrator. The article by Laurence Stessin reveals the position that the arbitrator is likely to take when called upon to hear and to rule upon union-management disputes. This article reveals some of the precautions that management can take to insure that it will have a strong case to present to the arbitrator should it be necessary to take a dispute to him for settlement.

36. UNION TRADITIONS AND MEMBERSHIP APATHY *

Bernard Karsh

The author is with the Institute of Labor and Industrial Relations, University of Illinois. He is grateful to Joel Seidman, Jack London, and Daisy Tagliacozzo for many of the ideas presented here. An elaboration of this material is contained in *The Worker Views His Union* (University of Chicago Press, 1957), on which he worked with the above.

The assertion that membership apathy is one of the determinants of the local union's power potential needs no documentation here. The ability of the local to achieve its formal objectives, it is said, is bound up with the support which the local's formal leadership receives from the membership. A measuring rod, often used by management and other students of industrial relations to gauge membership support, is attendance at membership meetings—and the universal cry in the labor movement is that attendance is poor. Some legislators, as well as others, assert that rank-and-file apathy leads to the monopolization of power by a handful of leaders and, therefore, increases the possibility that these leaders will abuse their power grant. Corruption, racketeering, and undemocratic practices are seen to be the result, at least in part, of membership apathy.

I propose here to examine some implications of such assertions by taking a look at a few aspects of the composition of the local union, its leadership, membership, and functions. My remarks may be most applicable to the local in the manufacturing industry, particularly the large one, though I think a good case can be made for applying these comments to many building trades locals.

The word "apathy" carries a number of implications, at least as applied to understanding the operations of the local union. To describe the membership as apathetic is to assume, in the first place, that the membership is a relatively homogeneous mass with respect to their conception of the union and of unionism. It assumes that

* From the *Labor Law Journal*, Vol. 9, No. 9 (September, 1958), pp. 641-646. Copyright 1958, Commerce Clearing House, Inc. Reprinted with permission.

all members, by virtue of their status as members, have or should have an equal or relatively equal set of reasons for becoming members and, therefore, should have an equal or relatively equal obligation to take an active role in the government of the union, the formation of its policies and programs, and the successful achievement of the local's professed objectives. In short, we often assume, and certainly the typical set of local union leaders assume, that local union members have or should have an undifferentiated set of motives for membership and obligations as members, and a uniform conception of an abstract union or unionism.

Rather than being a body of relatively undifferentiated individuals, each having by virtue of his status as a member a similar conception of what the union is all about and, therefore, relatively equally motivated in his behavior toward it, membership is differentiated in a number of ways. Obvious differences occur on the basis of age, skill, occupation, seniority, sex, family background, information about and experience with unions, and similar variables. These factors get summarily combined to produce a number of fairly distinct types of members, each differentiated from the other on the basis of differing sets of values with respect to unionism.

Seven types of local union members can be distinguished: (1) a fairly insignificant number of ideological unionists who see the labor movement as a vehicle for fundamental social, political, and economic change in society; (2) a solid core of "good union men" with whom I will shortly deal at some length; (3) a small group of members who, in most respects, are like the good union men but critical of either incumbent leaders and present policies or both; (4) a large proportion of "crisis activists" who, though accepting the union, by and large see it in a personal way as an agency to be used to protect and advance self-interest; (5) a relatively few members, in most part drawn from the skilled craftsmen, who accept the union but who adopt management's point of view to criticize some of its programs and practices; (6) a substantial number of "card carriers" or totally indifferent members; (7) on the outer fringe, a few unwilling unionists who, if left to their own devices, would not join a union, and if compelled to join would get out at the first opportunity.

Each of these types, and there may be still others, are ideal constructs or models and they differ from each other in their basic conceptions of an abstract union and the meaning which this word has for them. The crisis activist, probably constituting the largest proportion, is the fellow who hardly ever comes to meetings or volunteers for picket duty or committee work. He may or may not vote in elections, but he can be counted upon to present himself to his departmental steward when he has a complaint to make or to turn up at a meeting whenever an issue arises that he feels affects him directly and immediately. He would deny that his membership in the union obligates him to the same degree as the obligation faced by the leaders whom he elected. Like the card-carrier, or indifferent type, he may have come to the union movement almost completely ignorant about it or hostile towards it. He may subsequently learn that the union performs a set of functions which are useful to him, not in his status as a *union member*, but in his status as an *employee* of the company. He is interested in the union almost exclusively because it is for him an insurance policy against the day when he may get into trouble on the job.

The union, for this type of member, is essentially a policeman— a "cop on the beat" who is there in order to "keep the boss honest." He supports the union but without any kind of emotional involvement; he pays his dues willingly but views dues in the same way he views taxes which are collected to pay the police and fire departments. He hopes that he'll never have to call the cop (and even goes out of his way to avoid contact with him except when he's in trouble) and, similarly, he hopes that he'll never have need of the fire department. Essentially, he supports both as kinds of necessary evils.

The second most numerous type found in the local union membership is the card-carrier, the worker whose union membership is a matter of almost complete indifference. He is neither prounion nor antiunion; he joins because he has to. A compulsory membership clause or the pressure of co-workers has brought him in it. He carries a union card but has no sense of duty or obligation; he is both indifferent and uninformed.

Unlike these types, which probably comprise the largest proportion of members, the good union man (usually the elected officer or steward) is devoted to the union. He understands its generalized goals in a historical perspective and accepts them fully. Ideally, he tries at all times to protect and advance the union's prestige and power. More than anybody else, he disparages those who are critical of the union or view it as an agency through which their own self-interest may be enhanced, or who are indifferent toward it. He particularly discredits fellow members who do not "assume their union responsibilities as I do." He, more than any other type, considers that all members have an equal obligation to be good union men.

He often views the crisis activist or the card-carrier as somehow disloyal. In substance, he measures all other union members by his own standards, and when they fail to qualify he denounces their irresponsibility.

The good union man is the primary link between the historical tradition and values of the union movement and the present and future generations of workers and members. If the rank-and-file member knows any of his union officers, he is most likely to know his local union leaders, particularly his steward or grievance committeeman. Whatever sympathetic understanding he may have of the union movement is most likely to come in his contact with the good union man in his department. The good union man 'may have learned trade union values on a picket line or at the end of a policeman's billy club, or from an employer who paid substandard wages in exchange for a continuous speed-up and abusive treatment. It is in terms of these experiences that he came to the union movement and adopted its values. However, with the submergence of the depression-born militant unionism in the economic boom of the past decade and a half, the core of good union men is increasingly becoming smaller and increasingly ceases to be the transmitter of the union's heritage.

Consider what has arisen in many places to substitute for the abusive employer or the good union man in recruiting and proselytizing the new worker, the young fellow just out of school. Presently when the young worker enters an employment office to apply for his first job (and this experience may be repeated on subsequent occasions), he is typically given a number of forms to fill out by the employment officer—the personnel man or clerk. Among these forms may be an application for employment, a social security form, workmen's compensation or other health or insurance forms, an application for membership in the union and a dues checkoff authorization card. He will probably be told that his application for union membership will take effect 30 days hence and that he must pay $5 a month to belong to a union he never heard of and, at best, cares nothing about. However, he may be told that he has to join and to pay in order to work. The personnel clerk may also give him an elaborate multicolored, very attractively designed brochure which contains a list of the many benefits he will enjoy as an employee—the insurance program for himself and his family (company paid, perhaps), a comprehensive medical program, a pension plan, a cafeteria where he can buy his meals at reasonable prices, a plan which pays him benefits supplementary to the regular state unemployment compensation should he ever be laid off, paid vacations and holidays, and so forth and so on. He is probably not told that many of these benefits may have been the result of a long strike which the union mounted five years ago. He may be shown the clean locker rooms and washhouses but is probably not told that these kinds of improvements may have been the result of the constant pressure of the union. He is merely asked, as a condition of employment, to sign an application for membership in the union and a dues checkoff card. He has as yet no knowledge of the struggles and sacrifices which good union men may have made to win these benefits for him.

This is quite different from an earlier time when the newly hired was recruited to the union by a good union man. Nowadays, it is more likely that he'll be recruited to union membership by the company, not the union. Thus, there may be an immediate identification of the specific company as the bestower of all that is good, and of an abstract union that requires that he pay tribute for reasons which are not explained other than to join up and pay or look for a job elsewhere. At least two effects may result: (1) Our young worker gets the idea that the company is really a good outfit because of the high wages it pays and the many fringe benefits it gives and (2) in order to enjoy the company's beneficence, he must contribute to a union whose history, program, structure and function is vague, undefined and provides him with no specific guides for action. He may also get the notion that there is really no distinction between the union and the company anyway, since it was in fact an agent of the company that recruited him to the union.

The good union man in his department, as the principal link in the transmission of the union's values and accomplishments, is almost the only source of information that the new recruit has to establish the connection between the company's benefits and the payment of dues. However, our young worker's opportunity to interact with the good union man is infrequent and often ephemeral. It may only come when the new worker gets into trouble on the job. Since the cash nexus has already been established, he demands that the steward —the good union man—come through with a payoff for dues collected. If the steward is unable to get him out of trouble, the new worker's identification with the union is even more tenuous than before. He pays his dues for nothing, he may feel. If the new recruit feels sufficiently disturbed, he may attend the next membership meeting only to be confronted with a bewildering display of what appears as endless wrangling, parliamentary confusion, long and irrelevant reports and communications, and maybe even a heated debate between factional opponents about an issue which he doesn't understand and is even less interested. An initial indifference or apathy may be re-enforced.

Good union men are among the first to hold that members should play more active roles in policy formation and execution, and that this would make the union somehow more effective. Attendance at meetings is the crucial test. "He has as much of a duty to attend meetings and keep informed as I do," the local leader is apt to assert. "If he doesn't come to meetings, I'm not going to tell him what went on because then he'd know and he'd never come around." When the good union man is pushed to suggest some number of members which is required to have a good meeting, his estimate is apt to vary anywhere from 20 per cent, rather than the present 3 or 5 per cent, to 40 or 50 or 60 per cent. When he's asked to explain why 30 per cent of the members, for example, is needed to have a good meeting (rather than some other figure), he runs into a wall. There seems not to be any logical reasons. "It just seems good," he may say.

The problem of local union power does not turn on the number of people at a meeting but on *whom* they are. There is no magic in playing this "numbers game." The traditional value of participation is achieved if the *interests* of *all* of the members are represented. By and large this is what actually occurs.

The typical membership meeting is attended regularly by the elected officers, stewards, executive board members and committee chairmen. In the ordinary case, particularly when the local is composed of a heterogenous membership, many of the diverse membership interests are represented among the officers. Where local union elections are conducted on the basis of slates of candidates, the slate-makers are very likely to deliberately select candidates as representatives of particular interest groups. The political process in a local union is essentially no different in this respect from what occurs on our larger political scene. Thus, the solid core of routine meeting-goers is typically composed of the representatives of special interests inside the shop. Additional meeting-goers are typically drawn from the personal following of the elected leaders, a small number of workers who come to the meeting to plead special causes, and an occasional chronic dissenter or curiosity seeker.

When a contract or collective bargaining item is scheduled to come before the meeting, the number present grows substantially. However, it is generally the crisis activists who now come. They do so in order to protect or advance their status as *workers,* not necessarily as union members. The point here is that the union, as an institution, has the professed goals of serving the interests of its members as union members and as employees. However, the rank-and-file member is not much interested in the professed goal of service to him in his status as a member. He is much more interested in the service he gets by virtue of his status as an employee of the company.

There is a real question as to whether the democratic ideology of the trade union movement, as expressed in its rhetoric, is compatible with its function in an age of mass unionism—of locals with many hundreds of members and diverse interests. In such locals the meeting of all members is as poorly adapted to an effectively functioning decision-making body as the New England town meeting is to the needs of the modern metropolis. Once more then, several hundred persons and a large number of different interests are involved, it is no longer efficient—indeed, often impossible to transact business through mass meetings. The meetings of hundreds of people may serve other functions, like generating enthusiasm, demonstrating needs and loyalties, or transmitting information, but it is not a useful device for transacting business.

The simple fact is that a large proportion of members will not attend routine meetings because they feel no obligation to do so. The fact is that there would be no place to put them if they came, and that if a place were available the proper conduct of business would be impossible. The nature and function of the union meeting, shaped when the membership groups were small and homogeneous, need redefinition in an age of mass unionism. Indeed, it can be argued that the formal structure of government in the local union is a carry-over from an earlier time and is no longer appropriate.

One can conceive of the local union as embodying not one but two distinct governments, each performing a different function for which an appropriate structure has been built. One government, concerned with relations *within* the union, is formed to control the relationship between member and member. Its rules and regulations are provided in the constitution and bylaws. An executive board is elected to administer these rules and regulations. This government is essentially concerned with the worker in his status as a union member. The other government, concerned with relations with the employer, is symbolized by the collective bargaining agreement and the grievance procedure. Its functions are carried out by the stewards and the grievance committeemen who carry on collective bargaining. Essentially, this government seeks to establish rules and regulations for the worker in his status as an *employee*. Though the personnel executing these two functions may overlap, their roles are different. The second government, for the most part, carries on its business at the work place where the members are found, and is structured formally as a representative government and enlists the support, participation and interests of the workers to a far greater degree than does the first government.

The local of such size that its members can no longer interact as members of face-to-face groups might do well to abandon the rhetoric of the mass business meeting, based as it is on the assumption of a homogeneous membership and equal or relatively equal identification with, conception of and obligation toward the union in all matters. Rank-and-file control and, accordingly, leadership responsibility to an electorate can better be achieved if workers meet for the discussion of issues in relatively small and homogeneous units such as departments. Action on the discussed issues could be taken through a body of representatives, each of whom was chosen by and responsible to a constituency of fellow workers. Since those who attend routine meetings are usually stewards or other active members who legislate with the interests and views of the workers in their departments in mind, why not recognize this and accordingly, change the structure of the meeting. A formally constituted representative internal government, structured similarly to the formally constituted representative collective bargaining government, would not guarantee greater participation in decision-making. However, it might tend to safeguard the local against legislation enacted by a special interest group that packed the meeting or the domination by an organized minority that attended meetings regularly. It might also build into the system a formal channel of communication between the leaders and the members that is not now present except informally.

This raises the importance of keeping the membership informed of developments in the local. Often the officers insist that the meeting is designed to perform this function and that they have no further responsibility to members who fail to attend. This is another variation on the theme that members are undifferentiated and, accordingly, have equal responsibilities as members. Leaders who see the membership in their own image will usually insist that they have no further responsibility to members who do not come to meetings. Since few members do attend routine meetings, the result is usually a membership that is uninformed as well as inactive. Many devices are available to inform the rank and file—a local union paper which may be no more than a one-page mimeographed sheet, departmental meetings, locker room and lunch room informal discussions, and simply talking up the union in the shop might provide the member with an intelligent basis for re-electing or defeating officers at the next election. It may even persuade a card-carrier to become a crisis activist, on the whole a net gain. However, sometimes the good union man, in his zealous effort to safeguard the security of the union, as he sees it, is afraid to open channels of communication with his members outside the local meeting on the ground that the employer would learn too much about internal union affairs. However, the chances are that an alert management, with its many and diverse lines of communication, knows as much about what goes on inside the local as the leader does—maybe even more when his communication channels include a pipe line into the opposition group where it exists. The good union man might even be an officer in a local which elects inner and outer guards to the executive board, and he may still view the union as the semisecret body which in an earlier time required such guards to protect the business of the local from hostile eyes and ears. However, the business of the local union is now public business which operates with a grant of authority from a larger public body—a law.

When the good union man takes the position that the inactive or apathetic member can "stew in his own ignorance," he is likely to confirm the suspicion of the crisis activist or the card-carrier, however mistaken, that the local is a tightly controlled, close corporation, run by and for the "elite," the officers who have the company agents recruit him to membership, force him to pay dues to an institution he knows little about and doesn't understand, and who won't tell him when he does ask. The result, again, may be increasing indifference or increasing hostility.

The problem of communications and participation in the local's power structure and the matter of apathy all involve the following question: What kind of loyalty does the ordinary rank-and-file member have toward the union or the company? Rather than possessing loyalty to both institutions, as some writers have concluded, a large number of ordinary members, labeled apathetic, may possess dual apathy. The crisis activist or the card-carrier, not to speak of the unwilling unionist, may see the union as an agency seeking to impose a set of values upon him and the company similarly engaged.

He internalizes the original and professed goals of neither institution. A large proportion of factory employees work for the company because by doing so they are able to satisfy needs which arise outside the work place. Work is seen merely as a way to escape from the boredom of routinized, trivialized and repetitive labors. The worker who has this view, and the proportion is probably very substantial, may belong to the union because he is compelled to belong by the language of a contract whose meaning to him is obscured in complicated and legal terminology. He may belong simply because his fellow workers do and he doesn't want to be a deviate. In neither case does such a worker internalize the values of the union or the company. Each institution provides a different set of satisfactions for him; neither provides a value system with which he identifies himself or which he understands and accepts. However, he puts up with them and, hence, accepts them for reasons which are different from the values which each professes.

Studies of organization life have shown that running an organization generates problems which are not necessarily related to the professed or original goals of the organization. Indeed, the day-to-day behavior of individuals in groups becomes centered around specific problems and the achievement of immediate goals. These goals may often be different from the professed and original goals of the organization. Then, since these day-to-day activities come to consume an increasing proportion of the time and thoughts of the actors, from the point of view of actual behavior, the day-to-day activities become substituted for the intended goals. The highly abstract ideas intended to be conveyed by the notion of "unionism" simply do not specify sufficient concrete behavior to have very direct influence on the bulk of union members. The general idea of "union" may influence the action of members by setting the limits and defining the context for action, but only in a very general way. This is true not because the leaders or the ideals are evil or unintelligible, but because the ultimate ideals and the formal structures initially erected to effect the ideals are not very helpful in the constant effort of the worker to find proximate and immediate solutions to the specific problems which day-to-day factory living poses. Phillip Selznik has put it this way:

> Besides those professed goals which do not specify any concrete behavior . . . there are other professed goals which require actions which conflict with what must be done in the daily business of running an organization. In that conflict the professed goals will tend to go

down in defeat, usually through the process of being extensively ignored.[1]

How many of the newer entrants into factory employment will develop the attitudes and ideal characteristic of trade union traditions? The union movement of the future will be but a pale image of the present one, let alone of the new unionism of the middle and later 1930's, unless ways can be found to reach the large proportion of members, presently discredited as apathetic, who operate with a value system which is a departure from the intended or original values of the trade union movement. These are workers who see the union not as an abstract ideal, but through the cash nexus of the union shop, the checkoff and the payoff, that is, the satisfaction of personal and immediate shop problems. The professed ideals of trade unionism will disappear through ignorance or become transformed to make them compatible with the value system of the apathetic—or local union power will increasingly depend upon the formal structure of authority and the appointed or elected officials who exercise that authority from points of power which may be even more distant to the rank and file than the local union.

Questions

1. What bearing, if any, are differences in the members' background likely to have upon their enthusiasm or their apathy toward union administration?
2. How does the background of the typical "union activist" member differ from that of the "good union man"?
3. What are some of the reasons why many members today fail to develop any sense of loyalty toward their union?
4. What is the reason why a large portion of union members fail to attend their union meetings?
5. What effect, if any, does the support or the apathy exhibited by its members have upon the degree of democracy that exists within the union?
6. What changes in the traditional organization and administration of unions might help to reduce apathy on the part of their members?
7. Does this article support or reject the views expressed in Article No. 37 by Jones?

[1] Phillip Selznik, "An Approach to a Theory of Bureaucracy," *American Sociological Review*, 47-54 (1943).

37. THE FUTURE OF COLLECTIVE BARGAINING *

Dallas L. Jones

On every side one hears forebodings of doom concerning the future of collective bargaining. Although such gloomy forecasts are not new, they have increased as the result of the strife-torn years through which we have just passed. A general assessment has been that collective bargaining has failed to resolve our labor-management problems and that it will be less able to do so in the future.[1] I do not share this opinion. I believe the strife we have experienced resulted from changes in the status of the labor movement as compared to business, from economic and technological changes, and from a changed managerial approach to collective bargaining, rather than to gross inadequacies in the fundamental nature of collective bargaining. As a result of these changes, for reasons which I will advance, we may well be on the threshold of a new era of collective bargaining.

The period of the late 1930's was in many ways the "golden age" of the American labor movement. Business leaders, who had been dominant in the community during the 1920's, were in disrepute as a result of the depression. Labor leaders helped fill the vacuum thus created. Led by John L. Lewis, a group of young, militant leaders gave a new surge of life to a moribund movement. In every sense of the word, organized labor was a movement—it had a purpose and it had an ideological fervor. It attracted millions of unorganized workers and it received widespread support from intellectuals and from the public.

Today, these roles have again been reversed; businessmen, not labor leaders, are regarded as the leaders of the community. This does not mean that labor has no community influence (and of course there are differences between individual labor leaders), but the fact remains that as a group business leaders command more public

---

* From *Management of Personnel Quarterly*, Vol. 3, No. 1 (Spring, 1964), pp. 3-7. Reprinted with permission.

[1] *See* for example, Paul Jacobs, *Old Before Its Time: Collective Bargaining at 28*, Center for the Study of Democratic Institutions of the Fund for the Republic, 1963.

respect than do labor leaders. And even when there is a lapse of business morality, as in the case of the electrical company executives, public disfavor is brief when compared to reaction to similar cases involving labor leaders. Finally, if intellectuals have not entirely deserted the labor movement, they have become critical of it. Why has this change occurred?

The changing role of unions

Loss of some public and intellectual support was inevitable. The labor movement was initially supported because it was a part of the general protest movement of the times and in particular because it was dedicated to alleviating critical problems of workers in the work place. In this latter regard, the labor movement did yeoman's service. But in so doing, it sowed some of the seeds of its decline.

The negotiation and administration of collective agreements—agreements which became increasingly complex—began to require more and more of the time of union officials at all levels, and especially at the local level. As a consequence, labor leaders had less time for reform causes. Unions, in short, became service organizations with a basic philosophy not too unlike that associated with the old A. F. of L. Although the labor movement continued to support an ever broadening range of social legislation, the basic function of the union movement became and remained collective bargaining.

The American labor movement thus failed to meet the expectations of many intellectuals who hoped that it would develop into something more, at the very least a vigorous proponent at all levels of political liberalism. Moreover, the organized worker, with the great improvement in his wages and working conditions, has ceased to be the "underdog" in the eyes of the intellectual. This former ally of labor is also somewhat bothered by the constant seeking of "more," oftentimes, he believes, at the expense of the unorganized. The increased power of unions has also caused great uneasiness both on the part of the intellectual and the public. Equally important in accounting for the loss of public and intellectual support was the failure of the union movement to live up to expected standards of democracy and ethics.

Lack of democratic and ethical practices in many unions was apparent quite early, but it was widely held that this was simply a problem of growing up. However, with some significant exceptions, time did not bring much change. Although it can be argued that the union movement in this regard is no better or no worse than other organizations in society and that its leaders are just as honest, the fact is that more was expected; the labor movement did not live up to an envisioned ideal and disillusionment followed.[2]

Organizing failures

Significant also has been the failure of the union movement to organize important segments of workers—particularly the white-collar and technical groups. Whatever the causes for this failure, and many reasons have been advanced, it is certain that this group does not look with favor upon the union movement. The failure to organize this group has two important consequences: it reduces both numerically and financially the strength of the labor movement and the labor movement is faced with an ever increasing segment of the work force who are in opposition to it.

Internally, the union movement also has its troubles.[3] The union member of today is not the union member of yore—militant and dedicated to the union and its progress. The old militant who helped to organize the union is passing from the scene. He is being replaced by people who have entered the workplace in a new era of labor relations and who have little emotional attachment to the union. This is not to imply that present-day union members will not support their union in time of crisis—a mistake management too often makes —but that there is a difference in the quality of this membership. It weakens the union as a movement although not necessarily so as a collective bargaining agent.

There has also been a deterioration in leadership. The leaders of the 30's are growing older. Most unions have a great need for younger, energetic and capable leaders at all levels. In this regard, the union movement has a unique problem—it has to secure most of its leaders from within, and they must rise through the political process. The problem is much different today than it was in the 30's. Then there were opportunities for capable, ideal-oriented people to rise in the labor movement without spending a long period of time at the trade. Union positions at all levels were staffed with people

---

[2] A good example of this from a staunch supporter of unionism is Clark Kerr, *Unions of Their Own Choosing*, Center for the Study of Democratic Institutions of the Fund for the Republic, 1958.

[3] George Strauss has made a penetrating analysis of this change in his article, "The Shifting Power Balance in the Plant," in *Industrial Relations*, Vol. 1, No. 3 (May, 1962), pp. 65-96.

who saw the union as a cause and who willingly devoted their time and effort to it. There are still many of these people, but not enough. Younger people do not appear available in sufficient numbers to fill the gap. Moreover, it would appear that many of the present leaders have lost their zeal. Critics, as well as sympathizers, have noted the loss of dynamism, the adherence to old shibboleths, and the failure to formulate new goals.[4] Formulation of goals, as well as seeing that they are carried out, is a leadership function and many of the present leaders do not appear capable of providing that kind of leadership.

To sum up, the union movement as a force in society has, for various reasons, lost much of its public appeal. In this country, as in many countries abroad, the labor movement is not regarded as an organization which can constructively deal with the major economic and social problems of our time. Its proposals are not regarded as highly as those emanating from the business community. A case in point is the labor movement's proposal for a shorter work week to deal with unemployment. The same is true for many other issues. Thus, at the moment, the business community has greater public support than the labor movement. This has important consequences for legislation and other government policy affecting industrial relations, and it also affects collective bargaining.[5]

A new management approach

During the late 40' and early 50's, there appeared to be only token management resistance to union demands. In the tight labor market and the high demand market of those years, there was little incentive on the part of most companies to keep costs down. Not only was management providing little resistance during negotiation, it was highly susceptible to union pressures such as wildcat strikes during the term of the agreement—pressures which often expanded the agreement at the expense of work rules. The philosophy of many companies appeared to be "production at any cost."[6] There also

---

[4] *See* for example, Solomon Barkin, *The Decline of the Labor Movement*, Center for the Study of Democratic Institutions of the Fund for the Republic, 1961.

[5] Many might quarrel with this assessment in view of recent N.L.R.B. decisions regarding subcontracting, employer free speech, etc. I would point out that some of these decisions have not yet been upheld by the Supreme Court, and the only major legislation enacted within the past few years was the Landrum-Griffin Act which was directed at the union movement.

[6] In the case of suppliers, however, there was little that an individual management could do. If a strike occurred, the prime contractor would seek other sources of supply. This kind of pressure was difficult to withstand.

appeared to be a belief on the part of many managements that one could "buy" good industrial relations. Wage increases were often used as justification for higher prices.

By the mid-1950's, the economic situation was changing. Management began to encounter consumer resistance to higher prices. Competition with foreign products began to develop with the revival of industry in Europe and Japan. (One might also note that the marketing departments of many companies made some terrible forecasts regarding consumer tastes at this time.) Profit margins began to shrink even in cases where volume remained quite high. Vital industries such as steel were confronted with increased foreign competition as well as competition from substitutes such as aluminum and plastics as steel prices climbed. Economic pressures thus began to force management to re-evaluate its approach to collective bargaining. Rising labor costs also accelerated the process of technological change.

At the same time, there was an ideological change on the part of many managements.[7] The idea of getting along with the union for harmony's sake was discarded. Although this was in part a response to economic pressures, it was also a response to other important causes. Management seemed to realize for the first time the success it had achieved over the preceding fifteen years in leading American business in both war and peace to unprecedented heights. Businessmen also seemed to realize that they were no longer outcasts of society—a fact brought home very vividly with President Eisenhower's reliance upon businessmen for advice and his appointment of businessmen to important posts. This ideological shift was in part the reaction of a new generation of businessmen who were determined not to allow the unions "to run their business." It was a resurgence of a will to lead in labor relations as well as in other areas of society.

It was in this atmosphere that management's strategy and tactics toward unionism changed—strategy and tactics which have since been termed the "hard line." Whatever one calls this changed management approach, its purpose was clear—to reduce or to bring to a halt wage increases and to recover management initiative in directing its labor force—an initiative which management believed it had lost. This approach had two prongs—one in contract negotiation and the other in contract administration.

---

[7] Many writers have commented upon this development. *See* for example, "Roger Blough's Crusade," by Paul Jacobs in *Reporter*, Vol. XXI, (August 20, 1959).

To attain its purpose in contract negotiation, management set out to win public support and to reduce union power. For example, management started to sponsor advertisements in all sorts of publications setting forth its views concerning the "monopoly" power of the unions and "featherbedding." "Cost-push inflation" became a by-word of the times. The recessions of the late 50's and early 60's with ever-increasing levels of unemployment and higher prices seemed to verify management's assertions.

Management also moved to the attack on the political level. The managements of many companies began to urge increased political action and some companies set up political education courses. National business associations moved in the same direction. Support was given, both indirectly and directly, to "right-to-work" campaigns. Although many of these attempts failed, labor was placed on the defense.

To strengthen its collective bargaining position various types of alliances were formed. The steel industry grew closer together and bargained as one—at least until Kaiser bolted. The automobile companies, starting with the sharing of information in 1955, developed their system of "parallel bargaining." The airlines and other industries developed their systems of strike insurance—all for the purpose of offsetting union strength and the preventing of "whipsawing." But such tactics were only one part of a total program.

Instead of waiting for the union to make demands and then erect a defense, management began to put forth demands of its own. It was not only that management was putting forth demands that was important, but it was the way in which it was done. Demands were not advanced simply for the purpose of placing unions on the defensive but were for the purpose of making basic changes in the labor agreement. This required planning. Purpose and planning in negotiations, and in contract administration as well, was made possible by the professionalization of the industrial relations function and by the new role assigned to it.

Professionalization of industrial relations

If it is an exaggeration to say that many of the early industrial relations people were "happiness" oriented and that the industrial relations function was not regarded very highly by many companies, there is at least a germ of truth in the statement. Such a statement cannot be made now. In the past decade, there has been a quiet but

significant revolution; today, there is a new breed at the helm. They
regard industrial relations as a profession—many of them have college degrees in industrial relations or related areas—and they
approach industrial relations in a professional and capable manner.
This means careful research and policy planning—the same kind of
research and planning that would go into any other function of the
business. This group does not regard itself as a mediator between
union and management, as was often the case formerly, but as a part
of management whose function it is to carry out industrial relations
in a manner that will further the objectives of the company. Thus,
their intent is not to destroy the rights of the employees or to destroy
the union—it would not be in their interest to do the former and
impossible to carry out the latter—but simply that there is a different
emphasis and quality in their approach. In addition, the importance
of industrial relations was recognized and industrial relations people
were given a new status in the company hierarchy.

In contract negotiations this new approach has meant careful
study and preparation for bargaining. The current agreement is
meticulously analyzed and proposals for changes in problem areas
are carefully noted. There is no intention of making all the desired
changes at one time, but each modification becomes part of an overall
plan. By the same token, careful consideration is given to developments which might have adverse effects such as court and other
governmental unit decisions.[8] Many companies have also adopted
better communication systems with their employees in order to build
employee confidence in the fairness of the company offer and to avoid
the mistake of communicating only during a crisis.[9] Some companies
also take note of possible union proposals and prepare to meet them.
Backed by this type of advance preparation and purpose, management
enters into negotiations prepared to secure its own demands and to
resist excessive union demands even at the cost of a strike. Management has not always been successful, of course, but an assessment
of bargaining over the past three or four years certainly indicates
that management did secure the initiative and did make progress
toward its goals.

---

[8] For example, the 1960 Supreme Court decisions in *Warrior and Gulf, et al.*,
caused many managements to propose strengthened management rights and limited arbitration proposals to meet what many managements considered a real
threat. This statement is based upon a research project being undertaken by
Professor Russell A. Smith of the University of Michigan Law School and myself.

[9] This is, in effect, an approach based upon the General Electric program
but with adaptations to meet the circumstances.

This same sense of purpose and professionalization has extended to the administration of the agreement. Although many firms recognized the need for good contract administration very early in the game, others did not. In part, this was a concomitant of the "getting along with the union" philosophy, the problem solving techniques of the "human relators," as well as the lush economic conditions of the post-war period. Thus, as noted above, management was prone to surrender to pressure tactics which enlarged the agreement at management's expense. Management often found that it had given up as much through the administration of the agreement as through the negotiation of it.

But this situation has changed in the past few years as George Strauss has pointed out.[10] Led by the professional industrial relations staff and with full support from top management—i.e., willingness to resist union pressure tactics—there has been a tightening up in many plants. Costly practices have been slowly reduced or eliminated. Management at all levels are urged to take the initiative in order to make the contract "creep" for the company rather than for the union.

One area in which this approach of the professionals is most evident is in grievance handling and arbitration. Supervisors are thoroughly trained in the company's interpretation of the contract and are instructed to carry it out in that fashion. They are also given training in the importance of making thorough investigations and the compiling of evidence to support a position in the event the dispute is processed to arbitration. For the most part, management allows only those grievances which it believes are likely to be decided in its favor to be processed to arbitration—there are fewer "face-saving" grievances arbitrated. Although it is impossible to know the exact tally, my guess is that management is securing a favorable decision in a majority of the cases now being arbitrated—a reversal of the situation of a decade ago.[11]

The consequence of this new management approach, combined with the stagnation of the economy, and rapid technological change which intensified job security fears, inevitably led to the industrial

---

[10] Strauss, *loc. cit.*

[11] Strauss, *loc. cit.*, believes, and I think rightly so, that part of the success of management has come because of the internal problems of the union movement. There has been a decline in the number of representatives to handle the complex problems of contract administration. Increasing age, more demands of all kinds upon their time, and often less enthusiasm have caused many staff representatives to become less effective. Moreover, as noted above, many of the rank-and-file are less militant and therefore less willing to support pressure tactics—especially with the knowledge that management will unhesitatingly take disciplinary measures when such actions occur.

conflict of the past few years. Moreover, the various alliances which business had formed to counteract union power has, in some instances, tended to make work stoppages more critical. This has caused some people to express the belief that collective bargaining cannot meet the demands placed upon it. It has led others to advocate breaking up national unions or to advocate compulsory arbitration to deal with critical work stoppages. I am not yet ready to accept these solutions; in part because I am not sure that they will work and in part because I do not believe that collective bargaining is obsolete or that it has failed as miserably as is sometimes asserted. In addition, I think we are entering a new era.

The greater impact of collective bargaining

In the pre-1930's era, collective bargaining affected only a minor part of our economy. The widespread development of collective bargaining has come in a tumultous period—depression, war, and postwar boom. For most of this period, there appeared to be few restraints on what could be done—at least in the way of wages. It has been only in the past few years that the situation has altered significantly. Over the years, however, joint dealings became accepted. Some of the disillusionment with collective bargaining has come because too much was expected from it. Collective bargaining cannot solve all the problems of the labor market, although that is sometimes expected.[12]

Yet it can also be said that there was a lag in the growth of industrial relations maturity on the part of the parties—partly because there was no incentive to produce it. The need for maturity came quite quickly. Management reacted initially because it was the first to feel the pressures of changed economic conditions. The new management approach shocked the labor movement and it responded violently.[13] Out of this tumult, however, I think has come some good.

Both parties have come to realize that displays of economic power and public exhortation will not solve the problems which they face.

---

[12] As the Independent Study Group in *The National Interest in National Labor Policy*, Committee for Economic Development, 1961, pp. 33-34, pointed out, collective bargaining cannot provide solutions "for all the issues of the labor market and work process" yet there has been a general feeling that it should. This has, in my opinion, resulted in failure to take action in areas in which only the government can be effective.

[13] The labor movement believed that in some instances there was a deliberate plot on the part of management to destroy the union. This would not appear to have been generally true, but in some instances the charge did have substance.

But the recent period did show that both parties had economic strength that could be used to the detriment of each other as well as to the public, and that there were compelling reasons to discard old practices—reasons such as competition, declining profits and declining membership that stemmed in part from inadequate economic growth. And where it was not clear to the parties, the Kennedy Administration did so in various ways. Although the war of slogans still goes on at the AFL-CIO and NAM levels, I think there is real progress at the level which really counts—the negotiating level.

Thus at the private level we are witnessing many interesting experiments to prevent breakdowns in collective bargaining, and to resolve the perplexing problems of technological change. Among these innovations is the "human relations committee" in the steel industry as a means of exploring and solving problems that can accumulate and prevent settlements at negotiating time. Certainly the negotiations and the results of those negotiations this year and last are a far cry from past negotiations and results. Although it is too early to make a definitive judgment, the parties in this industry appear to have solved the problem of "crisis bargaining" as well as to have made some progress in dealing with other difficult problems.

The recent developments in the auto industry, the study committees, follow this trend. It is too soon to know what success this approach will have. And in the aftermath of the New York newspaper strike, the parties are studying means to prevent such an occurrence in the future. There has also been some experimentation with private mediation—the so-called "informed neutrals"—and this too offers interesting possibilities. Kaiser Steel is an example of this approach. The National Academy of Arbitration has also been considering ways in which it can offer its services without any intention of substituting arbitration for negotiation.

At a less grandiose level, in the smaller firms, one receives the impression that accommodations to the economic facts of life are being accomplished. Research has shown that "pattern bargaining" was never as widespread or as monolithic as supposed, but even the pressures toward it appear less intense. The union, as well as management, appear far more flexible than formerly.

There are also developments at the governmental level which are working toward a more public interest oriented bargaining atmosphere. The work of the President's Labor Management Advisory Committee has been helpful, if not spectacular, and it may develop into a body of even more importance. The early mediation techniques of the government have been, in my opinion at least, more helpful than harmful. The President has also made it known that not only is a peaceful settlement desirable, but the nature of that settlement is also important.

There has been, of course, great criticism of the government's actions—a criticism which takes as its basis the position that the government is intervening too much and that this is leading to government dictation. As Selwin Torff recently said, much of this criticism is misdirected—it should be directed at the parties because they have not lived up to their responsibilities.[14] I believe that there has been a change in the attitudes of managements and unions and that they are now taking a more responsible approach—in large part to avoid this kind of intervention.

In conclusion, therefore, I am hopeful for the future. The collective bargaining crisis, if crisis there has been, has created problems, but it has also made it possible for the parties to reappraise their positions and to take a more realistic view—a process that is still going on. I don't believe that we will attain the happy situation prevailing in Switzerland where there have been no strikes in 25 years, but I do think we may well be entering an era in which collective bargaining will become a viable tool which will serve our interests better.

Questions

1. Why, possibly, has the support of some liberals for the labor movement declined in recent years?
2. Do you feel that unions are having any difficulty in recruiting energetic and intelligent young people into leadership positions? Why do not more college graduates seek leadership positions in labor rather than in company organizations?
3. How have the attitudes and practices of management in the area of labor relations changed during the past decade?
4. Do you share the author's optimism regarding the future of collective bargaining? Explain.
5. What recent developments in labor relations offer some encouragement for its future?

---

[14] Selwin H. Torff, "A Reappraisal of the U. S. Collective Bargaining Process," *Personnel Administration*, Vol. 26, No. 1, pp. 5-94.

38. THE UNION CHALLENGE TO MANAGEMENT CONTROL *

Neil W. Chamberlain

One recent day at a small cement plant near Palo Alto, Calif., the boss strode up to one member of a two-man crane-operating crew. The boss asked if he'd step down off the giant machine now and then, walk a few paces to the side, and punch a button that would start or stop the conveyor belt being used to haul sand and gravel into the plant. The oiler complied.

A couple of days later, this matter came to the attention of a business agent for the International Union of Operating Engineers in San Francisco. The union speedily dispatched a representative to the scene. He instructed the oiler that henceforth he wasn't to set foot off the crane while on duty. Next morning an additional man appeared on the job to run the conveyor belt.

Incidents such as this—in which unions, rather than management, decide where workers are to work, and what they're to do—are provoking a management counterattack that's far broader than generally realized. While the battles over "featherbedding" in the steel industry, the railroad industry, and on the East coast docks have been grabbing the headlines, the fight also is being waged in a variety of other businesses, large and small across the country.[1]

The interpretation of management rights has become important as an arbitrable matter and the management rights issue is rising in prominence. In the immediate postwar days, when management rights clauses were being introduced in contracts, many observers believed these clauses to be window dressing. It seemed that acknowledged rights of management were being formally put into words, and this formalization had no value except possibly for public relations purposes.

Now it is being realized that perhaps there is greater substance in these clauses than was thought and that they do have a bearing on the interpretation of other clauses in the contract. Consequently, we may need to take a new look at what they mean. Indeed, there seems to be a feeling across the nation that rights which had once been conceded to the union are again under scrutiny, that privileges which unions thought had been won in the postwar decade are being

* From *Industrial and Labor Relations Review*, Vol. 16, No. 2 (January, 1963), pp. 184-192. Reprinted with permission.
[1] James R. MacDonald, "Work Rules Battles," *The Wall Street Journal*, November 4, 1959, p. 1, col. 1.

re-examined and subjected to hard bargaining. Assignment of work and subcontracting are just two of these controversial areas, areas which in their larger setting are generally referred to as disputes over managerial prerogatives and the unions' attempted invasion thereof.

What is involved here is a power struggle, a conflict of relationships which has gone on over the years, perhaps over the centuries. This phenomenon should be viewed in historical and philosophical perspective.

From this perspective what we are interested in are the points of similarity between the situation today and situations in the past. We are also interested in the ways in which today's situation may be distinguished from those involving the same kind of dispute, the same kind of argument over prerogative power relationships in previous years.

The issue of prerogatives

At the outset, it may be suggested that the issue of management prerogatives, of authority prerogatives, is as old as the master-servant relationship, and goes back a good many centuries. In fact, it might be fair to say that this issue of prerogatives is as old as the parent-child relationship. Wherever there is an authority which presumes to direct a subordinate and to determine paths of conduct and routines of behavior, and wherever this kind of authority is assumed, there will inevitably be protest from those to whom the assignment is made. There will be questioning by the subordinates of the basis for the authority, and of the reasonableness of its exercise. So let us not assume that this is an issue which somehow has suddenly been precipitated into our midst. It is one which has been experienced in human relationships in a variety of forms over hundreds and thousands of years.

This issue, too, studs the history of the union-management relationship. Every bit of progress the unions have made, every achievement they have won, has been realized in the face of charges that they were invading the prerogatives of others, that they were assuming authority which should be the proper preserve of some other group, generally a managerial one. Unions have become somewhat inured to this charge of invasion of others' prerogatives.

They were so charged when they sought to reduce the twelve-hour, indeed even the sixteen-hour, workday. They were so charged when they first attempted to have some say on so elementary a matter as wages. When they first attempted to bargain on these matters they were met by the counter-offensive that such matters were really in the hands of those who represented the workings of a systematic order, perhaps even in the hands of God. One need but remember some of the quotations which are part of the lore of labor relations from those who presumed that they were spokesmen of higher order, vessels of an authority which was greater than their own, and whose righteous position was being challenged by renegade, upstart, rebellious groups who really had no ground for such a challenge.

A typical illustration of this can be found in an editorial which appeared a little more than a hundred years ago, in the *Journal of Commerce* published in New York City.

On an occasion when the printers' union was attempting to negotiate on such matters as restriction of number of apprentices, the employment of women as compositors, child labor, and female labor (viewed as a threat to the position of the old established compositors), the editorial attacked the union in this fashion.

> Who but a miserable craven-hearted man would permit himself to be subjected to such rules, extending even to the number of apprentices he may employ, and the manner in which they shall be bound to him; to the kind of work which shall be performed in his own office, at particular hours of the day, and to the sex of the persons employed, however separated into different apartments or buildings. For ourselves we never employed a female as compositor, and have no great opinion of apprentices; but sooner than be restricted on these points, or any other, by a self-constituted tribunal outside of the office, we would go back to the employment of our boyhood and dig potatoes, pull flax, and do everything else that a plain honest farmer may properly do on his own territory. It is marvelous to us how any employer having a soul of a man within him can submit to such degradation.[2]

This is characteristic of the heights or the depths of feeling which can be stirred by such challenges to one's authority. It is interesting to note how this reference to the position of the plain honest farmer who controls his own destiny has always seemed to be an escape hatch for managements beset in this fashion. About a hundred years after the appearance of this editorial, Charles E. Wilson, then president of General Motors, was faced with a demand from his union for a union security clause. He replied: "I would not have a closed

---

[2] George A. Stevens, *New York Typographical Union No. 6*, Annual Report of the Bureau of Labor Statistics, New York State Department of Labor, 1911, Part 1, pp. 240-241.

shop. I am never going to sign one. When it gets around to that, it will make a farmer out of me." This thought of a return to the soil as a means of escaping the depredations of unions seems to have persisted over the years and has perhaps been a comforting reassurance to management that if the unions become too persistent, there is always a way out.

In certain respects the issues we are examining have continuities with the past and ties to history of which we can remind ourselves. But there are also elements of difference. One peculiarity of the present labor-management relationship is that, so far as I know, for the first time in history our society has given, not only legal sanction, but a measure of encouragement to those whose very function is to challenge a vested authority.

We realize that the very role of unions is to act as a challenge to management. Nonetheless, our society has since 1935 given legal protection to those seeking to attack the wielders of established authority in the business setting. This has been forcefully brought home to many managements in the form of NLRB decisions dealing with the duty to bargain over a large variety of issues.

We may recall the Circuit Court decision which upheld the National Labor Relations Board in its ruling with respect to the Phoenix Mutual Life Insurance Company.[3] In that case, a group of insurance salesmen had decided that the frequent turnover of the cashier in the office was a handicap to them. Consequently, they banded together in order to support the appointment of a new cashier after the latest one had left the company. They prepared a petition in which they urged the appointment of the person who was then acting as assistant cashier. This came to the attention of the office manager before the petition was formally presented, and the two ringleaders were fired.

This was an informal kind of action. No union was involved. But because it was considered concerted activity, a charge was filed with the National Labor Relations Board. The Board supported the two discharged men and ordered their reinstatement. A majority of the Circuit Court upheld the Board and said that the salesmen's interest in the appointment of the cashier was reasonably related to the conditions of their employment. This evoked a very strong dissent from one judge who said that the choice of a cashier was purely a management affair and that: "To put it bluntly, their grievance was directed

---

[3] *Phoenix Mutual Life Insurance Co.*, 73 NLRB 1463 (1947).

at a matter which was none of their business or concern." [4] He then went on to say that he supposed, under the construction given by the majority, the employees would have been protected if they had concerted regarding the naming of the company president, or directors of the company, or the general counsel of the company, or other officials who were important to the conditions of their employment. This is an interesting example of a case in which an arm of the government is protecting a group of employees who are contesting a managerial right or are at least seeking to influence a managerial prerogative of appointing company staff.

The issue has come up in numerous other ways. The appropriateness of stock options as a subject of mandatory bargaining has been upheld. The cases in which the Board has held a subject non-bargainable are surely rare.

Conflict in values

Now to examine the underlying value conflict that permeates this kind of relationship. Sometimes we feel that this attempted union invasion of management rights represents an aggressive, a novel, an intruding, a radical kind of approach—that it puts the unions in the position of urging radical institutional reforms. To some degree and in some respects one might defend that argument.

It could be said, using a sociologist's phrase, that this is an unintended consequence of purposive action. In fact, the union's actions have been motivated by a conservative point of view. The underlying rationale is one, usually, of trying to preserve a relationship rather than trying to establish a new one. The latter is sometimes present, but the former is much more prevalent.

This reminds us of the functions performed in this sort of controversy by management and union, and the conflict of values represented in their very functional roles. What I am suggesting is the conflict which is engendered by disputes over managerial prerogatives is not simply one of a right or a wrong in a particular situation, but is a conflict of values which is virtually inherent in the very functional roles which are played by the two parties.

We must remember that management in the performance of its function is necessarily an instigator of change, a responder to change. Management is operating in an economic environment within which

---

[4] *NLRB* v. *Phoenix Life Insurance Co.*, (C.A. 7th, 1948), 22 LRRM 2089 at 2095.

change is the rule. The pressures of economic competition force it to be responsive to changes that are occurring around it. Thus, for management, change is the law of life, whereas unions, on the other hand, very frequently are cast in the roles of forestallers of change. They are seeking to preserve positions involving security for their members.

In its role, management, almost of necessity, seeks to achieve certain well-focused objectives. It may be seeking to pass a competitor in total sales. It may be trying to bring a new product to the market before a rival does so. It may be trying to open up new territory, establish a new plant, or effect a merger with another company. These can be fairly large objectives, but they are almost always quite concrete in their execution.

On the other hand, unions are usually engaged in a drive for what may be termed satisfactory states of existence for their members— a morale-building relationship with supervisory foremen, the respect of others for good performance, a physical or a material situation which is comparable to that of their fellow workers or their neighbors. These are all satisfactory states of existence which they are seeking. They are not the pinpointed, well-focused objectives which management has before it.

And yet, both of these organizations must try to achieve these different objectives through the same medium; namely, the business, the firm, the corporation. Management is seeking to achieve its objectives, its pinpointed goals through the corporation. This involves change. It frequently involves a restructuring of the organization of the company in an effort to achieve what it is after. The union goals, on the other hand—the reaching and maintenance of satisfactory states of membership existence—very often require adherence to the status quo.

Even the vocabulary of the two organizations differs in ways that strikingly point up the values conflict. For example, management will regard efficiency as being a good word, a good objective, something which is conducive to the health of the organization. To the union, efficiency usually connotes some attempted means of chiseling the workers out of something which they have earned for themselves. Security becomes, in the union vocabulary, the desirable counterpart. But this very word, in reverse, usually chills management. It is not the kind of word to which management can respond.

Or take the word "ability." Again, to management this connotes a positive, affirmative quality, the kind of a criterion which should be used in the management of an organization. But to the union the term, ability, may represent the way in which management seeks to weasel some short-term employee into a position which is really due to the long-term employee. Seniority becomes, in their vocabulary, the preferable kind of attribute.

Or take the term "incentives." Again, for management this connotes something good, a driving force of which they are a necessary integral part; whereas, on the union side, incentives are usually tied up with rate busting, and undue pressures on the workers to achieve, or to produce. The responses are similar in connection with the term "scientific management," and the illustrations could be multiplied.

Hence, the vocabulary of these two groups reflects the inescapable conflict in values which is inherent in the very roles and the functions these two organizations perform.

Out of this background, and compounded by unremitting competitive pressure facing management (and size does not mean that companies can escape this competitive pressure; a General Electric or a General Motors cannot afford to rest on its oars simply because of its size) in the performance of its duties, one can understand management's view of unions as a force which interferes with management-espoused objectives. The union looms as an intruder which does not subscribe to management values and aspirations and which tends to frustrate the attainment of what management views as socially desirable ends.

In the light of this inescapable and continuous conflict between the parties, it is well to take brief note of the defense positions which each has prepared and the kind of rationale which each has mustered in defense of its attitudes.

Management and union positions

The issues have seldom been more sharply posed than in a discussion which took place some six years ago before the National Academy of Arbitrators between James Phelps of Bethlehem Steel and Arthur Goldberg, then of the Steelworkers' Union. Phelps rested his position almost exclusively on the doctrine of residual rights. The following quotation indicates the reliance which he placed on this argument.

The job of management is to manage. The operation of the enterprise at its maximum efficiency [one of the vocabulary words which is peculiar to management] is management's responsibility and obligation. If a management believes that, in order to discharge its obligations, it must retain in full measure the so-called prerogative of management, it has the right to refuse to agree in collective bargaining to restrict those rights. If the management should agree to limit its exclusive functions or even to delegate certain of its duties to a union, it can enter into an agreement that will clearly define how far it has agreed to go. To the extent the parties have not seen fit to limit management's sphere of action, management's rights are unimpaired by the contract.[5]

This is the doctrine of residual managerial rights which can only be given away by specific contract entered into in collective bargaining. Opposed to this is a philosophy which comes from a different set of values and which rests its argument primarily on the concept of consent of the worker, the basis for challenge of authority over history immemorial.

Arthur Goldberg said:

A backlog of rights and practices and precedents does develop as the collective bargaining relationship continues, based not on pre-union history but based on the period of the collective bargaining relationship.

. . . the practices which grow up during decades of a collective bargaining relationship cannot be swept aside . . . [they] inevitably represent the set of circumstances which formed the backdrop of the negotiation of the current agreement.

. . . To the extent that present conditions and methods for change are not revised, they are accepted. Therefore, each party has the right to assume that changes in wages, hours, or working conditions not provided for by contract can be made only by mutual agreement or by following practices for making changes which have existed during the collective bargaining relationship or [and this is a phrase which has always puzzled me] by virtue of management's exercise of an exclusive right (such as the introduction of new products, new machines, new material, new methods of manufacture, etc.). [The rationale for the inclusion of these specific items was never very apparent.] To suggest that management can make changes at will unless the contract specifically bars it is unfair and can lead to placing so many bars in the contract as to make successful negotiation increasingly difficult and operations less and less flexible, with detailed consideration of the facts and merits of each case replaced by precise rules and regulations.[6]

---

[5] James C. Phelps, "Management's Reserved Rights: An Industry View," *Management Rights and the Arbitration Process*, Proceedings of the Ninth Annual Meeting, National Academy of Arbitrators (Washington, D.C.: Bureau of National Affairs, 1956), p. 117. The phrase in brackets is, of course, mine, not Phelps's.

[6] Arthur J. Goldberg, "Management's Reserved Rights: A Labor View," *Management Rights and the Arbitration Process*, Proceedings of the Ninth Annual Meeting, National Academy of Arbitrators (Washington, D. C.: Bureau of National Affairs, 1956), pp. 125-126. Again, the bracketed comment is mine and not Goldberg's.

My view is that both of these represent indefensible extremes. On the one hand, Mr. Phelps would seem to be relegating the union to the role of a simple supplier, a supplier of services akin to the supplier of materials and having no more stake in the continuing operation of the company. But, of course, collective bargaining itself imposes continuing obligations, including obligations to consultation. The element of mutuality applies to the relationship, and it is not simply a matter of legal contract that is involved.

On the other hand, Mr. Goldberg seems to limit management initiative, with a few exceptions that have been given no rationale, to situations in which the union has given its concurrence, which is not, in my lexicon, initiative at all but a method of converting the individual firm into a kind of legislative forum. This, it seems to me, is an indefensible attack upon that necessary functional aspect of management, the right of initiation. Somewhere there must be a middle ground between these two positions.

One of the problems confronting us is how to establish that middle ground. What kind of resolution can we bring to a conflict which is necessary, inescapable, and continuing? The conflict is one which cannot be easily or permanently resolved. But perhaps something can be done to lessen the conflict, to smooth the relationship between the parties, to reduce the areas of tension and to build up areas in which the parties can effect an adequate working relationship.

Some mitigation of this inescapable conflict has come over the years. We have made progress, in part by improved understanding on both sides, management and union. Whether this can be ascribed to the development of the human relations philosophy which has had such wide circulation, one does not know, but it probably has had something to do with it. But certainly both sides have become much more enlightened in their dealings with each other. There is growing appreciation of the idea that both the simple demands of a democratic relationship—namely, consent of those over whom authority is wielded—and the realistic pragmatic necessity of getting something done require this accommodation. Thus it is only good management to seek to secure consent of the governed who could otherwise make it impossible for management to achieve the very objective which it has set for itself. This, it seems to me, represents a forward advance, and I do not think there has been an increasing degree of enlightenment and understanding of the human relationships involved in the process.

One of the really great instruments for resolution of the difficulties which have been pointed out here is the grievance procedure. Where the parties are willing to experiment with an increasing use of this device (not more frequent use, but a wider scope for its operations, a more flexible approach to it) and where there is a willingness to experiment with ways in which grievance procedure can be used, we may have one device which can, in the future, to a greater extent even than in the past, be made an instrument for resolving on an ad hoc basis the kinds of disputes we encounter as we move along.

It should be added that in this process the terminal role of arbitration will continue to be a necessary one, even though the role of the grievance procedure may spread beyond the simple adjudication of terms of an agreement. The grievance procedure can operate at its most effective level when there is recognition on the part of all the parties to the process that what is necessary to observe is both the logic of the rule and the logic of the situation. These two are not always the same.

There is a need for somehow effecting an adequate compromise between the common rule, which applies in all situations, and the extraordinary solution which may represent deviation, a deviation which does not destroy the rule but only keeps the rule flexible enough to preserve it. This sort of experimentation involves developing a philosophy of the grievance procedure along lines which I think still lie largely ahead of us.

There is room for a more extended and deeper delving into the functioning of the grievance procedure in the union-management relationship than has been done. We need to explore, perhaps in a clinical fashion, some of the differences between grievance procedures which are on their face quite similar; the differences that exist between, for instance, the UAW-Ford relationship when Harry Shulman was umpire and that at GM when Ralph Seward was umpire. An intensive examination of the differences in these two relationships, what each was able to effect, and the difficulties that each encountered might help us in seeing more clearly in the future the ways in which this extremely important device, this invention which is one of our truly great social innovations, can be made even more fruitful in the future.

I have suggested that there are elements of similarity with the past in the conflict over managerial prerogatives as the union seeks to exercise them, and that there are also elements of dissimilarity. I have suggested that one of the important dissimilarities is that of giving legal sanction to the invasion by one group of the authority of another. I should like, finally, to focus on another dimension of this. It concerns the interplaying roles of productivity and efficiency in our economic processes and brings in several avenues of discussion and controversies ranging over a very wide economic area. Galbraith's concept of the "affluent society" is pertinent here, as is the current dispute between the railroads and the Railroad Brotherhoods over featherbedding. It is the question of the relative importance of efficiency and productivity in our economic life.

Efficiency and productivity

In recent years there has been a tendency to take the position that we are sufficiently wealthy in this country to allow us to be unconcerned about waste as it accumulates. Daniel Bell has put this into the thesis that one of the fruits of increasing productivity is the ability to be wasteful.

There is a measure of truth in this proposition. It is true that we can be less concerned about the need of exacting every last measure of human effort from our people and from ourselves because of the increasing efficiency of our productive machine. But I am somewhat fearful that the doctrine of the "affluent society" has reached the point where it is sapping some of our needed interest in efficiency and productivity.

This, for two reasons. On the domestic scene we are reaching a position where there will be an increasing confluence of views from all shades of political opinion—over the next five, ten, fifteen years, it is difficult to say just when—that the affluence about which we speak is in the private sector, but that in the public sector we are really facing a pretty shabby and run-down society. Our housing situation, our transportation situation, our educational establishment, our recreational facility are but portions of our public plant which in many respects is operating at a very low level. It is not getting any better but is, in fact, deteriorating.

I would expect as the years move by we will find, not that we feel we are living in such an affluent society, but that we must recognize and give up an increasing measure of private wealth to enable us to put back in working shape and improve our public plant. This will mean that we are going to need the fruits of a productive and efficient economy, so we cannot afford to be wasteful in this respect.

Second, moving from the domestic to the international scene, there is similarity no doubt in my mind that as the years go by we will have imposed on us as a society inescapable responsibilities to help improve the economic lot of underdeveloped countries abroad. In the same way that we now take it for granted that citizens of New York, by a progressive income tax, are helping to improve the lot, let us say, of residents of Oklahoma, or of Montana, or of other less wealthy states, the same kind of a demand will be imposed on us for overseas assistance, and we will in time learn to accept this. But it is also going to impose strains on our productive efficiency and we will find that we do not have quite the degree of affluence we once thought if we are to turn out this mountain of wealth which is going to satisfy our private wants, our public needs, and the international demands upon us. We will find that we have to produce and produce effectively to meet all these requirements. This may also mean that, to the extent our national objectives of increasing the productivity of other countries abroad is successful, we are rearing up more effective competitors for our own economy. What we are trying to do seems almost quixotic from one point of view—attempting to create a more rigorous competition for ourselves. Yet, over the long haul, this is surely the only way to accomplish our aims.

If change is the law of life in industry, and if one of the functions of unions is to try to insure that change does not do damage to the morale and material security positions of its members, then it becomes increasingly incumbent upon all of us to find more effective means of resolving the inescapable conflict. The means developed to eliminate wasteful practices from the industrial scene must be such that they do not damage those who are a necessary and integral part of that scene.

I do not think we can go on indefinitely assuming that the union position must be always accepted when it claims that practices which have been developed in the past should be left untouched in the present. There may well be instances where the extraction of a greater measure of productive efficiency will require an increasing acceleration of innovation, new processes, and new methods in the industrial scene. But this only underscores the necessity of our turning a much more critical eye to the question of how we can make such changes come about without exacting a price from those on whom the burden will rest. In this process we must try to establish ways, procedures, and new devices by which we can meet the legitimate demands, the necessary functional position, of the union when it seeks to conserve the security and the position of its membership.

Questions

1. What is the underlying basis for the conflict between the company and the union over the issue of management prerogatives? To what extent is it affected by the roles that each side must exercise?

2. What determines whether or not a particular decision is a management prerogative?

3. What effect, if any, may our frontier environment have had upon employer reaction in the last century to demands of unions for increased security and for the opportunity to exercise a greater role in decisions affecting employees?

4. What was the significance of the Phoenix Mutual Life Insurance Co. case?

5. In what ways is the conflict over management prerogatives a conflict of values and semantics?

6. To what extent do you agree or disagree with the statement by Mr. Goldberg that is quoted in this article?

7. Do you share the author's concern over the effect that the failure of our country to utilize our country's productive capacity may have upon society in the future?

39. SENIORITY IN LABOR CONTRACTS *

Walter L. Daykin

Seniority rights of industrial employees is an important problem in labor-management relations. While years of service has given workers certain privileges in the past, seniority in the main stems from collective bargaining agreements or contracts.

Management and worker views

It is in the nature of our industrial society that in the application of seniority fundamental conflicts will arise. The employer desires the freedom to direct, place and retain a labor force in terms of his needs and judgment. Flexibility is essential to maximize production and minimize cost. This flexibility is due largely to the rises and declines in markets, to the consumer's demands for goods, and to the numerous technological changes that are being made in industry. Management often views seniority as being in direct conflict with its competency to manage, or with the recognition of merit.

On the other hand, workers are interested in job security, and seniority is a limited form of job protection. If it is applied in the area of layoffs and recalls, it provides senior employees with some degree of job safety. When employment is high and stable, seniority provides for job preference if the contract applies it to promotions and transfers. Unions contend that there is no basic conflict between efficiency and seniority because seniority develops morale which results in increased productivity. Furthermore, seniority is a good organizing tool or device used by the union during unionization campaigns.

Role of arbitrators

This article shows how arbitrators interpret or view the many aspects of seniority and solve the problems arising out of its functioning in industry. Some of these are the scope of seniority, i.e., company, plant, department, or craft seniority; how to attain and how

* From *Personnel Administration*, Vol. 23, No. 3 (May-June, 1960), pp. 36-44. Reprinted with permission.

to lose seniority; superseniority for union stewards; and the application of seniority. While the arbitrators are concerned with all the phases of seniority their main interest, by necessity, is with the application aspect, and the weight to be given to seniority in cases where a number of factors are involved. The major application is in the area of layoffs, recalls, promotions, and other job changes. In applying seniority to choice of shifts, to choice of vacations, layoffs and recalls, and to demotions and promotions the arbitrator is required to show the relationship between seniority and other important factors, such as past practice, the effect upon efficient plant operation, and the ability of the senior and junior employees to function adequately in the jobs in question.

Influence of the contract

In arbitration those responsible for making decisions are required to recognize the contract, especially its language or the way the various seniority clauses are worded, the past practices relating to seniority, and the federal and state laws regulating this behavior pattern. For example, the National Labor Relations Board has considered it a violation of the law for an employer to delegate to the union authority to settle controversies pertaining to seniority or to delegate to the union complete control over seniority because such power tends to illegally develop union membership (1).[1] Such reasoning has been sanctioned by a circuit court (2).

Departures from rules

Some contracts allow the departure from strict seniority rules to maintain or increase the efficiency of the plant (3). In some instances the contract may state that seniority is not controlling, or that it may not be applied in cases of temporary layoffs or promotions. However, if the layoffs or promotions assume a permanent nature, then seniority is to be applied. On occasions seniority may be disregarded in work stoppages resulting from emergencies even though the contract contains a broad clause regulating the application of seniority in all layoffs. For example, a contract containing a clause stating that straight seniority will control layoffs when practical does not prevent the employer from retaining junior employees whose presence in the

---

[1] Numbers in parentheses refer to articles listed in the bibliography at the end of the article.

plant is necessary to prevent numerous additional layoffs, especially if the work of the junior employees requires a training period of several weeks. It is obvious that it would be impractical to penalize the employer and other employees by the recognition of seniority.

Also, even though the contract states that seniority is to apply to both permanent and temporary layoffs, it has been ruled that it will not be applied or application can be delayed during brief emergency periods if such an application would be unreasonably burdensome or cause the company to lose money. However, it has also been decided that seniority does apply to temporary layoffs if there is no interference with efficient plant operations, and that even a one day separation from work is a layoff and not just temporary curtailment of operations.

Furthermore, where a contractual provision states that seniority does not apply to layoffs caused by emergencies, breakdowns, or stock shortages because of the difficulty involved in the application, the employer is not privileged to substitute work sharing for seniority during a period of stock shortages (4). Seniority often does not become controlling in promotions to supervisory positions from the bargaining unit. This selection is considered to be a necessary prerogative of management which has the responsibility for the behavior of supervisors, as well as the operation of the business (5).

Length of service

It has been established that legal collective bargaining contracts are to be respected and enforced. Consequently, if the employer agrees to a seniority clause he must keep a seniority list so that the clause can be maintained or effectuated (6). This respect for the contract as a device for industrial peace necessitates careful and intelligent construction.

Even if this is accomplished, many arbitrators are called upon to decide such issues as the meaning of length of service, loss of seniority, and the effect of transfers upon seniority rights. If the contract states that seniority is based upon service with the company, service is generally interpreted to mean the time from the date of employment and not the time worked minus layoff time (7). Seniority can be broken by a long layoff, or by certain behavior engaged in by the employees involved. For example, it has been ruled that seniority is broken after a thirty months' layoff (8). Employees can lose seniority for the violation of leaves of absences, such as overstaying the leave (9). However, a leave of absence of three months does not prevent the retention and the accumulation of seniority even if the employee obtains some work during the leave, if the leave is caused by physical handicaps and neither the contract nor past practices restrict outside work during a leave (10).

Seniority can also be broken by the violation of safety rules (11), and absence from work for three consecutive days without a reasonable excuse as designated in the contract. However, a person put in jail for thirty days has a reasonable excuse for absence and his seniority is not broken (12).

Failure to report for work within the specified time, as outlined in the contract after a layoff without a satisfactory explanation, is a sufficient and justifiable reason to break the seniority rights of an employee (13). It has also been ruled that a laid off employee who obtains an interim job without notifying his employer loses his prior seniority rights because he cannot accumulate seniority with two employers (14). Mergers of businesses which necessitate transfers do not cause employees to lose seniority (15), and in case of the sale of the company recalled employees retain their seniority (16). Also, employees who are transferred back into the bargaining unit after being assigned to jobs outside of the unit must be given credit for plant seniority from the original date of hiring (17).

Superseniority

Superseniority or preferential seniority for union officials or stewards must be respected and recognized if it is in the contract (18). Such superseniority grants them the right, if they are qualified, to bump others from their jobs during layoff periods (19). During a reduction of force superseniority does not give union stewards the right to retain their own jobs because preferred seniority is on an area rather than a job basis (20). Furthermore, while top seniority for union officials may not be limited by ability qualifications in seniority clauses, such a contractual right does not permit officials to choose jobs they are unable to perform, but it is controlling if they can do the job (21).

Shifts and overtime

In applying seniority rights to choice of shifts and overtime it is accepted that seniority is controlling if agreed in the contract. However, the employer is not required to assign overtime on the basis of seniority in the absence of contract provisions and an established history in the area of collective bargaining. Seniority rights come into existence because of the collective bargaining contract or stem from the contract. The employer possesses inherent and specific reserved rights to schedule work, and these rights remain intact unless limited by the collective bargaining agreement (22).

Layoffs and promotions

In dealing with seniority the most intense problems develop when it is applied to layoffs and promotions. An analysis of the arbitration decisions reveals that the majority of the contracts give more control or weight to seniority in determining layoffs and demotions than to promotions or advancements. Probably this is due to the recognition that layoffs endanger the employee's security, and to the feeling that promotion should be left more for management to decide.

The practice of bumping employees in case of layoffs in terms of seniority has created some problems. The decisions reveal that there is a difference of opinion among arbitrators relative to the bumping rights of senior employees. In the solution of these difficulties it has been decided that in the absence of contract limitations preventing it senior employees operating under a plant-wide seniority system are privileged to bump junior employees from their jobs (23). If an employer refuses to allow a qualified senior worker to bump a junior employee in terms of the contract provisions the burden is on the employer to prove that the senior worker is unqualified for the job in question (24). However, the past industrial practice of excluding women from production work prevents females from bumping men in such areas, even though the seniority provision incorporated in the contract does not distinguish between the sexes (25).

Also, if the right to bump in case of force reduction is regulated by such a qualification as ability to do the work, this has been interpreted by some arbitrators to mean that the bumper must be qualified to do the job immediately and no breaking-in period is to be allowed (26). Others have ruled that ability in bumping simply means the basic ability to do the job, and that the employee is entitled to a breaking-in period as distinguished from a training period on the job. The mere lack of familiarity with the duties of the job of the junior employee can not be interpreted as lack of ability (27).

Furthermore, it has been held that seniority rights permit the bumping of only the lowest ranking employees in an occupational group, or that seniority should be applied downward during layoffs (28). Other arbitrators reason that if the contract gives senior employees the right to qualify for other jobs in case of layoffs this does not refer only to jobs carrying a lower rate than their own (29). If the contract does not limit bumping rights of senior employees but allows for the exercising of plant seniority in any job for which they can qualify, upward bumping is permissible (30). Unless definitely limited by contractual relations where seniority is controlling in layoffs, senior employees must be given the job that they are qualified to fill. They can bump into lower rated jobs or higher rated jobs if capable of doing the work without a breaking-in period (31).

Upward bumping is not permissible if the contract does not specifically give this right to senior employees and if there has been no historical practice established (32). Some arbitrators have held that if the contract states that in case of layoffs employees can be transferred to jobs of comparable rates this does not give senior employees the right to bump into higher rated jobs (33). Even if the contract clause provides that seniority governs in layoffs qualified senior employees are privileged to bump junior employees in equal or lower rated jobs but they cannot bump into higher classifications (34). Also, where the contract specifically states that qualified senior employees can in case of job elimination or replacement displace junior employees in other classifications, they are not permitted to bump into higher classifications. It is reasoned that such upward movements amount to promotions, and that promotions are controlled by separate clauses and occur only when vacancies exist (35).

What is ability?

The trend is, when bargaining over the application of seniority to layoffs and promotions, to include a clause in the contract stating that length of service will be controlling if ability is equal or relatively equal. Thus, management attempts to formulate seniority rules so that plant efficiency can be maintained. This has created a number of significant problems. Some of these are the meaning of ability, who has the prerogative to determine ability, and the factors that can be used in the determination of ability. Ability is generally defined as meeting the demands of the position or ability for the job, or ability to learn the job in the normal training period and not to mean greater ability or efficiency (36). The minimum qualifications to do the job or the ability to perform the work in the shortest period of time are considered sufficient (37).

The employer is not privileged to by-pass qualified senior employees in case of layoffs and recalls in favor of more speedy and efficient junior workers because to permit such behavior would violate the basic and fundamental principles of seniority. The employer is required to determine ability on the basis of the particular job involved, or he must interpret ability to relate to the particular job sought without regard for general or potential ability to be promoted to more responsible positions, or the capabilities of progressing beyond the job, or without taking into consideration the possibility of job changes. He must compare employees on an individual and not on a group basis (38). Ability has been defined to mean capabilities to actually do the work or job and not just the ability to learn the job. In terms of this reasoning management has been permitted to select younger workers who have had experience and training for promotions over senior employees who only have the ability to learn to do the work (39).

It is generally conceded that management has the right to determine ability unless this prerogative has been limited in the contract. This means that the employer is initially the sole judge of ability to perform available jobs, and that his judgment cannot be set aside, unless he exercises this right arbitrarily, or discriminatorily (40). In determining the relative ability for promotion to supervisory duties, the employer may interpret this ability more liberally and broadly than in cases concerning promotion from one production job to another (41). While the employer can determine fitness and ability for layoffs and promotions to a particular job he is required to support his decision (42).

The burden of proving greater relative ability is placed upon the employer; so if he retains or promotes a junior employee, where the contract provides for the observance of seniority where abilities are equal, he must prove by clear, specific, understandable, and convincing evidence that the senior employee's ability to perform the job in question is not relatively equal to the ability possessed by the junior employee. In fact, the employer must prove by preponderance of evidence that the senior employee lacks ability. "Opinion evidence" is not acceptable. If there is a reasonable doubt concerning the ability of the senior employee, the employer is often required to grant him a trial period in order to demonstrate his efficiency (43).

Also, even if management possesses the sole right to determine ability of employees to do the jobs, the union is permitted to challenge the decision through the grievance procedure in case it accuses management of acting in an arbitrary manner, or acting in bad faith; but if the union challenges management's determination of ability, the burden is on the labor organization to prove that the employer acted arbitrarily or made an error in judgment (44). Consequently, management is permitted to retain younger employees in cases of layoff and select them for promotion if the choice is based upon valid standards and job criteria, and if his judgment is made in good faith. The employer can even fill vacancies by hiring outside qualified employees if his present employees must be given special training before being able to function in the positions (45).

Determining ability

Often arbitrators are required to decide upon the factors or devices that can be used by the employer to determine ability. In measuring ability much emphasis is placed upon the quantity and the quality of the work or the output of the employees involved because these factors show skill, effort, and knowledge (46). It is generally conceded that the employer can require employees to take reasonable written tests or formal examinations, such as aptitude tests, in connection with other standards to determine relative ability even if such measuring standards have never been used in the industry (47). However, the tests used must be fair and proper, must be related to the job requirements or based upon the job duties, must be those commonly used in vocational activities, and must be administered without any discrimination under proper conditions; that is, those taking the tests must be given plenty of time to answer and be permitted to ask questions. In other words, a recognized formal examination can be used as a verifying device but not as a hurdle. It is also emphasized that the results of such tests must not be given undue weight in determining ability (48). Ability cannot be determined by a casual interview, and merit rating plans which include such factors as cooperation, personal habits, and attendance are often not considered valid tests because ability to perform work is not the same as the willingness to respect rules (49).

In the determination of ability for layoffs and promotions employers have been permitted to use other factors than technical qualifications. For example, poor attendance records, disciplinary records, age and physical impairments, record of errors, and the attitude of the employees toward their jobs and the employer are considered significant or can be given some weight in the proving of equal or unequal ability (50). On the other hand, the employer has been denied the right to determine ability or competency on the basis that the employee had never discussed the problems connected with the job with the foreman, intermittent absences, or lack of qualifications to perform the human relation aspect of the position. It was reasoned that the determination of ability on the basis of such limited evidence was arbitrary and capricious (51).

Nor can an employer by-pass a senior employee for promotion on the grounds that he lacks interest. The lack of interest is not a measure of ability, particularly if it is only temporary and inconsistent with the usual attitude of the worker (52). Nor is the employer permitted to refuse a promotion to a senior employee because of a surly attitude unless this interferes with production. In fact, management cannot deny promotions or recalls to senior employees as a disciplinary measure if the contract bases these job changes upon seniority and ability. Therefore, the employer cannot determine eligibility for recall on the basis of past absences because this is a matter of discipline and should be handled when the absences occur (53).

Conclusion and summary

An analysis of the decisions rendered by the arbitrators reveals that many of the problems in industrial relations are created by the emergence of seniority rights. While seniority gives to employees limited security, it makes inroads into management's right to allocate workers in the plant. Most of the arbitrators have accepted the residual claimant doctrine and emphasize that seniority rights stem from the contract. It is obvious that arbitrators are called upon to settle such matters as the type of seniority, how to attain and how to lose seniority, and superseniority for union stewards. However, the most important problem is the determination of the application of seniority in such areas as layoffs and promotions. In order to safeguard management the ability clause is generally incorporated in contracts if seniority is applied to such labor changes. This necessitates the definition of ability, and the factors to be used in its determination.

In general, management can determine ability within a defined framework. The decisions demonstrate that arbitrators attempt to safeguard the rights of employees, and to protect the employer and other workers from unnecessary hardships if seniority is rigidly applied. It is also evident that while there are some differences of opinion among arbitrators relative to the correct way to settle the conflicts created by the application of seniority, there is a tendency to develop standards which are uniformly applied, or to establish precedents which will be controlling in future decisions.

References

1. Minneapolis Star and Tribune Co. 109 NLRB 727 (1954); North East Texas Motor Lines, Inc. 109 NLRB 1147 (1954); Kenosha Auto Transport Corp. 113 NLRB 643 (1955); Interstate Motor Freight System. 116 NLRB 755 (1956).

2. NLRB v Teamsters Union (Pacific Intermountain Express Co.). 225 F2d 343 CCA 8 (1955).

3. General Cable Corp. 3 LA 506 (1946).

4. A. O. Sutton Co. 29 LA 575 (1957); John Deere Des Moines Works. 24 LA 88 (1955); Pantasote Co. 2 LA 477 (1946); United Engineering and Foundry Co. 31 LA 93 (1958); Quaker Oats Co. 13 LA 529 (1949); Dow Chemical Co. 12 LA 763 (1949).

5. Duquesne Light Co. et. al. 11 LA 1023 (1948).

6. Libby, McNeill and Libby. 11 LA 872 (1948).

7. Standard Oil Co. 12 LA 693 (1949).

8. Link-Belt Co. 1 LA 530 (1946).

9. Clendenning's Inc. 7 LA 580 (1947); Brown and Sharpe Mfg. Co. 11 LA 228 (1948).

10. Goodyear Tire and Rubber Co. 5 LA 234 (1945).

11. John Deere Tractor Co. 5 LA 534 (1946).

12. Quaker Oats Co. 15 LA 42 (1950).

13. Standard Steel Spring Co. 20 LA 494 (1953).

14. Fairchild Engine and Airplane Corp. 3 LA 873 (1946).

15. City Packing Corp. 11 LA 358 (1948).

16. Shapiro Bros. and Gordon Co., Inc. 11 LA 481 (1948).

17. Cit-Con Oil Corp. 30 LA 267 (1958).

18. Bethlehem Steel Co. 12 LA 214 (1949); Denver Equipment Co. 14 LA 791 (1950); Davis Co., Inc. 2 LA 279 (1946); Brad Foote Gear Works, Inc. 2 LA 310 (1946); Sealed Power Corp. 7 LA 485 (1947).

19. Hendey Machine Co. 13 LA 185 (1949).

20. Deere and Co. 18 LA 780 (1952).

21. Wilmington Welding and Boiler Works. 3 LA 23 (1946); Brewster Aeronautical Corp. 3 LA 200 (1946); Ryan Aeronautical Co. 3 LA 725 (1946).

22. Crowe-Gulde Cement Co. 30 LA 177 (1958); Gorton-Pew Fisheries Co., Inc. 11 LA 15 (1948); Libbey-Owens-Ford Co. 31 LA 251 (1958); McQuay-Norris Mfg. Co. 1 LA 305 (1946).

23. Darin and Armstrong. 13 LA 843 (1950).

24. Bell Aircraft Corp. 25 LA 618 (1955).

25. Blaw-Knox Co. 31 LA 488 (1958).

26. American Lava Corp. 24 LA 517 (1955). Victor G. Bloede Co. Inc. 23 LA 779 (1955).

27. Shore Metal Products Co. 24 LA 437 (1955).

28. Ford Motor Co. 1 LA 362 (1945).

29. Branch River Wool Combing Co. 11 LA 346 (1948).

30. McNamara Boiler and Tank Co. 30 LA 886 (1958); Aetna Paper Co. 29 LA 439 (1957); International Harvester. 21 LA 214 (1953).

31. Bethlehem Steel Co. 16 LA 478 (1951); Borg-Warner Corp. 29 LA 629 (1957); Chrysler Corp. 12 LA 739 (1949).

32. Bethlehem Steel Co. 30 LA 815 (1958).

33. Continental Can Co. of Canada, Ltd. 31 LA 458 (1958).

34. Warren Petroleum Corp. 26 LA 532 (1956).

35. U. S. Rubber Co. 25 LA 417 (1955); International Harvester Co. 15 LA 891 (1950).

36. Rudigar-Lang Co. 11 LA 567 (1948); North American Cement Co. 11 LA 1109 (1948); Shell Oil Co., Inc. 4 LA 13 (1946).

37. Central Franklin Process Co. 19 LA 32 (1952); Pittsburgh Limestone Corp. 6 LA 648 (1947).

38. Cameron Iron Works, Inc. 23 LA 51 (1954); Kuhlman Electric Co. 26 LA 885 (1956); Universal Atlas Cement Co. 17 LA 755 (1951); Borden Co. 28 LA 104 (1957); Electric Boat Co. 11 LA 719 (1948); Bethlehem Steel Co. 24 LA 379 (1955).

39. Ohio Seamless Tube Co. 6 LA 309 (1947); Eastern Machine Screw Corp. 6 LA 977 (1946).

40. Stauffer Chemical Co. 23 LA 322 (1954); Sandia Corp. 31 LA 338 (1958); Ingram-Richardson Mfg. Co. of Indiana, Inc. 3 LA 482 (1946); U. S. Slicing Machine Co. 22 LA 53 (1954); Connecticut Power Co. 13 LA 459 (1949).

41. Butler Bros. 9 LA 458 (1948).

42. Bethlehem Steel Co. 5 LA 578 (1946).

43. Columbia Steel Co. 13 LA 666 (1949); Darin and Armstrong. 13 LA 843 (1950); Mole-Richardson Co. 12 LA 427 (1949); Linde Air Products Co. 25 LA 369 (1955); Ford Motor Co. 2 LA 374 (1945); Pacific Gas and Electric Co. 23 LA 556 (1954); Corn Products Refining Co. 25 LA 130 (1955); Rome Grader Corp. 22 LA 167 (1953).

44. American Air Filter Co., Inc. 6 LA 786 (1947); Merrill Stevens Dry Dock and Repair Co. 6 LA 836 (1947); International Paper Co. 19 LA

402 (1952); Durham Hosiery Mills. 12 LA 311 (1949); Hercules Powder Co. 10 LA 624 (1948).

45. Imperial Paper and Color Corp. 16 LA 346 (1951); Franklin Tanning Co. 12 LA 410 (1949).

46. Universal Mfg., Co. 13 LA 238 (1949); Worth Steel Co. 12 LA 931 (1949).

47. Standard Oil Co. (Indiana). 11 LA 810 (1948); Atlas Powder Co. 30 LA 674 (1958); Bethlehem Steel Co. 29 LA 710 (1957).

48. Wallingford Steel Co. 29 LA 597 (1957); Linde Co. 31 LA 757 (1958); Youngstown Sheet and Tube Co. 18 LA 413 (1952); M. A. Hanna Co. 25 LA 480 (1955); Standard Oil Co. (Indiana). 11 LA 810 (1948).

49. South California Edison Co. 15 LA 162 (1950); Western Automatic Machine Screw Co. 9 LA 606 (1948).

50. John Deere Tractor Co. 16 LA 790 (1951); Dewey and Almy Chemical Co. 25 LA 316 (1955); Norwich Pharmacal Co. 30 LA 740 (1958); Unit Rig and Equipment Co. 31 LA 42 (1958).

51. Alabama Power Co. 18 LA 25 (1952); Standard Oil Co. 16 LA 586 (1951).

52. Ford Motor Co. 7 LA 324 (1947).

53. Pan American Refining Co. 9 LA 47 (1947); Bethlehem Steel Co. 19 LA 186 (1952); Curtis-Wright Corp. 8 LA 706 (1947); Cleveland-Cliffs Iron Co. 24 LA 599 (1955).

Questions

1. Do you feel that the NLRB was correct in ruling that an employer could not delegate to the union the right to settle controversies pertaining to seniority?

2. In an arbitration case involving seniority, what factors other than the wording of the contract may serve to influence the arbitrator's ruling?

3. What is ability? How does it relate to the seniority provisions of a labor contract?

4. According to the article, can a lack of interest or a poor attitude be considered as one of the measures of a person's ability? What is your opinion on this subject?

5. What are some of the considerations that can complicate the administration of seniority provisions in a labor contract?

6. How do seniority provisions affect the issue of management control which is discussed in Article No. 38 by Chamberlain?

40. STRATEGY AND TACTICS AT THE BARGAINING TABLE *

Thomas G. Downing

Though the overwhelming number of union contracts are settled without resort to a strike, conflict is an almost inescapable condition of the bargaining process. Every organization is committed to the pursuit of certain objectives—a statement that applies to unions no less than to the companies with which they bargain.

Sooner or later, these objectives are likely to clash. At first, the difference may not be serious enough to affect the traditional relationship between the parties; but as pressures build up, year after year, finally one side or the other decides to bring matters to a head. Instead of a routine negotiation, the company representatives are then faced with a situation in which, in order to preserve the company's favorable bargaining position, it may be necessary to go to the brink of war.

When, for whatever reason, negotiations deviate from the normal and the routine, skillful maneuvering is required of the company representatives. In fact, a high degree of bargaining skill is required of the management negotiator if the company is not to come off second best in the final settlement. Unfortunately, there are no standard texts the inexperienced negotiator can turn to for guidance when the going gets rough. Nevertheless, there are certain pitfalls he can learn to watch out for and shape his strategy accordingly. This article will endeavor to pinpoint some of the more common union tactics and suggest ways of countering them.

Logically, we might begin by considering the somewhat special case of bargaining on an initial contract. This, of course, differs somewhat from usual contract negotiations in that the parties are starting from scratch. The importance of the first contract cannot be underestimated—it is the chance to start off clean, without being weighed down by prior encumbrances. If the company is a multi-plant organization, the union will often copy many of the favorable

* From *Personnel*, Vol. 37, No. 1 (January-February, 1960), pp. 58-63. Reprinted with permission.

clauses contained in other plant contracts. Alternatively, it may put forward standard clauses taken from the contracts of competing companies. If the international union has an active and aggressive research department, this may help the local to draw up the whole contract, which will then be submitted as the union proposal.

The first session

The first bargaining meeting is a crucial one—it marks the beginning of the collective bargaining relationship and may well determine the whole trend of subsequent negotiations. Above all, it is a good opportunity to clear the air, especially if feelings have run high before the election. When, as so often happens, a fair amount of antagonism has been generated during the organization period, the conflict is likely to spill over into the initial bargaining sessions. Hence the company will be wise to indicate that, despite earlier differences, it fully accepts the fact that the union has successfully established that it represents a majority of the employees in the bargaining unit. The management negotiator should make it clear that the company genuinely wants to negotiate in good faith with the employees' duly authorized representatives. As a general rule, the employer is well advised to make every effort to create a favorable atmosphere during these first meetings. He is going to have to live with these people from now on.

Now let us turn to the more common situation where the contract is up for renewal and management has reason to believe that it is going to be confronted by various unacceptable demands. At the first meeting, the usual approach is for the company representatives to ask the union committee to read through and clarify the union proposals to make certain that there is no misunderstanding as to what the union is asking for. Some unions will submit their proposals before the first meeting, thus giving the company a chance to review and analyze the demands and compute the wage and fringe costs. Either way, in most cases, the union prefers to see some visible reaction to its demands when the parties meet.

In such circumstances, the company negotiator may decide to use the first meeting solely for the purpose of clarifying the union's proposals. Alternatively, he can start the ball rolling by asking the union to explain the reason for each specific proposal. In any event, the company representatives should make it clear early in the game that it is up to the union negotiating committee to justify its position. Merely stating that it wants, say, an improved layoff procedure, is not enough. The tactic here is not merely to put the union on the defensive, but to test the logic and sincerity of its position. Suppose, for example, that the union wants to revise the layoff procedure on a plantwide instead of a departmental seniority basis, as before. First, it can be asked, can they cite any actual instances where some injustice has occurred under the present system, or is their position a purely hypothetical one? Second, if they can point to some hardship case, is this merely an isolated example which does not warrant revising the entire layoff procedure? Third, has anybody really been injured, financially or otherwise?

It is surprising how often a union's bargaining committee will have failed to think a proposal through. Management can be sure that, if the union has taken pains to justify the soundness of its position, it will come up with most of the right answers to any questions that may be asked. Some proposals, however, originate in the fact that the union has had a membership meeting and opened the floor to any dues-paying member who wanted to put forth a demand. In such circumstances, unless the proposals are subsequently screened by the union committee, the company may be faced with "shotgun demands." It is always a problem, therefore, to distinguish what is real from what is unreal in what the union is asking for.

The general practice is to start by separating the noncost items from the cost items and to defer the latter until agreement has been reached on all or most of the former. This is good common sense—when it comes to the question of wages and fringe benefits, you do not want to have seniority problems hanging fire. Most conflict situations revolve around money in one form or another, so it is better to wash out, if possible, all the noncost items before bargaining on money begins in earnest. Of course, there are some unions that "die hard" on every single proposal and persist in wringing the sponge dry. They will never give up on any proposal until they have been convinced that it is not in the cards. The only way to counter this attitude is for the company representatives to be equally tenacious.

The noncost items

In bargaining on noncost items, ultimately the stage is reached where everything has dropped out but a few proposals on which disagreement still remains. Here, there are no hard-and-fast rules—each situation is different, and the employer must decide how to act in the light of his particular relations policy. One possibility is to trade—to concede one proposal against the union's withdrawal of another.

Though it is a truism to say that labor peace cannot be bought, it is also worth bearing in mind that negotiations are not unlike doing business in the market place—management need not be ashamed of assuming a position or attitude of flexibility. Nevertheless, while compromise or retreat is permissible, the company should avoid giving any impression of weakness. It is good strategy to put the union in the position of having to reciprocate after management has moved to its bargaining position. One must always be conscious of whose turn it is to act. It may not be fatal for management to act out of turn, but it may result in some undesirable complications.

The heart of the matter

Now we reach the nub of the problem—money. What to do when, say, the union asks for 40 cents an hour plus additional fringe benefits? To ask, as well you might, "What kind of a bargaining proposal is that?" is futile—the union expects a counterproposal from you. Suppose the company figures the settlement is worth 10 cents. Any counterproposal with a chance of ending up at 10 cents would have to start with a cut of 20 cents in present rates—but just try it! This is exactly what the union committee wants you to propose. Now they can really steam up the membership. Other companies are giving raises and this skinflint management wants to cut your wages, the rank and file will be told. So you don't want to make an offer until the union comes in with a realistic figure. You want them to drop down to a point where you can work up to your proposed figure of 10 cents. Meanwhile, the union accuses you of being unreasonable because you haven't made an offer. You are now on the horns of a dilemma, and this is where you learn that patience is indubitably a virtue.

In the early stages of negotiations, the union will probe for some indication as to whether management is likely to accept or reject the proposal under discussion. The tip-off may come in the form of summary dismissal of the demand or strenuous arguments against it. Alternatively, the management representatives may show no particular repugnance to the proposal, or simply table it. All these are signals to the union indicating where management stands without its having made any formal commitment on the issue.

As a rule, both parties will be prepared to retreat from their original stands and can be expected to move toward their final positions as the negotiations proceed. This is particularly true in the case of wage demands. The union, for example, may ask for a 14 cents an hour wage increase, while actually it would be willing to settle for 9 cents. Here, the union has a bargaining cushion of 5 cents— the difference between 14 cents and 9 cents. Management, on the other hand, while willing to agree if necessary, to 6 cents, will advise the union that no wage increase can be expected this time around; its bargaining cushion, therefore, is 6 cents, that is, the difference between zero and 6 cents. Hence, the difference between the union's real or minimum figure of 9 cents and management's real or maximum figure of 6 cents is likely to be the area of ultimate bargaining.

Industry or community wage surveys may reveal that other settlements have been in the neighborhood of 6 to 9 cents. Let us suppose then, that the union has reduced its demand to 9 cents and the company has offered 6 cents. Both parties have now reached their real positions. Where to go from here? Faced with the threat of a strike, most managements will reappraise their original position. They must ask themselves: "Should we take a strike for 3 cents?" Of course, it must be remembered that the union also must decide: "Is it worth striking for 3 cents?" The ensuing deadlock is likely to result in a compromise somewhere between 6 and 9 cents. Or the company may offer a counterproposal—another holiday, more generous vacations, or an additional severance allowance—in order to achieve a settlement. Of course, this situation is not confined to bargaining on wage items. The skill of the company negotiator may be equally put to the test on such issues as seniority, union security, pensions, work assignments, and a host of other intractable items.

If negotiations appear to have broken down, or if the company is anxious to impress the union with the finality of its position, an outside third party, either from the Federal Mediation and Conciliation Service or the State Mediation Service, can be called in. In considering such a course, the company should remember the old adage, "Always save something for the mediator." Since it is the mediator's job to prevent a strike, his assistance in ascertaining the ultimate position of both parties can be invaluable.

A device often used by unions, especially after feelings have been strained from a series of heated exchanges, is to put on an act designed to give the impression that further negotiation is fruitless. This may take the form of the union bargaining committee's dramatically exploding in an emotional outburst and walking out of the meeting. Or, if management has taken the initiative by suggesting that the meeting be broken up, with the aim of indicating the strength of its position and the futility of the union's, the union representatives may try to give the impression that the situation is more serious than management had supposed. The veiled threat of a strike may be forthcoming from the more vociferous and militant members of the union bargaining committee. To further impress management that the negotiations are headed for a breakdown, the union may even start making overt preparations for a strike. There may be visits to the local banks asking for extended credit for union members on mortgage payments in the event of a strike.

The false alarm

Within a matter of hours, word of this filters back, arousing precisely the excitement and alarm in management ranks that was intended. The company may, at this stage, reconsider its position and come back with some concession. If it does, it must at the same time make it clear that its retreat is conditional upon the union's retreating from its position also. In response to this tactic the union may move within its bargaining cushion, asserting, of course, that this really is its final stand, which in all probability it is not.

At this precarious stage, the company has to take good care that a strike does not take place as the result of a false break-off point. There should be avenues of retreat to the final bargaining position, otherwise the employer may find himself either having to take an unwanted strike or in an embarrassing position in the eyes of the union and the employees.

Eventually, the parties reach their real positions—often during the final days of negotiations, when the contract is about to expire. At this stage, all the excess proposals and counterproposals should be off the table and the real positions exposed. Any threat of a strike at this time constitutes, therefore, a serious situation, and must be regarded as such by management.

Management's choices

Here the company has three choices: (1) concede, (2) compromise, or (3) hold firm. If it decides to hold firm, it can back up its position by impressing upon the union what the strike would mean in lost wages for various periods of time and how long it will take the workers to make up the loss. Management can also appeal directly to the membership in order to swing the tide in favor of its final offer. Such an appeal usually takes the form of letters to the employees' homes, coupled with meetings by supervisors with their people, with the aim of pointing out the reasonableness of what the company is offering.

Unions are well aware of the fact that, in most companies, some limits are placed on the authority of management's representatives at the bargaining table. Naturally, they are interested in knowing just how far the company negotiators are empowered to go, and make all kinds of attempts to find out. Quite often the union will start a war of nerves aimed at breaking down the company's position and obtaining greater concessions than management had intended.

In a situation of this sort, a strike vote may be taken by the committee as a tactical weapon. The bargaining committee will request the membership to arm them with a strike vote in the event they are unable to work out a satisfactory settlement.

A number of managements have succumbed to this form of pressure. Actually, the strike vote has not been taken on the company's last offer—the union is merely using the vote to prove its economic strength. This, like many other union weapons, is in reality a union attempt to by-pass the company bargaining committee and appeal to top management. Gloomy articles in union newpapers have the same aim in view. An experienced appraisal of the situation is required here. If a company succumbs every time the union flexes its economic muscles it may find itself yielding more than its competitors. On the other hand, such tactics must be considered in the light of the actual bargaining situation.

Certainly they are not to be taken lightly—unions have learned from experience that these weapons often succeed where conversation and persuasion fail.

Questions

1. What may be the value and purpose of asking the union to explain the reason or justification for each proposal that it wants management to accept?
2. The author draws a distinction between the cost items and the noncost items in a bargaining agenda. Actually, is there such a thing as a "noncost item" as far as management is concerned?
3. Under what handicap does management operate in making counterproposals to union demands for wage increases?
4. What is a "false break-off point" and what problems may it involve?
5. What types of psychological pressures can a union use against management?

41. IS THE ARBITRATOR YOUR FRIEND? *

Lawrence Stessin

In the no-man's land of employee discipline, visibility is very poor. Rules and regulations are of some help—but who can design a set of rules that will provide for every contingency? Who would have dreamed, for example, of making a rule that "Any employee who shoots his wife will be subject to immediate discharge by the company?" Yet three companies that tried to dismiss employees on these grounds wished that they *had* made such a rule when the arbitrators considered these cases as matters of social impropriety rather than as violations of company rules.

Actually, it's not practical to run a company or a department by rules or formulas so rigid that they deny the supervisor his necessary elbowroom.

What about the union contract? Isn't that a useful guide to discipline? Unfortunately, it's not as useful as it might be. Both management and labor usually see fit *not* to pinpoint the discipline process in a collective-bargaining agreement. Contract references to discipline are typically sparse and vague, giving management the right to punish for "cause" or "just cause," or including the right to discipline within the framework of the "management's-rights" clause.

The manager is, then, often left without specific standards by which to gauge his actions in employee discipline. It may be worth while to see if some useful standards can be discovered from a study of arbitrators' awards in discipline cases that have come to arbitration. This article is based on such a study of arbitration awards in 900 cases involving discipline over a five-year period.

Can the arbitrator help?

In discipline cases, the role of the arbitrator is not usually limited by a tightly negotiated clause such as those covering seniority, pro-

* From *Supervisory Management*, Vol. 4, No. 8 (August, 1959), pp. 9-16. Reprinted with permission.

motions, and layoffs. Rather, he has an implied mandate to roam freely, to indulge personal opinion and observation, and to take plenty of "think time" (at $100 a thought—or so, at least, it seems when the company gets the bill).

This lack of specific standards has disturbed many arbitrators. One man said, "About all that an impartial arbitrator can do is to decide the justice or injustice of the discharge in the light of common sense, common knowledge of generally prevailing industry standards for employee deportment, and common understanding." Another noted that an arbitrator in discipline cases brings to a hearing "the ethical teachings of his parents [and] religious advisers, the stereotypes of his friends. His experiences and attitudes toward life, be they hard or soft, may condition man in favor of or against tolerating particular offenses, and may motivate him for or against mercy or rigor." Still another commentator observed that the best he could do was "to decide what a reasonable man would do under similar circumstances and in that light decide whether the conduct of the disciplined employee was defensible or the disciplinary penalty just."

Is it reasonable, then, to look to the arbitrator for applicable standards or guideposts for employee discipline? I think so. Despite the personal nature of the arbitration award in discipline cases, the arbitrators, sitting in collective judgment over the thousands of discipline cases that are appealed to them every year, have created a pattern of standards, guideposts, and criteria. Although arbitrators continue to maintain that there can never be a framework of policy standards on discipline, a study of their awards reveals that one is, in fact, being established. Let us consider some of these standards.

The boss is the boss

Management demands that the arbitrator acknowledge, in cases involving refusal to obey an order, that *the boss is still the boss*. With this principle arbitrators agree: In none of the cases analyzed in this study has an arbitrator been "soft" on an employee who, when told to do a task, balked or argued or questioned the employer's right to give the order. As Harry Shulman, a pioneer arbitrator, said, "An industrial plant is not a debating society; it object is production. When a controversy arises, production cannot wait."

Arbitrators have, in some cases, supported employees who refused to obey orders because they felt that their safety or health might be endangered. But these decisions were based, not on the worker's right to refuse an order, but on the grounds that management was not behaving as it should.　Concern for the health and safety of an employee is a management responsibility, and the manager who subjects his work force to hazardous or unhealthy conditions cannot expect immunity.　However, the union view that an employee has the right to disobey an order because the boss is violating some contractual right has received short shrift from arbitrators.　Thus, the right of management to issue an order and have it obeyed with dispatch is so universally accepted by arbitrators that it is, for all practical purposes, an undiluted standard of discipline.

Don't shove the foreman

The power and authority to direct the work force go hand in hand with another attribute of management: status.　A worker who was fired for giving his foreman "a gentle shove," as the union called it, stayed fired after arbitration as surely as if he had hauled off and landed a haymaker.　Managerial dignity and status must not be tampered with, say the arbitrators, and even employees charged with abusive language against a supervisor have received severe penalties. In 1941, Whitley McCoy laid down the principle that "no business can operate efficiently if the supervisory force is abused," and there has been no serious divergence from this view.　Instances in which employees have been declared innocent in cases of assault or verbal abuse are so few that a common law may be said to exist for the support of management status by arbitrators.

The missing employee

A similar management orientation is evident in the area of absenteeism.　Many hearings on employee absenteeism bring to light touching situations of sickness or family responsibilities.　In the union's eyes, a worker who is forced to be away because of illness or family burdens should not be penalized.　But arbitrators have consistently recognized the needs of the business as overriding, whatever the plight of the individual.　As one arbitrator put it, "No matter how good the excuse for absence may be, the company is entitled to the attendance of workers.　When an employee is absent so much, *even for the best of reasons*, that his services are of little or no value to the company, he cannot remain in the company's employ."

There are, of course, many reversals of management action in cases of absenteeism—but these do not indicate any shift away from the principle that **management's job is, among other things, to protect** the company's pocketbook. Management actions are reversed in absenteeism cases only when management has failed to practice what it preaches. Management decisions should not be based upon whim, fancy, or exasperation. Thus, when a supervisor suddenly invokes a rule against absenteeism after long neglect, such hasty action is viewed by arbitrators as behavior unbecoming to a manager. They insist that management cannot enjoy the prerogatives of authority and control without making use of the tools. Employers who have devised specific rules providing for a gradation of penalties, accompanied by appropriate warnings—and who have enforced these rules —have had no problems at arbitration.

Who's incompetent?

To judge from the record of defeats of employers in cases involving employee incompetence or negligence, it would seem that arbitrators are seriously curtailing a basic demand: the right to a fair day's work. Actually, however, arbitrators don't question the right of management to deal severely with an employee who is not carrying his weight in production or is incompetent or sloppy; what arbitrators *do* insist is that management come to a hearing on incompetence with clean hands. They have laid down some very specific standards:

(1) Before an employee can be disciplined for incompetence, the employer must show that he actually has standards of performance. Further, to sustain such a charge, the company must have adequate records which can be produced upon request at the hearing.

A case involving discharge for incompetence must be well documented because, in such cases, it's harder to convince the arbitrator.

(2) Before being fired for incompetence, the employee must have been told of his shortcomings and given an adequate opportunity to improve. He must have been warned that continued unwillingness or inability to meet the standard would result in disciplinary action.

Length of service is a mitigating force. The arbitrator asks, Why did he *suddenly* become incompetent? Why was there no earlier action?

(3) Management has the right to tighten production standards, but the employee must be given a reasonable opportunity to meet a new standard.

(4) Discipline for incompetence must follow some pattern of past practice; sudden crackdowns without warning are frowned upon as inconsistent with sound managerial practices.

(5) Management cannot demote an employee who is merely care-less or negligent and expect this to be upheld at arbitration. Discipline is supposed to be a corrective measure, the arbitrator will hold, and the employee can be just as careless or negligent on the new job. If a man is careless or negligent over a period of time, he should be fired.

The high cost of walking out

Arbitrators most strongly show their managerial leanings when they render decisions involving strikes and walkouts. Arbitrators have allowed management every tool to curb and punish those who walk out in violation of their contracts, or who slow down rather than use the grievance machinery. The union usually argues that employees have walked out because management goaded them into it. "How much pressure can a man stand?" the union asks. To this plea, arbitrators have turned a deaf ear. As far as they are concerned, no matter what sins the manager commits, employees have no right to walk out during the term of the contract. They have their protective device in the grievance machinery. Whatever punishment manage-ment imposes on those who walk out, or on their leaders, has been approved in arbitration.

The union leader—shop steward or other official—has been par-ticularly hard hit in the evolution of this standard. Arbitrators insist that these men have much more than a passive responsibility in a crisis. They must take active measures to keep their men from walk-ing out—they must talk, threaten, cajole, and practically push the aggressive wildcatters back to their workbenches—if they want any sympathy from an arbitrator. Arbitrators do not take lightly the disruption of plant operations. They share with management the philosophy that time, properly used, is vital to the success of a busi-ness enterprise.

The long arm of management

In awards dealing with fights and altercations, arbitrators have carved out a set of criteria of considerable importance. What they have done is to extend the arm of management's control to areas out-side the workplace. The old "sacred" rule that a man can do as he pleases outside the plant without fear of censure from his employer is no longer valid.

A worker who ran into his foreman at a race track and hauled off and belted him one—and shortly thereafter found himself fired—

discovered that the argument of outside privacy was of no avail. If the worker's action had been motivated by the fact that the foreman had given him a bad tip on a horse, he might have contended it was none of the company's business. But as it happened, the employee had vowed to "get" the foreman as a result of a hassle in the plant earlier that day. In that context, the employer's authority extended to the very shadow of the two-dollar window.

Arbitrators have become equally aware of the fact that a modern business enterprise is a glass house. The worker is no 8:00-to-4:00 automaton; he is a member of the community. A loose tongue used indiscriminately at a bar or other community gathering place can be punished by management if there is some evidence that such exercise of free speech might have harmed the company's reputation.

These important expansions of management rights show up with a high degree of consistency in arbitration awards.

The right to reconsider

One area, however, in which arbitrators have contributed significantly to the erosion of managerial authority is that of quits and resignations. The power of management to refuse re-employment to a worker who decided too hastily to quit his job has been considerably watered down in awards.

By managerial standards, a worker who has quit and then comes back to reclaim his job may often be denied employment because his action has disrupted the smooth flow of the enterprise. Must management rearrange its plans to take back an employee who stalked off angrily saying he would not return? Arbitrators say yes. They do not feel that the inconvenience to the company is more important than the employee's right to reconsider an action taken under emotional stress.

The greedy few

Discipline for stealing presents the arbitrator with special problems. Any attempt to discover criteria in this area is beset by special difficulties, for management will often discharge employees for violating various company rules rather than openly accusing them of theft —and arbitrators succumb to the same temptation. Thus, an employee with a record of missing funds may be let out for "carelessness." Furthermore, there are few arbitration awards on the subject because few of these situations reach the arbitration stage.

Punishment for gambling encounters some of the same difficulties. When an employee caught gambling is part of a professional ring, of course, there is little need to ponder. Pay-day poker or dice games, however, do not strike arbitrators as serious, and a minor disciplinary layoff for the first offense is about all that management is permitted. The difficulty arbitrators face is not in deciding on the severity of the penalty for gambling, but rather in reaching some satisfactory conclusion on whether the people so charged have really participated. Are workers who are standing around in the locker room allegedly watching a card game "participants" or "spectators"?

Consider the following case: Four employees were discharged after two warnings, for shooting dice. When their case came to arbitration, each man was placed on the stand. The first one claimed he had taken up a collection for coffee for the group and was on his way out to get the coffee. The second maintained that he had just arrived for the second shift and was getting ready to change his clothes. He said he never gambled—didn't even know how to shoot dice. The third vowed sanctimoniously that he never gambled, and looked upon the practice as a vice.

Finally the arbitrator came to the fourth man, who had been caught with the dice. "All these other men say they weren't gambling. But you—weren't you caught with a pair of dice in your hand?"

"Yes sir, I certainly was," was the amiable reply.

The arbitrator followed up quickly, "Then you *were* gambling, weren't you?"

The worker looked up, startled. "Gambling?" he exclaimed with indignation. "With *whom,* sir?"

What's the answer?

Is the arbitrator the manager's friend in the area of employee discipline? As long as he behaves in the image of good management, the answer appears to be yes. Arbitrators agree that the manager's basic jobs are to plan, organize, direct, and control, and this recognition is indicated in their awards in discipline cases.

Arbitrators have carved out a whole body of criteria, standards, and guideposts in employee discipline. It is now possible for the manager, through a little research, to predict closely the outcome of his disciplinary actions in the event that they are appealed.

Questions

1. What is the purpose of arbitration in the grievance procedure? What percentage of cases would you estimate reach an arbitrator?
2. It was noted that the labor-management contract usually does not cover the discipline process in detail. Are there advantages and disadvantages in this procedure to management? to the union? Discuss.
3. Do you feel that the support of management status by arbitrators is desirable? Why?
4. What should management do before discharging an employee for incompetence? Do you consider the requirements of arbitrators in this type of situation reasonable?
5. Would it be desirable and/or possible for a nonunionized company to have some type of arbitration process for grievance cases that could not be settled by the management and employees? Discuss.

Additional Readings for Chapter 7

Aaron, Benjamin. "The New Labor Bill," *The Nation.* Vol. 189, No. 17 (November 21, 1959), pp. 373-377.

Black, James Menzies. "Collective Bargaining: The Positive Approach Pays Off," *Dun's Review and Modern Industry.* Vol. 68, No. 1 (January, 1957).

Blake, Robert R., and Jane S. Mouton. "Reactions to Intergroup Competition Under Win-Lose Conditions," *Management Science.* Vol. 7, No. 4 (July, 1961), pp. 420-435.

Cole, David L. "Government in the Bargaining Process: The Role, of Mediation," *The Annals of the American Academy of Political and Social Science.* Vol. 333 (January, 1961), pp. 42-58.

Davey, Harold W. "The Arbitrator Views the Industrial Engineer," *California Management Review.* Vol. 7, No. 1 (Fall, 1964), pp. 23-29.

Foegen, J. H. "Strikes: On the Way to Obsolescence," *Business Topics.* Vol. 13, No. 2 (Spring, 1965), pp. 53-59.

――――――――. "Has Collective Bargaining Degenerated?" *California Management Review.* Vol. 6, No. 4 (Summer, 1964), pp. 37-40.

Goldberg, Arthur. "The Rights and Responsibilities of Union Members," *Labor Law Journal.* Vol. 9, No. 4 (April, 1958), pp. 298-303.

Gotterer, Malcolm H. "Union Reactions to Unilateral Changes in Work Measurement Procedures," *Personnel Psychology.* Vol. 14, No. 4 (Winter, 1961), pp. 433-450.

Hazard, Leland. "Unionism: Past and Future," *Harvard Business Review.* Vol. 36, No. 2 (March-April, 1958), pp. 59-65.

Imberman, A. A. "Labor Leaders and Society," *Harvard Business Review.* Vol. 28, No. 1 (January, 1950), pp. 52-60.

Kuhn, James. "Encroachments on the Right to Manage," *California Management Review.* Vol. V, No. 1 (Fall, 1962), pp. 18-24.

McFarland, Dalton E. "The Scope of the Industrial Relations Function," *Personnel.* Vol. 36, No. 1 (January-February, 1959), pp. 42-51.

McKersie, Robert B., and William W. Shropshire, Jr. "Avoiding Written Grievances: A Successful Program," *The Journal of Business.* Vol. XXXV, No. 2 (April, 1962), pp. 135-152.

McLaughlin, Richard P. "Collective Bargaining—The New Trend," *Labor Law Journal.* Vol 15, No. 8 (August, 1964), pp. 499-518.

Metzler, John H. "Human Relations and Contract Negotiations," *Personnel Administration.* Vol. 24, No. 4 (July-August, 1961), pp. 51-56.

Newman, Louis. "Management Rights and Arbitration," *Personnel.* Vol. 33, No. 4 (January, 1957), pp. 318-326.

Peters, Edward. "Only Real Issues Count in Contract Bargaining," *Personnel Journal.* Vol. 32, No. 10 (March, 1954), pp. 367-373.

Selekman, Benjamin M. "Trade-Unions—Romance and Reality," *Harvard Business Review.* Vol. 36, No. 3 (May-June, 1958), pp. 76-90.

Shepard, Herbert A. "The Psychologist's Role in Union-Management Relations," *Personnel Psychology.* Vol. 14, No. 3 (Autumn, 1961), pp. 270-279.

Sibson, Robert E. "Handling Grievances Where There Is No Union," *Personnel Journal.* Vol. 35, No. 2 (June, 1956), pp. 56-58.

Solomon, Benjamin, and Robert K. Burns. "Unionization of White-Collar Employees: Extent, Potential, and Implications," *The Journal of Business.* Vol. XXXVI, No. 2 (April, 1963), pp. 141-165.

Stagner, Ross. "The Psychologist's Function in Union-Management Relations," *Personnel Administration.* Vol. 26, No. 1 (January-February, 1963), pp. 24-29, 53.

Stogdill, Ralph M., Omar S. Goode, and David R. Day. "The Leader Behavior of Presidents of Labor Unions," *Personnel Psychology.* Vol. 17, No. 1 (Spring, 1964), pp. 49-57.

Strauss, George. "Professional or Employee-Oriented: Dilemma for Engineering Unions," *Industrial and Labor Relations Review.* Vol. 17, No. 4 (July, 1964), pp. 519-533.

——————. "The Shifting Power Balance in the Plant," *Industrial Relations.* Vol. 1, No. 3 (May-1962), pp. 65-96.

Taft, Philip. "On the Origins of Business Unionism," *Industrial and Labor Relations Review.* Vol. 17, No. 1 (October, 1963), pp. 20-38.

Torff, Selwyn H. "A Reappraisal of the U. S. Collective Bargaining Process," *Personnel Administration.* Vol. 26, No. 1 (January-February, 1963), pp. 5-9, 23.

CHAPTER 8

Personnel Management:
Meeting Today's Problems

As a result of the progress that is being achieved in science and technology as well as in the social sciences, our society is in a constant state of change. The survival of any organization or institution within this society is contingent upon its ability to keep abreast of changes and to resolve successfully those problems that it may create. Probably no function in an organization is affected more by change than that of personnel management. Changes that are occurring in industry affect the nature of the work to be performed, the jobs to be staffed, as well as the policies, procedures, and functions of the personnel program. The program for the management of its personnel, therefore, must be dynamic if it is to serve successfully the needs of the organization. At the present time a number of developments are taking place which are of concern to the personnel manager. One of the most significant challenges confronting the personnel manager today is that of attending to the many problems resulting from automation and mechanization, both in the plant and in the office. The introduction of automation can affect nearly every phase of a company's personnel program. A report of one of the more significant studies pertaining to the effects of automation upon the personnel manager is contained in the article by Otis Lipstreu and Kenneth A. Reed. While the reader should be aware that the findings which are reported relate to a particular company, these findings are significant in terms of their possible application to other companies.

Automation and technological progress have resulted also in an increase in the proportion of professional and scientific personnel who are employed by many organizations. The article by Jerome M. Rosow discusses the role of such personnel and some of the special considerations that must be given to their management.

During the past decade, many companies have expanded their operations into foreign countries. Professor G. M. Oxley in his article discusses some of the special problems that a company has had to consider in developing a personnel program for employees who are sent to foreign countries. Another significant development relating to personnel management is the growth in the proportion of women who are being employed in the work force, and this trend has made necessary adjustments in certain personnel policies and procedures. Some of the psychological considerations that relate to this adjustment are covered in the article by B. von Haller Gilmer.

The last two articles in this chapter deal with the procedures for effecting change within an organization. The experiment discussed in the article by J. R. P. French, Jr., and his associates is a classical one dealing with the subject of effecting industrial change. It has been cited by many authors and provides a firsthand description of the experiment by those who conducted it. The final article in this chapter suggests how a reorganization may be accomplished without creating a crisis. Since some form of reorganization is inevitable in any company over a period of time, this article by Ewing W. Reilley offers some very practical advice on how to accomplish it.

42. A NEW LOOK AT THE ORGANIZATIONAL IMPLICATIONS OF AUTOMATION *

Otis Lipstreu and Kenneth A. Reed

In August, 1960, the *Journal of the Academy of Management* carried an article by one of the authors exploring the organizational implications of automation. The hypotheses developed were based largely on responses from top manufacturing executives of the largest industrial corporations in the United States.[1]

As a result of the information obtained from this "experience and opinion" study, the authors undertook to test empirically those organizational hypotheses that appeared most critical to the introduction of automation technology. Accordingly, a company was selected that offered the opportunity to observe a total organization undergoing a major technological change. The company (referred to hereafter as X) is a baking plant employing some 1,200 employees, slightly over one half being factory workers.

Management of the company proved receptive to our proposal for a 2-year study covering the transition period. There is little question but that the degree of change from an old mill-type plant to a new, highly automatic facility was as great in magnitude as most plant workers will ever experience. It represents what we believe will be the typical stage in automatic evolution. This then is a study of change to the partially automated plant, not to the automatic factory.

Effects of Automation

The research methodology employed included observation, interviews, attitude surveys and analyses of personnel statistics during a two-year period. We have chosen to follow the same general format used in the earlier *Journal* article for ease of comparison in order to

---

* From *Journal of the Academy of Management,* Vol. 8, No. 1 (March, 1965), pp. 24-31. Reprinted with permission.

[1] Otis Lipstreu, "Organizational Implications of Automation," *Journal of the Academy of Management,* August, 1960, pp. 119-124.

show the modifications of the previous research data in the light of empirical evidence.[2]

Automation reduces the number of supervisory levels

Authorities generally agree that automation reduces the number of supervisory levels.

The response of our operating executives provided ground for questioning unequivocal support of such a conclusion. No reduction in supervisory levels occurred because of automating in Company X. But this appeared to be a temporary plateau during reorganization. It was evident to observers and to management as well that the first level supervisors, whose authority span had been reduced, were having a difficult time adjusting, primarily because their function had become so nebulous. Bluntly speaking, they weren't needed since the production superintendent could perform easily their general oversight duties. The other tasks could be handled functionally by general maintenance technicians, whose duties overlapped those of the supervisors.

In addition, they were experiencing difficulty in adjusting to the new supervisory patterns. Consequently they were over-supervising to compensate for reduced span of authority and feelings of insecurity due to the nebulous nature of their new function. It appeared only a matter of time until this level of supervision might be eliminated.

Automation increases the amount of supervisory responsibility

Both authorities and operating officials supported this conclusion.

Whether or not the increased automation had increased the amount of supervisory responsibility in Company X cannot be answered in either the affirmative or the negative without some qualification. In the more highly automated departments the supervisory span of control over workers was drastically reduced; in the baking section, for example, from approximately 75 to around 25. In this instance, as in others, the responsibility for personnel has been reduced. But the responsibility relative to the consequence of human error was greatly increased due to the speed of the line and the tremendous cost of breakdowns. Formerly, supervisors had time to correct errors in

---

[2] For a full presentation of the transition and its effects on other areas of management, *see* Otis Lipstreu and Kenneth Reed, *Transition to Automation* (Boulder, Colorado: University of Colorado Press, 1964).

process, since there was time for, and assistance in, quality control feedback all along the line. Now, the increased speed of the lines and the restricted mobility of machine operators have significantly reduced opportunities to spot difficulties early enough to avoid substantial scrap. As a result, supervisory tension has been greatly increased.

Everywhere in the plant, it was clear that the expectations of higher management relative to supervisory performance had heightened.

Automation increases interdependence of work between supervisors at the same level

A majority of executives agreed with this statement and experts in the field concur.

There seemed little question that supervisor interdependency has increased under more highly automated conditions. But simply to say that there must be more coordination without preparation for it is little more than wishful thinking. The plain fact is that the degree of lateral communication and cooperation in most organizations is atrociously underdeveloped. (Company X was probably no better or worse than the rule.) When coupled with intensified pressure to get production up to standard, the new interdependency is apt to produce backbiting of the most vicious nature. In our estimation, this was minimal in X due to rather good horizontal rapport among supervisors prior to the change. Under conditions where a less positive atmosphere prevails, however, this new relationship can produce demoralizing results.

This area is a frontier in communication. Few formal methods for horizontal interaction presently exist and informal social pressures can impede effective lateral communication. Under changed conditions involving new technology, weak horizontal communications can be substantially more costly.

Automation increases ratio of supervisors to workers

An overwhelming amount of informed opinion from the plant and the university supported this conclusion.

At Company X, as previously indicated, no modification in the number of supervisory levels had been made some twelve months after the change; and a number of supervisory personnel from other plants have been absorbed. The outstanding instance of the accelerating supervisory ratio was in the Baking and Mixing Department, the area experiencing greatest technological change. Formerly, some 70 employees were supervised by a foreman and an assistant foreman. These 2, with the addition of another assistant foreman, supervised 25 men after the change. So, in this one department, a 35/1 ratio has become roughly an 8/1 ratio.

Though this was the extreme, in no instance in the plant had the ratio of supervisors to workers decreased. Contributing to the increased ratio, however, were a number of other logical and profit-oriented factors. In the first place, there has been a significant change in spatial relationships. Prior to the change, the baking and mixing functions were on the same floor in juxtaposition. A mixer had to walk only about 20 paces to see the baked goods. From two positions on the floor, all 70 workers could be observed. In the new plant, these operations were stacked above each other on three different levels. Complete surveillance of one work level was possible only on the two upper floors. On the ground floor, at best, only two employees could be seen from any one position, and these may be 300 feet away.

Other aspects to be considered were the nature of the work and the speed of product flow. The consequences of individual error were greater. The flow of the product was so much faster that in-process adjustments were far more difficult if not impossible to make. Consequently, the 8/1 ratio probably could be justified from an organizational standpoint. Furthermore, old distinctions between direct and indirect labor became exceedingly fuzzy under automated conditions.

Automation reduces the amount of direct communication required between supervisors and employees

This generalization was generally rejected by researchers and plant operating men as well.

In Company X, however, there was little doubt that the amount of direct communication between supervisors and employees had been drastically curtailed in the highly automated areas. This was largely true because the act of assigning work had been vastly simplified. The nature of the work content was more clearly delineated in advance and did not change except when a machine broke down. The pace of the machines, the reading of gauges, the flashing of lights, or the sounding of horns controlled individual work attention and effort. Composition of work teams, shifting of workers to compensate for absenteeism, and frequent checks on work progress was minimal. Thus, foremen did far less direct communication, but rather directed their efforts toward general oversight and trouble-shooting activities.

Automation leads to a greater percentage of indirect labor to total plant labor force

Scholarly speculation and practical operating experience supported this statement at a very high level of confidence. And to a corollary statement—automation requires closer attention by maintenance technicians, agreement was almost as high.

Company X's ratio of indirect labor to total plant work force changed from 1 to 6.73 before the change, to 1 to 4.12 after the change.

There appeared general agreement that many of the transitional problems in X could have been eliminated initially by more adequate and qualified staffing of the Maintenance Department to provide closer oversight of the operating process. (Yet the fact remains that most companies will experience the same problems of recruiting well-trained maintenance personnel.) Company X did not begin its search for such personnel early enough; did not provide incumbent maintenance personnel with enough up-grading training prior to the move; nor did it initially offer salaries that would attract well-qualified maintenance technicians. Management eventually moved to rectify the situation, but during the most critical change period, maintenance personnel had to learn the hard way—on the job, and largely by trial and error.

Automation reduces the size of work crews or teams

Experience and informed opinion upheld this conclusion.

In the automated areas of X, most of the work was done by machine monitors. The number of helpers had been reduced or removed entirely. The only teams were maintenance pairs. And there was no need for work teams except when machines broke down. The general pattern involved isolated stations and individual work. Automation not only reduced the size of work crews or teams in the more highly automated areas of X but almost eliminated them except for certain maintenance and repair activities.

Automation leads to increased isolation of workers

Again a high level of concurrence supported this hypothesis, and this condition was certainly true in X.

The increased isolation of workers undoubtedly posed real attitudinal problems. One of the most significant shifts in response for any question on the X morale survey occurred relative to the amount of time available for talking with fellow workers. As one might have suspected, the shift was overwhelmingly in the negative direction. Responses to two other questions—"What do you think of your job?" and "Do you feel your job is important to the company's ability to produce and/or sell a good product?" (both involving significant negative shifts after the change)—may also have been related to employee feelings relative to this new isolation.

Automation gives workers more freedom of movement away from their machines

Plant executives solidly disagreed with this generalization.

In Company X under non-automated conditions, machine operations (peeling and oven jobs, for example) required that employees engage in rather feverish continuous activity either proximate to their machines or in rather cramped work parameters. But they also enjoyed frequent rest periods which were not provided in the new work assignments. When the jobs in baking were automated, work positions became isolated, with machine tenders being assigned to monitor one or more machines within a limited area. During the debugging operation (at least 9 months in X), because of the numerous breakdowns, the strangeness of the machines, and the urge to manually override the electronic controls (as a new driver tends to oversteer an automobile), the machine monitor's freedom of movement was very limited. In every sense they were tied more closely to their machines. We had anticipated far more time to talk with employees on the job immediately after the change, but the reverse was the rule. After the debugging stage and when the employees gained more confidence in their machines, however, attention to machines became more leisurely, and, for the most part, some freedom to move a short distance out of orbit was enjoyed. But any real sense of freedom was illusory, since any failure to observe alertly the various gauges could have resulted almost instantaneously in serious product loss and/or costly machine damage.

Automation reduces the prevalence of informal worker cliques

Informal opinion and experience were divided on this statement.

In the old plant of X, although the informal organization was highly developed and rather easily identifiable, one aspect of the work process minimized informal activity: only during the 30-minute lunch period were machines and production lines inactive. Employees were relieved for rest breaks at varying times, depending upon their particular work station. Few rest period coffee cliques developed, although employees did sit with others from different departments in the lunchroom, proximate to the work area, on the second floor of the building. The rather minimal amount of talk time provided by the brief lunch period also reduced opportunities for widespread close interpersonal relationships. Thus, informal structure in X was not as strong, cohesive, or closely knit as in other organizations which we have observed.

Even so, from the postchange response, it appeared that opportunities for even this minimal amount of social interaction on the job had been drastically reduced. Work schedules and assignments in total had been modified to a considerable degree, producing a different composition of coffee "klatsches" and, for some more highly automated departments, luncheon groups.

In the Mixing Department, two unauthorized free-time periods enjoyed by employees both in the morning and evening had been eliminated, reducing the amount of interaction time by almost 20 minutes per day. Some of the machine monitors told us they seldom saw some of their old friends with whom they formerly enjoyed regular contact. Women in the non-automated areas reported even more dissatisfaction.

One department was discontinued, with the employees scattered throughout the remaining departments. Interviews with these workers supported by attitude survey responses indicated that their attitude toward the company and work satisfaction was the lowest in the plant. The informal social organization looked disoriented, relatively fragmented, and directionless; however, the process of restructuring appeared to have begun. (But, as cohesiveness increases, it seems unlikely that it will be as positively oriented toward management as formerly.)

Automation increases the need for stand-by personnel at the work level

Plant officials were equivocal and the literature of automation is vague concerning this issue.

In X, additional personnel were employed directly to good advantage for the first 3 to 4 months following the move. However, as so frequently occurs, when the staffing was reduced, the machines began to "act up," resulting in a very harried, frustrated group of employees. No easy solution exists here. While machinery is functioning properly no added personnel are required. And normal relief staffing is adequate. But, for example, when automatic raw-material feed mechanisms malfunction, operations revert to the manual shovel and lift activities.

Company X executives are considering the idea of developing a flying squadron of versatile trainees to fill any number of positions, yet to perform functions that might be postponed during emergency periods.

An example from the Mixing Department may highlight the stand-by personnel problem. Very careful manning documents were developed by management for this area on the basis of visitations to other plants in the organization. Problems were anticipated since X had some new machines not previously used anywhere else. Properly, the staffing was based upon a debugging period during which additional help would be needed, after which only the regular staff would be required. On the basis of this logical plan, things moved along on schedule. Everything seemed to be operating smoothly, and so the manning was reduced to normal requirements. This seemed to be fine although, as mentioned previously, the mixers did not have much if any opportunity to derive many of the old satisfactions from the work, and there was some griping. But then all hell broke loose. There is no other phase that so describes the temper of the situation. A mixer called for 100 pounds of flour on his electronic gadget—instead he got 200. Feverishly he attempted to shovel out the excess from the trough, while all the time the hungry machines below were fast running out of dough. Not much effort is required to imagine the deteriorating state of human relations when the supervisory group ascended to ascertain the problem.

Our point in relating this episode (and there were many others just as tense) is to point up the extremely complex aspects of staffing. When everything is operating properly, "clockwork" is an appropriate term and normal staffing is adequate. But there are few days of such utopian smoothness during the first few months of change. As a result of negotiations completed approximately 1 year after the change, the Mixing Department now has virtually the same staffing pattern initially visualized as necessary only during the debugging process.

Automation tends to increase centralization of authority in multi-plant companies

It seemed to us from the outset that some organizational modification involving centralization of authority would be mandatory if a multi-plant system was to derive the greatest benefit from added capacity. Diversification of product and/or freedom for decision-making within the system appeared inconsistent with optimal use of facilities under increasing technology.

This proved to be the case in Company X. Authority for product planning and scheduling was centralized. For example, the introduction of new product items was examined in terms of the total product line of the System, rather than just that of Company X. A greater degree of product specialization within the various plants in the organization is in the offing and should offer cost advantages due to longer product runs and fewer machine set-up adjustments.

The net results of the organizational modification can be summarized in a quote from an employee brochure—"When the Unification Program is completed, the System as a whole will operate in much the same way as any one of our Divisions is operating." The specific effect in Company X was the transfer of the President to the home office as a Senior Vice President of the System and his replacement in X by an acting resident manager accompanied by a centralization of functional control in the home office.

Observations and Conclusions

There can be little doubt that technological change will modify significantly the organizational environment of a considerable segment of the industrial world. From the foregoing limited study, it is nevertheless possible to identify and evaluate certain structural problems that will require careful planning if serious negative consequences are to be mitigated or minimized, if not eliminated.

• The previous conclusion that the supervisor will regain some of his lost discretionary authority still seems tenable. However, even more certain from our study is the fact that the number of supervisory jobs will surely shrink; the supervisor's job will indeed resemble that of middle management in that his span of supervision will be drastically reduced, and his function will be upgraded from that of "gang boss" to that of a general overseer, trouble-shooter, and coordinator.

• Although the supervisor should be able to do a better human relations job, our research indicates that he will not, at least initially, largely because his adjustment to his new managerial role will be one which he will find difficult to make because of insecurity and lack of training for his new job.

• Contrary to our former conclusion, the gross amount of direct, verbal interaction required between supervisors and workers will be greatly reduced. What communication there is will, as previously concluded, change in the direction of greater use of inter-coms, and the substance of the communication will be geared to more consultative team approach concerned with "keeping the line moving."

• We are even more convinced that the selection, training, and proper use of the maintenance technician requires far more research attention than it appears to be getting at present. We believe that many companies, like X, will suffer prolonged debugging, costly machine down-time, and reduced morale because of their failure to provide an adequate maintenance staff to service automatic machinery.

• The new isolation of work is real and poses a different pattern of psychological problems that require careful study. The social organization, after change, will tend to be less company-oriented and the entire company atmosphere will become more impersonal.

• The experience in Company X points up the complexity of the stand-by employee problems. It will be much more difficult than many have suggested to attain projected staffing norms long after debugging. It appears that what may be considered by management as excessive staffing will be typical for openloop automation processes. After the debugging operation, additional personnel may not be required except occasionally. When required, however, their nonavailability can result in rather fantastic materials and machine damage. Moreover, the added tension of operators who envision production irregularities that they cannot handle alone may produce indirectly man-caused, machine malfunctions. Consequently, it behooves management to anticipate such staffing problems, plan for them (flying squadrons appear to be the best of present alternatives), and develop job descriptions which utilize fully these auxiliary workers.

• Finally, centralization of managerial control appears endemic to increased automaticity of production, particularly in a multi-plant corporation.

Questions

1. In what ways were the supervisors in this company affected by automation?
2. How do you account for the fact that automation increased the interdependence of supervisors in performing their work?
3. Based upon the evidences gained from this study, what effect is automation likely to have upon employee morale and interpersonal relations?
4. Did automation tend to tie the worker more or less closely to his work place? What effect, if any, may this have upon the worker?
5. Do you feel that automation in this plant made it a more desirable place for employees to work?
6. Can you think of any effects besides those mentioned that automation might have upon personnel management?

43. THE GROWING ROLE OF PROFESSIONAL AND SCIENTIFIC PERSONNEL *

Jerome M. Rosow

There are seven and one-half million professional and technical people working in America today. By the end of this decade this number will have grown to over ten million. The growth rate is three times greater than in total nonagricultural employment. Although the professions have tripled in size during the first half of the century, the traditional disciplines of law and medicine have increased by only one-fourth. Engineers have increased four times faster than all other professional workers—a real confirmation of the technological explosion. Accountants and auditors have multiplied at about the same dizzy pace, reflecting the multiplication of records and the financial specialization in our society. These growth trends indicate in general terms the growing role of professional and scientific personnel in American companies.

Professionals are people just like you and me. They have no horns and no halos. In discussing them in special terms of reference, other major groups are excluded, but without any intention of glorifying the professional at the expense of many others who remain so vital in the labor force.

This discussion considers:

1. The characteristics of the professional.
2. The growing importance of the professional manpower component.
3. The problems and the prospects within three areas: organizational concepts, management development and personnel policies.

Characteristics of the Professional

As used here, the term "professional" is rather all embracing. It means practically every employee who is college educated has professional training and experience, and is working in the same or related field as his discipline of study. Scientists and engineers may predominate, but they are not the exclusive members of this broad category of personnel.

* From *Management Record*, Vol. 24, No. 2 (February, 1962), pp. 19-23. Reprinted with permission.

Deep investment in themselves

The professional has invested many years in education and preparation for his work. He has built up many hopes, expectations, and dreams which are identified with his career. Therefore, the *job* for the professional is his life's work. It's an inherent and vital part of his life—it's not merely a place to pass the hours or draw a pay check. This is in sharp contrast to many of the clerical and production workers who see the job as a source of income which provides leisure and off-the-job fulfillment. For the professional the commitment to work is deep and lasting; it places a strain on him and the organization. The problem isn't a desire to escape work—it's the high expectations for fulfillment at work.

A new labor force with high mobility

The professional labor market is new and highly competitive. The professionals' horizons stretch far beyond local geography. The best professionals are often the most restless, the most demanding, and the most mobile. National and international labor markets require employers to be more responsive to their economic and emotional needs. Each organization must appeal to the best by providing a more attractive environment than does the competition. This competition is not only within specific industries, but it is also from universities, government and consulting firms.

The professional's mobility and intelligence provide him with more strength in the labor market than the immobilized wage earner or clerical worker. When unemployment reached the 7% level in 1961, fewer than 2% of professionals were out of a job and most of this unemployment was frictional—in essence, job changing.

Basically self-regulating

No system can truly regulate or control the energy and drives of men at work. The degree of effective control is less and less as the work becomes more specialized, more individualized and more the product of the man. Men can be put to work to perform specific tasks in a controlled environment. This is organization and direction of men, but it is not motivation. A person basically must motivate himself—not only to work, but to strive, and to *want* to reach out beyond himself.

In terms of physical tasks we can measure utilization by units of output and call it productivity. But professional work is not easy to convert to conventional units. There is no mathematical method for measuring productivity in this area. Yet we worry about it all the time. We want to know if our high level manpower is "utilized." However, the professional is basically self-regulating; there are no standards of output which can be applied with consistency from occupation to occupation—or even for one complex occupation over time. Levels of effectiveness vary as much as men vary.

The professional and his work interact. They shape each other in a dynamic relationship. The man has almost absolute control over the degree to which he *engages* his work. He can go through the motions of his job without ever coming to real grips with the challenge—and no one is the wiser. Often he too remains sadly unaware of the superficial nature of his work habits.

His work must challenge him and he in turn needs to challenge himself. Once his energy, his spirit and his imagination are fired by these deep human drives the outcome becomes a challenge to the very organization itself. Then, of course, the need for regulation no longer exists. Many attempts to regulate are substitutes for a failure to motivate.

Recognition, involvement, and self-realization are vital

The professional is vulnerable and sensitive. He needs to be involved in the significant assignments and his special skills beg for recognition and use. Idleness and inactivity are not merely a waste— he often feels that they are slow-acting poisons which will destroy him. Once a man is actively involved in challenging problems he'll feel useful and important. Of course, the need then shifts from involvement to recognition. Involvement and recognition linked together create a sense of self-realization—a sense of hitting on all cylinders with mind, body, heart and soul.

Place extraordinary expectations upon the organization

The professional in an industrial setting is not a perfectly adjusted individual, but he is capable of performing at high levels. Very frequently his occupational choice was a combination of compromise and accident. Many of his first career choices were abandoned, often during his freshman or sophomore years. Although graduated as an engineer, he may have dreamed of becoming a scientist who aspired for the Nobel Prize. The routines of his engineering work in the organization may seem dull and second rate in relation to his youthful dreams. These frustrations, which were planted years ago, may now flower as a job problem. The organization becomes a ready scapegoat for every disappointment. He relates his unresolved personal conflicts to the job. He places both real and imaginary demands upon work—demands that are unrealistic and often impossible.

As a professional adjusts to organization life, he involves *himself* in both its failures and successes. He realizes that *even a single individual* can have a real effect upon results. Yet, the organization often represents a challenge to be met by emotional maturity. The professional who blames every problem, every disappointment and every project failure upon the corporation is only kidding himself.

The organization *cannot* accommodate to the needs of each of its many professionals. Therefore, each individual must adapt to the organization without losing his sense of purpose. If he does not, the individual must realize his own responsibility for withdrawal or half-hearted involvement.

Growing Importance of the Professional

The manpower mix has changed and the work force has developed a new look. This "professional look" has an investment side, a population aspect, and a growth trend. These, in turn, point to the need for new managerial systems.

Represent major investments

The fact that professionals represent a significant manpower investment has become increasingly apparent in terms of the following considerations:

1. The direct cost per capita averages from two to three times that of the production or office worker.
2. The indirect costs are substantial, in that professionals require a supporting staff. They commit facilities and money to long-term programs and they involve the time and effort of corollary groups. They are not "contained" human resources tied to a unit of production; rather, they are self-regulating programmers often on the sending end of the work process.

3. The selection, training and indoctrination time is greater. It's more costly and it adds to the investment in each individual even before he becomes fully effective.

4. Their proportion to the total labor costs in modern organizations is growing. In many cases it represents from one-third to two-thirds of the total.

5. At today's salary levels every new college graduate hired represents a potential minimum investment of $500,000. Visualizing a doubling of salary levels over the next 20 years, it is more realistic to consider each new man as a potential $1 million investment over a life's career of forty years. Add another 25% to cover benefit programs. Therefore, every 800 young professionals in your company represent a billion dollar investment. Think of it. The long-term manpower investment has become so significant as to place new meanings on the management of men. It casts a long shadow into the future.

Manpower is an asset

Manpower is an asset which *appreciates*—which grows over time. Machines are assets which *depreciate* with service and over time become scrap. A machine's maximum value is reached the day it is installed and begins producing. A man never reaches his ultimate value through his lifetime at work. As a man he is constantly able to change, to grow and to enlarge his value. Sometimes he does this in the face of continuing obstacles, more often his *appreciation,* his growth and value are slowed down or stunted completely when obstacles are thrown in his way.

The organization and its management must provide a climate where human assets can thrive and grow. Wasting human assets is a serious business—for the individual, for the company, for our country.

Dependent minority has become the majority

In the past, professionals were a select group who were a very small proportion of the total organization—now, they may be *the* organization, and they are the greatest single investment in manpower. The terms "burden," "overhead," and "staff" are outmoded in today's organization. Professionals are no longer the dependent luxury group who enjoyed a certain status but were of uncertain value to the organization. Their value and their high cost have become certainties. Their emotional commitment is not equally certain.

Rapid and uneven growth

The rapid and uneven growth of professionals has raced ahead of organizational adaptations. Not only scientists and engineers, but mathematicians, sociologists, economists, psychologists, accountants, lawyers, and an endless variety of specialists have multiplied in the organization. The new and strange variety of experts include many names which still have an unfamiliar ring to our ears.

The number of professionals required is difficult to foretell in the absence of standards for measurement. Different professions make inroads into various organizations at accelerating rates, while others lag far behind the requirements. *Rivalry* and *sectarianism* among professions create barriers and complicate the problem of adaptation.

Some fields of specialization are still searching for ways and means to bridge the differences between theory and practice. The application of the broad disciplines of knowledge to relatively narrow problems requires experience—both for the organization and the specialist. The professional is a resource. The realization of the potential of this resource is often more difficult than the exploitation of a physical resource in nature.

Needed—new managerial systems

The future of the enterprise depends increasingly upon the energy of its best minds. Brainpower is the energy source of industrial growth. The new work force is a necessity. It's an inescapable responsibility to attract brainpower. However, managing the minds of men is a new and strange art which is far different from organizing bodies or hands.

The sophistication of professional manpower imposes new responsibilities upon the organization. Each company faces the necessity of evolving managerial systems that recognize the need for a new kind of motivation and, at the same time, preserve institutional objectives. As stated previously, the professional's need for recognition and self-realization requires practical results. This blend means a new recipe of delicately balanced ingredients.

Problems and Prospects

The nature of the professional and the relationships of the organization to the new work force create problems and open prospects for change and accommodation. Three broad areas are described here: organizational concepts, management development and personnel policies.

Organizational concepts

Organizational structure dominates both purpose and people. These relationships can become so fixed that it is possible for them to stabilize individuals and groups in their functions and make them captives of the structure. In some cases organizational symbols have become ends in themselves and not really means of management. It must be understood that the specialization of knowledge and the speed of technological breakthroughs have antiquated the monolithic organization. Working through old channels of communication is no longer sufficient. Communication across lines of supervision, between line and staff, horizontally, vertically and diagonally through the organization is now normal and should be encouraged by the organization structure. This means creating new organization concepts—one of the most baffling and bewildering problems of any big institution.

Production line concepts of supervision persist. Results continue to be measured in physical units of output and the individual is subordinate to the process. What is required is the development of less control and regulation of the nonphysical units of mental effort. Organizations are searching for means of transferring the regulatory mechanism from the institution to the individual and the group. This means also an increase in the time span for results and a need to redefine effort as *programs* rather than as *pieces*. Supervision can't persist in the use of the clock, the desk, and paperwork. Supervision, as applied to professionals, means leadership.

Supervision has a new definition. Another side of this problem lies in the intellectual capacity of supervisors vs. professional staffs. The production foreman can see almost everything. He is either equal or superior in knowledge and authority to the production worker. By contrast, a professional often knows more than his "supervisor"— this is the reason why he was employed in the first place. Yet, the supervisor feels responsible for his "staff." He feels that he must demonstrate superiority by a greater personal knowledge of all technical problems. This is impossible in our present day world. It creates serious conflicts for supervision and produces insecurities which dig deeply into personality.

The professional needs intellectual freedom in an environment which is supportive. He needs a supervisor; he can't be cut free from all organizational moorings to drift about or bounce aimlessly at sea. The supervisor may be a catalyst, a bridge to higher management, a coach, a counselor, or even a critic. But, if the supervisor functions as a warden or turnkey, the professional resents rather than respects both the role and the person.

It's not simply a question of hard or soft supervision—sweet or bittersweet relationships; it's a question of creating a different concept of supervision. Here's the crux of the matter. The supervisor represents management. He has the power of life and death over the *ideas* of the men in his group. As the ideas become more important, these supervisory powers are intensified.

Cooperation assumes increased importance with size. Progress and organizational growth require harmony and happiness. The need for interpersonal co-operation is apparent if the organization is to avoid extreme personal conflicts and ultimate chaos. Yet, an over-emphasis on harmony obscures individuality. Thus harmony may smother healthy frictions which underlie change. Where progress is subordinate to harmony, co-operativeness may kill creation. The need for growth requires taking the risks and meeting the problems which come with disharmonious relationships.

Recent research has found that the groups which have been associated together for extended periods are less creative than the newer research teams. These studies also revealed that creativity diminishes in groups which have high identity, similar traits and interests and a homogeneous pattern. Although this is an oversimplification, it implies that harmony and accommodation produce high cooperation but low growth. The big organizations ordinarily avoid personal warfare, waste, and the bitterness which is produced by conflict. On the other hand, the "conflict of ideas" which sparks change and creates movement and progress is important. Obviously, a balance between conflict and cooperation is needed. Today's supervision has to learn what Douglas McGregor appropriately refers to as *the art of managing conflict.*

Management development

Indoctrination and imitation. The new generation of professionals and managers is being molded by the philosophies of existing executives. This provides continuity and conformity with past practices and traditions. In a real sense it is necessary in order to permit sufficient stability. Yet, the opportunity to experiment with new managerial methods cannot be denied. The organization must adapt to the new requirements of a rapidly growing economy. A spirit of change and progress needs breathing space. It needs an environment which encourages intellectually minded people. New managers, therefore, can't be poured into the same mold as managers who served the organization well in the past.

Promotions from within foster inbreeding. A promotion-from-within system links job security and company loyalty to opportunity and personal rewards. It is an "in-group" concept which has been developed with great effect and has produced a continuous system of personal development. It creates an inside market of talent and experience which is sheltered from competition and readily available as a resource to the company.

Yet this system is very difficult to maintain. It requires growth and expansion; a lead time adequate to train and develop people; financial resources sufficient to continuously reinvest in the long-term future value of people; a continuous reappraisal of the occupational mix to keep pace with market, scientific and technological changes; a relative balance in the age and service composition in all critical occupations without either heavy overconcentrations or vacuum areas; a free and open policy of competition, with strict limits on nepotism, favoritism and seniority; and above all the persistent ability to attract and retain outstanding people for a life's career. In the face of these requirements, the system may break down.

A further problem is that the professional's training and experience are contained within the four walls of the organization. This may mean a secure future for the individual, but not necessarily for the company.

Arch Patton recently discussed the relationship of inbreeding to executive compensation. Referring to higher paid industries, he notes: "As a group, they appear willing to reach 'outside' the company for executive talent rather than promote an inadequate man, and seniority usually carries less weight in promotional decisions. By contract, lower compensation industries have 100% promotions from within, emphasis on seniority, and job security." [1]

---

[1] Arch Patton, "What Is An Executive Worth?" *Harvard Business Review*, **March-April, 1961, pp. 68, 69.**

Company loyalty in a unilateral dimension. **Many of the profes-**sional's "outside" activities are viewed by the company as questionable, if not inimical to the goals of the enterprise. Naturally, managements are anxious that professional people devote themselves to company problems. They are jealous of the time, energy and even the ideological outlooks of key people. From a short-range point of view this attitude on the part of the company may be constructive. From a long-range point of view it weakens and lessens the professional's effectiveness. An individual plays many roles in life and has many loyalties. Loyalty to family, job and profession, though they appear to conflict, may reinforce rather than weaken each other.

Personnel policies

Manpower concepts must be redefined. The inroads of mass-production technology and the rise of labor organizations have focused our attention upon the wage earner. Today, managerial strategy continues to devote its primary attention to wage earners. Mention labor problems and labor costs and one usually thinks of the blue collar worker. Yet, wage earners are becoming a diminishing factor in American industry. This does not mean that production workers are not tremendously important. However, their relative importance has declined and will continue to decline in the future.

Automation and the rise in capital investment checked the growth of production workers in American manufacturing about ten years ago. Since then the demand for highly educated workers has increased over 60%. Current estimates indicate that the technical and professional sectors of the work force will be increasing at about 10% a year even though unemployment elsewhere in the work force remains a serious problem.

A pattern of homogeneity. In order to create industrial harmony, management has stressed equal treatment for all employees regardless of ability. Homogeneity has been accepted. It is easy to justify and, in most cases, has produced salutary results.

Yet heterogeneity is the spice needed to enliven an organization. When economic and psychic rewards are related to contributions, capacity and potential, employees are challenged and stimulated. When the organization loses its ability to differentiate, the result is apathy and the emergence of a phlegmatic approach.

High personal security systems immobilize the professional. **High** personal security, long tenure and life-time careers have been intertwined to weave the individual into an organizational web. While the organization seeks to build stability, it may be creating a lasting tenure among half-hearted men who have lost their sense of striving. Pensions, vacations, salary and other benefits are closely correlated to service and tend to reduce or eliminate job mobility. Personal security systems were built up in the belief that turnover is always a wasteful thing. But the absence of turnover means that an aging professional population remains in the organization. Employees are becoming more dependent, less agile, and too tolerant of their own limitations and the limitations in their work. Everything is biased toward a "don't rock the boat" attitude.

High mobility, particularly among the effective people, is clearly undesirable. But, *no mobility* among all of the people is even more undesirable. Just as the business operates in a competitive system in which it can move ahead or fall behind, so must the professional employee. The organization must keep the doors open for new people. It must also keep the exits open for its own professionals who can no longer apply themselves or who have drifted into dead ends without any clear way out. This need not mean discharge; it may merely mean reassignment. The firm should revalidate career management by applying the best in-service placement methods. Problem areas should be attacked quickly and directly in order to serve the interests of both the individual and the company.

Conclusion

The professional has come of age in America—and the professional age has become a reality in business. Modern organizations are striving for a successful working relationship with their professionals. New managerial systems are required to motivate professionals and, at the same time, further the goals of the enterprise and the total society. The problems and prospects are equally great. Those organizations who face the problems and divest themselves of their prejudices and outdated beliefs have the best chance for success.

Questions

1. How do professional employees differ from other employees in terms of their motivation?
2. What changes in the traditional concepts of supervision are necessitated by the growth in the proportion of professional employees who comprise an organization?
3. Is more group effort or more individualism required of professional employees than of other employees?
4. What conflicts, if any, may develop between the goals of the professional employee and those of his company?
5. Should the professional employee be extended the same security provisions as those that are granted to operative employees?

44. THE PERSONNEL MANAGER FOR INTERNATIONAL OPERATIONS *

G. M. Oxley

> Why pay an overseas premium for living in Paris? I'd like to
> live there myself!—V.P. *for Operations.*
> What—a cost-of-living bonus in Guatemala City? What for—to
> pay all those servants?—*Controller.*

As he attempts to formulate policies for foreign operations, the
personnel manager of the company that has just established a new
unit overseas fields such ticklish questions as these from his own
management every day. Nor do his troubles end there. An entirely
different set of questions rains down on his defenseless head from the
people being transferred or recruited to work abroad:

> Will you keep us supplied with baby food in Colombo?
> You mean to say you pay only a 15 percent premium for the
> sacrifice of leaving the United States?
> My daughter could live at home while she attends college—will
> you bring her back to the States and pay her living expenses?

The questions continue in their endless variety:

> Will you pay my way back to see my own doctor, if necessary?
> Will you move my new outboard cruiser?
> Will you move my mother-in-law to Buenos Aires with us? (This
> questioner, though, may secretly be hoping that the answer here will
> be a resounding "No!")

To the company newly beset with the problems of foreign
exchange and foreign taxes, the special problems of staffing an overseas unit come as an additional burden. And the books and services
available from the company library offer the personnel man little
in the way of support or solace. While most of the new problems
seemingly fit familiar categories, the 5,000 miles between the head
office and the new unit somehow add a touch of pathos to the plight
of the overseas employee. All of a sudden, the company's well-settled
domestic personnel policies are thrown out of kilter.

At this point in the planning for new operations abroad, several
alternatives are available to the company. It can:

* From *Personnel,* Vol. 38, No. 6 (November-December, 1961), pp. 52-58.
Reprinted with permission.

1. Hire a consultant familiar with the policies of experienced overseas companies.
2. Follow the familiar routine of surveying other companies to see how they handle the same problems.
3. Hire an additional personnel man with overseas experience.
4. Set about analyzing its own particular problems in an objective fashion.

The best cure is probably some combination of these alternatives. In any case, if more than one overseas unit of any size is being set up, the personnel staff will need a man to handle the particular problems of foreign and expatriate personnel. He can well be transferred from a domestic job. There are obvious advantages in having a man who is well grounded in the company's domestic policies, since these are the foundation on which its overseas policies will be built.

Let us assume that an experienced personnel man who is familiar with company policy is chosen to take charge of personnel matters for the international operation. His first task will be to school himself in the differences between his former domestic activities and what is now required of him in the international sphere. He must then begin to modify his regular procedures in light of those differences.

Differences between domestic and overseas operations

There are at least four major ways in which overseas operations differ from those at home. These four factors are generally present in foreign operations of any type, and each has a significant impact on personnel administration:

1. *Communications are more difficult.* It may be 5,000 miles from the head office to the first overseas unit. Later, a network of overseas operations extending throughout the world's continents, time zones, climates, and cultures may be built up. But long before that point is reached, communications will have become entangled in at least one foreign language.

2. *Social Security legislation is developed far beyond our own laws in many parts of the world.* From the pension rights of widows in France to the milk allowance for infants in Bolivia, nearly every type of employee benefit has been thought of and tried somewhere. In some countries, the benefits required by law amount to from 60 to 80 per cent of payroll. In others, such benefits and costs are either negligible or nonexistent.

3. *Cultural differences cause some surprising problems the first time around the course.* Complexion in Peru, religion in the Near East, social status elsewhere—each of these may impose specific limitations on the design of an organization. Then there is the special problem of "culture shock" for the families sent abroad from the United States. ("Culture shock" is the state of confusion and tension that often arises when an American discovers that many of his normal responses are not appropriate in a foreign culture.)

4. *Salary scales and benefit programs favor American employees over foreign country nationals.* This gives rise to morale problems when employees in both categories are working on the same or similar jobs.

Additional differences between domestic and overseas operations may, of course, arise from special conditions existing in the foreign country in question. Once the personnel man has established these various points of difference, how should he proceed?

His first reaction is likely to be to embark on the task of writing a new set of policies for the overseas unit or units. Extreme care must be exercised, however, when this impulse strikes. In Guatemala, for example, pensions for employees are not required by law. But in Peru, an employee who has worked 35 years for the same company is legally entitled to retire on full salary for the rest of his life. If the company is operating in Peru, or likely at some future date to be operating there, it had better not establish a blanket policy to the effect that no matter where they are located expatriate employees will receive the benefits of the company's domestic pension plan. To do so would require double funding of retirement provisions for expatriates in Peru. Some way of dealing with this requirement must be devised therefore, before any general policy on pensions for overseas employees can be laid down.

In fact, it is better not to try to formulate general policies until the company is thoroughly *au fait* with conditions in overseas locations. Even then, any statement of policy should be limited to specific countries.

It may be legally impossible, for instance, to ship an employee's automobile to Chile or to assume part of his income tax in Trinidad—practices that may be company policy elsewhere. On the other hand, special conditions in one area may make it advisable for the company to depart from its general policy to the extent, say, of providing the

employee with a house. Management must retain a greater degree
of flexibility in its overseas policies than is necessary at home.

Recruitment and selection

Recruiting people for overseas jobs presents no problems—at all
events, to the extent that there is never any dearth of applicants.
Picking the right candidate or candidates is, however, an unusually
difficult task.

As the personnel man well knows, it is often hard enough to
select the right candidate for a specific job at home. Now, however,
the problem is to find one who can perform on the job while he and
his family are adjusting to life in Accra or Zaragoza. This particular
avenue of selection is far from being a well-trodden path. There are
no tests that have proved satisfactory for this purpose as yet.

Nevertheless, there are certain accepted minimal standards: The
employee (and his family) must have "left home" psychologically.
To adjust to a new culture, he must have an inquiring mind; he
should be interested in the way things are done in other cultures and
not be predisposed to assume that customs which are different from
those at home are unenlightened or stupid. For most posts he should
have an aptitude for languages. For any distant post he must have
some degree of independence and a willingness to assume responsibility that may not be required of the employee who is buttressed
by the ample support normally available in the home office. In
addition to all these qualities, he must possess excellent health and
outstanding competence in his field.

Some companies minimize the risk of making mistakes in overseas selection by refusing to assign anyone abroad until he has
worked in the domestic operation long enough to be well known to
management. Others retain consultants to conduct depth interviews
and psychological tests. Companies with long-standing overseas
operations tend to rely more, however, upon multiple interviews conducted by men who have served where the job is located. This has
the double advantage of permitting the applicant to talk about the
potential assignment with people who have actually lived in the
country in question, and at the same time enabling the interviewers
to size up the applicant's personality in the light of their knowledge
of the kind of people who have adapted well to life in the location
under consideration.

Orientation

Orientation both to the new job and to the new location is important for the same two reasons, communications and cultural adjustment. The cost of sending the wrong man or one who is inadequately prepared for what he will face abroad is very high. The expense of moving a man, with his family and car, may, for example, run to between $30,000 and $35,000. An outlay of this magnitude justifies extraordinary measures in selecting and preparing employees, whether they be recruits or old company hands, for duty abroad.

Ideally, orientation would include a visit by the prospective employee and his wife to the area in which they are to live and work. A few companies do, in fact, follow this practice. Most, however, consider it too expensive—at all events, for candidates who are being hired from the outside. When a foreign transfer is being considered for an employee of proven caliber, a preliminary visit is easier to justify.

If such trips are not provided, some way must be found to acquaint the employee with the conditions he will face. He must know something of the host country—its people, customs, and traditions. He should be prepared for both the worst and the best he will find on the job and in his new home. He must be sent out prepared to be a good representative of his company and his country.

Much of the information he needs is available, of course, in any public library. Both the employee and his wife should be encouraged to talk with people who know the area. In addition, a number of universities, especially the American University and Syracuse, now offer orientation courses for Americans being posted overseas.

In short, the importance of proper selection and orientation can hardly be overemphasized—though perhaps the Foreign Secretary of the American Baptist Convention did carry matters a shade too far when he said in a recent speech, "Hereafter only seasoned missionaries will be sent to cannibal territories."

Compensation and benefits

In establishing compensation and benefit programs the company must draw a clear distinction between national employees, that is, citizens of the country in which the operation is carried on, and expatriates.

Nationals hired in the area of the foreign operation must, of course, be treated in accordance with the prevailing conditions in the labor market in question. They obviously cannot be hired at lower than going rates; nor can the company pay much higher rates or provide benefits noticeably better than are usual in the location. To do so would disrupt the labor market and incur the enmity of both local businessmen and other foreign operators.

Expatriate employees present far fancier problems. It is generally accepted among companies engaged in international operations that you do have to pay a premium to persuade an employee to move, say, from Akron, Ohio, to Paris. And you also have to pay a cost-of-living bonus if the living expenses in the overseas location are higher than the cost of living at your head office.

Practices are not uniform by any means, but there is a general pattern for the pay and fringe benefits of expatriates. Base pay should equal pay for a similar job at home. An overseas premium of from 10 to 25 per cent of the base pay is the only extra pay really needed to compensate for the inconvenience of giving up familiar surroundings, American schools, American doctors, and ease of access to relatives. The other extensive benefits that complete the overseas package are intended and computed to keep the employee on an even keel financially throughout his foreign assignment.

Typically, these additional fringes may include any or all of the following: an adjustable cost-of-living allowance; a housing allowance if housing is scarce or expensive or if the company wants its representative to live in a better house than he normally would have at home; educational benefits for the employee's children, such as the cost of a private school abroad or of travel back to the United States for attendance at college; longer vacations to give the employee time to get back to the United States (though jet travel is causing some rethinking on this one); and increasingly, a system of tax equalization whereby the employee does not have to pay higher income taxes than he would on the same salary at home.

Needless to say, the payment of such lavish benefits to expatriate personnel does not endear the company to the nationals hired locally, who, of course, receive nothing more than the local scale of pay. For this reason, some companies prefer to cut out most of the fringes and instead pay a flat salary to their expatriate personnel. The total amount paid will, of course, take into account the expenses the extras are intended to cover. Part of this total may be deposited to the employee's account at home.

While this device works well in smoothing the relations between national and expatriate employees, it creates other problems of its own. The payment of a flat salary that has been calculated to include an overseas premium and the rest can cause no end of trouble when the company wants to transfer a man back to the head office from an overseas post. The employee can't make much of a case for retaining his overseas premium when he is transferred back to Chicago. But if the extras have all been included in a single salary figure, he can make a tremendous fuss about being transferred to Chicago at a cut in salary—and after all that valuable overseas experience!

On balance, the better system seems to be to pay the long list of premiums and benefits while keeping an appropriate stateside base salary for the position. Since it is extremely expensive to pay expatriate personnel on either basis, the remedy is to train nationals and to replace expatriates, wherever feasible, as quickly as possible.

Training and management development

In the long run, the real profit potential in personnel administration in the international sphere lies in the training and development of employees hired locally, especially if the operation is located in one of the less-developed countries. Here the personnel man should project his labor force requirements for some years ahead and keep management constantly aware of the importance of having specific plans for the replacement of all personnel except essential expatriates. (The company may want to keep some key financial or technical jobs in the hands of United States employees, at least for the time being.)

Planning for the eventual takeover will, of course, necessitate the use of all the familiar elements of a systematic development program —organization charts, key man inventories and their periodic review, a performance appraisal system, and so on. Specific plans for the training and development of the nationals who are to be relied upon as replacements must also be drawn up.

To be effective, these techniques need not, at the outset, be highly formalized. Where there are only a few employees in one or two foreign locations that are frequently visited by someone from the home office, the job can quite well be done on a fairly informal basis. Later on, as the overseas staff expands, more systematic steps must be taken to insure that the financial man in Concepción, say, is not forgotten.

For the most part, the company wishing to develop managerial skills among its foreign nationals must expect to have to do most of the training within its own organization. However, outside facilities are becoming increasingly available. The American Management Association now has centers in Latin America and Europe. Several American universities run summer programs on other continents. Consulting firms are running seminars abroad. Finally, a number of foreign organizations dedicated to the advancement of management now offer short courses for middle and top management in their own countries.

Toward better management abroad

Educating a Brazilian or a Nigerian in the principles and practices of American management can, admittedly, be a costly project. Nevertheless, this practice offers the most practical solution to the problem of staffing a foreign operation. In any case, the outlay involved must be weighed against the cost of sending an American and his family to the area—and, in a high percentage of cases, the further cost of bringing them home and replacing them with another American family. Assuming that this amounts to something in the neighborhood of $30,000 per family, a company obviously can spend substantial sums on improving the managerial and technical skills of its foreign employees and still save money. Further, it has the satisfaction of knowing that, in so doing, it is also extending the international usefulness of its operations and serving the ends of the free world by improving the managerial effectiveness of the nationals of the countries in which it operates.

Questions

1. What departures from its personnel policies and practices may a company have to make for those personnel who are employed in a foreign country?
2. What uniform personnel policies are difficult to maintain when company branches are opened in a foreign country?
3. What added considerations must be taken into account in the selection of employees for jobs located in a foreign country?
4. What special fringe benefits may be provided for employees in a foreign assignment?
5. What are the relative merits of training the nationals of a foreign country to assume company management positions in a foreign country as opposed to sending its employees abroad to staff them?

45. PSYCHOLOGICAL ASPECTS OF WOMEN IN INDUSTRY *

B. von Haller Gilmer

Summary

The literature centered around the woman worker, the woman executive, and the professional woman in industry is fraught with conflicting opinions, pronounced prejudices, and almost a "mythology." Much has been written on the subject of women in industry and apparently this area is receiving attention of personnel people as never before. Our expanding economy is providing the impetus. This article attempts to pull together what has been written in journals, magazines, books, and government pamphlets about women's jobs, abilities, attitudes, interests, and productivity in industry. There is little "scientific evidence" to guide the practical decisions of personnel people. Here we hope to give a brief picture of what is known about the changing place of women in industry.

Introduction

With the ever expanding American economy, women are increasingly playing more significant roles as workers, as managers, and professionally. Almost one-third of the total labor force in our country is made up of women. There were 50 per cent more women at work in 1956 than in 1940, and working wives outnumbered single working girls more than two to one. In any good business year, women comprise about 90 per cent of the total labor reserve (18, 32, 33).[1] One study commission predicts that by 1975 the labor force will total about 90 million persons. Of necessity about half of the growth will have to be made up of women, largely from the married group in the 35-54 year age bracket. The percentage of single women now working is said to be near saturation (2, 23, 24).

* From *Personnel Psychology*, Vol. 10, No. 4 (Winter, 1957), pp. 439-452. Reprinted with permission.

[1] Numbers in parentheses refer to articles listed in the bibliography at the end of the article.

Women are now doing jobs once thought to be exclusively **for** men, both at the worker and at the professional level, yet they **are** not fully "accepted" in industry (31). Women workers have, in part, been responsible for many changes made in production equipment design and in the introduction of new safety methods. Women have caused changes in industrial training methods and made some of our theorizing on absenteeism obsolete (17). They have broken through barriers of industrial prejudices and have helped change the buying habits of a nation.

In this article, we shall trace briefly the history of the development of women's occupations, describe some psychological problems peculiar to the woman worker and manager, and try to give the reader a picture of where women are finding their place within the modern industrial environment. There is some risk in trying to give the "total picture" of women in industry, since so much has been written about the subject with so little "scientific evidence" to back expressed opinions. In this summary, the author will attempt to pull together what has been written in hundreds of articles, a few books, and from quantities of government statistics, some of those things he believes will be of interest to personnel men. The reader should be aware that this summary is in itself a highly subjective interpretation of what has been written about women's abilities, attitudes, interests, and productivity in industry.

Historical changes

The rapid growth of women in industry has been contemporaneous with the growth of our mass-production economy, with the vast strides made in marketing, no small part of which has come about through a better understanding of human motivations. The broadening of educational opportunities for women and the accompanying changes in customs and modes of living have been important in the growth of the numbers of women workers. The social revolution at the turn of the century which brought the young single woman into the office and gave her some economic independence created a host of new industries—the garment industry, beauty shops, women's magazines (33).

The industrial expansion in manufacturing, construction, and transportation industries was followed by growth of commerce, trade, and service industries. But the dramatic appearance during World War II of Rosie the Riveter, the woman welder, truck driver, and lathe operator into occupations formerly unusual for women directed attention anew to the extent of the abilities of the woman worker. Mechanical power has made difference in strength between the sexes less important in doing many jobs. For example, the use of fork trucks allows women to do much of the heavy lifting type of work once performed solely by men. In the three years following Pearl Harbor, over six million women entered the labor force for the first time (33).

Before World War II, it was generally accepted that "skirts were bad luck" in steel mills, this was the province of men. But by the height of the war, women were performing every job in ore mines, steel mills, and ship yards formerly done by men except those requiring heavy physical exertion or calling for many years of training and experience. During the year 1944, for example, about 40,000 of the total of 315,000 employees of one large steel corporation were women. Approximately 15,000 of these were in office occupations and 25,000 were working directly in war production. These women came from all walks of life—housewives, saleswomen, stenographers, teachers, musicians. One subsidiary of this large steel corporation listed 275 different jobs filled by women (9).

Women were found to be especially valuable where deft hands were needed. By "conveyerizing" operations one plant was able to increase its women employees to 48% of the total. Overhead cranes and electrically driven "dinkies" carried materials from department to department, thus obviating the need of lifting heavy material. Of the 153 crane operators in this plant, 79 were women. In the chemical laboratory of this same plant, 80 per cent of the personnel were women who had not gone beyond elementary chemistry, taken either in high school or college. They were given on-the-job training (9).

In a big sense women in steel mills broke tradition, gave to their sex a power status never before experienced in heavy industry. Their presence introduced other changes, ranging from installation of modern sanitary facilities to the employment of women counselors to guide new employees into the strange world of the steel mill.

In the half century period from 1910, women workers showed significant changes in terms of the socio-economic groups to which they were attached. While only about a quarter of all women workers were nonmanual workers in 1910, the proportion has risen to about twice this number at the present time. The number of women in non-agricultural work has increased nearly 100 per cent in the past half century. In part this increase has been due to changes in cultural attitudes as well as to economic influences. The breakup of the old middle-class pattern of "respectability," in which the wife does not work if her husband can afford to keep her home, has spread through society. There appears to be a "feeling of accomplishment" need on the part of the woman being invoked. In one survey 74% of working women said they would continue to work even if they inherited enough money to live comfortably. Work apparently fills a deep social need (2).

For many years, domestic service remained the largest single occupation for women workers. The rise in new mass-production industries and the vast technological changes taking place in more recent years have seen clerical positions and machine operators change this picture (38).

At the professional level teaching and nursing are still high, as always, for women although business, engineering, and the sciences are gaining in proportion as woman's status changes (32).

Various factors have affected a change in women's occupations. The change-over from an agricultural to an industrial economy expanded the need for a new labor supply which became available as women became less tied down with household duties (33).

The rise of our highly industrialized economy has been accompanied by social changes. During pioneer days most women directed their efforts in production and service for the family. Later, with invention, spinning, weaving, clothing manufacturing, laundering and many personal services were taken over commercially. As the "luxuries" of living became more and more "necessities," there was an increasing need on the part of the women of the family to help with the family budget. This raised considerably the status position of both the part- and full-time woman worker. Gradually women were offered more extensive opportunities to obtain education and specialized training. These changes have been coming about slowly and are still in process. Some companies claim that they put girls into jobs because of manpower shortage, to find later that special characteristics of women make them better suited to some tasks than men. One should use caution, however, in building up classifications of sex differences in such an informal manner. Whereas there are some data to substantiate the hypothesis that women have more finger dexterity than men, for certain tasks, it certainly has not been scientifically established that women have better depth and color perception, as has been claimed from the experience of one manufacturer (2).

With increases for public service and welfare, new opportunities appeared for women in such areas as social work and government offices. With little or no historical competition from men, these joined teaching and nursing as "women's work." Technology added to the picture with such inventions as the typewriter and telephone giving new kinds of jobs which went mostly to women. As automation increased, more new places were found for women. The traditions of long apprenticeships and prejudices against women in the craftsmen's occupations began to give way as machines began to replace the necessities for physical strength on the job. The attitudes on the part of the public and of employers, that certain types of work are not appropriate for women, have been changing gradually.

Some attitude differences

Of the several questionnaire type studies reported in the literature comparing men and women in job satisfaction, some indicate that women are more satisfied than men, others show the reverse, while still others show no differences (3, 4, 5, 6, 7, 11, 14, 20, 25, 28). On the more qualitative side, women seem to be more verbal in expressing themselves, either by written comments or in interviews, about such things as cleanliness of working conditions, pleasantness of social relationships on the job, and how their supervisors treat them. Women verbalize loyalty more than men, but show less interest in pay, benefit programs, and opportunities for advancement (12). The author had the opportunity recently to make a good comparison between the attitudes of men and women working together on the same types of jobs in a company employing about equal numbers of each sex. In response to a question of what do you "like least" about your job, two-thirds of the men mentioned low pay, but very few women mentioned money, in spite of the fact that their rate of pay was below that of the men. On an item concerned with cafeteria conditions, 600 women made a specific complaint which only two men mentioned. Reliable differences between men and women in their questionnaire responses were found in areas involving supervision and cleanliness in working conditions. The women were more sensitive than men. On questions involving a proposed installation of automatic labor saving machines, the men expressed fear of losing their jobs, but the women were apparently disinterested in the problem.

The employed woman who has to divide her energies between the working world and her traditional role as a woman brings about adjustment problems peculiar to the female. The married woman has both home and job responsibilities somewhat different from her male counterpart. The social and psychological pressures of the single woman toward marriage complicate her attitudes toward her job and her associates (25, 34).

Age differentials

There are changes in job attitudes with changing age in both men and women. In general, morale is high among young workers, it decreases during the first few years of employment, reaching a low point in the late twenties and early thirties. Studies indicate job morale climbs steadily from this low point until "middle-age revolt" sets in during the late forties (25, 36).

Women differ from men in their original attitudes toward work. Most young women today take a job until marriage or a few years after. The married women are most likely to leave the labor force during the time their small children require care. Many women workers return to jobs when their children are partly grown and no longer need constant attention. Because of the cycle, a larger proportion are in the labor force at the ages of 20 to 24 years than in older groups. The proportion of women in the labor force declines in age range of 25 to 34 years and increases again around 35 (38).

Statistical surveys show there is an increasing number of married women going into industry. Part-time work is more likely to be sought by women than men, since women frequently need to combine a paid job with household cares. Data show that 60% of all part-time workers are women, most of them married and over 35 years of age. They usually do the same types of work as full-time employees. Apparently, part-time work has resulted from the normal needs of management and is not merely a by-product of full employment. Women work part-time because of a need to increase or supplement income, or to have outside interests. Management uses them during busy periods, for relief schedules, or for temporary peak loads (11, 38).

Some female influences

Some of the initial work of "human engineering" in industry—fitting the machine or job to the worker—began with the female. Women being shorter than men had to use platforms when standing at machines. With the large influx of women into industry during

World War II many plant changes were brought about, good for men as well as women. More effort was made to substitute levers and pulleys for muscles. Rest rooms were modified and lunch rooms were improved. More safety practices were introduced. It has even become fashionable for the woman worker to dress to suit the job (9, 36).

Facts and opinions

A great deal has been written about the physical limitations of women for various jobs (1, 26, 27). For example, a Soviet Russia commission reports an investigation which revealed that almost three-fourths of the women required to do heavy lifting in such industries as coal and steel had menstrual troubles as compared with about half that number having similar troubles when engaged in lighter work. It has been generally assumed that women are more susceptible to fatigue than men. One finds statements that overtime work causes more accidents among women than men and that absenteeism among women is much higher, by as much as 100%, says one report of the National Association of Manufacturers (22). Such statements are often made without citation of valid statistical data, and one should caution in generalizing from these sources. Statements can be found that conclude that women are more accident-prone than men. Other writers claim the reverse. When specific studies are considered, the evidence points in the direction that in the areas of safety, absenteeism, and general adjustment to the job situation, factors other than sex differences often are the more important variables in human behavior. Those writers who maintain that woman's psychic dependence on man, and the feeling of superiority engendered by male domination which causes her to be less successful in the industrial world might better be thought of as opinions (8, 15, 16, 17, 27).

It is difficult to separate facts from opinions on what has been written about women workers. To say, as have several writers, that women are not as good long-term investments as men is giving way to overgeneralization. In some spots they have been shown to be better investments, for example in some kinds of clerical positions. To say that a smaller proportion of women in manufacturing qualify for upgrading, or advancement to supervisory jobs, than men may be true. But what are the criteria used here for upgrading or advancement? Maybe we have placed the woman in such a stereotyped role she cannot meet our standards for promotion (8, 13, 27).

Women's jobs

About two-thirds of all women employed in industry (21,000,000) are either in manufacturing, retail trade, or personal services. The largest numbers are employed in clerical and operative jobs, with only a few in executive positions. Somewhere around one-fourth of all women workers are employed in factories, primarily those manufacturing apparel, textiles, or foods. About one-fourth of the workers in the executive branch of the Federal Government are women (19, 36, 38).

There are still many prejudices and traditional discriminations against women in the factory type jobs, but enough "traditions" have been broken to show that changes can be made. Even such small things as changing physical working conditions and inducing schedules permitting the woman time to get her housework done can reduce absenteeism even below the level of men. In the more professional types of jobs (accounting, science, engineering, mathematics), once thought to be within the exclusive province of man, women are being better accepted in many quarters. Some writers feel that much of our manpower shortages of scientists and technologists can be lessened by selecting and training more women (32, 39).

Although women are going into many "men's" professions, the proportions are still small. Most female college graduates who work go into traditionally "women's jobs" where, for example, women constitute about 90% of all librarians, 60% of all welfare workers, and 80% of all public school teachers (36).

At the worker level, women have a hard time "fitting in" in some of the skilled trades. Although this may be due in small measure to lack of training facilities, mostly it is due to having to buck "tradition" and union politics," even at times of peak employment. For example, studies have shown that among tool and die makers two out of three men entered the trade via apprenticeship; among molders 57% entered this way. During the peak employment of the middle 50's there were only nine apprentices for every 100 journeymen tool and die makers employed in the metal working industries. Women apprentices in many trades are unheard of. In another way women have not quite fitted into the union picture. Whereas, in emotional situations like strikes, women may be aggressive and courageous, they take little interest in the day-to-day business routine of the union. They are apathetic to paying dues and fighting for fringe benefits. Some union leaders have expressed concern about the possible dangers to unionism in this feminine attitude, and well they might (31).

It apparently takes a long time to establish tradition within the higher level positions in industry favorable to the woman. In the home offices of insurance companies, women hold only about 20 per cent of the supervisory positions, and in banks the figure is even less. Both of these industries employ large proportions of women; two-thirds of all insurance company employees are women as are about one-half in banks (2, 32). Only in department stores does one find approximately an even distribution among women and men in the so-called higher level positions. Here women make up about two-thirds of all employees.

Women officers in industry run no more than 4%. Only a handful hold board directorships. In production operations in manufacturing, few women are found above the forelady level (2, 15). Aside from "prejudice," education and training have been cited as big reasons why women do not advance. One writer summed the problem up well by pointing out that the young woman does not take specialized training because she fears it will be wasted in a hostile market, and she has little chance to advance because she lacks training. This "circular dilemma" must surely be abated if our economy is to continue along its predicted course (39). The women in middle-management brackets with no more than a high school education are usually older than the general labor market and more of them are single. Women in personnel work, training, publishing business, job testing, social service, science and engineering are usually college graduates.

The opportunities for women at the administrative level are increasing in such positions as research analysts in banks and insurance companies, in merchandising, public relations, advertising and personnel work. However, very few women in any field occupy the top executive jobs. One business magazine estimates that not over 5,000 women can be found among the one-quarter million "real" executives (2, 15). A market analysis of women holding positions of responsibility in industry and commerce indicated that the way women *behave* on the job, rather than the way they *perform* the technical operations of their position, is a chief determinant of their acceptance as administrators (2, 10, 13). There is apparently the widespread belief that women are "too emotional," "too personal" to hold down supervisory jobs or executive positions. Most evidence, however, that seems to point in this direction is more subjective than objective.

Conclusions

Over all it is perhaps safe to say that there is no scientific proof that women differ from men greatly in most abilities, save where physical strength is a factor. In terms of sex differences in productivity, studies show that there are more important variables in operation than sex differences (12). What then of "attitudes," "preconceptions," "feelings," about women in industry?

There have been studies which show differences in attitude of men and women which affected production. For example, during the last war, research indicated that eye-strain could be reduced by blue-green lighting. Such lighting was installed in one war plant. The result was that the output of the male workers increased. There were many comments about less eye-strain from the men. Their attitude was very much in favor of the new lighting. But with the women employees, it was quite different. Output fell off, absenteeism hit its highest peak. Their motivation for production was gone. Why? Because the women felt that the new type of lighting made them look ghastly, which, in fact, it did (21).

Those studies which measure interests give evidence that there are differences between the sexes (29). This may well be related to our thinking that there is a "woman's world" and a "man's world." However, industrial experience during and following World War II indicates that these worlds may not be too far apart.

There is enough evidence to conclude that attitudes of women, and about women, can and do change. It may well be in our expanding economy it is the wise personnel man who takes a hard look to see just where he might better profit by employing women even though men may be available for the job. It may well be that the woman worker, the woman executive, and professional woman holds the key to our expanding economy.

Questions

1. To what principal factors can you attribute the significant rise in the number of women employed within industry?
2. What principal human needs does employment help to satisfy for many women?
3. What behavioral differences, if any, has research revealed to exist between men and women employees? What is the possible implication of these differences for the manager who employs or contemplates employing women in production jobs?

4. Some women claim that they would rather work for men supervisors than for women supervisors. What factors might account for this attitude?

5. If attitude rather than performance is the basic difficulty encountered in the employment of women, what approach should management follow in the supervision of them?

6. Should management provide any modification in its personnel policies and practices if it engages in the employment of women? If so, to what degree?

Bibliography

1. BAETJER, A. M. *Women in Industry: Their Health and Efficiency.* Phila.: W. B. Saunders, 1946. Pp. 344.

2. BELL, D. Women and Business: II. The Great Back-to-Work Movement. *Fortune,* 1956, July.

3. BENGE, E. J. How to Learn What Workers Think of Job and Boss. *Fact. Magmt. Mainten.,* 1944, 102 (5), 101-104.

4. BLOOD, W., HARWOOD, J., and VERNON, H. M. Discussion on Effects of Wartime Industrial Conditions on Mental Health. *Proc. Roy. Soc. Med.,* 1942, 35, 693-698.

5. CHASE, F. S. Factors for Satisfaction in Teaching. *Phi Delta Kappan,* 1951, 33, 127-132.

6. COLE, R. J. A Survey of Employee Attitudes. *Publ. Opin. Quart.,* 1940, 4, 497-506.

7. DAVIS, N. Some Psychological Effects on Women Workers of Payment by Industrial Bonus Method. *Occupational Psychol.,* 1944, 18, 53-62.

8. DEUTSCH, H. *The Psychology of Women.* New York: Grune & Stratton, 1944. Pp. 393.

9. FISHER, D. A. *Steel in the War.* New York: United States Steel Corp., 1946, 1-164.

10. FULLER, F. M., and BATCHELDER, M. B. Opportunities for Women at the Administrative Level. *Harvard Bus. Rev.,* 1953, 31(1), 111-128.

11. GADEL, M. S. Productivity and Satisfaction of Full and Part-time Female Employees. *Personnel Psychol.,* 1953, 6, 327-342.

12. GARDNER, B. B., and MOORE, D. G. *Human Relations in Industry.* Homewood, Ill.: R. D. Irwin (3rd ed.), 1955. Pp. 427.

13. GREEN, V. Women's Place in Management. *Amer. Gas Assoc. Proc.,* 1952, 178-184.

14. HABBE, S. Job Attitudes of Life Insurance Agents. *Jour. Appl. Psychol.,* 1947, 31, 111-128.

15. HAMILL, K. Women and Business: I. Women as Bosses. *Fortune,* 1956, June.

16. Industrial Research Board. Physique of Women in Industry. *Brit. Med. Jour.,* 1927, Feb. 5. P. 250.

17. KAY, E. An Experimental Study of Some Methodological and Psychological Aspects of Industrial Absenteeism. Unpublished dissertation. Carnegie Institute of Technology, 1956.

18. KEHOE, K. Woman's Place in Tomorrow's Workforce. *Amer. Mgm. Assoc.,* Personnel Series No. 165, 1955, 24-26.

19. KINKER, H. R. Women in Industry. Bibliography. *Industrial Arts & Voc. Edu.*, 1952, 41, 189-192.

20. LIVINGSTONE, E. Attitudes of Women Operatives to Promotion. *Occupational Psychol.*, 1953, Oct., 191-199.

21. MCGREGOR, D., and KNICKERBOCKER, I. Industrial Relations and National Defense: A Challenge to Management. *Personnel*, 1941, 18, 49-63.

22. National Assoc. Mfg. *Labor Relations Bulletin*, No. 41, 1942, May. P. 6.

23. National Manpower Council. *Improving the Work Skills of the Nation.* New York: Columbia Univ. Press, 1953, 1-203.

24. National Manpower Council. *Womanpower.* New York: Columbia Univ. Press, 1957. Pp. 371

25. Psychological Service of Pittsburgh. Job Attitudes: Review of research and opinion. Report No. 1. The Prevalence of Job Dissatisfaction. 1955, April, 1-67.

26. Russia: Medical Aspects of Women in Industry. *Jour. Akush. i. Zhensk. Boliez.* 1932, Vol. 43. (Abstract reference, original not seen.)

27. SCHEINFELD, A. *Women and Men.* New York: Harcourt, Brace, 1944. Pp. 453.

28. STOCKFORD, L. O., and KUNZE, K. R. Psychology and the Pay Check. *Personnel*, 1950, 27, 129-143.

29. STRONG, E. K. *Vocational Interests of Men and Women.* Stanford Univ. Press, 1943. Pp. 746.

30. SUPER, D. E. *Appraising Vocational Fitness by Means of Psychological Tests.* New York: Harper, 1949. Pp. 727.

31. U. S. Dept. of Labor: Bureau of Labor Statistics. Fact Book on Manpower. 1954, Sept., 1-88.

32. U. S. Dept. of Labor: Women's Bureau. Women in Higher Level Positions. Bulletin No. 236, 1950, 1-86.

33. U. S. Dept. of Labor: Women's Bureau. Women's Occupations Through Seven Decades. Bulletin No. 218, 1951, 1-260.

34. U. S. Dept. of Labor: Women's Bureau. Women Workers and Their Dependents. Bulletin No. 239, 1952, 1-117.

35. U. S. Dept. of Labor: Women's Bureau. Toward Better Working Conditions for Women. Bulletin No. 252, 1953, 1-71.

36. U. S. Dept. of Labor: Women's Bureau. 1954 Handbook on Women Workers. Bulletin No. 255, 1954, 1-75.

37. U. S. Dept. of Labor: Women's Bureau. Changes in Women's Occupations 1940-1950. Bulletin No. 253, 1955, 1-104.

38. U. S. Dept. of Labor: Statistical Branch. Women as Workers—a statistical guide. [1955] 1-111.

39. WOLFLE, D. L. *Commission on Human Resources and Advanced Training.* New York: Harper, 1954. Pp. 332.

40. ZAPOLEON, M. W. Working Girl. Bibliography. *Personnel & Guidance Jour.*, 1953, 32, 68-71.

46. EMPLOYEE PARTICIPATION IN A PROGRAM OF INDUSTRIAL CHANGE *

J. R. P. French, Jr., I. C. Ross,
S. Kirby, J. R. Nelson, and P. Smyth

Several years ago the management of a well-known men's apparel manufacturing company decided to modernize its production methods. In the past, programs to improve work methods had often provoked so much trouble in management-employee relations that the savings hoped for were largely offset by the costs of conflict. On the other hand, several small changes had been successfully introduced by having the employees participate in their design.[1] However, the modernization program to be reported here differed from these earlier innovations in that it entailed much more extensive change than anything that had been attempted with employee participation in the past. Furthermore, the general lines along which the methods changes were to take place had already been developed by the company's engineering consultants.

Management was aware that the attitudes and feelings of the workers toward the change were a matter of prime concern. It therefore decided to encourage their participation in the change process as much as possible within the limitations of the situation. This article will describe how management went about doing this and present some tangible evidence of the success with which the extended series of changes was carried out. Since few instances of successful plant-wide modifications have been reported in the literature, this account may be helpful to companies contemplating similar far-reaching changes in their present operations.

The changes were scheduled to take place in three of the company's plants, each producing similar garments. These plants are located close enough to each other to be effectively run by one management team. In these plants about 75 per cent of the production

* From *Personnel*, Vol. 35, No. 3 (November-December, 1958), pp. 16-29. Reprinted with permission.

[1] For the story of these earlier changes, see L. Coch and J. R. P. French, Jr., "Overcoming Resistance to Change," *Human Relations*, Vol. 1, No. 4 (1948), pp. 512-532. Reprinted in D. Cartwright and A. Zander (Eds.), *Group Dynamics: Research and Theory*, Row, Peterson, Evanston, Ill., 1953.

workers are women, highly skilled at their jobs. Two of the plants employ about 150 workers each and the third employs about 500. Wages are based on "production units," i.e., the worker is paid according to the number of units produced. While each worker does one small operation in the assembly of the product, there is sufficient work in process at each step for her to be seldom immediately dependent upon the productivity of the preceding operator to keep her pace.

The workers in these plants are represented by a strong, progressive labor union. Important issues of industrial relations are negotiated at the head office of the company, but all ordinary operating problems are usually settled by local management and local union representatives. In general, labor-management relations have been very good, and the fixing of working conditions and specific rates at the local level has proved to be satisfactory.

However, the workers had always manifested great resistance to any change in production methods. The decision to revise them was taken by management as part of its duty to keep the plants modern, progressive, and efficiently run. With rising labor costs, the introduction of labor-saving processes had become mandatory; otherwise, the company would not be able to maintain its competitive position. Its competitors had already begun to change their manufacturing methods, and were introducing a continuous-flow form of production in place of the older batch process.

Aims of the Program

The re-engineering program had these objectives: (1) to reduce the in-process inventory and to shorten the length of time it took to complete a particular garment; (2) to attain more flexible control of production; (3) to reduce manufacturing costs by introducing semi-automatic flow procedures; and (4) to improve the quality of the garments by better care of the material during manufacture.

The major innovation involved the transport of each batch of garments from station to station. Heretofore, each operator had obtained her work from a centrally located rack, returning the batch to the same rack when her job was done. The proposed change provided for more rapid movement of material, along with substantially less handling. Much lifting of the batches of heavy goods was to be eliminated. In several instances, two operations were to be integrated in a short production line. In addition, various work aids were to be introduced for folding, trimming, holding, and directing material. The sequence of operations was also to be rearranged. These changes would have the effect of altering the work of some operators to a considerable extent; others would be affected only by the new system of transporting the material along the assembly line.

In this type of factory, minor changes in methods of performing a job occur quite frequently. Now the differences between minor changes in work methods and major production changes, such as the re-engineering of an entire assembly line, are differences of degree rather than kind. In handling ordinary minor changes the management had firmly adhered to three principles, based partly on a recognition of the psychological factors involved and partly on legal considerations, inasmuch as these principles had gradually been incorporated into the pattern of labor-management relations over the years. The principles in question were: (1) Earning opportunities on the job should not be deliberately reduced for the purpose of adjusting rates when experience had shown to be too generous. In other words, management would carefully avoid actions that appeared to be any kind of disguised rate-cutting. (2) The worker should always be informed of an impending change in the job as soon as it was definitely decided upon. (3) If a change required relearning on the part of the worker, the cost of relearning should be borne wholly or partially by management.

In the case of relatively major changes, it was management's belief that the workers should participate in the definition of the change to the maximum possible extent. Of course, this does not mean that management was prepared to abdicate its responsibility for the growth, development, and operation of the organization. Management alone decided to make the changes in question here and —as has been said—their general nature was determined by management with the help of its engineering consultants.

What is to be gained from employee participation in a program of this kind? Above and beyond the general positive efforts on morale and labor-management relations, two highly practical benefits may be noted. First, the technical program develops more rapidly. Any problems encountered by the workers are early brought to management's attention so that adjustments can be made with a minimum of delay. The worker's suggestions can be incorporated into the new procedure before a scheme of payments is fixed. Through participation, it is possible to head off any misunderstandings that might arise. This helps to avoid any deliberate obstruction of the new system by the workers.

The second advantage of having the employees participate is that the new method becomes the brain child of the workers themselves. Its success gives them a feeling of pride and accomplishment. Their very desire not to fail at their own project exerts a major influence on its success.

Participation is also a form of communication. When a man's job has been changed, some of his skill becomes obsolete and it is easy for him to view management as frustrating him, and as unjustly and even hostilely cutting his earning opportunities. If management's reasons for the change are not hostile but are actually for the good of all concerned, the worker's participation in planning for the innovation is an appropriate way of explaining it to him and letting him know the real reasons for it.

One form of participation is interactive discussion between management and the workers. This type of discussion gives management the opportunity to communicate and to be challenged at the same time. Of course, where communication is only one way and the workers merely listen politely, no participation takes place at all. A minimum requirement of participative discussion is that the workers should ask questions and that management should answer them in a straightforward and honest way. Furthermore, the workers must feel free to raise important issues—questions that are perhaps impolite and that recognize the possibility of conflict between management and the workers. Discussions are not participative if the workers have no real opportunity to speak up. It should be added that "opportunity" in this sense is not merely a matter of providing adequate meeting time coupled with a polite request for questions. Management must deem it proper for the workers to ask hard questions at such meetings—and the workers must have the assurance that no reprisals will be taken against frank discussion. (In passing, it may be suggested that participation may perhaps be more readily obtained from workers in unionized shops because the employees feel that they have the union to fall back on.)

Admittedly, interactive discussion is a minimal form of participation. Naturally, it is better to have the workers actually share in designing the change, if this is possible. When, as in this case, the nature of the problem calls for skilled engineering, employee participation must necessarily take a more limited form.

Nevertheless, the main benefit of participation can be achieved even when there are practical limits as to how far the employees can actually contribute to the change. The goal is to have the workers feel that they are truly part of the company, that in some sense it is their enterprise as well, and that they are as dependent upon and responsible for its success as management is. But unless management really believes that the workers have such a place in the organization, it is extremely difficult, if not impossible, to communicate this message to them. Management must begin by considering the workers to be an integral part of the enterprise. This is a basic condition—without it, participation cannot be attained.

How the Change Was Introduced

At the outset, the precise changes to be introduced in the re-engineering of the production lines were not known; these were to be worked out experimentally within the plants. The methods proposed were as yet unproved; nevertheless, they offered great promise, and it was decided to develop them in the two smaller plants first. This strategy was based on various considerations—some technical, others having to do with employee morale. On the technical side, simpler and more standardized items were produced in the smaller plants. Since these two plants accounted for a smaller proportion of the firm's total output than the large plant, less risk was involved should serious production delays be encountered during the change-over. It was also felt that there was more personal communication between management and workers in the smaller plants. Furthermore, since the large plant had intra-union difficulties, the small plants were considered less sensitive places in which to try out the rather fundamental changes contemplated.

Group Meetings

The program was introduced to the workers by a series of meetings. Each group of operators performing the same operation in the same plant met with the local plant management. In the course of the program, approximately 80 such meetings were held, the number of workers attending varying from one to eight. When there were only a few workers on a particular operation, they were accompanied to the meeting by the shop steward.

At the first meeting, the proposed change in methods was announced and its general objectives were stated. Emphasis was placed on the need for the change and the importance of the program to both the company and the workers. The relationship of the company's success to steady employment was pointed out. No technical details were presented at this time, but the workers were assured that while the new methods were being developed their incomes would continue at the average level of the preceding six weeks. They were also told that when the new system was working well enough, new rates would be established and that a subsidy fund was being set up to help maintain their incomes until their skills were fully readapted. Frank discussion of these matters by all participants was encouraged.

Immediately after the initial meeting, things began to happen on the production floor. Machines were moved; new devices and small carts appeared. Experts gave demonstrations and instructions to individual workers in the new procedures. Engineers and supervisors watched, asked questions, and answered them. This gradual and outwardly tentative introduction of the changes was a deliberate policy. Only a few workers at a time were given revised tasks. Usually, it took several weeks before the whole garment was being made by the new methods.

Problems were solved as they arose. Many informal discussions of the new methods took place between engineers, supervisors, and workers. As the new methods were mastered, additional changes were made, sometimes at the suggestion of management, but often at the prompting of the workers themselves.

After the new system had been in effect long enough to be stable and was operating with some smoothness, another series of small group meetings was called to discuss revised wage rates. Separate meetings were held for each group of workers who were doing the same job in the same plant and who would experience the same changes in rates and the same revision of work procedures. After the workers were thanked for their help in developing the new system, they were given an explanation of how a time study had been applied to their jobs, along with the time allotted for each part of their operation. Time studies had been carried out on both the old and new systems, and this means of arriving at standards of time and pay was fully explained. While this technical discussion may have been beyond the understanding of many employees, its primary purpose was to show that management was not trying to hide anything, and that a rational method had been used to determine the new rates.

The Subsidy Program

At these meetings, management also said that the new rates would go into effect shortly and that the subsidy program promised at the first meeting would now start. The initial subsidy ranged from

10 per cent for those jobs which involved only minor changes to 65 per cent for those with the greatest changes. These amounts were decreased by 5 per cent each week until the subsidy ended.

In addition to protecting earnings during the readjustment period, the subsidy was also an indication of management's opinion as to how fast workers should recover a normal level of productivity after the disturbing effect of the change. The gradual reduction of the subsidy and its eventual termination was intended to provide a financial incentive for the workers to regain their normal production as soon as possible.

Many operators expressed satisfaction with the new rates. Some quickly did enough work in one day to attain their expected earnings. Others had obviously been holding back their production until the new rates were announced; when they saw that their earning opportunities had been protected and preserved, they, too, quickly recovered their former level of productivity. Although there were some expressions of dissatisfaction with the new scale, discussion of this was postponed until after the subsidy program had been given a chance to operate.

The workers also raised a great many complaints at these meetings, not all of which had anything to do with the new system. There were complaints about equipment, inaccurate cutting of parts, and other mechanical difficulties which are regularly experienced in factories. Management listened carefully and promised to investigate. This pledge was kept and the difficulties were subsequently remedied. (In a sense, these complaints were a favorable measure of the extent to which management was able to create a participative atmosphere. The workers did complain; they accused management of many shortcomings, and management on its part accepted the complaints as matters that merited its attention.)

The meetings at which the new rates were announced were the last such get-togethers for most operators. However, management continued to hold individual consultations on the production floor and to listen attentively to complaints. Problems and difficulties presented by the new methods were talked over and ironed out. A senior operator was given the job of interviewing other operators to find out what problems they were having and how they felt about the change. Through this channel management became aware of some technical problems that had not been raised at the meetings or during those times when its representatives were available on the production floor. By taking the initiative in establishing communication with the workers involved, management was able to solve these problems also.

After the new system had been developed and refined in the smaller plants, and the workers there were well on the way to reaching their former level of productivity, the change was finally introduced into the third and largest plant. The same methods of introducing the change were used here, but by now, of course, management was able to point to many examples of proven success with the new methods in the smaller plants. Development work in the third plant was limited to conditions arising from the manufacture of the many special items produced there. The whole change was carried out much more rapidly than the other plants because the best procedures had already been worked out and most of the rates had been set.

Reactions to the New System

After the rates were announced, there were two instances where a few workers tried to prove them unfair by deliberately restricting production. But most of the workers responded well to the innovations, gradually raising their output to satisfactory levels. In the two cases of deliberate restriction of production, a satisfactory recovery of output has not yet been achieved. These involved two machine operations performed by groups of four and six women respectively. One operator in each group made a satisfactory recovery. It is worth noting that each was the only one in her group who had thought the rate was fair when it was proposed. Though these two women were able to resist considerable group pressure on them to hold down their production, their successful examples were insufficient to win over their co-workers to their point of view. Management finally had to make adjustments on these rates so that its policy of maintaining earning opportunities might not appear to have been contradicted. The benefits of these adjustments have also accrued to the two productive operators, but at this writing the others are still limping along, still convinced that the new system has drastically cut down their earning power.

These two very similar instances were about the only ones in which the new method was not accepted. While they were only a small flaw in an otherwise resounding success, they emphasize the importance of the proper initial presentation of a program of change, and show how firmly people cling to their original reactions to it.

There were, of course, noteworthy examples of a happier kind. Thus, the job of an older worker with almost 10 years' experience under the old system was completely changed, and for a long time her attitude was one of discouragement and hopelessness. However, thanks to the correct engineering of the rate for her new job, coupled with continuous attention and encouragement from her supervisor, and a substantial relearning pay adjustment, her job improvement was constant. A year later, her earnings were higher than ever before and she was able to look back on her period of hopelessness with equanimity.

In any such change as this, the engineering problems are so complicated that it is impossible to present a uniform picture of future experience to the workers. Some will meet genuine difficulties, others will find difficulties where none exist; some will be better off, and some but not all of these will know that things are better. The success of the whole operation depends upon the distribution of these partly psychological assessments. If management has been honest, has done its computations fairly, and spoken openly, there should be enough successes to carry the operation to a good conclusion. Otherwise, difficulties and negative reactions will be so widespread that the entire project can result in failure.

At this point, it may be pertinent to present some rather more tangible evidence of the success with which these plant changes were introduced. This evidence takes the form of "before and after" records of productivity, turnover, and grievances in the three plants in question.

Productivity and Turnover

Of these three indices, productivity is, of course, the most direct measure of the degree of adjustment to change. In calculating productivity, workers producing the same item in the same plant were considered to have experienced the same change process. Since, in the two smaller plants, there were changes in the production of one item apiece, while two items were re-engineered in the larger plant, this gave us four groups, large enough to be statistically stable, whose productivity before and after the change could be compared.

The average productivity of these four groups for two six-week periods, one immediately before the change was introduced, and the other one year later, is shown in Table 1. (It should be added that only those workers who were still in the same plant and working on the same item are included in these figures. However, the average of all workers employed in the latter period is only slightly below that shown for workers who were employed both before and after the change.)

TABLE 1

AVERAGE PRODUCTION BEFORE AND AFTER RE-ENGINEERING

| Worker Group | | Average Production in Standard Units | |
Plant	Item	Base Period	One Year Later *
1	A	79	76
2	B	67	75
3	A	79	80
3	B	69	75

* The base periods differ for the several groups, being the six weeks just prior to the start of the change. In each case, the one year later is the same six-week period of the next year.

As will be seen, a year after the changes had been made, the general level of productivity had increased by about 10 per cent on Item B and stayed essentially the same on Item A. There was also a substantial gain of about 10 per cent less direct-labor costs on each item because of the engineering improvements.

While to some extent the changes involved the substitution of capital equipment for direct labor, the capital costs were modest in relation to the savings in labor costs.

It should be stressed that, thanks to a market for additional production, the workers were able to maintain their incomes even though direct-labor costs were being substantially reduced. New jobs were rated so that the workers could earn as much as before; and the change was introduced in such a way that the workers' motivation to produce was not disturbed.

Besides providing information about the final recovery of earnings, production statistics may also be used to chart the pattern with which that recovery took place. As had been expected, when the new methods were introduced there was an immediate and drastic decline in production. The program of subsidies was designed to maintain the workers' incomes as long as their production did not drop to an unreasonably low level, and modest progress was made each week. The expectations upon which the subsidy program was based are generally justified by the production curves shown in Chart 1.

As the chart shows, in three cases there was an initial drop and then a general upward trend toward the previous level of output. The trends are generally upward: the slight drops can be attributed to the normal fluctuation associated with different fabrics and other usual sources of variations in output. In the fourth case—Item A in Plant 1—production was more erratic in its progress toward recovery. This may be attributed to the fact that the new methods were first developed on this operation and there were a number of special difficulties to be overcome. It is interesting to note that the fluctations were least for Item A in Plant 3, the last operation to be changed. This would seem to indicate that the methods for introducing change had become routine and that their acceptance was less of a problem here.

The production records shown in Chart 1 are for all employees of moderate experience regardless of whether or not they worked in the base period before the changes were made. This accounts for the difference in the "one year later" results between Chart 1 and Table 1.

The second check on the success of the re-engineering process is provided by turnover statistics. It may be assumed that if the new methods were unsatisfactory to the employees, more than the normal number would leave in the period immediately following the changes, either because of dissatisfaction with their new earnings or because they felt frustrated in other ways. *No such increase in turnover occurred.* In fact, the turnover rate continued to decline right through the period of change. Table 2 shows the turnover rate by plants in terms of the ratio of resignations for 12 months to the average number on the payroll during the year.

TABLE 2

TURNOVER RATES BY YEAR

Year	Plant 1	Plant 2	Plant 3
1952	*	*	.703
1953	*	*	.623
1954	.618	.398	.320
1955	.545	.291	.282
1956	.380	.243	.248

* Data not available.
NOTE. The changes were begun late in 1954 and were completed in the first part of 1956.

It may be added that absenteeism also decreased during the period of the change. Since absenteeism and turnover are both generally regarded as indicators of frustration and dissatisfaction and neither increased during the period of the change, it may be assumed that the change was introduced without serious effects on morale.

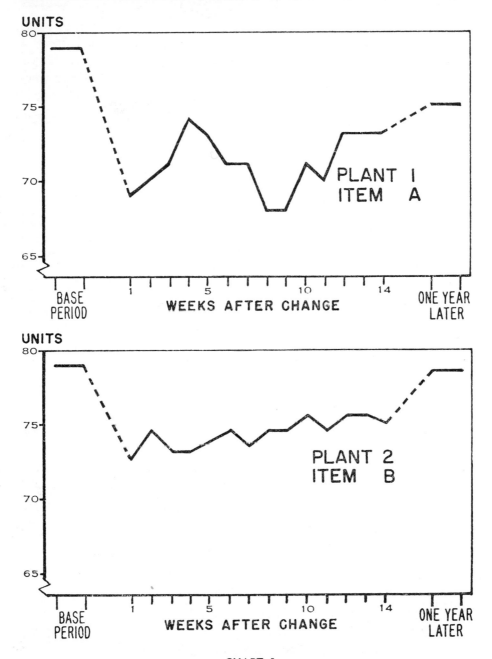

CHART 1

Productivity After the Change

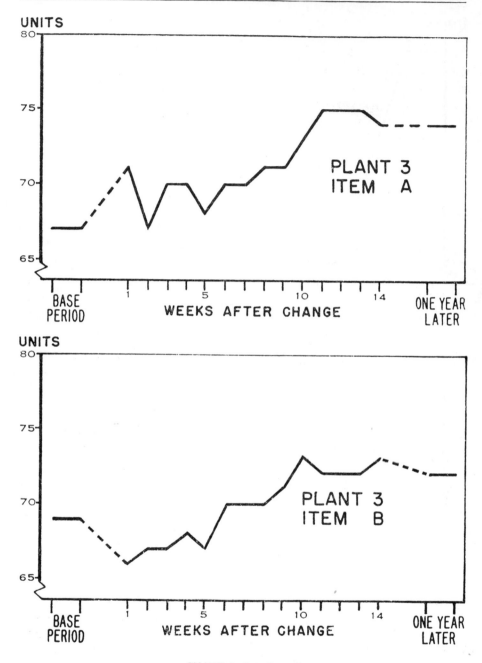

CHART 1 (continued)

Productivity After the Change

The Grievance Record

One remedy open to employees who are dissatisfied with their earnings is to file a rate grievance. Complaints about rates are, of course, sometimes due to causes other than dissatisfaction over money; but probably more than the usual number of rate grievances can be expected after any change in which a great many new rates are set.

Because of constant changes in styles and fabrics, as well as various minor alterations in the specifications of the garments being produced, the company has always had a fair number of rate grievances. However, after the change these increased quite substantially over the totals recorded for previous years. As can be seen from Table 3, there was an increase in all plants after the new method had been in operation for some time.

TABLE 3

NUMBER OF GRIEVANCES BY PLANT, TYPE, AND YEAR

Plant	Type	Year				
		1953	1954	1955	1956	1957 (5 mos.)
1	Rate	1	0	1	8	3
	Non-rate	0	0	0	3	0
2	Rate	1	0	4	21	3
	Non-rate	1	0	4	5	2
3	Rate	4	9	8	21	7
	Non-rate	24	31	16	14	11
	Total	31	40	33	72	26
All	Rate	6	9	13	50	13
	Non-rate	25	31	20	22	13

NOTE. The changes were begun late in 1954 and were completed in the first part of 1956.

Though, on the face of it, the 50 rate grievances recorded in 1956 would seem to indicate considerable dissatisfaction with earnings after the change, it must be remembered that approximately 1,300 rate changes were made. Compared with this total, the number of grievances may well be small. Nevertheless, it seems large when set against the usual number of complaints. However, many of these grievances were actually about long-standing issues which were again brought to the fore during the installation of the new system. Unfortunately, the record does not show how many separate issues lay behind the new grievances since, in resolving them, one decision generally settled many complaints. Also, the number of grievances includes complaints about the same issues that arose in more than one plant. Without going into an extended analysis of the precise nature of the grievances, it is impossible even to estimate the number of separate issues involved. It is best, therefore, to consider their significance not in terms of the number of grievances filed but rather according to the manner in which they were settled.

Disposing of the grievances called for intensive joint work between the company and union engineers. Most of the rates checked by the union were left at the same level set by management. In the few cases where management's figures were not confirmed by the union study, principles were agreed upon which increased the rates by 8 per cent. This amount was considered small since most of the increased rates were on special styles of garments and were connected with controversies that had arisen in principle before the re-engineering project began. In only two instances were the new rates adjusted on regular products.

In management's opinion, the number of grievances was not excessive in view of the number of new rates that had been set and the kind of issues raised in the majority of the complaints. The negotiations which settled most of the grievances were amicable and an acknowledgment of management's honest intentions.

Summary

The radical change in production methods described here brought about results that were highly gratifying to management. The cost of production was reduced; a better product was turned out; production time was shortened; and productive capacity was expanded without heavy overhead charges. Since the plants were highly engineered before the changes were effected, these gains cannot be attributed to any lack of efficiency earlier. These were substantial accomplishments which taken by themselves certainly justified the program. However, the achievements in the company's labor-management relations were also highly gratifying. To management the minimal nature of the difficulties met with during the change was at least as noteworthy as the economic gains. Indeed, the company's heads believe that the economic success could not have been obtained without the accomplishments in labor-management relations.

In addition to a sound beginning in production engineering, management attributes the program's success to the policies which it followed with its employees. These might be summarized as an honest attempt to maximize the participation of the workers in the change. Management considered the workers as part of the enterprise, with an interest in its success, and with the right to expect fair treatment. Hence management's plans were disclosed as early as possible before unfounded rumors got started, the workers' ideas were given attention, and their problems with new methods were investigated. In addition, their earning opportunities were protected and any economic loss brought about by the new methods was properly compensated for. Moreover, management was careful not to inspire resistance to the change by any action which appeared to be provocative.

Throughout the whole process, management did not lose sight of its right to make the changes it contemplated, but it was equally aware of what the changes meant to the employees. Basically, management laid down a policy of fairness and openness and stuck to it. The results continue to be highly satisfactory.

Questions

1. Would you agree with the authors' suggestion that employees in unionized shops feel safer in participating in discussions of work changes than those in nonunionized shops? Discuss.

2. What action with regard to earnings did management take during the change-over? Was this desirable? Why?

3. Describe the participative atmosphere created by management. What effect did this apparently have on reducing employee resistance to change?

4. The graphs reveal that in three groups there was a noticeable decline in production immediately following the change in work methods. How do you account for this? What action should be taken by managerial and supervisory personnel?

5. The company which participated in this study conducted a similar study over a decade ago. What would you conclude about the attitudes of its executives toward people? Do you know of similar studies that have been conducted by other companies?

6. Some of the findings from this study might have been expected. What purpose is served by conducting such studies? Are there any aspects of the study that could have been improved?

47. HOW TO REORGANIZE WITHOUT CRISIS *

Ewing W. Reilley

Whether you're reassigning duties, diversifying, or growing, these tips will save money, eliminate headaches.

Your business is changing. Growth, diversification, increasing competition are constantly forcing alterations in methods or structures.

The change may be as simple as a reassignment of duties, the opening or closing of a department. It may be as complicated as changing product mix, adding a new plant or revising the entire organizational setup that has served a company for generations.

Whatever the goal, the hoped-for benefits of change are seldom fully realized. Often it takes years for people to function effectively in the ways the revised plan calls for, and the costs of making the change, both in terms of lost profits and human anxieties are often very great.

The preliminary results of a study being made by the McKinsey Foundation for Management Research in collaboration with Dr. Eli Ginzberg of Columbia University and his colleagues Dr. Douglas Bray and Dr. John L. Herma, and Dr. James Thompson of Cornell University indicate this does not need to be so.

Proper handling can reduce the costs of change both in terms of lost profits and human anxieties.

Many factors contribute to the difficulties of making changes. They include the structure of the plan itself, compensation of executives, status changes, communications, systems. But the greatest single factor is that the people who make the decision to change do not realize that an organization consists of people whose capacities, psychological make-up, personal goals, informal relationships and value systems must be taken into account.

These human qualities do not belong to the rank-and-file alone. The executive—whether he is the foreman, division manager or com-

* From *Nation's Business*, Vol. 44, No. 7 (July, 1956), pp. 74-80. Copyright, 1956. Reprinted with permission.

pany president—has a personality structure, too. A plan which does not take this personality structure into account has little chance of success.

So, any proposed change that is to succeed must begin with an examination of

The chief executive

To achieve any goal requires paying some price. So it would be unrealistic to design a plan which required a price higher than the chief executive is willing to pay.

For example, an executive approaching retirement may be unwilling to undertake things that a younger man would do. Some executives are willing to risk delegating substantial authority to subordinates; others are more cautious. Some are willing to take steps that are contrary to the personal interests of even their closest friends if this is in the best interest of the organization. Others have such deep loyalty to individuals that they cannot bring themselves to act critically toward these individuals even when the good of the business calls for it.

It is also essential that the top man understand and be prepared to do what he must do to make the plan a success. If he does not carry out his part, resistance and inertia down the line will increase. In such cases, it would frequently have been better never to have undertaken the plan at all.

So, in making a change it is necessary to answer such questions as:

- How much change must the key executive make?
- Is he adaptable?
- Will he set a good example?
- Does he really understand and feel strongly about the new approach, or does he recognize the need for change intellectually without much disposition to pay a price personally to make it work? Is he an effective administrator, or does his ability lie in other directions?
- Will he enforce organization discipline? Does he have the ability to communicate concepts and ideas?
- Is he skillful at guiding subordinates?
- Does he have the loyalty and confidence of the organization?
- If he lacks the skills and interest to do certain parts of this job himself is he willing to delegate these and back up the executives to whom they are assigned?
- Is a suitable executive available?

Equally important, the planners must get the commitment of the chief that he will do the things needed to get the plan successfully launched. If he has to make speeches to management personnel or demonstrate strong interest and support of training programs, or handle staff meetings in certain ways, or apply disciplinary pressures to those who fail to cooperate, these things should be spelled out and his commitment obtained in advance. If this strong support is not obtained, people down the line will say, "If he isn't interested, why should we be?"

Key personnel

It is also important to take into account the capacities and limitations of other key personnel, and the impact of the change on them.

It is important to ask:

- What kind of abilities, skills, and judgment are required that the old plan did not require?
- How difficult will these be to acquire?
- Do present executives have the intelligence, breadth, attitude, maturity, to develop them quickly enough?
- If not, can additional personnel be obtained?
- How serious would the consequences of poor performance or failure be?
- Can these be guarded against?
- Can the transition from the old to the new plan be so phased as to minimize the risks of breakdown?

The planners must also consider how the proposed changes will affect the present status, prestige, and career ambitions of key executives. Will it expose poor performance they have been successfully camouflaging? Are there rivalry, cliques, and power politics in the management group? How will these be affected? Is the new approach adapted to the way key members of the management group operate best?

Sometimes the plan can be modified to deal with the human factor. A sales manager who is weak in planning and control may be reinforced by a strong product manager or a sales planning and analysis staff. Or suppose there is rivalry between the controller and the vice-president for manufacturing. It is doubtful that the latter will make effective use of a budget and cost analysis group reporting to the former. Under some circumstances it may be better to give the manufacturing vice-president his own departmental staff unit, even though this represents a theoretical duplication of activities.

Other management processes

The planners must be sure that all of the other processes on which the organization depends are aligned to conform to the new plan. For example, it is important that procedures for planning and the measurement of results be immediately aligned to conform with the new structure. This is generally the first thing a company does when it decentralizes. Otherwise delegation results in abdication and costs get out of hand.

It is also important that the compensation plan and management incentives implement the new philosophy of management.

If the new plan emphasizes the profit responsibility of executives and involves greater risk to the individual than the old one, the compensation plan should provide for greater earnings to individuals who are successful.

Incidentally, the more new things that have to be learned in order to make the plan effective, the greater will be the difficulty in getting it accepted and functioning effectively. A plan which requires the introduction of new management techniques such as budgeting and appropriation request procedures, measurement methods and the like will present greater difficulties than one which changes reporting relationships but calls for people to go about their jobs pretty much as before. The fact that the former change is much harder to put into effect should not be a deterrent, because over the long term the new methods can be very beneficial. However, the greater difficulties must be faced.

Timing

A frequent remark, when change is suggested is, "You can't act now because people are upset."

Even if people are not upset now, changes are frequently resisted because of the risk that they may upset people.

The fact is that changes courageously undertaken when people are upset not only succeed, they generally improve morale.

Generally, the greater the external pressures, the more changes it is realistic to undertake. For example, we have all observed that under the emotional stress of war it was possible to get people to do many things that they would not have done otherwise.

Alexander Leighton, an authority on social change, has pointed out that it is fairly well recognized in psychology that, in periods of great emotional stir, the individual can undergo far-reaching and permanent changes in his personality. When the pressure is removed, there is probably always some slipping back toward the previous status, but much of the new period is retained.

However, even if change is more difficult when things are going well, there is a great deal to be said for initiating change at a time when the company's trade position, profits, and financial condition are favorable to assuming the risks involved.

When setting up a timetable for change, the company should recognize that everything does not have to be done at once. It can establish a long-term objective and then phase its changes, depending upon the availability of qualified personnel, as well as other considerations. One company which planned to decentralize its central engineering department first organized the department into a number of separate self-sufficient groups, each serving a different operating division. After this arrangement had been operating long enough for top management to feel that the separate groups could stand on their own feet, the central department was broken up and each group was integrated into the division it had been serving.

Such considerations as these mean a certain amount of compromising with the ideal plan that represents management's long-term goal. But planners must establish definite limits beyond which they will not compromise. If they give sufficient attention to the next steps the amount of compromising can be minimized and the speed with which the full ideal can be obtained can be accelerated.

These next steps include:

1. Reducing resistance to change.
2. Introducing the plan.
3. Speeding the learning process to help all members of management function effectively under the new plan quickly.

Resistance to change

Resistance to change is not always bad. It may point up the need for adaptations in the new plan.

As Chester I. Barnard, a leading authority on management, has observed, resistance primarily grows out of fear of disrupting organization communications. Organized cooperation involves a complexity of subtle habits, attitudes, and standardized expressions whose smooth and more or less unconscious employment is essential to effective and comfortable collaboration. A new plan disrupts all this, makes collaboration difficult, and increases misunderstandings.

Kurt Lewin, who pioneered the subject of group dynamics, pointed out that once management has decided that changes are sensible it can deal with this resistance in one of two ways:

- It can increase the pressures for change.
- It can reduce pressures opposing change.

The latter is preferable. Increasing the pressures for change will result in a fairly high state of tension whereas reducing the forces opposing change accomplishes results under conditions of low tension.

For example, among the pressures opposing change are these human attitudes, one or all of which are almost always present when people fail to alter their habits:

1. They do not know what is expected of them.
2. They do not know it is important.
3. They do not know how to change.
4. They feel psychologically threatened.

These pressures can be reduced by:

- Presenting the new plan in a way that wins understanding and acceptance. This is the process of communication and persuasion.
- Helping people to change certain habitual ways of responding and to develop new responses and skills.
- Establishing an atmosphere of confidence.

But change is difficult and considerable pressure is usually necessary to get people to break deeply ingrained habits and develop new ones.

So discipline—pressure for change—is also required: uncompromising insistence that people do what they are expected to, reinforced by consistent use of rewards and penalties.

Introducing the plan

The methods used to introduce the plan should take into account the personalities of the company and its people.

For example, people have always recognized the importance of ceremony in effecting change. But it would be unrealistic to introduce the plan with a big show if the company is not used to doing things that way. Similarly, it would be unwise to rely heavily on consultative supervision and coaching by an executive who has not managed this way in the past.

This does not mean that efforts should not be made to introduce new communications methods into management processes. However, if they are relied on at the outset, key executives will feel uncomfortable and so will their subordinates.

Therefore, the results are not likely to be as good as they will be if the plan is introduced in the way that the people concerned do things most easily and well. When this way is determined, the first step is to get factual statements out ahead of rumors. Anyone who has ever lived through the period before a major reorganization knows how destructive of morale and productivity can be the period when it is known that something is going to be done but no announcement has been made.

This initial announcement is the hinge on which a major part of the plan's success will depend. Everyone involved is immediately going to wonder how the change will affect his present status and his long-range ambitions. So the first announcement must consider not only the logical, but also the emotional reactions of each executive. Therefore, it should be as explicit as possible both as to the over-all purpose of the plan and about the specific goals of each executive. It should spell out concretely what will be expected of each level of management and what the benefits and costs will be.

It is also important to point out the disadvantages of the old system. People can easily visualize disadvantages in the new plan, whereas its superiority over the old will probably seem less real. So it is important to make clear the benefits of the new plan, both for the company as a whole and for each level of management.

Every plan has disadvantages and difficulties, and these must also be pointed out. Not to mention them will reduce the credibility of the advantages, and people, fearing the unknown, will imagine the difficulties anyway. But they can face up to almost anything provided they know what it is. The more specifically the risks and costs are spelled out, the less frightening they are. Moreover, if the announcement does not prepare people for the inevitable difficulties, the ensuing disillusionment when problems are encountered may scuttle confidence.

The initial announcement should also deal with emotional considerations which are, subconsciously if not consciously, weighing upon many members of management. It should make explicit the nonpersonal reasons for the reorganization so that no executive feels it is the result of dissatisfaction with his personal performance. It should be made clear that no executive is losing financially or in status, if this is the case. Finally, the announcement should make clear that ample allowance will be made for honest mistakes during the transition period; that key executives will be given the necessary assistance, facilities, and authority to carry out their new responsibilities.

Since it would be unrealistic to assume that the planners can foresee all the problems, each man should have a chance to analyze his new situation and determine what he will require. Arrangements should then be made for conferences at which each executive can determine what others will require from him and what he can expect of others. This will develop new questions which, if not dealt with, can reactivate old doubts. So the first announcement should be followed shortly by additional opportunities for key executives to ask questions and get answers.

It is important to remember that people quickly forget almost all of what they hear or read, and that they are likely to misunderstand spoken or written material, no matter how clearly it is presented.

One way of increasing their understanding and retention of the material is to have key members of management participate in introducing the plan. For example, after the over-all plan is announced executives can be asked to describe their own roles. This requires them to think through their new responsibilities and increases their understanding. It also commits them publicly to their new roles.

To get even wider involvement, it is desirable, after the plan has been communicated, to break the meeting down into small discussion groups where the participants discuss how they will function under the new plan, what problems they expect to meet, how they propose to meet them, and raise questions.

The groups should meet without any higher member of management present so that they will be uninhibited. When the discussion groups reassemble, a spokesman for each reports the consensus of his group's discussion. This removes any personal onus that might arise from criticisms of the plan or embarrassment due to misunderstandings. Thus, all problems are laid out on the table so top management can answer them.

Learning

No matter how well the plan is introduced there is still a big gap between intellectual understanding and action.

Application of learning theory can contribute a great deal to effecting the desired changes fully, quickly, and smoothly. Psychologists tell us that learning has four elements:

1. DRIVES, or the motivating factors that induce a person to act.

2. CUES, or those elements in the situation that indicate to him that he should respond.

3. RESPONSES, or the resulting kind of behavior.

4. REWARDS, which represent at least partial satisfaction of the individual's drives as a result of giving the right response to the cue. Incidentally, these rewards do not have to be immediate, since an individual can be induced to make the proper responses by the expectation of future reward.

Also, learning typically requires repetitive action over a period of time until new habits are formed.

If management wishes to speed the learning process it must analyze the plan in terms of each of these elements. What new responses or ways of doing things does the plan require? What kinds of events, incidents, or actions are likely to cue these responses? How, realistically, can the correct responses be rewarded in terms of factors that appeal to the self-interest of the individual or group, such as through incentive compensation, advancements, or recognition? Have the desired new responses been spelled out in suitable form to facilitate learning? Have the proper conditions been established for learning these new responses? Have opportunities to practice been created?

In one company, preparing for decentralization, management set up product boards made up of the individuals who would have ultimately comprised the management of the various product divisions. These boards considered all the problems that they would consider if they were managing the division. However, they had authority to recommend only. Therefore top management could catch and correct errors before they were acted upon. When these boards demonstrated their ability to assume full responsibility, the company shifted to the divisional plan of management.

Learning will be greatly improved if ways can be developed to determine whether people are responding correctly. The importance of this is demonstrated by some research recently conducted by the Rand Corporation which developed some interesting methods for recording everything that took place in a management situation. The results were then played back to the participants who were able to analyze their own mistakes and figure out what they should do next time. As a result, the productivity of the participating units rose to three times what any unit had ever achieved previously. The conditions under which these experiments were conducted would be difficult to duplicate fully in a typical business situation. But this demonstrates how much a company can gain from providing people who are learning with some means to be informed of whether or not they are responding correctly.

Another key factor in learning is involvement. Experience confirms that behavior changes and acquisition of skills do not result merely from intellectual understanding and acceptance, but from thinking a problem through or doing things in a new way.

In addition to the contribution they make, executives who participate in the development of a plan have an opportunity to discover for themselves the reason why the change should be made, the benefits to be derived and how the plan is supposed to work.

During the transition from old to new ways there are bound to be rough spots, and temptations to revert to former methods.

You cannot cut people loose and expect them immediately to perform efficiently and display the judgment that comes with experience. Also, almost any sensible person trying to take over new responsibilities and do things in new ways is bound to feel insecure until he has mastered the new methods. Therefore, a good deal of hand holding is needed during the transition process.

The most important person in this process is the individual's boss. However, there are often practical limits as to how far he can go in meeting the individual's need. In the first place, he himself is probably affected by the change. So he may not understand the new concepts himself. Moreover, he, too, may feel quite insecure. Also, he may lack teaching skill. Finally, the dependency relationship between a man and his boss may create a psychological problem similar to those of a husband trying to teach his wife to drive. This underlines the need for staff or other outside help during the transition process.

The feelings of insecurity that accompany change underline the need for encouragement. The chief executive and others who participate in introducing the new plan must stress their confidence in the ability of individuals to do what is expected. It is also important that they demonstrate, by their own conduct, their belief that their subordinates can do the job. This includes, besides actual encouragement, refusal to entertain suggestions that the individual will not be able to do the job or to accept in advance excuses for possible poor performance. Obviously, commendation for work well done is also important. Confidence can also be built by consciously seeking opportunities for individuals to experience quick successes in applying the new concepts and by rewarding these in appropriate ways. These will get on the grapevine and build general confidence in the new plan.

In addition to conscious and logical considerations, human behavior is influenced by unconscious mental processes which follow an entirely different set of laws.

Unconscious forces influence behavior at all times. But we need to know how to recognize them during organizational change, and what, if anything, we can do about them. Clearly, every executive cannot become a psychoanalyst and every company president cannot have a psychiatrist at his side as he sets about a large-scale reorganization. But it is helpful for the executive to be alert to the conditions under which these unconscious forces may be present.

These unconscious mechanisms include:

DISPLACEMENT, or shifting reactions from the context in which they belong to one in which they do not. Anger felt toward the boss but taken out on a subordinate is an example of displacement.

PROJECTION, or unconsciously attributing one's own impulses to someone else. Thus, a politically minded individual may suspect political motives in others.

TRANSFERENCE, or shifting of one's attitudes toward persons who were important in one's early life to a current relationship. Thus, a man who was highly dependent on or rebellious toward his parents may adopt similar attitudes toward his boss.

NEGATIVISM, or the psychological term used to describe conscious or unconscious efforts to behave in a way which appears to be submissive to those in authority but which is calculated actually to defeat their purposes.

This manifests itself in the conscious or subconscious effort of people to resist change, even when the need is clear, the solution appears reasonable to objective people, and even after the individual has agreed to do what is required. For example, when a company shifted from a centralized functional plan of organization to a decentralized divisional type, the vice-president for manufacturing's authority was shifted from line to functional. Instead of discharging his new responsibility to advise and coach the inexperienced divisional personnel, he did nothing, even when they let things get badly out of hand. Apparently unconsciously he hoped that they would fail and that line authority would be returned to him.

We can recognize these unconscious mechanisms, psychologists say, because they are usually illogical and disproportionate to the situation that touches them off.

Discipline

Some psychologists question whether in most cases consideration of the psychological aspects of this behavior is either necessary or desirable. They believe that if management uncompromisingly insists that people do what they are supposed to do, individuals will generally solve these problems for themselves.

The psychiatrist of one of the country's leading companies contends that, after all reasonable efforts to deal with resistance to change and failure to do what is expected have failed, we can probably assume that the cause is unconscious negativistic behavior. Such behavior, he contends, cannot be corrected by reasoning. Therefore, we would waste time if we continued to try to change it by these means. When reasoning fails he contends we need to begin to discipline the individual. We need to give fair warning of what we are going to do and then do it.

This should not be interpreted as advocating fear of punishment as a primary means of effecting change. However, if other methods do not produce results, the administrator must be willing to apply penalties as well as rewards. Used sparingly and with discretion and care, penalties can have a salutary effect, not only on the individual involved, but sometimes on the rest of the organization also.

To an even greater extent than in the case of most other management processes, it is most important to provide for a continuing evaluation of progress during the installation of the plan and opportunities for executives to feed their problems back.

Since it is not possible to anticipate all eventualities in planning changes, the need for further change in structure or processes may develop. Also, since changes involve balancing many alternatives, some mistakes are inevitable; they should be admitted frankly and corrected promptly.

Such action will build confidence both in the plan and in the chief executive.

One company found that it had grown so rapidly that it was necessary to slice off a whole group of products for manufacture and marketing in a separate, integrated division. These products were all sold to the construction industry. The change was planned for more than a year and explained, step by step, to all concerned. But shortly after the plan had been put into effect, management observed that setting up separate manufacturing facilities for the new division had increased costs abnormally. Study showed that many of the division's products could have been made with existing facilities. It was not too late to admit the mistake. The new division was redesigned as a primarily marketing division, its manufacturing operations were absorbed by the parent organization, and all executives concerned respected management's courage and wisdom in rectifying an honest error in planning.

These appraisals of the plan's progress will also disclose human problems. For example, they may reveal that a key executive is not cooperating because he is still somewhat in the dark as to what the new plan implies for him or his subordinates. In that case some further indoctrination may cure the difficulty. On the other hand, his opposition may grow out of a deep-seated hostility to the plan so that he will remain in opposition until removed.

It may prove that the original program underestimated the extent of training required to assist personnel in mastering their new skills. If so, additional training will have to be provided and adjustments made in the time schedule.

When consideration is given to the things that should be done, the difficulties they present, and how little is really known about dealing with them, it is a wonder that changes ever get made. But lest the whole process seem so difficult that some managements hesitate to make needed changes, they should bear in mind the enormous adaptability of human nature.

Also, most businessmen know of reorganizations where every rule in the book was broken. It seemed that everybody would have quit. But they did not. And while morale and productivity were a fraction of what they might have been, they still got the job done, after a fashion.

There is no question that changes can be put into effect by brute force. It is happening every day. But it is doing it the hard way—hard on people and hard on profits.

Questions

1. One of the reasons why employees are reluctant to change is that they feel psychologically threatened. What is there about job changes that may be threatening to an individual? What can be done to minimize the threat?

2. While the authors do not advocate fear of punishment as a primary means of effecting change, they say that if other methods fail it should be used. Why is punishment not recommended as the primary means but as a last resort?

3. What effect is participation in planning for changes likely to have on those who will be affected by the changes made in an organization? Why?

4. Try to recall some of the situations in which you have been required to change your habits. What was your reaction? In what ways did others (boss, parent, teacher) help you or hinder you in your adjustment to the change?

5. How should communication be employed in a situation where changes affecting people are necessary? What should the communication process provide that might otherwise be overlooked by the goal-seeking executive?

Additional Readings for Chapter 8

Austin, Barrie. "The Role of EDP in Personnel," *Management of Personnel Quarterly*. Vol. 3, No. 4 (Winter, 1965), pp. 24-30.

Baumgartel, Howard, and Gerald Goldstein. "Some Human Consequences of Technical Change," *Personnel Administration*. Vol. 24, No. 4 (July-August, 1961), pp. 32-40.

Bell, Daniel. "Living with Automation: A Look Ahead," *Management Review*. Vol. 46, No. 1 (January, 1957), pp. 75-83.

Bennett, George. "Unemployment, Automation and Labor-Management Relations," *Personnel Administration*. Vol. 27, No. 5 (September-October, 1964), pp. 22-23.

Blum, Albert A. "America's Reactions to Technological Change and Automation: A Comparative View," *Management of Personnel Quarterly*. Vol. 3, No. 3 (Fall, 1964), pp. 12-16.

Brayer, Herbert O. "Automation and the White-Collar Worker: Fact vs. Fantasy," *Management Review*. Vol. 45, No. 4 (April, 1956), pp. 284-286.

Buckingham, Walter. "The Human Side of Automation," *Journal of the Academy of Management*. Vol. 3, No. 1 (Spring, 1960), pp. 19-28.

Davis, Keith. "Human Adjustment to Automation," *Advanced Management Journal*. Vol. 29, No. 1 (January, 1964), pp. 20-27.

Diebold, John. "Mental Barriers in Office Automation," *Office Executive*. Vol. 32, No. 12 (December, 1957), pp. 16-19.

Dinsmore, William F. "The Case for Evaluating Professional Jobs," *Personnel*. Vol. 41, No. 6 (November-December, 1964), pp. 54-60.

Gellerman, Saul W. "What's Behind Employee Attitudes Toward Change?" *Supervisory Management*. Vol. 8, No. 10 (October, 1963), pp. 4-8.

Gray, Arlen. "Problems of Adjustment in the Automated Office," *Personnel*. Vol. 41, No. 4 (July-August, 1964), pp. 43-48.

Habbe, Stephen. "Moonlighting and Its Controls," *Management Record*. Vol. 19, No. 7 (July, 1957), pp. 234-237.

Johnson, Richard A., and Walter A. Hill. "Management's Dilemma—The Professional Employee," *Journal of the Academy of Management*. Vol. 5, No. 3 (Spring, 1963), p. 37.

Kushner, Albert. "People and Computers," *Personnel*. Vol. 40, No. 1 (January-February, 1963), pp. 27-34.

Lawrence, Paul R. "How to Deal with Resistance to Change," *Harvard Business Review*. Vol. 32, No. 3 (May-June, 1954), pp. 49-57.

Lundberg, Craig C. "New Directors for Personnel Research," *Personnel Journal*. Vol. 41, No. 10 (November, 1962), pp. 497-504.

Myers, Austin S., Jr. "Personnel Management Overseas. I. Recruiting and Selecting Foreign National Personnel for Overseas Operations," *Personnel Administration*. Vol. 28, No. 4 (July-August, 1965), pp. 25-30.

Page, Robert M. "Motivations of Scientists and Engineers," *Personnel Administration*. Vol. 21, No. 5 (September-October, 1958), pp. 28-33.

Parnes, Sidney J. "Can Creativity Be Increased?" *Personnel Administration.* Vol. 25, No. 6 (November-December, 1962), pp. 2-9.

Schlesinger, Lawrence E. "Personnel Specialists and Change, Monks or Missionaries?" *Personnel Administration.* Vol. 28, No. 4 (July-August, 1965), pp. 3-5.

Schultz, Duane P. "R & D Personnel: Two Basic Types," *Personnel.* Vol. 41, No. 2 (March-April, 1964), pp. 62-67.

Shostak, Arthur. "Race Relations: Questions and Answers for Personnel Men," *Personnel Administration.* Vol. 27, No. 4 (July-August, 1964), pp. 12-22.

Speroff, B. J. "Automation and Human Relations: Some Problems and Predictions," *Personnel Administration.* Vol. 25, No. 2 (March-April, 1962), pp. 4-11, 54.

Stewart, Nathaniel. "Are They Ready for Changes? Gaining Support for New Policies and Methods," *Management Review.* Vol. 5, No. 10 (October, 1961), pp. 4-12.

Stieber, Jack. "Automation and the White-Collar Worker," *Personnel.* Vol. 34, No. 3 (November-December, 1957), pp. 8-17.

INDEX

Contributing Authors

Subject

A